Social Currents in Eastern Europe

Social Currents in Eastern Europe

The Sources and Meaning

of the Great Transformation

Sabrina P. Ramet

DUKE UNIVERSITY PRESS

Durham and London 1991

© 1991 Duke University Press
All rights reserved
Printed in the United States of America
on acid-free paper ∞
Library of Congress Cataloging-in-Publication Data
appear on the last page of this book.

This book is dedicated to
Janet Rabinowitch
and
Reynolds Smith,
my editors,
who have in countless ways helped me produce quality
and who have put me on the map
twice,
in friendship.

Contents

Preface

This book is concerned with social change in seven communist countries of Eastern Europe—East Germany, Poland, Czechoslovakia, Hungary, Yugoslavia, Romania, and Bulgaria—and with their transformation into pluralist or (in the cases of Romania and Bulgaria) pseudopluralist systems. I decided largely to exclude Albania from examination because until the latter half of 1990, it did not share for the most part in the patterns of change sweeping the rest of the area and has been largely cut off from any interaction with the other countries of the region. What little I have to say about Albania is in the final chapter of the book.

My idea in writing this book was that diverse social currents (mainly ethnic, religious, trade unionist, civic, feminist, musical-cultural, and youth) do not exist in isolation; on the contrary, they overlap, interact, and often follow parallel lines of development. I wanted to bring out this interrelationship and to show how changing social currents present political authorities with policy challenges, indeed with challenges that may bear on the fundamental questions of governance: system legitimacy and system stability. The phenomena described herein are of different levels of significance. To take the extremes, Solidarity has been a force for major system change in Poland, while Yugoslav feminists are relatively marginal. Both, however, are symptomatic of changing attitudes and changing behaviors.

Interviews have been important for the research for several chapters, in particular, chapters 2, 3, 5, 8, and 9. Interviews were conducted over an eight-year period, 1982–89: in Belgrade (1982, 1987, 1988, 1989), Ljubljana (1982, 1987, 1989), Zagreb (1982, 1987, 1989), Sarajevo (1982, 1989), Munich (1987), Rome (1987), Vienna (1987), East Berlin (1988), Leipzig (1988), Dresden (1988), Halle (1988), Erfurt (1988), Eisenach (1988), and Skopje (1989). I am indebted to the American Council of Learned Societies and to the International Research Exchanges Board (IREX) for providing funding for the 1982 and 1988 research trips, and to IREX and the Graduate School Research Fund of the University of Washington for providing funding for the 1989 research trip.

I am deeply indebted to László Kürti, who read the entire manuscript and provided helpful suggestions for its improvement. I am also indebted to Chris Bettinger, my research assistant, who assisted with the research for chapter 3, and to Robin Alison Remington, Darko Glavan, and Lawrence W. Lerner for their comments on earlier drafts of chapters 6, 9, and 13, respectively. I am also very grateful to Dan Beck and Clark Sorensen, who translated some material from Czech and Korean sources, cited in chapter 5. I also wish to thank Helena Ott, Piotr Jankowski, Carolyn Kadas, and Michelle Arneaux for checking the diacritical marks for Czech, Polish, Hungarian, and Romanian names, and to the Henry M. Jackson School of International Studies of the University of Washington for providing a small grant for that purpose. Finally, I would like to thank Whit Mason, who helped to proofread the final page proofs.

Earlier versions of chapters 2, 7, and 9 were previously published in *World Politics*, the *Canadian Review of Studies in Nationalism*, and *Survey*, respectively. A portion of chapter 8 was previously published as part of a study appearing in *Osteuropa*. I am grateful to the editors of these journals for their permission to reuse this material.

This has been a difficult book to write insofar as events in Eastern Europe have been moving at a breakneck pace recently. The initial drafts of chapters 1–10 and 13 were completed in October 1988, but of necessity had to be updated and revised. Chapters 11 and 12 were added in November 1989. When the book was finally cleared for publication in June 1990, I decided to update much of the text but to make only the slightest changes in chapter 1. Chapter 13 had to be substantially rewritten at that time, while chapter 14 is new.

Finally, a personal note: While working on this book, I have been wrestling with issues of my own. In December 1989, after years of recurrent depression and crisis, which reached a particular intensity at that time, I decided to begin the slow process of changing my physical sex in order to bring it into harmony with my psychic gender. While this has opened up feelings of euphoria and self-contentment surpassing anything I had ever experienced before, it has also presented me with continued challenges. Readers acquainted with the earlier incarnations of some of these chapters will associate them with the authorship of Pedro Ramet: Pedro and Sabrina are one and the same person.

Sabrina P. Ramet
Seattle, 12 June 1990

Abbreviations

CDU	Christian Democratic Union (West Germany)
CDU-East	Christian Democratic Union (East Germany)
CP	Communist Party
CPP	Czech People's Party
CPSU	Communist Party of the Soviet Union
FGY	Free German Youth (East Germany)
HDF	Hungarian Democratic Forum
HSWP	Hungarian Socialist Workers' Party
IPA	Independent Peace Association (Hungary)
KKS	National Strike Committee (Poland)
KOPP	Citizens' Committee Against Violence (Poland)
KOR	Committee for the Defense of the Workers (Poland)
KOS	Committee for Social Resistance (Poland)
KPN	Confederacy for an Independent Poland
LC	League of Communists
LCY	League of Communists of Yugoslavia
MKO	Interregional Commission for the Defense of Solidarity (Poland)
NOB	National Liberation Struggle (Yugoslavia)
NVA	National People's Army (East Germany)
OKO	National Resistance Committee (Poland)
PPF	Patriotic People's Front (Hungary)
PRON	Patriotic Movement for National Renewal (Poland)
PUWP	Polish United Workers' Party
SAWP	Socialist Alliance of Working People (Yugoslavia)
SAWPY	Socialist Alliance of Working People of Yugoslavia
SD	Democratic Party (Poland)

SED   Socialist Unity Party (East Germany)
SSOJ   League of Socialist Youth of Yugoslavia
TKK   Interim Coordinating Committee (Solidarity, Poland)
UDF   Union of Democratic Forces (Bulgaria)
VONS   Committee for the Unjustly Persecuted (Czechoslovakia)
WSN   Freedom-Justice-Independence (Poland)
ZSL   United Peasant Party (Poland)

I Introduction

1   Social Currents and Social Change

The pressure for change in Eastern Europe was building for years. It was unrelenting—as reflected in the perennial crises with which local communist elites had to wrestle in the postwar era. By the late 1980s the combination of economic deterioration, political decay, the growing strength of society, the long-term effects of urbanization, the accession of Mikhail Gorbachev to power in the USSR, and other factors made great change inevitable. An early symptom of the coming Great Transformation was the greater confidence shown by dissidents and religious activists throughout much of the 1980s. Finally, it was the flight of more than 225,000 East Germans to the Federal Republic of Germany in a matter of months in 1989 that spelled the final collapse of communism in Eastern Europe, with immediate effects in the German Democratic Republic, and ripple effects in Bulgaria, Czechoslovakia, Romania, and, in conjunction with everything else, Albania.

Some could see change coming. For example, in late 1987 Mieczysław Rakowski, a member of the Politburo of the Polish United Workers' Party (PUWP), wrote a sixty-page report arguing that the entire region was in political crisis and that the communist party would face serious threats unless it "finds the creative energy, courage, and imagination to free itself of useless ideas and outdated concepts. . . . [If it does not do so,] one can assume that in the future our formation will see upheavals and revolutionary outbursts initiated by an increasingly better educated populace."[1] Impending social and political change became inevitable, but when it arrived, it seemed sudden. After seeming, in the age of Brezhnev, to have succeeded in freezing time, the region now seems to be changing all the more quickly.

This book is concerned with the current dynamics of change in Eastern Europe and with the sources of change. I shall argue that social and political change is the product of social pressure and can best be understood through an examination of social currents—issue-oriented or group-centered patterns of thought and behavior—such as religious currents, ethno-nationalist currents, political currents among independent activists, feminist currents, and cultural currents among young people. I shall also argue that in several cases, the roots of change go back farther than is apparent at first sight and that the pressures for change are multifaceted, interrelated, and more or less comparable throughout the region. The changes which have occurred are no less than revolutionary. In Yugoslavia, for a variety of reasons having more to do with interethnic antagonisms and societal fragmentation, civil war has become a real danger.

In the following pages I shall outline the vulnerabilities of the area to destabilization and revolutionary change, as they emerged in the late 1980s. These vulnerabilities to destabilization and revolution were symptoms of social and political change and of ensuing structural distortions that put pressure on the system to find a new equilibrium.

Cultural Drifts and Social Movements

There has been a growing awareness in the past two decades that political change cannot be isolated from social change, and that changes in the group consciousness and behavior of people may be symptoms of pervasive changes in institutions, customs, and attitudes. A key element in such changes is change in people's values—what Herbert Blumer calls "cultural drifts."[2] Examples of cultural drift in recent decades include the increased value placed on health and exercise, the drive for the equality of women, and a heightened concern for the environment and for animal life. In Eastern Europe, examples of recent cultural drift would include a new openness to nontraditional religion (discussed in chapter 5), a new consciousness among urban women (discussed in chapter 8), a heightened value placed on "alternative culture" (discussed, in different aspects, in chapters 2, 3, 4, and 9), and a new drive for genuine pluralism, epitomized in the drive for independent trade unions and political parties in Poland, Romania, and elsewhere (discussed in chapters 3, 4, 12, 13, and 14). As cultural drifts occur, they give rise to popular self-conceptions which are at variance with social reality or in tension with political reality. This variance and tension provide the context in which new social movements arise.

Blumer defines *social movements* as "collective enterprises to establish a new order of life."[3] Social movements may be amorphous or highly organized, though they tend to lack organization initially and to acquire more organizational features as they evolve, including hierarchical structures and formalized routines. Social movements may be successful or unsuccessful: if successful, their program becomes accepted in society at large and may result in the restructuring of society; if unsuccessful, the movement may adopt a different program, evolve into a "sect," or fall apart. Social movements may be political, religious, or cultural in nature. They may also combine all three aspects like the Hussite movement in fifteenth-century Czechoslovakia and the Solidarity movement in contemporary Poland. Solidarity has spawned a rich art in which the themes and symbols of labor, pacifism, and religion recur.[4]

Angela Aidala notes that the exotic new religions which appeared on the American scene in the later 1960s responded to "the fragmentation of cultural symbol systems" and to a sense of drift among young people who felt they lacked clear standards for sexual, social, and political behavior.[5] They were thus symptoms of social stress associated with a particular phase of development.

Cultural drifts occur in specific social and cultural contexts, and may develop in diverse ways. They may reflect the influence of certain activist groups (such as feminists or human rights activists), or result from the dissemination of new information or understanding. They may reflect generational shifts due to different formative experiences. They may also be triggered by traumatic or energizing events experienced by the society as historical in a grand sense. An example of the latter is provided by the Albanian riots in Kosovo in April 1981, which triggered a Serbian national awakening and drove Serbs to look inward, bemoaning what came to seem like "hundreds of years of Serbian solitude,"[6] and to draw parallels between the Battle of Kosovo in 1389 (fought between Serbs and Turks) and the new battle for Kosovo in the 1980s (pitting Serbs against Albanians).[7] Again, cultural drifts may reflect an increase in society's confidence in its ability to determine its own fate (as occurred in Poland between July 1980 and August 1988). *Social currents*, which may be defined as processes of social and cultural replication and development, often serve as the vehicles of cultural drift.

A social current may thus be understood as a milieu in which social and cultural ferment is energized and focused. Social stress may be reflected in diverse social contexts of varying importance. To the extent that a cultural drift affects the perceptions or instrumentalities of basic social values, it may engender a politically relevant social movement that aspires to "revitalize" the system by changing aspects of its cultural and social order.[8] Sometimes in a society in stress, social questioning and the search for new solutions become so widespread that one may speak of the appearance of an "apocalypse culture."[9]

The appearance of revitalizing social movements is organically linked with the potential for revolutionary turmoil, but they are not reducible to each other. Social movements figure as one mode in which society mobilizes itself; social mobilization has revolutionary potential only when existing institutions are unable to channel disposable social energies into politically acceptable arenas.

When the development of political institutions is able to keep pace with the demands placed on the system, and when institutions are adaptable, the result is civic order. But when political institutions are unable to keep pace with social and economic change, political decay is the result. Political decay signifies that existing institutions have lost their capacity to process demands and to maintain order without resorting to force; as a result, in a system in which institutions lag behind rising participation —what Huntington and others have called *praetorian society*—"social forces confront each other nakedly," without the benefit of generally accepted, routinized intermediary bodies.[10] "In all stages of praetorianism social forces interact directly with each other and make little or no effort to relate their private interest to a public good."[11] A praetorian situation is potentially but not necessarily revolutionary: a praetorian society may continue to muddle along in political chaos with the apparatus in a state of partial decay, or it may succumb to a revolutionary upheaval leading to a restructuring of the system.

The Illusion of Stability

In the early 1970s some astute researchers thought that Eastern Europe had achieved a substantial degree of political stability. In a brilliant if wrong-headed article, Zygmunt Bauman argued that the communist systems of Eastern Europe had become "immune" to revolution due to the "ability and readiness of the government to deal with the basic social and economic issues"[12]—a claim that looks very odd today, given the record of the Gierek and Jaruzelski governments in Poland, the Ceauşescu government in Romania, and the eventual overthrow of communism throughout the region. In fact, in the early 1970s there was a tendency for Western observers to forecast continued stability for the foreseeable future, sometimes expecting change to emanate from the top down rather than from the bottom up. This book argues that change has emanated—and will continue to emanate —primarily from the grass roots. Elite changes in course have very often been responses to pressure from below.

Bauman developed an elaborate argument designed to demonstrate that none of the forms of *social dissent*—or *disaffection*, in the sense I define it in the next chapter—can be profoundly destabilizing or translated into revolutionary upheavals. Bauman's analysis thus specifically excluded the possibility that anything like Solidarity could appear.[13] His argument takes the form of an enumeration of seven categories of social dissent. Since his enumeration aspires to comprehensiveness, it will be useful both in furnishing insight into why Eastern Europe was once thought to be "stabilized" and in suggesting zones of social destabilization.

The first type of social disaffection identified by Bauman is simply maladjustment. Newly urbanized peasants experience difficulty in adjusting to their new environment but, Bauman confidently predicts, with the passage of time they acclimatize to city life and develop vested interests in their new status. Bauman's argument was misleading insofar as it suggests that urban life in communist states is largely serene and anxiety free (is it *anywhere*?). It is also incomplete in that it ignores the role of urban centers as the primary generators of "alternative culture." Hence, although in the short run "the susceptibility of a country to revolution may vary inversely with its rate of urbanization,"[14] in the long run social dissent is articulated and developed in urban settings. The recent history of Berlin, Warsaw, Gdańsk, Prague, Budapest, Belgrade, Zagreb, Ljubljana, and other cities amply demonstrates this maxim.

The second type of disaffection noted by Bauman is linked with a specific generation and is therefore by definition ephemeral. The "partisan" generation, whose members fought their way to power and consequently developed skills appropriate to the early utopian phase of the new order, becomes disgruntled when political developments leave them behind. A third type of disaffection is associated with the generation held back by these partisans. Bauman concedes the seriousness of this latter form of disaffection, and notes that the interfactional tension it generates has long-lasting negative consequences for the exercise of power at the center. Both types are resolved by time. Bauman's fourth category[15] is also associated with generational cleavage and involves social expectations stirred by the socialist revolution itself. In Bauman's view, "the critical period [comes] approximately twenty years after the social upheaval."[16] At this stage people become impatient to reap the expected benefits of socialism, and frustration sets in. His only comment as to how elites will deal with this challenge is to observe that they have moved away from ideals of social equity in the direction of a market economy.[17] On the whole, however, "Bauman seems to believe that after carrying out the demographic revolution socialist systems are more and more able to domesticate their working population, while the recent development reveals that the opposite is true."[18]

But this account omits the crucial role played by the late Stalinist terror and the post-Stalinist relaxation in defining generational attitudes and hopes. As Hungarian dissident János Kis has perceptively noted,

[I]n the early 1950s, mobilized people could not reap the fruits of the reorganization because of the terror and the general misery. . . . The generations that participated in the events following the crushing of the revolution and the concomitant terror were very deeply affected by it. The very deep [difference] between then and now was decisive for these generations. It was really an unexpected gift for them that the same power that had crushed them, later allowed them to reestablish a normal social life. As a result they didn't bother about putting pressure on the government. They simply didn't think in those terms.

But the last parts of these generations are passing away in this decade and new generations have since grown up for whom the Kádárian regime is already a precondition, not something they received as a present.[19]

The result is that generations respond to economic conditions not in absolute terms, as Bauman suggests, but, as Davies, Gurr, and others have noted, in terms relative to their experiences and expectations.[20] Kis's portrayal of generational differences is insightful in another respect: its presumption of generational exhaustion, which may have a cyclical quality.[21]

One final point about generational change should be made here: the generational gap, which sometimes gapes wide, sometimes relatively more narrow, is in part a function of generationally linked "cultural drift." Hence, when members of Eastern Europe's younger generation demand new ways of doing things, the older generation—and particularly members of the partisan generation—feel that their central values have been betrayed and react with fear and hostility.[22] This phenomenon is, of course, not unknown in the West.

Bauman's fifth category of social disaffection is labeled "trade interests." By this he means that people with specific job-related and career-related interests may at times find those interests to be at variance with the interests of the system as a whole, as defined by the political elite. This variance is so fragmentary and at such a low level of politics as to be marginal to the calculus of stability, as Bauman is, of course, aware.

His sixth category of disaffection is the yearning for national sovereignty among bloc states, and a consequent anti-Soviet orientation. But Bauman is quick to qualify this factor:

But to conclude from this that a major *social* revolution becomes more likely in any of the socialist states, judged in its own right, is to push one's imagination too far. . . . As a matter of fact we know [of] no single fact which would support such a conclusion. Whether the relationship of a given socialist country to the Soviets has been warm, lukewarm, or cool, whether the grip of Russian power remained firm, weakened, or disappeared entirely, there were no signs at all of the State retreating from its socialist path.[23]

Not, at any rate, in 1971, when Bauman wrote his essay. The difficulty is that communism in all the East European states except Yugoslavia and Albania was clearly an import imposed and maintained by Soviet power, and until recently resentment of Soviet colonialism was readily compatible with hostility to the system. Beginning in 1985, however, malcontents in East Germany, Czechoslovakia, and Romania applauded Gorbachev's program, hoping it might provide an antidote to the multifarious ills afflicting their respective societies.

Bauman's last type of social disaffection is "the intellectuals' demand for more freedom of expression." But Bauman writes off the intellectuals as an isolated caste, commenting on "the (at best) apathetic response which the intellectuals' manifestos win in the other strata of the nation" and on the impossibility of an effective alliance between intellectuals and workers.[24] Since Bauman intended his essay as a prediction, it is fair to point out that the record since 1971 has proven him wrong on both counts—for instance, the alliance between the intellectuals of the Polish Committee for the Defense of the Workers (KOR) and the workers of Solidarity in Poland. It is also necessary to keep in mind that ordinary citizens' responses to demands for freedom in conditions of dictatorship are apt to be conditioned by caution, fear, and circumspection rather than by apathy; the difference becomes politically important when power decays, because the hitherto circumspect can be mobilized for radical politics, while the truly apathetic cannot. Conformity is safe, while even so rudimentary a "protest" as removing the mandatory portrait of the leader from the shop window becomes a perilous, perhaps even reckless, act that can result in social ostracism by cautious conformists and reprisals from authorities.[25]

What is striking about Bauman's list is that the first four categories of disaffection are specifically transient (or seen as transient), the fifth is economic but narrowly conceived, the sixth is anticolonial but seen by Bauman as nugatory, and the seventh is limited to the desire for more "freedom of expression." The list excludes both traditional foci of discontent—religious, ethnic, and economic deprivation broadly conceived—which Bauman could have been expected to take into account, and newer foci—pacifism, environmentalism, feminism, and the campaign for free labor unions—which emerged only in the late 1970s.

Potential for Destabilization

When systems are able to handle the demands placed on them, they remain at equilibrium; when they cannot, the result is destabilization. Revolution is a possible outcome of destabilization; hence, in tracing certain ideas about the preconditions of revolution, I shall be indicating in the same breath the preconditions for destabilization more broadly.

Among the foremost theorists of revolution and destabilization is Crane Brinton. In *Anatomy of Revolution* he identifies certain uniformities in the Puritan, American, French, and Bolshevik revolutions.[26] First, these revolutions took place not in stagnant societies, but in societies with developing economies. Based on a study of Dorr's Rebellion of 1842, the Egyptian Revolution of 1952, the American Revolution, and the Bolshevik Revolution, James C. Davies concludes that revolutions are most likely when a prolonged period of economic growth with associated rising expectations is followed by a sudden economic downturn with associated frustration. In the Russian case, a period of growth in the late nineteenth century was followed by an economic slump (1904–17).[27] Ted Robert Gurr's theory of "relative deprivation" explains how the widening of a gap between expectations and actual benefits mobilizes the discontented and fuels destabilization.[28]

The second uniformity identified by Brinton is a change in the relationships of social classes and groups stimulated, as Charles Tilly argues,[29] by the mobilization of important new strata in the political arena (who may, in the process, acquire a new group identity) and characterized by a widening rift between the rulers and the ruled. The result is increased demands on the system and an intensified pressure for political participation.

Third, the desertion of the regime by the intellectuals is important because their defection signifies a more articulate and more focused political opposition. Fourth, the inability of the government to develop efficient means for channeling public participation and for processing public demands on the system leads directly to political decay and the disintegration of the system. As Huntington has also noted, when this occurs destabilization follows, and its translation into revolution may be the only route out of prolonged political chaos. Symptoms of governmental inefficiency include widespread corruption and the mobilization of nongovernmental groups on the streets.

Fifth, the financial failure of the government undermines its credibility in the eyes of the public and its ability to conduct effective policy. Factors 4 and 5 lead directly to the sixth uniformity, the loss of self-confidence on the part of the ruling class. This is expressed in intraelite polemics and infighting, recurrent purges, and repeated public breast-beating by office-holders. And seventh, the government's capacity to maintain order is seriously crippled if it displays ineptness in the use of force against rebellious elements.

The record of Eastern Europe's governments in these seven areas provides a useful barometer of the region's susceptibility to destabilization and, consequently, of the urgency of change. In the following pages I will discuss the situation in Poland, Czechoslovakia, Hungary, Yugoslavia, Romania, and Bulgaria as it relates to these seven factors. East Germany is discussed in detail in the next chapter, and that discussion will not be anticipated here. The entire scale of the problems has been much smaller in Albania and Albanian society has been generally weaker and more atomized; for that reason, Albania will also be excluded from the following discussion.

Economic downturn. The chief economic indicators reveal that the East European countries registered uniformly high rates of growth in the 1950s and, with the exception of Czechoslovakia, continued to register modest to high rates of growth into the 1960s and early 1970s. But the Polish and Hungarian economies lost their dynamism in the late 1970s, and the Czechoslovak, Romanian, and Yugoslav economies were clearly in trouble by 1981. In 1985 even the adaptable Bulgarian economy experienced a downturn. These trends are reflected in the data for national income growth (table 1) and in the data for growth of gross industrial output (table 2).

Similarly, in the agricultural sector there were difficulties. The region as a whole registered steady growth into the 1970s, but difficulties subsequently emerged, first in Poland, then in the agricultural sectors of the other countries (table 3).

The data in these tables suggest a close correlation between economic deterioration and social destabilization. In the Czechoslovak case, the low annual growth rate of 1.9 percent in national income in the early 1960s was one symptom of economic stagnation which contributed to the pressure for reform. More particularly, Poland in the late 1970s recorded minimal growth in national income (1.6 percent annually) despite party secretary Edvard Gierek's program of heavy borrowing from the West to finance ex-

Table 1   Average Annual Growth Rate of Produced
National Income, 1971–88

Year	Bulgaria	Czechoslovakia	Hungary	Poland	Romania	Yugoslavia
1951–55	11.2	8.2	5.7	8.6	13.1	17.9[a]
1956–60	9.6	6.9	6.0	6.6	6.6	13.9
1961–65	6.7	1.9	4.1	3.4	9.2	8.7
1966–70	8.8	7.0	6.9	4.6	7.5	6.3
1971–75	7.8	5.6	6.2	9.8	11.3	5.9
1976–80	6.1	3.7	3.2	1.6	7.3	6.5[b]
1981	4.5	0.2	1.8	−13.0	2.1–2.2	−0.4[c]
1982	4.2	0.2	2.6	−5.5	2.5–2.7	−0.2[c]
1983	3.0	2.3	0.3	6.0	3.4–3.7	−1.5[c]
1984	4.6	3.5	2.5	5.6	7.7	0.0[c]
1985	1.8	3.0	−1.4	3.4	5.9	−0.5[c]
1986	5.5	3.2	0.5	4.9	7.3	—
1987	5.1	2.1	2.0–2.5	—	4.8	—
1988	6.2	—	−1.5[d]	4.5–5.0	3.2	—

Source: See note 136.
Notes:
[a] Data for the period 1953–55.
[b] Data for the period 1976–79.
[c] Per capita data.
[d] Data for first six months of 1989.

tensive industrial investment. During the same period Polish agricultural
output actually shrank an average of 1.6 percent annually. By 1980 the Polish economy was clearly in crisis.

Of the six countries, Bulgaria is arguably in the best economic shape.
The adoption of the so-called "New Economic Mechanism" in 1979–80
was designed to head off problems through a combination of selective decentralization of decision making, greater emphasis on cost-effectiveness,
and enhancement of the autonomy of enterprises.[30] And Bulgaria's special-
ization in computers, electronics, transport industry, and nuclear energy
since the 1960s has earned it a reputation as the "Japan of the Balkans."[31]
Yet there are some problems. To begin with, growth rates in the major economic sectors sagged in the 1980s and, although overall growth rates in
industrial production were impressive, growth rates for "*marketable* industrial production" were more modest (4.3 percent in 1986, 4.1 percent in
1987).[32] In addition, repeated shortages of consumer goods like tomatoes,
clothing, and kitchen utensils eroded confidence in the system.[33] The weakest sector in recent years has been agriculture, where production plunged a

disastrous 9.0 percent in 1985, made a partial recovery in 1986, and dropped another 3.8 percent in 1987.[34] On the whole, however, this does not appear to be a cause for alarm on the part of the Bulgarian authorities. Moreover, Bulgaria's foreign debt ($6 billion in late 1988) was the smallest of the Soviet bloc countries.[35] Eventually, the Bulgarian press reported the outbreak of strikes in certain industries, but the strikes themselves were not enough to produce a destabilizing potential.[36]

Czechoslovakia is a different story. Industrial growth rates fell below 4 percent in the 1980s, sagging to a modest 2.3 percent in 1987. Even *Rudé pravo*, the official party organ, admitted that economic performance in 1987 was "in many respects far from satisfactory."[37] Some 26.8 percent of enterprises failed to meet their assigned production targets in 1986; 31 percent fell short in 1987. But in 1988 industrial growth was even slower—2.0 percent. More serious still were the qualitative shortcomings, with poor quality constricting sales on both foreign and domestic markets. In fact, Czechoslovak economic managers certified only about a third of new products as being of a "high technical standard." There were periodic problems with energy supplies, and supplies of meat and other food products. Servicing the foreign debt absorbed 20 percent of Czechoslovakia's export earnings,[38] and its economic performance became rather uncertain in recent years.[39] First-quarter economic losses in 1988 were twice as high as comparable figures for 1987.[40] But the main concern for the communist regime was how the Czechoslovak public would react to this economic uncertainty, and this hinged above all on the standard of living. In the early 1970s the standard of living rose steadily,[41] but in the 1980s it came under strain.

Hungary, long the economic success story of the Soviet bloc, also experienced economic stress. Economic growth was sluggish in the 1980s—consistently below 3.0 percent in annual growth rates of national income—and a combination of rampant inflation, climbing foreign debts, and trade deficits imposed new hardships.[42] The economy grew by a marginal 1.6 percent in 1987, while the budget deficit that year amounted to an estimated Ft43.5 billion (nearly $1 billion). Meanwhile, the country suffered trade deficits of $401 million and $361 million in 1986 and 1987 respectively, tallying a gross debt of $17 billion as of April 1989, or more than $1,600 per capita—the highest per capita debt in the bloc.[43] The increase in the standard of living in the 1970s stopped in 1984, and in order to keep pace with inflation at least half of the work force took a second job. Some people even worked three jobs. As part of a much broader effort to make the economy more competitive, the regime removed many price subsidies in 1988, but the immediate effect was to further damage the standard of liv-

Table 2   Average Annual Growth Rate of Gross
Industrial Output, 1971–88

Year	Bulgaria	Czechoslovakia	Hungary	Poland	Romania	Yugoslavia
1971–75	9.2	6.7	6.4	10.4	13.0	8.1
1976–80	6.0	4.7	3.4	4.6	9.4	7.1[a]
1981	5.6	2.0	2.3	−19.0	4.5	4.0
1982	4.7	1.9	1.9	−0.2	1.0	−1.0
1983	4.5	2.8	1.0	5.8	4.8	1.9
1984	4.3	3.7	2.8	5.5	6.4	5.7
1985	4.0	3.6	0.9	4.2	5.1	2.7
1986	4.3	3.1	1.8	4.4	7.7[b]	3.9
1987	4.1	2.3	3.7	3.4[c]	4.6[d]	—
1988	—	2.0	—	5.4	11.0–12.0[c]	—

Source: See note 137.
Notes:
[a]Data for period 1977–80.
[b]Data reflect marketable production.
[c]Data reflect planned production.
[d]Data reflect net production.

ing, which sank to the level of 1973.[44] The trend at the lower end of the wage scale has also been unfavorable. According to official government statistics, 24 percent of Hungarians now have incomes below the "social minimum" of Ft4,010 per month.

Studies by the Social Science Institute found that the number of those living in poverty increased 10 percent between 1982 and 1986.[45] The deterioration in the economy led directly to a decline in public confidence in the government, as the government itself openly admitted. In late 1987, for example, Prime Minister Károly Grósz, who became general secretary of the party in May 1988, said of the public mood: "The political atmosphere and public feeling are noticeably worse than a few years ago, even worse than is justified by the average living standards. The public mood is deteriorating as the living standards of considerable strata of society have stagnated over the last years and even decreased for a not negligible segment of society. Confidence in the leadership has dwindled, and sometimes the viability of socialism is put in doubt."[46] Ivan Volgyes, a noted authority on Hungarian affairs, highlighted the interconnection of political, economic, and social crisis in the country, concluding that the situation in 1987 was more dangerous than at any time since 1956.[47] The Hungarian socialists responded with a program of introducing income tax,[48] allowing unemployment to rise,[49] opening a limited stock exchange,[50] approving an austere state budget for 1988,[51] and drawing up plans for a transition to a market economy[52] in an effort to defuse the situation.

By contrast with Bulgaria and Hungary, Poland has been confronted with staggering problems. With a foreign debt of $32 billion to Western countries and $5 billion in transferable rubles to fellow COMECON states, as of late 1987, Poland was compelled to use 67 percent of its export earnings to service its debt.[53] Between 1981 and 1987 food prices rose 500 percent while wages rose only 100–200 percent, and authorities announced in advance their expectation that consumer prices would rise at least 40 percent in 1988.[54] Twenty-five to thirty percent of Poles were living in poverty as of 1985.[55] The figure today would be higher. Supplies of food and other staples are uncertain, and Poles have responded by hoarding food and other items. The flare-up of workers' strikes in several cities in May and in August 1988 was a reminder that the situation remained volatile.

In order to prevent the debt from rising even more, the Polish government slashed imports by 40 percent (1978–86) but this has hindered economic development. The general economic crisis has been compounded by an energy crisis and by difficulties in the agricultural sector (see table 3).

Along with Poland, Romania and Yugoslavia face the most serious economic challenges. In Romania the present economic morass had its source in the leadership's unwise decision in the 1960s and 1970s to try to establish major petrochemical, steel, and machine-building industries despite the absence of sufficient domestic raw materials, and to invest in advanced industries such as data processing, computers, and aerospace. By 1981 Romania's hard-currency debt had climbed to $10 billion (reaching $13 billion in 1982) and debt service payments were becoming difficult.[56] President Nicolae Ceauşescu decided on a radical policy of slashing imports and expanding exports in order to pay back the debt, and by 1989 had succeeded. A series of measures were introduced to reduce power supplies for domestic consumption and public services: the first cut of 20 percent came in 1979, followed by further reductions of 20 percent in 1982, 10–20 percent in 1985, another 20 percent in February 1987, and 30 percent in November 1987.[57] A forty-six-hour work week was introduced, and in 1983 the minimum wage was abolished, with earnings linked to the level and quality of production at the workers' enterprise.[58] Compulsory agricultural deliveries abolished in 1956 were reintroduced in 1983. Quality consumer goods and foodstuffs were marketed abroad, and Romanians were reduced to relying on a cornmeal mush called *mamaliga* as their basic nutrition source.[59] To prevent hoarding the state council issued a decree in 1981 establishing punishments of 6 months to 5 years in prison for persons who stockpiled more

Table 3   Average Annual Growth Rate of Gross
Agricultural Output, 1971–88

Year	Bulgaria	Czechoslovakia	Hungary	Poland	Romania	Yugoslavia
1971–75	2.9	2.6	4.6	3.7	6.5	3.2
1976–80	0.9	2.1	2.5	−1.6	3.8	2.2
1981	4.0	−3.4	0.0	4.0	−0.9	1.0
1982	3.0	4.4	7.3	−2.8	7.5	7.0
1983	−7.2	4.2	−2.7	3.3	−1.6	−1.0
1984	7.0	4.4	2.9	5.7	13.3	2.0
1985	−9.0	−1.6	−5.5	0.7	0.1	−7.0
1986	7.0	0.5	1.0	5.0	12.8	11.0
1987	−3.8	1.1[a]	5.0[a]	−3.0	2.3	—
1988	0.1[b]	0.9	—	0.6	6.0–6.5[a]	—

Source: See note 138.
Notes:
[a] Planned.
[b] Stock-breeding.

than a month's supply of food.[60] By 1988 social frustration had hardened
into deep hatred of the political leadership, especially Ceauşescu and his
family.

Yugoslavia has been faced with declining rates of growth in industrial
output (see table 2), a foreign debt of $20.5 billion in 1989,[61] a decline in
foreign currency reserves from $1.5 billion in December 1986 to $658 million in February 1988,[62] the necessity to devote 36 percent of exports earnings to debt servicing (for 1987, see table 4), unemployment in excess of 16
percent in 1986,[63] and runaway inflation projected at one point to run at a
staggering 11,000 percent in 1990.[64] One of the obstacles to economic reform is the absence of a unified Yugoslav market—a legacy of the decentralization of the 1960s and early 1970s—but any movement toward recen-
tralization has been firmly resisted by at least two of the six federal republics
(Slovenia and Croatia). Indeed, in May 1988 Slovenia and Croatia made the
first move to bring down the government of Prime Minister Branko Mikulić
by urging a vote of no confidence in the parliament.[65]

Wages have not kept pace with prices, and real wages in 1986 were said
to be on a level with 1967 wages. Yugoslavs survive financially through the
black market and a barter economy, and by exchanging services. A 1987
poll found that 95 percent of Yugoslavs did not think they could live normally on the basis of their regular income alone, and 50 percent believed
that their standard of living had fallen below the "existential minimum."[66]

Yugoslavia experienced a series of workers' strikes in 1987, including a strike by 1,400 miners of the Rasa coal-mining company at Labin in March in support of demands for a doubling of wages, and protests by 3,000–5,000 railway workers in Skopje in November against the government's wage freeze.[67] Further strikes in 1988 idled some 10,000 workers at a vehicle assembly plant in Maribor in June, a thousand textile workers in Paračin and several hundred workers at a tractor factory in Rijeka in August, and additional numbers at other locations during the year. In late June, between 4,000 and 10,000 Yugoslav workers gathered in front of the Federal Assembly in Belgrade to protest the government's ineffective economic policy and to demand the resignation of Branko Mikulić as chair of the Federal Executive Council.[68] Subsequently, in early July some 5,000 workers from Borovo and Vukovar came to Belgrade for similar protests.[69] There were several more protests by workers in Belgrade in July. Meanwhile, in November ironworkers in Bosnia formed their own "independent trade union."[70]

These developments were naturally unsettling to the authorities. Stipe Šuvar, the incoming chair of the League of Communists of Yugoslavia (LCY) Presidium, admitted in mid-July that the emergence of a "parallel trade union" could be averted only if the official trade union developed new, more effective methods of work.[71]

A poll taken in 1986 found that 37.83 percent of those surveyed blamed "the politicians" for the economic crisis.[72] A subsequent poll taken in 1987 revealed who these politicians were: 44 percent blamed republic and provincial authorities, while only 20 percent blamed the Federal Executive Council and 4 percent blamed the party as a whole or the party's central committee specifically.[73]

Jim Seroka argued in 1986 that Yugoslavia was most vulnerable to destabilization in the early 1980s, but that by 1986 the real danger of destabilization had passed.[74] Growth rate figures for produced national income (table 1) provide some support for this hypothesis, but the principal reasons why Yugoslavia was long able to postpone political breakdown, I would argue, are that (1) decentralization shifted politics to the federal units and fragmented the political arena,[75] and (2) social and political change proceeded "around" the federal government, so that there was no need to confront the federal government head-on.[76]

For a while the Yugoslav government's chief remedy was to freeze wages and increase food prices, as in November 1987.[77] The limited private sector has done well for itself,[78] and if Yugoslavia's 30,000 millionaires (1986 estimate)[79] were allowed to invest in profit-making enterprises, the entire economy might get a boost. Instead, the authorities insisted on keeping a

Table 4   Percentage of Export Earnings Assigned to Servicing
the Foreign Debt, 1987

Country	%	OECD Rating of Financial Vulnerability[a]
Bulgaria	41	slight vulnerability
Czechoslovakia	20	slight vulnerability
Germany, East	45	invulnerability
Hungary	50	vulnerability
Poland	67	high vulnerability
Romania	28	slight vulnerability
Yugoslavia	36	N/A

Source: See note 139.
Note:
[a]Based on an assessment of total hard-currency assets against current claims.

tight rein on ownership, and this available capital was spent on luxuries. This may change with the recent adoption of constitutional amendments that would open up new possibilities for private enterprise and encourage foreign investment. Yet bureaucratic resistance to reprivatization has remained stubborn. In June 1988, for example, a party conference in Slovenia, where support for reprivatization has long been strongest, concluded that "neither Slovenia nor Yugoslavia as a whole [is] sufficiently prepared for market orientation."[80] By 1989 economic duress had won new converts to marketization and even high-ranking LCY members talked about the necessity of moving to a market economy.

All these countries experienced rapid economic growth in the 1950s, 1960s, and in some cases into the 1970s, followed by economic downturns. This is the classic economic pattern preceding a revolution. Of the six countries discussed, Poland is quite obviously the country whose economy was in the most serious shape and which was the most vulnerable to political destabilization. Romania was an easy second. Seroka's optimism notwithstanding, I would list Yugoslavia just behind Romania on this factor, followed by Czechoslovakia, Hungary, and Bulgaria.

The basic problem in all these societies was the same: the absence of private enterprise, except on a small scale and in marginal areas. This suggests that there were (as of mid-1989) the following alternative futures: (1) social and political destabilization leading to prolonged chaos and praetorianism, with no clear resolution of the difficulties; (2) social and political destabilization leading to revolution and the forcible overthrow of communism; (3) the introduction of private enterprise on a large-scale basis (already begun in Hungary and Poland in the course of 1989 and proposed by some economists and other prominent figures in Yugoslavia), whether from above or below, leading to economic recovery; and (4) continued economic and social decline, leading to the steady disintegration of civilized society. Communist authorities regularly spoke of reforming the system, as if it were a distinct fifth alternative future. In actual fact, such reform could be subsumed under options 1, 3, or 4, depending on its particulars. Which of these four paths would be followed by any country has been, in each case, affected by other variables, and it is to these that we now turn our attention.

The Mobilization of New Groups into the System. When new groups appear on the political stage, or when old groups lose their meaning and group boundaries are redefined, the political game necessarily changes. The communists themselves encouraged the emergence of certain groups—Macedonians and ethnic Muslims in Yugoslavia, for instance—and through the propaganda of workers' democracy gave the working class a sense of political entitlement, a sense which proved to have unforeseen consequences (Solidarity being the most dramatic illustration to date). Social changes produced by urbanization, expanding education, changes in sexual ethics, and a combination of both organic and induced secularization have also kindled a new activism among young people, women, religious groups, and malcontents. William E. Griffith suggests that the importance of this "excess of mobilization over institutionalization" is that it is directly at the root of the major crises in postwar Eastern Europe.[81]

Hungary aptly illustrates what this can mean in practice. In 1976 László Szentirmay and a group of other students at the Karl Marx University of Economics in Budapest decided to organize a political discussion club (POLVAX). Its purpose, Szentirmay admits candidly, was to provide a forum for the free exchange of information, in recognition of the fact that "because of the limits and deficiencies of the official information distribution, there was an enormous hunger of the students for information. We considered it extremely important that frank debates should not be relegated to the hallways, messhalls, or even to some nearby saloons, but that an organized forum should supply the framework."[82] By 1984 the club had organized several hundred discussion programs touching on the situation in socialist countries, human rights, pluralism, the international communist camp, and issues in domestic Hungarian politics, and bringing in various luminaries and political dignitaries as speakers. The talks were regularly attended by some 500 persons, mostly students.

More recently, in spring 1988 thirty-seven law students at Budapest's

Lorand Eötvös University established the Federation of Young Democrats as a rival to the unpopular communist youth organization, and quickly signed up 1,000 members.[83] About the same time, a group of academic researchers and scientific workers set up an independent union, the Democratic Union of Workers in Science. The one-thousand-member union was said to have been formed in response to the government's decision in 1987 to cut funds for science and education. The union members felt they needed an independent advocate to represent their views to the government.[84]

Imre Pozsgay, the reflective head of the Patriotic People's Front, drew attention to the meaning of these symptoms: "The nature of the citizen has changed. The earlier common consent [which] was based on the resignation of citizens rather than on their active participation [is] over. Hungarians need new institutions in which they can exercise their rights as citizens."[85]

Environmental concerns mobilized special public groups into political action in Yugoslavia. In 1986, for instance, an independent ecology group was formed at the philosophical faculty in Zagreb, while a second group devoted to ecological, pacifist, and feminist concerns was established on citizens' initiative within the Zagreb-Trnje district conference of the Socialist Youth League of Croatia.[86] An antinuclear protest movement arose in Yugoslavia in the wake of the Chernobyl nuclear accident,[87] and in November 1986 "several hundred citizens marched through the streets of Kraljevo to express their disgust and indignation at the latest pollution of water in the city waterworks."[88] There are also citizens' initiative groups concerned with human rights, artistic freedom, and gay rights active in Belgrade, Ljubljana, and Zagreb.[89] The Yugoslav feminist movement, fragmented though it may be, is the most important feminist current in Eastern Europe today (this current will be examined in chapter 8). In addition, youth in Yugoslavia have acquired a new sense of group identity, and molded the leading youth periodicals—*Mladina* (Ljubljana), *Katedra* (Maribor), *Studentski list* (Zagreb), and *Student* (Belgrade)—into important forums for alternative ideas.

In April 1986 the League of Socialist Youth of Slovenia held its Twelfth Congress in Krško. The atmosphere at the congress was remarkable. The young participants did not bother to dress formally, and some were obviously from the rock subculture. The discussions were lively and often emotional, reflecting the defiant motto of the congress, "Words are no crime." Finally, the meeting adopted a resolution which said, in part:

Experience has taught us that nobody should have a monopoly over Truth, over revolution, that the true measure of revolution is the actual change in people's social position. We are not interested primarily in "internal" and "external" enemies . . . [but in the] democratic and self-management decision-making process regarding every aspect of future social development.[90]

The resolution also recommended the direct election of officials at higher levels, more independence for the press, acceptance of an alternative civilian service for conscientious objectors, and abolition of the legal obstacles to establishing small private businesses.

Finally, the Albanian and Serbian populations of Yugoslavia have been mobilized as interethnic relations in the largely Albanian province of Kosovo have deteriorated (see in chapter 7). The violent Albanian riots of April 1981 revived currents among Albanians for full-republic status for Kosovo as well as currents favoring Kosovo's annexation by neighboring coethnic Albania. The Belgrade government has never been able to regain control. Random and collective violence periodically shake the province, and a stream of Serbian and Montenegrin families has fled the province. Delegations of disgruntled Serbs trekked to Belgrade to confront the authorities and demand effective protective measures. On 31 August more than 10,000 Serbs staged a protest in the provincial capital of Priština against intimidation and harassment by local Albanians. The leadership, which once tried to hide behind optimistic phrases, eventually admitted that the situation in Kosovo was "worsening daily."[91] By 1988 people talked openly of the possibility of civil war.

In 1988 and 1989 alternative political parties began to appear in Yugoslavia (these will be discussed in chapters 12 and 14).

Even in Bulgaria there are some signs of mobilization. Specifically, in late 1985 Bulgarian émigrés in Paris obtained copies of a lengthy leaflet drafted by workers at a Sofia locomotive factory which called for passive resistance to the government's new economic policies and to its "exploitation and oppression."[92] In early 1987 a small group of Bulgarian dissidents founded Bulgaria's first known human rights organization, the Independent Association for the Defense of Human Rights. At least five of its supporters were arrested and interrogated after signing a collective appeal for freedom of movement and emigration, free choice of career, and objective information in the media.[93] There were also rumors that environmental groups were being organized in a number of municipalities; whatever their truth, some 2,000 people demonstrated in Ruse on 10 February 1988 against environmental pollution[94] (see chapter 11 for further discussion of social mobilization in Bulgaria).

The mobilization of new groups in Poland, Hungary, Czechoslovakia, and Romania will be discussed in chapters 3 and 4. But by way of a preliminary conclusion, we may say that in the forty-five years since World War II, various associational groups (women, youth, workers) and issue-oriented publics (pacifists, environmentalists) have acquired a sense of collective identity and shared interests. This process became farthest advanced in Poland, followed by Hungary, Yugoslavia, and East Germany, probably in that order. The Bulgarian and Albanian publics have been the *least* mobilized. The reunification of Germany promises to quicken the process in East German society.

The Defection of the Intellectuals. One aspect of the defection of the intellectuals is the appearance of critical dissent, and in this form the subject will be explored further in the next three chapters. Defection may also display a more moderate aspect in the form of critical forums and conferences, the publication in the regime press of interviews and essays critical of the regime, and so forth. This is sometimes viewed as a "safety valve" for critical opinion, but such safety valves have at times proven unsettling to the authorities, as the Petöfi Circles in 1950s Hungary and the *Praxis* journal in 1970s Yugoslavia illustrate.

An important segment of the Polish intelligentsia has been alienated from the regime for decades,[95] and after 1976 clearly joined the political opposition. The "Flying Universities" in Poland, like the "Flying Kindergartens" in Hungary,[96] were a symptom of both the regime's refusal to allow certain ideas to be discussed in state universities and the intellectuals' corresponding determination to discuss those ideas.

In Romania there has been considerable evidence of the defection of the intellectuals, ranging from the deep frustration of ethnic German writers in the Banat,[97] to the submission of proposals for reform to the Soviet embassy by engineer Nicolae Stancescu and architect Ion Fiştioc in 1987,[98] to the appearance of a string of essays by engineer Ion C. Brătianu in favor of classical liberalism,[99] to the human rights activism of mathematician Mihai Botez.[100] Esoteric communication is a popular form of protest by alienated intellectuals, since the adoption of Aesopian language seemed to confuse the censors. The weekly magazine of the Writers' Union, *Luceafărul*, has been a periodic vehicle for such critiques. An apt example is Mircea Micu's series of articles "Alone in Mongolia," published by *Luceafărul* in 1986.[101] Nominally about Genghis Khan, the series portrays a ruler cut off from his subjects, ruling in an arbitrary way, and advancing his son as his heir. A string of unmistakably pointed details highlighting similarities between Genghis and Ceauşescu serve as clues to the author's principal purpose.

In Yugoslavia academic criticism of the regime has become commonplace and is often sharp. In 1986, for instance, the Serbian Academy of Writers issued a famous memorandum bemoaning the fate of the Serbian people in Yugoslavia and criticizing the federal system for nurturing "egoism" in the constituent republics.[102] Yugoslav academics have repeatedly urged a change in the economic system (for example, in 1985 and 1986 at conferences held in Belgrade). In October 1987 Yugoslavia's renowned economist Branko Horvat urged full legalization of private enterprise in the country.[103] In Slovenia intellectuals have demanded greater freedom, including greater freedom of speech and publication. Intellectuals in Slovenia and elsewhere in the country have advocated the introduction of a multiparty system in Yugoslavia.[104]

Even in Bulgaria there have been some signs of alienation among intellectuals. Gorbachev's *perestroika* campaign has found receptive ears in these quarters, and some Bulgarian intellectuals have shown themselves eager to criticize past and present policies of the Zhivkov regime. By April 1988 Bulgarian party leader Todor Zhivkov decided that things had gone too far: he condemned the "negative attitude" being promoted by writers in certain publications and called for a purge to "get rid of those who lost their qualifications [as party members], the demagogues, and politically decayed people."[105]

Given the number of relevant variables, it is inevitably a subjective business to assess the comparative degree of alienation on the part of intellectuals in the region. Bearing this caveat in mind, I would suggest that the intellectuals became most estranged from the regime in Poland, Romania, Yugoslavia, and Czechoslovakia—possibly in that order, though it is only in Poland and Czechoslovakia thus far that contacts between dissident intellectuals and workers have become routine. Many intellectuals were clearly discontented with the system. But there was an ongoing dialogue between discontented Hungarian intellectuals and reform-minded members of the political establishment. This took some of the edge off their alienation. This is also, to some extent, true of Yugoslavia, except that what Yugoslavia has learned, and what the Hungarian Socialist Workers' Party (HSWP) did not learn until it was too late, is that such dialogue inevitably opens up channels for critique, which in turn feeds the critical attitude and ultimately reinforces estrangement.

Governmental Inefficiency and Corruption. Governmental inefficiency is a prime source of the loss of credibility among the population, and goes hand in hand with corruption, which figures functionally as an alternative channel for accomplishing basic tasks. The combination of inefficiency and corruption becomes especially dangerous when the government itself admits to problems. And hence, the launching of anticorruption campaigns, like those in the 1980s in Poland, Hungary, Czechoslovakia, and Bulgaria, not to mention the USSR, while offering some prospect of reform, entailed considerable risk, especially if the campaign was not perceived as effective.

In Poland the fall of Edvard Gierek in mid-1980 was followed by a string of revelations of ministerial corruption and judicial indictments. Wojciech Jaruzelski, the Polish general secretary from 1981 to 1989, tried to exploit his military background to inspire confidence that his government would be free of corruption. But corruption remained a massive problem, and the corruption of communist public officials is well known to Poles.

In Romania inefficiency and corruption are married to nepotism,[106] and there was no talk under Ceauşescu of any campaign to eliminate these problems. Romanians blamed Ceauşescu personally for much of their duress.

In Czechoslovakia corruption was a problem throughout the 1980s. As early as August 1980 the communist party weekly *Tribuna* acknowledged: "The facts are irrefutable. Bribery and corruption damage the development of economic and social relations and are contrary to socialist morality—but despite this they exist."[107] Slovak courts dealt with some 300 cases of bribery between January 1980 and June 1981, and on 29 April 1981 the Slovak regional government issued "a set of binding measures aimed at solving the problem of bribery and corruption in the Slovak Socialist Republic."[108] But this and other measures encountered difficulties and there were further corruption scandals in 1983,[109] 1985,[110] and 1986.[111] Those implicated in 1985 included Finance Minister Leopold Ler and General Director of Customs Ladislav Kusý, along with some 250 party members.

In Hungary several thousand party members and officials were dismissed or otherwise disciplined every year, as András Gyenes, chair of the Central Inspection Committee, openly admitted.[112] In Yugoslavia a financial scandal in 1987 resulted in the expulsion of forty-two party members, the resignation of Vice-President Hamdija Pozderac, and serious damage to the reputation of the regional Bosnian party apparatus.[113] The scandal sent a shock throughout the whole society, but the fragmentation of responsibility under the federal system probably helped to limit the most serious damage to the republic of Bosnia-Herzegovina.

Finally, even in Bulgaria the communist press openly admitted abuses of power and privileges. As early as March 1982 former Deputy Foreign Minister Zhivko Popov was sentenced to twenty years' imprisonment for corruption.[114] Under pressure from Gorbachev there was a gathering campaign against corruption in Bulgaria throughout 1986 and 1987, and an "unprecedented number of middle and senior ranking officials" were fired for corruption, mismanagement, or incompetence.[115] But when the trade union daily *Trud* published a series of four investigative articles in June 1987, alleging massive corruption by three generations of the same family in the town of Etropole, the party, after initially permitting the dismissal of those implicated, later reversed itself. The Central Control and Revision Committee of the Bulgarian communist party claimed that the articles in *Trud* had built up a misleading case on the basis of a "capricious" selection of facts and "tendentious" interpretation, and recommended the reinstatement of the officials. The author of the investigative series was fired from his job and expelled from the party.[116] Clearly, *glasnost* had its limits in Zhivkov's Bulgaria, where the leadership may have felt—correctly, I have argued—that the revelation of corruption might be more damaging than the corruption itself.

Loss of Credibility. Of the six systems under discussion, the Polish and Romanian regimes have by far the most serious problems of credibility, though Pozsgay conceded in early 1988 that "the [Hungarian] party's authority is very small and is widely mistrusted."[117] Surveys taken in 1983 and 1985 showed that the Polish United Workers Party (PUWP) commanded minimal credibility among the public,[118] while in Ceaușescu's Romania such surveys were not even published because they would not have commanded any credibility. The Yugoslav communist authorities do not command much more credibility, but the de facto liberalization which has unfolded there as a by-product of the weakening of the center has helped to alleviate some of this problem. In Bulgaria and Czechoslovakia, by contrast, apathy and resignation served to partially defuse or muffle this issue, while in Hungary the entire issue of credibility seemed to be up in the air in 1989, as the ex-communist party, renamed the Socialist Party, searched for a new formula.

The ruling parties of the Soviet bloc states tried to build credibility by controlling information,[119] but this tactic had its limits. As Daniel Nelson noted in 1981, apropos Romania,

as the Romanian population becomes more educated, more mobile, and more diverse occupationally, the wider and more rapid dissemination of information may pave the way for a broader range of interpretations by individuals regarding their social, economic, and political circumstances. . . . Notwithstanding propaganda and misinformation employed by the regime, citizens in a public sample evaluated events reported by mass media in ways quite distinct from that observable in an "elite" sample. The party's control over media content, then, does not appear to have assured a uniformity of interpretations in an environment of increasing socioeconomic diversity and complexity.[120]

Factionalization and Loss of Self-confidence. When leadership elites become polarized and turn upon themselves, their capacity to govern is weakened. Instances of factionalization within East European leaderships are well known.[121] Suffice it to say here that this problem has been most serious in the Yugoslav case[122] and, to a lesser degree, in the Czechoslovak, Hungarian, and Polish cases.

Loss of confidence is a related but distinct phenomenon that is deadly to a regime once it passes a certain threshold. The Polish communist regime in 1980 had clearly crossed that threshold, and it took a military coup in December 1981 to "normalize" the situation.

The first step in the direction of loss of confidence is often the admission of past error or mendacity. As Brinton once wrote, heaven help the prince who decides to confess to having made serious mistakes.[123] This is not a move Ceauşescu would make, but there are other reasons for loss of self-confidence among Romanian officials. On the other hand, both the Polish and Yugoslav parties made many telling admissions in the late 1980s. For example, the Polish communists, in tandem with the Soviet regime, finally admitted that it was the Soviets, not the Germans, who shot 15,000 Polish prisoners-of-war in World War II. They admitted that between 1939 and 1941 Soviet authorities not only deported many Poles to the USSR but also arrested, tried, and sentenced several Polish underground leaders for "anti-Soviet" activities.[124] They confessed that the purge of some 9,000 Polish Jews from official capacities in 1967 and 1968 was the result of anti-Semitism.[125] And they acknowledged the serious blunders and transgressions made by the party during the Gierek era (1970–80).

Similarly, the Yugoslav party admitted that many innocent people were imprisoned and tortured in the early years of communism, that Tito made serious mistakes in Kosovo and elsewhere, and that the self-management system has not worked.[126] Understandably, these admissions shook the credibility of the party and the self-confidence of the political leadership.

Inept Use of Force. The communist regimes of Czechoslovakia, Poland, Romania, and Yugoslavia resorted to the obtrusive use of force to maintain order in the 1980s—Yugoslavia in the case of Albanian unrest in Kosovo.

Bulgaria, of course, resorted to force as part of its campaign to "Bulgarianize" its Turkish population. Of these five instances, only in Poland could the use of force be construed as "partly" inept, though of course force always entails certain costs.

Expectancy of Change. Brinton's list is complete with the seven foregoing factors, but I would add one additional element to the list: the expectancy of change. When a population *expects* change, it behaves entirely differently from the way in which it behaves when it does not, even if the basic complaints are otherwise the same. This point is related to Davies's emphasis on the importance of public *mood.*[127]

The outbreak of new strikes in Gdańsk and Nowa Huta in May 1988 and in several locations in August 1988 drove home the point that Polish workers still expected change, in fact nothing less than the relegalization of their independent trade union. Lech Wałęsa, the symbolic head of Solidarity, told the striking workers in 1988, "If we do not carry out *perestroika*, if we do not make reforms peacefully together with the nation and with compromises, then we are threatened with a revolution, and a bloody one."[128] A survey conducted by the government's Public Opinion Research Center found that 70 percent of Poles considered the economic situation "bad" or "very bad," and 80 percent considered "the danger of serious social conflicts" as a result of economic failure to be very real.[129]

There has also been a high expectancy of change in Yugoslavia. A Slovenian intellectual told me in 1987 that he expected Yugoslavia to experience dramatic and far-reaching changes around 1990, arguing that by then advocates of change will have gained the upper hand. "The result," he told me, "will be a break with Titoism and its aftermath, a break analogous to and as far-reaching as what the Soviet Union has experienced between 1953 and 1985, i.e., from Stalin's death to the rise of Gorbachev." Not everyone has wanted to wait even that long. A member of the Alternative Movement in Belgrade told me, "Some people are only hoping for change. In the Alternative Movement, we are actively working for change. We hope it will not take another three years before we see fundamental change."

The expectancy of change has been arguably only slightly less in Romania, though it is infinitely more difficult to talk about this there than in Poland or Yugoslavia. Typically, articulate malcontents rely on esoteric communication to spread their message. An excellent example of this is an article published on 8 February 1986 in *Luceafărul*, reprinted from the 12 January 1889 issue of a Bucharest daily. The fact that it was addressed to a different era absolved it of the charge of having been *written* to criticize the

Ceauşescu regime. At the same time, the parallels between 1889 and 1986 were clear, revealing the deep expectancy of change in *both* periods. In a crucial passage, the article wonders:

> The problem is whether we are indeed on the eve of events that will bear a decisive influence on the position of the country as a civilized and constitutional state based on modern law and current requirements; whether we do still have the power to strengthen and improve the country's position from within by extensive reforms and other measures related to them . . . or whether the tendencies displayed by adverse groups with outdated aspirations, as well as the glacial egoism of their ambitious policies, will once more raise obstacles on the road to national development. . . . Let us hope that at least in the future and under a new legislation the habit of naming or dismissing officials only on the narrow basis of their political convictions will cease, because all party and personal considerations ought to be dropped in the appointment of state officials, a process that should rest on the interests of impersonal justice.[130]

Likewise, in Hungary there is widespread expectation of change, and just as in Yugoslavia, Hungary became engaged in a wide-ranging debate about reform alternatives.[131] The leading advocate of reform within the establishment was the popular Imre Pozsgay, at one time head of the People's Patriotic Front (PPF) and later a member of the Politburo. Convinced that change is inevitable, Poszgay pushed for an opening up of the system and a partial repluralization of Hungarian society. Pozsgay told a Budapest party meeting in early 1988 that the party would not be able to maintain its "present positions of power and [present] methods." But, he added, "If the party can guide the masses to modernize the country, then it will have the leading role. If not, it won't."[132] The string of workers' strikes in Hungary in summer 1988 and the multiplication of grass-roots initiatives (discussed in chapters 4 and 12) were other dimensions of this expectancy.

There was also a subtle shift in Czechoslovakia, where popular attitudes and behavior perceptibly changed around 1986. In Bulgaria, on the other hand, expectancy of change has been minimal to slight, although by early 1990 Bulgaria also felt the effects of region-wide change. For a while, communists hoped to devise a new approach, a new model: "A new model of socialism is rising up before our eyes," said Oleg Bogomolov, director of the USSR Academy of Sciences Institute of the Economics of World Socialist Systems in 1989.[133]

Table 5   East European Vulnerability to Destabilization
September 1988/November 1989

	Bulgaria	Czechoslovakia	Hungary	Poland	Romania	Yugoslavia	GDR
Economic deterioration	1/1	3/3	3/3	5/5	5/5	4/5	3/3
Mobilization of new groups	1/2	2/2	4/5	5/5	2/2	5/5	3/3
Defection of intellectuals	1/1	4/4	3/5	4/4	4/4	4/5	3/3
Inefficiency & corruption	1/1	3/3	3/3	5/5	5/5	4/5	2/2
Loss of credibility	1/2	3/3	2/5	5/5	5/5	3/5	4/5
Loss of self-confidence among elite & factionalization	0/1	3/3.5	3/5	4/5	4/4	3/5	2/5
Inept use of force	0/0	0/0	0/0	1/3	0/0	0/1	0/2
Expectancy of change	1/3	2/4	3/5	5/5	2/3	5/5	1/5
Score 1988:	0.8	2.5	2.6	4.3	3.4	3.5	2.3
Score 1989:	1.4	2.8	3.9	4.6	3.5	4.5	3.5

Key
5 = extremely serious
4 = serious
3 = partial
2 = slight
1 = minimal
0 = not detectable

Conclusion

This chapter has attempted to assess certain pressures for change in Eastern Europe and, in the process, to weigh the individual countries' vulnerability to destabilization on the eve of the Great Transformation. The results
are shown in table 5, where I have assigned numerical values to the degree
of vulnerability with respect to each of the eight factors examined. Though
these values do not have quantitative significance, I hope they are useful as

qualitative measures of tangible differences, including differences of degree. The average scores for each country are thus *indicative* values that summarize the trends across the eight values. In computing this average, no effort has been made to give greater weight to one factor over another, even though some factors are clearly more important than others. I have assigned two values in each case: the first reflects the situation in September 1988 and the second reflects the situation in November 1989. I have also added estimates for East Germany, although the discussion of that country is reserved for the next chapter.

The result is a picture which is quite differentiated. Poland, with a mean score of 4.3 in 1988, ranked between "serious" and "extremely serious" in terms of vulnerability to destabilization. The introduction of a coalition government in summer 1989 reflected that vulnerability but as of November 1989 the Polish system was not yet "in the clear." Yugoslavia and Hungary are the next most vulnerable, with Yugoslavia's failure to deal with its internal political problems making it extremely vulnerable. By contrast, while the reform wing of the ruling party in Hungary moved quickly to deal with the situation, because the expectancy of further change was high, the leadership was no longer able to control the process of change. At *this* point, Hungary's overall vulnerability to destabilization is now lower than Yugoslavia's. East Germany and Romania end up with the same average score (3.5), even though the situations in those countries were very different. In Czechoslovakia, vulnerability is "partial" (2.8). History has proven that these levels of vulnerability are quite sufficient. And finally, Bulgaria, with a mean score of 1.4, seemed to show only slight vulnerability to destabilization. Regardless of the precise numbers, in all seven countries, vulnerability to destabilization and the pressure for (further) change increased between 1988 and 1989.

The tempo of change in Eastern Europe has been quickened by another factor, what Fred Riggs has called the *diffraction* of social systems.[134] In a word, what it signifies is that the old social equilibrium is breaking down, and social life is fragmenting. In the political arena, this means the multiplication of discussion clubs, samizdat publications, even political clubs and parties. In the religious sphere it means a weakening of some of the traditional churches, typically with neo-Protestant groups as the chief beneficiaries, and the appearance of guru cults, Hare Krishnas, satanists, and other fringe sects. In the social sphere it means a restructuring of both gender and generational relations, with women and youth assuming different orientations toward the community and increasingly willing to organize autonomous groupings. In the musical sphere it means the fragmentation of musical taste and associated cultural suppositions and the fostering of an epidemic of subcultural currents including new wave, punk, heavy metal, and skags. And in high politics it signifies the passing of a generation: gone is the time when the cult of the personality could go unchallenged and from 1985 to late 1990 the Soviets themselves led the way with calls for new political thinking, assailing the fetishization of slogans.[135] The *ancien régime* is dead.

II Dissent and Parallel Society
in the 1980s

2 Disaffection and Dissent in East Germany

Fools, you search my suitcases!
You won't find anything hidden there!
The contraband I bring with me
Is in my head.
—Heinrich Heine, *Deutschland:*
Ein Wintermärchen

Communism traced deviance, disaffection, and dissent alike to alienation and presocialist forms of consciousness. Insofar as the building of communism was expected to bring about an end to exploitation and alienation, deviance, disaffection, and dissent should disappear with them. The persistence of disaffection and articulate dissent, as well as crime, delinquency, and social deviance generally, represented a failure of socialization and thus a failure of the system to live up to its own expectations. Communist regimes tended to be anxious, therefore, to deny the existence of crime, to expel dissenters, and to curb social deviance. Dissent and deviance were troubling in yet another respect: insofar as Marxism aspired to eliminate social conflict and traced it to differences in social or class interest, dissent and deviance may be taken to reflect the persistence of differences in perceived interest, whether "objectively" rooted in class differences or not.

Dissent has therefore been a central issue for communist systems and has accordingly been amply discussed in Western scholarship. Disaffection as an analytical category has been far less amply treated,[1] though, as I shall argue, it is as great a concern to communist regimes as is dissent. We may begin by drawing distinctions among the chief terms at issue.

Technically, *dissatisfaction* may be seen as discontent with the way in which certain parts of the system operate or with certain policies of the regime, without necessarily calling into question the legitimacy or optimality of the system. Hence, for example, when East Germany ran short of basic foodstuffs in late 1982, workers in Dresden went on strike and shouted, "We demand better supplies! We want meat and vegetables!"[2] The workers were clearly dissatisfied, and clearly blamed the authorities, but their protest, although of political importance, could scarcely be called "dissent."

By contrast, *disaffection* may be defined as discontent with the system itself without necessarily entailing a belief in one's ability to change the system, but possibly being expressed in social nonconformism or deviance. The pilferage of socialist property in Czechoslovakia has been a highly popular form of protest since the establishment of the communist regime there;[3] it reflected more than mere dissatisfaction, for pilferage was intended as a form of revenge against the system itself. Still, such activity would not ordinarily qualify as dissent.

Finally, there is *dissent* itself, which may be defined as discontent with the system, charged by belief in one's ability to effect change, however gradual or slight, and implying an external standard by which the system's performance is evaluated. The external standard is, of course, the heart of the matter and constitutes the core of the threat posed by dissenters to communist regimes. Obviously, all dissenters are disaffected and all disaffected are dissatisfied; but not all those dissatisfied are disaffected and not all those who qualify as disaffected are dissenters.

There are several reasons for broadening our focus to include not merely dissent but also disaffection:

(1) Disaffection is the seedbed from which dissent sprouts;
(2) It is both a broader and a more accurate measure of the problems, tensions, and dilemmas of a society;
(3) Both dissenting disaffection and nondissenting disaffection can have political consequences—the latter insofar as it engenders apathy, antisocial attitudes and behavior, and antiregime sympathies; and
(4) Disaffection is a more useful measure than dissent of the failure or limits of political socialization because it embraces a much larger portion of the population.

Disaffection may be expressed in different ways. Those disaffected may assert their potency to effect change and adopt a posture of dissent. Alternatively, they may conclude that they are unable to effect change in society and may resign themselves in a spirit of studied apathy. Finally, there is a middle ground in which they may tune out the regime and drop out, becoming in some sense deviant. Deviants may retreat into a counterculture such as punk rock, which will in turn sustain their deviance and reinforce their disaffection. Social deviance may thus reflect a fundamental rejection of the dominant values of the society—in this case, the official political culture of Marxism-Leninism—and East Germany's Socialist Unity Party (SED) accordingly viewed social deviance with consternation. It is for this reason that, as Paul Shapiro has noted, communist regimes treated dissenters as deviants;[4] it is equally true that communist regimes tended to treat deviants as potential dissenters.

There were four basic sources of disaffection in the German Democratic Republic (East Germany) in the 1980s:

(1) As resocialization failed, the population became susceptible to alternative cultures (such as Christianity or punk rock) that crystallized doubts about the system and reinforced disaffection by providing independent criteria for assessing the system.

(2) Specific policy shortcomings, insofar as they were viewed as both systemic and endemic to the system, could spark disaffection and dissent. The militarization of East German education, persistent abuses of human rights, environmental problems, neglect of women's rights, and lingering discontent among the small Slavic Sorb population could be grouped in this class.

(3) Marxism itself may have been a stimulus to disaffection and dissent as socialization instilled values that the regime flouted. The political radicalism of Robert Havemann and Rudolf Bahro, for example, stemmed from their acceptance of Marxist premises.

(4) the gradual economic erosion of the "East German economic miracle"[5] obviously resulted in growing discontent with the regime's capacity to "deliver."

These sources are of different character, weight, and importance. Categories 1 (the failure of resocialization) and 3 (the relative success in instilling new values) are attitudinal. The former affects members of society from diverse sectors, the latter becomes articulate only in the hands of intellectuals. The other two sources reflect regime performance, that is, specific policy shortcomings (category 2) and stagnation or erosion in economic performance (category 4). Policy shortcomings may affect only a particular group within East German society (e.g., the Sorbs) or may have a wider impact (though the environmentalist case reminds us that wider impact does not necessarily translate into wider concern). The effects of economic performance, on the other hand, are felt by the entire spectrum of society and thus have the capacity to excite other latent sources of disaffection—as the Polish case demonstrates quite clearly. Indeed, although any of these sources can play a catalytic role, the economic factor is perhaps the most potent. Hence, by converse logic the regime has hoped to "buy" political conformity.

Discussion of these several sources of disaffection invites a further observation. Insofar as we may find it useful to describe a society as passing through sequential or overlapping crises of identity, legitimacy, participation, distribution, and penetration[6] and, under certain conditions, to speak of a reversal of the developmental process and the onset of political decay, we may expect to find that the strength and importance of any given source of disaffection—as a category, and not merely in terms of specific instances —will vary from phase to phase, and that these categories will play different roles in different crises. Certain kinds of disaffection may be more easily contained in certain developmental phases, and more apt to be translated into dissent in others. For the regime this may signify that policy invariability, which communist parties perfervidly claimed to practice until Gorbachev's arrival on the scene, may be worse than an illusion: it may be a positive weakness. The whole point of *perestroika* was to adapt policies to changing conditions.

I propose to probe each source of disaffection, to come to a preliminary assessment of the pervasiveness, depth, and importance of disaffection in each category, to examine the extent to which disaffection has translated itself into dissent, and to estimate the untapped sources of dissent in each category of disaffection. The last of these four tasks will necessarily involve a degree of speculation. Finally I shall argue that, far from leading to the transcendence of alienation and the extirpation of disaffection, communist socialization and policy in East Germany multiplied the sources of disaffection and deepened the potential for dissent.

The Failure of Socialization

Communist systems may be understood in part as political engines for cultural transformation and resocialization. The dominant themes of East German resocialization were the superiority of socialism, the identification of socialism with peace, the need for unity among "progressive" forces, antinationalism, secularization, and anti-individualism.[7] Connected with the themes of both socialist superiority and antinationalism was the eventually abandoned effort to instill a concept of a "socialist German nationality" distinct from "bourgeois German nationality," linked to the broader policy of *Abgrenzung*.[8]

The steady erosion in the numerical strength of the Christian churches could be counted as a kind of "success" for SED policy, and some Western scholars even concluded that East Germans and West Germans were drifting apart in national consciousness.[9] Even these successes, however, were compromised by the very tangible resilience of the Evangelical church and its active role in both the independent peace movement and environmentalist concerns,[10] by continuing signs of identification among East and West Germans, and by continuing contacts between citizens of the two Germanys —for example, between the antiestablishment Green Party in West Germany and antiestablishment pacifists in East Germany. Moreover, in a survey authorized by the East German regime, young people overwhelmingly indicated that they viewed themselves as Germans first and as citizens of East Germany second.[11]

In other spheres of SED's resocialization program, the limits were even more tangible. The communist regime tried to foster a kind of *Systemstreue*, but failed to win the trust of the population or even, by some accounts, of the bureaucrats themselves, while the political sympathies of the population clearly lay with social-democratic ideas such as those propagated by the West German Christian Democratic and Social Democratic parties, as the eventual elections of 1990 so dramatically demonstrated. The regime also tried to foster a sense of collective responsibility and ethic and to erode the basis for individualism. Yet, ironically, individualism never flourished in East Germany as it did in the late 1980s, whether one looks to the withdrawal and consumerism of the working and middle classes or to the rejectionism and headlong assertive individualism of those youths caught up in the East German rock scene.[12]

The persistent flow of disaffected East Germans to the West (including, in 1984, the request for political asylum in West Germany by five relatives of East German Premier Willi Stoph),[13] the outspoken remonstrations by articulate East German intellectuals such as Wolfgang Harich, Robert Havemann, and Rudolf Bahro, and the continued incarceration of some 3,000 political prisoners in East Germany (as of April 1989)[14] are probably the best-known reflections of the limitations of East Germany's resocialization efforts. Equally troubling to the SED was its inability to control crime. In Marxist-Leninist thought, crime reflects social alienation, which is possible only in pluralist societies ("capitalism") or among persons retaining pluralist ideas ("bourgeois vestiges"). Unfortunately for adherents of this theory, crime was most prevalent among precisely that group which had been nurtured entirely under the socialist system, the youth. After the crime rate had risen for the fifth straight year in 1973, the SED stopped publishing crime statistics.[15] Alcoholism remained a persistent problem (linked to 30–32 percent of violent crimes) and arbitrary assaults by young "rowdies" rose dramatically. By spring 1980 the crime level was so high that East German authorities admitted that East German crime was rising tangibly.[16]

But whereas crime, alcoholism, and rowdyism represent inchoate forms of disaffection reflecting the failures of socialization in its *social* aspect, antiregime activity represents a more focused and more dangerous strain of disaffection reflecting the failures of socialization in its *political* aspect. In mid-1977, for instance, several hundred East German youths burned the blue shirts of the youth league (Free German Youth, FGY) in Pankow. Later, in October 1977 a rock concert degenerated into an anti-Soviet demonstration when eight people became trapped in a ventilation shaft. The crowd (some 500 youths) shouted "Russians get out!" and "Germany awake!" (*Deutschland erwache!*—an old Nazi slogan). Police used water cannons and batons to suppress the youth.[17]

More than a decade ago a Western observer could write that East German youth could no longer conceive of any alternative to the system established by the SED.[18] Recently, however, the generational gap in East Germany acquired acute political overtones, and the party itself eventually admitted that university students were fed up with the steady doses of required ideological training.[19] Three important catalysts of the estrangement of the youth may be mentioned—the rock counterculture, the militarization of society spawned by the SED, and the consequent attraction of the Christian churches as alternative foci of institutional loyalty.

Rock music will be discussed separately in chapter 9, but a few observations may be made in this chapter. First, rock lyrics have displayed a consistent and unmitigated *subjectivity*, refusing to cater to political parties or programs (East Germany's Dean Reed was an uncommon exception to this rule). As a result, rock lyrics have tended to be either egocentric or critical of social policy. Indeed, one of the roots of East German pacifism is the "make love not war" ethic associated with Bob Dylan, Donovan, and Joan Baez in the late 1960s. Even then the regime worried about the effects of their protest songs, and dance clubs that played too much protest music were reprimanded. Indigenous groups began to imitate the protest genre, however, and in 1965, at a performance of the Leipzig rock group Butlers, young people clashed with police and several were arrested.[20]

Second, the SED has feared that rock music, and especially disco music, reinforces tendencies toward individualism by accentuating private feelings and dramatizing individual perceptions. Rather than concentrating on relations between the sexes, disco music should be programmed to "contribute . . . to the development of socialist personalities by linking entertainment, sociability, topical information, and education."[21]

With Erich Honecker's accession to power and East Germany's eventual garnering of diplomatic recognition from most states in the international community in the early 1970s, East German youth hoped that the authorities would at last try to live up to their high-sounding ideals. In reflection of this hope, rock groups such as the Renft Combo became bolder in their lyrics. Renft, for instance, took up the subject of conscientious objection in its songs. The regime was not disposed to tolerate a proliferation of protest, however, even if "disguised" as musical diversion, and banned the Renft Combo in 1974. The banning of the prominent rock group was widely interpreted to signify that rock groups should eschew "negative" political themes. The subsequent expulsion of singer Wolf Bierman in 1976 seemed to confirm the accuracy of this interpretation.

Faced with the uncomfortable fact that young people were gravitating toward rock music and that regime hostility to rock music would only deepen the disaffection of youth, the SED decided in 1976 to loosen up strictures on dance clubs and to allow the establishment of carefully monitored discotheques. Under the guidance of the Ministry of Culture, "disco moderators" received training in ideology, and district academies conducted disco workshops. The communist regime watched East German rock groups closely, fearing not merely insidious political criticism but also the "moral decay" promoted by subjective individualism and ostentatious vulgarity. Thus, in march 1983 the East German cultural journal *Sonntag* criticized the "vulgar" lyrics of certain East German rock groups, noting that some rock musicians seemed to believe that the more vulgar their lyrics were, the better.[22] Politically provocative lyrics remained more troublesome than mere vulgarity, however, and occasioned the dissolution of the East Berlin rock group Freigang in 1983. The regime's apprehensive posture was balanced by a strategy of trying to channel rock music away from opposition; in an expression of this strategy, the FGY organized a successful rock festival attended by some 4,000 young people in October 1983.[23]

In the 1980s punk counterculture also penetrated the country, and by the mid-1980s a thriving punk rock scene had developed with adherents in all the major East German cities. Punk groups included Abwärts (Downwards), Juckreiz, and Chaiselongue in Magdeburg; Tapetenwechsel (Change of Carpets) and Pankow in East Berlin; Keks; Restbestand (State of Rest) and Ausfluss (Outflow) from Weimar; and Maulsperre (Locked Mouth) from Gera. Maulsperre was banned from giving concerts because of its name.[24] In its more consistent and articulate strains, punk is a species of cultural nihilism, repudiating as a whole all establishment values: the dissident dimension here is obvious. But even in its less articulate strains, punk culture is unmistakenly an antiestablishment pose in which, in the East German context, Marxism-Leninism, the SED, and the entire program of resocialization were rejected as foolish irrelevancies at best. This attitude is aptly captured in the slogan with which East German punks took to adorning public buildings—*"legal, illegal, scheissegal!"*[25] The regime was equally clear about its attitude toward the punk counterculture, which it described as "unmitigatedly hostile" to its program.[26] Students who came to school with multicolored hair and punk fashions were punished by having critical entries made in their permanent academic files; that these entries were intended to block future professional advancement is obvious. The East German security police (colloquially known as the *Stasi*) were likewise mobilized against punk adherents; they broke up punk gatherings in Leipzig of more than 100 persons in March 1981 and of some 400 to 500 punks in July 1982.[27] Ironically, one of the bands which had been scheduled to perform in Leipzig was called Unerwünscht (Unwanted).[28]

Cultural disaffection is the keynote of punk. A nineteen-year-old East German punk put it this way: "Philistinism turns me off. I am against Germanness. The German is, for me, a *petit bourgeois* and a philistine by nature. I am bothered by this whole pretense, by this mask which is there but which no one removes."[29] Disaffection with "this whole pretense" is the substratum underlying punk nihilism and, although it at present constitutes a dropout mentality, it could at some future time be catalyzed into more active dissent. In either case, this species of disaffection obstructed the resocialization program and hindered regime efforts to fashion a "new communist man and woman."

Pacifism and the Churches

As alternative social institutions with alternative value systems, the churches remained potent stimuli of nonsocialist thinking and ideas, sharpening the cognitive dissonance between normative standards and the socialist reality, and thus stimulating disaffection from the communist system. State Secretary for Religious Affairs Klaus Gysi recognized this and noted, in 1981, that "as long as the church remains a church, it must be independent. We are of the opinion that it will, in this fashion, never be fully integrated in our society as a social force."[30] It could not be fully integrated because it was alien to communism and because church and party offered competing value systems. The churches were also recalcitrant when it came to specific desiderata of SED religious policy. Thus, although the regime hoped at one time to reduce the churches to carrying out liturgical functions, neither the Evangelical churches nor the Catholic church was willing to accept this role.[31] Through the mouthpiece of the Christian Democratic Union–East (CDU-East), the regime urged at one time that "we Christian Democrats can ... only fulfill our social obligation if we penetrate even deeper into Marxism-Leninism and use Christian faith and atheism —as the instrument of our social work."[32] Neither church embraced this approach. Finally, the regime defined the terms of policy so that *by definition* the regime was a peace movement, the only pacifism worthy of the name was that which supported the regime, critical distance was disloyalty, and disaffection was the breeding ground of opposition. Instead of accepting the practice of "policy by definition," the Evangelical church, under the influence of the World Council of Churches, the Lutheran World Federation, and the Conference of European Churches, spoke out on the subject of peace with increasing frequency after 1968 and, although in 1981 the government threatened action unless the Evangelical church toned down its criticism and severed contacts with West German Evangelicals, the church refused to comply and became even more active in its engagement in public discussion of the theme of peace.[33] The Catholic church's approach to the subject of pacifism has been far more low-key, but the Catholic bishops did address the subject in a pastoral letter of 2 January 1983 condemning the militarization of East German life.[34]

Both the fledgling independent peace movement and church involvement in it must be traced to the steady militarization of East German society. From the beginning, the SED held that pacifism under socialism is "objectively" antipacifism.[35] Beginning in September 1978, ninth- and tenth-graders participated in formal "premilitary" training, which included a two-week period of intensive training at the end of the school year. Nursery school children were taught to sing songs about army life and to play martial games. In fourth grade, sports instructors introduced marching and military formation. In sixth and seventh grades, students took part in maneuvers organized by the Young Pioneer Organization in cooperation with officers of the National People's Army (NVA): in sports classes, these students were trained in the use of hand grenades and ran obstacle courses similar to those used in military basic training. In eighth grade, students began special military sports exercises that included the firing of hand arms and hand grenades, rope climbing, first aid, and air defense. Since 1 September 1981 premilitary and ambulance training were also obligatory for all eleventh-graders, with special twelve-day summer sessions. Beginning on 1 December 1981, all East German citizens between the ages of 18 and 65 were obliged to participate in civil defense training exercises, which often involved whole sections of a city.[36]

The accompanying sharpening of hostile stereotypes of the West provoked sharp reaction from Evangelical and Catholic clergy alike. In a series of sermons published in early 1982, for instance, Catholic bishop Joachim Wancke of Erfurt criticized the overemphasis on defense and defense readiness and the habituation of students to think in terms of *enemies*. Bishop Wancke also advocated the institution of a civil service alternative to military service—an idea increasingly popular among East Germany's disaffected.[37] Meanwhile, in April 1981 the "Church and Society" committee of the Evangelical church convoked a congress on the theme "Peace Today," and invited all interested persons to attend, in order to bring together for the first time the previously isolated groups and individuals in East Germany concerned with peace. Pacifist consciousness swelled, and between late 1981 and early 1982 small groups of pacifists appeared in many East German cities. In late 1981 young pacifists planned a peace demonstration to be held at the wreckage of the Frauenkirche in Dresden on the anniversary (13 February 1982) of the bombardment of Dresden. News of the demonstration spread by word of mouth (*Buschfunk*), and the church leadership in Saxony, fearing that the event could lead to open confrontation with the authorities, decided to coopt the demonstration and to try to keep it "within limits." Although only one short notice appeared in a local newspaper, *Buschfunk* worked well enough to turn out some 5,000 young people from all over the country. Many others were prevented from attending by police, who headed off many young people on their way to Dresden and who ordered some known pacifists to stay at home that day. At Dresden, speakers demanded the introduction of obligatory "peace education" in the schools, and in the months that followed, similar peace forums were held in Potsdam, Eisenach, and Burg (Spreewald), drawing in a total of more than 10,000 young people.[38]

The Reformed (Calvinist) church likewise took up the pacifist theme, and on 9 November 1982 issued a declaration to the effect that peace is a central question for the church, standing at the very center of the Gospel message.[39]

The Evangelical church has sponsored various lectures, discussions, and seminars on peace throughout the country and for the past several years has sponsored a ten-day annual peace conference. It called for arms negotiations in good faith, asked the Soviets to destroy some of their ss-20 missiles, and criticized the militarization of East German society. By April

1982 the SED regime decided that the emerging peace movement constituted a political opposition and banned the "swords into ploughshares" shoulder patch that had become the emblem of the movement; far from buckling under, however, the peace movement established contacts with the antiestablishment Green Party of West Germany. By the end of 1983 the regime was bent on isolating and emasculating the pacifist groups. Well over 100 East German pacifists were arrested during 1983, and many of these were summarily expelled from the country.[40]

The rising tide of pacifism could only be encompassed within the church since unregistered discussion groups were permitted only on church premises. The result was the steady spread of such groups, generally numbering five to eighty members, based in all the larger cities. Taken collectively, between 30 and 50 percent of group members were not Christian.[41] Of the groups themselves, some were genuinely church groups, while others were essentially secular groups which simply wanted to use church facilities. Some members of these groups were even openly hostile to the church.[42]

In spite of the invigorated opposition of these groups, the SED continued with its program of militarizing East German society, overhauling the educational system in the kindergarten in September 1985. Until then, kindergarten classes had stressed themes of friendship and solidarity; now, in common with other grades, kindergartens stressed the heroic role of the East German military and hatred of the "class enemy."[43] The program passed by the regime specifically noted that "the children should know that the Soviet people are our best friends . . . [and] should experience that there are people who are our enemies and against whom we must fight."[44] This program did not apply, of course, to church-run kindergartens, but for those pupils "friend-foe" thinking began only a year later, when they entered first grade in the state school system.

There have long been currents within the church which have felt that the church has not been bold enough. In June 1987 these currents burst into the open with the staging of an alternative church congress alongside the official church congress being held in East Berlin. Some 1,200 persons, mostly young people, attended this alternative congress and took for themselves the name "church from below." They criticized the church hierarchy for quiescence vis-à-vis the state, and declared that many people no longer felt that their interests were represented by the church. Ironically, the "church from below" in East Germany could not be entirely independent and had to approach Berlin Bishop Gottfried Forck for permission to use church premises to stage their alternative congress.[45]

Tensions in what had become a rather tranquil relationship between the Evangelical church and the state arose in the wake of the September 1986 church synod in Erfurt. In an unprecedented but unsuccessful gambit, the church demanded that there be a public discussion of nuclear energy in light of the nuclear accident in Chernobyl. The synod also tackled the issues of the militarization of education and aspirations for a substitute peace service. State Secretary Gysi actually promised to take up these issues in serious discussions with church leaders, but was evidently overruled, and nothing was done.[46]

Frustrated by their inability to obtain any compromise on matters of importance, church leaders adopted a steadily more critical stance in synods held from 1986 to 1988. A church synod at Görlitz in early June 1988, for instance, criticized the "glaring injustice of the division of our fatherland," called "democratization" the principal problem for East Germany, and volubly bemoaned the failure of the East German regime to adopt Gorbachev's policies of *glasnost* (openness) and *perestroika* (restructuring).[47] At the Halle synod in late June 1988 there were again calls for *glasnost* and *perestroika* in East Germany.[48] Twenty theses for domestic renewal were presented and discussed at that synod. At a church conference at Erfurt, local provost Heino Falcke, an influential voice in the Evangelical church, urged church and state to move beyond the "ritual of self-affirmation and self-appeasement" and to learn to accept criticism.[49] And at a synod in Dessau in mid-September 1988 Evangelical church spokespersons complained of "rash administrative actions and unreasonable decisions" on the part of state authorities, called for greater tolerance for dissident opinion, and urged that East German children be eligible to travel to the West.[50]

These were dangerous ideas in the regime's eyes, and in 1988 and 1989 it repeatedly banned church newspapers which sought to report on the synods. The authorities even banned an issue of the East Berlin paper *Die Kirche* in which the editor had planned to reprint an article on Soviet religious policy from the official Soviet newspaper *Moscow News*.[51]

This reached the point that in summer 1988 East Berlin theologian Richard Schröder wrote an article for the West Berlin journal *Kirche im Sozialismus* in which he criticized the East German church's formula "church in socialism" on the grounds that it suggested "that the church incorporate the theory of socialism in its self-image."[52]

April 1989 became a turning point for ecclesiastical engagement in social critique when, for the first time in East Germany, religious communities of different denominations assembled for an ecumenical conference in Dresden devoted to political questions. The Catholic church departed from previous practice to attend the conference, which was held on 26–30 April. The conference adopted twelve resolutions and, in the body of the text, provided "an account of how the communist party, during 40 years of rule, had succeeded in suppressing all popular initiative and creating a state in which conformity and opportunism were the norm."[53] The authorities were so disturbed by this that even before the conference was over, State Secretary for Church Affairs Kurt Löffler called Bishop Johannes Hempel of Dresden to an urgent meeting at which he told the bishop that he feared that the text would lay the basis for the establishment of an "opposition group." Löffler added that the text would place church-state relations under great strain. But neither the bishop nor the conference was deterred, and the draft text was approved. By September of that year church-state relations were strained as they had not been in years, and *Neues Deutschland* made a rare attack on the Evangelical church, accusing it of playing the role of a "Trojan horse" in East Germany.[54]

Policy Problems and Disaffection

Earlier in this chapter, five specific areas of policy problems were listed: the militarization of East German education and society, persistent abuses of human rights, environmental problems, women's rights, and discontent among the Sorbs. Disaffection with regime policy in these areas spawned groups of anywhere from five to one hundred persons in size, in various medium-sized towns and in all the larger cities. These groups lacked both the formal structure of the Christian churches and the stable behavioral diversions of the disco and punk countercultures. They also lacked, as a rule, an all-embracing *Weltanschauung*, and, in contrast to the disaffected analyzed under category 1 (failure of socialization), they tended to focus on more specific issues. There is, however, a grey area between categories 1 and 2 produced by the merging of some of these groups (specifically the environmental groups and some feminist groups) and the independent peace movement, as well as by the obvious fact that some of the disaffected in this category are active Christians. The impact of the militarization of East German education has already been discussed above.

Human rights issues ranged from conscientious objection and the desire for alternative social service (beyond the construction brigade)[55] to demands for freedom of conscience, association, speech, and assembly, as spelled out in a pamphlet distributed in East Germany in summer 1981. The authors of this pamphlet also called for the release of all political prisoners, a general amnesty, and free elections with free nomination of candidates and secret ballots. Human rights activist Dr. Werner Schädicke, a Leipzig physician, went to prison in 1974 for a six-year term for writing various letters and tracts calling on the regime to honor basic human rights, including the right to emigrate. Günter and Leni Prager and Bernd and Gerdi Sobe similarly received prison terms for transmitting information likely to tarnish the East German image abroad. The Sobes had written to the UN secretary-general and the UN Human Rights Commission about "serious violations of human rights in the GDR." In August 1980 Andreas Koburg received a four-year prison term in Potsdam for having asked the International Committee of the Red Cross to send a delegation to East Germany to inspect prison conditions. In a related case, Dr. Wilhelm Kock, whose concern for human rights in Poland had prompted him to send financial aid to the Polish independent trade union Solidarity, was imprisoned, as were other East Germans who expressed sympathy for Solidarity.[56]

Aside from occasional church sermons and synodal statements, human rights activism in East Germany remained the work essentially of individuals and embryonic groups until 1985. This picture changed slightly in 1985 with the creation of an independent movement called *Menschenrechte DDR* (Human Rights GDR), which sent an open letter to Honecker demanding freedom of speech, assembly, and movement, and freedom from discrimination on the basis of religion or ideology. As of 1986 the group was said to have "well over 100" activists and a larger circle of sympathizers.[57] Much more important—although primarily in terms of raising consciousness and stirring confidence—was the creation of the New Forum in 1989 by a group of intellectuals that included Bärbel Bohley and Sebastian Pflugbeil. With aspirations to promote democracy, the New Forum quickly registered thousands of supporters.[58]

From time to time the East German regime had recourse to expulsion as a way of dealing with human rights dissent. For example, in January and February 1988 the regime expelled a number of activists, including folk balladeer Stephan Krawczyk and his wife Freya Klier, and several members of the Peace and Human Rights group who produced the samizdat publication *Grenzfall*.[59]

The situation of the Sorbs is a specific human rights issue. Following the model of Soviet nationalities policy, East German policy toward the Sorbs was supportive in some respects and antagonistic in others. A Sorbian cultural movement, the Domowina, was reestablished with the blessing of Soviet occupation authorities in 1945, but in the mid-1950s, under SED pressure, the Domowina endorsed industrialization and collectivization in Sorb-inhabited Lusatia—measures that were very unpopular among the

Sorbs. As a result, the membership strength of the Domowina waned thereafter.[60] Despite the Sorbian-language instruction in kindergartens, primary and secondary schools, vocational schools, and business academies —supplemented by the Slavonic Institute of the Academy of Sciences of the GDR in Berlin, and the Sorbian Institute for Teacher Training and the Sorbian Ethnological Institute, both in Bautzen—the younger generations increasingly became detached from their own Slavic heritage and viewed themselves as immersed in a "German sea." The prize-winning Sorbian author Jurij Brězan captured some of the spirit of the dilemma in his book *Views and Insights*:

"My literary bilingualism . . . it seems to me very difficult to explain it. My mother tongue is Sorbian. I learned to speak it, the way one learns to speak it in the village. In school we learned the Sorbian alphabet and occasionally took dictation in Sorbian, but never were we assigned to write an essay in Sorbian. Throughout my 14 years in school, the German language was a major subject: here I wrote a hundred essays, read a thousand books—Goethe, Schiller, Lessing, Shakespeare, the Song of the Nibelungen, Cervantes, Zola, Tolstoy were all in German. . . . When I told my sisters stories, and soon after my friends as well, I related the stories in Sorbian. When I tried to write my first story, I wrote it in German. With the girl I loved I spoke Sorbian; when I wrote the first poem for her, I wrote it in German. The spoken word found sufficient room in my mother tongue. . . . The written word . . . could only be built on what I had read.[61]

Interestingly enough, the combination of German cultural engulfment with a general toleration of Sorbian culture[62] and heritage has produced, at least in one respect, an effect very similar among Sorbs to that produced by the civil rights repression among human rights activists—that is, atomization, a failure to organize, and a tendency to deal with the situation as individuals.

As of late 1989 there were nine Sorbian-language schools and eighty-five schools offering instruction in Sorbian in East Germany. There were also ten periodicals and one daily newspaper in Sorbian, one Sorbian-language radio station, and ninety-eight Sorbian mayors.[63]

But by late 1989, stimulated by the general opening up of East German society, Sorbs too became restless. Complaints were heard that the Domowina had not shown "the necessary commitment" to Sorbian welfare, a circumstance explicitly blamed on "political structures."[64] And in November 1989 the national executive of the Domowina convened in Bautzen and discussed proposals to transform the Domowina into an independent organization not beholden to any political party,[65] an eventuality that was inevitable at that point anyway.

The situation is dramatically different with regard to environmental and feminist concerns—probably in part because these have been traditional concerns of pacifists over the years and have thus drawn strength from the groundswell of pacifist sentiment in East Germany, and in part because environmentalism and feminism were "live" issues in West Germany, whereas human rights and Sorbian culture were not. Thus, contacts with West German Greens and other confrontations with the West German example (e.g., on television) could stimulate the former but not the latter (at least not in a straightforward manner).

The environmental issue is serious enough. Environmental destruction is said to be well advanced in five densely populated areas of the country, namely, Halle, Leipzig, Dresden, Karl-Marx-Stadt, and Berlin, and air pollution in Halle, Leipzig, and Zwickau is said to be more than twice the level of that in Chicago, Tokyo, or Düsseldorf. Young people started to become concerned about the environment in the late 1970s. As in the case of the peace movement, Evangelical pastors took the lead in acting as spokespersons for environmental concerns. In 1979 a regional synod at Mecklenburg-Schwerin held discussions on the environmental risks of nuclear power, and in some parishes environmental groups were formed. In November 1979 the first large-scale, volunteer tree-planting event was organized in Schwerin. Since then, annual tree planting and cycling events have figured in various parish programs.[66]

Organizers of tree-planting ventures, at least initially, tended to view their actions as having symbolic and educational rather than practical importance. Through their demonstrative actions they hoped to raise public awareness of the issue, to change public behavior, and to stimulate a dialogue about large-scale remedies to be undertaken at a higher level.[67]

The environmental movement received a major impetus in April 1983 when it succeeded in organizing a meeting in Wittenberg of more than thirty church-linked environmental groups, coming from Rostock, Potsdam, Berlin, Rotha, Leipzig, Dresden, Jena-Neulobeda, Karl-Marx-Stadt, and Naumburg. Two months later, at a synodal meeting in Rostock, the Evangelical church gave vocal expression to these concerns, and on 5 June, the day the regime itself had designated as the "International Day of the Environment," some 200 residents of Halle donned gas masks and rode bicycles through town to protest the pollutant Buna Chemical Works. The demonstrators were soon stopped and fined by security police, and five people, including the popular parson Lothar Rochau of Halle, were arrested.[68] There can be no doubt that in the case of environmental issues, disaffection has been translated into active dissent. Environmentalists demonstrate not merely against pollution but against the government planning that produces it. Moreover, various environmental conferences from 1983 to 1989 took place under the protection of the church and thus, implicitly, in opposition to the regime.

SED policy toward women, like its nationalities policy, followed the Soviet model: in practice this meant that economics rather than politics dictated policy decisions. Hence, although the German communist party had demanded the legalization of abortion as early as 1931, it was not until 1972 that SED legalized it. Similarly, the encouragement of women to enter the labor force and the consequent establishment of large numbers of daycare centers and kindergartens were designed primarily to build the economy rather than to advance women's equality—and in fact, only 30 percent of the SED and 12 percent of the members of the central committee of the SED were women (in the early 1980s).[69] Female participation in the work force was critical to East German productivity, and the East German constitution of 1968 proclaimed the duty as well as the right to work. Yet, although "East German women [were] not entirely happy with their lot,"[70] they lacked an organization to represent their interests—unless, of course, the regime-controlled Democratic Women's Federation of Germany counted as such. But as David Childs notes, the federation's main tasks were "to encourage more women to seek employment outside the home, to convince women of the correctness of the SED's policies, and to support the SED/Soviet line in international organizations."[71]

For all of the continued gender inequality, especially when it came to housework (a phenomenon scarcely unique to East Germany), it took the extension of military conscription to women to mobilize them into political opposition. An unfavorable status quo was tolerable, but a regime-dictated change for the worse was unacceptable and catalyzed inchoate disaffection into active dissent. A group calling itself GDR Women for Peace, led by Bärbel Bohley and Ulrike Poppe, was founded basically to press for recognition of a right to female conscientious objection to service.[72] Further, in autumn 1982 several hundred East German women signed a petition addressed to SED general secretary Erich Honecker protesting female conscription and emphasizing that military service would entail "entirely new duties" that would be "irreconcilable with the concept we have of ourselves." The letter added that the new law had nothing to do with equality since the signatories repudiated "the abstractions of 'enemy' and 'adversary'" and systematic training in "the destruction of human beings."[73] Subsequently, on 17 September 1983 a meeting of East German feminists took place at the Church of the Resurrection in the East Berlin district of Lichtenberg. Some 500 persons attended this first display of organized feminist action. An earlier attempt in 1981 to put together something similar had collapsed.

Clearly, disaffection in this second category had the potential of being translated into active dissent. But just as clearly, disaffection in category 2 was a *less* potent source of dissent than disaffection in category 1. Much of this has to do with the sheer dynamics of the situation. In category 1 there is a substratum of counterculture that provides a vantage point for an *active* orientation toward the system. Christians, like punks, define their roles in the system on the basis of external criteria. In category 2, on the other hand, the genesis is more *reactive*: it is only because the regime carries out a specific policy that individuals become disaffected and contemplate resistance. Because disaffection in this category is more narrowly focused and does not necessarily entail the application of articulated external criteria (such as the Christian moral code), it is both more apt to prove ephemeral and less potent a source of dissent, unless it becomes wedded to other sources of disaffection (as in the symbiosis of environmentalism and pacifism) or the regime provides an impetus by tinkering with the status quo in a fashion viewed as unacceptable (as in the case of female conscription). On a final note here, it might be supposed that the church's role in support of pacifists and environmentalists ought to be analytically comparable—that is, that these supportive activities ought not be listed in separate categories. But on the contrary, although the church's engagement with the peace issue is an organic dimension of its commitment to seeking alternatives to mass murder and violence, and thus a stance derivable from its core values, its support for the environmentalists seems to have a very different source, namely, the traditional role of pastors in representing and articulating the interests of their respective parishes.

Marxism as a Stimulus of Dissent

Marxism-Leninism combines Young Hegelian methodology with a system of empirical and normative theories. The normative element is implicit in the revolutionary project and is proudly admitted by the young Marx in *Economic and Philosophic Manuscripts*, but is stubbornly denied both by the later Marx (beginning with *The German Ideology*) and by the Leninists. The gap between the "ought" and the "is" is bridged by asserting that what is inevitable is progressive and that good communists must therefore work hard to make the inevitable even "more inevitable." This identification of the inevitable with the progressive has in practice also entailed an identification of *actual* policy with *best* policy, and a portrayal of *desired* results as *achieved* results. A disjunction between practice and theory cannot be admitted because this would open the way to considerations of alternative applications and realizations of the theory, thereby undermining the party's political monopoly. So, since "practice is the criterion of truth,"[74] what is true is what is practical, and Marxism-Leninism reverts to the Hegelian identification of the real (under "socialism") with the rational. Until the advent of Gorbachev, Marxist-Leninist systems thus commonly proceeded from positing what *ought* to be the case—no unemployment, classes, ethnic frictions, crime, or religious affiliation except among the elderly—to declaring that this already *was* the case. These strange avowals of utopia engendered widespread disaffection when people perceived the disjunction between what was declared to be and what really was, and also provided a basis for critique (dissent). *Glasnost* was slow to penetrate East Germany, and the SED was slow to admit problems. But when the critic in fact accepts the theoretical premises and the normative baggage of the system, the result is Marxist dissent, the third category in our typology of disaffection and dissent.

Because Marxism is so concerned with achieving economic equality and abolishing classes, this type of disaffection ordinarily rivets on the persistence of social and economic inequality and the existence of distinct classes under socialism. This form of disaffection is not limited to the intelligentsia—though they are the only ones capable of translating it into articulate theories of dissent—but may affect all those who come to feel betrayed by the revolution. This feeling of betrayal is a clue to the fact that this third strain of disaffection does not appear until after the lapse of a certain period of time—long enough to convince the discontented that the system has failed to live up to its promises. Zygmunt Bauman says approximately twenty years must pass before large numbers of people feel betrayed by the revolution—that is, enough time for the second generation to reach maturity, seek its place in the social structure, and discover that distributional equality does not exist.[75]

Given this analysis it could be expected that Marxist dissent would become more thorough and more encompassing as time passed. This is exactly what happened. To move from Harich to Havemann to Bahro is to move from criticism of the application of Marxism to a reassessment of certain central Marxist premises to a systematic examination of the Marxist concept altogether. Khrushchev's revelations about Stalin at the Twentieth CPSU Congress in March 1956 made a deep impression on Wolfgang Harich, a professor of social science in Berlin, and on philosopher Ernst Bloch. They responded by urging the democratization of the party and suggesting unification of the SED and the West German Social Democratic Party (SPD) as a prelude to the reestablishment of a united, neutral Germany. Harich did not question Marx's analysis but believed that the Stalinist model of political development was not merely a perversion of Marxism but might actually impede the development of authentic communist relations within a society. Indeed, the Stalinist endeavor to skip the "capitalist" stage of development represented a deviation from Marxism, and hence it was conceivable to Harich that the pluralist West might achieve "communism" before the collectivist East. Harich organized a group to work for the internal reform of the party, taking into account the contributions of Trotsky, Bukharin, Luxemburg, Kautsky, SPD theorist Fritz Steinberg, and the Yugoslavs. He urged the establishment of workers' councils on the Yugoslav model, a restoration of autonomy for the universities, an emphasis on raising living standards, and the complete abolition of the *Stasi* and the secret trials.[76] He also argued that the *Volkskammer* (Parliament) should be in reality, and not just in myth, the highest legislative organ in the land. Harich was imprisoned for a ten-year term, and Bloch was expelled from the party.

Physicist Robert Havemann gained notoriety in 1962 when he launched a series of lectures in Leipzig and East Berlin, denouncing the SED's ideology as neither dialectical nor materialist. Surprisingly, he was not dismissed from Humboldt University until 1964, after thousands of East German students had heard his lectures. Though he reproached the SED for deviating from Marxism, his dismissal was justified on the grounds that he had "gone beyond productive discussion to the point of radical divergence from the party line and Marxist-Leninist theory."[77] Subsequently, Havemann was expelled from the party, and in 1966 he was removed from the GDR Academy of Sciences. He spent his later years under virtual house arrest and eventually came to the conclusion that the SED had erred in abolishing parliamentary democracy. Havemann would demand the abolition of censorship, the establishment of independent media, and the release of political prisoners.[78] For Havemann, as for Harich, pluralism was not incompatible with Marxism but was in fact presumed by it; that is to say, where the SED had resolved the inner tension within Marx's thought between humanism and organized revolutionary force in favor of revolutionary force and revolutionary transformation, Harich and Havemann clung to the inchoate humanism most amply developed in Marx's early writings. Their critique thus challenged the very heart of the SED system.

Two books smuggled out of East Germany to be published in West Germany in the mid-1970s carried Marxist dissent one step further. In a work published in 1975, Peter Lübbe argued that socialism had become mired in a bureaucratism in which the state dominated and exploited the people, and concluded that a new revolution would be needed to correct the political subversion carried out by the Soviet and East European communist parties.[79] Two years later came the publication of Rudolf Bahro's *The Alternative*.[80] Bahro's critique proceeded at two levels. On the first level Bahro accepted the structure of Marxist analysis and marshaled it to upbraid Soviet-style systems for radical deviation. On the second level he turned a critical eye toward Marxism itself and revised some of its operational principles. Then, having developed a critique on two levels, Bahro moved on to a third level, spelling out his prescription for a Marxist-inspired reform of East European politics.

On the first level Bahro accepted Marx's argument that the transition from "the realm of necessity to the realm of freedom" required the abolition of the division of labor, but argued that this transition was impossible in Soviet-style systems because society under these systems was dominated by an entrenched bureaucratic apparatus. By establishing a political and informational monopoly, this bureaucratic apparatus produced a "false consciousness" that transformed Marxism from a revolutionary methodology into a legitimizing ideology. Indeed, as Hugh Mosely has noted, Bahro's analysis of Soviet-style systems evoked parallels with Marx's so-called Asiatic mode of production, in which the ruling class maintains its rule on the basis of its control of the ideological and administrative apparatus, not on the basis of private property holdings. Communist party rule had not, therefore, brought an end to human alienation, however much it might claim to have done so; it was in fact the chief obstacle to social progress in Eastern Europe. Yet, faithful to Marx, Bahro scorned political pluralism as backward and aspired to eliminate bureaucratic domination by expanding political participation from below in a new "cultural revolution." Since this new cultural revolution would provide a basis for eliminating fundamental social conflict, Bahro accepted the Leninist belief that there would be no need for labor strikes, and preferred to keep strikes illegal.[81]

Bahro looked to the attempted Czechoslovak reforms of 1968 for inspiration and counseled emulation of Yugoslav self-management. For Bahro, the fetishization of the plan did not serve the interests of economic rationality, as was claimed, but rather the political rationality of maintaining hierarchical subordination and party monopoly of the means of production.

On the second level Bahro took a critical look at Marxism itself and identified three fundamental errors. First, Marx and Engels

> profoundly misunderstood the nature of the modern state. It is not epiphenomenal to society; nor will it wither away; nor is it a means for social welfare and political articulation. Rather it is an apparatus with its own hierarchy and set of institutional interests, ruling and dominating the rest of society and in "tendentially antagonistic relationship to the immediate producers."[82]

As a result, the "noncapitalist" path to socialism produced a series of problems not anticipated by Marx, problems different from those he analyzed in nineteenth-century Europe.[83] Second, Marx believed that the elimination of private property and the erection of a system founded on "people's property" would suffice to eliminate alienation: he did not appreciate that even a "people's state" could foster alienation.[84] And third, Marx overestimated the capabilities of the working class, completely failing to perceive its fundamentally conservative and passive character. The working class could *never* dominate a "dictatorship of the proletariat," whereas the revolution is, from the beginning, apt to be administered by a professional elite—the party.[85]

The upshot for Bahro (as he moved to the third level of his analysis) was that the East European political systems were in serious need of restructuring. He proposed the legalization of extraparty opposition in East Germany and elsewhere; the elimination of privileges for governmental and party workers; the greater equalization of wages; the obligatory participation by all functionaries, managers, and intelligentsia in four to six weeks of low-skilled work in their own workplaces annually; the establishment of workers' councils modeled on the Yugoslav experience; and the creation of a multiregime League of Communists to spearhead cultural revolution throughout Eastern Europe. Bahro was thus aware of the tension in Marx between revolutionary force and humanism, but attempted to resolve it at a higher level. This "higher resolution" was of course no less than a challenge to the entire superstructure of Marxism-Leninism, a challenge all the more troubling to the SED because it took Marx as its starting point.[86] Bahro was arrested the day following publication in *Der Spiegel* in August 1977 of one of the chapters of his book. He was tried and convicted of espionage and sentenced to prison for eight years. In late 1979, however, on the occasion of the thirtieth anniversary of the founding of the GDR, he was granted amnesty and deported to the Federal Republic.

What Harich, Havemann, Lübbe, and Bahro have in common is that they had all marshaled Marxism to argue that East Germany had become too Stalinist and that in this way it had betrayed the revolution. A very different tack was taken by East German Stalinists. Although they agreed with the aforementioned Marxist dissidents that the SED had betrayed the revolution (and they routinely denounced the *Verräter am Sozialismus*), they believed that the problem was that East Germany was not Stalinist enough, and looked to the Albania of Enver Hoxha and Ramiz Alia for a contemporary model. The East German Stalinist opposition was active in the late 1970s and early 1980s, and grew to about 500 adherents in 1981, publishing a bulletin called *Der Rote Stachel*. Despite their hard-line attitude, the East German Stalinists have also been defiantly anti-Soviet, and thus presented the SED with an additional challenge. In 1981 eight to ten leading members of this opposition group were arrested, including twenty-eight-year-old Andreas Bortfeldt and thirty-year-old Manfred Wilhelm.[87] At the other extreme, there were reports of the emergence of a new fascist party in 1989, whose members wore Nazi uniforms, desecrated Jewish cemeteries, and celebrated Hitler's birthday.[88]

What strikes one immediately when considering this third category is that the translation from disaffection to dissent entails a challenge to the regime's interpretation and application of Marxism—that is, to both its theory and its praxis. This is a dimension of the practical orientation of Marxism as expressed, for instance, in Marx's famous thesis on Feuerbach, in which he insisted that the real point was to change the world, not to theorize about it.

The authorities seem to be particularly concerned about this form of dissent because it threatens to create splits within party ranks, to divide the ideology—sowing doubts and creating cracks in which a new form of pluralism might take root and diluting the fundamental operational code of political control. Marxist dissenters bring no external criteria to bear; on the contrary, they use the criteria internal to the official ideology to create an alternative to that ideology. Marxist dissent thus strikes at the very heart of the Marxist-Leninist system.

Economic Discontent as a Source of Dissent

The fourth and final category of sources of disaffection is economic performance. East Germans' expectations had been raised both in absolute terms, by the economic boom of the 1960s, and in relative terms, by the ideology of equality. Partly as a result of the general world recession and partly as a function of the structural limits to East Germany's developmental capacity and economic reforms, economic growth rates began to sag in the mid-1970s. East German planners adopted the solution of increasing imports of Western technology and goods in the effort to upgrade capital stock and reverse the economic slowdown. Instead, the debts spiraled and added to the pressures on the economy. East Germany's hard-currency debt to noncommunist countries rose steadily from $1.4 billion in 1970 to $4.8 billion in 1975, $11.6 billion in 1980, and $12.8 billion in 1982. By 1982 it had tallied the largest trade deficits in the Eastern bloc, and 40 percent of its hard-currency earnings went to servicing its debts.[89]

Meanwhile, disturbances in world oil and gas markets in 1978 and 1979 triggered a Western recession, which in turn resulted in an across-the-board drop in the demand for all East European exports except fuel. East German growth rates in national income, gross industrial output, and gross agricultural output were slashed by an average of 40 percent within seven years (1975–82), and nervous East German bankers repeatedly tried to reschedule their debts to the West, only to be turned down. Although East Germany recorded increases in growth rates in national income and industrial production in 1983, and even trimmed back energy consumption by 7 percent, East Berlin's planners were faced with rising unemployment and had to impose a drastic reduction in investments and imports in 1984, with a consequent negative impact on living standards.[90] Ordinary East German citizens routinely complained in the late 1980s that their standard of living was seriously deteriorating, and pointed to shortages of staple commodities.

The East German decision makers responded to these pressures by shifting their trade to the USSR (with whom East Germany conducted an estimated 40 percent of its foreign trade in 1985) and by turning to private entrepreneurs (granting some 30,000 licenses to start private businesses between 1976 and 1982). They were not, however, able to make headway against unemployment, and some East German workers came to interpret the dual-tier pricing system, wherein basic necessities were extremely cheap but other items exceedingly expensive, as supportive of a rigid class system in which the modestly paid workers lacked access to luxury goods except through black market dealings.[91] In 1977 this policy led to worker protests and strikes, after Honecker opened up the hard-currency Intershop chain to East Germans. Since the workers had no guaranteed access to Western currency, the move clearly favored the elite. In one district in East Berlin, workers protested vehemently, forcing the closure of one Intershop outlet. Elsewhere, striking workers demanded to be paid in hard currency. In other instances East German workers struck to protest the substitution of an inferior coffee blend for a preferred one, or to object to other irregularities in commodity supplies. Later, in summer 1981, stimulated by developments in Poland, East German workers in at least five cities staged strikes and clashed with police. Seven workers from four industrial enterprises were arrested for discussing ways of democratizing the East German trade union on the model of Solidarity, and, in response, a group of East German malcontents drew up a manifesto calling on East German workers to revolt and establish democratic rights of free speech and free assembly.[92] Traditional anti-Polish sentiment provided some insulation against contagion from Poland, and this was reinforced by some resentment over East German supplies to Poland to tide it through its period of economic chaos,[93] but the striving for democratization has a life of its own, and anti-Polish prejudice could not undermine its attraction in the long run.

By late 1982 supplies of meat, lard, milk, and vegetables were so unreliable that workers went on strike in Dresden, Boehlen, Espenhain, and in Premnitz, where factory managers used police to stop the demonstration.[94] The authorities admitted to being able to correct only 80 percent of the supply shortcomings, but enacted stiffer measures to deal with unofficial public gatherings, especially where young people were concerned.[95] There were credible and confirmed reports in January 1983 of an attempted assassination of Honecker that month. The regime's haste to deny these reports, offering in their place a strange and not very believable account of how a shot happened to be fired, betrayed a curious insecurity suggestive of latent vulnerabilities.[96]

After economic reverses in 1983 the East German economy rebounded in 1984 with a record growth of 5.5 percent in social product, exceeding the plan by 1.1 percent.[97] Economic performance in 1985 and 1986 seemed strong too, but there were some danger signs, and in 1987 economic growth was reportedly 0.9 percent less than planned.[98] In real terms the East German economy registered no growth at all in 1987, and some 80 percent of its industrial trusts failed to meet their output targets. In 1988 the government reported 3.0 percent economic growth, but for the fourth straight year the actual rate of growth was less than the planned target.[99] In order to make payments on its foreign debt East Germany diverted resources from domestic investment and industrial modernization; much of its industrial machinery had become obsolescent and susceptible to frequent breakdowns. By 1988 East Germany had slipped from its earlier position as the world's tenth leading industrial power to twenty-sixth place. Meanwhile, its agricultural sector also ran into trouble, and authorities began to search for ways to stimulate agricultural production.[100]

There are four preconditions for the translation of economic disaffection into widespread dissent: (1) a general perception of the situation as a problem (by comparison with past performance, performance in other countries, or promises held out by the leadership); (2) a widespread belief that the political elite is responsible for the problem and that it must be opposed (or even overthrown); (3) a diffuse hope; and (4) a belief in one's ability to effect change in one's own condition (sometimes called a "sense of political efficacy"). By late 1989 all four conditions existed in East Germany, although some members of the opposition worried that the opening of the Berlin Wall and the liberalization of travel might sufficiently calm the population so that the wind might be taken out of the sails of the movement for democracy.[101]

The Transformation of East German Dissent

In January 1988 East German authorities arrested at least seventy of the country's leading political activists, expelling them to West Germany. Those who remained were demoralized. Some feared that the authorities had broken the back of East German dissent. Almost exactly a year later, East German police were again arresting independent activists (and again in Leipzig). The police searched several apartments and confiscated various books and other materials. But this time the mood was different. Through all the difficulties imposed on them, including the expulsion of some of their most prominent adherents, independent activists had managed to continue their work and were increasingly encouraged first by Gorbachev's *perestroika* and subsequently by events in Hungary and Poland.

Much of what was occurring in East Germany in 1988 and 1989 remained below the surface—until the dramatic flight of 225,000 East Germans to the West forced the world and the authorities to take note. But disaffection was increasingly translated into dissent, as new opposition groups were founded. By August 1989 there were more than 500 grass-roots opposition groups in East Germany, including pacifist, environmentalist, democratic, and countercultural groups, and on 13 August representatives of these groups announced that they would establish a nationwide movement.[102]

Out of this initiative was born the New Forum, a group founded by Bärbel Bohley and Sebastian Pflugbeil among others and conceived as a pressure group for dialogue rather than as an embryonic political party. Within little more than a month, New Forum had 4,000 adherents. By mid-October, two weeks later, it had some 25,000 adherents. On 24 September opposition groups throughout East Germany decided that New Forum would be an appropriate vehicle to serve as an umbrella organization for dissent.[103]

Meanwhile, other opposition groups continued to arise, most prominently: the Citizens' Movement for Democracy Now (established in August or September), Democratic Awakening (established in September), and the reborn Social Democratic Party (established in October).[104] The creation of these groups reflected the broad transformation of the political mindset of East Germans in the course of the late 1980s. But that story belongs more properly to chapters 13 and 14, and will be taken up there.

Conclusion

Although disaffection and dissent are organically related, they remain analytically distinct phenomena. In functionalist terms one might say that, although disaffection serves the "negative" functions of creating a critical distance between the disaffected and the regime, and of undermining socialized expectations and behavioral patterns (the repudiation of military service, workers' strikes, and punk rock all reflecting different kinds of erosion of socialized behavior), the functions of dissent may be seen as "positive." These functions are: (1) the articulation and expression of the meaning of disaffection; (2) critical opposition to the regime and the defense of the right to think differently; (3) presentation of an alternative information source (in this regard the Evangelical church's mini-"think tanks" on disarmament and peace education served "dissenting" functions within East Germany); and (4) the demonstration of an alternative model.

The differing sources of disaffection are translated into dissent in different ways. Disaffection in category 1 (failure of socialization) is associated with countercultural options and has available transitory or stable institutional resources. It is thus likely to give rise to forms of institutional or "countercultural" dissent. Disaffection in category 2 (policy shortcomings) is apt to provoke discussion among affected persons and lead to forms of group dissent through emergent ad hoc groups of varying sizes. Disaffection in category 3 (Marxist revisionism) carries great risks for the person who speaks out publicly. The state ideology was the state's preserve and it did not allow individuals to chart their own courses through the Marxist-Leninist corpus, let alone challenge the SED interpretation in public. Disaffection in this category is therefore likely to be translated into individual dissent. And finally, disaffection in category 4 (economic malaise) showed that it has had the potential of being translated into social dissent, widespread protest, and even (for that matter) social disintegration.

Of course, the translation of disaffection into dissent is not automatic; if it were, the analytical distinction would break down and the two would have to be seen as, at most, two phases in a single phenomenon. The translation of disaffection into dissent requires several factors, however, among which are hope, the emergence of an alternative vision, a sense of political efficacy, and, often, a "trigger," whether a policy reversal on the part of the regime or a situational change.

Dissent as resistance to accepted or imposed social and political norms may arise in any society; the more narrowly those norms are defined, the broader the scope of dissent. Hence, the very approach taken by monocratic-dogmatic systems like that of the SED tends to subsume larger areas of activity under the term "dissent." But even given this point of departure, the SED hoped, in consonance with its Leninist presumptions, to extirpate both alienation and disaffection altogether, and in this way to banish dissent, except as an epiphenomenon of mental derangement. I have argued above that in fact SED policy multiplied the sources of disaffection and deepened the potential for dissent. The militarization of society produced a critical backlash, especially among youth, and consequently the Evangelical church became increasingly involved both in this area and in environmental concerns. Antinationalism has not worked and has only produced estrangement from the system, and after late 1982 the SED completely reversed this policy and belatedly set about to reclaim its past—Friedrich the Great, Martin Luther, Prussia, and so on.[105] In a related area East Germany's obvious subordination to the USSR, its participation in the 1968 invasion of Czechoslovakia,[106] and its fawning endorsement of the Soviet invasion of Afghanistan rankled German pride and excited anti-Russian sentiments that remained close to the surface. The ideology of equality encouraged workers to expect real equality and fostered disaffection in its absence. Marxism itself proved to be a potential seedbed for oppositional thought and opened new vistas for dissent. And finally, the generally repressive approach taken by the SED actually stimulated social deviance and dissent, whether one looks at the effect of political impotence in stimulating egocentric individualism both in supportive (acquisitional) and antagonistic (punk) guises, the politicization of counterculture produced by regime intolerance of either Christianity or punk, or the resistance engendered by human rights violations. In short, the effect of the SED's policy responses to disaffection and dissent turned out to be precisely the opposite of what it aspired to achieve.

Disaffection posed a curious and ambiguous threat to the SED and therefore proved in some ways more complex an issue than dissent. In 1989 East Germany was engulfed in a tidal wave of *disaffection*, not dissent. The increase of organized dissent was symptomatic of widening disaffection but, to a large extent, followed in its wake. Disaffection thus fueled popular pressure, which has been the engine of change in Eastern Europe.

3 Underground Solidarity and Parallel Society in Poland

The concept *parallel society*, like its surrogates *independent society* or *alternative society*, presupposes an *official society* to which it is parallel. The terms may be applied to any society but they will assume different meanings in different political contexts. In the West, if one were to speak of parallel society or alternative society, one might think of the rock counter-culture (perhaps especially of punk and heavy metal), drugs, prostitution, organized crime, and other collective behavior which defies the dominant culture and norms or seeks to evade the authorities. In Eastern Europe (at least until very recently) not only have there been official channels and institutions, but there was also an official culture as well as a strict definition of legitimate collective action. Accordingly, collective behavior which defied official culture and official norms *ipso facto* had to defy or evade the authorities.

Parallel society in this sense is a living part of any society. Its breadth varies in inverse proportion to the breadth of allowable open activity: where the political authorities let society organize itself, parallel society inhabits the narrow ravines of subculture, deviance, and crime; where the political authorities seek to impede society's self-organization, parallel society encompasses a much wider array of socially organic processes.

The term *parallel society* has an advantage over its alternatives in that society cannot completely ignore the official structures, the legal codes, and official economy: it cannot be fully "independent" or create a full-blown "alternative," though it self-consciously tends in that direction. As Václav Benda has noted, the term *parallel society* suggests the possibility of interaction, interference, mutual influence, and exchange with official society. It also leaves open the possibility of an eventual merger of the two, or as advocates of parallel society envisioned it, the swallowing up of official society by the freely self-organized structures of parallel society.[1] This is, in effect, what came to pass in Hungary, Poland, Czechoslovakia, and East Germany by mid-1990, as well as in Slovenia and Croatia.

Parallel society is not an entirely new phenomenon in Poland or Eastern Europe. There have been important independent currents in Poland through much of the postwar era.[2] But beginning in the early 1980s parallel society in Poland mushroomed and spread. There were three important impulses that produced the configuration of parallel society prevailing in Poland in the late 1980s. First, in the late 1970s intellectuals and workers grew in confidence and began to organize themselves, at first separately, and later in contact and coordination with each other. Second, the disintegration of the communist political infrastructure and concomitant rise of the legal independent trade union Solidarity in the period July 1980–December 1981 was accompanied by the efflorescence of independent associations of various kinds, including Farmers' Solidarity and the Independent Students' Association. Existing political structures such as the fraternal parties (the United Peasant Party and the Democratic Party) and the proregime clerical association PAX also began behaving in new ways in this period.[3] And hence the seeds which had been sown in the 1970s could now produce shoots. The third impulse came with the imposition of martial law on 13 December 1981 and the suppression of all legal independent structures. This "restorationist" impulse effectively forced independent currents into a *parallel* channel.

Although the evolution of parallel society in Poland was thus quite natural, opposition activists also viewed the promotion of parallel structures as a conscious strategy. Warsaw Solidarity activist Wiktor Kulerski, for example, sounded the keynote in early 1982: "This movement should create a situation in which the authorities will control empty stores but not the market; the employment of workers but not their livelihood; the official media, but not the circulation of information; printing plants, but not the publishing movement; the mail and telephones, but not communications; and the school system, but not education."[4] This aspiration entailed the creation of independent theater, concerts, newspapers, book publishing, education, and methods of circulating the products of an independent system. In the short run the goal was to force the authorities to allow freedom of association and freedom of speech, and thus liberalize the political system.[5] In the long run the aim was to erode the official structures of power and create a democratic system from below. The opposition largely succeeded in realizing this goal by late 1989.

Parallel society in Poland has been closely associated with Solidarity, which during the period December 1981–April 1989 was the single most important underground organization, although there were numerous other underground organizations of various political and cultural stripes. Even some underground organizations not linked to Solidarity were created on its initiative. Consequently, parallel society became strongest in those cities where Solidarity was best organized; it was weakest in the countryside, where Solidarity had little activity even in 1980 and 1981.

Parallel society is expensive. For example, most publishing equipment had to be obtained abroad.[6] Authors whose works were published underground received royalties. Printers had to be paid. These and other expenses were covered by contributions from Solidarity members, by sales of books, stickers, and other items, and by contributions from Western trade unions and foundations. Although some persons working in the underground were paid, most were not.

How many people were involved in parallel society? In August 1985 Zbigniew Bujak, head of the Mazowsze region of underground Solidarity and one of Solidarity's leading figures, estimated that 50,000–70,000 Poles were involved in writing for and publishing the underground press and in organizing underground groups and protest actions, and that another 200,000–250,000 provided "logistical support" for such activities.[7] If one were to add in those participating in independent theatrical performances or artistic exhibits, the self-education movement, independent youth movements, and independent social support organizations, the number would be several times as great.

Martial Law and Its Aftermath

The proclamation of martial law on 13 December 1981 ended thirteen months of legal existence for the independent trade union Solidarity. It culminated a period of active preparation by the authorities to crush the free trade union movement. As early as 24 August 1980, even before the registration of Solidarity as a legal entity in mid-November, Prime Minister Józef Pińkowski, General Wojciech Jaruzelski, Politburo members Stefan Olszowski and Mirosław Milewski, Central Committee Secretary Kazimierz Barcikowski (a reputed "liberal"), and Vice-Premier M. Jagielski met and first discussed a draft plan for the imposition of martial law.[8] Military preparations started on 22 October. The Soviets were impatient to see the restoration of the status quo ante, and Soviet military brass, including Marshal Viktor Kulikov, commander-in-chief of the Warsaw Pact, visited Warsaw in January and March 1981 to monitor Polish plans to deal with "the counterrevolution" and to warn General Jaruzelski that if he would not deal with the situation, the Soviets would do so.[9]

Solidarity was aware that there were hard-liners pressing for military action, but had not anticipated the form it would take. On the contrary, Solidarity's top leaders had expected that if things came to a head, the *Sejm* (Parliament) would vote to give the government extraordinary powers. Although Solidarity activists had hidden some weapons caches, they had largely presumed that they would be faced with openly promulgated legislation and thus remain in a position to use legal channels to resist.[10] The proclamation of martial law closed off all legal channels.

Thousands of people were detained. Communications throughout Poland were cut. Most public organizations, including Solidarity, Rural Solidarity, and the Independent Students' Union, were suspended (and subsequently banned, a few months later). The United Peasant Party and the Democratic Party were brought back into line.

Government spokesperson Jerzy Urban would later claim that the imposition of martial law was supported by two-thirds of all Poles, with the other third being largely indifferent. The existence of the underground gives the lie to this claim. More honest was *Polityka*'s admission in March 1985 that most of Poland's intellectuals were opposed to the Jaruzelski regime.[11] Later a survey conducted by the Public Opinion Research Institute in Warsaw in 1987 found that 80 percent of the Polish public had a negative opinion of the government, and that 60 percent believed that there were the makings of "serious explosion" and "open social conflict."[12] An opinion poll conducted on behalf of the party in 1988 found that the Jaruzelski government enjoyed the trust of only 5 percent of Poles.[13]

Arrests hurt the Solidarity infrastructure. In addition, the government confiscated most of Solidarity's printing presses.[14] As late as mid-January, citizens' militias were still uncovering secret stores of arms and ammunition that Solidarity supporters had hidden.[15] Underground Solidarity had to be reconstructed, first at the factory level, then on an interfactory level, and subsequently on a regional level. A former Solidarity leader recalls those difficult days:

> Part of Solidarity's infrastructure had been underground even in the period of the union's legality. But for a period, even this broke down. So the union had to be revived. My first task was to get in touch with the activists in my region. It was extremely difficult. I had to do it myself. I traveled by train and then looked for the people I needed to see. I often found people in very mundane places or even by chance. One man whom I needed to see, for example, I found in a cafeteria.[16]

There were two abortive attempts to set up national coordinating committees for underground Solidarity. The first, the National Strike Committee (KKS), located in the Gdańsk shipyard and led by Eugeniusz Szumiejko and Andrzej Konarski, fell apart when the shipyard strike collapsed on 16 December. A second attempt came when the National Resistance Committee (OKO) was formed in Gdańsk on 13 January 1982. This second organization was again led by Szumiejko. Solidarity activists in other regions, however, suspected that OKO had been infiltrated by the security police, a suspicion seemingly confirmed when a large number of OKO activists were arrested shortly thereafter.

Finally, on 22 April 1982 the Interim Coordinating Commission (TKK) Solidarity was formed jointly by activists from Gdańsk, Mazowsze, Lower Silesia, and Małopolska. The founding declaration was signed by Zbigniew Bujak (head of the Mazowsze region), Władysław Frasyniuk (Wrocław), Władysław Hardek, and Bogdan Lis (Gdańsk).[17] Lech Wałęsa, who personified the movement, was in detention, where he remained until November. Arrests of the leading figures (Frasyniuk in October 1982, Lis in mid-1984, and Lis's replacement Bogdan Borusewicz in January 1986) complicated TKK's operations.

Solidarity activists had little experience with underground work. Faced with the necessity of surviving underground, they contacted members of the older generation, veterans of the struggle against German and Soviet occupation during World War II, and learned the methods of underground work from them.[18] Imprisoned Solidarity activists learned from convicted criminals how to cope with prison life—how to do gymnastics in a tight space, how to get tea and cigarettes (the basic currency of the prison), and how to communicate with the outside as well as with different cells within the prison itself. Sometimes, for example, prisoners would tie rope to the window bars of two cells, linking them, and then pass messages along the rope. Or on other occasions, prisoners would use the pipes between floors, which carried voices very efficiently. The guards were aware of this activity but simply could not control it.[19] In this way imprisoned Solidarity activists maintained contact both with each other and with those outside.

Already by Christmas (less than two weeks after the imposition of martial law) pamphlets were distributed in Warsaw calling for the establishment of grass-roots Committees for Social Resistance (KOS) among circles of trusted friends. Underground newspapers appeared immediately, and developed very quickly. By early 1983 there were more than 500 underground newspapers in circulation.[20]

An underground embracing hundreds of Solidarity activists was soon built up in Gdańsk, led by Bogdan Lis and Aleksander Hall, an activist in the nationalist underground group Young Poland.[21] A strong Solidarity network was rebuilt underground in Wrocław[22] in the southwest and in other cities. In the early months of underground work, Solidarity leaders were fearful of being written off as defeated and of losing their following. The key to dealing with this lay in demonstrations of strength, resulting in repeated calls for strikes and demonstrations. A typical expression of this concern was Bujak's comment in August 1982: "If August passes peacefully, it will mean to the authorities that the society and the union are weak and broken."[23] Or again, Jacek Kuroń, a veteran of KOR, advised the underground union to prepare to use force against the government and to infiltrate the police and the army.[24] In July it was reported that underground Solidarity had some 70,000 activists, mostly young people, under arms in southern Poland, and that they were training in military combat.[25]

In July 1982 TKK Solidarity issued a five-point plan for reconciliation with the authorities, including lifting martial law, amnesty for all political internees including Lech Wałęsa, and restoration of all suspended trade unions. The authorities rejected the proposal and instead delegalized Solidarity in October. TKK responded by calling on its members to work for the creation of a "self-managed republic."[26]

General Secretary Jaruzelski's strategy was to recentralize decision making, to expel many of the regional party first secretaries, and above all to try to undermine and uproot underground Solidarity. On 13 January 1982 the authorities set up the Association of Clubs for Social and Political Knowledge under the leadership of former Politburo member Tadeusz Grabski. The association was supposed to work for "a return to true socialist practices [in public life] and a rejection of the deviations from the system that undermined socialism in Poland."[27]

In addition, a special "study bureau" under the Ministry of Internal Affairs was entrusted with the task of weakening Solidarity. Coordinated by Eligiusz Naszkowski, a young state security official who had at one time headed one of Solidarity's *voivodship* trade union groups, the bureau concentrated on spreading disinformation. Because morale was low even in the ministry at the time the bureau was established, it was necessary to disseminate disinformation not merely in society at large but also specifically within the Ministry of Internal Affairs. The bureau's work included psychological intimidation, character assassination, the dissemination of alarmist rumors, and the editing of tape recordings of Solidarity spokespersons' comments to change their meaning (some of the products of the tape division were broadcast over Polish radio).[28]

The Security Service also broadcast fake Solidarity programs. For example, on 20 July 1983 a fake broadcast in Warsaw urged underground activists to turn themselves in and claimed that an "elite underground unit" was being created which would replace Solidarity's network of couriers and supporters. The real Radio Solidarity broadcast a disclaimer soon after, and the fake broadcast had no evident effect.[29]

Security Service operatives also successfully infiltrated several underground Solidarity units, leading to the destruction of clandestine committees in Warsaw in 1982 and in Gdańsk and Bydgoszcz in February 1983. Security police also on occasion constructed "Solidarity" organizations of their own, drawing genuine activists into their net. The most famous of these was the Interregional Commission for the Defense of Solidarity (MKO), which was formed in thirteen regions in September 1982. Konarski, a veteran of KKS and OKO, headed the MKO and was suspected of being a police informant. MKO published a samizdat paper, *Bez Dyktatu*, in which it criticized TKK Solidarity. TKK in turn accused MKO of trying to split Solidarity. Within a week of the government's amnesty program, three of MKO's leaders turned themselves in and proclaimed the dissolution of their organization.[30] Anti-Solidarity groups were also created, which roughed up Solidarity activists in an effort to sow division and distrust.

The "study bureau" located and contracted a Wałęsa look-alike, who was filmed acting in an obnoxious and arrogant way. The bureau even considered arranging to have Wałęsa eliminated. "Lech Wałęsa would have been murdered long ago if he did not have the Nobel Prize," according to Naszkowski, a former bureau operative who defected to the West in 1985.[31]

But where Wałęsa was concerned, the regime had a parallel strategy, that is, to buy him out. They offered him an important-sounding ceremonial post in the Patriotic Movement for National Renewal (PRON). They offered him a post on the advisory council for trade union affairs. Other offers were broached. Gradually, as Wałęsa observed in his autobiography, it became clear "to them that what they considered interesting proposals had no interest for me. I was careful not to be disdainful, however, because I knew that there was only a narrow margin between the game we were playing and a much more savage one. The game being played was nonetheless exhausting: no one ever put all his cards on the table, and the constant bluffing kept us from ever reaching the moment of truth."[32]

In July 1983 martial law was formally lifted, but restrictions associated with it had been passed into law. In particular, "commissions for special order enforcement" were set up throughout the country beginning early in the year. The commissions were instructed to assure that persons occupying executive posts in administration, state enterprises, schools, universities, and other social structures carry out their prescribed functions in accordance with approved codes. The commissions obtained their powers under a law passed on 18 December 1982 that authorized them to issue warnings and to demote, transfer, or dismiss uncooperative officeholders.[33]

On balance, 1983 was a difficult year for underground Solidarity. On the plus side of the ledger, Wałęsa was able to elude his guards in April and attend a clandestine meeting with TKK Solidarity. The brief matter-of-fact two-sentence communiqué issued after the meeting so angered authorities that there were pointed reprisals. On May Day, in response to a call from TKK Solidarity, there were large demonstrations in twenty cities and towns throughout Poland, involving some 40,000 people nationwide according to Polish television, and some 40,000 people in Gdańsk alone, according to Western journalists.[34] But on the other side of the ledger, Solidarity was weakened by the arrests of Andrzej Konarski in March, Zbigniew Belz (a member of Solidarity's 107-member national commission) in April, and Józef Pinior (one of TKK's principal leaders) also in April. In addition, a limited amnesty persuaded other Solidarity leaders to turn themselves in. In July Ryszard Bogacz (a former member of Solidarity's national presidium) and two top local union activists, Andrzej Mazur and Jerzy Nowak, surrendered and appeared on state television. The following month, Władysław Hardek, another TKK leader, turned himself in. Appearing on Polish television, Hardek said that Solidarity's strategy had produced only hardship, and that society needed "normalization and calm." He closed with an appeal to his former TKK colleagues and other underground activists to "think over the purposes of any further activity."[35]

In spite of these arrests and surrenders, the Solidarity underground continued to function and parallel society continued to spread. Indeed, by 1984 it was clear to both the state and Solidarity that Jaruzelski's program of "normalization" had failed to achieve its objectives and that a vibrant and resilient parallel society had emerged.

The Jaruzelski regime responded to this situation by trying a new tactic: amnesty. This tactic had the advantage of gratifying both the church and the West, to whom the Polish government was financially deeply in debt. The amnesty became effective in late July 1984 and applied to common criminals as well as to political internees. The authorities hoped for three benefits from the amnesty. First of all, acceptance of amnesty technically implied an admission of culpability, which is why imprisoned KOR activist Adam Michnik tried to decline the amnesty and to insist on a public trial. Second, since the amnesty extended not merely to those already in prison but also to those who might surrender to the police, authorities hoped that Solidarity activists in hiding, especially Bujak,[36] might be lured into the open, where they could be placed under surveillance. Indeed, by 20 August ninety-three persons had turned themselves in, including twenty-four members of Wrocław's underground Solidarity branch.[37] And third, the amnesty law specified that amnestees who were subsequently rearrested for a future infringement of the law could be tried and punished not merely for the new infraction but also for those acts committed prior to the amnesty. This, according to Polish dissident Jan Lipski, lent the amnesty act the character of a probationary release.[38] Hence, a spokesperson for the Ministry of Internal Affairs expressed optimism that most of those amnestied would desist from returning to their old activities.[39]

By late August some 285,000 persons were said to have "benefited" from the amnesty, with 31,000 persons actually released from prison. Of the 652 political prisoners who were still behind bars on the eve of amnesty (many having been released earlier), 630 were freed by 24 August.[40] Among those released at this time were former Solidarity vice-president Andrzej Gwiazda; Antoni Pietkiewicz, chair of the Wielkopolska Poludniowa regional board of Solidarity; Andrzej Słowik, chair of the Łódź Solidarity organization; Jerzy Krupielnicki, the deputy chair in Łódź; Karol Modzelewski, Seweryn Jaworski, and Andrzej Rozpłochowski, other highly placed Solidarity activists; Jan Rulewski, a Solidarity leader from Bydgoszcz; KOR leaders Jacek Kuroń, Adam Michnik, and Henryk Wujec; and former TKK leaders Frasyniuk and Pinior. Before the month was out, warnings were issued to Rulewski, Frasyniuk, and Pinior that they were engaging in activities that might result in their rearrest and the withdrawal of amnesty. The latter two were in fact arrested on 31 August and sentenced to two months' imprisonment for disturbing the peace.[41]

Solidarity, on the other hand, clearly felt more confident now (even before amnesty), as shown on 1 May when Wałęsa and a large group of Solidarity supporters succeeded in infiltrating the official May Day parade in Gdańsk. Wałęsa and his adherents paraded defiantly in front of the stand where the party officials were seated, passing within ten feet of them. As they passed, Wałęsa turned to the party barons and flashed a V-for-victory sign at them. "The officials on the stand were stupefied," one witness later said. "They didn't know what to do."[42] Later, in complete disregard of the cautions and conditions that accompanied the amnesty, Solidarity staged 5,000-strong demonstrations in Warsaw on 31 July (to mark the fortieth anniversary of the Warsaw uprising) and 31 August (to mark the fourth anniversary of the birth of Solidarity).[43]

Far from being cowed by the authorities' threats of reimprisonment, the newly amnestied leaders of Solidarity hurried to make contact with each other. By the latter part of September there had been meetings between Frasyniuk and Bujak, Michnik and Bujak, and Wałęsa and all the released leaders of Solidarity and KOR individually, except for Marian Jurczyk.[44] Wałęsa now held the first Solidarity "summit meeting" since December 1981. Andrzej Rozpłochowski, Seweryn Jaworski, Jerzy Krupielnicki, Jan Rulewski, Andrzej Gwiazda, Marian Jurczyk, and Andrzej Słowik of Solidarity, along with Henryk Wujec and Zbigniew Romaszewski of KOR attended the meeting, held in the Jasna Góra monastery in Częstochowa.[45]

There was a new boldness among Solidarity leaders. Bujak talked of looking to the future with confidence and encouraged workers to set up independent unions in their factories, creating faits accomplis which the government would be forced to accept.[46] Wałęsa declared his confidence in the utility of stepped-up organizational activity.[47] Frasyniuk called for the Solidarity leadership to switch to open activity, while Michnik highlighted the importance of open opposition activity.[48]

This gravitation in the direction of open opposition received impetus at year's end from an unexpected source — the brutal slaying by security police of Father Jerzy Popiełuszko in October (discussed further in chapter 6). The widespread sense of tragedy and loss was accompanied by a feeling of outrage. Grass-roots monitoring groups called Citizens' Committees Against Violence (KOPPS) arose in reaction to Popiełuszko's murder, in Wrocław, Kraków, Warsaw, Łódź, Poznań, Lublin, Gdańsk, Wałbrzych, Szczecin, Toruń, Częstochowa, Słupsk, and the village of Ciepłowody (in Wałbrzych province).[49] The authorities banned the new groups, arranged for the dismissal from work of some of their members, arrested others, and advised foreign journalists that they risked imprisonment for up to six months if they took part in press conferences organized by the new human rights groups.[50] Sociologist Jacek Szymanderski, one of KOPP's founders, explained the philosophy inspiring the new committees, in an interview with the samizdat periodical *Czas*:

> Lawlessness can and should be opposed through open and not clandestine activities. Open demonstrations of opposition to lawlessness are, in fact, the only effective method. Society must overcome its fear of open activity. Open forms of resistance and public activity force the authorities to take a stand, to admit . . . [that] they are governing against the national will. . . . We want to encourage people to form open committees, and not only ones similar in character to ours. Such organiza-

tions must arise everywhere—on the shop floor, in places of residence, in schools—[and] they should monitor compliance with the law, not only with the laws the authorities issue, because they can issue any regulation, but also the compatibility of fresh legislation with that already in force and, primarily, with international agreements. Such committees should ensure the observance of human rights everywhere.[51]

The Ideology and Structure of the Political Underground

After the imposition of martial law, Solidarity activists considered three alternative strategies. Kuroń, looking back to the strategy adopted from 1976 to 1980, urged the formation of a unified resistance movement which would prepare for a confrontation and force a showdown with the government. Bujak favored setting up a decentralized underground network that would confound the regime in the long term. Kulerski argued for a more evolutionary approach that would sap government institutions of their strength. The second and third strategies proved to be compatible and came to form the foundation of underground Solidarity's strategic thinking in the late 1980s.

Underground Solidarity was very much a grass-roots movement. Solidarity strategists believed that its network of clandestine union cells in factories constituted a wellspring from which a future system of factory self-management,[52] similar in some ways to the Yugoslav conception, could develop. Unlike Yugoslav practice, however, Solidarity wanted at that time to couple self-management with trade union pluralism. This presumed the dismantlement of the communist system in Poland and the attainment of independence from the USSR—both essentially realized by mid-1990. Symptomatic of Poland's new independence was the fact that by June 1990 the Polish army, like other East European armies, was no longer under the authority of the Soviet General Staff but was effectively under *national* command.[53]

Solidarity inspired the creation of various other groups, opened the way for others, and in some cases, gave birth to others, as a result of ideological and strategic differences of opinion. The result is that the underground political landscape in Poland in the 1980s became richly diverse. This, I would argue, was a strength, not a weakness.

The Underground Structure of Solidarity. When Solidarity first emerged in mid-1980, it had more of the character of a movement than an organization. Its structure was largely amorphous, it had few regularized procedures, and it had no network of offices with clearly delineated jurisdictions. During the roughly seventeen months of its open existence (thirteen as a legally registered organization), it started to institutionalize itself, to establish procedures and jurisdictions. All this was effectively destroyed in mid-December 1981, and since Solidarity had made no preparations for continuing work underground, the organization essentially had to be rebuilt. Under the circumstances of illegality, new structures were created for which there had been no precedent during the period of legality.

In some areas the new underground structures first appeared at the factory level and the organization was rebuilt from the bottom up. In other areas regional bodies appeared first and coordinated the creation of union cells at the factory level. Of the thirty-eight regional committees which Solidarity had operated prior to December 1981, twenty-three were successfully reestablished by mid-1986. As of 1985 there was no organized regional commission in the Koszalin and Słupsk regions.[54] The Gdańsk, Wrocław, and Warsaw organizations were among the strongest in the country. By contrast, the organization in Upper Silesia and Zagłębie was said to be less active, in part because many of the workers were migrants from other parts of the country who had come to the region in order to make money and enjoy a higher standard of living than average; as such, they were considerably less interested in politics.[55]

TKK Solidarity operated on the basis of a network of specialized cells. Among the most important was "the bureau," which kept track of the whereabouts of Solidarity leaders and newspaper editors, and coordinated contacts between other cells. The cell for interregional contacts handled materials and correspondence to and from the regional commissions. An information cell maintained a file of information that could be useful to the organization, including, for example, the names and addresses of people willing to let their apartments be used for clandestine meetings. A financial cell kept a budgetary record of the income and expenses of the underground. An instructions cell obtained equipment needed for activities and prepared contacts for large-scale operations. A legalization cell forged official seals and stamps and produced fake documents. And a control cell investigated people offering their services and checked on all other vital information. TKK also had a special cell which maintained a communication system independent of the state-owned telephone and telex systems.[56]

Fighting Solidarity. Based in Wrocław, Fighting Solidarity split off from the main Solidarity organization in June 1982 in order to develop a more militant strategy. As of 1986 the organization claimed to have several hundred active members plus additional supporters and sympathizers, with centers of activity in Wrocław, Poznań, and Katowice.[57] Fighting Solidarity spelled out its fundamental premises in three manifestos published in its biweekly newspaper *Solidarność Walcząca* (which had a print run of 1,200 to 2,000 copies): "Solidarity Manifesto" in December 1982, "Our Visiting Card" in September 1983, and "The Ideological Principles and Program of Fighting Solidarity" in June 1987.

Fighting Solidarity rejects Western pluralism because it allegedly "treats the interests of the whole community as the sum of the interests of individuals." At the same time, it rejects communism because the kind of equality it generates is an equality in poverty and because it "realizes the interests of the Party and state at the expense of the individual."[58] In their place, Fighting Solidarity preaches "solidarism," which cares for the individual, emphasizing at the same time the communal bonds which tie individuals together. These ideas are traced in part to the general philosophy of the original Solidarity movement, but also to Christian social doctrine and the traditions of Polish independence. The final goal advocated was a "Polish Republic of Solidarity" founded on principles of self-management, with a market economy but safeguards to prevent the amassing of huge personal fortunes.[59] Such a republic would be characterized by parliamentary government, an independent judiciary, and safeguards for civil and minority rights.

Fighting Solidarity has been strongly supportive of independent youth movements and independent peace initiatives. In February 1984, for example, the organization's newspaper printed a short manifesto from the newly formed Peace and Solidarity pacifist group. Fighting Solidarity has also issued appeals in Russian and Ukrainian directed at Soviet citizens on Poland's eastern borders. In June 1987 *Solidarność Walcząca* published a Polish translation of a sympathetic letter from Soviet citizens in Moscow and Leningrad.

Despite its reputation for militance, Fighting Solidarity has eschewed terrorism or social violence. Moreover, it has fostered good relations with other opposition organizations, including mainstream Solidarity, Niepodległość, and the Confederation of Independent Poland (under Leszek Moczulski). It has also cooperated closely with KOS.

Because of the constant danger of arrest, Fighting Solidarity took the precaution of naming a substitute for every person holding an important position in the organization. Andrzej Kołodziej, for example, was the designated substitute for Fighting Solidarity leader Kornel Morawiecki.

The organization suffered a serious setback in November 1987 when security forces in Wrocław arrested Morawiecki. Kołodziej, who then assumed the leadership post, was in turn arrested in January 1988. In early May both Morawiecki and Kołodziej were given the option of flying to Rome for needed medical treatment. Although the church had "guaranteed" them the possibility of returning to Poland, Morawiecki's subsequent attempt to do so failed, his passport was confiscated at Warsaw airport, and he was deported to Vienna. Kołodziej's designated successor, Andrzej Lesowski, was expected to take over leadership responsibilities. Subsequently, in September 1988 Morawiecki succeeded in returning to Poland under a false passport, passing himself off as a member of a Canadian human rights delegation.[60] Like other opposition organizations, Fighting Solidarity remained proscribed for a while even after the relegalization of TKK Solidarity.

Niepodległość. In January 1982 a monthly political journal began appearing under the title *Niepodległość* (*Independence*). With a circulation of 5,000 and a readership that is probably much wider, the journal became a forum for political debate of a critical nature. The periodical became the nucleus of a political organization. In October 1983 *Niepodległość* published a draft party program, which was revised and finalized in April 1984. Subsequently, on 11 November 1984 the group announced its formation of a political party (the Liberal-Democratic Party "Niepodległość"). The group has branches in Warsaw, Kraków, and Katowice, and representatives in France and Sweden. Standing outside the mainstream of opposition thought, the group nonetheless exerted tremendous impact on the opposition.

Niepodległość is critical of gradualism and reformism; since it (correctly) identifies these strategies with Solidarity, it was also highly critical of Solidarity, which it saw as passé. Niepodległość also disagreed with KOS over tactics and programmatic objectives.

Niepodległość's program outlines a vision of a pluralistic parliamentary democracy based on a modified version of the constitution of March 1921. More specifically it has advocated a bicameral legislature, a president elected by both houses of the legislature, an independent judiciary, a free market economy, and constitutional guarantees to minorities. The centrally planned system would be dismantled and the factories turned over to the workers, leaving them free to sell shares of stock if they should so choose. There would be no state support for factories or other enterprises, and private business and foreign investment would be encouraged.

Unlike most other groups which emerged in opposition, Niepodległość accepted Poland's present borders unconditionally, thus renouncing any possible claims to the eastern territories annexed by the Soviet Union in 1939. The party spelled out a bold vision for Eastern Europe: the overthrow of communism throughout the region (including in the USSR), the reunification of Germany, and the breakup of the USSR, with independence for its component nationalities.[61] Niepodległość ruled out the possibility of fundamental change in Poland except in association with change throughout the area and therefore encouraged Poles to help democratic opposition movements in other communist countries.

Tactically, Niepodległość initially called for the creation of a clandestine revolutionary party to overthrow the system by force. Later, it placed its emphasis on encouraging passive resistance, the rejection of appeals to work harder, and the organization of strikes, demonstrations, and other disturbances.

The Committee of Social Resistance (KOS). Formed immediately after the proclamation of martial law, the Committee of Social Resistance (KOS) occupied a unique niche on the Polish opposition landscape. Unlike most of the other opposition groups, which spelled out in detail their political aspirations and worked out explicit political programs, KOS limited its ideology to a demand for independence and pluralist democracy. KOS's focus was much more on the tactics of struggle, since that was the task at hand. In this context KOS denounced any form of collaboration with the communist regime, advocated the ostracism of collaborators, and urged the sabotage of economic sectors that did not produce goods and services needed by the community. With its emphasis on the tactics of struggle, KOS came to place an inherent value on struggle per se. "Each initiative," the group's journal wrote in 1982, "each situation in which a group of people takes into its own hands some fraction of responsibility for itself . . . each such act is an act of liberation in the real sense of the word and the realization of the goal of our fight, which is for people to regain their self-determination and dignity."[62]

Given KOS's eschewal of programmatic statements, it is not surprising that it united people of many different political viewpoints. Furthermore, KOS's journal frequently reprinted statements by various other opposition groups including the Independent Peasant Movement, Peace and Solidarity, and Freedom-Justice-Independence (WSN). It also issued joint statements with Fighting Solidarity and the National Committee of Resistance of Private Farmers.

KOS involved thousands of people in its work. Its principal publication was the fortnightly journal, *KOS*, which had a print run of 6,000–15,000 copies, although more than thirty KOS periodicals appeared in various parts of Poland, including at least eight in Warsaw and seven in Kraków.[63]

Freedom-Justice-Independence (WSN). Most of the opposition groups active in Poland in the late 1980s were formed in 1982 during the harshest days of martial law. Freedom-Justice-Independence (WSN) was no exception, having been established in August of that year in Warsaw. WSN's first programmatic statement boldly called for the establishment of an "underground state" based on self-management bodies in the factories and the local communities. The reference to self-management is a clue to WSN's socialist orientation. Indeed, the group traces its genealogy to the old Polish Socialist Party and in its founding declaration placed itself in the "tradition of the Polish Left, based on Christian, absolute ethical principles."[64] Like all the opposition groups, it advocated independence from the USSR and the overthrow of the communist power monopoly. Like most of them, it advocated a mixed economy, individual freedom, and the establishment of a parliamentary democracy.

Based in Warsaw, WSN was probably quite small. It does not seem to have had any organized branches elsewhere in the country. Its monthly journal *Idee* started appearing in February 1984. It has also published a second journal, *Nasz Komentarz*, on an irregular basis.

Polish Socialist Labor Party. Likewise looking back to socialist roots, the Polish Socialist Labor Party was formed in September 1981 with headquarters in Szczecin. Its founding program took as its starting point the thirteen demands of the Szczecin strike committee formulated during shipyard strikes in 1971. Only one of the demands—for an independent trade union —had, at that time, been granted.[65] There has been little, if any, recent reportage of the Polish Socialist Labor Party and it is not clear if it is still active.

Polish Socialist Party. A recent creation, the present Polish Socialist Party was called into being by forty-two activists in Warsaw on 15 November 1987. Its initial meeting was broken up by police, who cut off the electricity and detained several participants, as well as nine Western journalists.[66] The authorities argued that the organization, and hence its meeting, were illegal. The new Socialist Party challenged this by noting that there was no law in Poland requiring the registration of political parties. Spokespersons also cited an internal document of the central committee's Information Department which, curiously, says that "because of the special role of political parties in the process of shaping the form and contents of the state system, they are not subject to the same formal and legal limitations as other associations. This is intended to emphasize their sovereign existence in the country."[67] The intent of this provision, with respect to the communist party and its "fraternal" parties, is easy to surmise, as is the use to which the Polish Socialist Party would like to put it. The director of Warsaw's Social and Administrative Department rejected the party's appeal, however, on the grounds that it had not observed the procedures prescribed by the *1932* [*sic*] Law on Associations!

The Polish Socialist Party sees itself as a revival of the party of the same name that was absorbed into PUWP in 1948 and declared its intention in May 1988 of working for organizational unity with the émigré Polish Socialist Party and of cooperating with it in drawing up a unified program. In its (re)founding declaration, it stated that its right to an open, legal existence was grounded in international law. It indicated its awareness that forty years of communist party rule had dulled popular enthusiasm for anything labeled "socialism" but insisted on retaining the term. In spite of that, its founders claimed that their thinking was closer to the social teachings of the Catholic church, above all Pope John Paul II, than to Marxism.[68]

Its founders include Jan Józef Lipski, Zuzanna Dąbrowska, Andrzej Malanowski, Jan Kostecki, Grzegorz Myszka, Józef Pinior, and Władysław Goldfinger-Kunicki. The party claimed to have 500 members at the time of its founding, and to represent Poland's future. "This is a party of young people," Pinior told a *New York Times* reporter. "There is a young angry generation in Poland with a bleak future, and we want to offer a political path for this young generation. We have to secure political influence for these young workers."[69] Piotr Ikonowicz, who is also associated with the Socialist Party, charged the Jaruzelski regime with "Thatcherism." "We are used to many forms of social security," he explained. "And the present program of change is less and less socialist, according to the character of the society we now have."[70]

In February 1988 four of the party's leading members—Lipski, Goldfinger-Kunicki, Malanowski, and Marek Nowicki—resigned, claiming that the party had been infiltrated by security police. The move created a crisis in the young party that it struggled to resolve. A commission was appointed to investigate the matter, and its findings were later accepted by the four, who rejoined the organization in June.[71]

13 Grudnia. *13 Grudnia* (*13 December*), named for the date on which martial law was imposed and trade union pluralism suppressed, is a journal,

not a political movement. It is included here because it provides a sharp contrast to most of the preceding groups. Published in Kraków, *13 Grudnia* expounds the free market economy and Western-style laissez-faire, and places its emphasis squarely on individual liberty. One of its leading contributors is Mirosław Dzielski, who has criticized Solidarity for failing to understand the importance and centrality of individual freedom. His argument is that the Polish opposition had been so socialized by the system that it continued to think in socialist/communist terms, to accept socialist/communist concepts as to what the state should deliver, and therefore remained trapped within the premises of a false ideology. Most of the Polish opposition, according to Dzielski, limited their ambition to making the state deliver on the promises held out by Marxist ideology (equality, self-managing democracy, material progress, guarantees against exploitation, and an end to alienation). Dzielski argued that the promises of a false ideology were themselves false, and challenged the notion that the state should be expected to deliver *anything at all!*[72] For Dzielski, the principles upon which policy should be based have been developed and put into practice in the West by Ronald Reagan, Margaret Thatcher, and Helmut Kohl.

Wyzwolenie. Several of the foregoing parties and organizations have underlined their determination to function as open, legal parties. Wyzwolenie (Liberation) is different. Founded in Warsaw in early 1984, Wyzwolenie is a clandestine cadre organization whose members take a secret oath of loyalty and discipline. Its organizational structure, membership, and activities are all secret.

In spite of these differences, Wyzwolenie has some things in common with other underground groups. Like Niepodległość, it believed that Polish independence was a prerequisite to democratization, and that change throughout the Soviet bloc was a precondition for independence. Like Niepodległość and WSN, it favored the establishment of a parliamentary system. Like mainstream Solidarity and Fighting Solidarity, its vision embraced a role for self-management councils. Like Solidarity, Fighting Solidarity, and WSN, it favors a mixed economy. And like most of the foregoing groups, it advocated broad cooperation among opposition groups. Its overall political coloration is thus social-democratic.

Confederation for an Independent Poland (KPN). KPN was formed in September 1979 under the leadership of journalist-historian Leszek Moczulski. It is thus one of the few active groups in the underground that predates Solidarity. KPN was in fact the first underground organization in recent years to call for the overthrow of communism and the establishment of genuine independence: initially these aspirations were viewed by many others in the opposition as "radical" and "unrealistic"; eventually these demands became widespread.

Already in February 1979 Moczulski had launched the underground newspaper *Gazeta Polska*, which became the mouthpiece of the KPN. In its first year of activity KPN set up branches in Warsaw, Lublin, Łódź, Kraków, and Wrocław. In late 1981, despite an earlier decision by KPN to suspend its activities, up to 80,000 new members joined the organization; most of these left when martial law was declared.[73] KPN assisted Solidarity by setting up Committees in Defense of Prisoners of Conscience.

In September 1980 Moczulski was arrested on charges of having slandered the Polish People's Republic; specifically, in an interview with the West German magazine *Der Spiegel*, he predicted that the authorities would eventually ban Solidarity.[74] He remained in prison until amnestied in 1984. In March 1985 Moczulski was rearrested with four KPN associates. They were eventually tried a year later in March and April 1986. Moczulski contracted mycosis and suffered an impairment of his hearing while in prison; the other defendants also developed health problems while in prison. The defendants pleaded not guilty to the charge of operating an illegal organization, arguing that the Polish constitution does not bar the formation of political parties. Eventually, the court convicted all five, handing down a four-year prison sentence to Moczulski, and sentences of two to two-and-a-half years to the other four defendants.[75]

KPN was conceived as a self-consciously conservative movement, proud of its ideological bond with traditional Catholic ethics. Every year KPN organized a pilgrimage march from Kraków to Kielce in honor of Marshal Piłsudski's troops, who made that march during World War I.[76] The Polish communist authorities viewed Piłsudski as an "enemy of socialism." Despite its hostility to the system, KPN declared its intention, from the beginning, of employing only legal means to overthrow the system. Throughout the trial in 1986 Moczulski and his associates insisted that their organization had never broken the law. On the other hand, Moczulski charged the Polish government with violating its oath, specifically in not holding the free elections promised at Yalta: these, he suggested, could be held now.

KPN held its third congress in Warsaw on 4 February 1989 with 150 delegates representing 40 districts. Moczulski (freed by then) addressed the gathering, which was broken up by security police before it could complete its work.

Freedom and Peace Movement. On 18 December 1984 Marek Adamkiewicz was sentenced to two-and-a-half years in prison for refusing to take the military oath. Adamkiewicz said he was willing to perform military service but would not take an oath of loyalty to a foreign power. The section of the oath to which Adamkiewicz objected read as follows:

> I swear to serve the Fatherland with all my strength, to defend steadfastly the rights of working people, which are guaranteed by the Constitution, to safeguard peace *in fraternal alliance with the Soviet Army and other allied armies.*[77]

In April 1985 a group of outraged young people led by Jacek Czaputowicz established the Freedom and Peace Movement to protest Adamkiewicz's imprisonment. The movement adopted a loose federal structure with branches in eleven cities (Warsaw, Kraków, Gdańsk, Wrocław, Szczecin, Gorzów, Katowice, Bydgoszcz, Częstochowa, Kołobrzeg, and Poznań), with six publishing their own bulletins. By 1987 the movement claimed an active cadre of one to two hundred and a following of perhaps 30,000 sympathizers.[78] The movement focused its attention on the military oath, conscientious objection more broadly, peace and environmental issues, and human rights. It had no formal membership or hierarchy, and relied on friendship and dedication to give it strength. Opposed to violence and force, it shunned the use of these means to further its objectives, preferring more peaceful expressions of will, such as sit-ins and hunger strikes. The following passage from an early programmatic statement was characteristic of Freedom and Peace's approach:

> Experience teaches that political changes, generally demanded as absolutely necessary, are not sufficient. They do not yet amount to an assurance that love and truth will prevail in human relations. . . . The basic tool in our struggle against evil is nonviolence. This is the most difficult but also the most just way for society to secure its rights. We must find ways of nonviolent action, effective in conditions of communist totalitarianism. . . . Basic human rights, such as freedom of speech, of association, full religious freedom, are a precondition of any thoroughgoing social reforms. The political system under which we are living negates these rights and violates them at every step.[79]

Although Freedom and Peace did not maintain a membership roster, all its actions have been open: hence, the more than 10,000 sympathizers who have signed petitions in support of those imprisoned also noted their addresses.[80]

In 1987 Freedom and Peace organized protests against torture in Afghanistan, arrests in Czechoslovakia, Hungary, and Yugoslavia, air and water pollution from the Siechnice steelworks near Wrocław, the construction of a nuclear plant in Żarnowiec, and the use of old Wehrmacht bunkers in southwest Poland for the storage of nuclear waste.[81] The movement also championed the rights of Jehovah's Witnesses to conscientious objection. And in May 1987 it conducted a three-day conference on "International Peace and the Helsinki Agreement," attended by about 215 persons from more than a dozen countries including Czechoslovakia, Poland, Yugoslavia, the United States, Great Britain, Italy, and West Germany.[82]

The communists seem to have been particularly angered by Freedom and Peace's campaign to honor and popularize Otto Schimek, a Wehrmacht soldier who refused to participate in the liquidation of Poles in World War II, deserted his squad for that reason, and was subsequently executed by his own side. Freedom and Peace saw the Schimek case as a means of overcoming the deep distrust and hatred between Poles and Germans which it accused the communist regime of actively fostering. As if to prove the accuracy of that charge, authorities cordoned off the roads to Machowa (where Schimek is buried) when Freedom and Peace tried to organize a pilgrimage there in November 1986, beat up several participants, and arrested some.[83]

The steady pressure from Freedom and Peace seems to have had an effect. In June 1988 *Trybuna Ludu* announced that a bill had been submitted to the *Sejm*, providing for "substitute service" for conscientious objectors "in specified enterprises for the benefit of the natural environment, social welfare, the communal economy, and the water economy."[84] The bill was subsequently passed into law.

In December 1988 Freedom and Peace endured a split in its ranks, when a group around the paper *Czas Przyszly (Future Tense)* broke away. The split was described as relatively amicable. In a programmatic statement issued soon after, the splinter group declared its intention to work for a restriction of the military budget, a curtailment in the length of military service, greater rights for Poland's national minorities, and better environmental safeguards. In a striking passage, the Future Tense group asserted,

We intend to take an active part in the renaissance of political life in our country. We wish to support and create new forms of civil society, such as local self-government, education, culture, information, and public opinion independent from the state, and economic enterprise[s]. The main task of this movement is to build social, economic, and political pluralism.

We see the legalization of Solidarity as the first step towards the systemic reform in Poland. Continuing the tradition of the Independent Students' Association of 1980–81 and the Freedom and Peace Movement of 1985–88, we want to express the views and interests of our generation.[85]

The statement went on to call for gradual, proportional disarmament in Europe, leading to a united Europe.

The Orange Alternative

Question: What does "happening" mean?
Answer: Happening is just what happens to happen.
Question: Do you set up happenings in order to expose the totalitarianism of the system under which we live?
Answer: I do them because I do them.
Question: But one does things because of [some reason], or for something.
Answer: Well, yes. When I was preparing for the gnome happening, I assumed that we would have a good time, with sweets and streamers.[86]

As the foregoing dialogue suggests, the Orange Alternative is no ordinary group. The brainchild of Waldemar Frydrych, alias "the Major," the Orange Alternative is an inchoate Dadaist group which took to staging mock celebrations of the system in order to make the communist authorities look foolish. When Solidarity asked Poles to boycott the government's referendum on 27 November 1987, the Orange Alternative issued a manifesto exhorting the citizens of Wrocław (where it is based) to vote *twice*—and make Wrocław "the city of 200 percent turnout."[87] On another occasion, the Major drilled his adherents for two weeks, then assembled 5,000 students dressed in red by the orangutans at the zoo to sing Stalinist hymns and wave red flags.[88] On another occasion, the Major dressed his followers in Santa Claus outfits and led a parade; the santas carried a banner: "Santa Claus—the hope of the reform."[89]

Banners and slogans are the pabulum of political mobilization, of course, as the Major knows. Among those hoisted by the Orange Alternative:

More People's Councils—fewer hospitals![90]
The Warsaw Pact—an Avant-Garde of Peace![91]
Let's try to make our town outdo Los Angeles—let's dress colorfully![92]
Toilet paper R.I.P.—We can also wipe the government's![93]
Molotov, yes! Ribbentrop, no![94]

In June 1988 a thousand young people gathered with trumpets and horns and after an appropriate amount of noise elected Jaruzelski "King of Poland." Pleased with that accomplishment, they staged another election for "Mister Poland," electing a policeman. His election was greeted by the Orange Alternative flock with gleeful shouts of "Down with the opposition!"[95]

The Orange Alternative loved to "celebrate" the police. On Policeman's Day, the Orange Alternative brought an eighteen-foot "flower" to police headquarters, serenaded the police with guitars, festooned patrol cars and officers with flowers and decorations, and even danced for them while singing "Happy Birthday." On another occasion, after the Orange Alternative had celebrated the Bolshevik Revolution and its participants were released from prison, they smiled sweetly at their jailers and shouted "Thanks for a nice evening" and "All the best."[96]

The Major, who has a degree in the history of art, once described Polish communism as "socialist surrealism." His aim, he said, was "to treat the [communist] political system of Poland as a work of art."[97] Or, as he put it on another occasion: "It is not a question of political changes, but of psychological change."[98] If people mock the police and laugh at the government, they will lose their fear of the authorities.

This approach may have been contagious, for in October 1988 a group of Warsaw University students not connected with the Orange Alternative attired themselves in red (some down to their socks) and marched to Dzierzhinsky Square bearing portraits of Lenin and procommunist banners. Once there, they proceeded to plaster posters of Lenin on public buildings. Riot police attacked them and tore down the posters, to which the students responded, "Long live the police!" and "The party's fighting, and it's a winner!"[99] The following month several hundred students in Warsaw celebrated the seventy-first anniversary of the Bolshevik Revolution by staging a pantomime "storming" of department stores in the city center (redubbing the largest of them "the Winter Palace"). The pantomime revolutionaries came equipped with a cardboard model of the cruiser *Aurora*, which had fired the first shots to signal the start of the revolution in 1917. Rafel Szymczyk, one of the students, became the first Pole since the war to be arrested for carrying a portrait of Lenin in a public demonstration.[100]

Other Groups. There were various other active groups in the Polish political underground, some more important than others. The number would include the Independent Students' Union, Rural Solidarity (virtually nonexistent by 1987), the Congress of National Solidarity, the Worker Political

Group, the Polish Politics Group, the Alternative Society Movement in Gdańsk, the Movement for Real Politics, and, allegedly, at one time, cells of Young Piłsudskiites.[101] There have also been environmental groups, such as the Polish Ecological Club and the Polish Ecological Party, both based in Kraków, with overlapping memberships.[102] In what may have been an abortive attempt to set up a Stalinist-Maoist party in Poland, Kazimierz Mijal, who had escaped to Albania in 1966 to set up a "rival" Communist Party of Poland with a Maoist accent, tried to sneak back into Poland in November 1984 using fake documents. He was apprehended at the border.[103]

Parallel Society as Civil Society

Not all independent associations arose on independent initiative; some were outgrowths of official associations which refused to knuckle under in 1982. With the proclamation of martial law, all unions, associations, and professional organizations were suspended, but some refused to shut down. In early 1982, for example, the suspended Association of Polish Journalists issued guidelines for its members:

> If you can continue your journalistic work in the way you did before martial law, do so without bad feelings; your audience will back you up.
>
> If you praise martial law and try to win for it social acceptance, if you attack those who cannot defend themselves, if you provide false or biased information . . . be sure that you will lose face and your reputation in the eyes of your audience. . . . Besides, don't be surprised if you'll have to face consequences one day.[104]

In March 1982 the regime dissolved the Association of Polish Journalists and replaced it with the Association of Journalists of the People's Republic of Poland. Forty percent of the earlier association's members joined the new association. The suppressed Association of Polish Journalists continued its work underground.

In response to martial law, actors and performing artists boycotted officially sponsored shows, and in retaliation the regime banned the Association of Polish Plastic Artists on 20 June 1983. The government replaced it with a series of specialized unions for sculptors, graphic designers, painters, and so on, which most potential members refused to join.

When writers produced a code of conduct urging authors who published in official channels to demand that changes made by the censor be marked in the text, the regime dissolved the Polish Writers Union (on 18

August 1983), and created a replacement association with the same name. Writers who refused to join the new PWU were subject to higher income taxes than members; even so, most of the members of the new association were party members and unknown writers.

In early 1982 a group of professors at the University of Warsaw likewise issued a code of conduct, suggesting in particular that scholars refuse to accept official prizes, decline to participate in official events, ostracize newly appointed school administrators, and refuse any research collaboration with the new appointees.

Musicians and composers also issued a code of conduct in spring 1982, stating among other things: "We also must immediately start to create an unofficial circulation of music. It is possible and realistic, and it is also realistic and possible to create a financial basis for this activity. . . . Our professional activity does not have to be organized in the offices of the rulers."[105]

In this way, the cultural intelligentsia withdrew from the system and set the stage for the development of a lively underground culture parallel-ing the underground political scene. It is important to stress that the pri-mary impulse for the creation of the underground cultural scene was the desire to preserve the nation's integrity and to defy the moral torpor of the regime.

By 1988 there was perhaps no part of communal life in which parallel society had not penetrated, whether one speaks of education, science, pub-lic health, or the arts.

As early as April 1982 the Independent Education Team was formed in Warsaw. With help from KOS, the team organized the publication and distri-bution of educational materials, established independent networks of lec-turers for self-education groups, and began training lecturers for these groups. Later, on 19 July 1982 the National Education Council was formed at Soli-darity's suggestion, although the body was not affiliated with Solidarity. Its functions were similar to those of the Independent Education Team. About the same time, the new samizdat magazine *Tu i Teraz*, devoted exclusively to independent education, began appearing in Warsaw, with a circulation of 3,000–6,000.[106] The self-education movement has involved hundreds of study circles and attracted people from all sectors of society—workers, peasants, students, even schoolchildren.[107] It has been strongest in Warsaw, Lublin, Wrocław, and other towns where Solidarity had been well entrenched. Underground libraries also developed, by and large set up spontaneously.

Closely linked to the self-education movement was the independent Social Committee of Research, founded in spring 1983 with Solidarity's endorsement. The committee encouraged and provided financial support for research on subjects not supported by the regime, including the humanities, ecology, medicine, sociology, and economics.

Where public health is concerned, certain physicians in Kraków published a report on injuries inflicted by the police on participants in the early demonstrations against martial law. Some physicians became involved in efforts on behalf of political prisoners. In February 1984 the Social Commission on Health emerged as an independent representative of medical personnel. The commission established a quarterly journal, *Zeszyty Niezależnej Myśli Lekarskiej*, with contributions from some of the top medical specialists in Poland. The journal has also published some classified documents about public health.[108] The Social Commission on Health and the Social Committee of Research jointly established the Working Group for Environmental Protection, which devoted the first issue of its samizdat bulletin *Zagrożenie* (5 May 1986) to the Chernobyl disaster.

But in some ways it was in the arts where independence and experimentation went the furthest. The internationally renowned composer Krzysztof Penderecki had already provided a model by composing a choral work, *Lacrimosa*, on commission for Solidarity in 1980. But independent culture need not have operated on this level. There were independent art exhibits in private apartments (illegal in view of the law prohibiting unregistered gatherings of more than six people). Other artists resorted to "suitcase art," painting suitcase-size pictures and packing them for impromptu exhibition at the next social gathering.[109] Similarly, home theater filled a vacuum: as a precaution, the prospective audience arranged to arrive at a staggered pace in groups of twos and threes. Independent repertory groups were also established on a legal basis in Warsaw, Kraków, Lublin, and Poznań. Other theatrical performances were presented in churches.

An underground music scene also developed. One underground music ensemble, the Traugott Philharmonia, was named for one of the leaders of the 1863 Polish uprising, hanged by the Russians.

Videocassette recorders also gave life to an underground film market. Some underground films were originally made with official sanction, only to be banned by the authorities when they saw the final product. In May 1985 the underground publisher NOWA created a video division, and between 1985 and 1986 released five movies made officially but subsequently banned, including Ryszard Bugajski's *The Interrogation*, which deals with repression and torture in a Stalinist prison.[110]

Most of the independent culture scene was a spontaneous, grass-roots affair. But the Committee for Independent Culture, formed in the winter of

1982–83, tried to stimulate and encourage independent culture with financial support. This support included subsidies to independent publishers.[111]

Finally, some mention should be made of the efforts by students to obtain legalization of the Independent Students' Association. Such an association was registered in 1981, and as of April 1981 it claimed that 25 percent of Polish university students were members. During its period of legality the union pushed for expansion of the autonomy of universities. It was banned on 5 January 1982. After that it remained dormant until January 1987, when activists from nineteen Polish institutions of higher learning met in Warsaw to revive the association. The resurrected Independent Students' Association staged demonstrations in February 1987 and February 1988 in Kraków, in March 1988 in Warsaw and Kraków, and, with university permission, in October 1988 in Warsaw, Kraków, and Wrocław.[112]

On occasion the Jaruzelski government was willing to register public associations established on independent initiative. In July 1987, for instance, government spokesperson Jerzy Urban announced that registration would be granted to an economic association in Warsaw and to an industrial association in Kraków; both associations proposed to act as consultants for private entrepreneurs. In October 1988 an independent political club called Dziekania led by former *Sejm* deputy Stanisław Stomma was registered.[113] All the same, however, when registration was sought for a Polish-U.S. Friendship Society in early 1988, permission was denied.

Underground Publishing

The importance of underground publishing for the maintenance of parallel society should not be underestimated. Underground publications were the vehicles for self-education, the arenas for strategic and tactical debate, and the conduits for news and useful information for everyday life. One can safely say that without underground publishing, there could have been no parallel society.

It has been estimated that some 1,100–1,300 different underground periodicals appeared in Poland during the years 1981–86, with some surviving only briefly, and others running as many as 400 or more issues.[114] Most underground periodicals were sponsored by Solidarity or one of its subsidiary bodies. The underground press also included about forty newspapers published by secondary school students and a women's newspaper, *Amazonka*, which appeared in Bydgoszcz. About 20 percent of underground papers were weeklies, another 20 percent were biweeklies, perhaps 35 percent were monthlies, and most of the remaining 25 percent were bimonthlies and quarterlies.[115] Their average circulation was between 500 and 2,000, although *Tygodnik Mazowsze*, which during the era of Solidarity's illegality was widely treated as the official Solidarity organ, reached a peak of 80,000 copies a week in 1985.

In 1981 and 1982 many in the opposition hoped that the underground press would in time *replace* the official media as a source of information for Poles. But a Solidarity poll taken in 1985 found that some 80 percent of Poles relied on the state media for most information—leaving the underground press the tasks of supplementing and correcting the official media.[116] Initially the underground press devoted almost all of its attention to internal affairs, above all union affairs, news about the opposition, and the presentation of political viewpoints. In time, however, the underground press devoted a greater portion of its pages to discussing more general national affairs and even to reporting on international developments. "It's amazing," reflected one of *Tygodnik Mazowsze*'s senior editors, "in that we've been writing far more about developments in the Soviet Union than [is written] in the official media. People are reading *Tygodnik Mazowsze* to learn about Gorbachev's reforms."[117]

The communists fought back in various ways. Arrests and confiscations were one method.[118] Another was to fabricate underground periodicals, inserting one or two forged texts with disinformation.[119] Still another method was to offer concessions: a rather signal concession came in 1987 when the regime authorized publication of the first independent secular journal in communist Poland, *Res Publica*. Though critical of the government, *Res Publica* advocated cooperation with the Soviet Union and was, in any case, subject to censorship.[120]

Underground book publishing was also important, bringing some seven to ten titles to the public each week, or about 400–450 titles annually in the late 1980s.[121] The average print run was 800–2,000 copies, but some books were published in editions of 5,000–7,000 copies, with a few editions running to 10,000 copies. In addition to publishing original works of documentation, political and economic analysis, history, poetry, prose, and instruction booklets, underground publishers also issued reprints of books and essays by Polish writers in exile, and translations of works by Russian, Ukrainian, Czech, and Yugoslav dissidents. These books often enjoyed a wide circulation. In addition, the existence of the underground press prompted state publishing houses to publish books they would not otherwise have published, such as Maurycy Mochnacki's *History of the Polish Insurrection, 1830–1831* and George Orwell's *1984*.

Ted Kamiński estimated that between 10,000 and 30,000 people were involved in underground publishing in the late 1980s.[122] Since Polish law required that all citizens hold (legal) jobs, work in this sector was strictly after-hours, and those involved said that sheer fatigue was a greater problem than actual police intervention. Still, precautions were necessary. Some publishers frequently changed their names to confuse the police, or published books without the date of publication. Members of the editorial staff of *Tygodnik Mazowsze* "never, but never, use[d] telephones."[123] For those underground publishers who were unfortunate enough to be discovered, there existed the Insurance Fund for Independent Publications, founded in early 1986, which helped insurees get reestablished upon release from prison or in the event of the confiscation of equipment or issues.[124]

Underground publishing is expensive. Some financing came from Solidarity, thus from union dues; probably the bulk came from abroad: Polish émigré communities and associations such as the Polish-American Congress, the Brussels Solidarity Committee, Western trade unions, and Western foundations.[125]

Underground Solidarity's Continued Struggle, 1985–88

The amnesty act of 1984 did not reflect a change of strategy on the regime's part, but a new tactic in a war of nerves. This was clearly shown by the fact that security forces continued to arrest and interrogate Solidarity leaders in 1985. Early in the year, seven Solidarity activists were arrested after a meeting with Wałęsa and charged with undertaking activities aimed at public unrest. Three of them (Bogdan Lis, Adam Michnik, and Władysław Frasyniuk) were subsequently tried,[126] and sent to prison for two-and-a-half to three-and-a-half years. Lis had been released from prison only the previous December under the amnesty.[127] Jacek Kuroń and Henryk Wujec both received three-month jail sentences in May for participation in a May Day counterdemonstration. Kuroń's sentence was subsequently overturned, but in October he was arrested on new charges, along with Zbigniew Romaszewski (head of Radio Solidarity) and Janusz Onyszkiewicz (a former Solidarity press spokesperson).[128] In June a member of Solidarity's underground leadership, Tadeusz Jedynak, was apprehended. Wałęsa himself was threatened with a three-year prison term if he continued his activities.[129]

In late April Solidarity leaders across Poland were taken in for questioning, presumably in an effort to prevent a mass demonstration by Solidarity on 1 May. If that was the intent, the effort failed. Some 10,000 Solidarity supporters marched in Warsaw on 1 May, with a similar demonstration in Gdańsk as well. The May Day parade sparked three days of demonstrations in which nearly six hundred persons were arrested.[130]

With the decline in the Polish standard of living, the economy remained high on the agenda for both Solidarity and the regime. In August 1985 Solidarity released a five-hundred-page analysis of the state of the nation, detailing its views on law, repression, economic policy, education, and cultural policy. Wałęsa contacted the authorities and proposed a meeting to discuss it. The reaction from the authorities was "scornful." By year's end Wałęsa was despondent: "The effectiveness of our work is not very great," he admitted. "Until now we were fighting with the authorities. Now we are looking for different methods, but we don't have any. If we find some, they must be better orchestrated and better understood. . . . I am faithful to my ideals, but for others, if they think other methods are more effective, I don't have any more arguments for stopping them."[131]

Although the boycott of the *Sejm* elections in 1985 represented a successful show of strength for underground Solidarity, the opposition increasingly felt stunted and in need of a new strategy. The underground journal *KOS*, for instance, wrote in August that Polish public opinion was dominated by two views that produced deep pessimism: ". . . nothing can be done, and things cannot go on this way. This first view is very widespread and expresses concisely the belief that the opposition is powerless. The second, no less widespread, derives from an appraisal of the present state of the nation and its prospects."[132] The samizdat monthly *Replika*, published by Fighting Solidarity, echoed this appraisal, arguing that underground Solidarity had to adapt to a changed situation and, in particular, to encourage more individual initiative in the opposition and less reliance on directives or suggestions from the Solidarity leadership.[133]

Wałęsa himself concluded that "a new situation" had emerged in Poland and that it demanded a new strategy on Solidarity's part. The new situation was a product of several factors: first, the feeling in the opposition that mere survival was not enough and that it was necessary to find ways of pressing for the legalization of pluralism; second, the increased international stature of underground Solidarity through its affiliation with the International Confederation of Free Trade Unions and the World Confederation of Labor, and the bestowal of the Robert F. Kennedy Memorial Prize on Bujak and Michnik, both events transpiring in 1986; third, the release of the remaining 225 political prisoners in September 1986, including Bujak (who had been arrested only on 31 May) and Michnik;[134] and fourth, the unfolding of a new political context in Gorbachev's USSR.[135]

Underground Solidarity settled on a new strategy by the end of September, with the decision to establish the Temporary Council for open operations. The council consisted of the following members: Borusewicz and Lis from Gdańsk; Bujak from Warsaw; Frasyniuk and Pinior from Wrocław; Jedynak from Katowice; and Janusz Pałubicki from Poznań. By coming into the open without dismantling any underground structures, Solidarity hoped to force the government into a new position.[136] The underground journal *KOS* explained the strategy in the following way:

> The recent about-face in the East bloc leaders' strategy has given us an opportunity that can only be exploited one way: by embarking on a policy of faits accomplis. We must create social facts that the authorities will be forced to accept in the name of the peaceful strategy that they now advocate, or they will be forced to counter with violence, which would automatically reveal their true intentions. We must exploit the present cease-fire to create overt opposition centers and legal groups that would exert pressure on the authorities; we ought to implement our human and civil rights with all the means at our disposal. The creation of the Provisional Council of Solidarity is the first step along this path.[137]

Predictably, the authorities reacted by declaring the new council illegal and by summoning its members for questioning.

Within Solidarity, however, there was criticism of the new council. One high-ranking Solidarity activist called the move "premature" and fretted that it would create a dualism in leadership with the TKK.[138] Some lower-level activists drew the same conclusion and complained that the underground union no longer had a "coordinated leadership." This, in turn, was causing the leadership to lose touch with its grass roots.[139] Solidarity's advisers drew the obvious conclusions and told the leadership that unless it changed its modus operandi, it risked losing its influence.[140] By October 1987 these doubts had reached the point of provoking an organizational crisis. This was resolved by disbanding the two governing bodies of Solidarity (the underground TKK and the public Temporary Council), replacing them with the National Executive Council. The following members were named to the council: Wałęsa (chair), Bujak, Jerzy Diuzniewski, Frasyniuk, Stefan Jurczyk, Lis, Andrzej Milczanowski, Pałubicki, and Stanisław Węglarz.[141]

Under Polish law, a newly formed association was required to file an application for registration. If this was turned down by the regional court, the decision could be appealed to the Supreme Court. During this entire period the association was legally entitled to operate. Even if the application was ultimately turned down by the Supreme Court, however, it could resume the process from scratch and reapply for registration, thus giving itself a new breathing spell of provisional legality. This legal loophole inspired a new Solidarity strategy, and when strikes broke out at the Gdańsk shipyards in May 1988, Solidarity militants were able to circulate freely in the shipyards to discuss the situation with the disaffected workers.[142]

Solidarity leaders were also looking for other methods of struggle. Beginning in 1984 the government mixed an increasing dose of liberalism into its political recipe: select private initiatives were allowed; certain private associations were registered; long-suppressed books were published by state publishing houses; and even the regime press started printing articles highly critical of aspects of the regime's policies. A journalist from *Tygodnik Mazowsze* explained the dilemma: "It was simple to fight repression. Now the direct goal has somehow disappeared. It's difficult psychologically. The heroism isn't called for."[143]

Perhaps the best way to explain the country's mood vis-à-vis Solidarity at the close of 1987 is to say that while Solidarity continued to enjoy broad support and popularity, that support was often passive and tempered by doubts, despondency, and a sense of futility. The strikes of April and May 1988 changed this picture—first, by demonstrating that passivity was not tantamount to the evanescence of support; and second, by reinvigorating the underground union.

There were hints of trouble early in the year. In January, after the government raised food prices 40 percent (the sharpest price hike since 1982), some 3,000 Poles demonstrated in Gdańsk.[144] Five weeks later Kraków was the scene of confrontation between students and police as the former rallied to commemorate the twentieth anniversary of the 1968 campus disturbances; similar rallies were held in at least three other Polish cities.[145] But the strikes that were to shake several larger cities in early May were, ironically, triggered by Poland's *official* trade union, which in its first strike action ever shut down bus and tram service in Bydgoszcz for twelve hours on 25 April in an effort to obtain higher wages. That strike ended when the authorities granted the strikers a 63 percent pay increase.[146]

But that action evidently ignited the strike that broke out the following day at Nowa Huta's Lenin steelworks.[147] Those strikes erupted spontaneously, and even Solidarity's leaders were caught by surprise. Strike organizers reported that between 12,000 and 18,000 of the plant's 32,000 workers supported the strike.[148] The strikers demanded a 50 percent pay increase as well as a 6,000-zloty increase in the monthly checks for all pensioners and health workers in Poland. In the following days further strikes broke out at the Dolmel electronics plant in Wrocław, the small Bochnia steel mill east of Kraków, and the Lenin shipyard in Gdańsk, while an effort to organize a strike at the Ursus tractor factory in Warsaw petered out.[149] In addition, workers at a steel and armaments plant in Stalowa Wola went on strike on 29 April, but accepted a government pay offer the following day and resumed work.[150]

The authorities tried to settle with strikers in Nowa Huta and Gdańsk with offers of pay increases, but strikers at both plants refused because the authorities failed to grant other demands, in particular, the release of four detained Solidarity activists and the relegalization of Solidarity.[151] At one point the government seemed to accept the Catholic church's offer to send mediators to work for a solution. But even while seeming to accept this offer, governmental spokesperson Jerzy Urban accused the strikers of "terrorist activities" and said that Wałęsa was threatening the nation with "bloody revolution."[152] And as the church-appointed mediators began their difficult task, security forces attacked the steel mill in Nowa Huta and crushed the ten-day strike there by force. In Gdańsk the authorities withdrew their offer of a pay increase, ringed the shipyard with security forces, and threatened reprisals unless the strike was terminated. The number of strikers at the shipyard had declined in the interim, and on 10 May the remaining thousand Gdańsk strikers left the plant peaceably.[153] Meanwhile, the government passed a new law forbidding the official trade unions from calling strikes without permission from their central leadership in Warsaw.[154]

Yet the strikes of April and May transformed the national mood. Shortly after the strikes ended, the underground weekly *Przegląd Wiadomosci Agencyjnych* commented, "What took place at the end of April and the beginning of May is only the rumbling of thunder as the storm approaches."[155]

The strikes were accompanied by a new Solidarity membership drive in Nowa Huta, where a large number of membership cards were handed out. The strikes had been spearheaded by young workers and thus both brought new blood into the union and gave it a renewed sense of drive.[156]

Both the new sense of drive and the plummeting standards of living contributed to the outbreak of more serious strikes in August. These began when coal miners at the July Manifesto mine near Jastrzębie went on strike on 16 August, inflamed by the sudden and unilateral withdrawal of a pay raise granted after the May strikes.[157] The miners now demanded not only the restoration of their bonuses but also the relegalization of Solidarity. Strikes quickly spread to four other Silesian coal mines, Szczecin's port and public transport systems, and, on 22 August, to the Lenin shipyard in Gdańsk and three smaller shipyards nearby. By 23 August strikes had spread to twenty locations, idling 75,000 to 89,000 workers. In the first nine days the strikes were estimated to have slashed Polish coal exports for 1988 by 148,000 tons, costing the government some $7.4 million.[158] There were of course additional losses entailed by the strikes at the ports and other enterprises, and authorities fretted about the possibility of a permanent diversion of cargo traffic from Polish ports to "more reliable" transit points.[159]

At first the government struck a tough pose. "The phantom of self-rule and anarchy is being born again,"[160] General Czesław Kiszczak, minister of the interior, said in a televised address, as he imposed special security measures on three regions and sent large convoys of police vehicles in the direction of the main trouble spots. Police broke down the barricades at the Mieszko coal mine and ended the strike by force. In Szczecin police occupied a striking bus depot and forced its occupiers to surrender. Riot police also used force to end strikes at the Moszczenica mine at Jastrzębie, the Morcinek mine at Kaczyce, and the Mysłowice mine near Katowice.[161] At the Lenin shipyard in Gdańsk masses of police ringed the shipyard in a dramatic show of force. But even as a number of strikes ended (some peaceably), new ones broke out, and the central demand was always the same —the relegalization of Solidarity, a demand the regime branded "totally unrealistic."[162] As in April and May, the August 1988 strikes were spearheaded by young workers who had been too young to participate in the 1980 strikes. The older generation seemed burned by the experiences of December 1981 and its aftermath and in many cases offered passive approval rather than energetic support.[163] But this should not be overdrawn; all generations in Poland agreed that "things cannot go on like this."

On 18 August Jaruzelski declared himself willing to meet with strikers at the port of Szczecin. On 22 August the Council of Ministers met to review the situation. On 28 August the central committee approved a resolution to initiate roundtable talks with the opposition. This led directly to two rounds of talks between Wałęsa and Minister of the Interior Kiszczak. At the same time, the official magazine *Konfrontacje*, which airs views not likely to be found elsewhere in the official press, published an interview with Wałęsa. Using this forum Wałęsa suggested that Solidarity might agree to a compromise formula, agreeing to changes in Solidarity's organizational form in exchange for legalization.[164] In a simultaneous demonstration of his good faith, Wałęsa summoned his authority and charisma to defuse the few remaining strikes in the first week of September.

Is trade union pluralism politically conceivable in a communist system? That question was addressed by Nikolai V. Shishlin, head of the CPSU central committee propaganda department, in an interview with *Le Monde* on 6 September. Shishlin maintained that there was no incompatibility between communism and trade union pluralism, and endorsed the Kiszczak-Wałęsa meetings as a sign of "realism" on the part of the Polish leadership.[165] These meetings eventually bore fruit in April 1989 with the relegalization of Solidarity. Other hitherto underground groups were also granted registration. Gradually, parallel society achieved legality, official society withered away, and hitherto parallel society became coterminous with society itself. Some groups were still underground as of mid-1990, but their number and importance are considerably less than before.

Conclusion

Strikes, demonstrations, and other protest actions have a dramatic quality, and therefore tend to seize headlines. But they are only the tip of the iceberg. Specific grievances would frequently be registered—for the withdrawal of price increases, for pay hikes, for the release of specific persons from prison, and so forth. But the limited nature of some of these demands should not distract one from the central point, which is that such actions were increasingly either organized by or came to involve underground organizations, especially Solidarity. Protest actions proved one method of struggle on the part of a self-aware parallel society which had been consciously and deliberately encouraged by leading figures in the underground. And, just as the underground hoped, that parallel society provided the nucleus of an emergent noncommunist society in Poland. Kulerski put it this way in 1986:

We have achieved something unprecedented in the history of communist systems: we have created a civil underground that is campaigning without violence and that has now been in existence for many years, and we must not give it up.

It ought to have the broadest scope and be as varied as possible. A uniform, hierarchical structure is much less able to resist police operations; it is far less mobile and active; and, above all, it corresponds far less to the needs of society. Poland needs independent labor unions and a variety of different social centers that would be concerned with the observance of law, cultural matters, education, and health. Political groups are necessary as well as organizations such as Freedom and Peace [bodies representing] ethnic minorities, and youth associations. Such variety is normal in a democratic society; and if we are to build such a democratic society for a future independent Poland, then we must start to lay the foundations now—in the form of an underground society.[166]

4 Independent Activism in Czechoslovakia, Hungary, and Romania

Independent activism in Eastern Europe has taken different forms over the years. In the immediate postwar period, when noncommunist parties continued to exist in most of these countries, legal activism concentrated on trying to maintain a parliamentary form of government. The experiences of Poland, Czechoslovakia, Hungary, and Yugoslavia provide examples of this.[1] Others tried to resist communist rule through armed insurgency (for example, in Poland), while Kosovo's Albanians resisted reincorporation into Yugoslavia for ethnic rather than political reasons.[2] The "old dissent" was thus anticommunist or irredentist. As a result of the terror of the Stalinist era, independent activism largely disappeared in the 1950s and 1960s, leading Zygmunt Bauman to conclude that the possibility of dissent was largely evaporating in Eastern Europe, that dissenting intellectuals could not expect to evoke anything but apathy among the general public, and that the communist systems in the region had developed an "immunity" to revolutionary upheavals.[3]

When independent activism revived in the 1970s it had a new content. Activists no longer aspired to overthrow the communist systems: the lessons of 1956 and 1968 were very clear. What they sought, thus, was more limited, in two senses. First, as Vladimir Kusin notes, most East European dissent in the 1970s and early 1980s was defensive in character, seeking to safeguard basic human rights and equality of treatment.[4] Second, it tended to be issue-oriented, as seen in the efforts to obtain alternative service for conscientious objectors (in East Germany),[5] pressure the authorities to take effective measures to halt environmental damage (in East Germany, Czechoslovakia, and Hungary), and obtain price hikes and social benefits (for workers in Poland and Romania).

When Polish workers went on strike in late July 1980 it was clear that

something dramatic was taking place. The demand that Solidarity be registered as an independent trade union was, to be sure, issue-specific, but it
augured far-reaching changes throughout the system. As a direct result of
Solidarity's emergence and under the impact of its influence, independent
activism in Eastern Europe began to change—drawing encouragement in
Czechoslovakia and Romania from the Gorbachev tide to the East. It changed
in three chief respects. First, activists were increasingly inclined to zero in
on what they saw as the fundamental issue—the democratization of political and social life in their countries. Second, activists across issue spheres
increasingly maintained contact with each other, resulting in an alliance
among environmentalists, pacifists, feminists, and human rights activists,
and, to a certain degree, a fusing of their energies.[6] And third, since 1978
there have been periodic contacts between and repeated instances of cooperation among dissident activists in East Germany, Poland, Czechoslovakia, and Hungary.

The situation in Czechoslovakia (until very recently) and Romania has
been quite different from that in Poland: independent activists in these
countries could not mobilize large numbers of people, as Solidarity demonstrably could and can. The same was true of Hungary until late 1988; hence
the opposition there, as in the other countries, concentrated on pointing
the way to alternative thinking. János Kis, a founding editor of the Hungarian
samizdat journal *Beszélő*, conceded as much in a 1986 interview.

> I do not think that the role of the opposition in Hungary is to marshal
> social forces. . . . The main thing to understand about the Hungarian
> opposition is that its conceivable role in the near future is not parallel
> to that of the Polish one in smaller dimensions. When the Polish oppo
> sition organized in the middle of the 1970s, there was a clear polariza
> tion of power and society and clear decomposition of the power struc
> ture. In that situation the opposition could really marshal the majority
> of the politically attentive and active public behind it. In Hungary, the
> general mood, although rather pessimistic about the capacities of the
> government to overcome the crisis and to put serious and important
> reforms into effect, is that of a strong attachment to stability due to
> Hungary's special situation. . . . This means that social movements
> begin to form in Hungary not behind the opposition, but between the op
> position and the government. So the aim of the opposition is rather more
> to try to elucidate the situation, to show alternatives, to stimulate dis
> cussion and political thinking. It is rather more like an effective inde
> pendent press in the West than a social movement or an organization.[7]

This analysis also aptly describes the situation in Czechoslovakia and Yugoslavia in the closing years of the 1980s, and to some extent that in Romania at that time, where independent activism has been much less developed. In Czechoslovakia, for instance, Charter 77 activists talked about organizing informal discussion meetings in which citizens could talk about political and social issues in a frank manner: this was seen by advocates as laying the groundwork for a free-thinking "civil society" which could push for broader changes at a societal level.[8] In Bulgaria, by contrast, dissident activity was much weaker (and much newer, insofar as it was not until 1988 or later that most of the present independent organizations came into existence).

Thus, what we have witnessed in the late 1970s and the 1980s is the repluralization of East European society from below. Distinct social interests began asserting themselves more volubly—sometimes legally, sometimes illegally, most often in the grey zone of extralegality. The communist regimes recognized this repluralization for what it was, and fashioned diverse strategies ranging from repression (Czechoslovakia) to toleration (Yugoslavia). And in Hungary in November 1987, the reform-minded secretary of the People's Patriotic Front, Imre Pozsgay, called for recognition of the right of citizens to establish autonomous associations while Hungarian legal experts endorsed this position and declared that their founders were entitled to register them without political preconditions.[9] Ultimately, the dissident movements in Czechoslovakia and Hungary provided the nuclei of emergent political parties, thus graphically demonstrating the importance of dissent.

This chapter will explore the rise of the "new dissent" in three East European countries and will outline the growing international cooperation among independent activists in the region.[10]

Czechoslovakia:
Being Normal in a "Normalized" Society

On 3 August 1976 Ludvík Vaculík, a Czechoslovak writer banned from publishing in his own country, recorded a curious conversation which he had in a Prague cafe. He and two friends had fallen into brief conversation with a man from Baghdad, who had previously spent time in Greece. Vaculík asked the visitor which he preferred—Czechoslovakia or Greece—and to his astonishment, the Arab visitor declared for Czechoslovakia, explaining, "There's more freedom here." After a somewhat stunned silence, one of Vaculík's associates blurted, "Oh no, this isn't real!" But later, Vaculík reflected on the fact that free thinking and free action may exist under any regime, and may indeed have greater weight in more closed systems.[11] Or, to put it another way, being *normal* in a pluralist society is not a particular accomplishment, while in *normalized* Czechoslovakia, one may speak of the endeavor to be *normal* as a politically charged project.[12]

One of the earliest dissident actions in post-Dubček Czechoslovakia was the samizdat issuance on 21 August 1969 of the Ten-Point Manifesto signed by several reformers. The fourth point of the manifesto remonstrated against the banning of the Society for Human Rights, which had been active during the Prague Spring of 1968. In the early 1970s small dissident groups appeared, often led by expelled party members, and tried to press for political reform. The best known of these groups was the Socialist Movement of Czechoslovak Citizens, which included several prominent would-be political reformers. This movement published its Short Action Program in early 1971; the group collapsed in summer 1972 with the arrest and subsequent trial of several of its leaders.[13] Other reformist groups in the 1970s included the Student-Worker Coordinating Committees, the Movement of Revolutionary Youth, Communists in Opposition, the Czechoslovak Movement for Democratic Socialism, and the Civil Resistance Movement. None of these have survived.

In the 1980s the most important currents of independent activism in Czechoslovakia were the human rights group known as Charter 77, the Committee for the Defense of the Unjustly Persecuted, the Jazz Section, and religious activists (mainly Catholic). Other groups included the Preparatory Committee for the Foundation of Free Labor Unions, the Revolutionary Action Group, the Legal Defense Committee of the Hungarian Nationality, and the Democratic Initiative.

Charter 77. The oldest and (up to the collapse of communism) the most important activist group in Czechoslovakia was Charter 77.[14] In September 1976 the Prague authorities decided to try the members of a rock band, Plastic People of the Universe, for musical nonconformism and social subversion. The band contacted playwright Václav Havel, already renowned for his 1975 "Open Letter to Husák" pleading for more tolerance in political and cultural life, and asked for his help. Havel and others sympathetic to the accused became involved in the controversial trial, and out of this milieu Charter 77 emerged. The original document was drafted in December 1976, and was made public on 6 January 1977. It bore 243 signatures, including those of Havel, Pavel Landovský, and writer Ludvík Vaculík, who wanted to deliver a copy to the federal assembly but were arrested while en

route to that body. This first document defined Charter 77 as "a free, informal, and open community of people of different convictions, different faiths,
and different professions, united by the will to strive, individually and collectively, for the respect of civic and human rights."[15] Charter 77 was never
a formal organization, having scrupulously avoided such things as rules,
statutes, or membership lists. It was represented to Czechoslovak society
by three spokespersons selected annually.[16]

The initial signatories of Charter 77 included writers, academics, journalists, former party functionaries, technicians, students, and even some
blue-collar workers. Over the years additional persons have signed the charter, and by 1987 there were some 1,300 signatories.[17] Despite intense regime pressure, as of 1985 only fifteen persons had withdrawn their
signatures.[18]

The chartists decided to spurn clandestine work and to function openly,
disclosing the names of all signatories. They also declared themselves open
to "constructive dialogue" with the government and committed themselves
to act within the framework of the law. They disavowed any specific agenda
or political ambitions, and began issuing a series of expository essays. From
the beginning, Charter 77 focused on human and civil rights, and stressed
its interest in promoting legality. Some of the earliest Charter 77 documents were analyses, covering discrimination in the educational system
documented by instructions from the Ministry of Education regarding the
political criteria to be applied for admissions (January 1977); economic and
social rights in Czechoslovakia (March 1977); freedom of belief (April 1977);
and discrimination against writers, documented by a list of 130 Czechoslovak writers who were wholly or partially banned from publishing in the
country.[19] Many of the early Charter 77 documents were concerned with
violations of legal procedure by the authorities, for example during the
November 1977 trial of four of the founding members.

But it proved impossible for Charter 77 to maintain this focus, and
from its origins as a human rights lobby group it developed in the 1980s
into a body concerned with a wide array of political, economic, social, and
cultural issues. Its documents trace its evolution. In January 1978, for example, Charter 77 protested the government's violations of its own labor
legislation. In July 1978 it addressed internal Soviet affairs for the first time,
requesting the immediate release of human rights activists Aleksandr
Ginzburg, Anatoly Shcharansky, and Viktoras Piatkus. The following month
it sent a letter of solidarity to human rights activists throughout Eastern
Europe and the Soviet Union. Later that same year it issued communiqués
addressing the safety of nuclear power stations and the status of Gypsies in

Czechoslovakia. Charter 77 supported East German critic Rudolf Bahro, Soviet dissident Andrei Sakharov, and the Polish independent trade union Solidarity.

Charter 77 devoted relatively little attention in its first five years to freedom of religion. Indeed, of the 181 Charter 77 documents compiled by Vilém Precan for the years 1977 to 1981, only one dealt with freedom of religious belief. But in 1982 Charter 77 addressed this subject on three occasions, broadening its concerns simultaneously with statements concerning price increases of basic foodstuffs, solidarity with the East German independent peace movement, and the state of academic research in Czechoslovakia.

By 1984, with the release of "The Right to History," Charter 77 had even taken up the defense of historical memory from the depredations of the regime, thus embracing a dimension of nationalism. This important document charges the regime with severely restricting access to historical archives, especially those relating to the years since 1918, and with smothering research into entire epochs, such as medieval times. The document continues:

> It is typical of the totalitarian manipulation of history that it eventually must lead to history's gradual eradication, because the eradication of politics, public opinion, morals, and other social values cannot be consistently undertaken without the elimination of the historical dimension. We are witness to a great leap backward, before the earliest origins of our culture, a renunciation of all culture, which cannot exist without a memory and a meaning. We believe that this "process of forgetting," which the state authorities find so desirable, must be actively opposed. None of us ought to allow the death within himself or herself of the memory of justice and injustice, truth and falsehood, good and evil, the memory of reality altogether.[20]

Charter 77 also made a contribution to sustaining independent culture in Czechoslovakia by promoting private concerts, exhibitions, theatrical performances, and independent lectures in private apartments (usually by academics barred from teaching), and by creating an educational program for young people barred from the university. This has come to be called Patočka University, after philosopher Jan Patočka, a Charter 77 signatory who died in 1977 after intense and grueling interrogation by the police. To no one's surprise, some of these classes were disrupted by the police. Participant Julius Tomin, a philosopher, was assaulted by "unknown" thugs, and other leading figures in the educational initiative were likewise harassed.[21]

At first there was considerable controversy within Charter 77 along lines similar to those that would divide Polish Solidarity during 1981. At the time of its formation there were five groupings within the organization: *reform communists*, who tended to believe the system was reformable and who did not want Charter 77 to develop into a political organization; *democratic socialists and independent liberals*, such as Rudolf Battek, some of whom criticized the reform communists for excessive moderation or wanted to develop a political organization; *self-styled revolutionary Marxists* led by Petr Uhl, who wanted a revolutionary program of action; *religious activists*, whose influence has increased over the years; and an assortment of *unaffiliated intellectuals*, including Havel and young people from the cultural-musical underground.[22] With time these early differences lost their importance and the prevailing approach—eschewing any effort to build a mass movement in favor of concentrating on educating the public and on stirring the public conscience—gained in credibility.

The authorities were unequivocally hostile toward Charter 77 from the very beginning. On 7 January 1977 the government began a big press campaign against Charter 77, thereby giving it far more publicity and visibility than it otherwise would have had. The government also pressured workers to sign anti-Charter resolutions, but typically the workers asked first to see what they were asked to condemn. When the authorities refused to make the text available, the workers refused to sign. The police were assigned to harass and threaten coworkers, associates, and neighbors of Charter 77 signatories in an effort to ostracize all signatories. These tactics were relatively successful in the small towns and villages, and signatories in those places usually moved to larger urban centers.[23] The authorities have repeatedly arrested Charter 77 spokespersons, and in 1981 pessimistic Czech émigré sources concluded that the human rights group had been "broken."[24]

Czechoslovakia's independent activists lived in nervous anticipation and fear that the secret police were going to search their apartments and confiscate their manuscripts. Vaculík playfully alludes to this fear in a feuilleton written in 1975: "Someone rings my doorbell, so I quickly remove the paper from my typewriter and hide it before going to open the door. It was the rent collector. What a pleasant surprise!"[25] Similarly, Havel was long afflicted by fears that his manuscripts would be seized before he could finish them and smuggle them out of Czechoslovakia. His solution was to hide multiple copies in the apartments of friends and, of course, to hide pages in progress whenever the doorbell rang.[26]

In 1988, under the impact of the faint breeze of hope inspired by Gorbachev, Charter 77 boldly proposed the erection of a monument to the victims of Stalinism.[27] In a separate action, two signatories of Charter 77, Rudolf Bereza and Tomáš Hradílek, brought a legal suit against central committee secretary Vasil Bilak for "high treason" because of his role during the 1968 Soviet invasion of the country. Gorbachev would subsequently force Bilak's retirement from politics, as Bilak continued to show himself antagonistic to reform.[28]

Charter 77 aspires to be the social conscience of Czechoslovak society, not its leader. Even so, not everyone in Czechoslovakia, even leaving aside the political and coercive apparatus, has supported Charter 77's efforts. Some viewed Charter 77 as counterproductive, threatening to evoke broad repression. Some were suspicious of any movement that included former communist officials. Others simply preferred the safety of political passivity and were troubled by Charter 77's activism. And still others either had not heard of Charter 77 or had no clear idea as to what it was.

Having said that, it seems to me that Charter 77 was an important political phenomenon in at least two respects. First, it addressed issues which were of wide interest to the population, from environmental deterioration to discrimination in education and hiring to religious freedom; and it contributed to the sustenance of a lively underground publishing scene and an equally lively underground culture. Second, it signaled the defection of at least part of the intelligentsia, and this, as was noted already in chapter 1, is one of the central ingredients not only in political decay but in any emergent revolutionary situation, regardless of its final outcome.

The Committee for the Unjustly Persecuted. Usually known by its Czech initials (VONS), the Committee for the Unjustly Persecuted was created on 24 April 1978, on the inspiration of Charter 77. In December 1978 VONS became affiliated with the International Federation for Human Rights based in Paris, which is in turn associated with the UN. Between 1978 and mid-1986 VONS prepared and issued more than five hundred communiques and other materials on state repression in Czechoslovakia.[29] Authorities arrested and tried ten VONS leaders in May 1979 and sentenced six of them to prison terms in October of that year. Repression proved ineffective, however, as new members assumed the roles played by those imprisoned.

The Jazz Section. Unlike most of the groups discussed here, the Jazz Section began quite legally. It was born in 1971 when a group of jazz enthusiasts obtained permission to form a special interest section within the Czechoslovak Musicians' Union, on the model of the Music Critics' Section. Under guidelines issued by the Ministry of the Interior, the Jazz Section was limited to a membership of 3,000.[30] The Section started the members-only bulletin *Jazzbulletin* that ran for twenty-eight issues, held jam sessions, and sponsored annual jazz festivals in Prague. It organized trips to jazz festivals and concerts in East Germany, Poland, and Hungary, and launched the *Jazzpetit* book series which included titles on Czech art, John Lennon, and living theater, an anthology of rock poetry, a history of rock music in Czechoslovakia by Vladimír Kouřil, a two-volume dictionary of American rock musicians, and the 1984 Nobel Prize acceptance speech by Czech poet Jaroslav Seifert.[31] Passed from hand to hand, the 3,000 copies of *Jazzbulletin* reached at least 100,000 readers. As Josef Škvorecký notes, "It was not exceptional for one especially appealing title to be read by the entire student body of a high school (as well as most of the teachers) even if only one of its students was a Section member."[32]

In 1980 the Jazz Section's annual "Prague Jazz Days" were banned on the pretext that the event, for which some 15,000 fans had purchased tickets, might become the occasion for "public disturbances." The ban came on the eve of the event and a large crowd of musicians and fans gathered in Prague unaware that the festival had been canceled. The Jazz Section calmly informed the fans of the cancelation, refunded their money, and paid the musicians. But in seeking redress, the Jazz Section disregarded the possibility of appeals through channels and instead mobilized its many supporters. To the control-minded Czechoslovak bureaucracy, this signaled that the Jazz Section had become a "dissident" organization. Shortly thereafter, the Jazz Section applied for membership in the International Jazz Federation (an affiliate of UNESCO) and was admitted.

In early 1983 the regime decided on a headlong assault on popular music, taking in everything from punk rock to jazz. The authorities initially pressured the Czech Musicians' Union to dissolve its Jazz Section, and when these efforts proved unavailing, the authorities simply dissolved the entire union in fall 1984.[33] By that point, the Jazz Section numbered some 7,000 members—4,000 more than that permitted by the Ministry.

At that point Karel Srp and Vladimír Kouřil, the chair and deputy chair respectively of the Jazz Section, had a choice. They could simply accept the orders from above as a fait accompli and disband. Or they could seek some way of resisting the decree, an alternative that would convince the regime that the Jazz Section was literally *out of control*. Srp and Kouřil chose the latter option, and with the assistance of attorney Josef Průša, appealed the decree in the courts. But despite 130 letters, Srp and Kouřil were unable to obtain any answer, let alone an explanation. Later, at his trial in March 1987, Srp would ask, "Why did the Liquidation Committee not answer the letters we were sending?" The ministry official offered this Orwellian reply: "We could not answer letters from an organization that did not exist."[34]

Finally, in September 1986 the authorities arrested and jailed five leaders of the Jazz Section—Srp, Kouřil, Josef Skalníck, Čestmir Hunat, and Tomáš Křivánek. Průša continued as defense counsel, only to find his car badly damaged by "unknown hooligans."[35] They were ultimately convicted in March 1987 of engaging in an "unauthorized business venture." Srp received a sixteen-month prison term which he completed in January 1988, and Kouřil a ten-month term, while the other three defendants received suspended prison sentences and were put on probation.

Ironically, the Jazz Section's greatest "crime" may have been that it had established great credibility[36] with its constituency. For a specialized branch of a totally illegitimate bureaucratic apparatus to achieve credibility suggests a fundamental difference of orientation between the branch and the central apparatus, and that difference was most certainly apparent to all concerned.

Religious activists. The Catholic church, which accounts for about two-thirds of all believers in Czechoslovakia, was always singled out for special persecution in communist Czechoslovakia.[37] Not surprisingly, religious activism has been strongest among Catholics. Such activism took two forms. The first, with a history going back at least to the mid-1970s, was the underground church—called the "catacomb church" by its apologists and the "secret church" by its communist foes. The underground church was no more than that part of the regular church network of priests, nuns, and even bishops driven underground by police repression and the withdrawal of state licenses. The religious samizdat that developed was simply the church press driven underground.[38] This form was defensive and sought only to continue the spiritual life of the community. The second form, which was slow to develop, was the mass petition, and sought overtly to change the regime's policy vis-à-vis religion. The new confidence among Catholics in Czechoslovakia probably had roots in the election of the Polish pope in 1978, and no doubt the more resilient stand taken by the once-docile Cardinal Tomášek of Prague encouraged believers. After the Vatican's March 1982 declaration condemning priests' associations which supported specific ideologies,[39] a declaration generally seen as aimed specifically at Czechoslovakia's Pacem in terris association, Cardinal Tomášek, who celebrated his ninetieth birthday on 30 June 1989, condemned Pacem in terris explicitly and denied that the regime-controlled newspaper *Katolické noviny* spoke for the church. Tomášek gave further encouragement to believers concerned about the government's policy when he told the Prague World Peace Assembly in a brief address in summer 1983 that true peace presumed a respect for truth and a respect for religious liberty. Subsequently, Czech and Slovak Catholics circulated a petition asking the authorities to approve a papal visit to Czechoslovakia; the petition gathered some 28,000 signatures.[40]

Believers were also encouraged by the mass gathering (100,000–200,000 strong) at Velehrad, Moravia, in July 1985 to celebrate the 1,100th anniversary of the death of St. Methodius, bishop of Moravia. And in July 1987 100,000 Catholic believers assembled at Levoča for a pilgrimage, and members of the Franciscan and other orders donned their habits in defiance of a government ban. Fortified by the reawakening sense of religious community and encouraged by the changes being pushed by Gorbachev in the USSR, a group of Catholics in Moravia drew up and circulated a thirty-one-point petition in November 1987.[41] Cardinal Tomášek gave the petition his blessing, and by late February 1988, in addition to the 300,000 Czech and Slovak Catholic signatures, it was starting to attract Protestant and Jewish signatories.[42] By May there were half a million signatures. Among other things, the petition called for an end to state interference in church organization, the nomination of bishops, the appointment of parish priests, and the selection of students and instructors at theological faculties; the reopening of the theological faculty at Olomouc; permission to establish independent lay associations and to reestablish religious orders; unlimited access to religious publications; and an end to discrimination against Christians in schooling and on the job.[43]

By the mid-1980s there was a new determination among Catholics in Czechoslovakia, a new spirit of defiance. In March 1988, for instance, 2,000 Catholics gathered in front of Bratislava's National Theater for a candlelight rally that had been proscribed by the authorities. Jan Carnogurský, a rally organizer, told an Austrian radio interviewer, "It was a new form of civil protest in this country after forty years," and added that a demonstration of citizens that had been announced beforehand "has practically never taken place here before."[44]

Other groups. Organized dissent was slower to develop in Slovakia than in the Czech regions. Almost all the organized dissident groups were, in fact, essentially *Czech* groups. In the early 1980s the creation of a new dissident organization was a relatively unique event; in the late 1980s the pace quickened, with at least five new groups emerging in the course of 1988.

Among the earlier groups one should mention the Preparatory Committee for the Foundation of Free Labor Unions, which was established in June 1981 under the influence of Polish developments. It issued two statements in support of Polish Solidarity, but declared that for the immediate future it intended to concentrate on trying to democratize the existing communist labor unions. The group remained clandestine but claimed members in Prague, Pilsen, and Kladno in Bohemia, and in Ostrava and Brno in Moravia.[45]

A more militant organization calling itself the Revolutionary Action Group was likewise created in 1981, taking shape within two weeks of the imposition of martial law in Poland. In January and February 1982 police detained several individuals suspected of being associated with this clandestine group. A trial followed in December 1982, with four persons, including Václav Soukup and Jan Wunsch, being accused of printing and distributing subversive materials.

The Legal Defense Committee of the Hungarian Nationality is a self-defense group in Slovakia, where ethnic Hungarians constituted 11 percent of the population in 1984. As its name implies, it has been primarily concerned with the civil and cultural rights of the Hungarian minority in Slovakia. In March 1987 it reported several incidents reflecting what they believed to be officially condoned animosity toward ethnic Hungarians in Slovakia.[46]

At least at one time there was an embryonic independent environmentalist group. But a Western report in 1985 said that Czechoslovak police had used a combination of threats and interrogations to demolish the group.[47] Subsequently, the independent Ecological Initiative was revived in Prague.

One of the most important activist groups was an organization called the Democratic Initiative, which sought the overhaul of the system. In a petition to General Secretary Miloš Jakeš, the Democratic Initiative spelled out four key proposals: the overhaul of the economic system to take into account consumer interests; the abandonment of the party system of appointments and promotions (nomenklatura); the establishment of a free press; and political and religious tolerance. This last point was taken to mean amnesty for all political prisoners, the freedom to establish independent organizations and cultural societies, and an end to state supervision of churches.[48] On 5 March 1988 the police detained twelve members of the group, but released them shortly thereafter.

Steady police pressure forced the Democratic Initiative to suspend its activities in mid-November 1988 (at which time it had an estimated 200 members). The organization resumed its work the following year, however, convening a constituent congress in Prague on 16 September. In a programmatic statement adopted on that occasion, the group called for the creation of a pluralist democracy based on the market economy and a new constitution that would abrogate the leading role of the communist party.

The Independent Peace Association (IPA), established by five Czech citizens on 16 April 1988 is a different story, since the Jakeš regime would eventually decide to engage in dialogue with its leadership. The IPA initially called on the authorities to "demilitarize society, promote overall *glasnost*, and make efforts to strengthen peace and confidence among nations."[49] Among other things, the association supports the right of conscientious objection to military service. In June 1988 the association collaborated with Charter 77 in attempting to hold an international peace seminar in Prague. The police prevented the event from taking place.[50]

Finally, among the several new groups established in 1988 and 1989 one is worthy of special mention: Obroda, A Club for Socialist Restructuring. Inspired by Gorbachev's reforms in the USSR, Obroda is the creation of several former senior party officials who had been purged from the party after the Soviet invasion of their country in 1968. Founded on 16 February 1989, Obroda called for a pluralist social democracy based on a market economy and an end to the communist party's power monopoly.

Publishing Activity. Aside from these specific groups, there should be some mention of independent publishing activity in Czechoslovakia. The best-known underground publisher is Edice Petlice (Padlock Editions) created by Ludvík Vaculík in 1972, which issued more than 250 titles before it was shut down in 1983. Edice Kvart (Quarto Editions), started by Jan Vladislav, put out some 120 books. Other underground publishers have included Edice Expedice (Expedition Editions) created by Václav Havel, the short-lived Edice Popelnice (Ashcan Editions), and religious editions such as Život (Life), Přátelé (Friends), and Cesty myšlení (Paths of Thought).[51] All told, independent publishers were probably producing more books as of 1985 than the official publishing houses, according to Jiří Pelikán.[52]

There were reportedly between forty and sixty samizdat journals as of 1987, dealing with such spheres as literary criticism, music, philosophy, theology, history, culture, sociology, and politics. Two of the more recent were the Slovak literary journal *MAR.3–1 K 1987* (the meaning of the title is anyone's guess) and the sociological journal *Sociologické Obzory,* both launched in 1987.[53] The independent newspaper *Lidové Noviny* (*People's News*) was launched in January 1988 with uncensored material about such topics as East-West disarmament talks and the Soviet role in Afghanistan.

Edited by Václav Havel, Jiří Roml, Jiří Dienstbier, and Josef Zverina, *Lidové Noviny* published original interviews with Michael Dukakis, George Bush, Alexander Dubček, and Milovan Djilas, and was probably the most prominent samizdat periodical in Czechoslovakia as of March 1989.[54] Other samizdat periodicals include *Revolver Review*, which published its ninth issue (248 pages) in summer 1988 and has been extremely popular among young people; *New Junk*, a magazine likewise aimed at young people; *Jazz Stop*; *Ecological Bulletin*, published by the Ecological Initiative; and *Bulletin of Czechoslovak-Polish Solidarity*.[55]

Summary. Until the blossoming of democracy in the closing weeks of 1989, independent activism in Czechoslovakia was the preserve of a small minority. To what extent did this activity reflect broader social malaise? In a recent essay which appeared in the West in 1988, Václav Havel suggested that there is a fundamental point of agreement between independent activists and the general public: "the belief that the only meaningful cure for the economy is real pluralism of economic enterprise and that the only meaningful alternative to the present political system is political pluralism (without which, in the last instance, economic pluralism is unthinkable)."[56]

A clandestine poll taken among 342 Czechoslovak citizens in 1986 found that 37.7 percent of respondents took part (occasionally or regularly) in unofficial concerts and theater performances, 35.3 percent took part in unofficial lectures and seminars, 30.6 percent watched private film shows, 18.4 percent took part in religious gatherings, and the "overwhelming majority" preferred a pluralist democracy and foreign policy neutrality.[57] Participation in unofficial events was a form of "positive" dissent. There was also "negative" dissent or protest which amounted to a kind of collective sabotage. As Ladislav Hejdanek, a former Charter 77 spokesperson, explained in 1985, a person engaging in this form of protest

> undermine[d] measures from above, so that it look[ed] after only two or three weeks as if these measures had never existed. In a factory a hundred people regularly show[ed] up late, but some fellow workers work[ed] the time clock for them. Management [found] out about it and set up a special check at the gate. For a couple weeks perhaps, the loafing [would] stop. Then suddenly other "difficulties" crop[ped] up somewhere else in the factory. The checkers [were] transferred there, and the old cycle start[ed] over.[58]

The widespread and evident disaffection among Czechs and Slovaks proved, I would argue, to be a measure of the resonance that independent activism has with the general public.

Hungary: The New "Greek Agoras"

The dividing line between officialdom and opposition in Hungary became increasingly blurred in the 1980s. For instance, communist authorities permitted the establishment, by twenty-two elderly persons in April 1986, of a self-help organization called the Retired Persons' Cultural and Self-Assisting Association.[59] Authorities also permitted émigré George Soros to set up a private cultural foundation in Budapest in 1984, which in 1987 disbursed some $4 million to support private educational and research projects, musical groups, museums, and amateur theaters.[60] In the early 1980s the government let independent environmentalists publish their views in the official environmental journal and invited them to give lectures. Again, in 1987, the regime daily *Magyar Nemzet*, organ of the Patriotic People's Front (PPF), published in full the founding declaration of a nascent dissident organization. Indeed, the PPF's general secretary, Imre Pozsgay, sounded as critical as any of the opposition when he told an interviewer, "People need greater freedom, civic autonomy, and participation in [making] decisions, that is, a situation in which government for the people is replaced by government by and through the consent of the people."[61] On the other side, the independent Peace Group for Dialogue, though critical of the regime's concept of peace, hoped to cooperate with the regime and engage in constructive dialogue with the authorities. The Peace Group found itself unwelcome.

The political atmosphere in Hungary has been relaxed all along—especially when compared to Czechoslovakia or Romania—and between summer 1987 and autumn 1988 a string of independent noncommunist associations ranging from student groups to a forum of intellectuals appeared, many of them seeking legal recognition.[62] Still, for all that, most of the authorities were, at first, not entirely serene about these developments, as a "strictly confidential" Politburo document of July 1986 amply reveals. Leaked in early 1987 the report had been intended for distribution to about forty high-ranking officials, and fretted that cooperative links both among Hungarian independent activists and between them and other activists abroad had grown "significantly" since 1982.[63] But by early 1989 the atmosphere was significantly more open, and according to one estimate there were already several hundred independent associations and political groups.[64]

The pressure for change came from *mass* strength, and was typically manifested in the proliferation of mass rallies and demonstrations. When some 75,000 people marched in Budapest on 15 March 1989, the 141st anniversary of the Revolution of 1848, it was clear that society had become politically aware.

Until the late 1980s the major currents of independent activism in Hungary were the Budapest School, the Peace Group for Dialogue, the Blue Danube Circle (an environmentalist group), and miscellaneous intellectual circles and initiatives. Between 1988 and 1989, however, a number of political groups and embryonic parties were established, including the Hungarian Democratic Forum, the Association of Young Democrats, the Smallholders' Party, the Szárszó Front, the Christian Democratic Party, the Liberal Party, and the Social Democratic Party.

Early Independent Activist Groups.

The Budapest School. One of the earliest initiatives was the Budapest School, a group of nonparty philosophers and sociologists gathered around András Hegedűs (the former premier), Mihály Vajda, János Kis, and György Markus, who wanted to return to the "original" ideas of socialism. Their influence in Hungarian society was always somewhat marginal at best, and at their peak they probably enjoyed a greater following in the West than in Hungary itself. Now, in the heady atmosphere of the 1990s, the Budapest School is completely irrelevant. The School's idea of a pluralized Marxism was important in its day, to be sure, in roughly the same manner as the Yugoslav Praxis group, but by the late 1980s the Budapest School was completely overtaken by events. Almost no one in Hungary is very interested in Marxism anymore, even a "pluralized" Marxism, except for some of the people in what used to be the communist party, the Left-Wing Alternative Association, the Ferenc Munnich Society, and the János Kádár Society, all of which were established in or after October 1988.[65]

The Peace Group for Dialogue. Apart from the Budapest School, the early independent initiatives in Hungary tended to be issue-specific. For example, pacifism provided an early impulse to independent activism. Thus, in November 1981 the student parliament of the arts faculty of the University of Budapest set up a ten-member peace group with the idea of spawning a network of such groups throughout the university's student community. When other facilities failed to follow the lead of the arts faculty students, the plan proved stillborn.[66] But pacifism assumed a more organizational form the following year when a group of Budapest students and artists formed the Peace Group for Dialogue in July. The Group sought dialogue with the authorities and even spoke of wanting to cooperate with the official Hungarian Peace Council. Adopting a posture that might seem to have been gratifying to the authorities, the Peace Group, led by Ferenc Kőszegi, argued that peace and political freedom were distinct and *separable* issues. In January 1983 the Peace Group actually held talks with the official Peace Council. But the Group insisted that East and West bore equal responsibility for the arms race, and was therefore unacceptable to the regime.

In November 1982 the Peace Group numbered 200 to 300 adherents; by spring 1983 it may have claimed the loyalty of some 3,000 members. In May 1983 the Peace Group mobilized a bloc of 500 members to take part in an official peace demonstration in Budapest.[67] In July the Peace Group had planned to conduct an international "peace camp" in Debrecen, but authorities outlawed the event and sent the police to put pressure on the Peace Group. The following month, in the face of police pressure, the Peace Group dissolved itself, while pledging to continue to work "informally."[68]

The Blue Danube Circle. Another issue-oriented group begun in the early 1980s is the Blue Danube Circle, whose concerns have centered on protection of the environment. By contrast with most other independent activist groups in Hungary (but very much like Charter 77), the Blue Danube Circle owed its birth to a specific development, in this case, the decision on the part of the government to pursue plans for a hydroelectric plant and dam on the River Danube, the Gabcikovo-Nagymaros project. Initially there was an effort to establish an "Association for the Protection of the Danube Region" along legal guidelines, but the authorities disallowed it. Then, in 1981 fifteen young scientists and intellectuals, disquieted by the severe environmental damage they expected the dam to cause, organized the Blue Danube Group and began writing articles about the environmental issue, many of them published in the regime press. They also circulated a protest petition signed by some 10,000 Hungarians, and launched a samizdat journal, *Vízjel (Watermark)*. *Vízjel*'s editor, Ferenc Langmár, later ran unsuccessfully for National Assembly on an environmentalist platform.[69]

Subsequently, the Blue Danube Circle was awarded the Nobel Prize for peace, which the embarrassed authorities tried to persuade János Vargha, on behalf of the group, to turn down. Vargha refused, so the authorities did their best to make the award seem like an award to Vargha as an individual rather than to the group per se.[70]

In early 1986 some 2,655 citizens signed a request for a referendum on the project, noting that the Hungarian constitution permitted the citizenry to request referenda on policy issues. The authorities replied that there was no need for a referendum since the issue had already been decided by experts. But the authorities could not ignore the pressure and halted construction of the dam until an official commission could assess potential environmental damage and make recommendations. In May 1986 the commission finished its work and proposed the expenditure of some $75 million in environmental safeguards. Blue Danube continued to protest, however, claiming that the safeguards were inadequate. Meanwhile, Blue Danube broadened its critique to nuclear power. In 1987 Vargha warned that "by promoting nuclear power, we are substituting one danger for another. We don't even have the proper devices to measure radioactive emissions."[71] Only a year earlier another Blue Danube Circle leader, Iván Baba, had thought, "Nuclear power is a taboo. It is built with the help of the Soviets. That makes challenging it like asking the Soviets to take their troops out of this country."[72] In early 1989 the Blue Danube Circle collected more than 100,000 signatures in protest of the Gabcikovo-Nagymaros dam and forced the Hungarian government to finally withdraw from the project.

Recent Political Groups. As civil society has reemerged in Hungary, diverse cultural and political currents have also come into focus. Western press accounts sometimes made it appear that there were only two alternatives in Hungary: old-style communism and Western-style parliamentary democracy. In reality, Hungarians even now see many possibilities, and today there are not only liberal tendencies in the Western meaning, but also radical-democratic tendencies (looking to workers' self-management as a model), tendencies associated with concern for social justice and support for some kind of welfare state, humanists concerned about the erosion of morality and high culture, Marxist loyalists, antireform currents associated with concern for law and order and economic efficiency, and populist-nationalist tendencies.[73] Populist-nationalist thinking is heavily oriented toward questions of "national destiny," including the decline of the population, the fate of Hungarians abroad, the growth of the Gypsy population, alcoholism and suicide, and the threat posed by Western consumerism.

There is thus a fundamental tension between populist-nationalist thinking, which abhors consumerism and worries about moral decline, and liberal-democratic thinking, which welcomes consumerism and sees no threat in the Westernization of values. These two tendencies are embodied in two of the leading organizations in the opposition: the Hungarian Democratic Forum (HDF) and the Association of Free Democrats. The latter, which was founded on 13 November 1988 and which had some 3,800 members in thirty-five chapters as of July 1989,[74] takes constitutional freedoms as the starting point. The HDF (17,350 members in August 1989) places its emphasis elsewhere. István Csurka, one of its leaders, made this clear when he noted that in the organization's name, "Hungarian" is the more important adjective.[75] Predictably, friction developed between the two groups.

The Hungarian Democratic Forum. The roots of the HDF can probably be traced to a mid-June 1985 meeting of forty-five writers, actors, sociologists, historians, and economists at a campsite near the village of Monor (thirty miles southeast of Budapest). Drawing on at least four different currents of thought—populism, nationalism, economic reformism, and political radicalism—the meeting focused on discussion of the nation's future, and heard writer István Csurka lament, inter alia, that "the culture of today's Hungarian society is the culture of a defeatist, agonizing, . . . self-exploiting, and neurotic society, a kind of quasiculture if you will."[76] Another activist, philosopher János Kis, sketched out a program for radical political change, including more enforceable legal guarantees of civil rights.

Csurka and Kis were among the 150 to 160 Hungarian intellectuals who convened in the small town of Lakitelek in southeastern Hungary in September 1987. They met in the backyard of the populist writer Sándor Lezsák for a meeting that lasted from 10:30 A.M. to about 7:00 P.M. Among those present were Miklós Vásárhelyi, the former press secretary of the executed prime minister Imre Nagy, writer György Konrád, and PPF secretary Pozsgay. The meeting produced an agreement to create a body (the Democratic Forum) dedicated to helping solve the nation's problems. Those present also adopted a formal statement, which said, in part:

> The Hungarian nation has drifted into a serious crisis in its history. Its national strength has been broken, its self-confidence and bearing have been shaken, the bonds of its cohesion have been tragically loosened, its self-knowledge is startlingly insufficient. It is anticipating possible economic collapse. . . . In the course of the discussions, mention was made of the socioeconomic crisis shaking the country, the lack of democracy, the inadequacies of the institutional political system, the worsening problems of public morality, the alarming symptoms in cultural life and public education, and the worries about our survival. . . .
>
> Filled with a feeling of responsibility for the fate of the country and of the Hungarian nation, those assembled felt it necessary and timely to establish a framework that would permit the members of society to participate as true partners in the creation of a social consensus. . . . The present system of political and social organization does

not provide any guarantee for the expression of autonomous and independent views. This is why [we] propose the establishment of a Hungarian democratic forum as an arena for sustained public discussion.[77]

Discussion was lively and critical. Political scientist Mihály Bihari called the communist system a "self-complacent dictatorship." Writer Gábor Czákó claimed that Hungarians had been used as human guinea pigs in unwarranted medical experiments, and compared the practice to the Nazi experiments under Josef Mengele.[78] Author Béla Horgas agreed that change was desirable but despaired of achieving it as long as those responsible for the current failed policies remained in office. Pozsgay, who was cultivating a reputation as a liberal reformer, seemed to encourage the discussion, urging the formulation of an explicit alternative program and advising that the government was prepared to consider it.

Three months later the new organization held its first meeting in Budapest's Jurta Theater, with five hundred people in attendance. Among other things they discussed parliamentary democracy, the role and prospects of the National Assembly, constitutional revision, and creation of a constitutional court. György Konrád sang the praises of parliamentary democracy, and the HDF eventually adopted a resolution which concluded that the only path out of political crisis and rising social tension was to establish a functioning democracy in Hungary, including guarantees of individual liberty and an independent, effective parliament responsible only to the electorate. The National Assembly, the resolution said, should be in permanent session instead of eight days annually, should permit the formation of parliamentary "factions" (parties), and should permit a secret vote of confidence in the government on the initiative of any deputy.[79]

The formal establishment of the HDF and the adoption of statutes followed in September 1988. Pledging to abide by the existing constitution, the HDF also promised to work for the introduction of a multiparty system in Hungary and to nominate candidates to contest parliamentary seats in future elections. In addition, the HDF established an organ, *Hitel*, with official permission from the authorities, electing two of its inner leadership, Zoltán Bíró and Sándor Csoori, to serve as editor-in-chief and chair of the editorial board respectively.[80]

It should come as no surprise that the communist regime press hastened to repudiate the self-assigned watchdog role of the HDF. *Magyar Hírlap* fancied that "the age of the Greek *agoras* was over."[81] But the appearance of these new "Greek agoras" was itself a revealing symptom of the sociopolitical impasse and general mood of crisis in Hungary.

Other Groups. A number of the new organizations underline the importance of Hungarian sovereignty and advocate neutrality. The Social Democratic Party, for example, urged the dismantlement of both military blocs followed by a declaration of Hungarian neutrality. Somewhat more boldly, the Republican Circle established on 23 April 1988 urged Hungary's unilateral withdrawal from the Warsaw Pact.

Most of the new groups advocated a multiparty parliamentary system. The Association of Free Democrats, for example, sees itself very much in the Western liberal tradition. It also urged the "democratization" of Warsaw Pact structures. The Federation of Young Democrats, founded in spring 1988 and claiming some 5,000 members by the end of 1989, combines advocacy of parliamentary democracy with a deep concern for human rights and a conviction that only a strong society can guarantee democracy. The group stated this concisely in a programmatic statement issued in November 1988:

> We do not believe that any new organization attaining power would by itself bring about human and civil rights. This is because the ultimate guarantee and repository of democracy is a democratic, politically aware society, not the State. [The] existence of political parties vying for power is an essential, but not sufficient, condition [for democracy]. Our task is not to grasp the power to govern; rather to promote grass roots organization in the hope that the reborn society, building on its own communities, will be able to choose its own government.[82]

Resurrected on 18 November 1988 after forty years and with an estimated 6,000–7,000 members by June 1989,[83] the Independent Smallholders' Party likewise aspired to free elections and political neutrality. As a peasant party, the organization emphasizes the revitalization of agriculture.

Pacifism, one of the earliest impulses to lead to organized dissident activity in the 1980s, is also an important component inspiring the Republican Circle. In a document on military service and disarmament issued on 23 June 1988, for example, the Republican Circle urged:

> Except while in pursuit of armed criminals, the police should not carry weapons.
>
> Children should be taught not to use force. Therefore, all textbooks and other educational materials should be reviewed with regard to this issue; also, the Pioneers' Union should be dissolved.
>
> Paramilitary groups, such as the Young Guards, Workers' Guards, and the Hungarian National Defense League should be abolished.[84]

There were at least three independent youth groups active by the end of 1989 (the other two being the Szárszó Front and New Generation), as well as the revived Christian Democratic Party, the revived People's Party, the Party of Hungarian Gypsies,[85] and two fiercely anticommunist parties, the Hungarian October Party and the Hungarian Radical Party, both established in mid-1989.

Three more groups worthy of mention appeared in 1988. First, several hundred Hungarian intellectuals established the Openness Club in July to promote freedom in publishing. Interestingly enough, the initiative seemed to enjoy the support of the PPF. September brought the creation of an independent grouping of intellectuals similar to the Club of Rome that called itself the New March Front in order to suggest a spiritual unity with the prewar March Front that had sought to promote democracy in Hungary.[86] Among its founding members were Rezső Nyers, then a member of the Politburo and now chairman of the ex-communist party, Sándor Fekete, editor-in-chief of *Új Tőkőr*, and Szilárd Ujhalyi, one of the founders of the original March Front. The New March Front described itself as a "spiritual" movement rather than a political party. Yet its purposes were clearly political. Nyers himself noted that the founders were motivated by a "sense of danger and [a] sense of responsibility, along with the idea that the party must renew itself. In my opinion, at the same time we also thought that it is not sufficient to try to advance or to resolve social renewal merely with party politics and via party politics."[87]

And finally, 1988 brought the creation of the Network of Free Initiatives, formed in Budapest's Hági restaurant on 1 May as an umbrella organization for sundry independent activist groups.[88]

Historical Consciousness. Europeans are, in general, far more conscious of their history than Americans are of theirs. But even by European standards, Hungarians seem particularly history-conscious. Anniversaries of the Hungarian revolutions of 1848 and 1956[89] have the potential to ignite social unrest, at least in the nation's capital. On 15 March 1986—the 138th anniversary of the outbreak of the revolt against Austrian rule—Hungarians marched through Budapest, only to be dispersed by police wielding truncheons and tear gas. The following year some 2,000 Hungarians marched arm-in-arm through Budapest on the 139th anniversary, singing, chanting, and applauding calls for democracy and freedom of the press. The crowd formed at noon at the monument to Sándor Petőfi, the nineteenth-century poet whose name is identified with the 1848 Revolution and with Hungarian resistance to foreign rule. The marchers later converged on a shrine erected in memory of Lajos Batthány, a Hungarian leader executed during that same revolution. Dissident György Gadó delivered an oration there, drawing comparisons between Batthány and Imre Nagy, executed by the Soviets in 1958. Another dissident, Tíbor Pak, called for the withdrawal of Soviet troops from Hungary.[90] The nationalist component was unmistakable, as was its close link with the pressure for democracy.

On 15 March 1988 an even larger crowd commemorated the suppression of the 1848 Revolution. Some 10,000 Hungarians marched through Budapest chanting "Democracy" and carrying banners reading "Real Reform," "Freedom of Assembly," "Freedom of the Press," and "Free Elections." The crowd stopped to lay wreaths and hear speeches at monuments to the heroes of 1848—Petőfi, Batthány, President Lajos Kossuth, and Polish general Józef Bem (who fought with the Hungarians). As before, the procession was nationalist and liberal in orientation. And as Western news agencies noted, the mood of the demonstrators was "festive and confident."[91]

Romania: The Breakdown of Civil Order

Social Unrest. Partly because of the ruthlessness of the Romanian *Securitate* and partly, perhaps, because of the country's lower level of development, independent activism in Romania has been more important in its anomic forms than in the form of formal dissident bodies.

In the early years of the Ceauşescu dictatorship, there was a tendency for Romanians to "forgive" the regime for its Stalinism, taking a certain pride in Ceauşescu's ability to chart a course somewhat independent of the Soviet Union. But in the course of the 1970s there were increasing symptoms of discontent among workers, intellectuals, ethnic minorities, and religious groups. In response to the Polish workers' riots of December 1970, which toppled the government of Władysław Gomułka, Ceauşescu called for a program to improve the work of the trade unions and encouraged the workers to participate in discussions in this regard. Vasile Paraschiv, a worker at a petrochemical plant in Ploieşti, responded to this by sending a letter to the central committee in which he proposed the creation of trade unions independent of party control and run by the workers themselves. The regime's reply to Paraschiv's letter took the form of his forcible incarceration in a psychiatric clinic. In 1977 he was allowed to leave Romania.[92]

The regime of Nicolae Ceauşescu (1965–89) was confronted by periodic social unrest for more than a decade. The first chapter in this story was written in August 1977, when coal miners in the Jiu Valley went on strike and demanded to see Ceauşescu personally. The immediate cause of the strike was the announcement of a string of changes in social legislation that would adversely affect the miners and their families: the miners' workday was to be increased from six to eight hours, the retirement age was raised from fifty to fifty-five, various categories of sickness benefits and disability pensions were curtailed or abolished, and workers were informed that there would be new financial penalties for failures to meet production targets.[93]

Even before strikes broke out on 1 August there were rumors throughout the valley that preparations for a strike at the Lupeni mine were under way. Shortly after the strike was proclaimed at Lupeni, it spread throughout the valley, with miners from other mines converging on Lupeni in a show of solidarity.

Three strike leaders took charge: a mining engineer from the Lupeni mine, named Jurcă; the pit brigade chief from the Paroşeni mine, named Dobre; and a woman who may have been a local party or youth activist.

The miners issued demands for the restoration of the status quo ante in social legislation, the guarantee of adequate food supplies and medical care, the establishment of workers' commissions at the enterprise level empowered to dismiss incompetent or corrupt managers, and a pledge that there would be no reprisals against the strikers.

Ilie Verdeţ, a Politburo member, was sent to the Jiu Valley as the head of a delegation of high-ranking party and state officials. But when Verdeţ arrived the morning of 2 August he and the other high-ranking officials were imprisoned by the strikers. Verdeţ was compelled to telephone the vacationing Ceauşescu and summon him to Lupeni; Ceauşescu arrived the following day.

After an initial, hopeless attempt to order the strikers back to work, Ceauşescu promised to grant all of the miners' demands. The miners thereupon released Verdeţ, agreed to return to work the next day, and even offered to make up the time lost during the strike. The concessions held long enough for the authorities to break the organizational backbone of the resistance. The three strike leaders disappeared permanently in September.[94] Other miners who had been outspoken during the strike were rounded up piecemeal over the following months and dispersed to other parts of the country. Eventually most of the concessions were withdrawn and the eight-hour workday imposed, although this was not made official until 1983.

While the authorities thus contained unrest in the Jiu Valley, a symbolically important precedent was set in early 1979 when a group of fifteen workers and several intellectuals from the industrial center of Turnu Severin in southwestern Romania set up the Free Trade Union of Romanian Workers. The union made a number of bold demands, including the legalization of independent trade unions, the abolition of privileges for high party officials, changes in the retirement system, the abolition of censorship, and an end to compulsory "patriotic labor" on weekends. The authorities moved quickly before most Romanians were aware of the union's existence, and most of the known founding members soon "disappeared."[95]

There was further unrest in October 1981 among mine and quarry workers in the Motru basin, in September 1983 among miners in Baia Borşa, Gura Baia, and Toroioaga, in November 1983 among one thousand workers at the Braşov Steagul Roşu truck factory, in February 1985 among workers in Timişoara, in August 1986 among transport workers in Arad in western Romania, and in November 1986 among factory workers in Cluj and Turda in Transylvania. In both of the latter two instances, as in September 1983, pay cuts and poor food supplies triggered the stoppages.[96] The unrest in November 1986 was sparked by the official announcement that the bread ration in Transylvania would be reduced to 300 grams a day and pay at several major factories would be cut dramatically for nonfulfillment of the plan. On 1 November graffiti and leaflets in Romanian and Hungarian appeared, demanding meat, bread and "milk for our children," and condemning the "Ceauşescu dictatorship."[97] Strikes broke out at the heavy equipment and refrigeration machinery plants in Cluj, and at the glass factory in Turda. The strikers demanded improvement in the food supply and a retraction of the pay cuts. Authorities replayed the tactics used in 1977 — granting concessions at first, then questioning the workers, dismissing the suspected organizers, and gradually withdrawing the initial concessions. Along the way, some twenty-five organizers of the strike disappeared without a trace, leaving even their families uncertain of their fate.[98]

After permitting the Romanian national debt to climb to $13 billion in 1982, Ceauşescu decided on radical belt-tightening to bring down the debt. Residential consumption of gas and electricity was forcibly cut by 90 percent between 1979 and 1987.[99] Food was rigidly rationed. Imports were sliced, while anything exportable was sold abroad. Noncompetitive industrial products were sold at prices below production costs.[100] These radical measures bled the country but succeeded in halving the debt. In the midst of all this privation, Ceauşescu indulged in an architectural megalomaniacal fantasy, bulldozing a large section of historic Bucharest in order to create a permanent "monument" to himself, half a mile wide and ten miles long. The main plaza is spacious, framed by rigid rows of neoclassical buildings in the grand style, complete with Roman columns, fake arches, and gargantuan balconies.[101] All of this only deepened the general hatred for Ceauşescu.

February 1987 saw renewed unrest in Iaşi, Moldavia, among workers and students, with the latter ostentatiously burning textbooks on "scientific socialism." But this unrest was completely overshadowed by the dramatic demonstrations in Braşov in November 1987. Angered by new wage cuts and persistent food shortages, several thousand workers from Braşov's Red Flag truck factory staged a protest march to party headquarters on 15 November. During the one-hour march they sang a revolutionary song ("Awake, Romania") from the Revolution of 1848 and chanted "We want bread" and "Down with dictatorship." Other townspeople joined them and soon there were up to 20,000 people protesting. Upon reaching party headquarters some demonstrators forced their way inside and hurled furniture, files, and portraits of the *Conducator* out the window. Other demonstrators found the exclusive party shop storing special food provisions for party officials, and, amid great indignation, brought the foodstuffs to the public square.[102]

Romanian police arrested some 400 persons,[103] and troops were sent in to patrol the streets.[104] But there was no mention of the riots in the Romanian press, although *Scînteia* somewhat elliptically reproved local officials, urging the importance of "fruitful cooperation between citizens and elected officials."[105]

Crane Brinton, it will be recalled, identified several uniformities in the emergence of revolution, including the financial failure of the government, governmental inefficiency, class antagonism and the alienation of the people from the government, the abandonment of the regime by the intellectuals, and the loss of self-confidence on the part of the governing class.[106] All these elements were present in Romania at the close of the 1980s, including the loss of self-confidence within the elite itself.

There were various signs of this, including a purge at the upper rungs of the Defense Ministry in the wake of rumors of army resistance to Ceauşescu's policies.[107] Later, in the wake of the Braşov riots, Romania's former ambassador to the United States, Silviu Brucan, publicly compared the situation in Romania to that in Poland in 1980, adding that "a period of crisis has opened between the communist party and the working class." To make matters worse, he called on the leadership to make "a sincere effort to come to terms with [the public's] legitimate grievances" and declared that the "overwhelming majority" of the party itself agreed with his assessment of the situation.[108] Brucan was later forced to retract his statements, but meanwhile Ceauşescu was compelled to postpone the party's national conference for a week, evidently in order to make sure his internal opposition was muzzled.[109] Criticism of Ceauşescu even came from the eighty-five-year-old former Romanian prime minister, Ion Gheorghe Maurer.[110]

Independent Activist Groups. It is the depth of social malaise and the recurrence and deepening of anomic unrest that suggested that Romania was the most vulnerable to revolutionary upheaval of the three countries surveyed in this chapter. Because of the relative lack of organized dissent, however, it was the last of the three to begin the transition to "post-communism." But there have been *some* forces for social change, which fit more properly under the rubric of "independent activism."

Democratic Action. In late 1985 thirteen pseudonymous signatories signed a manifesto announcing the creation of an opposition movement dedicated to the establishment of democratic pluralism in Romania and inspired by Christian ideals. Calling their movement Democratic Action, the signatories swore "to undermine and destroy the communist regime in the course of time and to uphold the idea of democracy."[111] During 1987 the group distributed three manifestos emphasizing the importance of private property and individual initiative as prerequisites for economic prosperity, and calling for the establishment of a parliamentary system on the West European model, with guarantees for ethnic minorities.[112] In 1988 Democratic Action drew up a twenty-two-page "Green Report" on the environmental situation, criticizing the Ceauşescu regime for irresponsible mismanagement and complaining of the general secrecy in which information about the Romanian ecology was shrouded.[113]

Free Romania. Most of the members of Free Romania were white- and blue-collar Romanians concentrated in the Banat region. A small number of Romanians linked with this group moved to Budapest, and maintained contact with members inside Romania.[114] The movement was implacably hostile to Ceauşescu and called for his overthrow; it was necessarily clandestine. At the same time, however, unlike the anticommunist Democratic Action, Free Romania advertised its fidelity to the bloc, praised the Gorbachev line, and called for the introduction of *glasnost* and *perestroika* in Romania. The group even made contact with the Soviets at a Soviet embassy (presumably the embassy in Budapest, since access to the Soviet embassy in Bucharest was well guarded and monitored). But the Soviets told the Romanian malcontents that Romanians must resolve their crisis by themselves.[115]

In April 1988 the Budapest wing of the organization launched a Romanian-language samizdat periodical, *România Liberă*, with the intention of distributing it in Romania. The Free Romanian group was able to use the printing facilities of the Hungarian democratic opposition.[116] Meanwhile, in Romania itself, Ceauşescu's sweeping plans to physically destroy seven to eight thousand villages in Romania impelled Romanian and minority malcontents to form a "coalition" and to draw up a protest.[117]

In November 1988 *România Liberă* published an appeal to Romanians calling for the release of political prisoners, freedom of religion, an end to censorship, cancellation of Ceaușescu's rural resettlement program, equality for all nationalities, trade union pluralism, and freedom of movement.[118]

National Peasant Party. Outlawed in 1947 after winning nearly 70 percent of the vote in the 1946 elections, the National Peasant Party once championed the interests of the peasantry. After the communist takeover, party leader Iuliu Maniu and tens of thousands of other party members were imprisoned, many until 1964. The party seemed to have disappeared, but small groups of survivors, including once prominent leaders, began meeting in private, and some of them issued political statements in the name of the National Peasant Party in 1983, 1984, and 1985. In the last instance, the party issued a comprehensive political platform drafted by sixty-seven-year-old Ion Puiu, once a party youth leader. The platform called for respect for constitutional guarantees of individual rights, the abolition of party privileges, the dismantling of the *Securitate*, the separation of the labor unions from communist party control, the depoliticization of education, the restoration of the former (precommunist) role of the Grand National Assembly, and complete freedom of religion.[119] More recently, the National Peasant Party's former leaders have attracted a following among young people and have established a human rights organization (1986) with branches in Bucharest and Transylvania.[120]

An Expanding International Network?

One of the earliest efforts on the part of independent activists to establish cooperation across borders came in 1978, when signatories of Czechoslovakia's Charter 77 and members of the Polish KOR held two meetings somewhere along the Polish-Czechoslovak border. Cross-border contacts could be useful for sharing experiences, exchanging ideas, and possibly coordinating common strategies and joint actions. The issuance of joint manifestos could also serve to underscore the weight of the protest.

Gorbachev's drive to export reform to Eastern Europe made such coordination among independent activists more attractive than ever.[121] "With Gorbachev's reforms," János Kis said in October 1987, "you have a region ready for great change, even ferment. It only makes sense to develop a common strategy."[122] Technological advances also helped, as Janusz Onyszkiewicz, the former spokesperson of Polish Solidarity noted in January 1987: "There has definitely been a change. Psychologically, there was always the will to cooperate across borders but the technical capabilities lagged behind."[123] Direct-dial telephoning has been pivotal in this regard, even with bugged lines.

Pacifists and human rights activists were in the forefront of efforts to build an activist network. In 1984 activists from Czechoslovakia's Charter 77 and the East German independent peace movement issued a joint declaration showing their agreement on two key issues: the deployment of new Soviet nuclear missiles in their two countries endangered peace, and the inseparability of peace from respect for human rights.[124] The declaration was signed by seventeen East Germans and sixteen Czechoslovaks. Later, on 23 October 1986, dissidents from four Soviet-bloc countries—Czechoslovakia, East Germany, Hungary, and Poland—issued a joint statement to which three Romanian dissidents later subscribed. The statement commemorated the thirtieth anniversary of the Hungarian Revolution, noting,in part:

> [T]he essential demands of the revolutionaries have not been satisfied. On this anniversary, we call on all our friends in the world to join us to commemorate the 1956 Hungarian Revolution. We proclaim our common determination to struggle for political democracy in our countries, for their independence, for pluralism founded on the principles of self-government, for the peaceful unification of a divided Europe and for its democratic integration, as well as for the rights of all national minorities.[125]

The coordination was unprecedented, and the text itself suggested a new confidence in the possibility of change.

Recent years also saw a joint protest by Polish and Czech environmentalists (1987), a joint appeal for the right of conscientious objection to military service signed by more than 400 activists from throughout Eastern Europe (1988), and a joint memorandum signed by hundreds of pacifists and environmentalists in both Western and Eastern Europe (1987), which called for freedom of travel, legalization of independent publishers in Eastern Europe, and an end to restrictions on the import of books, journals, and tapes intended for the use of the traveler.[126]

From mid-1986 through early 1988, sundry groupings of independent activists in Eastern Europe began establishing regular contacts and organizing clandestine strategy sessions, joint declarations, and independent conferences.[127] Such conferences were held in Warsaw and Budapest.[128] Inevitably such cooperative contacts assumed an organizational dimension. For instance, in May 1986 four "special interest sections" associated with underground Solidarity contacted Charter 77 with offers of cooperation in specific areas: the sections concerned were the Social Commission for Health, the Social Committee for Science and Scholarship, the Group for Independent Public Education, and the Helsinki Committee in Poland.[129] Again, in July 1987 thirty-four Polish and Czechoslovak activists announced the creation of a joint committee, the Circle of Friends of Polish-Czechoslovak Solidarity, for the exchange of information and coordination of activities.[130] Shortly thereafter, the organization met and issued a statement. In a key passage, the twenty-one signatories noted:

> All our endeavors so far have been based on the conviction that the widening of civil liberties, and a better life for the societies of the Soviet bloc, depends above all on these societies themselves, namely, on what they themselves attain through active work. This conviction of theirs has not been changed by the onset of the Gorbachev era. Today, too, we want to rely first of all on our own strength. We are aware, at the same time, that the policy of the Gorbachev leadership is creating more favorable conditions for the self-emancipating efforts pursued in the countries of the Soviet bloc. . . . Those attending the meeting have once again acknowledged and affirmed that, no matter how different the situation is in the various European countries of the Soviet bloc and no matter how diverse their own approaches are to the resolution of the problems of their societies, the fundamental ideals of all those who take independent public action in these countries are essentially identical.[131]

In addition, the steadily deteriorating economic conditions of Romanians provided a special focal point for intergroup cooperation. In Romania the excesses of the Ceauşescu regime prompted Hungarian dissidents in Transylvania and Romanian dissidents to support each other's struggles.[132] And in January 1988 Charter 77 called on all Europeans to demonstrate against Ceauşescu on 1 February.[133] The result was a series of solidarity protests in Czechoslovakia, Hungary, Poland, and the Soviet Union, as well as demonstrations by East European émigré groups in London, Paris, Bonn, Munich, and other West European cities. Although police broke up the demonstrations in Warsaw and Prague, the Czech police even arresting some of the demonstrators, the police in Budapest restricted themselves to removing banners displaying slogans like "Human and Civil Rights for All Romanians" and asking the crowd to disperse.[134]

By spring 1988 Polish-Czechoslovak Solidarity operated more or less openly, publishing a monthly newsletter and organizing conferences and demonstrations.[135] It also issued a joint protest against reprisals in East

Germany as part of a coalition of Poles, Czechoslovaks, Hungarians, Yugoslavs, and Russians.[136]

Polish-Czechoslovak Solidarity provided a model for a similar cooperative committee involving Czechoslovak and Hungarian activists. The HDF and Czechoslovakia's Democratic Initiative took the lead in this regard and on 26 August 1989 established the Committee for Czechoslovak-Hungarian Democratic Cooperation.

The growing mutual support among independent activists signified, on one level, a growth in "genuine internationalism of the peoples in the region," as the Hungarian samizdat journal *Beszélő* put it in December 1987.[137] It also signified a new confidence among activists and a growing sense that real change could be effected. The Czechoslovak playwright Václav Havel put it this way in early 1988:

> I am convinced that this chasm between ideology and the basic power-political principles on the one hand and the authentic beliefs of society on the other will continue to deepen for a long time but not indefinitely. The growth of the chasm is acquiring the dimensions of an ever more important political fact that sooner or later must translate into political change.[138]

III   Religious and Ethnic Currents

5 Religious Change and New Cults in Eastern Europe

Religious change has its sources in *secularization*, which changes the relationship between religious institutions and society, and *cultural drift*, which is associated with changes in religious needs, cultural distortion, and general social stress. As traditional religious institutions cease to be seen as repositories of answers to emerging questions, the receptivity of society to new religious movements increases, both in specific subcultures and in general. The result is that both religious innovation and the importation of religious creeds from foreign lands are more successful. And as new cults and religious movements find fertile soil and sprout, social and cultural fragmentation is reinforced and the traditional sense of *Volksgemeinschaft* is further undermined.

Secularization has been variously defined. One useful definition equates it with "a societal process in which an overarching and transcendent religious system is . . . reduced to a subsystem of society alongside other subsystems, and the overarching claims of which have a shrinking audience."[1] In its early stages secularization involves the decline of religious content in art, literature, music, and philosophy. Later secularization takes the form of the creation of a political sphere autonomous from the religious, and the gradual demystification of the community's understanding of the universe.[2] The expansion of scientific knowledge steadily reduced social reliance on religion for explanations of natural phenomena. In later stages secularization is associated with a shift in the focus of communal life, which ceases to revolve around the church. Insofar as no other institution is capable of assuming the church's traditional role, the life of the community becomes fragmented as different sectors look to different institutions and different activities to satisfy primary associational needs. In this connection, Thomas Luckmann's comment linking secularization with the "dissolution of the traditional, coherent sacred cosmos"[3] is apt. Secularization necessarily fosters social stress, which in turn fuels religious revival and religious innovation.

The starting point for this chapter, then, is that secularization is part of a broader syndrome organically associated with religious revival in traditional religion, confessional change where mainline churches fail to adapt, and the appearance of new religious cults. One may even say that the latter phenomena are *manifestations* of secularization.[4] These aspects will be examined in sequence.

Secularization

Secularization in Western Europe has been a spontaneous process that has unfolded despite the protective attitude of some governments (e.g., Spain and West Germany). Secularization in Eastern Europe was a conscious goal of the communist authorities from the beginning. Prior to the communist takeover, religion was included in the school curriculum in each of these countries. The communists removed religious instruction from state schools, nationalized most religious schools, and set in motion antireligious campaigns, and, in Czechoslovakia and Yugoslavia, attempted to link Catholic clergy with the wartime fascist puppet states. Atheist Circles were established among schoolchildren in Czechoslovakia. Among their activities were the viewing of antireligious films and field trips to museums and exhibitions of revolutionary traditions. Communist youth organizations became vehicles for "atheization," and a youth initiation ceremony (*Jugendweihe*) was introduced in 1954 in East Germany as an atheist substitute for Christian confirmation. Young people often grew up without any knowledge of religious doctrine, teachings, or history.

Secularization was also implemented by making social advancement dependent on party membership and party membership dependent on the rejection of religious belief, although by the late 1980s there were known to be crypto-Christians in several of the ruling parties in the region, including the Czechoslovak,[5] East German, Polish,[6] Romanian,[7] and Yugoslav.[8] (In 1989, the Hungarian party passed a decree allowing believers to join the party.)

Finally, churches were financially undermined by the confiscation of landholdings, hospitals, old-age homes, and so forth. This policy was not applied in East Germany, where churches always owned a large number of such institutions, but elsewhere these confiscations deprived churches of independent income and forced them to accept state salaries for clergy.

The regimes thus found themselves in the position of being able to with-hold or lower salaries to obtain ecclesiastical cooperation and to reward cooperative clergy with larger salaries.

The combined result of these policies was that church attendance dropped off in most of the countries, reaching the lowest levels among East Germans, Czechs, Serbs, and Bulgarians. In Albania the government sim-ply closed all churches and mosques in 1967 and declared religion "abol-ished." Gradually the number of registered adherents dropped.

Secularization proceeded fastest among the Bulgarians and the Czechs. As early as 1962 nearly 65 percent of the Bulgarians declared themselves nonreligious[10] according to one report, while another source reported that about 45 percent of the population were believers in 1978.[11] In Czechoslo-vakia the historical legacy of anticlericalism in Bohemia and Moravia[12] facilitated the process, and official statistics recorded a sharp fall in the number of believers. In 1946, for instance, 64 percent of the population believed in God and only 12 percent did not; as of 1963, only 34 percent said they believed in God, while 38 percent said they did not. Church at-tendance also declined, with only 13 percent attending regularly in 1963 (versus 20 percent in 1946), and 51 percent never attending (versus 24 per-cent in 1946). The differences in the experiences of the component nation-alities were reflected in the fact that while 31 percent of the Czechs were said to be atheists in 1963, only 13 percent of the Slovaks were so described.[13] Surprisingly, official statistics from 1984 show little change among those over the age of fifteen: 36 percent remained religious believers (51 percent in Slovakia and 30 percent in the Czech lands).[14] Since the church has traditionally been weak among Bulgarians and Czechs, state authorities found less resistance to atheization programs.

The church seemed much stronger in East Germany, but by 1983 mem-bership in the Evangelical-Lutheran church had been reduced from 15 mil-lion in 1946 to 7.7 million, and, counting in the other religious organiza-tions, only 56 percent of the population were believers in 1983 (as opposed to 99 percent in 1946).[15]

Elsewhere, secularization proceeded more slowly. In Yugoslavia 70.3 percent of the population were believers as of 1964.[16] But a comparison of recent survey data from Belgrade with earlier surveys reveals an interesting trend: the numbers of both believers and atheists have recently been de-clining, with increasing numbers declaring themselves agnostics.[17]

In Hungary between 76 and 81 percent of the population are nominal believers, and at least two-thirds of adults avail themselves of some reli-gious ceremonies. But less than 20 percent of Hungarian adults attend Sunday services regularly. To some extent, religious adherence in Hungary has become hollow and superficial.[18] Religious affiliation is also negatively correlated with television ownership and urbanization; accordingly, those most active in religion are often the least involved in the sociopolitical life of the nation.

In Romania fully 81 percent of the population were recorded as believers in 1984,[19] and party theorists expressed their frustration with their relative lack of success in this area, attributing it in part—and with justification—to the ability of certain Christian organizations to adapt to social changes and to thus "revitalize" themselves.[20] There have been interconfessional shifts, to be sure, but actual atheization seems to be less tangible, judging from other figures, than in most of the countries of the region.

Finally, in Poland 93 percent of the population are baptized Roman Catholics and 83 percent of the population are believers.[21] The long association of the Catholic church with Polish nationalism is part of the explanation of this intense religiosity.[22] But the relatively greater anthropocentrism of Polish religiosity, focused on the Virgin Mary and the saints and placing a greater premium on communal relations rather than on the individual's relationship to God, also helps to explain the evident immunity of Polish society to secularization. As Barbara Strassberg explains,

> Since [Polish] religious culture is not really based on a knowledge of the doctrine and the church's teaching, it is not threatened by the dissemination of the scientific approach towards the natural and social world. Not caring very much for dogmas, people do not apply scientific criteria to them. . . . [Furthermore,] if secularization can be understood as a process of detheocentrization and of anthropocentrization of culture, then it becomes obvious that in a sociocultural context in which religion itself is anthropocentric, the change leads to a deeper "penetration" of religion into the entire national culture rather than to its "functional separation," "individualization," or "privatization."[23]

Secularization is not merely a question of a decline in formal adherence and actual participation in rituals; other processes are involved as well. In the first place, secularization tends to introduce doubts about specific church doctrines and teachings. Depending on the nature of the teaching thrown into question, the believer may even decide to retain some teachings while rejecting others, or may leave the church, possibly gravitating to another religious body. About 30 percent of Polish Catholics, for instance, evince selective religiosity in this sense, while only 13 percent of Hungarian believers say they are "religious according to the teaching of the church."[24]

This latter option is in turn reinforced by a second, parallel process—the relativization of affiliation. Traditionally, believers were taught that their church was uniquely holy and that all other churches were debasements of God's will. Confessional pluralization contributes to the erosion of this confidence, and believers tend to have a lower threshold of resistance to other denominations. Since the Second Vatican Council, this applies also to the Roman Catholic church. The result is that "the former rigid barriers between the denominations have become and are becoming permeable."[25] Third, secularization brings with it pressures for the laicization of the church as laypeople demand more active roles in church life. The basis communities of the Catholic church are a graphic illustration of this process, and will be discussed below.

Religious Revival in Traditional Religion

That there has been ferment in certain traditional churches, above all the Catholic church, has been clear for some time.[26] It is characteristic of religious revival that its principal impetus comes from the grass roots—this is its source of strength. Revival operates by the selective scuttling of old traditions, creative innovation of new traditions, and the harnessing of existing traditions in new ways; thus, religious revival is transformative. The challenge that this poses to communist party cadres was noted, for instance, in a decree issued by the Georgian party central committee on 18 September 1979, which warned that "in training atheistic cadres we must keep in mind that religious worldviews [and] cults are undergoing modernization, and are becoming more flexible, trying to adjust to present circumstances. Under such conditions, the tasks of atheistic indoctrination are becoming more complex and impose new requirements on atheistic cadres."[27]

Religious revival has been strongest in Hungary and Yugoslavia, though neighboring Ukraine shares in the syndrome. In Poland and (perhaps) East Germany it may be more accurate to speak of religious adaptation, since neither religiosity nor respect for the institutional church was ever seriously in danger. Impulses toward religious revival in the traditional (Orthodox, Catholic, Lutheran, Calvinist) churches in other countries of the region are weaker.

The East German context has already been discussed in chapter 2. Suffice it to add here that the impulses drawing both the Evangelical and the Catholic church into greater engagement in pacifist, environmental, and other social concerns *came from below*, and that the positive church response to these pressures led to a strengthening of their presence (at least temporarily)—especially in the case of the Evangelical-Lutheran church.[28]

In the Polish case the traditional nationalism of the lower clergy and the anthropocentrism of Polish folk piety gave the Catholic faith an uncommon resilience. The church also displayed adaptive capacity in establishing new rituals on the national level, which in turn heightened the consciousness of the Poles as a Catholic nation.[29] In addition, the Oasis and neocatechumenate movements, which have developed their own religious rituals, have reinforced Polish religiosity. Independent religious youth organizations were technically illegal in Poland until early 1989, but Oasis, which emerged in stages in the latter 1950s as a renewal movement for Polish youth, thrived from the the 1960s through the 1980s. Attracting more than 45,000 young people for its summer retreats, the movement sees itself "as an evangelistic movement, dedicated to leading people to accept Christ as Savior and Lord."[30] It has also preserved the Marian cult. The election of Kraków's Karol Cardinal Wojtyła as pope in 1978 only reinforced an already resilient religious feeling among Poles.

In Hungary transformative processes are perhaps as far advanced as anywhere in the region. Hungarian sociologist of religion Miklós Tomka says flatly that traditional religiosity in Hungary is finished.[31] Its replacement is a heavily laicized religiosity in which believers experience their faith as a personal quest for understanding rather than as subordination to clerical authority. To some extent both the Catholic and the Protestant churches have already accommodated themselves to this current, but grassroots pressures sometimes go farther than the respective hierarchies are wont to allow.

The Catholic basis communities are a case in point. The movement can be traced to the creation of the Regnum Marianum in 1903. In the late 1950s there were already many small basis communities operating in Hungary, albeit illegally. In 1976, however, two important changes occurred that affected the church-state relationship. The first was the conclusion of a church-state accord following László Lékai's succession as archbishop of Esztergom and primate of Hungary. The second was the passage of a statute pursuant to Hungary's ratification of the Helsinki Accords, which allowed private citizens to meet in private homes for religious purposes. The result was a "boom" in the founding of basis communities, and by 1987 there may have been as many as four or five thousand.[32]

The basis communities revive the sense of communal bonding which gave early Christianity its great strength, and permit members to talk to each other about questions that concern them. There are at least five major currents among Hungarian basis communities (not to mention various smaller currents): the Charismatic, Focolari, Taisei, Regnum Marianum, and Bush networks. All but the last enjoyed untroubled relations with both hierarchy and the communist state. Bush, led by the inspiring Father György Bulányi, differs from the others in seeking "radical change in the structure of the church, which would involve a redefinition of the roles of the laity, the priesthood, and the bishops,"[33] and in opposing obligatory military service. The Hungarian bishops have refused to support Bulányi's advocacy of conscientious objection, and have even suggested that it is contrary to the teachings of the church.[34] State authorities have likewise been discomfited by the pacifism of Bush, with Imre Miklós, chair of the State Office for Religious Affairs, reportedly telling Vatican officials that "the way will be made green" for the Bush, provided only that it abandon its pacifism.[35] But what concerns us here is not the controversy between Bulányi and both secular and ecclesiastical authorities, but the general striving of the entire basis community movement to "restore" what they see as "authentic" Christianity, and the specific aspiration of Bush to restructure the church.

The Lutheran church in Hungary has also been touched by the winds of change. Long tied to a "Diakonia theology" which preached unambiguous church support for the political system,[36] the Lutheran church has now seen the emergence of internal criticism. In April 1986 nineteen pastors and laymen sent a letter to Bishop Gyula Nagy and all of the country's Lutheran parishes urging "radical inner renewal," including the election of church leaders not subservient to the communist regime. In January 1987 members of the unofficial reform group met with the church leadership and produced a joint statement calling for extensive discussion of the church policy of cooperation with the state and for more open discussion of church problems. The bishops balked, however, at the reform group's call for decentralization of the church's judicial structure.[37] Before the end of the year, Bishop Nagy promised that his church was on the threshold of a "new era" and that the issues raised by the reform group, including its challenge to Diakonia theology and its demand for the restoration of a Lutheran grammar school, would be discussed in an open way. He gave symbolic expression to this resolve by partly rehabilitating the reputation of the deceased Bishop Lajos Ordass, who had been imprisoned by the state. Not surprisingly, Imre Miklós used a ceremonial occasion to warn the Lutheran church not to stray "from the path hitherto followed."[38] With the opening up of Hungarian politics, by 1989 Diakonia theology was dead.

In Yugoslavia and Ukraine impetus to religious revival has come from a very different source—reports of miraculous apparitions of the Madonna that produced a wave of pilgrimages and a marked rise in expressive religiosity among Catholics. In fact there have been a rash of such apparitions in Eastern Europe since 1981: first in Bosnia-Herzegovina, then in Dalmatia (in Gala in 1983,[39] and in Split in 1987[40]), in Poland and Czechoslovakia (where the reported apparitions evoked little response), and in western Ukraine in 1987.[41]

The best known is the apparition of the Madonna seen by six youths in the village of Medjugorje in Herzegovina on 24 June 1981. The youths continued to experience apparitions on almost a daily basis for several years, and four were still reporting apparitions in 1988.[42] Meanwhile, pilgrims started to arrive by the thousands, and Franciscan fathers came to say mass and hear confessions. By mid-1987 there had been 290 reported miracle healings. More than 50,000 pilgrims would arrive on some holy days, mostly Croats or other Yugoslavs, but also increasing numbers of foreigners. Yugoslav Airlines added several flights to cater to Medjugorje pilgrims, expecting some 25,000 foreign tourists to come to Medjugorje in 1987. Local officials belatedly gave permission for Yugoslav tourist agencies to build a big tourist complex in Medjugorje.[43] The swarm of pilgrims has contributed to a feeling of deepened piety among many in Herzegovina and has visibly strengthened the position of the Franciscan order in that region.

More recently, in April 1987 a young Ukrainian girl named Maria Kizyn reported that she had seen "a light in a long-closed church, looked inside, and saw a shining female figure surrounded by radiant light and carrying a child."[44] Since then, as many as 45,000 pilgrims per day have traveled to the village of Grushevo, where Kizyn reported the apparition.[45] Unlike Medjugorje, where the vision has been restricted to the six young people, many people at Grushevo have reported seeing the Madonna. These "sightings" have energized the devoutly Catholic population of western Ukraine and revived hopes of relegalization.

The Madonna's "message" at Medjugorje is a clue to the meaning of these apparitions: pray, repent, and think of God. The message is absolute simplicity with no adornment whatsoever. The receptivity of Yugoslav Croats and west Ukrainians to the apparitions signifies the desire of many in these countries to find a simple piety with simple answers that will cut through the complex challenges posed by contemporary life. These expressions of folk piety necessarily risk serious distortion of the church's rather more complex teachings; thus, the Vatican has reacted very slowly and cautiously, and at this writing has still not pronounced final judgment on either of these alleged miracles.

Finally, the Serbian Orthodox church has experienced a kind of revival, albeit a secularizing one fueled by Serbian nationalism. The outbreak of

Albanian nationalist riots in the Serbian province of Kosovo in April 1981 and subsequent incidents set thousands of Serbs and Montenegrins to flight and provoked a Serbian nationalist backlash. Serbian Orthodox church clergy spoke out about Kosovo, and the church newspaper *Pravoslavlje* began running articles on national themes, celebrated the anniversary of Serbian orthographer Vuk Karadžić, and even published poetry about Kosovo. All of this found resonance among Serbs, and even nonreligious Serbs started to take an interest in "their" church. A poll was taken among the citizens of Belgrade in 1987, revealing that one out of every five respondents "agreed with the statement that the Serbian Orthodox church was the *most* lasting and the *most* dependable Serbian institution."[46]

Confessional Change

Religious revival changes the character of religious organizations. Confessional change affects the balance between religious organizations. People leave churches for different reasons. Some, of course, leave because they cease to credit the supernatural claims of religion. Others transfer their loyalty from one denomination to another. The transferral process, or *confessional change*, has taken two forms in Eastern Europe: movement between traditional churches (typically as a result of confessional intermarriage or the unavailability of the services of one's original church in a particular community); and conversion from a traditional church to a "neo-Protestant" church (chiefly Baptists, Pentecostals, Plymouth Brethren, Congregationalists, Mormons, Seventh-Day Adventists, Nazarenes, and Jehovah's Witnesses).

Leaving aside Albania (for which no data are available), these dual processes have been occurring in *all* the countries of the region. They are weakest in Poland, although even there neo-Protestants are winning converts. Neo-Protestant conversions are most numerous in Romania and Hungary, as young people especially abandon the Romanian Orthodox church and the Hungarian Reformed church.

In fact, most traditional Protestant churches in the region, as well as the Bulgarian and Romanian Orthodox churches, declined in the 1980s, due largely to the subservience of their bishops to communist state authorities.[47] The major exception was the Evangelical-Lutheran church in East Germany, which experienced a revival, but that church's association with pacifist dissent was also exceptional.

The Bulgarian and Romanian Orthodox churches, like some Protestant churches, came to agreement with the communists soon after World

War II. Typically they agreed to support the internal and foreign policies of the regimes, endorse Soviet bloc peace propaganda, and remain silent about internal injustices. In exchange, the churches would be granted state salaries for clergy, and the opportunity to operate seminaries and theological institutes, and to publish church periodicals. In Romania, in fact, the accommodation of Patriarch Justinian (1948–77) to the regime provoked open mutiny among some bishops and believers in the early part of his reign.[48] By the 1970s disgusted Orthodox believers were switching to the Baptist and Pentecostal churches. Beginning in 1973 the former grew at a rate of about 13 percent per year.[49]

In Hungary, as in Latvia, the ratio of Protestants to Catholics steadily declined as dissatisfied Protestants left their quiescent churches for the more outspoken Catholic church or, at least in Hungary, for smaller sects. The Reformed (Calvinist) church is by far the weaker of the two mainline Protestant churches in Hungary. Presided over by Bishop Károly Toth, the Reformed church signed a major capitulary agreement with the state in 1948, by which it abided until the collapse of communism; the agreement set the limits within which the church could operate. In 1987 the Reformed church signed another agreement that regulated religious education on church premises. Keston College reported that the agreement was "designed to guarantee that the church's Christian education program develops in harmony with the interests of the state."[50] But during 1987 Christian reformers within the church repeatedly criticized the 1948 agreement and called for a new legal basis. Bishop Toth addressed this question in his report to the synodal council in December 1987, but rather than embracing the idea of reform, he called instead for the strengthening of his church's "alliance" with the state.[51] In the same report, however, Toth conceded that church numbers were declining and that Church funerals outnumbered baptisms two-to-one in 1987. The Church was also *qualitatively* weak, with only about 5 percent of its young people participating in religious instruction.

In most countries in the region, the Baptists constitute a nominal presence: 22,000 in East Germany,[52] 7,000 in Poland,[53] 4,000 in Czechoslovakia,[54] 2,000 in Yugoslavia,[55] 1,000 in Bulgaria,[56] and 20,000 in Hungary.[57] In Romania, by contrast, the Baptists have been able to establish a more perceptible presence. As recently as 1980 there were only 120,000 Baptists in Romania,[58] a number far ahead of the other Baptist communities; but by 1986 the Romanian Baptist church numbered 200,000 members with an additional constituency of 100,000 and was the fastest-growing Baptist church in Europe.[59] Fired with enthusiasm, Romania's Baptists attracted the attention of the regime. Various Baptist pastors were imprisoned and harassed, and some Baptist churches were bulldozed. Whereas Orthodoxy and Catholicism are priest-centered churches, the Baptist movement is more believer-centered and prides itself on its democratic structure and lay participation. The fact that this movement is experiencing high growth in Romania is a clue to undercurrents of political attitudes.

Pentecostals are present in the Balkans, with about 200,000 in Romania[60] and about 10,000 in Bulgaria.[61] Like the Baptists, the Pentecostals have had constant problems in Romania. In a well-publicized case in 1974, for instance, Pentecostal activist Vasile Rascol was given a two-year prison sentence for the illegal distribution of Romanian-language religious literature printed abroad, specifically, 150 Bibles and books, including Romanian translations of Billy Graham's *The Secret of Happiness*, John Bunyan's *Pilgrim's Progress*, and C. H. M.'s *Thoughts on Leviticus*.[62] Despite various forms of harassment, the Pentecostal church in Romania continued to grow, and it opened a seminary in 1976. The combined number of converts to the Baptist, Pentecostal, and Plymouth Brethren churches in Romania comes to about 15,000 to 20,000 per year—a statistically significant figure that points to cultural stress in Romanian society.

Despite its small size, the Bulgarian Pentecostal church is the largest Protestant denomination in that country (10,000 members and 120 churches in 1980). From 1944 to 1976 this church experienced little growth, but in the latter 1970s its ranks were augmented, chiefly by young people. Alongside the registered Pentecostal communities, there are also unregistered Pentecostal communities like the "Tinchevists," which add roughly 4,000 believers to the total.[63] Pentecostal pastors by and large prudently avoided politics in their sermons, but the intensity of their religious feeling attracted the state's hostility.[64]

Among fundamentalist Christians the best represented in Eastern Europe and the fastest growing are the Seventh-Day Adventists and the Jehovah's Witnesses. Both groups are present throughout the region. The largest Adventist congregation is again the Romanian, with an official membership between 55,000 and 60,000, and a constituency of between 80,000 and 100,000 "affiliated" sympathizers.[65] There are also 11,300 Seventh-Day Adventists in East Germany,[66] 10,000 in Poland,[67] 7,000 in Czechoslovakia,[68] roughly 11,000 in Yugoslavia,[69] 3,000 in Bulgaria,[70] and a small number in Hungary.[71] Adventists believe that the Second Coming of Christ is close at hand and that their primary task is to prepare for that event. As such, their orientation is distinctly other-worldly.

Relations between the Adventist church and the Catholic church in

Poland are distinctly hostile. Stanisław Dąbrowski, president of the Polish Seventh-Day Adventists, told a Polish journalist in 1985, "The Roman Catholic Church has not rid itself of its hegemonist tendencies and practices vis-à-vis adherents of other faiths, and . . . its clergymen, contrary to spectacular assurances, often can't resist temptations leading to discrimination against a religious background."[72] In October 1987 the trans-European division of the Seventh-Day Adventist church organized a mission in Gdańsk. More than 1,500 people attended the nightly meetings, with some 6,000 turning out for the New Life program conducted over a two-week period. Dąbrowski concluded that "people, especially the young, are looking for alternatives to their present day lifestyle and aspirations."[73]

The outspokenness of the Adventists earned them difficulties in several countries, though probably nowhere as great as in Romania, where they are strongest. In 1984 Romania's Adventists had 526 congregations served by 143 priests. At one time there were nine churches in Bucharest alone. But by late summer 1986 only five of those churches remained,[74] the others becoming victims of Ceauşescu's urban planning program. Still, until Ceauşescu started demolishing churches, the Romanian Adventists had little difficulty with the regime.

I shall omit separate discussions of the Plymouth Brethren (45,000 in Romania), the Mormons (4,700 in East Germany, less than 250 in Hungary),[75] and the Congregationalists (1,000–2,000 in Bulgaria) and pass immediately to the discussion of the Nazarenes and the Jehovah's Witnesses. Unlike the other groups discussed here, the Nazarenes and the Jehovah's Witnesses have had some difficulty obtaining legal status. The Nazarenes have long been legal in Hungary and Yugoslavia, but were banned in Ceauşescu's Romania.[76] They are convinced pacifists and refuse to bear arms; in Hungary they obtained official dispensation as conscientious objectors, but in Yugoslavia[77] and Romania their refusal to perform military service brought them only trouble. The Nazarenes were also vocally critical of the communist social and political order, refused to let their children attend state schools, and take a millennial view of the Second Coming of Christ, which they believe is close at hand.

But as Earl Pope notes, "the most feared group, with their vehement criticism of ecclesiastical, social, and political institutions" has been the Jehovah's Witnesses movement.[78] The Jehovah's Witnesses enjoyed legal status in Yugoslavia for many years, but were relegalized in Poland in 1989 and in East Germany in 1990. The largest concentration of Jehovah's Witnesses may be in Poland, where there may be as many as 100,000 adherents.[79] There are reportedly between 25,000 and 30,000 active

Jehovah's Witnesses in East Germany[80] and 10,000 in Yugoslavia,[81] with additional adherents in Czechoslovakia, Hungary, and Romania. Their refusal to bear arms landed many Jehovah's Witnesses in jail in Hungary,[82] Poland,[83] and Yugoslavia.[84] In spite of that, Yugoslavia's community is able to publish *Kula stražara* (*Watchtower*) in more than 32,000 copies in four linguistic variants.[85] In July 1987 Poland's community organized a three-day assembly in Lublin attended by 12,000 people,[86] an indication that the regime was turning a blind eye toward this "illegal" organization. Moreover, in summer 1988 Poland introduced alternative social service for conscientious objectors,[87] and granted the Jehovah's Witnesses legal registration on 12 May 1989. They subsequently hosted the massive World Congress of Jehovah's Witnesses in Warsaw on 11–13 August, attended by 60,000 people from thirty-seven countries.[88] In Yugoslavia in 1987 authorities released one Jehovah's Witness from prison after serving less than two months of a five-year sentence, with no official explanation, and acquitted another later that year on the grounds that his pacifism made him "mentally unfit" for military duty.[89] The Jehovah's Witnesses' radical millennarianism and their energetic efforts to proselytize made them particularly unwelcome to the communist states.

Finally, something should be said about Dragan Marjanović, the so-called "messiah from Veliki Mokri Lug." His early life was unexceptional, but in 1973, the thirty-seven-year-old Marjanović left his wife and children and began to change his life. By 1987 he was holding open-air meetings before hundreds of Yugoslavs, dispensing miraculous cures and inspiring rumors that he was Christ incarnate.[90] A year later he had disappeared from sight; I was told that the authorities had pressed him to curtail his activities.

The high-growth sects discussed above have been recruiting mainly from adherents of the Orthodox church in Romania, Bulgaria, and Serbia; the Reformed church and, to a lesser extent, the Lutheran church in Hungary; and from among vulnerable agnostics. To a lesser extent, the Catholic church has been vulnerable, especially in Poland and Hungary, while the Evangelical-Lutheran church in eastern Germany probably holds the largest pool of potential recruits for the neo-Protestant sects in that country. Interconfessional conversions have become much more common since the 1960s; thus, interconfessional boundaries have become somewhat fluid.

The mainline churches have started to become concerned about losses to these newer organizations, especially the Jehovah's Witnesses. For example, Hungarian bishop József Cserháti of Pécs issued a pastoral letter in January 1987 warning about the growth of that sect in the previous three years. Similarly, the East German Protestant weekly *Glaube und Heimat* called on church members and clergy to be on guard against Jehovah's Witnesses. The Vatican even commissioned a study of sects and new religious movements from its Secretariat for Promoting Christian Unity, in collaboration with the Secretariat for Non-Believers and the Pontifical Council for Culture.[91]

The Appearance of New Cults

In contemporary Eastern Europe, as in the United States of the 1960s, the explosion of new cults has been chronologically associated with a flourishing of social and political protest as symptoms of a single syndrome. Underlying both religious innovation and social protest is the deepening of social stress and the breakdown of traditional associational channels for coping with stress. Cult recruits are typically people who have had difficulty in adjusting to society or to changes in society.[92] Edward Tiryakian has highlighted the transformative impact of social change on the "normative structure" of society, which suggests a connection between social change and the rise of new religious movements.[93] Individual stress may arise from any of a number of sources, including the diminution of the status and presence of traditional churches (Stark and Bainbridge suggest a direct negative correlation between the strength of traditional churches and the growth of cults),[94] change in gender roles,[95] and alienation from materialism and the work ethic.[96] Cults may, of course, develop in different ways and may satisfy sundry needs on the part of individuals.[97]

Eastern Europe has suddenly become fertile ground for cults. Some related symptoms are readily visible, such as the recent boom for psychoanalysis in Hungary[98] and the astrology and faith healing fads in the USSR.[99] Other signs of cultural fragmentation and symbolic innovation remain below the surface.

One may differentiate among four types of cults in Eastern Europe today: Oriental and neo-Oriental (Buddhism, transcendental meditation, yoga, and Hare Krishna); occult (spiritualism and satanism); pseudo-Christian (the Unification church of Sun Myung Moon); and atavistic/mystic (theosophy, Bogomilism, and Danovism). While highly diverse, these cults are all *oppositional movements* reflecting the total rejection of the dominant culture of the given society.[100] The Unification church ("Moonies") aims at no less than the total transformation of the world and its unification in subordination to the personal authority of Reverend Moon, who is viewed as the new redeemer.[101]

Transcendental meditation (TM) and yoga probably enjoy the greatest exposure in Eastern Europe, with bookstores openly displaying books on these subjects. There have been yoga circles in Poland at least since 1985, and in Belgrade, Yugoslavia, since 1987.[102] By 1989 there were some 30 TM centers with an estimated 26,000 adherents in Yugoslavia. TM gathered steam in Romania in 1982, winning adherents among university faculty and students, when a Romanian émigré teaching at the Bucharest Education and Psychology Research Institute began to propagate it. In winter 1982 he was fired, the institute was closed, and several prominent officials lost their jobs.

There is also a yoga commune in Hungary in the town of Vagot Puszta, in the Mecsek Mountains just north of Pécs. The commune conducts meditation sessions twice a day and urban dwellers typically drive there for the weekend, using it like a retreat house. The commune has incorporated elements of Hinduism into its practices and prayers are recited in Sanskrit. Although that is the only such commune in Hungary, Joshi Bharat (a Hungarian married to an Indian woman) teaches yoga in Gödöllő, a far suburb of Budapest. Hungarians have also become interested in mental telepathy.[103]

In Bulgaria, by contrast, TM and yoga benefited from the active support of the one-time minister of culture, Lyudmila Zhivkova (1942–81), the daughter of party leader Todor Zhivkov. Zhivkova, who traveled widely and read voraciously, seems to have been familiar with the writings of early twentieth-century Russian mystics Georgi Ivanovich Gurdjieff and P. D. Ouspensky. In the process of reading their and other works, she developed her own synthesis of Marxism-Leninism and Eastern mystic traditions. As minister of culture, she became involved in the National Program for the Harmonious Development of Humanity, presenting periodic celebrations of outstanding "Titans of the Spirit." In 1978, celebrating the work of Russian artist Nikolay Roerich (1874–1947), whose work shows a blend of neomedieval romanticism and Buddhist mysticism, she gave an address, citing, in passing, "the Fiery Sign and the Fiery Sword, the Temple of Light, the Himalayas [which] pulsate and vibrate in the Heart of our Universe, [and] the beauty of psychic energy radiating from the heart."[104] The following year a central course in yoga was established in Bulgaria by the Committee on Culture, under Zhivkova's personal supervision. An Indian guru also came to Zhivkova's home for an unspecified duration to initiate her into yoga. Since her time, the practice of TM and yoga have spread in Bulgaria, with textbooks circulating in photocopies.

Bulgaria has also seen the recent revival of two domestic movements.

The Danovist Cult, or White Brotherhood, founded between the wars by Bulgarian philosopher Petar Danov, has reemerged lately. The Danovists blend Hinduism and Orthodox Christianity. In 1980 they were reported to have established a central society in Sofia, with branches in twelve provincial towns. Highly secretive about their organization, the Danovists have conducted open-air rituals at sunrise and at sunset, often on Mount Vitosha or at Danov's grave near the Soviet embassy in Sofia.[105]

The Bogomil movement, which can be traced back to the ninth century and which owes its theological origins to Mesopotamian Manichaeanism, is also experiencing a revival. On 25 June 1985 the provincial newspaper *Haskovska Tribuna* reported that Bogomil groups were winning converts in the towns of Dimitrovgrad, Lyubimets, and Merichleri, and in the villages of Dobrich, Krum, Stalevo, Garvanovo, and Levka.[106]

Buddhism has also won converts in Bulgaria, Czechoslovakia, Poland, and Estonia (where there were about one hundred Buddhists as of early 1988),[107] and secret Oriental devotional societies have been set up in Bulgaria and Yugoslavia. Interest and belief in reincarnation has also mushroomed.[108]

Buddhism came to Poland in 1972 when a Korean monk called Sung San Son Sa (literally, the Zen Master of Sung Mountain), visited Warsaw and Kraków at the invitation of Antoni Szoska and converted sixteen persons. In 1979 two Poles spent time in Korea studying Zen Buddhism, returning to their native country at the end of the study program. By 1981 Polish Buddhists had established the Zen Culture Society and registered it with the state. Temples were established in Kraków (1978), Warsaw (1979), Gdańsk (1979), Łódź (1980), and Lublin (1981), and study groups in nine other cities. As of 1988 there were 1,000 Korean-style Zen Buddhists in Poland.[109]

Eastern religions and extrasensory perception groups have gained popularity in Lithuania at the expense of its traditional religion, Catholicism. The two leading figures in this trend have been Abay and Mirza, two self-proclaimed gurus from the Karakalpak ASSR in Uzbekistan. In 1985 the journal *Svyturys* published an article by Juozas Jurevičius about Lithuanians making pilgrimages to the Karakalpak ASSR to visit Mirza. According to Jurevičius, Mirza and his translator extracted sex and money in exchange for training in the ways of attaining spiritual contentment.[110] Initiates then returned to Lithuania and set up "personal liberation" camps.

A large number of Oriental and pseudo-Oriental cults have also won adherents in Yugoslavia, including the conspiratorial group Ananda Marga, founded in India in 1955, which seeks the revolutionary transformation of the world.[111] The Ananda Marga cult was introduced into Yugoslavia in 1972 when one of its gurus made a visit to Zagreb. He won a number of sympathizers and a branch of the cult was subsequently set up in that city. Within a few years Belgrade had its own thirty-member branch, while Ljubljana claimed an even larger number.[112] Ananda Marga sends missionaries to Yugoslavia on a regular basis, including a missionary visit in 1983 and a visit by guru Judasil in 1987. The cult seeks to promote world government, envisages the development of a single world language based on English, and portrays feminine energy as negative, masculine energy as positive, signifying the cult's desire to move women into a more subordinate position.

With the newfound interest in Oriental religion comes a receptivity to the Hare Krishna consciousness movement. Indeed, by early 1982 the Hare Krishna cult numbered 3,000 adherents in the USSR and additional numbers in several East European countries, including Yugoslavia. The Krishna cult, which originated in India but floundered in that hostile domestic terrain,[113] came to the USSR in 1971 when spiritual leader Bhaktivedanta Swami Prabhupada visited Moscow and initiated a young Russian into Krishna teachings. One Russian who joined the cult later recalled: "We would meet in the homes of members of the group, prepare vegetarian dishes in accordance with the Vedas and invite people in—just people off the street—some would always accept. . . . We would view films and slides about India, about the Hare Krishna movement, illustrations to the sacred texts, chant mantras. So the circle of devotees gradually expanded until the repressions began."[114]

The cult repeatedly filed for registration as a legally recognized community (for example, in Riga in mid-1987), but for a long time it was turned down. As one Soviet official put it, the Council for Religious Affairs considers the cult "ideologically deviant." As of early 1986 fifty members of the Krishna cult were in Soviet prisons or psychiatric institutions; yet the cult showed defiance by holding a *kirtans* (spiritual chanting) in Moscow's Arbat shopping center on 16 August 1987.[115] By the mid-1980s there were also relatively large Krishna groups in Bulgaria and Poland.[116] Finally, in May 1988 the Hare Krishna community in the USSR was informed that it would be permitted to register as a legal religious organization, to build a temple, and to import religious literature.[117] As of late 1989, however, the sect was still experiencing problems.

In Yugoslavia the Hare Krishna cult dates its presence from 1980, when Vladimir Radek returned from London and organized the first Krishna group in Split with fifteen members. Additional branches were established in

Zagreb, Pula, and Belgrade. The Krishna cult began issuing books and bro-chures, mostly authored by Swami Prabhupada. By 1984 the Krishnas had established a firm foothold in Yugoslavia and the cult grew more tangibly over the next three years, expanding into Slovenia under the name Society of Hindu Assemblies (with about fifty members and several hundred sym-pathizers as of early 1987).[118] Like the Ananda Marga cult, the Krishna cult advocates the "superiority" of males over females. The Yugoslav weekly magazine *Danas* described the Hare Krishnas as the most male-chauvinistic of all guru cults.[119]

The Polish religious scene has also become quite diverse. Aside from the Hare Krishna groups, yoga circles, and Buddhists, Poland has recently seen the emergence of Zen and Hindu communities, Rastafarians, and faith healers of various stripes.[120]

Religious change came more slowly to East Germany, but even here there was an awakened interest in the new religions, as reflected in the 1984 publication of an important sociological treatment of the subject by Helmut Obst.[121]

Specialists on religion in the communist world have now started—as did specialists in the West earlier—to try to sort out the reasons for the sudden attraction to Oriental and pseudo-Oriental cults and artifacts. For example, *Nauka i religiia* reflected as early as 1976:

> [I]nterest in the Far East, its history, philosophy, religion and art, has been growing in our country in recent decades. A number of studies have appeared as well as translations of original works such as the Dharmapada, the Ramayana, and the Mahabharata. This is a positive development, to be sure, but it has drawbacks. The literature is not always interpreted critically, for one thing. . . . False, antiscientific, mys-tical ideas may be learned in some cases. . . . Religious and mystical teachings creep into our fiction. The heroine of Valeria Alfeyeva's short story "House and Garden" [*Novy mir*, no. 3, 1976], for instance, keeps the Bhagavad Gita on her table and consults it regularly as a guide to living. She has great reverence for it, in fact, and finds it a source of revelation and consolation. Such sayings [which she ponders] as "Act selflessly, as does the Ruler of the world" and "Reason is only one of the energies given to us" . . . surely are detrimental to readers' materialist upbringing.[122]

The Theosophist Society, which holds that religious heterogeneity de-rives from semantic confusion and which claims to have tapped the essen-tial truth of all religions, has adherents in Yugoslavia too. Founded in 1875, the society spread to Yugoslavia in 1924, after establishing chapters in Germany and Austria (Vienna). The first chapter in Yugoslavia was set up in Zagreb with Valerije Mayerhoffer as secretary, but the society soon established chapters in Belgrade and Ljubljana, and later in other cities. Some of its early members were also Masons. By 1927 the Yugoslav Theosophist Society was publishing the journal *Teozofija*, which continued on a regular basis until World War II. Of Yugoslavia's sixteen prewar Theosophist chapters, fourteen survived the war. At the end of the 1970s a young and energetic Emilio Trampuz set about "modernizing" the society and attracting new members. Two new journals were launched: *Teozof* and *Mladi teozof*. At the outset of the 1980s the society experienced a crisis when Franjo Miličević's efforts to establish an internal guru cult following polarized the society. The crisis was finally resolved when Miličević was expelled from the society in March 1981.[123]

Finally, the occult has started to attract a following in Eastern Europe and the Soviet West. The "Eastern" occult revival was, as is well known, presaged by a similar revival in the West in the late 1960s and early 1970s, and takes in everything from astrology to spiritualism to satanism. The lure of the occult is the lure of the arcane and the bizarre, the ambivalent fascination of the alien and potentially threatening. For those desperate to escape their mundane world, the occult offers a possible path.

Of the different strains of occult revival, the most innocent is astrology. As Marcello Truzzi noted some years ago, among the factors which reinforce the fascination with astrological prediction and advice are: the fact that they cater to the ego and provide ego-gratifying attention; the element of the esoteric, which also gives it a quality of entertainment; the ambiguity of astrological forecasts, which imparts an air of mystery and permits multiple interpretations; and the self-fulfilling nature of some astrological prophecies.[124] Astrology probably has adherents throughout the region.

Spiritualism is a far more serious affair. Founded in the United States in 1848 and introduced into Great Britain in 1852, the spiritualist movement believes that the survival of the human personality after the death of the physical body is a provable fact, and attempts to make contact with the deceased; thus, its primary activity is not worship but the séance.[125] Spiritualism came to Eastern Europe in the early years of the century but spiritualist groups have recently grown and spread in Bohemia, Hungary, and Yugoslavia (chiefly in Belgrade and Zagreb).[126]

Satanism exists in various strains from a largely fashion-oriented fad to the glorification of evil and positive worship of its incarnation in Satan.

Among the former one might mention the satanic theatrics of the Polish rock group Kat. But in 1987 and 1988 various reports emerged of the existence of violence-prone satanists in Leningrad,[127] Czechoslovakia, Hungary, Poland, and Yugoslavia. There are also satanists in the East German city of Leipzig.[128] From these reports it is clear that theatrical satanism and satanist fashions have stimulated the engagement in satanic rituals and even violence. What is not clear is how many people actually believe in Satan, let alone worship him.

The Polish case is probably a clue to regional trends. There was, for instance, a satanist fad among the Polish elite classes in the interwar period, complete with a functioning Church of Satan, books about satanism, and elements of satanism reflected in the poetry of the period. None of this survived World War II and it was not until the 1980s that satanism once more entered Poland, this time on the coattails of the heavy metal rock scene.[129] In 1986 a large group of rock fans showed up for the annual rock festival at Jarocin attired in black outfits emblazoned with the number "666" and the devil's pentagram, wearing studs and chains and an upside-down cross. One night during the festival they celebrated a "black mass" by engaging in the ritual slaughter of a dog and the desecration of a grave.[130] "Sacrificing animals, desecrating graves, violence, and even forcing persons into prostitution are all part of satanism in Poland," according to Ewa Smolinska-Borecka.[131] How many young people are involved in the satanist scene? Reverend Dr. Czesław Cekiera, an assistant professor at the Catholic University in Lublin, estimates that they may number as many as 10,000 in Poland as a whole.[132]

In 1987 the Czech samizdat periodical *Informacé o cirkvi* cited evidence of satanic practices in Czechoslovakia:

> Reports from Bohemia, Moravia, and Slovakia are now multiplying about the presence of this dark reality. It is mainly students who are becoming addicted to satanism. They wear upside-down crosses, invoke the name of Satan in prayer, conduct perverse rites and hold "black masses," and vow to perform an evil deed every day. They fanatically avow all power to Satan over this world, which must be destroyed.
>
> Members of this movement vary. Some join out of curiosity, others due to a mistaken romanticism, others out of defiance or the feeling of frustration, some from unbelief, and, finally, there are those who join due to a genuinely dark, demonic wrath.[133]

In Yugoslavia the suicides of a twenty-two-year-old girl in 1986 and of a thirteen-year-old girl in 1988 were tied to satanism, and satanic graffiti (including the number "666") were painted on a wall in Split in March 1988. A satanic movement called Dark is alleged to have existed in that country for several years and to promote "mystic death" as a means to "rebirth." It has received relatively little mention in the press, although a brief flurry of press attention in March 1988 linked the group to a string of suicides in Zagreb over the course of the 1980s.[134] As in Poland, satanism in Yugoslavia has been linked to the rock scene, with adherents allegedly listening to Bauhaus and Joy Division.[135] In 1989 a small publishing house in Šabac published a thin book entitled *The Solution of the Mystery 666*, which, among other things, predicts that the apocalypse will come in the year 2333.[136] Likewise in Hungary, there are reports of a satanist movement. As in the other countries, it is, at this point, restricted to young people.[137]

Astrology, spiritualism, and satanism do not qualify as religious in any usual understanding of the word. But they clearly may substitute for and displace conventional religion (at least in the case of spiritualism and satanism). Truzzi has suggested an alternative conceptualization: that is, to view them as *pop religions*. What is distinct to pop religion is that it preserves and in some ways even exaggerates some of the externals of religiosity, especially when it comes to ritual behavior, but scuttles concern with the moral and theological content. Pop religion thus demystifies religion and is a symptom of secularization. But as Truzzi points out,

> [I]t is precisely because we no longer believe in the fearsome aspects of the occult that we are willing to experiment with them. Most of those who would willingly draw a proper pentagram on the floor to invoke a demon would do so precisely because they do not really believe that some Devil's emissary who might just pluck their souls down to Hell would possibly ever visit them. If we fully believed in demons, we certainly would not want to call them up.[138]

Closing Thoughts

In communist aspirations, secularization was supposed to eliminate popular belief in the supernatural and to cut the institutional umbilical chord with Tradition, that obstacle to orthodox communist resocialization as it was conceived in the decades prior to Gorbachev. But as Peter Berger noted more than two decades ago, the principal effect of secularization is to bring about "a demonopolization of religious traditions [which] thus, *ipso facto*, leads to a pluralistic situation."[139] Hitherto unchallenged spiritual and normative explanations are challenged in the course of secularization; this, combined with social change and culture contact, increases the likelihood that alternative explanations may find receptive audiences.

The religious phenomena examined in this chapter are highly diverse, but they have some things in common. First, they are *symptoms* of change, whether it be change in the strength of traditional religion, in the expectations and needs of people, or in the relations between generations and their distinct orientations toward popular culture. Second, they figure as *reactions* to social and confessional change and to social and confessional stress. And finally, they are, at least potentially, *forces for further change*, whether in the sense that one or more of these phenomena may produce or evolve into a major new religious organization, or in the sense that both separately and collectively these phenomena may have diverse effects on a society by compelling the response of other organizations or by stimulating debates and discussions which might otherwise not have arisen.

6 Church and Dissent in Praetorian Poland

After a decade of communist rule, the Polish review *Przegląd kulturalny* published an article by Jan Szczepański warning that the formal political institutions were "comparatively inefficient and only superficially established."[1] The warning was not heeded, however, and Poland's communists failed to develop valued political institutions. The result was weakness of the party, perennial problems with corruption, and inconsistencies in the application and execution of the laws. In this political setting social groups came to face each other without widely accepted channels for mediation and political power itself became fragmented. In this context organized institutions such as the military, students,[2] labor unions, and churches have behaved in a more politicized way. Samuel P. Huntington has called this syndrome *praetorianism*.[3]

The church is a logical player in the praetorian syndrome: it is hierarchically organized, commands an independently recruited cadre, lays claim to the loyalty of all or much of the population, and has financial, psychological, and political ("the power of the pulpit") resources at its disposal. In the early phases of the slide into praetorianism the church also has the advantage that society is in some ways still simple, insofar as the incipient stages of praetorianism may coincide with a break with traditional politics (in some sense of the word). But, as Huntington notes,

> [A]s the praetorian society becomes more complex and differentiated, the number of social groups and forces multiplies and the problems of coordination and interest aggregation become increasingly complex. In the absence of effective central political institutions for the resolution of social conflicts, the military [like the church too] become[s] simply one of several relatively insulated and autonomous social forces. Their capacity to elicit and to induce cooperation declines.[4]

From a functionalist perspective one might say that certain functions need to be carried out in a society, and that when the "normal" channels are unavailable for certain purposes, other institutions (in this case, the church) take up the slack. The church's recurrent role as mediator between striking workers and the government during the May 1988 strikes in Gdańsk and Nowa Huta illustrates this point. But as society becomes more complex, its functional needs become more complex. In this context the church finds itself confronted with tasks which are not only more complex, but may even be at odds with each other.

It has become fashionable in recent years to think of the Polish church as the unfailing and constant ally of dissent and underground labor. This portrayal is misleading in two respects. First, the church's attitude toward dissent has not been constant over the years, and has been affected by a number of factors, including the appearance of opportunities for cooperation with the government. The church, after all, has its own institutional needs in mind: this is certainly true where the decisions and policies of the hierarchy are concerned. This in turn suggests my second point: it is to some extent inaccurate to generalize about "the church" and dissent, insofar as different members of both hierarchy and lower clergy have taken rather different attitudes toward dissent. Bearing these two caveats in mind, I propose to argue in this chapter that the traditional social role of the clergy as nurturer of culture, community, and sometimes civil liberties[5] has been transformed by the political mobilization of the Polish public, with the result that long-standing ambivalences within the church are reflected in new ways. Whereas the nineteenth-century hierarchy worried about offending the royal monarchies and upsetting the delicate forms of *modus vivendi* established in partitioned Poland, and felt ambivalent about nationalism insofar as Poles were clearly a "Catholic nation," Polish primates Stefan Wyszyński (1948–81) and Józef Glemp (since 1981) have cautiously built up and safeguarded various prerogatives for the church, including Catholic deputies in the *Sejm*, Catholic intelligentsia clubs, and, since the early 1970s, generous allowances for the construction of new churches. They have therefore been loathe to see these threatened by reckless advocacy or by the headlong destabilization of society. Far better, then, that people "keep calm. Do not drive our country to still greater disaster. Only self-control and the maintenance of calm can save the country and the Church which fulfills her mission in it."[6]

Primate Glemp has at times seemed to shy away from a political role. Part of the reason may well be his evident belief that the politicization of the church might sap its moral authority.[7] But in conditions of praetorianism, the Polish church ultimately found it impossible to skirt politics, both because the church is *already* political in the articulation of its core values, and because those discontented with the system look to the church for succor.

As of 1988 the Catholic church in Poland had 98 bishops, 23,432 priests, 23,711 nuns, and 9,038 seminarians; it operated 10,719 churches, 1,835 chapels, 2,506 convents, 447 monasteries, 12 high schools, and the Catholic University at Lublin with faculties of theology, philosophy, law, the humanities (including modern languages), and social sciences.[8] According to the episcopate's figures, the church publishes 35 mass periodicals (out of a total of 2,943 Polish periodicals total).[9] And in April 1987 the church established an agricultural committee, with more than $10 million in funding from abroad, in order to fund water and sewage projects in the 2,200 Polish villages which still lack modern water and sewage systems, provide private farmers with the opportunity to buy machinery normally unavailable in Poland, and conduct limited programs in farm education.[10] These resources give the church real strength in both the city and the countryside.

Despite the formidable strength and the legendary fervor of the Poles for their church, communist regime spokespersons regularly referred to religion as a "private affair," suggesting that the church steer clear of social questions. Alternatively, the daily newspaper *Trybuna Ludu* argued in 1986 that part of the clergy bases its attitude toward pluralism on its misconstrual of pluralism "as a system of relations that guarantees Catholicism exclusiveness in every field."[12] Such a characterization may be appropriate to a discussion of Polish Catholicism in the 1920s and 1930s, but it does not reflect the present reality.

The church has in fact nurtured pluralism in several areas—and under communism, pluralism was often tantamount to dissent. First, after the 1981 suppression of Solidarity, the church dramatically expanded its role in education. Church schools throughout the country began offering classes across a wide range of subjects from European history to pig breeding. One of the most formidable schools is the Institute of Christian Culture in Lubochnia headed by Reverend Mirosław Mikulski, which offers classes at all age levels from preschool to age nineteen, with extensive adult education in subjects like Christian ethics and the Bible. During the 1987–88 academic year, the adult education curriculum at Lubochnia included lectures on "Noncommunist Resistance in World War II" and "Citizens' Protection under the Law." St. Maximilian's Church in Konin organized a meeting of opposition journalists, who discussed their views of the Iran-Iraq war and the 1988 American presidential election, and criticized the Polish government's economic policies.[12]

Second, the church has actively backed "alternative culture" in Poland by sponsoring art exhibitions, poetry readings, theater groups, and film festivals. In 1975 the Warsaw Campus Ministry launched its annual Week of Christian Culture, embracing lectures, concerts, poetry, discussion groups, and meetings with noted scholars, writers, and artists. A related event, the Sacro-Song Festival, has attracted both Polish and foreign performers since its inception in 1968 and draws tens of thousands of listeners, mostly young people.[13] Ernest Bryll's play *The Circle*, which deals with the feelings of despair experienced by Christ's apostles in the period between the Crucifixion and the Resurrection, was banned by the authorities, but was staged by Andrzej Wajda at Easter 1985 in the ruined church on Żytnia Street in Warsaw.[14] On another occasion, in late 1984, the Week of Christian Culture brought together forty-four Polish novelists, including Marek Nowakowski, A. Braun, and Wiktor Woroszylski, and staged a number of plays, including one by Halina Mikołajska, known for her sympathies for KOR. On 10 December 1987 a Warsaw church played host to a human rights seminar attended by Jacek Kuroń, Leszek Moczulski, Czesław Bielecki, Bronisław Geremek, Janusz Onyszkiewicz, Zbigniew Romaszewski, and other well-known dissidents.[15] "Our churches no longer are just churches in the religious sense," Catholic journalist Krzysztof Śliwiński commented in 1987. "They are full-fledged community centers."[16]

Third, the independent Catholic newspaper *Tygodnik Powszechny*, edited for more than forty years by Jerzy Turowicz, offers an outlet for dissenting opinion. During the anti-Semitic campaign of 1968 Turowicz resolutely continued to publish Jewish writers, and when the Polish-Jewish poet Antoni Słonimski was blacklisted for criticizing official anti-Semitism, Turowicz invited him to join the staff of *Tygodnik Powszechny* as a contributing editor. On another occasion Turowicz devoted an entire issue of the weekly paper to a short story written by a Protestant whose work might otherwise have gone unnoticed. In the 1960s and 1970s *Tygodnik Powszechny* published the works of various dissidents, most of them agnostics, and after the suppression of Solidarity in mid-December 1981 the journal published poems by a jailed member of Solidarity and regular columns by jailed dissidents.[17]

Fourth, the church developed a network of services, including child day-care centers, pharmacies, and summer camps. Through the Rural Pastoral Communities established in early 1983, the church organizes religious retreats and pilgrimages in the countryside, finds legal counsel for private forums, and organizes self-help among the peasants (for example, care of the sick and the elderly). The Pastoral Service to Workers, reorganized in April 1982, is a parallel organization which caters to the needs of factory workers. The Primate's Relief Committee for People Deprived of Liberty and for Their Families was established in 1981 to organize aid such as food and medical supplies for political prisoners. In the cultural field, the Organization for the Pastoral Care of Artists is worth mentioning. Closely affiliated with the Week of Christian Culture, the organization is under the supervision of Monsignor Jan Oblak of Olsztyn. And finally, the church has maintained active student centers in Kraków, Warsaw, Poznań, and elsewhere, organizing student pilgrimages to Częstochowa and holding philosophical symposia and public discussions.[18]

The Wyszyński Years

The church in Poland was divided from the beginning. In the early postwar period, two lay Catholic currents emerged: a loyalist current centered in Kraków that aspired to reflect the views of the church authorities loyally; and an opportunist current centered in Warsaw and associated with Bolesław Piasecki's PAX group, which was prepared to make greater accommodations with the regime and which in time came to see itself as a kind of mediator between church and state.[19] For its part, the hierarchy supported both the land reform bill of 1944, even though the large estates expropriated under that measure included some of the church's landholdings, and the communist nationalization of industry.[20] There were tensions between church and state in those years, but in April 1950 the Polish episcopate signed an agreement with the government in which it pledged to teach Catholics to respect state authority and to seek Vatican recognition of the Oder-Neisse line as the western border of Poland in exchange for a guarantee of religious education in schools, the continued operation of the Catholic University of Lublin, and state recognition of the ecclesiastical supremacy of the pope.[21] A year later in Rome Archbishop Stefan Wyszyński explained Polish views on the western territories to the pope and obtained his acquiescence to the naming of Polish bishops on a permanent basis in those territories.

Despite this agreement, various priests were arrested and imprisoned in the years 1951–53, often on charges of collaboration with subversive organizations. On 9 February 1953 the Council of State issued a decree unilaterally reviving selected sections of the previously abrogated[22] Concordat of 1925—specifically the provisions that only Polish citizens could be appointed in the church hierarchy, that church leaders were required to take an oath of loyalty to the Polish government, and that prior approval of the government was mandatory for all appointments, removals, or transfers in the hierarchy.[23] After this the government frequently interfered in church appointments, and in a number of dioceses the office of vicar-general was assigned to a "peace priest." On 8 May 1953 the episcopate addressed a lengthy letter to the Polish government, protesting the authorities' failure to live up to the 1950 agreement. The government replied by putting Bishop Czesław Kaczmarek of Kielce on trial and arresting Wyszyński. The latter remained in prison until 1956.

These harsh measures were designed to weaken and tame the church. Instead, they ensured that the church would be seen as the innocent victim of an illegitimate, Soviet-imposed regime. Indeed, in the late Stalinist period Wyszyński came to be called *Interrex*, a reference to the tradition in prepartition Poland wherein the supreme power of state would be temporarily vested in the Polish primate between the death of the monarch and the election of his successor. Wyszyński also came to view himself as the spiritual father of the nation.[24]

Although Wyszyński's release from internment in October 1956 was followed by some improvement in church-state relations, the waxing association of the church and dissent belongs more properly to the Gierek years (1970–80). During the first secretaryship of Władysław Gomułka (1956–70), there was little in the way of organized opposition in Poland and the church itself still felt very much on the defensive. Where the communists were concerned, moreover, this era began with a flourish of optimism in that Gomułka's limited opposition to Soviet *diktat* made him immensely popular. Even in the early Gierek years it was still possible for the communist party to hope for an eventual, partial legitimation in the eyes of the people.

Wyszyński quite properly viewed the situation as potentially perilous for the church: between communist efforts to foment division and discord within the church and steady efforts to whittle the church down directly, there was room for uncertainty as to the outcome. Wyszyński's solution was to assert his personal authority as primate—sometimes implicitly bypassing both the Vatican and his fellow bishops.

It is generally acknowledged that Cardinal Wyszyński's strong and fearless exercise of authority played a crucial role in the church's survival and successful resistance to communist efforts to destroy it. On more than one occasion, this meant bypassing normal canonical procedures to remove from office duly elected leaders of religious congregations, summarily silencing or transferring outspoken clerical critics, unilateral rendering of decisions, and other markedly authoritarian actions. But in the final analysis, it is widely believed that it was this strong hand of authority that saved the Polish church.[25]

Wyszyński drew two complementary lessons from this experience: the chaos produced by intrainstitutional freedom can produce weakness and uncertainty, leaving the institution vulnerable to assault; and the vigorous assertion of authority builds power and institutional strength. These lessons were not lost on Wyszyński's understudy, the present pope.

Both Wyszyński and Wojtyła outspokenly criticized the anti-Semitic campaign of 1968, and the episcopate lent strong support to the groundswell of opposition to the proposed changes in the constitution in 1975. The subtle transformation in the church's social presence in the mid-1970s mirrored the broader systemic changes occurring at that time: in particular, the 1976 riots in the Ursus tractor factory and in the city of Radom were followed by the creation of KOR and the mobilization of intellectuals in a critical role. From its very inception, the intellectuals involved in KOR maintained contacts with the church hierarchy, and the two began to coordinate their criticisms of the regime. The hierarchy commented favorably on KOR's work for human rights on several occasions.[26]

The tensions which developed between church and state in the later Gierek years were a symptom of the church's new strength and the greater recognition it had won from the state. Meanwhile, Polish society was changing, the economy was slipping, the workers were becoming impatient,[27] and the dissident sector was becoming organized. The church was no longer thrust on the defensive; on the contrary, it was able to speak out on issues confronting Polish society. Taken collectively, these phenomena were symptoms of Poland's slide into praetorianism. Poland's church was becoming a "praetorian church." It follows that this ecclesiastical praetorianism was not a factor of Wyszyński's personality or a matter of the hierarchy's choice; on the contrary, the phenomenon had systemic, structural roots.

Praetorianism in Full Bloom

What happened in summer 1980 is that the political superstructure crumbled and society sprouted a vast array of independent organizations, from the independent trade union Solidarity, to the farmers' union Rural Solidarity, to the new Independent Students' Association created in early 1981. Existing structures began acting in new ways: the normally docile Democratic Party (SD) and the United Peasant Party (ZSL) suddenly started to convene meetings independently, to adopt resolutions without coordinating them with the PUWP, and to respond to their natural constituencies.[28] PAX, by then led by Ryszard Reiff, took a position strongly supportive of Solidarity, and shortly after the Catholic intelligentsia clubs set up a committee to advise the workers in fall 1980, PAX did likewise.[29]

The leaders of Solidarity looked to the church for consultation and mediation from the beginning, and the church easily assumed its new role as mediator between the newly organized Solidarity and the badly shaken and increasingly disorganized secular authorities. In autumn 1980 Wałęsa sought Wyszyński's advice as to whom to nominate as editor-in-chief of the trade union's weekly, *Tygodnik Solidarność*; on the primate's advice, he named Tadeusz Mazowiecki, the former editor of the Catholic monthly *Więź*.[30]

Popular participation had been suppressed for so long that the opening achieved in August 1980 inevitably fueled general excitement and stimulated new and more ambitious aspirations. Archbishop Józef Glemp, who succeeded Wyszyński as primate of Poland upon the latter's death on 28 May 1981, was clearly fearful that Polish society might dissolve into social chaos and conflict and hence urged restraint.[31]

The suppression of Solidarity on 13 December 1981 and the concomitant proclamation of martial law put the church under great stress. Glemp's initial reaction, like that of Wyszyński to the nationwide strikes of summer 1980, was to urge moderation and the avoidance of violence. In a message auspiciously carried on Radio Warsaw on 13 December, Primate Glemp told his flock:

> It does not matter if someone accuses the church of cowardice. The church wants to defend each human life; and therefore, in this state of martial law, it will call for peace wherever possible; it will call for an end to violence and for the prevention of fratricidal struggle. There is nothing of greater value than human life. That is why I myself will call for reason, even if it means that I become the target of insults. I shall plead, even if I have to plead on my knees: do not start a fight of Pole against Pole.[32]

Glemp's sermon did not refer explicitly to Solidarity and did not condemn Jaruzelski's coup. The Vatican's reaction was likewise restrained, and both Agostino Cardinal Casaroli and the pope evidently feared the eruption of a major conflict in Poland; yet within a few days the Episcopal Main Council issued a somewhat tougher statement, condemning the curtailment of rights and demanding the release of all political prisoners and a revival of Solidarity's legal activities.

The primate was not content, however, to give the regime a blank check. When the regime started to require loyalty oaths of all state employees, Archbishop Glemp sent an open letter to Jaruzelski condemning the oaths as incompatible with constitutionally guaranteed rights. At the same time, Glemp seemed to want to distance himself from those in the political underground who had been radicalized by the suppression of Solidarity.

> The consequences of standing up for the truth are enormous. Firstly, one must not, in the fervor of conflict and struggle, slander either the rulers or the ruled, utter falsehoods about them, exaggerate flaws, pass over merits, make them look ridiculous. Secondly, one must demand honest information from the mass media, both domestic and foreign. Thirdly, there must be demands that people deprived of freedom or dismissed from their place of work should know why they are being given such a punishment.[33]

Glemp went further, and declared that Solidarity shared culpability with the state for the ultimate course of events—an assessment that alienated many Poles. Subsequently, on 13 April 1982 the primate's Social Council, as advisory body of twenty-eight lay Catholics, issued a report urging Solidarity to critically reexamine its own culpability in the attendant crisis.

There were violent clashes in several Polish cities in the first week of May 1982, but, perhaps surprisingly, in his sermon on the feast of St. Stanisław a few days later Glemp seemed to endorse the regime's line that underground Solidarity had planned the clashes in advance. Glemp later appealed for calm on the second anniversary of Solidarity; his appeals were ignored, and more than 4,000 demonstrators in dozens of towns were arrested. Glemp was increasingly criticized, often in the context of unfavorable comparisons with his predecessor. Typical of such criticisms is a letter written on 24 April 1982 by Anka Kowalska, a writer, poet, and former member of KOR. In this letter she protested that the report issued by the primate's Social Council on 13 April in effect endorsed martial law and justified the state's criminality. She continued,

> We all turn our eyes and hearts towards the church. Why does she not raise her voice against those traders peddling human souls? How can the church suggest instead that this tortured and betrayed society admit to being naughty and behaving improperly and show understanding for its hangmen who lost their temper?[34]

Meanwhile, the traditional gulf between the hierarchy and the lower clergy was becoming once again evident as priests like Jerzy Popiełuszko, Mieczysław Nowak, and Kazimierz Szklarczy began delivering fiery sermons in defense of Solidarity. Popiełuszko and Reverend Teofil Bogucki (Popiełuszko's spiritual mentor), both assigned to the parish of St. Stanisław Kostka, began celebrating "masses for the fatherland" in 1981; from April 1982 on, Popiełuszko recited special prayers for the victims of martial law, including the imprisoned Wałęsa. Popiełuszko's criticisms of the government were direct and unflinching, as he hammered away at the positive contributions of Solidarity.[35] Similarly, in a June 1982 sermon Szklarczy denounced martial law as "evil," praised Solidarity as "immortal because it represents justice," and told his listeners that Christianity's confrontation with communism is a war of good against evil, love against hate, truth against lies.[36]

Against these bold words, Glemp sought more modest concessions. Soon after the proclamation of martial law, the regime made a small concession to the church, issuing a decree which permitted hospitalized children to obtain weekly religious instruction if requested by the parents. Later, in August 1982 he registered three requests: that Wałęsa be released from prison, that the remaining internees be released and trade union work recommenced "at least in stages," and that a date be established for the pope's second visit to Poland.[37] On 8 October the authorities formally banned the suspended trade union. Exactly a month later Archbishop Glemp met with Jaruzelski and confirmed the second papal visit for June 1983, prompting some to say that Glemp had concluded that the prospects for Solidarity's relegalization were nil and that it was pointless to continue to defend the now-banned organization. At any rate, when the coordinating committee of underground Solidarity called for antiregime demonstrations on 10 November, Glemp sharply criticized the planned demonstrations.[38]

The following month, two hundred priests, angered by Glemp's soft approach to the regime, paid a three-hour visit to the archbishop. In reply to criticism, Glemp charged that too many priests were behaving like "journalists and politicians."[39]

In early 1983 Polish police reportedly gave Glemp a list of sixty-nine "extremist priests" who needed to be reined in. Aside from Popiełuszko, Nowak, and Szklarczy, the list probably included Bogucki, Henryk Jankowski (an adviser to Wałęsa), Stanisław Małkowski, Rufin Abramek (a Pauline monk), Tadeusz Zaleski-Isakowicz (well known for his pro-Solidarity sympathies), and Zenon Ziomek. All were either beaten, tortured, or harassed, some were vilified in the press, and the homes of Popiełuszko and

Małkowski were ransacked on orders from above.[40] Glemp tried to accommodate the authorities by transferring Nowak from his parish in the Warsaw working-class suburb of Ursus to a remote parish, provoking vociferous protests,[41] and rebuked the outspoken Popiełuszko for displaying Solidarity emblems at his fatherland masses, for his contacts with Solidarity activists, and for allegedly neglecting his official duties in order to devote his time and energy to his fatherland masses.[42] Later, after Popiełuszko was murdered by Polish secret police, Glemp suspended Małkowski from preaching in Warsaw—perhaps to protect him, but perhaps to pacify the authorities, who had been assailing Małkowski in the press.[43]

Glemp sometimes appeared to be the most timid of all of Poland's prelates. Whereas Glemp now argued that Solidarity had lost its meaning after it went underground, and that "the Solidarity now in existence has moved a great deal away from its principles,"[44] bishops Tadeusz Gocłowski of Gdańsk, Kazimierz Majdański of Szczecin, and Andrzej Śliwiński of Gdynia, and Henryk Cardinal Gulbinowicz of Wrocław all struck more radical poses. Gocłowski, for instance, commemorated the fifteenth anniversary of the riots of December 1970 by reminding his listeners of the shooting of the defenseless citizens by security forces.[45] Majdański and Śliwiński both conducted solemn masses on the fifth anniversary of the imposition of martial law, the former raising pointed questions about the Szczecin agreement of 1980 on another occasion.[46] Bishop Damian Zimon of Katowice seemed even more radical, reassuring tens of thousands of Polish workers gathered at Częstochowa in September 1987 of their right to their own "independent and self-governing trade unions."[47] And Cardinal Gulbinowicz, who became Poland's third cardinal in 1985, openly encouraged pro-Solidarity sentiment at an open-air mass at the shrine of the Black Madonna in September of that year and sent a joint telegram with Wałęsa to the pope in the name of the Polish workers.[48]

In addition, Jan Sikorski, a Warsaw parish priest at St. Joseph's Church, played a highly visible role. In September 1984 he said a special mass to honor the critics of the regime, particularly Jacek Kuroń and Adam Michnik; thousands attended. In December 1985 he described the period of Solidarity's legality as "a time of joy when we won back our freedom and dignity." And in December 1986, on the fifth anniversary of the imposition of martial law, he led a solemn procession of thousands to St. Joseph's Church for a special memorial mass. On that occasion he said of his congregation, "These are the people who did not give up the struggle for the ideals that are alive in Poland. And to defend them, to allow them to meet, is the permanent role of the church."[49]

But Cardinal Glemp (by now "Comrade Glemp" to his critics)[50] was basing his strategy on his desire to obtain government approval for a church-sponsored fund to help private farmers (achieved in 1987) and enactment of a bill guaranteeing the church's legal status in clear and unambiguous terms (achieved in May 1989). In addition, according to Tadeusz Kamiński, a professor at the University of Hamburg, Glemp may well have felt that during the Jaruzelski years (1981–89) Poland was threatened primarily by the West which, in its desire to weaken Soviet communism, might be willing to "sacrifice" Poland by inciting a sanguinary anti-Russian revolt.[51]

Opposition Views of the Church

The imposition of martial law led directly to the fragmentation of Solidarity, as rival factions split apart and formed autonomous underground organizations. Predictably, the diverse para-Solidarity groups developed rather diverse attitudes toward the church.

Głos, a more or less formal organization which traces its roots to the National Democratic Party of Roman Dmowski in the early twentieth century but which actually emerged in 1977 from the ranks of KOR, is firmly pro-church, and has defended Glemp from criticism.[52] (Dmowski, incidentally, was well known for his belief that the primary danger to Poland came from the West, not from Russia.) Polityka Polska, which views itself less as a formal organization than as an arena for political expression, has published an analytical journal since autumn 1983. It too views itself as an ally of the church. By contrast, the Committee of Social Resistance (KOS) was more critical. KOS's attitude toward the church is basically positive, but when Glemp transferred the popular parish priest Mieczysław Nowak to a remote parish in early 1984, KOS warned that "the policy of conciliation with the regime, which has been forced through by the primate apparently with support from the episcopate, has brought the church perilously close to the point where it must lose social support. The church's successive concessions to the demands of the authorities have not brought the fulfillment of any of society's more significant demands, or even of the church's own, purely religious, demands."[53]

Much less sympathetic to the church is Fighting Solidarity, a radical underground spin-off from the original Solidarity. Created in June 1982 in Wrocław by Kornel Morawiecki and others, the organization sought the violent overthrow of the communist system and the establishment of an independent republic. Fighting Solidarity was not sympathetic to Glemp's Occidentophobia but more generally believed that the church did not have a role to play in politics, not even in defending human rights.[54]

Of all the underground organizations—and there were far more than I can enumerate here—Niepodległość (Independence) was among the least sympathetic to the church. Functioning underground since at least early 1982, it advocated militant underground organization as a preliminary to the overthrow of the communist regime. Niepodległość viewed the church with skepticism, believing that its institutional interests must necessarily compel the church to seek forms of modus vivendi with the government, entailing elements of cooperation rejected by Niepodległość.[55] On the whole, there was an important current of thought in the underground which held that the church cannot help the resistance. As one Solidarity spokesperson put it in 1984, "The church will drift away from us and it should. Let Cardinal Glemp and the pope concern themselves with the souls of Europe and let Bujak lead the revolution in Poland."[56]

The Second and Third Papal Visits

The Polish pope has played an ambivalent but effective role in the triangular relationship of church, regime, and opposition. On the one hand, the pope has repeatedly signalled his support of the cautious Glemp, most symbolically by elevating him to the College of Cardinals in January 1983. On the other hand, the pope's own comments have been defiant and, for the opposition, often exhilirating. Pope John Paul II's first papal visit to Poland in 1979 is now widely credited with having contributed to the social revolution of 1980. His second visit in June 1983 came at a time of widespread despondency, and the pope hoped to use his visit to lift Polish spirits.

The keynote of the pope's second visit was his emphasis on Poland's right to political sovereignty and self-determination, and his calls for dialogue were always placed within the context of the need for self-determination. He called for amnesty for all political prisoners, and endorsed Polish aspirations to establish authentic, self-governing trade unions.[57]

There were rumors on the eve of John Paul II's third trip to Poland in June 1987 that the tone of the visit would be more subdued and that the visit itself would be more purely pastoral. On the contrary, the pope, now able to travel to Gdańsk, Szczecin, and Lublin (unlike in 1983), used the visit to express church support for the relegalization of Solidarity and Rural Solidarity, and for the principles of the ill-fated Popiełuszko. At Tarnów on 10 June the pope quoted from the memoirs of Wincenty Witos, one-time leader of the prewar Peasant Party and prime minister of the prewar Polish Republic, calling on the government to respect its 1981 agreements at

Rzeszów and Ustrzyki and relegalize Rural Solidarity.[58] At Kraków later that same day, he told the hundreds of thousands of Poles present to resist disillusionment and to continue their "patient fight" for freedom; he repeatedly praised the goals and ideals of Solidarity.[59] At Gdańsk on 12 June the pope told a crowd estimated at one million persons that workers have the right to organize "independent and autonomous trade unions." There, and elsewhere, he frequently repeated the word "solidarity," always with great emotional impact.[60] And in Warsaw on 14 June, the final day of his trip to Poland, the pope paid a visit to the Church of St. Stanisław Kostka and prayed at the grave of Popiełuszko. Throughout the trip he spoke of the nation's right to determine its own fate, of the importance of religious freedom, and of the right of the workers to independent trade unions.[61] Understandably, underground Solidarity expressed considerable satisfaction with the papal visit.[62]

From time to time the Polish communist press attacked the pope.[63] In so doing, the press betrayed the regime's fear of the Polish pope and his command of the hearts of Poles. For in his sermons in Poland, the pope eloquently endorsed every major demand of the democratic opposition in Poland.

The Great Transformation

The Catholic church was unremitting in its support for the relegalization of Solidarity. In September 1987, for example, Bishop Damian Zimon of Katowice told a crowd of tens of thousands at Częstochowa that the church supported the people's "right to their own independent and self-governing trade unions."[64] In August 1988 Dominican friars in Gdańsk organized a pro-Solidarity rally involving some 3,000 persons.[65] And on 20 October 1988 representatives of Catholic intelligentsia clubs from across Poland issued a nine-point statement calling, among other things, for the relegalization of Solidarity and the establishment of a parliamentary democracy.[66] In the most concrete way, the church helped Solidarity by making facilities at St. Brygida's Church in Gdańsk available to the trade union for use as its headquarters while it remained illegal. And the Vatican insisted on the relegalization of Solidarity as a precondition for the restoration of diplomatic ties—something Warsaw wanted.

Poland's bishops collectively issued a programmatic pastoral message on 26 August 1988 that spelled out their support for trade union pluralism and described the wildcat strikes as a symptom of a lingering disease afflicting the sociopolitical system.[67]

Toward the end of 1988, at the same time that preparations began for roundtable talks between Solidarity and the government, there were also signs of an impending "great transformation" in church-state relations. Talks were continuing between the Vatican and the Polish government, and in late October Warsaw made a serious bid for the restoration of diplomatic ties. Meanwhile, Polish authorities legalized the Catholic opposition group Dziekania, whose 100 members had been pressing for political and economic pluralism since the group's founding in 1984. They also agreed to register Catholic student unions in Częstochowa, Lublin, Warsaw, Gdańsk, and other cities.

Subsequently, on 17 May 1989, after the relegalization of Solidarity, Parliament passed three laws which, for the first time since the war, guaranteed the church's legal status, guaranteed religious freedom, and extended state health coverage and pensions to Catholic clergy. Under the new law, the state recognized the legal status of the Catholic University of Lublin and the various theological academies and seminaries. These bills granted the church the right to organize radio and television programs, guaranteed freedom for the church press, and allowed the church to resume control over the Caritas charity, which it had lost in the 1950s. The new legislation also allowed the church to establish and administer hospitals, old people's homes, schools, and orphanages, and, in an especially surprising provision, the government agreed to return church property seized in the 1950s or, in the event that the church no longer wished to regain certain property, to pay appropriate compensation. In addition, the formation of new dioceses, construction of new church buildings, establishment of new convents and monasteries, and staffing of personnel posts in the church would no longer require regime approval. The legislation abolished military obligation for seminarians and novices. It also provided for the restoration of religious instruction in the school curriculum (with registration at the discretion of the parents). And finally, it confirmed 1 January, All Souls' Day, Christmas Day, Easter Monday, and Corpus Christi as nonworking holidays, and added an additional one: 15 August, the Feast of the Assumption of Mary.[68] Exactly two months later the Vatican announced that it had established full diplomatic relations with Poland and that it would be appointing a papal nuncio to take up residence in Warsaw. Subsequently, in October 1989 the government submitted amendments which would abolish the state Office for Religious Affairs. Taken collectively, these developments signify a dramatic change in the situation of the church in Poland, promising more security for church personnel and church life generally.

On the other hand, some mention should be made of the fact that three pro-Solidarity priests were brutally murdered in the course of 1989: Stefan Niedzielak of Warsaw, known for his intense devotion to his congregation, whose badly battered body was found on 21 January;[69] Stanisław Suchowolec of Białystok, whose asphyxiated body was found on 30 January;[70] and Sylwester Zych of Krynica Morska, who had served four years in prison (1982–86) for having allegedly sheltered two men convicted in the murder of a policeman and whose body was found on 11 July.[71] If one assumes that state security police were behind these murders—and there is no other reasonable explanation—then one is led to the conclusion that some elements in the political establishment were militantly hostile to any normalization of relations with the church.

The relegalization of Solidarity in April 1989, the passage of new religious legislation in May, and the appointment of a Solidarity prime minister (Tadeusz Mazowiecki) in August resulted in a dramatic change in conditions for society broadly and for the church specifically. These developments may spell the end of Poland's praetorian era and lay the basis for Poland's emergence from praetorianism.

Within a matter of months, the Polish Catholic church switched to the offensive and began pushing hard for the reintroduction of religious education in the schools—despite voluble protests from Protestants, Old Catholics, Orthodox, agnostics, and nonbelievers.[72] At the same time, the Catholic Church applied heavy pressure on the Polish legislature to ban abortion, even though public opinion polls show that most Poles oppose such legislation.[73]

Conclusion

Ecclesiastical articulation of institutional and social interests is not unique to praetorian systems. The Catholic church in the United States, for instance, has taken part in the public debate about the Strategic Defense Initiative.[74] The distinguishing feature of praetorian systems is the failure to build or sustain legitimate and effective political institutions capable of channeling rising public awareness of political issues. As a result, instead of functioning as an interest group as in effective pluralist systems, the church in conditions of praetorianism becomes more politicized.

Scot Paltrow has argued that the church could not have acted more timorously or more timidly in the 1980–81 period without undue risk to its fundamental interests,[75] and the argument might be extended to the entire period since 1980. Certainly the advocacy of church-state dialogue is a matter of necessity in many minds. But the very concept of dialogue is telling: one would not dream of talking about church-state dialogue in pluralist systems, because church and state do not confront each other there as antagonists. The concept of dialogue is appropriate to a meeting of erstwhile foes, rivals who view each other with distrust, but who may nonetheless have some common interests in pursuing cooperation. In such circumstances, as *Sejm* delegate Zbigniew Zielinski put it in 1985, "An attempt at mutual trust and good will is necessary."[76]

At the same time, the church has often been bold in the defense of its own institutional interests. In September 1986, for instance, Poland's bishops issued a statement advising the necessity of "establish[ing] the constitutional possibility for people to organize themselves without conditions based upon party membership. The lack of such possibilities impoverishes public life."[77] That this possibility would extend to Catholic social organizations was understood. Two months later, Reverend Alojzy Orszulik, director of the church press office in Warsaw, wrote an article for the weekly newspaper *Tygodnik Powszechny*. Orszulik contended that there was nothing in Polish law which prohibited workers, farmers, women, young people, and lay Catholics from forming associations outside communist control.[78] The article deplored the fact that Polish Catholics had been "pushed onto the sidelines of public life" and that many Catholic lay organizations had been suppressed, and suggested that this was partly to blame for the political apathy of the Polish public.[79] The article was banned by the censors.

But only a month later—in December 1986—another church newspaper, *Niedziela*, published a more moderate but no less explicit defense of the church's right to establish lay associations. Their purpose, *Niedziela* said, was to "imbu[e] the secular order with Christian spirit."[80] More to the point, *Niedziela* declared,

> The laymen's right to set up, lead, or join apostolic associations has its source in natural law; all the people have the right to set up associations corresponding to their genuine well-being. This is among the fundamental rights of a human being. Therefore, such right may not be denied to laymen by any human authority, whether secular or ecclesiastic, as long as the aims and activities of such associations comply with the canon law and the constitutional order.[81]

Earlier, in 1984, Solidarity cofounder Kazimierz Świtoń went on a three-week hunger strike in an effort to obtain authorization to set up Catholic trade unions like those that existed prior to World War II. He finally ended his hunger strike at the urging of Monsignor Bronisław Dąbrowski on behalf of the Polish episcopate.[82]

Huntington once wrote that "the primary problem of politics is the lag in the development of political institutions behind social and economic change."[83] Throughout the 1980s Poland was confronted with this problem, and this fact was, in itself, a powerful determinant of the political behavior of the church. But praetorianism—which is the result of that lag—is inherently unstable, and this generates pressure for a new equilibrium. When that new equilibrium is reached, the role of the church will inevitably change as well. Indeed, it has already changed.

The province of Kosovo is one of eight federal units in the federated republic of Yugoslavia. It is by far the poorest of the eight units, has the second
smallest population (ahead of Montenegro), and, as one of two autonomous
provinces lying within the republic of Serbia, has more constraints on its
autonomy than the six full-fledged republics. Yet since the turbulent days
of early April 1981 when the province was shaken by widespread rioting,
Kosovo has increasingly preoccupied party leaders in Belgrade and aroused
fears that the country may be sliding toward civil war.[1] In the resulting
uncertainty, the authorities abandoned their once-conciliatory posture vis-
à-vis the dissatisfied Albanian residents of Kosovo and adopted a hard line,
even while the situation slipped ever further out of control.

Whether the largely Albanian population wants merely to obtain the
fuller prerogatives associated with republic status, as some observers have
speculated,[2] or whether the majority now view any continued association
with Yugoslavia with distaste, as others believe and as official Yugoslav
spokesmen have continued to claim up to the time of this writing (June
1990),[3] is, even now, a complex question. Certainly Kosovar perceptions of
the Stalinist regime in Albania provide a deterrent to secession, even as
Belgrade's unimaginative policy seems to foreclose constitutional concessions to the discontented Albanians of Kosovo. Obviously, the longer Serb-
Albanian frictions remain at the pitch maintained between 1981 and 1990,
and the longer Belgrade persists in jailing advocates of republic status for
Kosovo, the less likely it is that a negotiated, peaceful accommodation can
be reached. The continued violence in Kosovo and neighboring districts in
Macedonia excited a Serbian nationalist backlash, undermined communal
stability in both Kosovo and Macedonia, provoked the exodus of some 45,000
Serbs and Montenegrins from the province between April 1981 and January

1990,[4] and seriously strained interrepublican relations, most especially between Slovenia and Serbia, but also between Croatia and Serbia.[5] Moreover, Serbian maneuvers to reduce the prerogatives of the autonomous provinces inevitably produced repercussions in Vojvodina. The Vojvodinan connection to the Kosovo crisis was graphically demonstrated on 9 July 1988 when some Serbs and Montenegrins from Kosovo went to Novi Sad (the Vojvodinan capital) to demand that the Serbian government's proposals to reduce the power and jurisdiction of the provinces (Kosovo and Vojvodina) be accepted and to protest Vojvodina's resistance to these proposals.[6]

What is clear is that the eruption of violence in Kosovo in spring 1981 and the continued underground antiregime activity there have exploded the Yugoslav authorities' bold claim of the 1970s to have "solved" the national question and shaken the foundations of Yugoslav nationalities policy in general. The latter claim may seem bold, at first sight, but a comparison of the Yugoslav handling of Kosovo with the Spanish handling of the Basques, the Swiss handling of the Jura secessionists, and the Belgian handling of Flemish-Walloon relations suggests enough reasons for Yugoslav self-doubt.

The Nature of the Problem

In one respect at least, the Kosovo problem could best be compared to the Palestine problem: two ethnic communities with distinct languages and religious traditions lay claim to the same territory with competing historical arguments as evidence. The Albanians claim to be descended from an Illyrian tribe named "Albanians" that inhabited the eastern coast of the Adriatic in the second century and to have maintained a presence in Kosovo preceding the advent of the Serbs; they also cite the role of Albanian patriots such as Isa Boletino, Hasan Prishtina, and Bajram Curri in the history of Kosovo. The Serbs, by contrast, claim to have migrated into the region as early as the sixth and seventh centuries, maintain that the Albanian presence in Kosovo cannot be documented further back than the 1070s, describe twelfth- and thirteenth-century Kosovo as "purely Serbian," and view the province as the ancient heartland of the Serbian kingdom.[7] The fact that it was in Kosovo in 1389 on the Field of the Blackbirds that the Serbian kingdom made its last great stand against the Ottomans has contributed to the view, widely held by Serbs, that Kosovo is "sacred ground." Kosovo is, in a sense, the Serbian Jerusalem.

Kosovo was initially part of the independent Albania that first emerged in 1912, until the Great Powers intervened and, under Russian pressure, turned Kosovo over to Serbia. Hence, when the Kingdom of Serbs, Croats, and Slovenes (Yugoslavia) was created at the end of World War I, Kosovo lay within its jurisdiction. This fate was, however, fiercely resisted. In 1919 Kosovar Albanians formed a political organization, Dzemijet, which held annual congresses and published the newspaper, *Moudjaeda (Struggle)*. Albanian uprisings against the Serbian monarchy between 1918 and 1919 were ruthlessly crushed by the Serbian army, and the local population was disarmed. Forced expulsions helped to cut the Albanian population in Kosovo in half between 1918 and 1921, from between 800,000 and 1,000,000 to 439,657.[8] According to one participant, however, the alleged "Albanian uprising" of 1920 was no longer an Albanian initiative, but, on the contrary, a regime provocation, enabling it to liquidate untold numbers of unwanted Albanians.[9]

The authorities shut down all Albanian-language schools in 1918 in order to "Serbianize" the Kosovar population. Later the authorities decided that the Albanians would only use their education to fight the regime, and adopted a policy of discouraging any public education for Albanians in order to keep the Kosovar Albanians ignorant and illiterate.[10] The Albanians, a Serbian official wrote in 1921, "will all remain backward, unenlightened, and stupid; nor will they know the state idiom [Serbian], which would help them to fight against us. It is in our interest that they remain at the present level of their culture for another twenty years, the time we need to carry out the necessary national assimilation in these areas."[11] This "assimilation" was to be accomplished through Serbian colonization of Kosovo. Indeed, between 1918 and 1940 the Belgrade regime seized 154,287 acres of land in Kosovo, turning 57,704 acres over to new settlers, mostly Serbs, and keeping other land for the army, the police, state schools, and other state agencies.[12]

Not surprisingly, when Kosovo was appended to Italian-occupied Albania in 1941, many Kosovar Albanians greeted the occupation as a "liberation."[13] The Italian occupation was generally supportive of Albanian culture, and ejected some of the Serbian settlers brought in by Belgrade. One source estimates that between 70,000 and 100,000 Serbs were forced out of Kosovo during the war.[14]

As of November 1944, as German troops were being driven out of Kosovo, an Albanian nationalist organization called Balli Kombetar resisted reincorporation of the province into Yugoslavia and even succeeded in infiltrating the new government being set up in Kosovo-Metohija. In Metohija a Ballist resistance assumed the proportions of an uprising, centered in Drenica. Armed operations against the uprising were launched in

December 1944, with two brigades from the Albanian National Liberation Struggle participating on the side of the Yugoslav communists. Fierce battles took place in January and February 1945 between the Ballists and the Yugoslav communist army, and the state of war continued in Kosovo until July 1945.[15] Even after the suppression of open resistance, however, Yugoslav authorities remained suspicious of the Kosovar Albanians, and later, between the beginning of 1955 and the middle of 1957, the state security service conducted house-to-house searches throughout the province, confiscating all the weapons it found. At the height of this process, state security organs arrested a group of Albanians said to have been dispatched by Albania to incite rebellion in Kosovo. They were tried and convicted in the famous Prizren Trial of 1956.[16]

Incorporation into Yugoslavia had a retarding effect on both the cultural and economic development of Kosovo. On the one hand, "the teaching of Albanian cultural traditions, literature, folklore, and history was severely constrained, and emphasis on the past unity of the Albanian nation was strictly prohibited."[17] On the other hand, although Kosovo was economically the most backward region in the country, it was excluded from any special treatment as an underdeveloped region until 1955, and even after that it received less investment, which in any case was targeted mainly into the region's extractive industry. During the 1945–56 period, gross investments in Kosovo were 36.0 percent of the Yugoslav average, rising to 59.1 percent in the 1957–65 period. As a result, despite certain tangible economic achievements,[18] per capita income in Kosovo shrank from 42.0 percent of the average of the four richer federal units of Yugoslavia in 1953 to 28.0 percent in 1971.[19]

Belgrade's policy toward Kosovo remained restrictive until July 1966, when Aleksandar Ranković, head of the state security service, was stripped of his posts. In the wake of that development, federal policy became more accommodating toward Albanian interests, and after violent demonstrations in Kosovo and Albanian-populated parts of Macedonia in late 1968, the federal government introduced constitutional changes that greatly expanded the prerogatives enjoyed by the regional party barons in the autonomous provinces, and made a number of concessions designed to appease Albanian national sentiment, including the establishment of an independent university in Priština. Although the Albanians were better represented in provincial political echelons after that, renewed unrest broke out repeatedly in Priština throughout the 1970s.

While at least some Kosovar Albanians certainly desired separation from Yugoslavia, it was obviously impossible to use official forums (such as the legal press or party meetings) to vent this idea. But even full-republic status, which at times could be broached in public, was foreclosed. *Borba*, for instance, in its 10 April 1968 issue, reported former minister Mehmed Hodža's pained question as to why 1.2 million Yugoslav Albanians could not have full autonomy when 370,000 Montenegrins had their own republic.[20] Shortly thereafter, Rezak Šalja, a former member of the provincial committee of the League of Communists (LC) of Kosovo, declared himself "categorically and unambiguously" in favor of establishing a republic for Albanians in Yugoslavia, which would also enjoy the formal right of secession.[21] Similarly, Mahmut Bakalli, who became provincial party chief in Kosovo in June 1971, warned federal authorities that the situation in Kosovo could blow up if the province were not granted wider autonomy. Serbian republic leaders resisted this idea, and Bakalli developed the tactic of going over their heads to resolve provincial issues at the federal level. This tactic contributed to an incremental slackening of ties between the autonomous province of Kosovo and the Serbian Republic, of which it is juridically a part; yet even in 1977 the provincial leaderships of Kosovo and Vojvodina would join in complaining that they did not have enough autonomy.[22]

Federal authorities proved willing to turn a blind eye, in the late 1970s, to the extraconstitutional augmentation of Kosovo's autonomous powers, but remained unwilling to grant the province republic status. The authorities feared that allowing jurisdictional changes partially based on demographic shifts would open up discussion of the possible allocation to a Kosovo republic of Albanian-populated districts in Montenegro, Macedonia, and Serbia proper.[23]

The Economic Quagmire

Economic development in Kosovo can be assessed from different perspectives yielding somewhat different conclusions. From the perspective of gross development, infrastructure, and the provision of medical care and educational facilities, there have been major strides since the war. The provincial capital of Priština in particular shows the benefits of ongoing urban improvement. From the more political perspective that assesses Kosovo's relative standing vis-à-vis the other federal units across a string of economic measures over time, however, the picture is disappointing for Kosovars: Kosovo has slipped steadily further and further behind the other federal units. Bakalli himself complained (somewhat euphemistically) in 1980 that "the resources set aside in the last medium-term plan [for 1976–80] obviously were not sufficient to ensure ... developing Kosovo as rapidly as possible."[24] Clearly, as the developmental gap separating Kosovo and the rest of Yugoslavia widens, Kosovar Albanian bitterness and frustration can only deepen. Finally, from the perspective of actual economic conditions in Kosovo there are a number of serious, unresolved problems, the most important of which is unemployment. Already in 1971 provincial unemployment stood at 18.6 percent. By 1981, on the eve of province-wide rioting, this had risen to 27.5 percent. As of 1987 the figure stood at 55.8 percent in the province, compared with 15.8 percent for the country as a whole.[25] Despite efforts to create new jobs in Kosovo, the birthrate continues to outpace growth in the economic sector. Hence, as *Borba* observed recently, the Kosovar economy will be unable to absorb the annual influx of new entrants into the available labor force even by the year 2000. And by then, Kosovo is projected to become the fourth most populous federal unit in Yugoslavia, with 2.5 million inhabitants (from 1.6 million in 1981).[26]

Part of the reason for Kosovo's economic backwardness must be traced to the inadequacy of labor-intensive investments and of economic assistance generally. But part of the reason lies also in the misuse of funds that *were* allocated. Unproductive investments account for part of the problem. In addition, in a flagrant abuse of the assistance program, Kosovar authorities allegedly used some federal developmental funds to buy land from Serbs and turn it over to Albanians.[27] Alex Dragnich and Slavko Todorovich note, further, that "the Kosovo Albanian authorities were also anxious to break up the compactness of Serbian areas. To do this they would, for example, build a factory in a solidly Serbian settlement. Under the population key of the Yugoslav government, 80 percent of the workers in that factory had to be Albanians, who then would be brought in, and thus break up the compactness of the Serbian settlement."[28] Given such politically motivated policies, it became all the harder to show tangible economic results.

The 1981 Demonstrations and Aftermath

With the long history of Kosovar-Albanian aspirations for union with Albania, Serbian suppression of Albanian culture from 1918 to 1966, provincial economic stagnation, and armed uprisings against Belgrade in 1918–20, 1945, and 1968, it is difficult to understand why Belgrade failed to see signs of the gathering storm in the late 1970s. It is true that by the 1970s the Albanian-dominated provincial committee was withholding much of its intelligence about underground organizations from authorities in Belgrade. Moreover, much internal information in Kosovo was published only in Albanian, rendering it virtually useless for most non-Albanians, whether in Kosovo or in Belgrade. But there was enough material in open, Serbo-Croatian sources as of spring 1980 to suggest that trouble was brewing; for that matter, Edvard Kardelj, Tito's right-hand man, warned in 1977 that in the absence of resolute action, Kosovo would eventually see large-scale violence.[29] His warning was ignored at the time.

In April and May 1981 the province was convulsed by antiregime demonstrations involving tens of thousands of persons. The regime boosted the local security forces from 1,200 to 1,500, declared a state of emergency, and sent in the army. Eventually, about a third of the Yugoslav army was stationed in Kosovo.[30] Instead of offering new concessions, as it had after the 1968 riots, the regime relied on a combination of armed force and the promise of economic stimulus to regain control of the situation. In the initial phase after the riots, however, the developed republics actually scaled back plans for joint investments in Kosovo and insisted on a credit relationship in economic transactions with the province; investments in Kosovo declined 40 percent between 1981 and 1982. As of this writing, authorities have been unable to reverse negative economic trends in Kosovo. That leaves coercion (and "differentiation of cadres") as the central means of stabilization.

Between spring 1981 and September 1987, according to official figures, criminal charges were brought against some 5,200 Kosovars of Albanian extraction, with 990 being sentenced for "political crimes" between 1981 and 1984.[31] According to the London *Sunday Times*, however, some 35,000 Albanians had been tried for "counterrevolutionary" activities by mid-1985, with more awaiting trial.[32] These trials proved controversial and some provincial judges evidently refused to be a party to the proceedings: between March 1981 and June 1983, 124 judges in Kosovo left the judiciary, 110 at their own request.[33]

Some 1,800 members of the Kosovo LC were expelled from the party. Among the 1,600 Albanians was provincial party chief Bakalli, who was given a twelve-year prison term. Some Albanian members of the Tetovo party organization in Macedonia were also expelled from the party.[34] More than 200 faculty members of the University of Priština were fired, along with the editors of the radio and television stations in the provincial capital. Between 1981 and 1984 the enrollment at the university was reduced from 37,000 to 20,000.[35]

Month after month there were fresh reports of the surfacing and suppression of new underground groups, many of which were described in the official Yugoslav press as Stalinist in orientation and almost all of which were said to be succored by the Albanian regime in Tiranë. Between April

1981 and March 1986 ninety-six irredentist organizations were discovered and broken up.[36] Their membership typically fell between 20 and 120.

Among these groups were the National Movement for the Liberation of Kosovo and other Albanian Districts in Yugoslavia, which had proclaimed itself in favor of union with Albania (suppressed in 1982);[37] the Communist-Marxist-Leninist Party of Albanians in Yugoslavia, whose goal was the union of all Albanian-inhabited regions into an enlarged Kosovo republic within the Yugoslav federation (suppressed in 1982);[38] the Call for Freedom organization based in Tetovo, which maintained contacts with Albanian exiles in Western Europe (suppressed in 1983);[39] the Front of National Liberation and the Kosovo Party of Struggle, both of which advocated creation of a Kosovo republic within the framework of the Yugoslav federal system (both suppressed in 1984);[40] the secret Movement for Liberation, which included a number of ethnic Albanian military officers in the Yugoslav national army among its members and had informants in the provincial security apparatus (suppressed in December 1985);[41] and the Marxist-Leninists of Kosovo, whose members were sentenced in spring 1986.[42] The Movement for Liberation was among the best organized and equipped and was said to have amassed considerable quantities of arms and ammunition, obtained communications and printing equipment from Albanian exile communities in the West, and operated the six medium-sized illegal radio stations captured at the time.[43]

Albanian irredentist organizations also appeared in the Albanian-inhabited districts of western Macedonia, in particular Vinica, Kičevo, Tetovo, and Gostivar. The irredentist organizations in both Kosovo and Macedonia were said to be engaged in weapons smuggling and illegal dealings in gold and drugs.[44] In addition to these irredentist organizations, 216 subversive cells were discovered within the Yugoslav national army between 1981 and 1987. According to Fleet Admiral Branko Mamula, minister of defense, their program included "killing officers and soldiers, poisoning food and water, sabotage, breaking into weapons arsenals and stealing arms and ammunition, desertion, and causing frequent nationalist incidents in army units."[45]

Despite this patent evidence of dissatisfaction with the status quo, the central committee of the League of Communists of Yugoslavia (LCY), meeting in December 1983, reaffirmed its policy of "no negotiations with the Kosovars and no concessions to them."[46] This remains Belgrade's policy today. Since advocacy of constitutional reform is treated as tantamount to treason, Kosovar Albanians are left with two choices: submit or resist. Similarly (and in a typical copycat syndrome), certain elements in Vojvodina began to talk of republic status for that province—to be dubbed "the republic of Hungarians, Croats, Serbs, and other nationalities." *Politika* was quick to denounce the idea as "reactionary" and "extreme."[47]

Stirrings Among the Serbs

The 1981 riots and their aftermath completely polarized Kosovo. In an open expression of this polarization, Serbs and Albanians took to walking on opposite sides of the main promenade (*corso*) in Priština.[48] Albanians had allegedly attacked and destroyed part of the ancient patriarchal building at Peć, prompting the Serbian Orthodox church newspaper *Pravoslavlje* to publish an "Appeal for the Protection of the Serbian Inhabitants and Their Holy Places in Kosovo." Signed by twenty-one priests, the "appeal" assailed regime policy in Kosovo, which was portrayed as the Serbian "Jerusalem."[49] In the church's view, the Serbian nation itself was vitally threatened. Meanwhile, Serbian and Montenegrin families were pouring out of Kosovo, raising the specter that the Serbian Jerusalem might become totally Albanian in composition.

Serbs began to talk of these developments as a "national" issue. Some Serbs countered the slogan "Kosovo—republic" with the wry "Serbia—republic," an expression which implied that Serbia was being milked and exploited by ungrateful autonomous provinces. In October 1983 a survey of 1,000 Belgrade residents found that 50 percent favored reducing economic assistance to Kosovo and other less developed regions.[50] Typical of the Serbian backlash were the comments made by delegate Dragan Gligorić at a joint session of the Serbian assembly's three chambers.

> "Serbia proper"—this clumsy, ridiculous, and humiliating term that has come into official use—unfortunately and to our political shame reflects the true state of affairs and Serbia's real status as a republic. On the other hand, everything has been done to make Kosovo a de facto republic. Irredentists are asking for what they already have, but are doing it so that tomorrow they can demand that Kosovo secede from the SRFY.[51]

With rising Albanian consciousness and occasional disorders also in Macedonia and Montenegro, there have been reports of nationalist backlashes among Macedonians and Montenegrins, and of the appearance of separatist currents among the Montenegrins.[52]

In both Kosovo and Macedonia there were reports of Albanian pressure on the local population and of Albanians buying up land from non-

Albanians. Reports of violent assaults on Serbs, the killing of cattle owned by Serbs, and attacks on Serbian property contributed to a sense of urgency. In 1984, moreover, two Albanian judges were accused of causing an unwarranted delay in the prosecution of Albanians charged with crimes against Serbs.[53]

As early as 1982[54] local Serbs from Kosovo drew up a petition asking federal authorities to adopt more effective measures to restore order in the province; seventy-nine Serbs signed the petition.[55] But little was done, and the out-migration of Slavs continued. Between April 1981 and December 1987, 24,209 Serbs and Montenegrins left Kosovo, often to live in Serbia proper, reducing the Slavic component in Kosovo's population from 14.9 percent to less than 13.5 percent.[56] With official encouragement, 3,000 Serbs and Montenegrins returned to Kosovo between September 1982 and June 1987, but of this number only a small portion found work upon their return. When an organized group of Yugoslav journalists came to Kosovo in December 1985, however, they were told that "over a longer period of time the characteristic trend is one of permanent improvement."[57] The provincial authorities have been anxious to minimize the involvement of republic and federal officials and have therefore tried to present the situation as under control.

But it is not merely a question of the activity of illegal organizations. Kosovo's administrative infrastructure itself remains unreliable, despite repeated shuffling of personnel. Four and a half years after the April riots, the editorial board of the Albanian-language Priština daily *Rilindja* was still said to be wayward, and the Association of Journalists of Macedonia complained that *Rilindja* was issuing "tendentious disinformation." Several persons were subsequently weeded out of *Rilindja* and Radio-Television Priština for "hostile" points of view.[58] And while in February 1986 Sinan Hasani, a prominent Kosovar politician and then vice-president of the SFRY Presidency (later president), continued to insist that the organizational center of Albanian irredentist activity was *outside* Yugoslavia, he noted, in an interesting phrase, that it was "wrong and unacceptable to look for the enemy *exclusively* within the LC ranks."[59]

A second citizens' petition submitted at the end of 1985 was signed by 2,011 Kosovar Serbs and Montenegrins. In this petition they vented their frustration at the continued deterioration of the political situation in the province. Provincial authorities in Priština denounced the petition as "subversive, unacceptable, [and] extremely nationalistic." The signatories had anticipated this kind of reception in Priština, and had addressed their petition to the organs of the Socialist Republic of Serbia—a fact that, according to Sadri Godanci, a provincial party Presidium member, demonstrated that "the signatories did not have faith in the political structure of Priština and Kosovo."[60]

In January 1986 a group of 212 Serbian academics, writers, artists, physicians, and engineers addressed a petition to the Federal Assembly, complaining that the Albanians of Kosovo were pursuing a policy of "genocide" against non-Albanians.[61] This petition declared, in part:

Under the guise of the struggle against "greater Serbian hegemonism," the Serb nation and its history have been subjected for decades to a show trial. . . . All those in our country who are not indifferent have long since realized that the genocide in Kosovo cannot be halted without deep social and political changes in the whole country. Such changes are impossible without a change in relations between the Socialist Autonomous Provinces and the Socialist Republic of Serbia, or indeed [in] the whole of Yugoslavia. No genocide can be stopped by means of [the] policy which had made it possible in the first place, i.e., [the] policy of a gradual handover of Kosovo to Albania, capitulation with no capitulation being signed, [a] policy of national betrayal.[62]

Subsequently, in March 1986, ninety-five Kosovar Serbs turned up in Belgrade and asked to be received by the Federal Assembly. There they complained that Albanians were buying up property in Kosovo, and that Serbian communities were being encircled by Albanian ones. They alleged that sex crimes against non-Albanian women had been ignored by provincial police, that the police had undertaken illegal actions where non-Albanians were concerned, and that provincial bodies had ignored the complaints of Serbs and Montenegrins. One citizen openly charged that the political situation in Kosovo was actually worse then than five years earlier.[63] The group demanded greater protection by the authorities from attacks by their Albanian neighbors. As if to confirm the truth of the Serbs' allegations, the provincial authorities arrested the organizer of the petition, Kosta Bulatović, upon his return to Kosovo, and charged him with having engaged in "hostile propaganda."[64]

When the thirteenth party congress convened in Belgrade's Sava Center in late June 1986, several hundred Serbian villagers from Batusae and other communities near Priština decided to march to Belgrade to bring their plight to the attention of the congress. Kosovo authorities dispatched the provincial police, however, who blocked the road and prevented the marchers from crossing the Kosovo-Serbia frontier.[65]

In such circumstances it comes as no surprise that a Belgrade meeting of ex-partisans from Kosovo raised questions as to whether leading functionaries of the Kosovar apparatus had been in secret contact with the Albanian communist party.[66] The veterans claimed that former federal information minister Ismail Bajra had engaged in talks in Tiranë at least three times a year prior to 1981 without ever reporting his presence at the local Yugoslav embassy, and demanded that both he and former state president Fadilj Hodža be brought to account for pro-Albania sympathies.

In early 1986 Miodrag Trifunović, president of the federal chamber of the Yugoslav Assembly, described the Slavic emigration from Kosovo and the deteriorating atmosphere in the province as the most serious political problem currently facing Yugoslavia. Irate Serbs in Kosovo demanded, *inter alia*, that the Socialist Autonomous Province of Kosovo be eliminated as a juridical unit and that the use of the Albanian language and Albanian national symbols in Kosovo be suppressed.[67]

The Limits of Yugoslav Socialist Patriotism

Until 1987 and the rise of Slobodan Milošević in Serbia, Yugoslav officials claimed to base their nationalities policy on "brotherhood and unity"—a vague Titoist formulation that embraces a federal system based on ethnic differences, guarantees for the language and culture of the sundry nationality groups, and a ban on noncommunist political organizations (described as inimical to brotherhood and unity). For much of Yugoslavia's postwar history it has also involved the significant decentralization of political powers to the eight federal units and a "population key" mandating fixed quotas for specific ethnic groups in federal and republic appointments and in other spheres.

Closely related to this broad concept is the notion of "Yugoslav socialist patriotism," described in one publication as "the consciousness of, feeling, and love for the socialist self-managing community."[68] Since there is no Yugoslav nationality per se, Yugoslav socialist patriotism is not, according to its advocates, related to nationalism. Indeed, it is described as diametrically opposed to particularism and localism, which allegedly represent forms of collective egoism.[69] On the other hand, Yugoslav spokespersons would claim that far from negating the values, traditions, and interests of the component national groups (such as Serbs, Albanians, and Montenegrins), Yugoslav socialist patriotism presumes them.

Since Yugoslav socialist patriotism was long presented as a norm for public and private behavior, it follows that the actions and policies of the regime must conform to that norm if it is to have any prospect of success.

There have been various inconsistencies between theory and practice over the years, but the most serious, arguably, have been manifested in Kosovo. To begin with, the Albanians view Yugoslavia (literally, Land of the South Slavs) as a Slavic country, and hence consider Yugoslav socialist patriotism an attachment to what is, in cultural terms, a predominantly Slavic community. Second, since Albanians now outnumber both Macedonians and Montenegrins, and will no doubt outnumber Slovenes in the next census, excluding them from full-republic status while allowing Macedonians, Montenegrins, and Slovenes that privilege can only be justified on the grounds that they are a minority diaspora from a neighboring state —Albania. But this in turn implies that Albanian national sentiment is not on a par with Serbian, Slovenian, and other Slavic attachments, and that while the latter are "presumed" by Yugoslav socialist patriotism, the former is tantamount to irredentism. Third, while the slogan "brotherhood and unity" suggests a policy supportive of mutually tolerant cohabitation by distinct ethnic groups, in summer 1986 Yugoslav authorities took the unusual step of legally barring any Albanian settlement in the few ethnically homogeneous Serbian villages left in Kosovo—a measure which Viktor Meier called Yugoslavia's "little 'apartheid.'"[70]

Finally, despite the population key, Serbs and Albanians in Kosovo continue to argue over appointments. Each side accuses the other of enjoying unfair advantage. In June 1985, for instance, the Belgrade news agency Tanjug released a report of a session of the federal conference of the Socialist Alliance of Working People of Yugoslavia (SAWPY), in which complaints were registered that almost all managerial positions in culture, education, and the media in Kosovo were reserved for Albanians.[71] Radio Priština offered a very different picture, however, citing statistics to the effect that 68.4 percent of those employed in the social sector were Albanians (though they accounted for more than 80 percent of the provincial population by 1986), while Serbs held 22.5 percent of such jobs and Montenegrins 3.3 percent (though together they accounted for less than 9.0 percent of the provincial population in 1986).[72] The national composition of the Kosovar party organization as of June 1985 seemed to bear out Radio Priština's viewpoint: despite the population key, only 67.0 percent of the Kosovo LC was Albanian, versus 22.4 percent Serb, 5.3 percent Montenegrin, 2.8 percent Muslim, 0.88 percent Turk, 0.61 percent Gypsy, and 0.95 percent other.[73]

The Party's Analysis

Despite underground actions, sabotage, pamphleteering, trials, riots, polemics with Albania, expulsions of party members, and controversies between the Serbian and Kosovar party organizations, the authorities wavered until early 1987 between portrayals of the situation as stabilized and improving and frank admissions that interethnic relations in Kosovo were "far from satisfactory."[74] One of the first Tanjug releases in April 1981 optimistically stated that "the broad masses of citizens, youth, Albanians, and members of other peoples and nationalities of Kosovo and Yugoslavia, sharply condemned [the antiregime demonstration in Priština], realizing its hostile background."[75] In 1983 *Borba* claimed that "during the 21 months since the first demonstrations in Priština, the enemy [has] lost battle after battle."[76] Later, Tanjug reported that the "situation in the Yugoslav province of Kosovo is constantly improving, security is strengthening, and political conditions are more stable," though that release conceded that "antiYugoslav activity is still intensive."[77] And in April 1985, repeating what had by then become part of the routine formula, Tanjug declared that "the political situation in Kosovo is improving from day to day."[78] Occasionally, certain Yugoslav politicians protested retention of this formula. At a SAWPY meeting in 1985, for instance, Ilija Djukić urged abandonment of clichés "that no longer correspond" to the truth, such as "the situation is good."[79]

Yet the party was distinctly uneasy about any public discussion of Kosovo, initially tried to circumscribe media reportage of the demonstrations,[80] subsequently imposed an embargo on press reportage of the Kosovar Serbs' petition to the Federal Assembly in March 1986,[81] and developed a "schematic framework" to which party spokesmen and media were obliged to adhere. Olivija Rusovac alluded to this in a 1985 report, commenting that "today's debate on the emigration of Serbs and Montenegrins from Kosovo has in many respects gone beyond the schematic framework according to which the situation in Kosovo is better but emigration has not been curbed."[82] SAWPY delegate Milan Rakas was even more explicit:

> What is at stake above all is the standardization of some assessments and attitudes referring, above all, to the political security situation. We have had various views about the situation in Kosovo; they range from the situation being fairly poor to the other extreme of being very favorable. . . . Now this assessment has been standardized and is as follows: The political security situation in Kosovo is favorable if one proceeds from the grave consequences left by the counterrevolutionary events . . .[83]

What this meant for the media was abundantly clear: "Journalists must not fall into the trap of daily upsets and disagreements about controversial issues and concrete solutions."[84] On the contrary, "It is the duty of Communists and other forces in Kosovo to direct the interpretation of specific provisions of the constitution of the Socialist Republic of Serbia,"[85] not to mention of Albanian demands in Kosovo.

In a word, between 1981 and early 1987 the authorities tried to impose a party line involving the following elements. First, every nationalism was dangerous. Second, the demand for republic status for Kosovo was a smokescreen for efforts to mobilize forces to bring about the secession of the Albanian-inhabited districts of Yugoslavia and engineer their annexation to Albania. Third, because of this, the autonomist aspirations of Albanians were in essence "irredentist" and threatened the territorial integrity and cohesion of the Yugoslav federal state. And fourth, Albanian activists in Kosovo sought an ethnically "pure" Kosovo, free of Slavs.[86]

This is a curious list—curious, first, because each element is an oversimplification or exaggeration that conceals and confuses more than it illuminates, and second, because an appreciation of the seriousness of the situation does not require that *any* of these claims be maintained. Were the party to have yielded on these points, however, the result would have been to grant that the Albanian activists have some reasonable demands, an acknowledgment that would suggest a policy of compromise. In short, the party line, was not designed to illuminate the situation, but to block any compromise by uniformly portraying all Albanian discontents as "extremists." The reasons for refusing to consider compromise will be explored later.

By the end of 1986 the party line began to change. In November a third deputation of Kosovar Serbs created a furor in Belgrade by telling authorities that if the police could not defend them, they would defend themselves.[87] During a two-day informational meeting the following January, Azem Vllasi tried to reassure the federation that Kosovar authorities had stabilized the situation, but, as the Zagreb newspaper *Večernji list* commented a few months later, far from improving, interethnic relations in Kosovo had worsened even within the provincial party apparatus.[88] By then the party's assessment had become bleak. Slovenian politician Franc Šetinc called developments in Kosovo "the deepest crisis in new Yugoslavia," and blamed it on "big, fateful errors in the developmental policy of the province,"[89] Marko Orlandić, a member of the presidency of the LCY central committee, admitted that the situation in Kosovo was steadily worsening, and that this threatened the stability of Yugoslavia and stirred discontent among the broader Yugoslav public.[90] And in a speech to the party committee of the Yugoslav national army on 23 September 1987, Defense Minister Mamula warned that "problems in Yugoslavia are rapidly increasing to a level beyond the . . . leadership's ability to control [them]."[91]

In June 1987 the central committee of the LCY held a two-day session devoted to Kosovo in which it passed a resolution calling for measures to halt the emigration of Slavs from the province and to restore law and order. In October, after admitting that organized irredentist activity in Kosovo had increased to the point that public security was seriously undermined, the state presidency placed Kosovo's security under federal control and authorized the dispatch of militia from the Federal Secretariat of Internal Affairs.[92]

In late 1987 Serbian party chief Slobodan Milošević emerged victorious from a power struggle with rival Ivan Stambolić and proceeded to transform the weekly magazine *NIN* and the daily newspaper *Politika* into mouthpieces for his political ideas.[93] Kosovo lies at the core of Milošević's political program. Milošević, who built up a charismatic following among Serbs, believed that Serbia had to take a hard line in dealing with Kosovo —what Yugoslavs call the *čvrsta ruka* (strong arm).

Despite the tough talk in summer 1987 and Milošević's emergence as the leading political figure in the Serbian republic, when the Serbian assembly convened in late June 1988 it found that no effective measures had been adopted for dealing with the situation in Kosovo, which was therefore deteriorating.[94]

Milošević triumphed over his rival Stambolić in a political contest that centered on policy in Kosovo. Milošević contended that Stambolić's policy amounted to empty rhetoric and that it was necessary to restructure the relationship between Serbia and its provinces. To achieve this end, Milošević established the Committee for the Organization of Protest Meetings of Kosovar Serbs and Montenegrins, under the leadership of his lieutenant, Miroslav Solević.[95] This committee organized mass rallies involving tens of thousands of Milošević supporters in Vojvodina and Montenegro, forcing the resignation of the leaders of those regions in October 1988 and their replacement by Milošević loyalists. In late 1988 it also appealed for the organization of similar protest actions in Bosnia.[96] But the committee concentrated on the organization of large-scale demonstrations in Kosovo and in Serbia proper.

September 1988 saw mass demonstrations involving 10,000 or more Milošević supporters in Zvecan, Leposavić, Zubin Potok, Ranilug, Sremska Mitrovica, Titov Vrbas, and other locations, with smaller rallies (3,000– 5,000) in Lebane, Nova Pazova, Koretiste, Rakovica, and elsewhere. Demonstrators typically carried Milošević's portrait and sang patriotic songs such as "Comrade Tito, we swear to you that we will not deviate from your path." They also sang certain lines from a hit song by the rock group White Button (*Bijelo dugme*):

Yugoslavia, on your feet and sing!
Whoever doesn't listen to this song,
Will hear a storm![97]

Protesting Milošević's populist strategy, Slovenia's Franc Šetinc and Vojvodina's Boško Krunić resigned from the party presidium in October 1988. The resignations sent ripples through Yugoslav society but did not deter Milošević.

Milošević forced the adoption of Serbo-Croatian as the official language in Kosovo (making Albanian henceforth unacceptable for official use),[98] forced the resignation of Azem Vllasi and Kolj Široka from the Kosovar leadership, promoted Provincial Interior Secretary Rahman Morina to the presidency of the Kosovar provincial committee, and authorized the preparation of a series of amendments to the republic constitution designed to disembowel the autonomous provinces. Within Kosovo itself, the polarization between local Serbs and Albanians was reflected in the very different treatment given to these amendments in their respective media. *Jedinstvo*, the Serbian-language daily published in Priština, took a basically neutral position on the proposed amendments. By contrast, *Rilindja*, the Albanian-language daily, especially in the second half of November and in December, bitterly attacked the proposed amendments, which, it said, threatened the autonomy of the province.[99]

In February 1989 the amendments were adopted, eliminating the province's authority to pass its own legislation and making the Serbian Supreme Court the highest judicial court of appeal for Kosovo prior to appeal to the federal level. Jubilant Serbs celebrated the "elimination" of borders between Serbia and its autonomous provinces. Albanian workers and students replied with a wave of strikes across the entire province, leading some Serbs to demand that the army send units into Kosovo. Army units in Kosovo were in fact placed on combat alert, and large columns of tanks and other army vehicles were reported on roads entering the province.[100]

To complete his victory, Milošević had Azem Vllasi and fourteen others arrested and tried for treason ("counterrevolution") and ordered extensive revisions to the party statutes of the Kosovar party organization. These measures did not ensure calm, however, and a meeting of the Provincial Committee of the Kosovo LC in November 1989 admitted that the activity of Albanian nationalists was undiminished and that there had been armed attacks on army installations and units and on members of local security organs.[101]

A New Wave of Tensions

By early 1990 discontented ethnic Albanians increasingly looked to political pluralization as a way out of the impasse. Three new alternative movements in particular championed the idea of pluralism as the key to solving the crisis. These were the Democratic League of Kosovo (which urged restraint on both sides), the Popular Movement for the Republic of Kosovo (which also highlighted the importance of full-republic status), and the Social Democratic Party of Kosovo (which was founded in February 1990).

On 18 January 1990, after many years of resisting pressure to negotiate, Kosovo's communist leaders finally sat down with representatives of the Kosovar opposition. Šakir Maksud, a member of the Kosovo party leadership, readily conceded after the first round of talks: "It is evident that the main aim of the alternative groups is the abandonment of the single-party system."[102] And indeed, speaking on behalf of the alternative movements, former journalist Veton Suroi insisted that "political pluralism is the only way to solve the problems of Kosovo."[103]

But the talks broke down, and on 24 January some 40,000 ethnic Albanians took to the streets of Priština, demanding free elections and the immediate resignation of provincial boss Rahman Morina, a Milošević ally. Those disturbances ignited several weeks of violence in which Albanian demonstrators fought with police. On 31 January there was even an open-pitched battle between armed groups of Albanians and Serbs in the village of Srpski Vrševac, near Lipljan.[104] Tens of thousands of Albanians took to the streets in towns across Kosovo. Meanwhile, back in Belgrade, thousands of disconsolate Serbs gathered on the Square of the Republic, shouting insults against the late president Tito and demanding an end to communism. The protestors shouted "Tito—criminal!" and "Tito—Ceauşescu!"[105]

The federal authorities sent in armored vehicle units of the Yugoslav People's Army; the death toll exceeded nineteen.[106] Meanwhile, Yugoslav president Janez Drnovšek proposed a birth control plan to slow the rapid population growth among Kosovo's Albanians.[107]

By this point, the Serbian party press had become accustomed to shrillness in its reportage of Kosovo, and routinely blamed troubles in Kosovo on "terrorists" and "separatists." In February 1990 the Belgrade daily *Politika ekspres* described Fadil Hoxha, the former Yugoslav vice-president, as the mastermind of "terrorist actions" designed to advance his alleged "insane fascistic plan to create a Great Albania."[108] Such rhetoric only helped to alienate other republic leaderships, and the longer the Kosovo crisis continued, the more isolated Serbia became.

The Slovenian and Croatian leaderships both criticized Serbia's policies in Kosovo, and Slovenia called for a lifting of the state of emergency in the province. The Bosnian leadership warned that time was running out for finding a solution in Kosovo. Of the five other republics, only Montenegro stood by Serbia.[109]

Kosovo has thus become a powerful factor for change in Yugoslavia for several reasons: it is the scene of the complete deterioration of interethnic relations, it has massively contributed to the breakdown of dialogue among the republics, and its economic dilemmas have ultimately created a serious pressure on the entire region. A fourth way in which developments in Kosovo have reinforced pressure for change is through the spawning of independent civil and political initiatives such as the Kosovo Committee for the Protection of Human Rights, the Association of Independent Journalists of Kosovo (established in February 1990), and the aforementioned alternative movements. Political pluralization has of course been farther advanced in Slovenia, Croatia, and Serbia; but all the same, the pressures for pluralization generated by interethnic tensions in Kosovo have independent importance.

Why Albanian Irredentism Will Not Go Away

It is worth remembering that rioters in both the 1968 and 1981 demonstrations were heard to chant "Long live Enver Hoxha!" Nor is there any reason to doubt Yugoslav reports that some underground organizations in Kosovo have had contacts with Albanian exile organizations in the West and perhaps also with officials in Albania. At this stage, however, it is doubtful whether many Albanian activists see the necessity of choosing between an *autonomist* program (republic status within Yugoslavia) and an *irredentist* program (secession followed by annexation by Albania). What matters is that Kosovar Albanians are fed up with the status quo, increasingly alienated from the Serbs and the Montenegrins, and face a deteriorating economic situation that cannot make the prospect of remaining within Yugoslavia seem by any means easy.

Most Kosovar Albanians simply want the situation to improve. Some are basically autonomist, most basically irredentist, and many for autono-

sails of support for the transfer of some of the provinces' jurisdiction back to the Serbian republic, with the result that the Serbian amendments were passed in early 1989. And third, by confronting Yugoslavia with the possibility of localized civil war, the continued political instability in Kosovo contributed to the more general pressure on Yugoslavia to rethink the political and structural premises of the system.

IV A New Generation

8   Feminism in Yugoslavia

"Now," said I, "take the male and the female sex; if either is found to be better as regards any art or other practice, we shall say that this ought to be assigned to it. But if we find that they differ only in one thing, that the male begets and the female bears the child, we shall not take that difference as having proved any more clearly that a woman differs from a man for what we are speaking of; but we shall still believe that our guardians and their wives should practise the same things."—Plato, The Republic, *Book V*

Blaženka Despot opens her 1987 book *The Woman Question and Socialist Self-Management* with a challenge: if, as Marx and Engels say, the ruling ideas of any epoch are the ideas serving the ruling *class*, then one may add that they are also the ideas serving the ruling *sex*.[1] It follows that if the radicalization of the working class is only the first step toward the overthrow of the old system of class relations, then the radicalization of women is only a first step toward the overthrow of patriarchal society and its complete replacement with something else.

Despot is one of a small but vocal number of feminists who since the late 1970s have been trying to change the way Yugoslav society thinks about the sexes and their roles in the family, society, and politics. Yugoslavia's feminists are concentrated in three cities: Belgrade, Zagreb, and Ljubljana. For the most part they are non-Marxists. Most of them are young professionals and academics born since World War II. Like their counterparts in the West, they have faced a combination of challenges. On the one hand, they have had to live with the scorn and self-righteous anger of people who grew up with patriarchal values and who therefore consider any challenge to those values as impudence at best, sacrilege at worst. Further, they have been confronted by suspicion from the party, which considered the implication that the "woman question" was not being resolved an affront to its own authority, and feminist activity an intrusion into its political sphere. And finally, they have been challenged by the older generation of women, the partisan generation, many of whom fought against the occupation forces in World War II and rose to positions of responsibility in the postwar apparatus. For this generation, the partisan experience and the mobility they personally experienced after the war were proof that socialist society in Yugoslavia had made a decisive move toward restructuring the relations between the sexes on more egalitarian lines.[2]

When the partisans first took power, they proposed to "solve" this question within the framework of a power monopoly.[3] The 1946 Constitution included a clause guaranteeing equality of the sexes both before the law and in social life, and when the Fifth Party Congress passed a new program in July 1948, it underlined the need for work "in educating women in the spirit of socialism, in achieving greater mobilization of women for the building of socialism, for strengthening the equality already attained, by means of a constant solicitousness for their cultural and political advancement . . . and for the more massive inclusion of women in all areas of social and economic life."[4] Further resolutions were passed at each succeeding congress. The Eighth Congress (1964), for instance, urged basic organizations of the LCY to devote more attention to the advancement of women's status and in particular to the promotion of greater numbers of women to positions of responsibility and authority in administration, while the Tenth Congress (1974) entrusted communists with particular responsibility for ensuring the ever greater participation of women in the political life of the country.[5]

Dramatic results were achieved in mobilizing women into the industrial labor force,[6] and, for a time at least, the proportion of women occupying seats in women's councils, on enterprise boards of directors, and in councils of agricultural collectives steadily grew.[7] Moreover, there is little question that, in comparison with women in many other countries, Yugoslav women have been as well or somewhat better represented in the echelons of power.

But the passage of the Economic Reform in 1965 resulted in a reversal of trends toward bringing larger numbers of women into positions of political and managerial authority. For example, the number of women elected as deputies in the federal assembly fell dramatically, from 15.2 percent in 1963 to 6.3 percent in 1969, as did female representation in the republic assemblies (from 16.1 percent to 7.5 percent) and in the district assemblies (from 14.2 percent to 7.9 percent).[8]

The Ninth Congress of the LCY (March 1969) expressed concern at this trend, interpreting it as an indication of a loss of momentum and stagnation in the sphere of women's equality, and admitting positive *regression* in the years immediately prior.

Some momentum was later regained, and by the mid-1970s many indicators showed that women had retrieved the position they had had in elective bodies in the early 1960s.[9] Yet in 1976 there was only one woman among the fifty members of the presidium of the LCY, two women among the fifty members of the presidium of the SAWPY, thirty-three women among the 144 members of the presidential council of the League of Trade Unions, eight women among the thirty-nine members of the presidium of the League of Socialist Youth, two women among the twenty-two members of the presidential committee of the veterans' organization, and two women among the thirty-two members of the Federal Executive Council.[10] In June 1975 only 41 (5.2 percent) out of the 792 highest ranking federal functionaries were women. In a final irony, the number of party members who are women was proportionately smaller in 1979 (about 20 percent) than in 1945 (about 25 percent).[11]

In 1987 a small controversy erupted over female representation in the Federal Secretariat for Foreign Affairs, when several magazines and newspapers received letters charging that the secretariat had demanded that the executive councils of the federal units remove all women candidates from their lists of names proposed for appointment in the secretariat. A tabulation of positions showed that only 28.8 percent of secretariat officials were women, and that, as of early 1987, only two of Yugoslavia's ambassadors were women—Ana Jovanović in Denmark, and Ljiljana Todorova in Guinea.[12]

But problems run deep. Illiteracy is three times as great among Yugoslav women as among Yugoslav men (14.7 percent versus 4.1 percent in 1981). Women are still in a clear minority among recipients of higher degrees (in 1984, 659 females out of 2,138 M.A. recipients, 185 females out of 820 doctorates). As of 1981, Yugoslav women's average wages were 16 percent less than that of men.[13] Unemployment has also been more serious among women, with 19.0 percent of females registered as unemployed in 1986, versus 10.4 percent of males.[14]

In March 1981 *Politika* conducted a survey of Yugoslav women that asked if they felt they had achieved equality. Many women refused to answer, while a large number expressed confusion about the notion of equality itself. Of those who did answer, there were some who answered that socialism had fulfilled its promise. Others, however, denied that they had achieved anything even close to equality either at the workplace or at home. Interestingly enough, when *Politika* approached a sample of men a week later with the same question, there was unanimous agreement that Yugoslav women were definitely *not* equal, with some respondents adding that that was the way it should be.[15] The difference in response reflects a well-known syndrome that women are less inclined to "admit" their subordination than are men.

Nataša Djurić stated the Yugoslav women's case clearly in a 1980 article for *Borba*: "A lot has been accomplished, but we want more. We want women to be more fully included in sociopolitical life," she wrote. "Where cadres policy is concerned, for example, everyone will agree that women are 'second-rate citizens' or a reserve work force."[16]

The LCY openly admitted its failure to achieve the goals it set in this area, and conceded that proportionally few women were involved in self-managing bodies, executive organs, or delegate assemblies, or occupied leadership positions in the society. Worse yet, the party apparatus had failed to heed the resolutions of its own party congresses, and the presidium of the LCY central committee felt obliged to concede in spring 1980 that the basic party organizations had been occupied only in a sporadic and unorganized fashion with advancing the position of women in Yugoslav society.[17]

The Cultural Problem

In the late 1970s various voices challenged the notion that bureaucratic resistance and "liberal" tendencies were entirely to blame for this persistent foot-dragging. Radivoje Iveković, Mirjana Poček-Matić, Gabi Čačinović-Vogrinčić, and others now called for a reassessment of the role played by the familial division of labor and by the persistence of "petit bourgeois" and religious consciousness, admitting that their tenacity and importance had been drastically underestimated. One observer even declared that Yugoslavia had failed to do away with the bourgeois family. Negative traditionalism, it was now argued, had to be attacked head on.[18]

A group of feminist scholars in Zagreb started to meet on a regular basis in the late 1970s to exchange ideas. Their meetings took on the character of seminars in which research findings on the past and present role of Yugoslav women were presented and discussed.[19] Long-standing traditions were identified as only part of the problem, which they saw as aggravated by the commercialization of the female body. They reached the conclusion many Western feminists have reached, that the cheap novels and television serials only imitate the television commercials in their depiction of women as stereotypes. In commercials for cars, cosmetics, and a host of other products, every woman is beautiful, sensuous, and full of life, computerized, and programmed for the game of sexual relations with men. Woman's beauty is portrayed exclusively as there for the satisfaction of men. In commercial after commercial, woman's body is glorified, not for itself, but to sell commodities. The mother sells dishwashing detergents, and smiling two-children families sell toothpaste, vacations, cereal. Human relationships become reduced to what they can sell or buy.[20]

The Zagreb circle published essays about feminist concerns in the secular press, and stirred some public awareness. The LCY began to take a second look at primary school readers, television programs, and so forth. In March 1981 *Komunist* even condemned the "women's press" (represented by such magazines as *Praktična Žena* and *Bazar*) as a reservoir of patriarchalism that catered to the "traditional interests of women"—cooking, child-rearing, room decoration, makeup, and fashions.[21] The "woman and family" page, which featured mostly articles on childcare, fashions, cosmetics, cooking, and family relations, with an occasional article on the subject of women's equality in Yugoslav society, disappeared from *Politika* in 1983.

The Feminist Challenge

Feminism first emerged in Yugoslavia in the mid-1960s, when a group in Zagreb tried to capture *Žena*, the journal of the Croatian Conference for Women, and transform it into a forum for feminist ideas.[22] After three years of exertions, the attempt petered out; by 1968 local feminists had given up this idea. For a while they were dispirited, but the early 1970s brought new blood into the feminist movement.

By the mid-1970s groups of professional women in Zagreb, Ljubljana, and Belgrade were becoming politically mobilized. They believed that the Conference for the Social Position of Women (established in 1961) had remained marginal. They felt that SAWPY was unwilling to take up the important question of family relations and was not satisfying the needs of women's equality. They were concerned that women in Yugoslavia were not even taking advantage of their legal rights because of cultural traditionalism, and they saw that women were typically reluctant to assume leadership positions in the party or governmental apparatus.[23] They felt that the most important task was to work toward changes in upbringing and education. After analyzing Yugoslav textbooks, they identified a pattern of systematic stereotyping, with women portrayed as passive by nature and inherently masochistic.

Out of this milieu came Woman and Society, a group formed in Zagreb in 1979 with a membership consisting principally of sociologists and philosophers. They have met two to three times a month since then, with a core membership of twenty to thirty. Their focus is academic, with members often presenting the results of historical research. One member, the late Lydia Sklevický, for instance, was deeply involved in researching the history of the women's movement in Yugoslavia.[24] Although viewed with suspicion by many in the apparatus, they have made themselves heard—through guest lectures at universities, public talks, and articles published in *Argumenti, Danas, Delo, Dometi, Duga, NIN, Pitanja, Start, Studentski list,* and other leading periodicals.

About the same time, feminist intellectuals in Belgrade were also beginning to meet and exchange ideas. The challenge, as they saw it, was above all *cultural.* As one of the leading members in the Belgrade circle told me in 1987,

> We have good laws. In fact, under the law we have full emancipation. But in life it is a different situation. We have a very progressive family law, for instance, also for divorce and for other things. But our men are very primitive. It is difficult to find civilized men in Serbia. The men and boys are very irresponsible; this is their style. The boys don't take school seriously, while the Serbian girls tend to do much better than the boys. Wife-beating is very common in Serbia.[25]

The Belgrade circle decided to organize an independent international conference on the subject of women's equality. The resulting conference, held in Belgrade 27 October–2 November 1978, was attended by feminists from Poland, Hungary, France, West Germany, Great Britain, and Yugoslavia, with an especially large contingent from Italy.[26] Perhaps surprisingly, the conference did not catalyze any further organization, but served chiefly to impress upon participants the weight of the difficulties which they were facing.

Later, in 1981, three Belgrade intellectuals—Sophia Trivunac, Lina Vušković, and Sonja Drljević—started to meet on a regular basis for discussions at the Student Cultural Center. Eschewing the formal organizational framework of the Zagreb circle, the Belgrade feminists deliberately kept things informal. The group was built up through friendship channels. The organizers telephoned people to remind them of meeting times. As many as two hundred people would come to their meetings. The group was active for about two years, and when it became dormant, it was succeeded by a new group, created in 1986 by Lepa Mladjenović, a Belgrade psychologist.

In the meantime, a second, less institutionalized and less academic Croatian feminist group was formed in the Trnje district of Zagreb by Katerina Vidović in 1985. This new group attracted younger women in their twenties who were not professionally interested in feminism or in the history of the women's movement. It concentrated on consciousness raising, and established a phone line for battered women. With a core membership of twenty to thirty activists, including some men, the Vidović group issued leaflets on exhibitions and other events considered chauvinist: one example was a photo display of nude and seminude women.[27]

Finally, a feminist organization called Lilith was created in Ljubljana in April 1985 by researchers of the faculty of sociology. Unlike the other groups, Lilith was consciously created to serve two quite different purposes —practical work and recreation. Lilith puts out its own magazine on an occasional basis (with four or five issues by summer 1987); the magazine is about twenty-four pages typed and xeroxed, and looks like some kind of samizdat, but it obtained support from the Student Cultural Center and therefore a legal basis. The magazine's circulation is 300–400 copies. "Something happened in the atmosphere when Lilith emerged," a member told me. "Lilith started to be talked about in the media. The various women's magazines had interviews with Lilith members. There was a certain interest generated in Lilith. People took notice."[28] In 1986 and 1987 Lilith members took the initiative in organizing open-air "protest celebrations" in which feminist, pacifist, and environmentalist concerns were brought together. The second of these, which included a peaceful march to the center of town, was timed to coincide with the first anniversary of the nuclear accident at the Soviet nuclear station at Chernobyl.

Hostile to the ideas of hierarchy and subordination, Lilith has no formal leadership, although Mojca Dobnika has served as the informal spokesperson of the group.

Besides Lilith, there is a second group in Ljubljana which is also active in this field, the Group for Women's Movements, originally attached to the Republican Conference for Youth. This was an officially sanctioned body, rather than a grass-roots organization, but it organized protests against sexism and demanded political quotas, suggesting that 50 percent of the leadership positions in the youth organization at both the federal and republic levels be reserved for females.

Zagreb, Belgrade, and Ljubljana are clearly the centers for feminist activity in Yugoslavia, where feminism is very much an urban phenomenon. But there are also some unassociated feminists in Novi Sad, and a Sarajevo sociologist, Nada Ler Sofronić, is well respected among feminists. Feminism is still small in Yugoslavia, but several feminists told me that the current is gaining adherents and projected that it would be able to play a more visible role in five to ten years.

Reactions of the Authorities

If taken seriously, feminism is fundamentally revolutionary, because it rejects the existing social order, of which the political order is one dimension. The feminist movement in Yugoslavia did not, of course, speak of overthrowing socialism, but it does speak of the need to overthrow patriarchy and of the failure of socialism to do so.

But for all that, the political establishment has reacted quite diversely. As already mentioned, most if not all of the leading periodicals have opened their pages to feminist writings. *Start* magazine, in particular, has been warmly supportive of the feminists, and the staff members of *Start* maintain contact with members of the Zagreb circle Woman and Society.[29] One member of the establishment, herself a member of the partisan generation, told me in 1982 that she had told women in Kosovo that they needed a special organization to advance the interests of women—a recommendation which goes beyond the usual recommendations of the party. She felt that promoting the organization of women in the villages could be a step in the right direction.[30] In Slovenia the authorities felt vaguely threatened by Lilith at first, but later they became more relaxed and would call up Lilith members to talk to them.

On the other hand, the gulf between the feminists and the official women's organization remains great. One feminist put it this way: "Our official women's organization is really a joke. They are doing nothing useful but they are very, very afraid of the feminist organizations because we are doing their job for nothing, and they are worried that soon people will see that their organization is unnecessary. . . . They are afraid for their salaries, but they are masking that fear in ideology."[31] And in June 1982 Branka Lazić, representing the Yugoslav Women's Conference, told the Twelfth Party Congress that it was necessary to fight against feminism with all available forces. Five years later, that same women's conference, while still hostile to the feminist movement, organized a conference on feminism in Yugoslavia and invited feminist writer Slavenka Drakulić-Ilić to present a paper. The topic Drakulić-Ilić chose for herself: do we need a conference on women and what purpose does it serve?

Visions of the Future

Jugo-feminizam is very much under the shadow of the West. Yugoslavia's feminists have read the major works of Western feminists, follow social and cultural trends in the West with deep interest, and are conscious of the fact that their small groupings are not at all comparable to the institutionalized feminist organizations of the West. Like Western feminists, those in Yugoslavia reject as both undesirable and impossible the idea of replacing patriarchy with matriarchy; they do not aspire to promote "female civilization" —which, as one astute feminist noted, could only be accomplished through totalitarian measures[32]—but rather a truly "human civilization." The chief problems they identify are gender role stereotypes; social, economic, and political inequality; the myth of female weakness; and the relationship of false history to ideology.

Of these, the most serious may be the first, fueled by social pressure to conform to stereotyped standards of appropriate behavior for one's sex. "Sex roles are one of the means of estrangement not only between the sexes," a Belgrade-based psychotherapist noted, "but also of limiting a person's development. They make a person less free."[33] Sex roles are perpetuated in the family, the school, films, and the media, and persons who reject these stereotyped roles do so at the risk of being ridiculed and branded as deviant.

Feminists have responded by organizing study groups to monitor and report on school texts and curricula, films, and television programs. One five-year study found that Yugoslav kindergarten teachers were preventing communication between the sexes by organizing separate study corners for girls and boys. The researcher, herself a trained psychologist, made the teachers conscious of their chauvinism, and as a result of her influence some of Belgrade's schoolteachers now encourage joint games for girls and boys. The researcher argues that division is the first step toward the subordination of one group to the other, and of both to constricting mythologies of the past. "If we are divided as sexes and cannot form the same language of communication, then we can be easily ruled."[34]

Similarly, Yugoslav studies of school textbooks have found that children

read school books that encourage boys to fight back, girls to withdraw. They teach girls to be neat, to cook, wash, iron, sew, and play with dolls, and teach boys to climb trees and not to cry or play with dolls or cook. Stories show mothers cooking dinner, ironing, washing, and caring for their appearance (makeup, dress) to be sexually attractive; fathers carry coal, do outside tasks, drive and repair automobiles, do home repairs, shave, and read the newspaper. Even a study of secondary schools in Croatia, in 1970–71, found the school handbook of rules defining gender differences in dress: "Students, *and especially the girls, must dress neatly and in keeping with their age.*"[35]

Yugoslavia's well-known cultural differences are also reflected in gender relations. Among the Albanian village populations of Kosovo, women are said to be treated as subhumans less important than farm animals. Elsewhere the situation is not as extreme: the status of women in Slovenia and Croatia is on a par with neighboring Austria and Italy. The status of Yugoslav women is closely correlated with the level of economic development in the region in question.

The second problem, that of social, political, and economic inequality, has already been discussed in earlier sections. The starting point for any remedy is, of course, good information, and Yugoslavia's feminists have devoted considerable energy to establishing the facts. In an important study published in 1985, Željka Šporer, a researcher at the University of Zagreb, showed that there were statistically significant correlations between the feminization of Yugoslav professions, on the one hand, and their prestige and remuneration on the other.[36] The inescapable conclusion is that underlying cultural prejudices must be eradicated before the opening of specific professions to women can be expected to produce real equality.

Another important work is Vjeran Katunarić's *Female Eros and the Civilization of Death.* Katunarić despairs of the utility of quotas or campaigns to improve the political representation of women, arguing that their efficacy is undermined by the characteristic "authoritarian attitude toward women." He also denies that women have any less interest in politics than men, citing research conducted in Slovenia. Before any progress can be made, he warns, it is necessary to steer clear of the pitfalls of *false universalism*, which denies there is a "woman question" and thereby reduces everything to an oversimplified humanism, and *instrumentalism*, which is interested in the status of women only as it relates to other problems and issues.[37]

Instrumentalism is well illustrated by a controversy centering on the problem of rape. The penalty for rape (five years in prison) has long been considered too light by feminists. But after the Albanian nationalist riots in Kosovo in 1981 (see chapter 7), Albanian men allegedly began vindictively raping Serbian women. There was a huge public outcry in Serbia, which spilled over into the television and magazines, but oddly, its focus was on the suffering of Serbian women as *Serbs*, not as women—that is, it was treated as an interethnic issue and not as an intersexual issue. Eventually, in March 1987, the Serbian republic passed a law doubling the penalty for rape when another nationality is involved—meaning, of course, that rape is considered less serious if it is between Serbs! Local feminists were outraged by this implication and protested loudly.[38]

The myth of female weakness underpins and reinforces the previous two problems. According to feminist writer Drakulić-Ilić, this myth is used to buttress a phallocracy that tells women that their subordination is natural and reflective of their allegedly inferior abilities.[39] The celebration of 8 March as International Women's Day is seen by Yugoslav feminists as a dimension of this phallocracy: the absence of a corresponding day for men suggests that they do not need it. Or, as a Belgrade feminist put it, "March 8, Women's Day, is a stupid day and a stupid idea, because if you have 364 days a year without respect for women, what good is one day?"[40]

This myth is even carried over into legislation. In Croatia, for instance, women were long compelled to retire five years before men. Finally, in the early 1980s a group of women professors appealed this law to the Supreme Court. Their petition was supported by Croatian feminists. Their pressure paid off when the law was changed in 1984 to give women the option of working the extra five years.

The myth also reflects familial relationships. Sophia Trivunac, who has counseled women and men with marital problems, relates that

> Women are unaware that they are persons. They spend their whole lives serving everyone, and sometimes they do not see this as a problem. The pay-off is to be viewed either as a victim or as a "good woman."
>
> Women often have phobias. They are afraid of the outside world. When they cannot use the world for their pleasure, they retreat back into their phobia. They feel guilty if they are virgins. They feel guilty if they are promiscuous. They feel guilty if they have only a few lovers. They feel guilty if they have many lovers. The Yugoslav woman—and, of course, not just the *Yugoslav* woman—typically feels like a sex object. Her body is not for her, but for display. She becomes alienated from her own body.
>
> It often takes a long time before women see the problem. Then it takes a *very* long time to convince the husbands that there is a problem.[41]

And finally, the fourth problem addressed by Yugoslav feminists is the relationship of false history to ideology. This was a central concern of historian Lydia Sklevický, who struggled to keep alive the memory of noncommunist feminist currents in prewar Yugoslavia and to debunk the myth that Yugoslav feminism is somehow a Western export. On the contrary, she emphasized, feminism has a long tradition in Yugoslavia.[42] The key distinction between the "bourgeois" feminists and the left-wing feminists in precommunist Yugoslavia lay in the fact that the former insisted on organizational autonomy, while the latter were prepared to see their activity integrated broadly within the framework of the party.[43]

Another feminist put it even more forcefully: "Leftist culture is basically *macho* culture. Marx and Lenin are very thin on women. Even the New Left doesn't have much to say on the subject. Sexism is built into socialism. In Serbo-Croatian they write 'Žena i čovjek [woman and humanity],' which means that women are excluded from the human race."[44]

In mid-December 1987 about a hundred Yugoslav feminists from Belgrade, Zagreb, Ljubljana, and Sarajevo (two from Sarajevo) gathered in Ljubljana for a conference. That some of them were afflicted by doubts was clear. One current held that feminists had done enough "theorizing" and that it was time for action. Another view held that feminism had remained divided and inconsistent and that the time had come to move toward some form of unity.[45] One opinion registered in the press held that feminism was in crisis, and that Yugoslav society had already moved into a "post-feminist" period.[46] Others were not so gloomy, and forecast a consolidation of the feminist movement in Yugoslavia over the next few years. Optimists could take encouragement, at any rate, from the founding in March 1990 of the Zagreb-based League of Women in Croatia, an independent political party which aims to promote women's rights.[47]

The emergence and persistence of feminist activism in Yugoslavia reflects the passing of a generation and signifies a search for new solutions and new approaches. It is symptomatic of the "structural distortion" identified by Blum, and reflects incipient cultural drift. The feminists aspire to accelerate that cultural drift and realize that the task of changing social attitudes is a long one, which needs to be attacked from below as well as from above.

Why Yugoslavia?

Yugoslavia is the only country in Eastern Europe in which a coherent feminist movement has developed. At first sight this is surprising, not only because the problems women face in Yugoslavia appear to a greater or lesser degree in all the countries of the region (and the world), but because there have been a number of articulate feminist intellectuals in several East European countries. In Poland, for example, sociologist Magdalena Sokolowska has devoted much of her life to arguing the case for female emancipation,[48] and in 1980 there was even an attempt to set up a feminist group in Poland, but it foundered for lack of interest.[49] East German and Hungarian women have also written cogently about the situation of women in their respective countries, but in neither case has a feminist movement developed. Instead, as in Czechoslovakia, socially aware women have become involved in other forms of dissident activity, chiefly pacifist groups or, in the case of Czechoslovakia, Charter 77.

Poland at the dawn of the 1980s looked like propitious terrain for feminism. Women were staging protest marches,[50] women's organizations were becoming more active,[51] and the number of women elected to the central committee in early 1981 rose sharply; a woman was even elected to the party Politburo.[52] Around this same time, a group of women at the University of Warsaw drew up a list of demands, which included the publication of feminist periodicals, a feminist theater, feminist art galleries, independent meetings and seminars devoted to feminist concerns, the establishment of a central pool of information about all feminist movements and about the situation of women in Poland and worldwide, and the establishment of links with feminist movements in other countries. The signatories claimed that they had already established cooperative links with feminists in West Germany, France, and the Soviet Union.[53] But the erosion of the economy and the introduction of martial law quickly reversed these incipient trends, and a 1986 article found that although the number of women obtaining higher education was growing faster than the corresponding number of men, they continued to find it more difficult to obtain responsible professional jobs.

Independent women's organizations were set up in Czechoslovakia, Romania, and Bulgaria in early 1990. In Czechoslovakia an organization called Public for Family—Women's Party emerged in mid-January. Its chief organizer was Viera Pospisilova.[54] In Romania the National Women's League was established in Bucharest on 30 January with Smaranda Ionescu as chair. In Bulgaria the Alternative Women's Union was founded in mid-March; it was advertised as a successor of the original (noncommunist) Bulgarian Women's Union, established at the beginning of the twentieth century.[55] A second independent women's organization in Czechoslovakia—the Confederation of Women and Family Initiatives of Czechoslovakia—came into being at the end of September 1990, and stressed its intention to act as a lobby group representing women's interests before the government.[56] In Poland there were several independent women's organizations by the end of 1990, including the Democratic Union of Women, the Committee for the Defense of Women, and the League of Polish Women. They faced their first major policy struggle in protesting a planned law (backed by the Catholic church) that would ban abortion.[57] To what extent these organizations can function as effective feminist forums remains open to doubt. In the German case, for example, as the two Germanys finalized their move toward reunification, Brunnhilde Fabricius, chairwoman of the West German Women's Council, complained, "Half the population is being shut out of the unification process. In the second state treaty [on social issues] there is no perceptible concept of women or children's issues."[58]

There are several factors which account for Yugoslavia's uniqueness in this regard. First, the Yugoslav system was long the most open system in the area, with the greatest tolerance for autonomous groups. Elsewhere in the region, only churches were allowed to engage in fully autonomous activity—until the dramatic changes of 1988–89. Second, because of the system's greater openness, the society was more permeable by Western influences, and women intellectuals in Yugoslavia were much better situated to obtain and read Western feminist materials or to travel to the West to attend feminist meetings. Third, Yugoslav women had already developed a feminist movement in the interwar period. This movement promoted women's interests through strikes and other actions, and spearheaded a grassroots campaign for women's suffrage. As Barbara Jancar has observed, "The demand for women's suffrage mobilized women from every national and social segment of society, and culminated in a mass demonstration for the right to vote in 1939."[59] And fourth, women's participation in the wartime partisan struggle had a potent effect on women's consciousness in Yugoslavia.

But for all of this the mobilization of feminist consciousness and strength in Yugoslavia has been relatively limited and is by no means irreversible. In Serbia the nationalist revival promoted by Slobodan Milošević since 1987 has been associated with a new patriarchalism and retrogressive changes in intergender relations.[60] As a by-product of these changes, Belgrade's feminists became increasingly cut off from other intellectuals, and by 1989 felt that they lived in a kind of ghetto in intellectual isolation. But such changes are not restricted to Serbia. On the contrary, there is a rebirth of neoconservatism throughout Yugoslavia that emerged as a reaction to deep social crisis and which proposes a return to "traditional" values—meaning that women will do all the housework, obey their husbands, and stay out of politics.[61] Significantly, pictures of Serbian peasants demonstrating in support of Milošević from 1987 to 1989 show large crowds consisting exclusively of males.

The emergence of feminist groups is one measure of the *strength* of a society. It is one symptom of a broader process of self-organization through which society gains the strength to criticize and challenge the existing order. The more diverse the independent groups, the more diverse and all-encompassing the pressure that society can bring on the system. Feminism is one sign of a transformation of social consciousness and of what Gabriel Almond once called the "sense of political efficacy."

9 Rock Music and Counterculture

Any musical innovation is full of danger to the whole State, and ought to be prohibited; when modes of music change, the fundamental laws of the State always change with them. —*Plato,* The Republic, *Book IV*

Rock music is an organic inseparable part of the sociocultural consciousness and activity of a society. Rock music, therefore, both reflects *and* contributes to the ideas of the age and the changes taking place in consciousness and behavior. In the context of Eastern Europe more specifically, rock music played a role in reinforcing the steady growth in the demand for freedom and in providing outlets through which alternative political ideas could be expressed and nurtured. As Goran Bregović, leader of the Yugoslav rock group White Button, told me in 1989, "We can't have any alternative parties or any alternative organized politics. So there are not too many places where you can gather large groups of people and communicate ideas which are not official. Rock 'n' roll is one of the most important vehicles for helping people in communist countries to think in a different way."[1] By the same token, the passage of communism has created a crisis for rock musicians in the Soviet Union, Poland, Czechoslovakia, Hungary, and, for as long as it still existed as a separate entity, East Germany.

This chapter will trace the dissenting role played by East European rock in the 1970s and 1980s, and suggest some reasons why the tolerance level for rock music differed from regime to regime during those years. It will close with some thoughts about the present status of rock music in the region.

Students of political culture are fond of reminding us that the self-perpetuation of systems is contingent upon the successful socialization of the young. Political culture—"the system of empirical beliefs, expressive symbols, and values which defines the [context] in which political action takes place"[2]—is the attitudinal environment in which governments function, and may be either supportive, corrosive, or indifferent to authority. The superstructure of communist regimes is attuned to the task of molding a "new communist man and woman," that is, to the task of transforming political culture and instilling specific values and attitudes in the younger generation.[3]

The task of "building communism" signified that communist regimes saw themselves as the managers of programmatic and purposive social change. While there may be some dispute as to whether there was any purposive social change being pursued at all in Poland, Hungary, and Yugoslavia by the early 1980s, in the abstract the cultural goal pursued under communism would embrace both behavioral and attitudinal patterns; therefore, any alternative culture or set of patterns would be unwelcome. Archie Brown argued in 1977 that changes in culture generally and political culture in particular are likely to be accomplished by changes in social structure, thus confirming Plato's observations in *The Republic*.[4] This says nothing about causality, which presumably would operate in both directions, but it does underline the fact that neither aesthetic nor attitudinal variables are politically innocent. The interest demonstrated by Soviet, Bulgarian, Romanian, and other communist regimes until the end of the 1980s in encouraging the development and spread of a common culture and political culture[5] indicates that at least some communist elites operated on that premise.

Differences in regime levels of toleration of rock music seem to roughly parallel differences in toleration toward religion, ethnic subcultures, dissent, and the scope of autonomy allowed to writers and journalists. These differences may be traced, as Andrzej Korbonski has observed, to the presence and extent of six background conditions:

(a) alienation of intellectuals and youth;
(b) political reforms;
(c) economic difficulties;
(d) divisions within the party;
(e) contacts with the West; and
(f) anticommunist attitudes.[6]

Rock music is clearly relevant to variables (a) and (e), and arguably also to (f)—all variables relevant to political culture and socialization. Rock music may thus express and articulate the alienation of youth, with the danger that articulation of disaffection will serve to sustain and deepen it. Moreover, rock music overtly promotes contacts with the West: directly, when Western rock groups tour Eastern Europe; indirectly, when indigenous groups sing Western songs and imitate Western styles; and vicariously, through the proliferation of Western rock records and associated paraphernalia from Michael Jackson sweatshirts to punk fashions.

Finally, while there is nothing intrinsically anticommunist in rock music, despite occasional charges to the contrary in the bloc press, rock music has, empirically, often served as the vehicle for protest—a feature that is scarcely unique to the communist world. The evidence for this statement will be provided later, but by way of an explanation of this phenomenon, there are several aspects that in fact make music in general an *ideal* vehicle for social criticism and political protest. First, music is a kind of esoteric language whose messages, however clear to the target audience, may be excused as "entertainment" where unsympathetic listeners are concerned. Second, music creates a feeling (whether limited or intense) of collective solidarity among concert-listeners: Woodstock serves as an obvious example, or the "Polish Woodstock" at Jarocin as a less well-known one. Third, music has always served as a kind of escape valve (as the blues genre exemplifies), with the possibility always existing that an escape valve may be transformed into a beacon for mobilizing opinion.

Counterculture may be defined broadly or narrowly. Broadly defined, any culture which challenges the party's official culture, which is premised on the concept of a single, legitimate general interest, can be seen as a *counterculture*. More narrowly defined, counterculture could be seen as a set of ideas, orientations, tastes, and assumptions which differ systematically from those of the dominant culture, recognizing that *dominant* culture and *official* culture are not the same.[7]

Under the broader definition, one can identify four broad categories of counterculture, at least within the context of communist politics: political dissent and opposition, including peace movements, feminists, and ecological groups;[8] religious alternatives, insofar as religious organizations propound alternative explanations of the purposes and meaning of social life;[9] criminality and social deviance, chiefly insofar as these represent and further stimulate the desocialization of their practitioners;[10] and foreign culture importations, usually via youth.[11] This chapter is concerned with a specific aspect of the last of these.

Music will be treated here as symbolic language—that is, as a medium of communication of given meanings. In some ways music is less precise than a spoken language; in other ways it is more precise. The nature of the communication process may in fact differ, but it is communication all the same. As such, music depends on conventions to convey its meanings.

These conventions may be specific to a given culture, subculture, or group, and those outside the reference group or lacking familiarity with its conventions will not be able to understand the music except as opaque confusion. To put it another way, those who listen to rock music habitually and those who avoid it necessarily *hear* rock differently.[12]

The Politics of Rock

The political effect of rock music depends on explicit (or perceived) messages in the lyrics and includes reinforcement of political attitudes through reference to the peer group.

Music has always lain within the sphere of the politically relevant for communist regimes. When the Bolsheviks first seized power, they were convinced that it would be necessary to create "a totally new culture, one that would eventually permeate every aspect of life and art."[13] Symptomatic of this orientation were the establishment in 1923 of the Association of Proletarian Musicians for the purpose of spawning ideologically approved music, and the activity of the Blue Blouse movement between 1925 and 1929, which, under director Boris Yuzhanin, took party views on events and issues of the day and set them to dance and song.[14]

Soviet wariness of popular music began with the fox-trot, which, like jazz, was seen as a "capitalist fifth column" aimed at subverting the forces of progress. The Soviets changed their minds, however, when the Nazis condemned the genre. If the Nazis hated it, the Soviets rationalized, perhaps it was not so bad after all; and besides, they were starting to develop a liking for jazz.

The emergence of rock 'n' roll in the 1950s confronted the Soviets and their allied East European regimes with a new challenge. The Soviets feared that the overt rebelliousness of rock 'n' roll would have deleterious effects on the political consciousness of the young, and rock music was banned. "When the Beatles craze hit Russia in the mid-sixties, efforts to reinforce the ban were strengthened."[15] This proved untenable. A constant refrain —repeated by Soviet Politburo member Konstantin Chernenko in June 1983—was that through Western rock, "the enemy is trying to exploit youthful psychology."[16] As recently as 1988 the ultraconservative journal *Rabochaya gazeta* wrote that rock was "the devil's work, morally corrupting, antinational and ideologically subversive."[17] In orthodox communist eyes, Western rock seemed to encourage the withdrawal from social engagement to a focus on personal feelings; the glorification of the West; the infiltration of political skepticism, if not outright dissidence; the introduction of cultural standards, fashions, and behavioral syndromes independent of party control; and a general numbness thought to foster political indifference and passivity.

The focus on personal feelings, encouraged by songs about "feeling good" and "doing your own thing," was clearly unwelcome in the more strident regimes of Czechoslovakia, Romania, Bulgaria, and, until Gorbachev, the Soviet Union. Curtis notes that in the process of obsolescing big bands, rock 'n' roll encouraged "a new sense of the singer as an individual," a sentiment that after 1964 would grow into adulation of specific rock figures. This symbolic individualism also has its psychological counterpart in the stimulation of narcissism noted by Curtis.[18] The Prague newspaper *Tribuna* commented, in this vein, that "individualization of life as a program does not have anything in common with a socialist way of life. It is motivated by old egotism; it is accompanied by petit bourgeois mentality."[19] Similarly, *Sovetskaya Kultura* attacked rock idol Michael Jackson in June 1984 for being "apolitical in the extreme, a vegetarian, sentimental, and a religious believer,"[20] while *Literaturnaya gazeta* blasted Donna Summer for singing songs full of "vulgar sexual shrieks," describing her as a "marionette" of the "ideological masters" of the United States.[21] The Soviets' refusal to issue a visa to Boy George in mid-1984 probably reflected a related concern —that is, that Boy George's transvestism might stimulate transvestism in the Soviet musical scene.

Glorification of Western culture is a latent feature in Western rock when transplanted to the communist world. Even if not consciously, Western rock promotes certain values and behavior which are associated with Western society, and there is a historical tendency for urban youth throughout the world, and perhaps especially in Eastern Europe and the Soviet Union, to be attracted to things Western, and to believe that the West is culturally superior. As an intellectual position, this orientation has a long history in Russia.[22]

East European youth, including members of official youth organizations, commonly wear blue jeans, and sometimes stars-and-stripes emblems and crucifixes. The East German government forbade the wearing of blue jeans,[23] viewing the fashion as a potential "Trojan horse." American university sweatshirts became so popular, moreover, that by the late 1970s the Yugoslavs were making their own facsimiles and selling them in the stores. In Romania, however, the popularity of American university sweatshirts and of T-shirts with pictures of American pop singers was seen as evidence of "moral pollution."[24] Similarly, in Czechoslovakia, an official commentator warned that Western paraphernalia in music and fashion convert their buyers into "walking advertising pillars for Western companies" and thereby "shape and nourish illusions about the Western way of life and the superiority of the capitalist social system and impede the shaping of a socialist life-style."[25] In Bulgaria, where only about a third of "pop music" broadcast on Bulgarian television and radio was native (the rest being mostly American or British), young people started making and wearing exact facsimiles of Western military uniforms in the early 1980s, American and British being the most popular.[26]

The infiltration of political dissidence is a more serious problem, however, and East European rock groups repeatedly drifted toward social criticism and political commentary. One of the best-known rock groups in Eastern Europe was a Czech group, Plastic People of the Universe. This outspoken group was put on trial in 1976 after releasing an album titled *Egon Bundy's Happy Hearts Club Banned.*[27] The album came with a sixty-page softcover booklet entitled "The Merry Ghetto," and included a song with the message, "war is hell." The album was banned by the authorities.[28] A similar fate befell the East German Renft Combo (see chapter 2).

Among rock groups of the 1980s, the now-defunct Yugoslav band Pankrti (Bastards), based in Ljubljana, was one of the more daring. In open mockery of the partisan mythology, the group proposed to release an album showing a young man hugging a war monument, and to call the album *The Bastards in Collaboration with the State.* The producer circumspectly disallowed the title and refused to run a picture using any monument from World War II. The Bastards therefore staged the same pose using a monument from World War I, and titled the album *Bastards—Lovers of the State.*[29]

The fourth epiphenomenon associated with rock music is *the propagation of cultural standards, fashions, and behavioral syndromes independent of party control.* To the extent that they persist in spite of party antagonism, they become implicitly antiparty, quite independently of any political messages being propounded. Punk and heavy metal countercultures penetrated the USSR, East Germany, Poland, Czechoslovakia, Hungary, and Yugoslavia, imposing a cultural specificity in fashion with rejectionist and nihilist overtones. In the Yugoslav republic of Slovenia, punk brought cultural neonazism in tow, with the now-defunct Slovenian punk group 4-R (Fourth Reich) appearing attired in Nazi uniforms.[30] The Albanian party paper *Zeri i popullit* put it this way:

> To accept the extravagant bourgeois and revisionist mode of dress is to create an appropriate terrain for undermining socialist attitudes, behavior, and convictions. To think that long hair and narrow pants or

miniskirts have nothing to do with one's world outlook, one's ideology, is as naive as it is dangerous. Not to fight alien fashions means to give up the fight against the penetration of the degenerate bourgeois and revisionist ideology.[31]

Finally, rock music is seen to produce a *general numbness,* blurring concentration. Party spokesmen sometimes argued that the passivity and retreat into indifference fostered by certain bands was a deliberate ploy by "the bourgeois manipulators of thought, ideologues, and subversive centers" of Western capitalism.[32] Czechoslovak communist newspapers compared the "new wave of rock" to a drug, arguing that the "deafening noise, monotonous tunes, and primitive, often vulgar texts" are well chosen to *inculcate* nihilism and cynicism.[33]

The bottom line for more orthodox elites, as phrased by Albanian communist spokespersons, was that liberal attitudes in arts and fashion (underpinned by an ultraliberal philosophy expressed in songs) lead to liberal attitudes in morals, which in turn lead to liberal attitudes in politics. Political liberalism thus undermines communist rule, which could lead to the overthrow of the communist power monopoly.[34] It seemed only logical for Vladimir Makarov, writing in the Krasnodar youth newspaper *Komsomolets Kubani,* to link Western rock with a CIA master plan to subvert the communist bloc. Indeed, claimed Makarov, Allen Dulles once "said that if we teach young Soviet people to sing our songs and dance to them, then sooner or later we shall teach them to think in the way we need them to."[35]

The Polish Rock Scene

Rock music and fashions have hit every East European country to one extent or another (probably even including Albania). Their most tangible impact has been in Poland, East Germany, Czechoslovakia, and Yugoslavia.

The three most popular rock countercultures in Poland in the late 1980s were punk, popper, and hippie (possibly in that order). The Polish punk scene is diverse. There were at least seven types of Polish punks, including punks and skins, skanks, Krasowcy, skinheads, and others. There were probably well over three hundred active rock groups in Poland in 1984, including numerous punk bands, in such cities as Warsaw, Gdańsk, Nowa Huta, and Kraków.[36] Polish Radio broadcasts as much as twenty-four hours of *Western* rock per week on channel 3, and ten hours per week on channel 4. And a survey conducted in 1982 by Leszek Janik found that listening to rock music was the most popular form of recreation for young Poles, and that more than 70 percent of Polish high school students were "well acquainted" with rock music and culture.[37]

Polish rock is infused with politics, and many of the leading rock bands have taken overtly political names, such as Delirium Tremens, The Fifth Column, SS-20 (renamed, under pressure, The Deserter), Pathology of Pregnancy, Verdict, Crisis, Shortage, Paralysis, and Protest. Other well-known groups include TSA, Republika, Perfect, Kombi, Exodus, and Turbo. Where punk is concerned, this trend may have been reinforced, in particular, by the despondency created by the suppression of Solidarity and numerous other independent structures in December 1981. The regime is especially sensitive to punk, but uncertain how to cope with it.

In August 1984 the fifteenth annual Jarocin rock festival attracted nearly 19,000 youth to listen to sixty Polish groups perform. Three hundred groups had applied for regime permission, but only sixty were approved after submitting their songs for clearance. The uncertainty in such a procedure is illustrated by the case of the approved group, Perfect, which had properly submitted the texts of its songs to the authorities. At the concert, the approved line "we want to be ourselves" was replaced with "we want to beat ZOMO,"[38] and the approved line "don't be afraid of anyone" was replaced by "don't be afraid of Jaruzelski."[39] The group was subsequently disbanded by the authorities, but staged a comeback at the 1987 Jarocin rock festival.

Most new wave bands were unable to obtain official clearance to cut a record, but private tapes of garage performances proliferated. Although Polish punk is a Western import, Polish punks felt they represented a purer, even superior, strain of punk culture. "Those in Britain sing 'no future,'" said a leading Polish punk vocalist. "But I'd like to be on welfare payments there! If you want to know what is 'no future,' come to Poland!"[40]

This bleakness colored the lyrics sung by Polish punk bands in the mid-1980s. The punk band WC, for instance, offered a nihilistic vision in one song:

Posers, fetishists—destroy them all!
A generation of conformists—destroy them all!
Your ideals—destroy them all![41]

And in another song, WC mocked the coercive foundation upon which the post-Solidarity regime was built:

I am a tank, I am a tank.
I am strong, I am healthy.
I can only beat everyone . . .

I can go only [straight] ahead
And I do not need to eat.
I am afraid of nothing,
You are tight—so what[!][42]

Other bands, with names like Cadaver and Clinically Dead, projected despair that deepened into resignation and apathy. Another band, Manaam, won critical acclaim in 1983 for the release of an album called *Night Patrol*. One of its songs was set against the background of wailing sirens and the sounds of breaking glass, and, in a dispassionate falsetto, described daily life in martial-law Poland in these terms:

Shadows in the dark city
Linger through the night.
Danger lurks by your doorway,
Don't turn out the light . . .
Don't go out alone
Evil is prowling . . .
Night patrol's alert
Making sure that you're OK
That you don't get hurt,
Anxious to protect you.
Everything's all right.
Shadows in the sad city
Bleed through the night.[43]

Lyrics like these have drawn charges of "fascism" from the party dailies *Żołnierz Wolności* and *Trybuna Ludu*.

Manaam's lead singer, Kora Jackowska, was among the most outspoken, and won prizes from the youth weekly *Sztandar Młodych*, and the magazine *Jazz Forum*. Jackowska also came to the regime's attention, and for good reason, since she has not shied away from searing commentary. In one criticized song, for example, she sang:

Treason, treason
Cunning, cold, calculating . . .
Broken promises, broken light,
White is black and black is white . . .
Don't talk back, turn the other cheek . . .
Talk out of line if you dare.
Don't make me look, I don't want to see.

Is everyone a traitor or is it just me?
Treason sneaks into your bed.[44]

What happened in Poland, as this song reflects, is that the nihilism and skepticism of much of rock, and of punk especially, became more focused, more clearly antigovernment. Rock culture in Poland was thus overtly political.

In the early 1980s Polish rock had an antiregime edge, and tended to blame the regime for society's pathologies. By the late 1980s rock groups began to sing a new song: people were responsible for their own problems and had enslaved themselves.[45]

To deal with the groundswell of "social pathology" (as the regime called it) among Polish youth, Warsaw issued directives in January 1984, advising school teachers and administrators to compile lists of punks, hippies, "fascists," and social "misfits."[46] These lists were turned over to the police, and those thus identified were placed under surveillance. In addition, the Ministry of Education drew up a set of "social preventative and resocializing measures" aimed at "eliminating the causes of poor social adaptation" and "protecting children and young people from the effects of social pathology."[47]

In the West, punk is already passé. Not so in Poland, where punk became a favorite vehicle for expressing youth's complete despair of the system. The punk group Insects, for instance, boasted that it took the name "because you can't kill off all the insects." Another group, Göring's Underpants, combined a coquetry with nazism with outright ribaldry—an odd combination. Their motto: "the underground must piss against the wind." Another group took the name Trybuna Brudu (Dirt Tribune), which rhymes with *Trybuna Ludu* (*People's Tribune*), the communist party paper. General Secretary Jaruzelski confessed on Polish television that he did not understand all this "screechy youth music."[49] So much the better, as far as punks were concerned.

Aside from punks, a satanist movement has also emerged within the Polish rock scene. The rock group Kat, which revels in satanic imagery and whose most recent album (1987) is titled *666*, is in part responsible for this trend. Polish satanists dress in black adorned with satanic emblems (such as 666 or the devil's pentagram, a star within a circle), and wear chains and an upside-down cross pendant. A group of one hundred satanists attended the 1986 Jarocin rock festival, where they burned a large cross and celebrated a black mass.[49]

Straight-laced in Czechoslovakia

The Czechoslovak rock scene presented a striking contrast to that in Poland. In communist Czechoslovakia, the kind of noisy defiance displayed by Polish groups was out of question. Lyrics had to be more subtle if the band planned to stay out of prison, and the singers had to be content with irony or, at most, ridicule and ambiguous sarcasm. An untitled Czech number from the early 1980s illustrates this quite clearly:

Women leave me unmoved
Emotions I scorn
I'm well liked at work
My record stays clean.
I welcome after-hours chores:
The bosses always get my vote.
I ask for extra duties free
And hope they will take note . . .
I'll miss [my] date
But not the meeting—
Union of Youth, you know.
Sessions and lectures
All day long.
Friends of Cremation
Have asked me to call.[50]

By contrast, the Czechoslovak group Šafrán produced a song entitled "Prison," in the late 1970s:

As we eat our bread in prison,
each of us can be certain,
that he has perpetrated terrible things
and therefore sits behind bars.
Leave me in peace with politics,
I am a criminal:
I could not keep my mouth shut,
Now I am a prisoner.[51]

These lyrics clearly went beyond irony and ambiguity, as did the regime's response. Šafrán members Jaroslav Hutka and Vlastimír Třešňák were arrested, abused by the police, brought to trial, and eventually deported to the West, despite thousands of letters of protest from young fans.

Rock music arrived in Czechoslovakia in the early 1960s and quickly took hold. The Comets, a Prague-based group, gave Czechoslovakia's first major rock concert in spring 1962, and in 1963 Czechoslovakia saw the launching of *Melodie*, the country's first rock magazine. By 1964, there were 115 big-beat groups in Prague alone, and by 1985 more than 1,000 such groups country-wide. In Bratislava a young man who called himself George L. Every put together the James Bond Club, whose members, generally twenty-year-old university dropouts, wore jeans, let their hair grow, and gathered together to listen to rock music.[52]

During the liberal phase of Dubček's rule in 1968, a Prague psychedelic band called the Primitives graduated from "fire-and-light" shows to generally crazy "animal happenings" in which the musicians had special costumes and everybody pelted everybody else with fish and birds. During the "Fish Fest," band and audience also hurled water at each other, so that the extramusical elements finally became more important than the music itself.[53]

The end of the Dubček era meant the end (until 1989) of liberalism in official policy toward rock, among other things. For twenty years, the Prague regime was to remain suspicious of *all* rock music. Yet certain groups were the beneficiaries of official sanction, such as Olympus, Abraxus, and Catapult, though the last of these was banned in 1983 from performing in central Bohemia, including Prague. Another group, the Yellow Dog Band, changed its name in 1983 to The Musical Entertainment Group of O. Hejma, and adjusted its repertoire in order to stay off the blacklist. The straight-laced Czechoslovak regime thus forced the more daring music underground.

Yet even among those groups that received official support, lyrics could be provocative. If they had not been, it is difficult to see how they could have established any credibility among youth. An example is the rock band Bronz, which performed a rock opera in Prague with official support. One of its songs included the line, "Our master is king; his name is heroin."[54]

The 1976 suppression of Plastic People of the Universe and DG-307, two of the most popular groups in their day, was followed by a general clampdown on the rock scene.[55] From 1976 to 1981 Czechoslovak authorities kept a tight rein on rock music. The bureaucrats decided what was permissible and what was not, though these decisions were not taken on the basis of aesthetic training or expertise. As a rule, authorities were most concerned about lyrics, but two talented musicians, Vladimír Merta and Vladimír Mišík, ran into trouble after authorities decided their music was "too inventive and interesting."[56]

In the late 1970s avant-garde groups like Electrobus, Extempore, Stehlík (Goldfinch), and Žába (Frog) began to strain the prescribed limits in

thropy, altruism, religion, law, government, and morality.[67] Stirner's incantations—"The people is dead—Up with me!,"[68] "Everything sacred is a tie, a fetter,"[69] "My freedom becomes complete only when it is my might,"[70] and "All truth by itself is dead. . . . Of itself it is valueless"[71]—find resonances in contemporary punk. It may be further noted that a nihilist-anarchist movement in Germany in the 1890s was heavily influenced by Stirner's ideas.[72]

Rock music "invaded" East Germany in 1957, when young people at an unprecedented Leipzig concert heard the music of Little Richard, Fats Domino, Bill Haley and the Comets, Peter Kraus, Hazy Osterwald, and Ted Herold.[73] But it was only in the 1963–64 period that East German rock music, as such, got off the ground. In the meantime, authorities had passed a resolution concerning "Appearances of Decadence and Decay." The regime press and media attacked rock music sharply for several years, but the genre was never expressly forbidden. Only in the late 1960s did the authorities' attitude begin to soften;[74] yet, as early as 1960 the regime had given its approval to an initiative from Canadian Perry Friedman to stage a hootenanny in Berlin's Sports Hall. The event proved a success and was repeated the following year. It became an annual event, and in 1966 led to the creation of the national Song Movement within the framework of the Free German Youth (FGY) organization.[75] The new beat could, authorities calculated, add vigor to "progressive" impulses.

With Erich Honecker's accession to the SED leadership in early 1971 came a new approach, embodied in the newly developed concept of "youth dance music" by which authorities now proposed to refer to rock. The ministry of culture explained that young people clearly wanted a new dance genre, but insisted that this genre could be developed without overlays of "Western decadence."[76] The annual Festival of Political Song was launched in 1971, and over the years has drawn folk, pop, folk rock, and rock groups from all over the world, including the West. At the fifteenth Festival of Political Song in 1985, for example, the Polish rock duo Urszula and Budka Suflera sang a song about Auschwitz taken from a larger rock song cycle, while the eighteenth Festival in 1988 included a song dedicated to Sandinista Nicaragua.[77]

Rock music remained political in East Germany. In 1974, for instance, the Dresden-based Lift put on their "Solidarity Concert" for the people of Chile on the first anniversary of the military coup that overthrew Salvador Allende. That same group produced the symphony-length "Che Guevara Suite" in 1978. There have also been a number of rock concerts for peace.[78]

The banning of the Renft Combo in 1974 (see chapter 2) may have sent a chill through the East German rock scene, but it neither stifled musical creativity nor ended the careers of that group's component musicians. Renft members Peter "Caesar" Glaser (vocals, guitar, flute) and Jochen Hohl (keyboards) went on to found the highly successful rock quintet Karussell, which received a variety of state awards and decorations, including the FGY Prize for Art and the Diploma of the Ministry of Culture.[79]

Indeed, despite the close watch of the authorities, East German rock groups occasionally sent out subtle messages, albeit typically with restraint. The mood was one more of resignation, however, than of protest. Take, for example, rock composer Kurt Demmler's lines,

They deny me any laughter
They deny me any song
They deny me land and life
Which passes me by.[80]

The mood is one of helplessness. Or again, there is the musically innovative group Silly, considered by many to be one of the best groups in East Germany. On a 1985 album, *Liebeswalzer*, the group sings,

I look so fondly in the distance
with my binoculars.
I look so fondly in the distance,
that makes me happy.
The distance is a nicer place
though when I'm there, it turns its face.
The distance is, where I am not.
I walk and walk and do not get there.[81]

For a nation divided in two, with families split by a political boundary and condemned to follow West German events on television, this text was not so innocent.

The best-known East German group is probably the Puhdys. With fifteen albums to their credit by 1988, including one of 1950s American rock favorites sung in English, the Puhdys were one of East Germany's longest lasting groups (established 1965) and one of its most decorated, having won the National Prize for outstanding artists in 1982.[82]

Rather than turning its guns on all rock indiscriminately (like the Czechoslovak communists), East German communists tried to encourage *tame* rock, and to put it to use. A decree on discotheques issued in 1973 required "discothequers" (disc jockeys) to enroll in a course on ideological and political thinking. Once they graduated, discothequers were expected to ensure that at least 60 percent of the music they played originated from the bloc, and to intersperse topical information and "positive" political commentary between hits.[83] The FGY operated 5,000–6,000 discotheques in the early 1980s, and most discothequers were also functionaries of the youth organization. The FGY even organized a major public rock concert in October 1983. For as long as the communists held power in Berlin, it would appear that their policy paid off. In contrast to neighboring Poland and Czechoslovakia, there was a sense that rock music was not bad in and of itself. In fact, by the 1980s East German educators included selected rock "classics" in their lesson plans in order to teach youngsters about an important aspect of social and cultural life.[84] This qualified acceptance of certain kinds of rock—though not of punk—created a "grey zone" in which many East German youth found it possible to function.

The Yugo-Rock Scene

Of the remaining East European countries, it is clearly Yugoslavia which has the liveliest rock scene. It is also politically the most innocent, partly because of the tangibly more liberal disposition of the regime in the cultural sphere. Much of the "Yu-rock" scene is either new wave or a local synthesis of "old wave," new wave, and indigenous innovations. Croatian groups like Dee Dee Mellow (which has made use of Peruvian and Indian folk melodies) and Psihomodo-Pop, and the Slovenian group Videosex, serve up a lighter fare—though Videosex's explicit treatment of lesbianism, sadism, and voyeurism created a sensation. In the mid-1980s break dancing (brejkdens) hit Yugoslavia too.[85] A Belgrade group called In Trouble became one of the most popular rock groups in the country by pointedly shunning social messages and scandals. In Trouble's lead singer, Milan Delčić, disarmingly confessed to Vjesnik, "We wanted to escape the [Balkan shock] style and be just an ordinary rock group."[86]

The degree of acceptance of rock in Yugoslavia is implicit in the wide coverage given to rock music in Yugoslav periodicals. The Zagreb free-lance writer Darko Glavan started a regular column about rock music for Vjesnik in 1972, and Politika began similar coverage a few years later.[87] Borba, Politika ekspres, and the Macedonian newspapers Nova Makedonija and Večer have also established regular columns devoted to rock music, with occasional articles appearing in the magazines Start (Zagreb), Danas (Zagreb), and Mlad Borec (Skopje).

There are also numerous magazines catering to the rock audience. The best known is *Pop-Rock* (formerly *Rock*, Belgrade). *Disko Selektor* (Skopje) appears in three languages: Macedonian, Serbo-Croatian, and English. A third magazine, *Ritam*, began publication in February 1989. Teenagers have a special magazine of their own—*Ćao* (which replaced the now-defunct *ITD*).[88] There are also regular rock columns in *Iskra* (Split), *Val* (Rijeka), *Valter* (Sarajevo), *Naši dani* (Sarajevo), *Polet* (Zagreb), *Studentski list* (Zagreb), *NIN* (Novi Sad), *Mladina* (Ljubljana), *Ekran Revija* (Skopje), and *Una* (Sarajevo). Rock records have also become big business, and most major cities (including Sarajevo, Skopje, and Split) can boast local groups.

As of 1982 there were roughly three thousand professional and amateur rock groups in Yugoslavia. As of 1987 there were thirty to fifty professional rock groups in the country, and perhaps as many as five thousand amateur groups.[89] Among these groups one finds a wide variety of subgenres ranging from rockabilly (Tonny Montano) to punk (Pankrti, now defunct) to industrial rock (Borghesia) to protest rock (Fish Soup) to heavy metal (Wild Strawberries) to folk rock (Plavi orkestar) to various strands of new wave and hard rock, and a specifically Vojvodinan strain called "šogor rock," which blends traditional Hungarian folk music with a soft rock beat.[90]

The most controversial rock group in Yugoslavia today is surely Laibach, a Slovenian group with a greater following in the United States and Western Europe than in its native country. The members of Laibach wear nazi-style brown shirts, uniforms, and jackboots in their concert appearances, festoon the halls with banners bearing the hammer and sickle, the red star, the swastika, and the iron cross, and distribute maps showing an enlarged Slovenia. Their music is unabashedly fascistic in inspiration, imitating nazi music-making and Wagnerian music drama. Their lyrics are often nonsensical or tautological, as in the nearly endless repetition of the refrain "Life is life" in the song of that title (on the album *Opus Dei*, released in 1988). Their performances are not designed to be entertaining but to appeal more directly to the psychic space where the libido comes into contact with the superego, and accomplish this through evocative cult celebrations of the collective.

In a 1984 "Resolution" Laibach alleged that its purpose was to contribute to the construction of a world totalitarian system:

> Laibach takes over an organizational system of work after the model of industrial production and totalitarism—which means, not the individual, but the organization speaks. Our work is industrial, our language political. [Laibach's] organizational activity is an intense agitation and a constant systematic ideological offensive. Any social activity

affects the mass. Laibach functions as a creative illusion, with a censored program. Laibach's musical approach is a move to the area of pure politicization of sounds, a means of manipulating the masses. When, in politically and economically complicated situations, the antagonisms in society become strained, only force remains as the ultimate *ratio* of social integration. [This] force must take the form of systematic physical and psychic terror. For the totalitarian government, the systematic terror becomes a constitutional instrument of authority.

Through the mystic, erotic, mythological sound, constituted in an ambivalence between fear and fascination, which rudimentarily affects the consciousness of people, through stage performances of ritualized demonstrations of political power, and through other manipulative means, Laibach practices systematic psycho-physical terror, in order to effectively discipline [the masses], which results in a state of collective aphasia, which is the principle of social organization. By darkening the consumer's mind, [Laibach's music] drives him into a state of humble contrition and total obedience. By destroying every trait of individuality, it melts individuals into a mass, and mass into a humble collective body.[91]

Although the resolution was melodramatically overstated to the point of suggesting tongue-in-cheek, Laibach's music unmistakably evokes an interest that is not purely satirical but is best seen as a sublimated form of "pop fascism" enabling aggressive instincts to be channeled innocently, rather than as the literal instrument of a real fascist movement, as Laibach pretends. At any rate, the liberal-minded local authorities in Slovenia have taken all this in stride. Whether Laibach intends its message as a critique of communism or as an advocacy of fascism or as thought-energizing art, the authorities (both communist and postcommunist) have felt comfortable knowing that Laibach is unlikely to stir up a neofascist movement.

The Serbian group Fish Soup has far greater resonance among the Yugoslav public and treats political themes in a way that reflects Yugoslav thinking much more accurately. Led by published poet[92] and "master of verbal terrorism"[93] Bora Djordjević, Fish Soup does not shy away from politically provocative themes. In its 1987 album *Ujed za Dušu*, the group sings a satirical song equating the communist party with the Mafia.[94] Djordjević hurls himself headlong into controversy, whether in his songs, his poems, or in regular columns for the magazine *Duga*. In one of the latter he tackled the sensitive problem of Kosovo, offering an independent perspective. His poetry is often scatological, sexual, or political. In one poem he assailed the mythology of the National Liberation Struggle (NOB):

> Some were really in the NOB,
> but by now they are all buried.
> Those who are concerned with the NOB today
> are only concerned with themselves.[95]

Djordjević has also been outspoken in numerous interviews with the press, predicting civil war in Yugoslavia on at least one occasion.[96] In 1987 Djordjević provoked the authorities with a fifteen-minute reading of some of his provocative poems before an audience of four thousand that included the mayor of Belgrade and other party dignitaries. He created a stir, and was later taken to court on charges of three verbal misdemeanors. The judge threw the case out of court, praising Djordjević as a "true poet, who loves his people."[97]

Among male solo vocalists in Yugoslavia, one may mention Oliver Mandić, a Belgrade musician who created a small storm in the mid-1980s by appearing in drag, and Rambo Amadeus, a kind of PDQ Bach of rock music, who once created a concert piece for twelve vacuum cleaners.[98] The best-known female solo vocalist is Snežana Mišković Viktorija, a Belgrade-based musician who was named top female vocalist by *Pop-Rock* readers in a 1988 survey.[99]

Among other groups in the Yugoslav rock scene one should mention Leb i Sol (based in Skopje and generally recognized as the best instrumental ensemble in the country), Bijelo dugme (Sarajevo, the "Beatles" of Yugoslavia), Belgrade groups Bajaga and YU-Group, Indeksi, and the now-defunct bands Azra and Korni group. The newest sensation in 1988 was YU-Madonna, alias Andrea Makoter of Maribor, who began imitating her Western namesake, copying everything from singing style and mannerisms to makeup and attire.[100]

Increases in the popularity of heavy metal have also been noticed,[101] but neither the old LCY nor the postcommunist elites have betrayed any serious concerns, either with this subgenre or with rock music in general. The consensus among the elite seems to be that rock music is merely an innocent diversion, at worst an ineluctable form of escapism. Besides, Yugoslavia has long been open to Western cultural penetration to a far greater extent than other countries in Eastern Europe; hence, the specter of a new strain of influence is intrinsically less threatening in the Yugoslav case.

Elsewhere in Eastern Europe

In Romania and Bulgaria, by contrast, a true rock scene has been slower to develop. Discotheques have become popular in both countries,[102] and groups like Sphinx in Romania and Crickets in Bulgaria have built up enthusiastic domestic audiences. By the mid-1980s even punk rock had penetrated Bulgaria and Romania.[103]

The Bulgarian communists were not friendly to rock music, especially Western rock records. Hence, the Bulgarian Council of Ministers issued a decree on 17 February 1984 aimed at Bulgarian radio and discotheques that popularize Western music,[104] Georgi Dzhagarov, vice president of the State Council and chairman of the Standing Commission on Spiritual Values, went so far as to declare that "the whole country has been disquieted by the muddy stream of musical trends sweeping away all the true values of music."[105] The solution, as the Bulgarian Communist Party saw it at that time, was to revive Bulgarian folk music and dances.

Bulgaria's earliest rock 'n' roll groups—Bandi's Boys (Bandaratsite) and the Silver Bracelets (Srebarnite Grivni)—were inspired by British bands, especially the Beatles and the Searchers. These groups continued to be influential in the Bulgarian rock scene well into the 1970s.

The leading Bulgarian bands today are the Crickets (established in 1966), FSB (Formation Studio Balkanton, composed of session musicians who obtained permission to put together a group), Tangra (formed in 1982), LZ, Diane Express, Factor (a hard rock group), and Signal. Dr. Doolittle (a progressive rock group from Varna) and heavy metal groups Lucifer (also from Varna) and Era (from Sofia) are also popular.[106] The Crickets created a commotion at a 1980 concert at Sofia's University Hall with their song "Wedding Day," which lamented the loss of freedom. Exactly what kind of freedom the group *really* had in mind was insidiously suggested by the fact that the lyrics were set to the melody of the old Beatles' song, "Back in the USSR." The audience became wild, the police told the audience to sit down, and when the audience failed to respond, the police turned on all the lights in the hall. In protest, the Crickets abandoned their approved program and played only Rolling Stones and Beatles for the rest of the night, forcing the police to retreat to the sidelines. After that concert, the Crickets were out of sight for some time, possibly as a result of an "administrative" decision. Similarly, Signal fell afoul of the authorities in 1982 by stirring up "excessive excitement" at a concert in the Black Sea port of Burgas.[107]

Perhaps surprisingly, in 1987 *Narodna kultura* (a magazine published by the Committee of Culture) and *Pogled* (the weekly organ of the Journalists' Union) ran articles stating that emergent informal groups of punks, heavy metalists, rockers, neo-hippies, and *discari* (disco fans) should not be seen as pathological, and that party officials and schoolteachers should accept young people on their own terms and not engage in sterile monologues.[108]

One of those associated with this tentative liberal view of rock culture was Vasil Prodanov, a professor of philosophy. In an article for the 24 July 1987 issue of *Otechestven Front*, Prodanov warned that in the absence of tactical liberalization, these informal groupings could develop into centers of opposition to the party.[109] The party daily *Rabotnichesko delo* seconded this suggestion with a prominent article by Dragomir Dakov and Mariana Mihaylova, which cited the opinions of experts on youth policy and rock performers, including members of heavy metal bands Lucifer and Era. As Stephen Ashley notes, *Rabotnichesko delo*

> entirely supported Prodanov's plea for tolerance and concluded with a series of recommendations that would revolutionize party policy toward hard rock music and "informal" youth groups. It called, in short, for official acceptance of heavy metal and punk music and for the relaxation of youth club regulations to abolish membership schemes, drop entrance charges, and permit a more diverse range of nonpolitical and recreational activities. The authors proposed that television and radio allot more time to hard rock music and encourage amateur Bulgarian groups. It advocated the establishment of a national rock concert agency to organize performances throughout Bulgaria on behalf of professional, semiprofessional, and amateur musicians. Lastly, it called for the improvement or construction of facilities for performing rock music in every region of the country.[110]

It is vital to keep in mind that this is a form of tactical liberalization, in which the *instruments* and *methods* of policy are changed in order to ensure the best chance of realizing an unchanged policy *goal*—in this case, the effective socialization of Bulgarian youth. In line with this new thinking, Bulgaria's cultural czars allowed the punk group Kontrol to record an album with the state-owned Balkanton label in 1989,—the first time a nonprofessional rock band in Bulgaria was granted that opportunity.

This tactic notwithstanding, Bulgarian rock performers have become more outspoken about social issues since 1986, and have sung about such topics as AIDS, drug abuse, ecological problems, the powers of the bureaucracy, adolescents' conflicts with their parents, and young Bulgarians' frustrations over the lack of personal and economic independence.[111]

In keeping with its general neo-medievalism, the situation in Romania was much more difficult for rock groups while Ceauşescu was in power. During Romania's "mini-Cultural Revolution" in the late 1960s and early 1970s, Ceauşescu suppressed the rock scene wholesale.[112] Subsequently the rock scene reemerged, but it was drawn into "patriotic" currents supportive of Ceauşescu's cultural line. Ceauşescu dreamt of witnessing the creation of a specifically Romanian rock genre that would underpin his official policy of national chauvinism, but a 1975 Romanian study found that young people were increasingly drawn to American-style folk music rather than to traditional Romanian music.

The leading Romanian rock bands in the 1980s were Phoenix and Post Scriptum (both symphonic rock ensembles), Sphinx (which evolved from symphonic rock to "sympho-pop"), and Progressive TM (a reference to the once-proscribed practice of transcendental meditation). There are also heavy metal bands in Romania, specifically Domino, Compact, and Iris.[113]

Ceauşescu's twenty-four-year rule was deadly to Romanian rock music. It was bad enough that high-quality instruments were unavailable except through the black market or overseas, but Ceauşescu's energy conservation plan was especially deadly. As one Westerner observed, "How could you expect roll-and-roll to survive in a country where there is barely enough electricity to power a light bulb, let alone drive an electric guitar?"[114]

With the fall of Ceauşescu in December 1989 Romania opened up somewhat. Between January and March 1990, Hungarian rock groups crossed the border repeatedly to perform for their ethnic kin in Transylvania. Meanwhile, in February 1990 several Yugoslav rock groups staged a mammoth three-day rock festival in Timişoara before 20,000 enthusiastic fans. Among the groups performing were Valentino, Viktorija, Galija, Bajaga and the Instructors, and Fish Soup.[115]

Finally, there is the more relaxed atmosphere in Hungary, which brought in the film version of *Jesus Christ Superstar* in June 1983, staged a mammoth rock concert in the village of Pilisborosjenö in August 1983 (in connection with the filming of a rock horror film, *The Predator*), and premiered the first Hungarian rock opera, *Stephen the King*, on 20 August 1983, St. Stephen's Day.

Disco had already become big business, with some four hundred licensed youth clubs in Budapest by early 1982, and additional dance clubs in almost every town and village.[116] But it was *Stephen the King* that stirred the most discussion. Based on the play by Miklós Boldizsár, the opera relates the story of Stephen's founding of the Hungarian kingdom in 1001 and his conversion to Christianity. It opened to an impressive crowd of 10,000 spectators. The opera is unabashedly nationalistic and "ends with a poignant scene in which the music celebrating the newly crowned king changes almost imperceptibly into the national anthem, and a large Hungarian flag appears over the crest of the hill. A provincial daily reported that the applause that followed [one performance] lasted for 45 minutes."[117] The production drew an emotional response from Hungarian audiences, and the work was quickly contracted for performances for both record and film. And while dramatist Boldizsár denied any interest in using the opera as a vehicle for commentary on the present,[118] opera director Gábor Koltay told an interviewer that part of the opera's popularity is attributable to the continued relevance of its themes: "the question of how a small nation finds its way to survive is always valid."[119]

Only four bands were able to achieve national acclaim in the three decades from 1960 to 1989: Illés, Omega, Metro, and Locomotiv GT. These commercially successful bands eschewed politically delicate or socially critical subjects, and stuck to safe lyrics about love and sex.[120] Groups like Beatrice and Coitus Punk Group filled the void where lyrics were concerned.

New groups emerged in the 1980s, and "teeny-bopper" groups like R-GO, Hungaria, Dolly Roll, Kft, and P. Box drew large crowds of young fans.[121] Heavy metal bands such as Edda Works, P. Mobil, P. Box, Von Band, and Piramis have consciously modeled themselves on West European bands. Also worth mentioning is the art rock group Solaris, which in 1984 issued a rhythmic and strangely fascinating album entitled *The Martian Chronicles*. Composed by Solaris members Róbert Erdész, István Cziglán, and Attila Kollár, *The Martian Chronicles* is arranged in six movements as an instrumental suite.[122]

In the context of Hungary's more relaxed atmosphere, the groups which attracted the most criticism from the communists were those playing punk, described by certain Hungarian authorities in 1983 as having a "pernicious effect on the morals of the young."[123] Hungarian punk groups have at various times insulted the dignity of Romanian party leader Nicolae Ceauşescu (a favorite Hungarian pastime anyway), expressed the desire to indulge in corporal dismemberment, evoked a phrase calling forth the defecatory bombardment of the planet, and endorsed extermination of the Gypsies. It was the punk group Mosoly which, in an unadvertised appearance at a February 1983 concert, expressed the latter sentiment:

The flame thrower is the only weapon
    with which I can win;
I destroy every Gypsy, adult and child!

Annihilate them altogether;
When we have dispatched them,
    we can put up a sign:
Gypsy-free zone![124]

In a country which still retains lively memories of World War II, such lyrics have a positively nightmarish quality. Worse yet, that nightmarish quality is deliberate.

The two best-known punk groups in Hungary are still Beatrice (which broke up in 1981) and Coitus Punk Group (whose members were given eighteen- to twenty-four-month jail sentences in 1984). Beatrice addressed the everyday concerns of young people and consciously rejected any prefabricated values, including those of the regime. Beatrice sang about waiting for an apartment, relating to one's boss, official peace demonstrations, and the economy. And its audience responded. During concerts Beatrice habitually threw bags of milk at the audience; the practice was utterly devoid of symbolic content, but was a huge success with audiences. The authorities tried to buy out Beatrice with offers of promotion and an album, but its members did not want to be tamed, and when the group folded in 1981, it did so without having released a single album.[125]

Coitus Punk Group (CPG) was a more difficult case from the authorities' point of view since, unlike Beatrice, it wanted, very deliberately, to be provocative. Instead of bags of milk, CPG would tear apart live chickens on stage and throw the bleeding chicken parts at the audience. Instead of merely reflecting on social reality, CPG passed judgment on it. The very titles of their songs—"Rotten Angels," "Our King Is a Puppet," "Pigsty," and "Everyone Is a Louse"—were designed to be provocative. And their lyrics clearly strained against the limits of the allowable. In "Everyone Is a Louse," for example, CPG sang:

I will be free.
What I want is this:
Not to be governed by a stupid beast.[126]

In the same song, the group predicts the coming of anarchism; the political context is quite explicit. Again, in "ss-20," CPG challenged the taboo against anti-Soviet "propaganda":

The Soviet atom is also an atom,
I can't stand this totalitarianism.
The police is always hassling me.
We have ss-20s in the East,

They have the neutron bomb in the West.
SS-20, SS-20, SS-20 in the East.
In the East and in the West,
The almighty power is the test.[127]

Those lyrics were obviously unacceptable, as CPG itself clearly knew. It could only be a matter of time before the authorities would move to silence the group.

But CPG did not stop there. In "Standing Youth," the group used the nonsense word *duli* to adorn some explicitly anticommunist lyrics:

In the meadow a young shock-worker is standing.
He had just come from a Communist Saturday meeting
Duli-dul-balalajka, duli-dul-balalajka.
Statues, pictures—you schematic bandit,
The workers' hero has to play along with it.
Duli-dul-balalajka, duli-dul-balalajka.
Rotten stinking communist gang—
Why has nobody hanged them yet?[128]

While singing this song, the group's leader tore up the familiar chicken and slashed his own face and arms with a razor blade. This was too much for the authorities and led directly to the group's trial and imprisonment in 1984. Three band members received two-year sentences, while the fourth received an eighteen-month jail sentence.

Yet the case of Coitus Punk Group is exceptional. Although there are punk groups and heavy metal groups and other "outlandish" fashions in contemporary Hungary, seeking above all to express their rejection of the world as it is, the authorities by and large take a disinterested view. Even where punk is concerned, the Hungarian political establishment is, at most, divided over the best policy response, if any should be needed.

The first attempts to politicize rock music in the mid-1970s ran into trouble. Spions was forced to disband after a 1976 concert which touched on political subjects, while Galloping Morticians was frozen out of the major concert circuits after a similarly sensitive concert in 1978. Attila Grandpierre had signalled the tone of the 1978 concert when he told his audience: "We are not here to entertain you. Don't even think that you'll be having a good time at this concert. If you want to have a good time, get lost. Go home and watch TV. Now you'll have something different."[129] Not good times, but politics. By the 1980s the new "political" music was increasingly prominent in the Hungarian rock scene.

Conclusion

I am very much inclined to agree with László Kürti that there was a direct connection between the growing decay of communism in Eastern Europe and the emergence of politicized rock in the late 1970s and 1980s. The former led directly to the latter, and the latter applauded and reinforced the former. Rock music offered itself as a form of counterculture, an alternative reference point, which shifted the terms of discourse.

Of course, not all rock music is conceived as counterculture per se. New wave, for instance, seems better described as self-assertion; on the other hand, the whole point of punk is to reject everything that civilized society offers. A Polish punk explained punk philosophy in these terms:

> Sometimes I am a pacifist; other times I am a vulgar cad. I provoke through my appearance. I want others to feel that here is still a bit of freedom. [The adults] want to profit from us, to organize us, and I do not want to be a prisoner. I am going to evade them. . . . I joined the punks to protest against constraint.[130]

The spread of rock counterculture in the communist states of Europe has, as in the West, been associated with increased drug abuse, outlandish fashions, and a self-conscious striving to be "socially deviant."[131]

The collapse of communism throughout much of Eastern Europe by mid-1990 had consequences for all spheres of social activity, including rock music. In Poland, Hungary, and Yugoslavia, record sales slumped drastically—in Yugoslavia, primarily for economic reasons, in Poland and Hungary for both economic and sociopolitical reasons. With the success of the popular rebellion, there is no need for the music of rebellion; hence, Eastern Europe's musicians, especially those in Poland, Hungary, and Czechoslovakia, are groping their way to a new commercialism.

The East Berlin industrial band Pankow, which built its reputation on songs about alienation and pollution, disbanded in 1990. Pankow's lead singer, Andre Herzberg, explained, "We are no longer relevant. I'm not sure what I'm going to do now."[132]

In Poland, the Riviera-Remont Club, which once hosted punk rock concerts, now offers its space to computer fairs and flower markets. Many Polish rock musicians have either left music or left Poland. Others have taken jobs playing soft-pop at the Marriott Hotel. "Rock is dead in Poland," said Zbigniew Hołdys, band leader of Perfect, in sadness. And for the time being, that assessment may be accurate.

In Hungary and Yugoslavia, attendance at rock concerts is down, and as a result, rock bands are not able to schedule as many concerts as before.

Rock has lost much of its political role in Eastern Europe in a matter of months. But in the annals of rock history the 1980s will go down as a heroic age in both Eastern Europe and the Soviet Union. The spirit of the age is perhaps best captured in the famous "Get Out of Control," first sung by the Leningrad rock group Televizor at a 1986 concert:

> We were watched from the days of kindergarten.
> Some nice men and kind women
> Beat us up. They chose the most painful places
> And treated us like animals on the farm.
> So we grew up like a disciplined herd.
> We sing what they want and live how they want.
> And we look at them downside up, as if we're trapped.
> We just watch how they hit us.
> Get out of control!
> Get out of control!
> And sing what you want
> And not just what is allowed.
> We have a right to yell![133]

10   Young People: The Lost Generation

In the villages,
The sound of the bugle is ringing,
Calling the young men to join the army,
And people do not hurry to meet it.
Nobody believes any longer
In the calling of the bugle.

The new generation . . . listens to the bugle
And does not understand . . .
How shall we call each other to battle?
How shall the alarm be given?
The bugle has become outdated . . .

—Adrian Păunescu, *Let's Make Love On Cannons*

"Savka" is a twenty-one-year-old student at the Philosophy Faculty. She has been engaged for three years to a young worker, but they are postponing their marriage until they can find an apartment. Meanwhile, she lives with her parents. Although she is majoring in architecture, she was required to take courses on dialectical materialism, atheism, and the history of the communist party. She took the classes in 1988, but usually skipped these lectures, which she found boring, and sometimes even missed the exams. When asked to identify Karl Marx, she thinks he was probably a Russian "philosopher." She joined the communist youth organization at one time, but found the organization so dull and so tediously political that she remained completely inactive. As for politics, she had contempt for the communist political authorities, whom she described as basically corrupt and self-serving, holds the party responsible for most of the country's problems, and until recently saw little hope for the future. Even now, she cannot view the future with confidence. For the time being, she has enough money, thanks to pocket money from her parents and to the government's student stipend, to buy the clothes she likes; her aspirations seem limited to the acquisition of consumer items, often on the black market. Where social and political issues are concerned, she has long been apathetic because she felt there was nothing she could do. She felt like part of a "lost generation."

"Savka" is a composite, not a real person. But the syndrome I have described is broadly typical of young people in Eastern Europe. In the communist era, apathy derived from the combination of deep frustration with a sense of powerlessness. Now the situation is changing totally and, for the interim at least, young people are able to find new possibilities. But the long experience with stultification and apathy has left a certain feeling of bitterness about the past.

When the communist parties took power in Eastern Europe, they conjured before their minds' eyes a vision of the youth of the future, a youth dedicated to the communist party, socially engaged, atheist, obedient, enthusiastic about socialism, and hard-working. In addition, the elites hoped that young people would imbibe the jargon of Marxism, coming to think in Marxist categories, and trust the political authorities. On every count the party was disappointed.

Pacifism was an early problem for East European elites. The communist party talked of class war, internal enemies, and the threat of world imperialism; the people, however, remembered World War II vividly, their offspring grew up amid ruins and the task of rebuilding, and the younger generations were infected by feelings of pacifism. This was especially true in East Germany, where the introduction of general military service in January 1962 stimulated pacifism and conscientious objection among some young people.[1] By the 1980s pacifist movements had also appeared in Poland, Czechoslovakia, and Hungary.

But pacifism actually engaged only a minority of young people. Pacifism is still a form of activism, of commitment, and, as a general rule, East European youth under communism were inward-looking and politically withdrawn. "Many young people feel convinced that in general they have no influence over what is happening around them," Polish sociologist Grzegorz Nowacki said in 1986, "particularly whenever national or regional issues are concerned. The principal . . . reason why the commitment and eventually activism of youth are deficient is precisely this feeling of lacking influence [over] what is happening."[2]

If today's youth feel less capable of affecting their environment than did previous generations, it is at least in part because their circumstances are different. Today's youth in Eastern Europe live with and remain partially dependent on their parents for longer than did earlier generations. At home their responsibilities are minimal, with parents usually satisfied if their sons and daughters do well at their studies. A Polish writer suggested that "that is why there are so many children in their twenties that do not at all feel like adults. These are grown-up boys [and girls] with infantile personalities and no feeling of responsibility for their behavior. As when they were children, they expect only pleasure from life and no responsibilities or restrictions."[3] Diminished personal independence sows the seeds of frustration. But it is only one source.

In the late 1940s and 1950s, when entire classes were despoiled or incarcerated and vast numbers of Germans were expelled from Poland, Czechoslovakia, and Yugoslavia, there were great opportunities for social mobility. The so-called "partisan generation" grabbed up important posts and, for a while, talented young people (and even untalented young people) could afford to be ambitious. In the 1960s and 1970s the economies of Eastern Europe started to slow down, and the channels for mobility were gradually choked off. One of the reasons that the rock protest of the 1970s found resonance in Eastern Europe was that young people were starting to feel a deepening frustration and the evanescence of hope.[4] Some looked to personal connections to get them established, while still others retreated behind a protective shield of indifference.

Young people became obsessed with the West, and yearned to visit or even to move there. For example, when a 1968 poll taken among Czechoslovak youth asked in what country they would ideally live, only 7.4 percent named a "socialist" country (a result possibly inflated by the inclusion of Yugoslavia in this category), while 13.1 percent named a "capitalist" country (typically, the United States, West Germany, Australia, or Great Britain), and 66.8 percent named a "neutral" country (Sweden, Austria, or Switzerland).[5] While the results of similar polls in Poland were less dramatic, the trend was toward declining commitment to reside in Poland: whereas between 82 and 85 percent of young people chose Poland as their first choice for permanent residence in surveys conducted from 1959 to 1978, only 62 percent did so in a 1983 survey, meaning that more than a third of Polish youth would prefer to live abroad—obviously, above all, in the West.[6]

East European youth are sometimes described as "pragmatic" or "rational." What this means, in practice, is that their aspirations center on private pleasures—friends, fashions, and material possessions. This consumerism very naturally became linked with the aforementioned admiration for the West because of the higher quality of Western commodities. And given the region's tight regulation of quality imports, this naturally fed the black market in all countries in the region (though in Yugoslavia to a lesser extent). A seventeen-year-old Romanian high school student gave vivid expression to this syndrome: "I was the first one in my class to have a Walkman. . . . I bought it with a lot of money from a foreign student from Mozambique. When I showed up with the earphones in the morning in the classroom, the whole class crowded around me. . . . It passed from hand to hand. Everybody looked at me with envy and admiration."[7] Similarly a nineteen-year-old Romanian student confessed: "Frankly, girls are crazy about Western clothes; they know that if you have these clothes you are rich and the target of envy. Do you know what it means to give a girl a pair of stockings from Italy, or a bottle of bath oil from West Germany?"[8] Predictably, the party press has attacked such consumerism both for its relationship to social withdrawal and for its association with Western commodities.

Social Pathology

But consumerism cannot serve as a universal escape valve, for one thing because only a few young people are sufficiently well off to be able to satisfy a consumerist mentality. Some young people seek release in rowdyism. A Bulgarian publication described this "solution" in a 1984 article:

> You will see them sitting on the steps of monuments or half lying at the main entrances of universities, public offices, and railroad stations. They smoke, chew [gum], munch and spit noisily, and look down upon the world with bored eyes. They shuffle around in scruffy shoes and torn socks, they are filthy, their clothes untidy, and bags of various kinds with all sorts of emblems and pictorial signs hang from their shoulders. Every now and then they shout out a senseless and vague protest—it does not matter against whom. . . . They loaf about in coffee houses, pastry shops, day bars, and clubs until their hour strikes: the hour of discos, dance halls, video arcades, the hour of an all-encompassing spitting at everything and everyone outside the gang.[9]

Others respond by adopting the language and attire of fascism. Young people sporting fascist insignia and giving vent to racist sentiments have been reported in East Germany, Poland, Czechoslovakia, and Hungary, as well as in Yugoslavia, where this has concerned above all pro-*Ustaše* sentiments among young Croats.[10] In April 1982 Polish police broke up an eighteen-member group calling itself the Fascist Organization of Renewal;

all but two of its members were between fifteen and seventeen years of age.[11] On the other hand, Hitler's continued "popularity" in Eastern Europe—if one may call it that—was often a reflection of the fact that young people saw the expression of pro-Hitler sentiments as the most potent provocation they could sling at the communist regimes. The punk movement is appealing for roughly the same reason.

And for those who could not find an appropriate release, there was the risk of lapsing into mental illness. In Hungary, at any rate, the steady increase in the number of mentally sick young people has become a cause for concern.[12]

Finally, in most of the countries of the region, there have been the growing problems of alcoholism, drug abuse, juvenile delinquency, and criminal activity. In East Germany, for example, alcohol consumption among young people is twice what it is among *West* German youth, and young people are turning to alcohol at ever younger ages. Crimes of violence have become everyday events, and there have been growing problems with vandalism and the wanton destruction of public facilities.[13] Skinheads became a social problem in East Germany, Poland, and Hungary; in the latter, skinheads have terrorized the local Gypsies, forcing them to arm themselves.[14] In Bulgaria, as of 1988, two-thirds of all criminal offenders were under thirty years of age and were responsible for 86.6 percent of all rapes, 87.3 percent of robberies, 85.3 percent of all house break-ins, and 92.9 percent of all car thefts. Bulgarian girls have turned to prostitution at the age of twelve or thirteen.[15] And in Czechoslovakia the rise in social problems among youth gave rise to serious discussions within the Socialist Youth Union.

Youth Slang and Jargon

Eastern Europe has not yet experienced a generational conflict parallel to what existed in the United States in the 1950s and 1960s, but there has clearly been a rift between young people and officialdom. Nowhere is this more clearly expressed than in the development of a special language peculiar to young people, or to particular subcultures among youth, such as punk, the disco crowd, and so forth. In the late 1970s, for example, a specific subcultural argot called "Disco-Deutsch" appeared among young Germans in both Germanys; it was heavily influenced by the rock and disco milieu.[16] Other jargon expressions favored by East European youth developed within the criminal subculture. For example, in Poland *Grypsera*, the jargon of the self-designated "good guys," was developed originally in juvenile penitentiaries. *Grypsera* gradually acquired a certain currency and ultimately left traces in the more general youth slang.[17] In part, thus, youth slang has grown organically, drawing inspiration from sundry milieux. But in part it is also a more or less conscious reaction to the "other jargon"—what East German young people called "party Chinese."

Slang typically multiplies synonyms for oft-needed meanings. For example, one study of Bulgarian youth slang found fifty-one synonyms for *stupid*, twenty-nine for *hit*, eighteen for *beautiful*, eleven for *dissemble*, ten for *steal*, and seven for *money*.[18] Slang is also used to convey judgment, as in the Bulgarian *machilishte* (literally, torture) and Romanian *la Bastille*, both used to refer to school. Similarly, the Polish slang words for adults —*ramole* (weak heads), *mumie* (mummies), *ekshumy* (exhumates), and *nietoperze* (bats)—leave no uncertainty of the user's attitude toward the adult world. Young Poles refer to a demanding teacher as a piranha and to the school faculty collectively as the *inkwizycja* (Inquisition), while Bulgarian students employ twenty-five synonyms for sexual intercourse.[19] More than a decade ago, Polish writer Zbigniew Mentzel commented,

> Linguistic inventiveness most fully reveals itself in certain areas of life, and in the jargon of students this concerns such things as the relationship to teachers, the erotic, and friends. It is similar with the language of adults, where the relationship to employers, promotion or advancement, and money somehow achieve a linguistic double-life. Researchers and publicists have long ago noted that in the language of a given society, most surrogate expressions arise from situations and themes which are especially taboo in this society. . . . Precisely in the case of taboo themes, the language [of the subculture] brings group complexes and frustrations to the light of day.[20]

Many words used specifically or primarily by young people are derived from foreign sources. In Bulgaria, Turkish is a source of many loan words in the youth subculture. English loan-words are, of course, widespread throughout the region. Rock music has been the conduit for some of these, bringing the words *available, background, blue, challenging, competitive, concerned, generous, impressive, loser, mellow, motivated, outspoken, pusher, responsive, self-made, single-minded,* and *trip* into common use among Polish youth. In Romania, the English words *actually, business, eventually, grapefruit, knockdown, knockout, smash, tennis player,* and *updated* have achieved currency. In Yugoslavia, the words *biznes, brejkdens, hit, new wave, ritam mašina, rock bend, sendvić, sintisajzer,* and *star* have all come into common use. In addition, Polish young people have also assimilated a few German expressions, such as *Schadenfreude* (gloating) and *Sitzfleisch* (perseverance with desk work), as well as a select set of Russian expressions, such as *molodets* (good going).

As Wolf Oschlies has noted, the flourishing of youth slang and jargon is an important indication that young people do not passively assimilate the values and conventions of the adult world, but in fact actively confront those values and categories with values and categories of their own.[21] Slang and jargon, of course, also serve another purpose, that is, to isolate one group from another.

Attitudes Toward Politics

If young people want to isolate themselves from the adult world, it is in part because they already feel cut off from it. An eighteen-year-old Serbian student, Sladjana Andjelković, stated the case quite simply: "We are neither dumb nor stupid; yet we are silent." Another young Serb, Vigor Majić, elaborated, "The first words one learns are *mommy*, *daddy*, and *shut up*. We have not been taught to speak. On the contrary, we are systematically taught to be silent—in the family, school, youth organization, [and] League of Communists."[22]

Pushed thus into a passive role, young people were later criticized for their passivity. Having forced young people to study Marxism-Leninism, mouth communist slogans, and take part in communist pageants such as Youth Day, party elders subsequently seemed taken by surprise that the natural rebelliousness of youth should turn against *them*.

In fact, however, the frustration of East European young people with the system goes far beyond the mere question of "natural rebelliousness." In some cases, elites have to reckon with the partial failure of socialization and the alienation of a generation fed up with the disjunction between theory and practice. In Poland, political training has largely broken down,[23] and in several countries (most certainly Poland, Hungary, Yugoslavia, and Bulgaria) the youth organizations were either in crisis by the late 1980s, or were evolving new roles which departed radically from traditional patterns.

This phenomenon is relatively new—at least in its present form. As recently as the early 1970s young people in Romania and Yugoslavia had largely positive attitudes toward their systems or about the attitude they should adopt toward their systems.[24] And in the case of Poland, of course, the imposition of martial law in 1981 and 1982 had a severe negative impact on young people's orientations toward political authorities.[25]

As of the mid- and late 1980s, the political attitudes expressed by young people gave the authorities cause for concern. In Hungary, for instance, a 1987 survey found that a majority of young people had "no confidence" in the communist party and preferred to introduce a Western-style democratic system.[26] An earlier survey in the same country found that less than half of responding students felt it was safe for people to express their opinions on political and economic subjects, roughly 75 percent felt that Hungarian political life was "not more democratic than before," and 40 percent declared that the political system was undemocratic.[27]

A 1982 survey of young Croats found that only 28.6 percent of respondents endorsed the delegate system, while 18.3 percent criticized it as undemocratic, with another 55.1 percent declining to answer. In that same survey, only 39 percent gave unconditional approval to the one-party system, while 6.7 percent said they were opposed to one-party rule under any circumstances, and 39.5 percent said they did not know or had no opinion.[28] A 1989 survey among 5,000 Yugoslav youth found that roughly 65 percent felt they needed to act outside the framework and programs of official political organizations, 42 percent declared themselves in favor of a multiparty system, and 20 percent favored abolishing the communist party altogether. In Slovenia 84 percent of young people favored a multiparty system, while 60 percent considered the communist party obsolete; the corresponding figures for Croatia were 65 and 33 percent, respectively.[29]

Until very recently, East European youth typically believed that, while some form of socialism would be ideal, their own systems had failed to realize the *potentials* of socialism. An eighteen-year-old East German student put it this way:

> The face of GDR socialism could also have looked different. It is not necessarily this way. But it has a lot to do with us ourselves. The roots of many erroneous developments lie in the history of the Germans. One simply cannot overlook that. One cannot try to trace all the explanations and solutions of the day to the errors of Marxism.[30]

This impressionistic picture is confirmed by survey data from Poland and Yugoslavia. In Poland, for instance, a survey was conducted among 1,082 young people. Asked whether they thought the world should develop in the direction of socialism, 49.8 percent answered in the affirmative, while 28.1 per cent answered in the negative; the remainder "did not know" or refused to answer.[31] In Yugoslavia, the previously cited survey of 1,100 Croatian youth found that most respondents rejected social equality—the central value of socialism—as negative.[32] Of the chief values propounded by these regimes—the superiority of one-party rule, social ownership of the means of production, equality for all nonbelievers, the standardization of thought, the myth of steady progress and "democratization" under communism—the social ownership of the means of production was the most generally accepted (for instance, by nearly 75 percent of young Poles in a 1984 survey). Other values tended to be rejected by the majority of young people, especially the standardization of thought. A 1986 poll showed that young people in Czechoslovakia were overwhelmingly convinced that people should be able to think as they please, while university students in Hungary demanded extensive changes in the curriculum in order to include the teaching of "bourgeois and religious philosophies."[33] In fact, by the mid-1980s Hungarian youth became highly critical of party policy in general and increasingly willing to speak their minds. Hard hit by unemployment and housing shortages, young Hungarians saw substantive change as urgent.[34]

An opinion poll conducted by the central council of the Socialist Union of Polish Students in early 1982 among high school and university students in Warsaw revealed some interesting statistics. For example, only 3.5 percent of university students and 2 percent of high school students said that the introduction of martial law was "completely justified." A somewhat larger number (15 and 17 percent) said the move was "correct in principle." Most respondents described it as either "completely unjustified" (48.5 and 34 per cent) or "wrong in principle" (20.5 and 38 percent). Asked about their appraisal of the role played respectively by the party, the church, and Solidarity in 1981, 72.5 percent of university students and 70.5 per cent of high school students appraised the party negatively, 67 and 84 percent approved of the church's role, and 67.5 and 64 percent gave Solidarity positive marks.[35]

Young people are thus generally disillusioned with the system, and as the 1980s drew to a close, they wanted to see it overhauled at the very least. "The young blame the older generation and want to modernize socialism, make it more open and efficient," said Tomaz Mastnak, an independent Slovenian sociologist.[36]

This disillusionment is reflected in the heroes adopted by young people. Few of these countries publish or even conduct such opinion polls. But in Yugoslavia and Poland, Pope John Paul II placed high, at least among Catholics, far outdistancing local party bosses. In a 1985 Yugoslav poll conducted among 750 high school students in Split, Mother Theresa (the Albanian nun from Yugoslavia) was the most admired of twenty-four persons listed, with the pope in third place, and Lenin in last place, with only thirty-seven votes. In a similar poll taken twenty years earlier, Lenin had rated very highly, while Pope Paul VI had ranked fifth.[37] On the other hand, a

1988 survey in Poland found that Gorbachev was the most widely respected personality among young people, with a 45.7 percent rating. Pope John Paul II claimed another 29.7 percent, leaving only 9.5 percent for the nation's leader, Wojciech Jaruzelski.[38]

The youth organizations were supposed to deal with this challenge. The charter of Yugoslavia's League of Socialist Youth (ssoj) was probably representative of the underlying formal ideology:

> The ssoj is a united and mass-based political organization. As the broadest democratic front of the young generation in Yugoslavia, the various interests, aspirations, and creative energies of the youth are expressed and directed toward socialist self-management in and through this organization.
>
> The ssoj is committed to developing and strengthening the organized ideological-political unity of the young generation; it concretely prepares the youth for their active and direct participation and involvement in our self-managed organizations and its structures, in the delegate system, and in the political organizations and social life in its entirety.[39]

But in fact, by the latter 1980s the East European youth organizations were everywhere in crisis. "My comrades are not interested in self-management by the students. They prefer the discotheque, excursions, sports. They come to ssoj meetings only when we put under 'miscellaneous' on the agenda—dance," said Milan Dočić, a Yugoslav eighth grader.[40] In Romania leading officials of the youth organization admitted in 1985 that they had been unable to respond effectively to the aspirations of members.[41] Csába Hámori, first secretary of the Communist Youth League in Hungary, admitted in 1986 that his organization's influence among young people was in decline; in an effort to deal with the problem, extensive administrative changes in the organization were carried out in 1988.[42] In Bulgaria there have been calls for "new approaches in the organization and leadership of the movement for fostering creative thinking in young people," "qualitative changes . . . in the style and methods of work," and, in general, "greater perspective, initiative, and tenacity."[43] And in Poland, so serious did the situation become that the regime authorized the creation of a second organization in 1982, the Polish Students Association, hinting that it would enjoy considerable practical independence. But Polish students were not won over, most viewing the new organization as "just another politicized and politicizing party bureaucracy."[44] As a result, young people stayed away.[45]

One clear alternative was for the youth organizations to evolve into something more than mere transmission belts. On this score, the youth organization in Yugoslavia was a pacesetter. Several years ago the Yugoslavs redesigned the annual Youth Day festival. No longer was it to be a drab affair with long columns of athletic youth parading with banners in hand while a military-style band plays patriotic marches. Now the centerpiece of the festival was rock music, and the entire event was redesigned to appeal to the membership. The "House of Youth" (*Dom omladine*) found in many cities became a true meeting place for young people, with provocative books on sale and rock concerts and dances in the evening. In 1987 the slick new magazine *Potkulture* (*Subcultures*) was launched, devoted entirely to alternative lifestyles.

Politically the youth organization in Yugoslavia has also changed. In Slovenia, for instance, the youth organization has opened its doors to alternative movements, allowing them to use ssoj facilities to carry on their more or less opposition activities; in this way, the youth organization in Slovenia has come to play a role parallel to that of the Evangelical-Lutheran church in East Germany.

Indicative of the new tone in Slovenia in particular was the twelfth congress of the League of Socialist Youth of Slovenia held in Krsko on 4–6 April 1986. Of those in attendance, only guests from other political organizations came formally attired; the majority were casually attired, some even wearing punk or heavy metal fashions. Many wore badges from the alternative movement in support of peace, ecology, feminism, and free speech. The congress itself opened with a rock concert. At the end of three days of lively discussion, the congress issued a document declaring, "in our opinion, the pressures toward conformity of thought that accompany the polarization of wealth and poverty are one of the weapons for maintaining the polarization of ruling and submission."[46] The congress called for a radical departure in official policy toward alternative thought and for the pluralization of politics and cultural and social life.

Two years later, in the wake of the highly controversial trial of three journalists and an enlisted man in Slovenia for publishing an article accusing the military of plotting a coup, the youth organization took another bold step. It declared its intention to monitor the work of "individuals who in its opinion are not trusted by the public and should leave their functions."[47]

In essence, what started to happen in Yugoslavia and, initially, in Slovenia, is that young people took over the youth organization, making it responsive to their needs and aspirations. Ultimately, the radical young members converted the Slovenian youth organization into a political party (Liberal) and fielded candidates in the 1990 elections as part of the Demos coalition.

Illegal and Underground Activities

Illegal and underground activity usually involves a minority of young people. The dropout syndrome is much more widespread. As a Czechoslovak publication noted in 1987, "the majority [of young people] are preoccupied with their own private concerns, such as partners and friends, while 'social involvement' . . . is rated at the bottom of their list [of priorities]."[48]

When young people do become politically involved, it is sometimes in organizations of their own creation, organizations toward which the communist authorities take umbrage. One of the earliest illegal youth organizations was a secret political organization called *Ruch* (The Movement) among Polish high school students in the early 1970s. The organization was uncovered in 1971, and its leaders were given seven-year prison sentences.[49]

The tendency toward self-organization is probably strongest among young Poles and weakest among young Romanians and Bulgarians. In the Polish case there have been recurrent reports over the years of different underground youth groups. In 1982, for example, three clandestine youth groups were uncovered among secondary school students in the Katowice *voivodship*. They were said to have been involved in hostile pamphleteering and in scribbling antiregime graffiti on public walls.[50] Earlier, in 1981, the Movement of School Youth was formed in the Tri-City region (Gdańsk, Gdynia, Sopot), and there was a renewed attempt to revive a "democratic" youth organization in Kraków.

Polish youth in fact became relatively active in the opposition beginning in 1981. High school students became involved in dissident activity: for example, a group of students in Gorzów Wiełkopolski started a journal, *Sokół (Falcon)*; nine were subsequently arrested in March 1985. Altogether at least thirty underground publications produced by Polish youth reached the West after 1981. In Warsaw, for instance, the Independent Youth Organization published *Gnom (Gnome)*, while the Lower Silesian regional council of the Solidarity Youth Resistance Movement in Wrocław publishes *Wolna Polska*. Kraków was the organizational center for Promieniści (Rays), a group which has published a journal under the same name since September 1982. It claimed a circulation of 3,000 in 1986 and covered a wide array of social and political topics.[51]

One of the best-known underground youth organizations in Poland was the Independent Students' Association, originally registered as a legal association in February 1981, but subsequently suppressed. Despite illegality, the Association continued its activities, albeit on a limited scale, and convoked its "second congress" on 10 January 1987 in Warsaw. The congress drew student representatives from nineteen universities and other institutions of higher education in Warsaw, Wrocław, Kraków, Łódź, Katowice, and Radom. The association was overtly hostile to communism, basing its activity on the Christian ethical tradition and pledging itself to work for an independent and democratic Poland.[52]

But even in Czechoslovakia there were some stirrings among young people. The scouting movement, which was resurrected in 1968 during the evanescent Prague Spring, continued to operate underground.[53] And in 1984 a human rights group based in Slovakia and calling itself the Young People of the CSSR sent a letter to President Gustáv Husák demanding, among other things, the restoration of the Slovak double-barred cross on the state seal of Czechoslovakia.[54]

And in Bulgaria too, alternative youth organizations appeared, by the end of the decade. The best known is the Federation of Independent Students' Unions (FISU), which was founded in the wake of Zhivkov's ouster as general secretary and which claimed a membership of 6,000 at the end of December 1989.[55] Despite its nonparty status, FISU won endorsement from a Bulgarian CP faction called The Bulgarian Road to Europe, which called for Bulgaria's social, political, cultural, and economic integration into mainstream Europe. Another alternative youth organization, Youth for European Socialism, was set up at Sofia University and declared its support for the Bulgarian Road concept.

Attitudes among young people vary considerably, of course, and among those who are criticized as "passive" are many who are simply disinterested in politics. In surveys of Yugoslav youth, generally 60 percent (but sometimes 75 to 80 percent) have been broadly supportive of the system or of its principles, at least until recently. Some 15 to 30 percent (mostly unskilled workers, poor peasants, and the unemployed) have been classed as "dogmatic-etatistic" types—which is another way of identifying working class authoritarianism. Only 10 to 15 percent have liberal-democratic values and orientations.[56]

The Values and Hopes of Youth

The chief determinants of the value system of young people, according to a Yugoslav sociologist, are their social and economic position—with low status tending to reinforce antisystem tendencies because those concerned have little hope of bettering their lot *within* the system—and the dominant ideological and cultural currents.[57] The latter may of course include exposure to rock music and Western cultural trends. To these one may add the family, which plays a crucial formative role. On this subject an East German research institute concluded in 1980 that "the vast majority of children and young people base their world view upon that of their parents. An average of 88 percent of pupils in grades 6 to 10 and 75 percent of job apprentices set for themselves, with certain restrictions to be sure, the goal of always following the advice of their parents, 'because it is usually right'. . . . The father and mother rank far above all others on the list of recognized authorities."[58] Television may also play an independent role, judging from the high rate of TV watching among East European youth.[59] But Western shows like *Dynasty* and *Dallas* were long much more popular among youth than the more didactic programs preferred by authorities.

There is a broad consensus among East European youth that the most important ingredients for happiness are a happy marriage and family life, and privacy. Other values frequently cited in polls taken in Romania and Yugoslavia include health, friendship, personal independence, material sufficiency, professional success, leisure, and respect. A mere 0.5 percent of Romanian respondents said that "achieving a high position in the hierarchy" was important for personal happiness, although some 15.8 percent of Yugoslav respondents listed "power" among the ingredients of happiness.[60]

But levels of interest in politics and the specific rankings of values are susceptible to external pressures. As the economic and political systems of Eastern Europe came under greater stress in recent years, the level of interest in politics rose, and data on political interest from one year may be of little indicative value a few years later. Until the dramatic political changes in Hungary and Poland in 1989 and the opening up of borders in the course of that year, young people throughout most of Eastern Europe felt a combination of resentment against the system, frustration with the limits of their travel possibilities and opportunities for social mobility, and, in the case of Poland, Romania, and Yugoslavia, an apprehension linked to the sense that things could not go on as they had in the past. In fact, young Poles have long been the most pessimistic in Eastern Europe. One young Pole, for example, commented in 1983, "People don't believe in anything any more.

They don't believe in a speedy emergence of Poland out of the crisis. They don't believe there will be any improvement in supplies."[61] Or, as another young Pole put it, "Aside from crises, socialism has given us nothing."[62]

The younger generation in Eastern Europe ultimately played a role in the revolutionary transformation of the region. But from August 1968 (a symbolic date) to the end of the 1980s, young people were gripped with a sense of powerlessness and a consequent apathy. Until the end of 1989, it was a lost generation that looked on the world of politics with frustration and bitterness. The Polish rock group Turbo gave expression to this mood in "Grown-up Children":

> They taught us rules and deadlines,
> Beat it into us what's allowed and what is not,
> Convinced us what is good or bad,
> Absolutely nothing could be forgotten.
> Only that we no longer know
> How we should live.
> Grown up children feel sadness
> With the wretched recipes for this world.
> Grown up children feel sadness
> Because someone has stolen
> So much of their lives.[63]

V Current Trends

Political awareness in turn requires a certain level of information. A society without information is necessarily weak. It can become strong only by developing reliable sources of information. In addition, opposition structures must either have independent channels for communication or be able to use official channels to communicate their ideas.

And finally, the defection of intellectuals is important because the intellectuals bring various skills—above all communication skills.

All told, Brinton's analysis suggests at least five components of a strong society: a modicum of information, the ability to organize, the defection of skill-bearing intellectuals, access to channels of communication, and mobilization of the public. These factors, I shall argue, either have not been present in Bulgaria or have been only faintly present. As a result, for the entire decade of the 1980s Bulgarian society was not merely not radicalized; it was actually, and still is to a large extent, *weak*. This is the key to understanding the political quiet which prevailed up to late 1989 in that country.

Information. The Bulgarian press and other media have long been virtually barren and unreadable; this is symptomatic of a regime policy to monopolize information. The result is that information becomes a prized commodity. There are several associated problems. First, the list of those things which qualified as state secrets in Bulgaria in the 1980s was quite long. In 1980, for example, the list of facts and information which were state secrets was expanded, and the new listing included, *inter alia*, information on Bulgarian trade protocols with bloc countries, credits to and from other countries, foreign currency credits for imports, the annual and quarterly plans for exports and imports, crude oil imports, and deposits of nonferrous and precious metals.[1] Other facts, such as those relating to the Macedonian minority, were likewise suppressed.

A second problem is that even when statistical information has been published, its quality and reliability have often been low, and certainly less reliable than comparable data from all other East European countries except Romania and Albania.[2]

Third, there is the system of censorship itself, which has regulated what may or may not be published. Books which offended the authorities were simply banned altogether; works by Bulgarian authors were screened and their authors subjected to the "method of persuasion" in order to obtain desired prepublication revisions in the text. Meanwhile, excessive press censorship was so demoralizing to Bulgarian journalists that there were indirect admissions that they suffered from low morale and even, at times, offered "passive resistance."[3] In Bulgaria the publication of information on the incidence of neurosis in Bulgarian society in 1984 was itself a newsworthy event.[4]

Fourth, the state publishing monopoly distorted the selection of titles for publication and ignored market demand. The result, as *Bulgarski Zhurnalist* admitted in 1983, was that funds were often diverted to luxury editions of works for which there was little or no demand, and which therefore sat on bookshelves unsold.[5]

A similar situation prevailed in science. In 1977, for example, Sofia hosted the International Conference on Space-Time Absoluteness, which set itself the task of debunking Einstein's theory of relativity.[6]

Recently, the Bulgarian regime gave lip service to the need for more openness in the press, and there were some striking reports in the Bulgarian press in the past few years. But the Zhivkov regime, which finally collapsed on 10 November 1989, was clearly unenthusiastic about any major change in media policy. Hence, for example, when the sixth congress of the Bulgarian Writers' Union, meeting in Sofia in March 1989, gave vent to spirited criticism of official policy on the media, press reports were generally unilluminating. The party daily *Rabotnichesko delo* reported that the speeches had been "lively," but said little about their content. The union's own paper, *Literaturen Front*, published a nebulous account that gave no information linking speakers and topics, and admitted that "a number of recommendations" had been made without saying what they were.[7]

One looked in vain in the Bulgarian press for criticism of official policies, for debates, for probing analyses of relevant issues, or, until November 1989, for opinion polls on government performance.[8] And when in June 1987 the trade union daily newspaper *Trud* published an exceptional four-part series exposing the corruption of the influential Mihaylov family in Etropole, the Central Control and Revision Committee ordered the expulsion of journalist Georgi Tambuev from the party, his dismissal as head of the Economic Department of *Rabotnichesko delo*, and a review of the incumbent editor, Damyan Obreshkov.

If it were not for Radio Free Europe and other foreign broadcasts, citizens of Bulgaria would long have been in danger of being cut off from the realities of their own society.

The Ability to Organize. Until its abolition in early 1990, the Bulgarian control apparatus (including the secret police) was singularly effective in containing would-be opposition organizations. Thus, for example, the first unofficial human rights group, the Society for the Protection of Human Rights in Bulgaria, came into existence only in 1988. Even then, of its two dozen members, only four dared to sign the group's founding document, and shortly thereafter one was placed under house arrest, another was sent to internal exile, and a third was expelled from the country.[9]

As of March 1989 there were reportedly nine independent (dissident) organizations active in Bulgaria.[10] The Discussion Club for the Support of Glasnost and Perestroika was formed in November 1988 and unsuccessfully applied for legal papers. In May 1989 eleven members were temporarily arrested after appealing to the National Assembly for democratic reforms. An independent association devoted to the defense of religious freedom and known as the Committee for Religious Rights, Freedom of Conscience, and Spiritual Values was set up under the chairmanship of Fr. Hristofor Subev on 9 March 1989. It declared its intention to campaign for an end to state interference in religious life and discrimination against believers in public and professional life, the legalization of religious instruction for the young, and freedom of religious information. The Holy Synod of the Bulgarian Orthodox church appealed to the state judiciary not to grant legal registration to the new committee. Meanwhile, the group's foreign representative, Fr. Blagoy Topuzliev, was immediately expelled from the country, and Subev himself was imprisoned for more than a month, even though no charges had been lodged against him.[11]

There are also small groups of environmentalists. In late 1988 a group announced that they were setting up the "Green" Party. The Greens later established a branch in the town of Burgas.[12] And in December 1989, armed with 4,000 signatures, environmental activists in Plovdiv established the Youth Association for Ecology and Environmental Protection, affiliated with Plovdiv University.[13] An earlier organization called the Ruse Committee had attracted a lot of intellectuals, but was suffocated by the authorities when it became too voluble. Some Ruse members joined the Eco-Glasnost Movement that emerged in March 1989. This new organization sought legal registration but was predictably turned down.

Finally, there is an independent trade union, Support, founded in February 1989 under the chairmanship of Konstantin Trenchev. As of August 1989, it claimed sixty members.

These groups are small and weak, and there are in any case very few of them. By comparison with the weakness of the opposition, the regime showed itself strong enough to convoke a mass meeting of ethnic Turks in support of its policy of annihilating Turkish culture in Bulgaria. Specifically, in September 1989 the regime organized a meeting of some 800 Bulgarian expellees turned back by Turkey under the motto, "Bulgaria: Our Homeland, Fate, and Future." As if to mock those attending the meeting, speakers told them, "It is high time that people in Bulgaria and around the world become aware of Pan-Turkism as a dangerous resurgence which is inconsistent with new political thinking and which poses a threat not only to Bulgaria [but also] to many other countries."[14]

Until the closing months of 1989, discontented Bulgarians displayed very little ability to organize themselves successfully, and such groups as have taken shape are all of extremely recent vintage.

The Intellectuals. Until late 1989 opposition among the intellectuals was an individual affair. One of the most striking instances of opposition on the part of the intellectuals came in July 1989, when the Discussion Club for the Support of Glasnost and Perestroika issued a declaration protesting the regime's treatment of the Turkish minority. The Bulgarian Writers' Union, as already noted, has become a particular focus of intellectual ferment, and in May 1989 some members of that union drafted an appeal for democratic reforms in Bulgaria, addressing it to the national assembly. Significantly, several of the points in the appeal dealt with access to information and to communication channels, and the right to organize. In particular, the appeal called for the declassification of all information not directly harmful to national security and of all files older than twenty-five years, the elimination of secret shelves in the state libraries, an end to the banning of works of literature and art, free access of citizens to the media, and the right to organize independent groups and associations, with the permission of the government.[15]

There is evidence thus that Bulgarian intellectuals are becoming politically aware. Yet, at the same time, their opposition is inchoate and it is too early to speak of a "defection" of the intellectuals, although depending on what Bulgaria's first "freely elected" communist regime does, this may only be a matter of time.

Communication. In a society in which the state asserts a monopoly over all media, printed information, and organizations, independent communication is a formidable challenge. In such a society word-of-mouth communication takes on much greater importance than it would have in an open society, and friendship networks function as de facto conduits of information.

The problem of communication is organically connected with the question of independent organizations. The very modest presence of independent organizations means that independent communication enjoys only modest organizational resources. Even the Orthodox church, the largest religious body in the country, was kept under the thumb of the communist regime, and its publications merely supported the regime line. The same is true of the hierarchy of the Islamic community.[16]

Mobilization of the Public. As a result, the public as a whole was not mobilized and the regime was long able to pursue policies calculated to alienate specific sectors of the society.

The entire campaign against the Turks poignantly illustrates both the virtual inability of the Bulgarian public to mobilize itself effectively in opposition to the regime's policy and, more broadly, the general weakness of Bulgarian society.

As early as the late 1940s and early 1950s the Bulgarian government pressured its Turkish minority to emigrate.[17] In the late 1950s all Turkish-language schools in Bulgaria were closed. Later, particularly since the 1970s, Turks, Muslims, Gypsies, and Pomaks (ethnic Bulgarian Muslims) came under strong pressure to assimilate.

In late 1984 the Bulgarian regime launched a new campaign to assimilate the Turks. It closed down Turkish-language media, banned the use of Turkish in public, restricted certain Islamic religious practices (such as circumcision), and forced indigenous Turks to assume Bulgarian names. In late 1984 and 1985 there were armed clashes between Turks and Bulgarian army and police units, in which hundreds of Turks and dozens of soldiers and police lost their lives. But that was only the first phase of the Bulgarianization campaign.

Despite international outcry, especially in Turkey and the Islamic world, there was no effective resistance offered within the country. There were protests and violent outbursts on the part of Bulgaria's Turks in May 1989 in several towns. In the northeastern village of Todor Ikonomovo, twenty to twenty-five ethnic Turks were killed when troops opened fire on a crowd of about two thousand people. Tanks, helicopters, and heavy security surrounded the towns of Razgrad and Šumen, where demonstrations were also taking place. In Razgrad (100 miles east of Sofia), four to five thousand protesters clashed with police, who arrested two hundred people and cut telephone lines to Razgrad.[18] The regime now decided on the expulsion of ethnic Turks who were resisting assimilation and engaging in protest actions. Between 6 May and 7 June, almost three thousand Turks were deported to Turkey. By 22 August Turkey had closed its border pending an emigration agreement, but about 310,000 Bulgarian Muslims (mainly Turks) had already crossed into Turkey, reducing the Turkish population of Bulgaria by as much as a third.[19] Among those expelled by the government were Ismet Ismailoglu Emurlah (secretary of the Association for Vienna '89, a human rights group), Avni Veliev (chairman of the same association), Mustafa Yumerov (chairman of the Democratic League), and Ali Ormanliev and Sabri Iskenderov (two secretaries of the same league). Shukri Sherifov, an ethnic Turk who had written an open letter appealing for minority rights, was arrested and sentenced to prison on charges of inciting unrest and spreading falsehood.

In mid-August 1989 there were fresh disturbances and deaths in several villages near Gotse Delchev. The renewed unrest was sparked by the authorities' decision that many ethnic Turks and Pomaks who had changed their names in 1984 or 1985 would have to change their names a second time because the names were "insufficiently Slavic." Hundreds of villagers filed for passports, but ironically, despite Zhivkov's televised public announcement in which he granted the Muslims the right to leave, local officials declared that Zhivkov's decision did not apply to the Sofia and Plovdiv regions and blocked their emigration.

The mass exodus resulted in an acute labor shortage in several regions in which the emigrants had been concentrated, and this new shortage had a knock-on effect in other parts of the country too. Production dropped in 121 municipalities—particularly, in Razgrad by 10.5 percent, in Haskovo by 8.5 percent, and in Varna by 3.7 percent. A few thousand Turks returned to Bulgaria but they were not necessarily given much of a welcome. In Varna oblast, for example, the labor collective resolved that Turks "who have left of their own free will should not return to their former workplaces. Proof is needed that they are really aware of their mistakes and guilt."[20]

The officially recognized Supreme Religious Council of Muslims remained cowed, and at an enlarged session in late August 1989 the council adopted a declaration stating that Islam enjoys complete freedom in Bulgaria, and benefits from the respect and assistance shown by the authorities.[21]

With the fall of Todor Zhivkov, there were stirrings among the Bulgarian public. On 17 November, for example, about 100,000 Bulgarians gathered in front of the National Assembly building in Sofia to show support for *perestroika* and to shout slogans against demagogy and corruption.[22] At a rally called by the nine independent associations at Aleksandr Nevsky Square the following day, there were calls for freedom of speech, pluralism, and free elections.[23] The regime started to feel a need to make concessions. It therefore met with members of the democratic coalition (the Union of Democratic Forces in Bulgaria), promised to hold free elections and end censorship of the press, and on 29 December rescinded its earlier decision imposing Bulgarian names on local Turks.

12 Strong Societies:
Hungary, Poland, and Yugoslavia

In 1956, in the wake of Khrushchev's famous "secret speech," Hungary and Poland revolted against Stalinism and demanded the restoration of authentic leaders—Imre Nagy and Władysław Gomułka. Thirty-three years later, these same two countries were again stirring. The Hungarian communist party renamed itself a *socialist* party and pledged itself to introduce a genuine multiparty system. The Polish communist party was forced to legalize Solidarity and to accept a Solidarity member as prime minister. This consistency may be attributed to the *strength* of these societies, as defined in the preceding chapter.

The Yugoslav situation is rather different. Viewed as a whole, Yugoslav society shows many signs of strength. But taken in its regional parts, it is clear that the diverse ethnic publics that make up this multiethnic state are quite distinct. The Slovenian, Croatian, and Serbian publics are organized and articulate, and have developed independent communication networks that by-pass and make use of official networks. The Albanian population of Kosovo is mobilized, but on a number of measures Kosovar society is weaker than Slovenian or Croatian society. In Slovenia, Croatia, and Serbia, independent associations for the protection of human rights and artistic freedom, environmental concerns, feminism, gay rights, and peace have been operating since the early 1980s, and a number of new fledgling political parties arose by 1989. In Macedonia, Montenegro, and Bosnia, alternative politics is of much more recent vintage, and basically dates from about 1988. In Kosovo the only independent initiatives which were undertaken until late 1989 and early 1990 were linked with local Albanians' striving for self-determination. Since then, however, several other associations have been set up, including the local Social Democratic Party. The Kosovo associations are described in chapter 7.

The relative ethnic homogeneity of Hungary and Poland have also been a source of strength, insofar as the sense of crisis has served to bring these nations together. In Yugoslavia, by contrast, the deepening crisis has driven the composite nationality groups apart, and increased distrust particularly between Serbs and Croats, Serbs and Albanians, and Serbs and Slovenes.

Across the five measures of societal strength outlined in the preceding chapter, Hungary, Poland, and Yugoslavia rank high. When it comes to *information* (the first measure), the Yugoslav press, in particular, has long been lively and informative, and has often presented opposing sides of controversial questions. But the Polish and Hungarian presses have also been informative, albeit sporadically—the former especially during the crisis of 1980–81 and later, after about 1984 or 1985, when the Jaruzelski government concluded that it needed to compete with the samizdat publications circulating in Poland. By contrast, the East German, Czechoslovak, Romanian, Bulgarian, and Albanian communist presses were always remarkably dry, uninformative, and propagandistic.

In terms of published statistical material, Hungarian data ranked as the best in the region, followed closely by Poland and East Germany.[1] Polish sociology is ranked among the best worldwide, and both Hungary and Yugoslavia have produced some excellent sociological studies.

The educational revolution of the postwar era is directly relevant to the question of information available to the broad public. In postwar Eastern Europe there was a big push to expand educational opportunities. In Poland alone the number of university graduates increased from 80,000 in 1945 to more than a million in 1980. Among those employed in the state sector, the proportion of those with either secondary school or university education rose from 24.2 percent in 1945 to 75 percent in 1986. The working class is also better educated: in 1958 only 10.5 percent of Polish workers had more than a primary school education; by 1986 almost 50 percent of workers had secondary school diplomas.[2]

In terms of the *ability to organize* (the second measure of a strong society), Polish society has consistently rated high, but especially in the years after 1980 when an underground "independent society" was in essence constructed from the grass roots. In Yugoslavia, by contrast, the growth of independent society in the 1980s was completely in the open and, for the most part, legal. In Slovenia independent associations often obtained legal protection by registering as "activities" of the Socialist Alliance of Working People of Slovenia (SAWP-Slovenia) or of the League of Socialist Youth—a convenient legal fiction which did not compromise their independence in the least. In Croatia the local SAWP organization played a similar role, while in Serbia the Serbian Association of Writers and the Serbian Academy of Sciences took some of these independent associations under their wings.[3] And in Hungary independent society was a sporadic affair until the mid-1980s, but in late 1988 the regime threw the doors open, stimulating the headlong repluralization of Hungarian society.

The role of the intellectuals (measure #3) has been more diverse. Only in Poland and, in a certain way, Yugoslavia can one really speak of the "defection" of a part of the intelligentsia, although the Praxis group in Yugoslavia, along with alienated nationalist and democratic-minded intellectuals in Slovenia, Croatia, and Serbia, have certainly provided a source of rival intellectual energy. One need only think of the role played by Serbian novelist Dobrica Ćosić to appreciate how Yugoslav intellectuals have challenged the ruling elite to rethink the premises of its policies.

Communication networks (measure #4) have been available to alternative ideas, especially in Poland and Yugoslavia. In both countries the secular media have been open to alternative ideas: in Yugoslavia, for example, the Zagreb magazine *Start* and the Ljubljana magazine *Mladina* became renowned as forums for alternative and even dissident ideas. Again, in both countries, the press of the Catholic church offered itself as an arena for the articulation of alternative ideas (although this did not apply to Hungary). And in both Poland and Hungary there were a number of underground publications in circulation by the mid-1980s.

Finally, in terms of the *mobilization of the public* (measure #5), the growth of independent associations was directly correlated with this phenomenon, to the extent that one may speak of an awakening of civic consciousness in these societies in the 1980s. The development of an independent society and of independent networks linked to Solidarity gave the Polish opposition a unity and an ability to mobilize the public that could not be compared with anything elsewhere in the region. But in each case, mobilization was to some extent spontaneous.

This brief introduction has already suggested that in many ways Polish and Yugoslav society seemed "stronger" than Hungarian society, at least up to 1988. And yet it was Hungary that, between late 1988 and late 1989, underwent the most radical change. The question is: why Hungary?

Hungary: Toward a Multiparty System

In retrospect, it appears that the critical months for the transformation of the Hungarian political landscape were from November 1988 to April 1989. It was during those months that the Hungarian Council of Ministers approved new laws which allowed the establishment of independent political parties and trade unions, that the Soviets sent repeated overt signals that they would not interfere to obstruct Hungary's evolution toward political pluralism, and that the Hungarian party ousted four conservative leaders from the Politburo: chief ideologist János Berecz, senior administrator János Lukács, Minister of Health Judit Csehak, and agricultural specialist István Szábo.

Pressure for transformation came from many sides: from the ultimate failure of the economy; from pent-up aspirations for democracy stimulated by Gorbachev's reforms to the east; from the withering away of the semilegitimacy once enjoyed by János Kádár and the failure of his successor, Károly Grósz, to win the trust of the population; and from a gathering sense that change was in the air, a sense that infected ever greater numbers of people until change became inevitable.

The transformative crisis can be dated to October 1986, when Kádár publicly admitted that living standards were declining and that the reason lay in the party's failure to implement appropriate economic reforms in the 1970s. Aware that the situation was becoming volatile, Kádár tried in March 1988 to regain control of the situation by expelling four of the most popular liberals from the party, including liberal economist László Lengyel, writer Zoltán Biro (a founder of the Democratic Forum), and Zoltán Király, a parliamentary deputy "who became famous for demanding to know, at a session of Parliament, what the forty billion forint expenditure in the budget marked 'miscellaneous' was—the only larger item in the budget was the deficit—and no one could explain it to him."[4] Kádár hoped to undermine the reform wing in the party and put Imre Pozsgay on the defensive. Instead, the move provoked a reaction: at the party conference in May 1988 Kádár and most of his closest associates were removed from the Politburo, while Pozsgay and Rezső Nyers, a liberal economist closely identified with the economic reform of 1968, were promoted to the Politburo.

Nyers, a founding member of the New March Front, had spelled out his views on democracy in a 1986 article for *Acta Oeconomica*. In his view, the problem of economic inefficiency is organically linked to the curbing of democracy; hence, economic revitalization presumes democratic reform.

I am of the opinion that, in the course of the development of socialism, it is impossible to lastingly curb the development of democracy, since otherwise the necessity of later political reforms would become so urgent that only the elimination of restrictions could bring a solution. . . . It should be obvious that the achievements of bourgeois democracy cannot be refused in their entirety, since certain parts of it are products of the development of humanity and do not merely serve the bourgeois class.[5]

In the course of 1988 there were two parallel developments that created great pressure on the party to accept systemic change. The first was the rapid formation of new independent associations (detailed in chapter 4). The second was the proliferation of mass demonstrations. The first demonstration took place on 5 February, when five hundred people gathered in front of the Romanian embassy to protest Romania's treatment of its Hungarian minority. A month later, on 15 March, there was a large demonstration to commemorate the 1848 uprising. Demonstrators shouted "Democracy!"; it was the only demand. On 17 June there was yet another demonstration, this time in honor of Imre Nagy; unlike the others this demonstration was violently dispersed by police. But just ten days later, 50,000–100,000 people turned out in response to appeals from twelve independent associations to protest Ceauşescu's program of eradicating village life in Romania.

By May the central committee of the Hungarian Socialist Workers' Party (HSWP) was reviewing opposition demands for legal guarantees of freedom of assembly and association. In mid-July the central committee unanimously approved a proposal to authorize the National Assembly to draft appropriate legislation, but Politburo member and CC Secretary János Berecz cautioned that the proposed guarantees would be within the framework of the one-party system and that any modification of the party's monopoly would have to await passage of a new constitution.

Until November, it was by no means certain that party liberals would triumph over party conservatives, or that this proposed legislation on freedom of assembly would really move Hungary much closer to political pluralism. Grósz, a middle-of-the-roader, was threatened not merely by liberals like Pozsgay and Nyers, but also by a conservative faction led by Berecz, the chief ideologist. Berecz's strategy was to limit the new legislation, hold fast to the principle of democratic centralism in party life, and infiltrate new groups such as the Hungarian Democratic Forum so that reliable communists could influence them from within.[6]

Ultimately the conservatives proved too weak to hold back the tide, and on 10 November 1988 the Hungarian Council of Ministers adopted revised draft laws on the rights of assembly and association which extended broad guarantees for the formation of political parties, trade unions, mass movements, interest groups, and other organizations. Nyers commented that the legislation provided a basis for the development of "a *natural* political system" in Hungary.[7] Subsequently, on 15 December the HSWP committed itself to the introduction of a multiparty system and promised that independent parties would be able to contest the parliamentary elections in 1990.[8]

It is important to understand that these concessions came as a response to political pressure from below, and that without such pressure, political pluralization would not have been on the agenda in the first place. This is suggested by the party's hesitations and doubts as it contemplated the possibility of being voted out of power and devised strategems to avoid that result. One such strategem was a proposal by Zoltán Király under which new political parties would have to recognize the leading role of the HSWP within the framework of a parliamentary system, accept Hungary's membership in the Warsaw Pact, and agree to the retention of some form of socialism as preconditions for legalization.[9] This formula for a "limited multiparty system" seemed in part reminiscent of the Mexican system, and was based on the assumption that the new parties would enter into a coalition with the HSWP. The entire formula was a case of too little too late.

About this time, Mátyás Szuros, a central committee secretary of the HSWP, commented that the question of political pluralism would be decided by society itself, not by the party.[10] This was already clear enough, and subsequent events continued to bear this out. To begin with, independent political parties continued to grow. By January 1989 the Hungarian Democratic Forum numbered 10,000 members; the Federation of Young Democrats (FIDESZ) could claim 2,500 members; the relatively young Ferenc Munnich Society, which advocated communist orthodoxy, almost 6,000 members; the Social Democratic Youth Circle, then barely six weeks old, had 100 members; and the Independent Smallholders Party, which resumed activity on 18 November 1988, had 3,000 members (22,000 by November 1989). The Federation of Free Democrats founded in November 1988 did not report membership figures, but had succeeded in organizing five rural branches and two urban branches by January 1989.[11] Meanwhile, a series of independent trade unions and professional organizations were set up, including the Democratic Trade Union of Teachers, the Democratic Trade Union of Scientific Workers, and the Federation of Young Professionals. And in January 1989 Inform Studio Ltd., a private company launched on 2 January with a starting capital stock of F7.2 million, announced that it would publish the independent political weekly *Jelenlet* (*Presence*) from Debrecen beginning in March. Later, in February, in a telling move, the Union of Metallurgical Workers, Hungary's largest union, set up a

party's membership was far more radical than its leadership.

The problem was particularly acute within the HSWP: by April liberal reformer Pozsgay was threatening to split the party in two, setting up a rival, more liberal communist party to challenge the older, more orthodox one.[21] The liberals captured the day, however, causing the inevitable split in the other direction when a group of hard-line communists led by forty-three-year-old filmmaker Roland Antoniewicz set up a rival organization which they chose to call the János Kádár Society. In October 1989 Antoniewicz demanded the resignation of the government, the establishment of a true "revolutionary worker and peasant government," and the surrender of all party property to the János Kádár Society. Maria Kádár, widow of János Kádár, issued a statement to the effect that she was "appalled" that her husband's name was being used by a group with goals so much at variance with those of her late husband.[22]

Until April 1989 the ruling party continued to lay great stress on the preservation of socialism, and any endorsement of multiparty democracy was always within the context of the maintenance of a socialist order. In April, however, Foreign Minister Gyula Horn said that the party recognized no difference between "bourgeois and socialist criteria for democracy and human rights" and that the leadership wanted to adopt a system of government in the West European tradition.[23]

One of the cardinal principles of any communist party has been a ban on the formation of factions. That ban notwithstanding, liberal reformers within the party put together a factional grouping in April 1989, calling it the Eger Reform Circle of the HSWP. Imre Pozsgay took part in its founding session.[24] The following month, in an unusual departure from customary practice, the party daily Nepszabadsag gave space to Grósz's liberal critics, who accused him of presenting his personal views in an interview as those of the party.[25]

A public opinion poll conducted in April 1989 showed a dramatic decline in confidence in the party since 1985. In 1985, 66 percent of the respondents believed the HSWP was concerned about and represented their interests; in 1989 the figure was 24 percent. In 1985, 70 percent of respondents expressed confidence in the National Assembly; in 1989 the figure was 44 percent. And if free elections had been held then and there, respondents in April 1989 indicated the following party preferences: HSWP, 36.0 percent; SDP, 13.0 percent; Democratic Forum, 11.4 percent; Association of Free Democrats, 5.6 percent; Independent Smallholders Party, 5.4 percent; and Christian Democratic Party, 4.4 percent.[26]

Democratization could not, of course, be achieved without free access to the media or without openness about the past. Both of these areas were confronted in spring 1989. A party plenum on 29 March proved the occasion for an intense discussion of new legislation to govern the media, since all concerned recognized that a genuine multiparty system was impossible as long as one party monopolized the media. Under the "blueprint" adopted by the party on that occasion, any Hungarian citizen was entitled to establish a newspaper or commercial radio or TV station, to own or use printing equipment, and to distribute the material printed. In addition, increased amounts of foreign capital were to be allowed to fund joint ventures in the media. Some examples of joint media ventures include the successful newspaper *Reform*, and the prominent daily *Magyar Hírlap*, long the official organ of the Hungarian government, which was purchased by a group of private British investors (including Robert Maxwell) in February 1990. Three weeks earlier, Maxwell's rival, Robert Murdoch, invested $4 million to buy half-shares in two new Hungarian tabloids.[27]

Openness about the past meant, above all, openness about the Hungarian Revolution of 1956, and the rehabilitation of Prime Minister Imre Nagy, whom the Soviets had executed in 1958. Hungarian society had never accepted the official propaganda that Nagy was a counterrevolutionary or that the United States was heavily involved in the events of 1956, and on 6 October 1988 some three hundred demonstrators gathered in downtown Budapest to demand the political rehabilitation of Nagy.[28] In September a member of the Hungarian Politburo had proposed that a monument be erected to Nagy.[29] Meanwhile, Pozsgay started referring to the events of 1956 as a "popular uprising," rather than a "counterrevolution" as prescribed by official parlance.[30] In early February 1989 the central committee convened a special session to review differences between Grósz and Pozsgay, and agreed on a compromise formula on 1956, declaring that it was both a popular uprising and a counterrevolution, and conceding for the first time that it had had positive aspects.[31]

In early May 1989 Radio Budapest rebroadcast Imre Nagy's speech of 4 November 1956, in which the prime minister announced the Soviet invasion of Hungary. The broadcast broke a taboo of more than three decades.[32] Before the month was out, the party had decided on the full rehabilitation of Nagy and had conceded that his execution had been illegal. Finally, on 16 June, thirty-one years after his execution by the Soviets, Imre Nagy was given a state funeral with full honors.

The new openness also affected relations with the church. The old State Office for Church Affairs, long headed by Imre Miklós, was closed down and replaced on 1 July by the new Secretariat for Church Policy headed

ended, Kiszczak confided to a Polish magazine editor that he had tendered the offer because he was convinced Wałęsa would not be able to sway the strikers."[50] Instead, Wałęsa was able to persuade, cajole, harangue, and convince the striking workers to return to work. This paved the way for talks.

But the government now raised repeated objections. First, the authorities demanded of Solidarity a declaration of loyalty to the political system. Then they demanded that the union sever all links with trade unions and other institutions abroad. And finally, they objected to the inclusion of human rights activists Michnik and Jacek Kuroń among Solidarity's negotiating team. Solidarity refused to concede anything on these points.[51] In October a document surfaced, which was alleged to be a secret directive to local party cells; the document described Solidarity as a "major threat" to the party's rule and said that Solidarity had to be combatted by all means available, and that any agreements signed with Solidarity should be considered invalid in advance. Wałęsa chose to dismiss the document as a spurious provocation—though not without warning the authorities lest it be authentic—and the party immediately distanced itself from the document.[52]

Finally, after a series of preliminary meetings, the two sides agreed to start formal roundtable talks on 6 February 1989, and organized separate working groups to discuss economic reform, political reform, and trade union pluralism. Solidarity spokespersons were quite open about their goal to democratize Poland and understood that the realization of such an objective required that key levers of control be restructured. Solidarity adviser Bronisław Geremek outlined the union's strategy in an interview with an Italian newspaper. In order to set in motion what he called the "locomotives of change," it was necessary to guarantee the independence of the judiciary, freedom of association, the right to establish independent media, and the autonomy of local authorities.[53]

When the government and Solidarity finally reached an agreement on 5 April, much of Solidarity's program was in fact realized. Specifically, the agreement relegalized Solidarity and Rural Solidarity, liberalized provisions for establishing independent associations and political clubs, granted Solidarity permission to publish a daily newspaper with a circulation of 500,000 (the party weekly *Polityka* only had a circulation of 400,000) and pledged that local government would enjoy greater autonomy than in the past. The agreement restored the upper house (Senate) of Parliament, with 100 members to be elected in free and open elections, and granted Solidarity 35 percent of the 460 seats in the lower house (*Sejm*). The agreement also established the new office of president of the republic. On the other hand, a government offer to end all censorship was firmly rejected as premature by

Solidarity's negotiating team. "We realized that we needed preventive censorship to protect ourselves," explained Krzysztof Kozlowski, a Solidarity negotiator. "We don't have an independent judiciary like you in the West. Our authorities could just decide they don't like what we write, indict us for liberalism [or apply charges under the vague provision of violating state security], confiscate our newspaper, and destroy us financially."[54]

Elections to the parliament were scheduled for 4 June, and a noisy campaign was soon got under way. The party daily *Trybuna Ludu* ran a series of attacks on Solidarity, accusing it of trying to overthrow communism. Simultaneously, the government intervened at one point to cancel Solidarity's weekly television campaign program. The courts also refused to legalize the union's student movement, which Solidarity spokespersons claimed was inconsistent with the accords. Solidarity also alleged that the communists were playing "dirty tricks" in the campaign. When election day arrived, voters were handed at least four separate ballots, but not a single candidate was identified by political affiliation. Despite all these difficulties, Solidarity won a resounding victory, capturing 92 of the 100 Senate seats outright, along with 160 of the 161 seats it was allowed to contest in the Sejm. On the average, its candidates won with comfortable margins of 70–80 percent. By contrast, the communist party did not win a single seat, even where its candidates ran unopposed; to win their seats, they needed to obtain at least 50 percent of the vote, and many received only 10 per cent or less. Two weeks later, in runoff elections, Solidarity captured seven more seats in the Senate, winning 99 of the 100 seats in that chamber; the one exception was an independent self-made millionaire named Henryk Stoklosa, who spent Zl.20 million (or 200 times what the average Pole earns in a month) to finance his campaign. Shortly thereafter, Wojciech Jaruzelski won confirmation as president of the republic, with the parliamentary vote at 270 in favor, 233 against, and 34 abstentions —the bare minimum he needed. Jaruzelski resigned as party general secretary, a position now taken by Mieczysław Rakowski, one-time editor of *Polityka* and heretofore prime minister.

Although Solidarity won a clear mandate in the elections, Jaruzelski initially declined to offer the prime ministership to Solidarity, arguing that the USSR, East Germany, and Czechoslovakia "would look at this askance."[55] Instead, he asked General Kiszczak to form a government. For his own part, Wałęsa repeatedly underlined Solidarity's preference to remain in opposition, even when Kiszczak proposed a "grand coalition" in which Solidarity would participate.

But Kiszczak, Wałęsa's jailer and the man who had once guided the suppression of Solidarity, was an unacceptable choice for prime minister as far as the opposition was concerned. By early August Solidarity was engaged in an effort to lure the United Peasant Party and the Democratic Party away from their traditional alliance with the communist party. By the end of the first week in August, the ice was beginning to crack; first the Peasant Party (76 deputies) and then the Democratic Party (27 deputies) defected. Together with Solidarity's 161 deputies, they now constituted a majority (against the communists' 173 deputies). Moscow issued a statement underlining that it would not tolerate any change in Poland's status in the Warsaw Pact.[56] But when Wałęsa issued a statement promising to respect Poland's alliance commitments and assuring that the communist party could retain control of the ministries of defense and internal affairs, Moscow praised Wałęsa and declared that it was up to the Polish people to solve their own problems.

In mid-August Kiszczak resigned as prime minister, having failed to put together a working coalition. Solidarity was asked to form the government, and submitted three names to Jaruzelski as candidates for the prime ministership. From among those names, Jaruzelski selected sixty-two-year-old Tadeusz Mazowiecki, editor of the Solidarity weekly, to serve as prime minister. Lech Wałęsa declared that the Solidarity-led government would attempt to take Poland "from a communist system of ownership to capitalism. Nobody has previously taken the road that leads from socialism to capitalism. And we are setting out to do just that, to return to the prewar situation, when Poland was a capitalist country."[57] Mazowiecki said of himself, "I'm a Christian, a Catholic, who follows the social teachings of the Catholic church, which emanate from the instructions of Pope John Paul II."[58] The Soviet Council of Ministers promptly sent a note of congratulations to Mazowiecki, promising that "the traditional relations of friendship and all-around cooperation" would continue with the new government.[59] But Mazowiecki called for a new tone in foreign policy: "We want our relations to be dominated by ties between people and between states, rather than offices, enterprises, parties, and so on."[60]

Confirmed by 378 votes (with 41 abstentions and only 4 negative votes), Mazowiecki set up a coalition government in which Solidarity took six portfolios (finance, industry, housing, labor, education, and culture), the United Peasant Party received four portfolios (agriculture, justice, health, and ecology), the Democratic Party received three portfolios (internal trade, technology, and communications), and the communist party received four (internal affairs, defense, transport, and foreign trade).

Throughout this period there were strikes, demonstrations, and other outbreaks of public disorder. For example, there were strikes and demonstrations by students in several cities demanding registration of an independent students' union.[61] There were demonstrations in December 1988 on the anniversary of martial law, spontaneous antigovernment demonstrations by young people in Gdańsk in March 1989, sporadic strikes at various enterprises throughout much of 1989, and anti-Soviet demonstrations in Kraków in May and in Poznań in June. Even as the new government of Mazowiecki began its work, the Confederation for an Independent Poland, Fighting Solidarity, and other independent groups staged a big demonstration in Katowice in September, chanting "Soviets go home!"[62] Throughout all of this, Wałęsa appealed for calm and patience.[63]

Yet these disorders probably contributed to the final outcome because they exerted a constant pressure on the communist party, reminding it that society had grown strong and had a mind of its own.

In fact, the political landscape of Poland continued to change at the grass-roots level too, as new independent institutions took shape and, in some cases, obtained official registration. In April, for example, an independent Democratic Youth Union was registered in Lublin, while officials granted permission in September for the publication of an independent weekly in Poznań, called *Wielkopolska Gazeta Handlowa*. It was described as "the first private regional weekly published by independent publishers and journalists since the war."[64] In February 1989 the Polish Labor Party, a center-right, Christian democratic organization, was established by a mixed group of former members and new adherents. And in August the National Party revived activity, even as the Green Party convened its first regional meeting in Szklarska Poreba. The communist party's control of the youth movement also came under challenge, as independent scoutmasters became emboldened and set up a Scouts' Union of the Republic based on the original principles of Baden Powell, rather than on communist party principles.

As for the United Peasant Party, it showed its new courage in other ways, passing a motion for the full rehabilitation of Stanisław Mikolajczyk, its early postwar leader and briefly deputy prime minister. The UPP also raised the issue of reclaiming its earlier name, the Polish Peasant Party.

Meanwhile, as independent society continued to grow, official society atrophied. Most obviously, *Rzeczywistość*, a doctrinaire party weekly set up in May 1981 to attack all manifestations of liberalism both in society and in the party, was shut down on 30 April.

The new government quickly adopted constitutional amendments designed to strengthen rights to own and inherit property, and outlined a two-phase plan for effecting a transition to a market economy. In the first phase, to be completed by the end of 1989, the government would begin the process of dissolving state ownership of property, breaking up state monopolies, reforming the budget and banking system, setting up a system of unemployment benefits to cushion the inevitable side effects, and increasing the efficiency of state enterprises.[65] In the second phase, to be launched in 1990, the government would reform the tax system, curb inflation, convert many state-owned enterprises into private enterprises, and create a stock and bond market. The Polish government also started to consult with Jeffrey Sachs, a thirty-four-year-old Harvard economist who urged Warsaw to clamp down on the money supply, eliminate all price and wage controls, free imports and exports, and make the zloty convertible against Western currencies.[66] By late October 1989 the communist party was becoming chagrined at Solidarity's evident rush to dismantle the communist system and issued a statement alleging that the government lacked a popular mandate to carry out such radical measures.[67]

Yugoslavia: A House Divided

The repluralization of Yugoslavia got off to a more promising start in the early 1970s, but was stifled by two factors: the Titoist (and post-Titoist) system of institutionalized deadlock and the very considerable regional differences. By one estimate there were some one hundred independent grassroots organizations and ten independent political associations in Slovenia alone in February 1989.[68] But no other republic could duplicate that, and in some republics (in particular, Bosnia-Herzegovina and Macedonia) there was almost no independent activism until early 1990.

From the beginning of the 1980s a large number of independent activist groups were created in Yugoslavia, mostly in Ljubljana, Belgrade, and Zagreb. By summer 1989, for example, there were independent pacifist and environmentalist groups in Ljubljana, Belgrade, and Zagreb; independent feminist groups in Ljubljana, Belgrade, and Zagreb; independent human rights groups in Ljubljana, Belgrade, and Titograd; the Association for the Advancement of Democratic Processes in Nikšić; the Association of Unemployed in Bijelo Polje; the Committee for the Protection of Artistic Freedom in Belgrade; the Committee for the Defense of Freedom of Thought and Expression in Belgrade; a gay rights movement in Ljubljana; and independent multimedia artistic groups in Ljubljana (*Neue Slowenische Kunst*), Osijek (*Metropolie Trans*), Skopje (*Aporea*), Zagreb (*Novi Evropski Poredak*), and Ruma (*Autopsia*).[69]

Existing institutions have also changed and, in the years since Tito's death, have increasingly acted in an independent fashion. Most important in this regard are the Serbian and Slovenian Writers' Associations, various media, most especially the youth press (*Mladina* in Ljubljana, *Katedra* in Maribor, *Polet* in Zagreb, *Student* in Belgrade, and *Valter* in Sarajevo), and certain other periodicals, such as the fortnightly magazine *Start*. Radio Student in Ljubljana was, of course, established by the students themselves as their own, independent radio station.

From mid-1988 social pluralization expressed itself also in the formation of embryonic political parties, first in Slovenia, and subsequently in Croatia. The process was ignited by the controversial army trial of Janez Janša, Ivan Borstner, David Tasić, and Franci Zavrl for having published military plans to suppress the movement for democratization in Slovenia. In particular, the article they printed in *Mladina* revealed that General Svetozar Visnjić, a Serb and chief of the Slovenian army district, had met with Slovenia's minister of police, Tomas Ertl, in March 1988 to inform him that the army would soon start arresting people in Slovenia and that they had drawn up a list of two hundred persons to be incarcerated. *Mladina* published these plans in April 1988 and the four were arrested soon after. The trial inflamed the Slovenian public, who turned out in the tens of thousands for big protest meetings in downtown Ljubljana. On 3 June 1988 the Committee for the Protection of Human Rights was created, which circulated petitions on behalf of Janša and his codefendants, gathering more than 100,000 signatures.[70]

If the trial galvanized the Slovenian public, the formation of the Committee for the Protection of Human Rights set off a chain reaction that soon resulted in the creation of the Slovenian Peasant Alliance, the Slovenian Democratic Union, the Social Democratic Alliance, the Transnational Radical Party, the Green Party, the Slovenian Christian Socialist movement, and the laissez-faire oriented Republican Alliance. By summer 1989 there was even a small anarchist club that mysteriously called itself AAAA and talked with outsiders on the basis of complete anonymity.

By December 1987, to be sure, France Tomšić, one of the organizers of the workers' strike at the Litostroj metalworks, had proposed the founding of a social democratic party to a meeting of 1,500 workers.[71] About six months later, Tomšić, Dimitrij Rupel (a professor of sociology at the University of Ljubljana), psychologist Hubert Požarnik, writer Rudi Seligo (president of the Slovenian Writers' Association), and other Ljubljana intellectuals began talking about taking practical action. The original idea was that they form a *single* social democratic party, but a combination of political and personality differences led to a split and the creation of two parties: Tomšić's Social Democratic Alliance, which was the more labor-oriented of the two (2,500–2,600 members as of September 1989), and Rupel's Slovenian Democratic Union, which espoused laissez-faire economics and politics (3,000 members as of September 1989).[72]

The Slovenian Democratic Alliance spelled out its aims in a preliminary program released to the press in January 1989. The alliance pledged to work for a new constitution based on human rights and on Slovenian national sovereignty, and emphasized the necessity of introducing a parliamentary system and an independent judiciary, and of joining the European Economic Community.[73] The linkage of the demands for democratization and for Slovenian sovereignty was not coincidental, but rather reflected the belief that the concept of democracy implies and includes the idea of self-determination of compact nations. This belief became increasingly widespread in Slovenia during 1988 and 1989, and led to the September 1989 passage by the Slovenian Assembly of constitutional amendments that declared that Slovenia had the right to secede from the Yugoslav federation, that only the *Slovenian* Assembly (hence, not the Federal Assembly) had the right to declare a state of emergency in Slovenia, and that the army could not be deployed in Slovenia in peacetime without the consent of the Slovenian Assembly.[74]

The Slovenian Peasant Alliance established in February 1988 grew rapidly, and by September 1989 it had registered 25,000 members in 100 branches throughout the republic—making it numerically the strongest independent party in Yugoslavia. Encouraged by its example, the Independent Peasant Union was set up in Subotica, Vojvodina, in August 1989.[75] In particular, the Slovenian Peasant Alliance sought to raise the ceiling for the size of private farms from 10 hectares to 30 hectares (and this latter figure was written into the proposed constitutional amendments).

Parallel with this, but entirely independently, members of the Slovenian League of Socialist Youth began to talk about reorganizing themselves as a political party and fielding candidates in the May 1990 parliamentary elections. In the place of a political youth organization, they proposed the creation of a ministry for youth affairs. The youth organization started to meet with the new alternative parties and to be counted as an alternative party itself. Public opinion polls in summer 1989 indicated that the youth organization was potentially the most popular political organization in Slovenia, with especial strength in the urban centers.

The proliferation of alternative parties created pressure on SAWP-Slovenia to adapt. The leadership of SAWP-Slovenia understood that if the process of democratization continued, their old function as a transmission belt of communist party directives would become irrelevant. They had to find a new formula, or face the possibility of organizational extinction. The choice was obvious, and by summer 1989 the leadership of SAWP-Slovenia talked about severing its connection with the communist party and fielding candidates as an independent party. "SAWP-Slovenia does not want to be a transmission belt any longer," one of its leading figures told me in September 1989. "We want to have our own candidates in the upcoming elections, and to run them against the communist party's candidates."[76] The SAWP-Slovenia leadership removed the reference to the vanguard role of the LCY in SAWP from its statute, thus taking a first step in the direction of loosening its relations with the other regional branches of SAWPY.

Similar processes were taking place in Croatia, where in 1989 the Yugoslav Democratic Initiative, the Croatian Social Liberal Alliance, and the Croatian Democratic Community took shape. All of these organizations, like the independent parties in Slovenia aside from the Peasant Alliance, were the creations of intellectuals—in this case, mostly academics associated with the University of Zagreb. Among all of them, only the Yugoslav Democratic Initiative truly looks to the Yugoslav arena; the others aspire to appeal to the Slovenian or Croatian publics only.

The Yugoslav Democratic Initiative was created on 2 February 1989. Unlike some of the other parties, the Initiative refused to register as an "activity" of SAWPY, and this immediately created problems for its registration. Initiative members applied initially for registration in Croatia, Bosnia, Serbia, and Slovenia, claiming a modest 600–700 members in all of Yugoslavia in September 1989.[77] By November the first three republics had turned down the Initiative's application, and it was awaiting a decision only in Slovenia (which was affirmative). Like other independent parties, the Initiative wants a democratically elected parliament and the creation of a multiparty system.

Although the Initiative clearly looks to Western models for inspiration, the other two Croatian parties are even more firmly grounded in the liberal tradition. The Croatian Social Liberal Alliance was established in May 1989 as a coalition of Croatia-oriented confederalists and more traditional laissez-faire liberals. With about a thousand members in August 1989 (almost all in Croatia), the Croatian Social Liberal Alliance insisted on the necessity of working for the dismantlement of the bureaucratic party apparatus. Operating in a grey zone of semi-illegality, the party leadership described its activities as "semisecret" and its connections in Belgrade and Vojvodina as "private" and "clandestine."[78] In a programmatic declaration issued immediately after its founding, the Social Liberal Alliance described the individual as the "highest value," underlining the need to protect individual rights and liberties from state encroachment. The Social Liberals declared their support for freedom of association, social equality of the sexes, a multiparty parliamentary system, reprivatization and the establishment of a free market economy, and freedom of trade union activity.[79]

Within a month of the founding of the Social Liberal Alliance, the Croatian Democratic Community was set up under the presidency of General Franjo Tudjman, the famous human rights activist. The Democratic Community was the most Croatia-oriented of the three and the most enthusiastic in its endorsement of confederalization. Its programmatic declaration emphasized many of the same points stressed by other parties, including guarantees of civil rights without regard to national or religious affiliation or political conviction, the right of association, the sovereignty of the Croatian people including their right of secession, and the necessity of debureaucratization. Among its specific goals, the Democratic Community demanded the revival of Matica hrvatska, the Croatian Literary Society shut down by Tito in December 1971.[80]

The echo in Serbia has been fainter, at least partly because the rise of Slobodan Milošević to power in that republic in late 1987 on the basis of a fusion of populism and Serbian nationalism has produced an atmosphere not conducive to the establishment of explicitly political independent associations. The outspoken Serbian Writers' Association, however, has increasingly functioned as a surrogate alternative party. Its weekly, Thursday night seminars have become the forum for lively discussions of controversial subjects. Its publication, *Književne novine*, has been in the forefront of the movement for democratization and has loudly championed Serbia's rights in Kosovo. In May 1989 the association issued a seven-point appeal for radical changes in Yugoslavia, including the introduction of a multiparty system. In a key passage, the appeal demanded "that people be allowed to exercise their rights in free political associations and to defend their programs through general, secret, and direct elections; in other words, the introduction of a multiparty system with an opposition, without which there can be no true democracy and also no modern socialism."[81] The appeal also drew an unfavorable comparison with Hungary and Poland, claiming that Yugoslavia, "which was the first socialist country to criticize Stalinism and to have liberalized itself, has been passed on that road and is now watching passively while other countries, such as Poland and Hungary, overtake it in political freedom."[82]

The alternative political scene in Yugoslavia is very much a product of three cities—Ljubljana, Zagreb, and Belgrade. What makes this politically significant is the national question, insofar as the parties created in these cities can appeal only to the Slovenian, Croatian, and Serbian publics. Meanwhile, the echoes of alternative politics have been much weaker in the other republics of Yugoslavia. Pressure from below is thus geographically and ethnically defined in Yugoslavia.

Even so, the power of contagion has assured that the question of a multiparty system has been taken up also within the League of Communists itself, and by the end of 1989 high-ranking members of the Slovenian, Croatian, and Macedonian parties had, on different occasions, suggested that the adoption of a multiparty parliamentary system had become inevitable.[83]

Similarities and Differences

In all three countries, similarities are evident. Pressure from below forced the question of a multiparty system onto the political agenda. Problems of political legitimacy forced the ruling party to enter into dialogue with the opposition, while in Poland and Yugoslavia, the partial defection of the intelligentsia fueled alternative politics. Issue-oriented associations were set up independently in recent years, thereby demonstrating the ability of these societies to organize themselves. There was a gathering consensus that the economic future lay with a free enterprise economy and that some form of reprivatization was essential. Finally, there was a general debunking of the past; this was particularly clear in Hungary, where the failures of the late Kádár era were highlighted, but much less clear in Yugoslavia, where in the late 1980s, for example, Tito was attacked and criticized in Serbia, defended and praised in Croatia, and ignored as irrelevant in Slovenia.

Yet there are also some obvious differences among these societies. To begin with, while Hungary and Poland are members of the Warsaw Pact and therefore had to be concerned about Soviet reactions to political changes in their countries, Yugoslavia is not a pact member and has therefore not had to worry in this regard. In Hungary, where there has been no central organizational focus in the opposition, the party seemed for a while to maintain a semblance of control of the process of pluralization by identifying itself with that process. In Poland, Solidarity became the focal point of the opposition, while the party, far less successful than its Hungarian counterpart, reached the point in mid-1989 of having to share power with the opposition. In divided Yugoslavia, Slovenia comes the closest to the Hungarian model, Croatia and Serbia are politically mobilized (although not along the lines of either the Hungarian or the Polish model), and Macedonia showed much weaker signs of change in early 1990, and came closer, if anything, to the Bulgarian model. Montenegro was largely dominated by adherents of Serbian party chief Slobodan Milošević, while Bosnia remained so internally divided between Serbs, Croats, and Muslims that serious alternative politics remained, at least for the time being, impossible.

13 Dominoes: East Germany,
Czechoslovakia, and the Future of Europe

When I visited East Germany in the summer of 1988, I was struck by how persistent and consistent the complaints were. One after another, people complained about wanting to travel to the West, about the deteriorating standard of living (hidden behind triumphant-looking but ultimately mis-leading statistics), and about the low quality of production under socialism ("in West Germany they have the BMW; what do we make—the Trabant!"). The discontent, even disaffection, among East Germans was well known. Their *Sehnsucht* for the West was well known. The fact that East Germans continued to risk their lives to flee to the West was well known. The fact that on 14 March 1989 the Hungarians had signed a UN protocol promising not to force refugees to return home and that they had dismantled the barbed-wire fence along the Austrian border in May 1989 was well known. The fact that East Germans could still travel to Hungary was well known. Less well known was the fact that by 1988 East Germans not only com-pared their economic system unfavorably with West Germany, but were also starting to look at the Hungarian standard of living with jealousy.[1] The calculus was straightforward: they wanted to leave, they could leave, they *would* leave.

Yet, when tens of thousands of East Germans started to pour into Hungary and from there into Austria and West Germany, and subsequently to scale the West German embassy compounds in East Berlin, Warsaw, and Prague, Western observers were surprised. Not so the Soviets. More than two months before the first East German refugees slipped across the Hungarian-Austrian border in August, the Soviet foreign ministry had reached the conclusion that a serious political crisis in East Germany was inevitable, and the Soviet government let it be known that it had no inten-tion of interfering.[2]

among other things, that long-term economic deterioration played an important role in mobilizing mass discontent. Chapters 2 through 4 traced tendencies to organize independent structures, whether for purposes of defending the civil rights of particular groups or individuals or in order to support cultural and educational initiatives independent of party control and censorship. These tendencies developed fastest in Poland, Hungary, and Slovenia, where one may speak of the emergence of "civil society." Chapter 5 outlined the penetration of new religious groups and cults in the region, a phenomenon associated with cultural drift in the population and possessing the potential to influence social attitudes and behavior in many areas.

Chapter 6 challenged the standard interpretation of the role of the Catholic church in Poland, which holds that the church is above all a traditional institution, defending traditional values against an imported communist system. I would not dispute the traditionalism of the church, but I would shift the emphasis elsewhere, and therefore argue that the political role assumed by the church in Poland in the late 1970s and 1980s was primarily a symptom of the emergence of "praetorian society" in that country. Samuel P. Huntington saw praetorianism as a prelude to and symptom of social chaos.

Ethnic frictions have long played an important role in Eastern Europe, but the weight carried by any particular ethnic conflict has not necessarily stayed even over the years. At the present time, the most explosive ethnic problem in the region is the Serb-Albanian friction in Kosovo, which has brought Yugoslavia to the brink of civil war. As a result, Chapter 7 argues, Kosovo has become a factor in the larger political debate, and has generated impulses for system change.

Chapters 8 through 10 trace the emergence of a new generation in Eastern Europe, a generation which is more Western, more disillusioned, and more materialistic than earlier generations. This generation has also seen the rise of small feminist groups in Yugoslavia and the growth of female activism in East Germany and elsewhere.

Finally, in Chapters 11 and 12 I developed a theory of societal strength and weakness on the basis of Crane Brinton's broader theory about revolution, and argued that while Hungary and Poland have been stronger societies, Bulgaria has been a weak society, and the picture in Yugoslavia is mixed and complex. The strength of a society may change over time. Indeed, this book has charted the processes by which all of the societies of the region —including Romania—have become stronger in the 1980s.

Taken together, these strands reflect different aspects of both modernization and decay—a dangerous combination. Adriano Guerra, the

Italian communist party's leading expert on Eastern Europe, put it very well:

> What we have here is not a crisis due to circumstances but the simultaneous emergence in all countries, with varying intensity but not in different forms, of a fundamental and completely new contradiction: that which has developed between the economic, social, and cultural development reached through such radical processes of transformation and growth, on the one hand . . . and, on the other hand, the persistence of the old centralizing structures of bureaucracy and authoritarianism.[5]

It must be emphasized that there are important differences among the countries of the region. Differences in economic solvency, the role of the church, and ethnic relations are among the most important. But in all these countries, the "contradiction" to which Guerra alluded had emerged by the end of the 1980s, and the illness to be "cured" (Poland, Yugoslavia, Romania, and arguably Czechoslovakia) or avoided (East Germany,[6] Hungary, and Bulgaria) was political decay. It was precisely this danger to which Gorbachev addressed himself.

The Gorbachev Effect

If there was already a reform agenda in several countries in Eastern Europe, the entire agenda was made to appear more urgent and indeed was made more urgent by the example set by Gorbachev in the USSR. Soviet *glasnost* (openness), *perestroika* (restructuring), and *novoye myshleniye* (new thinking) quickly exerted a fascination throughout the region among all sectors of the population, adding internal pressure to the external pressure being exerted by the Kremlin.

In his first three years in office, Gorbachev succeeded in opening up discussion of practically every policy sphere in the USSR and in engineering several symbolic changes. The centerpiece of his program of reform has been the drive to reinvigorate the economy. So far this has taken the form of giving local enterprises greater latitude and encouraging a small degree of private enterprise and workers' cooperatives.[7] In addition, in August 1988 Soviet authorities approved new legislation to remove the barriers to private farming and make farm land available on fifty-year leases. Some of Gorbachev's advisers have been urging more radical measures. Tat'yana Zaslavskaya, a sociologist who enjoys access to the general secretary, proposed a restructuring of GOSPLAN so that the agency would give up its tra-

joined the general chorus of exomologesis and in mid-February 1990 published a report in which it conceded that it had executed 750,000 people as enemies of the state between 1930 and 1953.

Meanwhile, scores of hitherto forbidden materials have now become available. In 1988, for example, 6,000 book titles hitherto locked away in special collections were made available to the general public, including works by Lenin, Kamenev, Preobrazhensky, Kropotkin, Trotsky, Savinkov, Milyukov, Bukharin, Rykov, Rozengolts, and Chernov, as well as the memoirs of Kerensky, Krasnov, and Denikin, and Tsar Nicholas II's abdication.[21]

Works of Trotsky have also been published recently in the USSR, as has Khrushchev's famous "secret speech" of 1956.[22] The Soviets also undertook to publish Robert Conquest's *Harvest of Sorrow* (which deals with the forced famine of 1930–31) in translation, and Alexander Solzhenitsyn's *Gulag Archipelago*. In August 1989 the Soviets even acknowledged—after years of denials—the secret protocols concluded between Molotov and Ribbentrop exactly fifty years earlier, which divided Poland between them.[23]

As if that were not enough, in February 1988 Gorbachev told members of the central committee personally that some of the fundamental teachings of Marx and Engels were outdated and no longer relevant. In Gorbachev's words, "It is necessary to remove the rust of bureaucratism from the values and ideas of socialism . . . The party has to literally fight for perestroika . . . in the spiritual sphere.[24]

Soviet historians have also begun to break out of the isolation imposed by their own system, and in 1986 and 1987 began to publish works by American and other Western scholars in their journals, and to allow long-banned Westerners such as Robert Conquest and Reverend Michael Bourdeaux to return as honored guests. In April 1990 the Soviets took the dramatic step of inviting fifty leading Western Kremlinologists and historians to participate in a conference sponsored by the Soviet Academy of Sciences.[25]

In social and cultural policy, Gorbachev's impact has been tangible. Among the early signs of change in the literary scene was the publication of Valentin Rasputin's novella *The Fire*, which describes the damaging impact of breakneck industrialization. One of the targets of Rasputin's criticism in the novella is the economic planning system, which he suggests should be scuttled. In October 1986 came the decision to permit publication of Anatoly Rybakov's searing indictment of Stalin, *Children of the Arbat*. The decision to permit publication was allegedly taken at the "highest levels of the Kremlin."[26] Rybakov himself explained his philosophy in this way: "A society that wants to build the future must know its past, its real past, as it was. A society that wants truth and openness must be truthful and open about its past, however it was. Only then will it be insured against the errors of the past."[27] Boris Pasternak's long proscribed *Dr. Zhivago* has now been published in the USSR.[28] In addition, many Soviet writers who had been expelled from the Writers' Union for unorthodoxy have been readmitted to the union and allowed to return to the cultural mainstream. Soviet theater has become sharply critical and has satirized both past and present political figures. One of the most daring has been Mikhail Shatrov's play, *Dal'she . . . dal'she . . . dal'she* (Onwards, Onwards, Onwards), which depicts Stalin constructing a society based on antisocialist principles. While this clearly pushes the limits of the permissible, the play was published in the literary journal *Znamya* in its January 1988 issue.[29] Nudity has also hit the Soviet stage. In rock music the old distinction between official and unofficial groups has been scuttled and groups which once had difficulty reaching the public are now tolerated and in some cases are obtaining re-cording contracts from Melodiya.[30] The Soviet fashion industry has a new, chic, occasionally risqué quality.[31] Reflecting on the sudden liberalization, the Soviet rock group Time for Love composed a song in which they worry about the permanency of liberalization:

And now that we are not afraid of anything,
they have given us freedom.
Have they given it forever?

New legislation is being drafted across a number of areas, including religious affairs, where religious organizations were finally authorized to buy and own property. In the religious sphere, the Russian Orthodox church was at first the chief beneficiary of the "new thinking." Since Gorbachev's accession to power, that church has been able to register hundreds of new parishes. Several monasteries confiscated under earlier leaders have been returned to the church, and authorities have begun to treat registered reli-gious groups with greater tolerance.[32] The Russian Orthodox church hopes to be able to open church hospitals as well.

Unsanctioned "informal groups" have likewise been shown a new tol-eration spawning a welter of politically oriented groups across a broad spec-trum, including the Russian nationalist *Pamiat'* with neo-Stalinist and anti-Semitic features;[33] the Western-oriented Democratic Union, which has tried to promote better relations between the USSR and the United States;[34] and the Perestroika Club, a "new left" grouping which supports Gorbachev's program.[35] In Estonia the Green Party, which is concerned about protecting the environment and expanding Estonia's administrative autonomy, has been tolerated.[36] For a while, Soviet authorities even tolerated the daring, independent magazine *Glasnost*, which published a detailed discussion of the KGB in one of its early issues.[37]

The new openness in the Soviet Union had reverberations in the non-Russian republics, where resentment of linguistic and cultural Russification had long been simmering. In Armenia and Azerbaijan there were demonstrations and riots, with Armenians demanding the return to Armenia of the Nagorno-Karabakh Autonomous Oblast and the Nakhichevan ASSR, and Azerbaijanis opposed. In March 1984 Soviet authorities had to use military force to quell rioting in the Azerbaijani city of Sumgait. And in June of that year the Armenian legislature actually endorsed the demonstrators' demand—a move that did not, however, produce the desired effect.

There were also nationalist disturbances in Estonia, Latvia, and Lithuania in 1987 and 1988, involving thousands of people. In August 1988, for example, 100,000 Lithuanians gathered in the squares of downtown Vilnius to mark the thirty-ninth anniversary of the armed annexation of Lithuania; some of the demonstrators demanded independence. Complaints about Russification in neighboring Estonia have grown markedly more voluble since the proclamation of *glasnost*. In August 1988 an Estonian newspaper became the first official Soviet publication to admit and describe the secret Nazi-Soviet protocol of 1939 which ceded the independent Baltic republics to the Soviet "sphere of interest."[38] At first, nationalists in the Baltic republics felt constrained to underline that independence was not a realistic possibility. But in the course of 1989 ever greater numbers of Balts expressed support for secession and independence. And in May 1989 the Lithuanian Supreme Soviet unanimously passed a resolution that declared that the republic wanted its independence from the USSR.[39] Farther south, young people in western Ukraine organized clandestine nationalist groups, possibly of a secessionist nature. In the ostensibly dormant republic of Belorussia, a political demonstration in Minsk on 1 November 1987 drew 200 people; among other things, participants condemned the "genocide" of Belorussians in the 1930s.[40] And in Moldavia, where the Soviets had long insisted that the Moldavian language (written since World War II in Cyrillic) was distinct from the Romanian language (written in the Latin alphabet), the local communist party admitted in early 1989 that Moldavian is the same as Romanian and began the costly process of reversion back to the Latin alphabet.

Even the old mechanisms of control were subjected to "restructuring." The Soviets admitted to abusing psychiatry,[41] rigging elections and routinely falsifying election returns,[42] and maintaining undue secrecy about information which could have been useful to Soviet citizens.[43] In a particularly striking development, the September 1988 issue of *Kommunist* published an article by a leading KGB official that argued that the maintenance of tight secrecy about basic facts had been used "irresponsibly and uncontrollably in the narrow interests of small groups of people."[44] In the same month, Viktor Chebrikov, then head of the KGB, told *Pravda* that a new law was being drafted which would make the KGB more accountable to the public.[45] The party began to trim the sails of the KGB: Chebrikov was replaced by Vladimir A. Kryuchkov, a new decree stated that no one would be subject to criminal proceedings merely for criticizing the state,[46] and in November 1989 KGB chief Kryuchkov publicly acknowledged the Stalinist KGB's brutality and arbitrary cruelty and pledged on national TV that this would never happen again.[47]

When Gorbachev first came to power, Czech wits used to joke: "What's the difference between Dubček and Gorbachev?" "None. Only Gorbachev doesn't know it yet." That pessimism notwithstanding, the joke suggested not merely a commonality of program but also a kinship of spirit. At an early stage, Dubček publicly endorsed Gorbachev's reforms. In turn, the Soviets rehabilitated him in late 1989, and in token of that he was interviewed on Leningrad TV in early November 1989.[48] The Soviets meanwhile repeatedly affirmed that they would never again send armed forces against their European neighbors.

Contagion in Eastern Europe

Taken in sum, Gorbachev's "new thinking" sent a surge of hope throughout Eastern Europe. The respective governments reacted very differently, however. The communist governments in Poland and Hungary backed Gorbachev's reform package, the latter realizing that in many respects Gorbachev was merely adapting solutions already tried by János Kádár. The Bulgarian government initially dragged its feet, then made bold promises of a Bulgarian *perestroika*, and later backed off again, dropping Chudomir Alexandrov, the strongest advocate of Gorbachev's ideas, from the Politburo.[49]

The authorities in East Germany, Czechoslovakia, and Romania tried to impede the penetration of *novoye myshleniye*. Gorbachev's speeches were censored in these countries, and reportage of Soviet developments was generally restrained. While the Soviets released Tengiz Abuladze's stirring film *Repentance*, which pokes fun at Stalin's autocracy, the East German paper *Junge Welt* criticized it for "defam[ing] the reputation of Marxist-Leninist historiography."[50] *Neues Deutschland* showed itself willing to admit that mistakes were made in the Soviet Union in the 1970s,[51] but not to admit that any mistakes had been made in East Germany. It is true that East German newspapers gave fairly extensive coverage to the Soviet party conference in June 1988 (though no front-page reportage); yet a subsequent report in *Neues Deutschland* highlighting the Soviet population's discontent with *perestroika* (quoting *Izvestiia*) suggested that the East German authorities remained cool toward Gorbachev's program.[52] In Czechoslovakia, in a similar spirit, delegates to a 1987 meeting of the Czechoslovak-Soviet Friendship Society were cautioned to be "on guard against the populace's excessive and unwholesome interest in Soviet developments."[53]

Finally, in Yugoslavia there was at first a broad consensus that that country had progressed far beyond the Soviet Union and could not look to Gorbachev for a model, and later a growing sense that the USSR was at least taking steps to solve its problems and that the Yugoslavs could not be smug about the Russians' continued deadlock and deepening crisis. But whether one talks about Gorbachev's repudiation of earlier Soviet claims to be the "leading center" of the socialist community, his advocacy of limited private enterprise and private farming, his tolerance of informal groups, his policy of openness in the press, his stress on legality and toleration in the religious sphere, his endorsement of greater economic autonomy for the constituent republics of the USSR,[54] his condemnation of Stalin, or, most obviously, his early endorsement of workers' self-management, Gorbachev seemed, in so many ways, to be merely adopting the old Titoist policies.[55] Only later did Gorbachev move beyond this.

Gorbachev's dual policies of *glasnost* and *perestroika* clearly contributed to the political transformation of the region. Gorbachev's original objective with respect to Eastern Europe was to effect a reinvigoration of the bloc.[56] Along these lines he initially promoted an intensification of intra-COMECON cooperation, although this was done within the context of greater integration and cooperation with Western Europe. By 1989 there was a shift in the wind, and the ever-flexible Gorbachev readjusted his sights and began to think in terms of endorsing the self-determination of the East European states—in effect dismantling the Soviet empire.[57]

Alternative Regime Strategies in Eastern Europe

The communists were never able to solve the question of political legitimacy. But in the late 1980s the question was posed in new ways by newly mobilized groups with new resources at their disposal, within a new political context created in part by economic crisis and in part by Gorbachev's *novoye myshleniye*. The legitimacy question had four levels. First and foremost, legitimacy is very much tied to economic performance. A society enjoying prosperity is apt to forgive many transgressions or errors on the part of its government. But all the countries of the region, including even

East Germany, experienced declines in the standard of living in the 1980s, with three of them (Poland, Yugoslavia, and Romania) functioning like Third World economies. As a result, legitimacy has been very much in question on this first level.

Second, communist rule throughout the region was not introduced democratically and had never been made the subject of an honest referendum. Underground and public polls have repeatedly confirmed that if free elections were held, the communist party would be swept out of power. A 1981 poll in Czechoslovakia, Hungary, and Poland, for example, found that only 3 to 7 percent of the adult population in these countries would vote communist if free elections were held.[58] Most people would prefer to vote for a social democratic or christian democratic party. (For data on the popularity of the communist and other parties in Hungary, Poland, and Yugoslavia, see the appendixes.)

Third, Soviet domination remained deeply resented in the five countries concerned and further eroded any possibility of legitimation. This factor was irrelevant to Romania and Yugoslavia. As of early 1991, the Soviets have lost their former means of control in the region and can only hope to rebuild relations based on mutual interest, emphasizing mutually profitable trade.

And fourth, in certain countries there are ethnic minorities which reject the government in question. Chapter 7 outlined in detail the problems confronting the Yugoslav government in the now largely Albanian-inhabited province of Kosovo. There are at least two other instances in which nationalities issues complicate the legitimacy issue, Romania and Bulgaria.[59]

The sundry changes traced here have variously contributed to the long unresolved crisis of legitimacy (as in the case of economic deterioration and the deterioration of ethnic relations in Kosovo), affected the context in which the illegitimacy of the regimes bore on party-populace relations (as in the case of the development of parallel society in Poland, the emergence of socially engaged churches in East Germany and Poland, and the rise of independent activism in Czechoslovakia, Hungary, Romania, and, for that matter, Yugoslavia), or reshaped social dynamics in such a way as to make irrelevant earlier party strategies (in the case of the appearance of new religious movements, the development of feminism, and the spread of rock counterculture and Western styles among young people). The relationship of this third phenomenon to the larger political context has too often been either ignored or downplayed. But the breakdown of the women's and youth organizations and their increasing self-doubts in the late 1970s and into the 1980s are measures of the impact of changing social identities on the political mechanisms for mobilization and socialization.

The Dam Breaks

There was a shift in the wind in East Germany around 1986 or 1987. This was the time when Evangelical-Lutheran church leaders started to demand Gorbachev-style reforms and East German citizens began to turn to the church in large numbers for help with emigration. Berlin's Bishop Gottfried Forck was even accused in 1988 of operating a de facto emigration office out of his chancery. The pressure for emigration was constant. In March 1989, for example, several hundred East German citizens demonstrated in Leipzig for exit visas to go to the West.[60]

Until early 1989 East German, Czechoslovak, and Bulgarian authorities were able to resist the tide because their people believed that resistance was pointless. As the winds of change penetrated first the USSR and then Hungary, East German authorities banned the Soviet magazine *Sputnik* and the lively Hungarian newspaper *Budapester Rundschau* in November 1988. Subsequently, East German authorities also banned a March 1989 issue of the Soviet magazine *Novoye vremya* because it contained an interview with Lech Wałęsa. The SED stated that it had no need to copy the Soviets, but at party meetings, members spoke out against the banning of *Sputnik*.[61] There were, to be sure, some critical articles published in East Germany.[62] But until May 1989 the pressure for change—leaving aside the periodic synods of the Evangelical-Lutheran church—remained muted. Then on 7 May local elections were held, and large numbers of people took the trouble to vote "no" on the single-candidate slate. When the official press reported that only 1.1 percent of the voters had voted "no," the reaction was outrage. From then until September there were repeated protests against the election fraud, and arrests of protesters.[63]

In September the picture changed virtually overnight. On 10 September Hungary opened its border with Austria. Within forty-eight hours, some 12,000 East Germans vacationing in Hungary crossed over into Austria. The East German government protested, briefly considered clamping down on travel to Hungary, and finally watched helplessly as 225,000 East Germans fled by the end of October. The average age of the East German refugees was twenty-seven, and an economist at the University of Halle estimated that the GDR would lose 0.12 percent of its national income for every 10,000 East Germans who left. The massive exodus was a powerful signal in and of itself, but it also served to catalyze massive demonstrations in East Berlin, Leipzig, and Dresden, where week after week, tens of thousands of people took to the streets in peaceful demonstration of their discontent. Among the larger demonstrations were those in Leipzig on 16 October (100,000 participants), 23 October (300,000), and 30 October (about 300,000), and in East Berlin on 4 November (up to 500,000). The protesters chanted "Ecology instead of economy!," "We are the people!," "Legalize New Forum!," "Gorby! Gorby!," "We want new leaders!," and "Stop the blah-blah-blah!"

The Evangelical-Lutheran church synod at Eisenach in September 1989 drew up a resolution demanding fundamental reforms, including freedom to travel and the introduction of a multiparty system, and sent a note to Honecker demanding democratization and proposing church-state talks on political and social reform. The SED rejected the church's proposal with the comment that it had "taken note of" the church's suggestion.[64] East Germany's usually silent Catholic bishops also took up the refrain, urging serious dialogue and a change in political structures.[65] By mid-September members of the CDU-East also began to demand serious reforms.[66] Professional organizations such as the Union of Writers and the national association of lawyers also issued strong statements in favor of change. The East German newspapers *Junge Welt* (organ of the youth organization), *Der Morgen* (organ of the Liberal-Democratic Party), and *Berliner Zeitung* published letters demanding self-criticism and reform on the part of the regime.

In mid-October the seventy-seven-year-old Honecker, in poor health after a gallstone operation, was removed from power and replaced by fifty-two-year-old Egon Krenz, Honecker's handpicked successor. On his first day, Krenz met with Bishop Werner Leich, chair of the Evangelical Church Federation, and pledged to conduct "a sincere dialogue with society, which will not exclude anyone."[67] Most of the old Politburo was forced to resign, and the size of the Politburo was reduced from twenty-one members to eleven.[68] The regime also promised to release all political prisoners,[69] and agreed to form a coalition government, assigning at least eleven of the twenty-seven ministries to noncommunists. The regime also lifted all travel restrictions and, in a highly symbolic move, opened the Berlin Wall. New Forum was promised registration. And the regime talked of holding free elections.

The East German changes sent shock waves throughout the region, exciting mass protests in Czechoslovakia and Bulgaria. Of course, in Czechoslovakia matters had been coming to a head in any case. Thirty new independent associations were created there in the course of 1989 alone, and pre-existing structures also started to behave in a new way. Within the Union of Czech Writers, for example, there were calls in late 1988 for the rehabilitation of some banned Czechoslovak writers and for greater creative freedom. Within the Czechoslovak People's Party there were signs of revived political consciousness in spring 1989, taking the form of the circulation of petitions. In June sixteen members of the party wrote a letter that criticized their long-slumbering party and called for a renewal of its Christian character.[70] Similarly, Jan Skoda, general secretary of the Czechoslovak Socialist Party, called for a stronger role for his party and the other "fraternal" noncommunist parties in Czechoslovakia, linking the demand to a stress on the need for democratization.[71] Meanwhile, the communist party was showing signs of depressed morale, pessimism, and nihilism, partly as a result of members' lack of confidence in their leaders to lead the country out of crisis.

On 10 September 1988 the Independent Peace Association (IPA) issued a nine-point petition, calling for:

(1) the withdrawal of Soviet troops from Czechoslovakia;
(2) the condemnation of the 1968 invasion of Czechoslovakia by those countries which had participated in it (the USSR, East Germany, Poland, and Hungary);
(3) a truthful reevaluation of the Prague Spring of 1968 and its aftermath;
(4) free elections with the possibility of independent candidates;
(5) freedom of the press and the abolition of censorship;
(6) the observance of basic human rights;
(7) the release of political prisoners;
(8) the right of independent associations to engage in public activities without government interference; and
(9) the right to publish this statement complete and verbatim in the public press.[72]

Four months later, three representatives of the official Czechoslovak Peace Committee met with five members of the Independent Peace Association for an hour-long discussion about issues ranging from the imprisonment of IPA members to problems of military service. Significantly, the two sides agreed to hold further meetings and to exchange materials.[73] Meanwhile, public opinion polls found increasing impatience among working people with the slow pace of perestroika in Czechoslovakia.[74] As *Rudé pravo* put it, "More and more people are getting the impression that everything is somehow taking far too long—restructuring is proceeding too slowly."[75]

Meanwhile, there were ever more frequent and bigger demonstrations in Czechoslovakia. In August 1988, for example, 10,000 people marched in protest through the streets of Prague to mark the twentieth anniversary of the invasion. Just two months later, about 5,000 people assembled at Wenceslas Square on the seventieth anniversary of Czechoslovak independence and demanded political change and more freedom. In December 1988 there was another demonstration to mark International Human Rights Day, and 5,000–6,000 protesters took part. "The courage to criticize is expanding," said Václav Maly, a dissident priest and Charter 77 member, at that time. "Fear no longer rules. Instead of just talking behind the closed walls of apartments, people now are criticizing in the trams, the buses, and the public squares."[76]

No wonder that the party was looking nervously over its shoulders at events in Poland and Hungary. As Miloš Jakeš, the party general secretary, euphemistically put it, "A certain role is also played by anxiety over the developments in Poland and Hungary, where serious changes are taking place. This naturally arouses concern."[77] By summer 1989 Czechoslovakia was already ripe for change and vulnerable to any "trigger."

That trigger came with the East German exodus; some of the East Germans even escaped via the West German embassy in Prague under the very noses of the already disaffected Czechs. On 28 October 1989 some 10,000 protesters took to the streets; the police dispersed the demonstrators, detaining 355 of them. Prague subsequently announced that it would ease travel restrictions and that Czechoslovaks would no longer require formal exit visas to travel to Yugoslavia and the West. They hoped that this would defuse some of the discontent. The Soviets were skeptical, however, and sent a high-level message to the Prague regime in early November, warning against further delay in introducing political reform. (The Soviets sent a similar message to Bulgaria's Todor Zhivkov at this time, which is credited with having persuaded Zhivkov to resign.)

But society had crossed an important threshold and there were repeated mass demonstrations in November, culminating in a march by 200,000 protesters through the streets of Prague on 20 November. There were similar marches the same day in at least three other cities—Bratislava, Brno, and Ostrava. The following day Czechoslovakia's communist leaders held talks for the first time with representatives of the opposition, while more than 200,000 people continued to demonstrate in the fifth straight day of protests. People shouted for an end to communist rule and for democratic freedom. Eighty thousand students also went on strike throughout the country, and three small provincial teachers' colleges were the only institutions of higher learning to remain open. By 23 November the crowd on Prague's streets had grown to an estimated 250,000. Václav Havel, the distinguished Czech playwright, addressed the crowd, saying, "We want to live in a free, democratic, and prospering Czechoslovakia, returned to Europe, and we will never give up this ideal."[78] Alexander Dubček, increasingly the subject of speculations centering on a possible return to politics, called for the resignation of the government and, on 23 November in a short address to about 70,000 demonstrators in Bratislava, gave his support to the resistance. The enthusiatic crowds chanted "President Dubček!"

Even Bulgaria felt the ripples from the East German exodus. After some 5,000 people took to the streets, seventy-eight-year-old Zhivkov resigned and fifty-three-year-old Petar Mladenov took the reins as the new general secretary. Promising democratic change, Mladenov organized a street rally to smash pictures of Zhivkov and muster support for his promises of reform. Some 10,000 people took part, but when the official program was over, 150 went to communist party headquarters and shouted "Democracy!" and "Freedom!" In taciturn, passive Bulgaria, that was itself an unusual occurrence. Bulgaria's Mladenov seemed to have in mind largely cosmetic changes, but it is noteworthy that immediately after his accession, a government prosecutor told the Supreme Court that a lower-court ban on the independent environmentalist group Eco-Glasnost was politically motivated and legally unjustifiable.[79] Registration of Eco-Glasnost would be a first step in the direction of the pluralization of Bulgaria. Meanwhile, changes in the structure and organization of the leading bodies of the Bulgarian CP were in preparation.[80]

Only Romania's Ceaușescu held back, seemingly oblivious of the turmoil unfolding on all sides. Romania predictably condemned the exodus of East Germans to the West, calling Hungary's abrogation of its earlier agreement to return refugees to East Germany "an instance of open interference in the internal affairs of the GDR."[81] The party daily *Scînteia* published a lengthy article defending Romania's separate path and arguing for the superiority of Romania's "worker democracy" over Western-style multiparty systems.[82] But Ceaușescu did not stop at that. On the contrary, in a speech to a plenary session of the central committee of the Romanian CP on 28 June 1989 the Romanian president revived the Brezhnev Doctrine, restating that the fate of socialism anywhere is the concern of the entire bloc:

> We feel seriously concerned about certain issues arising in various countries, because we want all socialist countries, all our neighbors, to make sure that they proceed firmly on the path of socialism. We therefore take the view that it would be of great importance for the countries of the Warsaw Pact, and for the socialist countries generally, to analyze jointly the current issues of socialist construction and to devise more

effective means for joint action in order to overcome the difficulties and to ensure that the socioeconomic development of each people proceeds on the path of socialism.[83]

In keeping with this doctrine, Ceauşescu tried to mobilize the Warsaw Pact in August to prevent the transfer of power to the Solidarity-led coalition government in Poland.[84] High-level Romanian officials also made vague threats against Hungary, announcing that Romania now had nuclear capability, while the Romanian army chief of staff intimated that the 1920 Treaty of Trianon, which stripped Hungary of Transylvania, was "unjust" because there were still regions in Hungary which included ethnic Romanians.[85] The chief of staff did not mention that with the constant flight of Romanians out of Romania, the Romanian contingent in Hungary had recently been augmented. Romanian discontent was already legendary, but the population was frightened, cowed, and careful. " 'We watch Bulgarian television, we listen to short-wave radio, we know about the developments [in other parts of Eastern Europe],' a young Romanian said, phrasing words that, even if overheard, would at most sound ambiguous. 'It is all very interesting.' "[86]

The Future of Europe

"The political situation is not stable. A new balance is emerging. . . . The real challenge is to change people's mind set."[87] So said Mieczysław Rakowski, the Polish communist party chief in October 1989. At this writing (June 1990), the future seems to promise at least four areas of major change.

The Restoration of Private Enterprise. Reprivatization is a high priority item in Czechoslovakia, East Germany, Hungary, Poland, and Yugoslavia, and a lesser one in Romania and Bulgaria. Popular pressure combined with economic constraint has forced all these countries to confront the question of reprivatization. Even in once-proud East Germany there has been a different tune. For example, Hans Modrow, who served briefly as premier from November 1989 to May 1990, said, "The GDR is open to suggestions by our capitalist partners that earlier were handled gingerly or fell on deaf ears. Joint ventures, direct investment, profit transfers, pilot projects to preserve the environment are no longer foreign words to us."[88] In Hungary, national bank officials foresaw that within a matter of a few years, the private sector could account for up to one-third of the social product.[89] In Poland a recent law made possible the conversion of public-sector enterprises into private concerns—a process to be accomplished in part by distributing shares to the workers themselves. Joint ventures are a key ingredient in the new rush to free enterprise economy. As of late 1989 Yugoslavia had about 400 joint ventures, Hungary had more than 300, and Poland about a hundred. Salgótarján Glass Wool, a Japanese-Hungarian joint venture, started operations in October 1989. The Hungarians have also pursued talks with Japan's Suzuki Motor Company and with the Ford Motor Company.[90] In addition, in November 1989 General Electric took advantage of new laws in Hungary to buy out the Tungsram light-bulb company for $150 million. Where East Germany is concerned, West Germany's Deutsche Bank AG, Volkswagen, the AEG AG technology group, and the Schering AG chemical group are among the concerns poised to enter the new market.[91] As of early 1989, there had been only 562 joint ventures between Western companies and companies in Eastern Europe, excluding East Germany. By the end of June 1990, the number of joint ventures in the region had risen to 5,070.[92] Within ten years the economies of most of the East European states may not look very different from the economies of Sweden or Austria (the examples usually cited by East Europeans).

The Integration of Europe. The process of reprivatization will in turn encourage the reemergence of Europe—what Gorbachev has taken to calling "our common house." Already Hungary has applied for admission to the Council of Europe, and the word is out that both Hungary and Yugoslavia are interested in joining the European Economic Community (EEC), if given the chance.[93] There are other forces at work too, such as the Alpine-Adriatic group, which brings together parts of West Germany, Hungary, Italy, Austria, and Yugoslavia in regional economic and infrastructure cooperation. Moreover, Italy, Austria, Hungary, and Yugoslavia met in Budapest in mid-November 1989 to discuss a special arrangement for regional economic cooperation.[94] The result was the creation of the Danube-Adriatic Community. The new organization held its second conference in Bratislava in May 1990, at which time Czechoslovakia adhered to the grouping. At the organization's third conference in Venice in August 1990, problems of ethnic minorities and human rights were discussed—an indication that the organization would not restrict its interests to narrow economic and ecological questions.[95]

The integration of Europe necessarily means more regional groupings that transcend the old East-West division, more political, economic, and cultural cooperation, and a shift in trade. Hungary, for example, has moved to put its trade with the USSR on a hard-currency accounting basis and to shift more of its trade to the West, and in May 1990 announced that it would open talks with the EEC about the question of Hungary's entry.[96] Leaders of Czechoslovakia, Poland, and Yugoslavia have also been concerned about integrating their economies into the rest of Europe. Czechoslovakia has pursued ties with Austria with particular vigor.[97]

The End of COMECON and the Warsaw Pact. The emerging integration of Europe had an immediate impact on perspectives on COMECON and the Warsaw Pact. By June 1990 the Warsaw Pact had returned the armies of the East European states to national command and its members had agreed to study ways to transform the pact into a "democratic alliance." The Czechoslovak government seemed to want to retain the Warsaw Pact, arguing that its preservation would prevent the isolation of the USSR from Europe and provide a balance to U.S. and/or German influence. The Hungarian government, by contrast, demanded the dissolution of the pact and announced its intention to withdraw from the pact by the end of 1990. The Polish government likewise let it be known that it had no use for the Warsaw Pact. In February 1991, the Warsaw Pact was officially dissolved, and, in that same month, ministers from Poland, Czechoslovakia, and Hungary signed a political club, citing the need to counter the continuing Soviet threat.[98]

As for COMECON, a two-day meeting of COMECON representatives in January 1990 produced an agreement to appoint a working group to study ways of restructuring and redesigning the trade group. The official headquarters of COMECON was to be closed down, and the December 1990 meeting in Budapest was said to be the organization's "last" meeting. There was talk of a successor organization, to be based on strictly voluntary membership. In February 1991, COMECON was likewise dissolved.[99] Meanwhile, bilateral trade agreements between ex-bloc countries or between them and a reunited Germany continue to increase in number and importance.

And finally, the various multilateral coordinative meetings through which the Soviets have long monitored policies in the economic sphere, youth affairs, church-state relations, and so on have already withered away. They could not but do so.

Germany. Then there is the German question, a question which has two faces: German reunification (suddenly discussed in late 1989 after years of repression), and West Germany's role in the new Eastern Europe. The complete collapse of the facade of East German legitimacy, carefully cultivated in the 1970s and 1980s, inevitably reopened the question of reunification. Germans on both sides of the border have always resented the division of their country and looked with longing toward the idea of eventual reunification. In surveys taken in October 1989, 79 percent of West Germans and 71 percent of East Germans said they favored reunification.[100] Almost overnight, German reunification moved from being impossible to being absolutely certain. By July 1990 currency union was achieved as a first step toward unity. Perhaps surprisingly, the Great Powers went along with the idea.

The Soviets at first tried to suggest that German reunification be put to a world referendum. This rather unprecedented proposal failed to obtain any Western support and by February 1990 the Soviets signalled their acceptance of the principle of reunification. The question remained as to the status of the two Germanys in the rival military pacts. At first the Soviets categorically rejected the idea that a reunited Germany could be a member of NATO, as West German Chancellor Helmut Kohl wanted. Later Gorbachev proposed that Germany be a member of *both* pacts. When this was rejected by Kohl and U.S. President George Bush, Gorbachev returned with a new compromise, suggesting that "West" German troops could remain in NATO without "East" German troops playing a corresponding role in either the Warsaw Pact or NATO. Reunited Germany would enjoy full membership in NATO and associate membership in the Warsaw Pact, and, according to Gorbachev's vision, honor all obligations deriving from both alliances. This idea was likewise immediately rejected by Kohl as "unacceptable because it completely misunderstands the purpose and foundations of NATO."[101] A NATO spokesperson added, "A united Germany must have the right, recognized in the Helsinki Final Act, to choose to be a party to a treaty of alliance, without the establishment of constraints on its sovereignty."[102]

By June German reunification appeared unstoppable. There was, to begin with, huge pressure for reunification from the population itself, especially in the east. Second, all the Great Powers had sanctioned reunification, at least in principle. Third, East Germany was by then governed by Christian Democratic Premier Lothar de Maizière, who owed his election to his image as a loyal ally of Kohl's and a firm advocate of reunification. And fourth, the two Germanys were moving with dispatch to achieve currency union, and by February Bonn earmarked $4.1 billion in economic aid to shore up East Germany's sagging economy.

On 16 July the USSR agreed that united Germany could be a full member of NATO, and that the 860,000 Soviet troops stationed in what was then East Germany would be withdrawn over a period of three to four years. The following day, Poland declared itself satisfied with German guarantees of its western borders. These agreements removed the last obstacles to German reunification. Later, in September, the West German and Soviet governments signed a twenty-year friendship treaty, under which the Germans extended a DM3 billion interest-free loan to Moscow to cover the costs of maintaining Soviet troops in the eastern part of the country and of withdrawing them to the USSR.[103] On 3 October 1990 the two Germanys were united as one.

Even prior to the reopening of the reunification issue, West Germany was already playing a greater role in Eastern Europe by 1989, and prospects looked good for growth in Germany's role. On the one hand, the West German government extended generous credits to Hungary, Poland, and East Germany in 1989. And on the other hand, West German businessmen have quickly made contacts in Hungary and East Germany, and the 1990s are apt to see the rapid spread of German industrial capital throughout much of Eastern Europe.

Conclusion

When I started writing this book in the fall of 1987, it was already clear that Eastern Europe was in a phase of transition. The gerontocrats were approaching their biological limits. Gorbachev was sending out loud signals that the East European elites had to reform and that reform was urgent. And among the societies of the region, multifaceted changes in cultural outlook and social behavior were transforming the political consciousness of people. The sundry associations of independent activists contributed to this process by providing independent sources of information and critical analysis.

In 1987 it was also clear that the old political formulae has exhausted their practicability everywhere, except perhaps in Albania and Bulgaria (and Bulgaria did not look quite so clear by 1989). As early as 1984 the signs of erosion in East Germany were clear. As I wrote at that time,

> There are four preconditions for the translation of economic disaffection into widespread dissent: (1) a general perception of the situation as a problem (by comparison with past performance, performance in other countries, or promises held out by the leadership); (2) a widespread belief that the political elite is responsible for the problem and that it must be opposed (or even overthrown); (3) a diffuse hope; and (4) a belief in one's ability to effect change in one's own condition. . . . The first condition exists in East Germany, and perhaps also the third. Moreover, there is ample material suggesting that many East Germans hold

the regime responsible for some of the economic problems (and of course for the militarization of society and the tight political controls). [At this point] it is far from clear, however, that there is anything like a general consensus that the regime "must be opposed"—and actually some evidence to the contrary. . . . [But] economic malaise has the potential of being translated into social dissent, widespread protest, and even—in theory—social disintegration.[104]

The signs of pressure for change were even clearer in Hungary, Poland, and Yugoslavia, although the ethnic factor in Yugoslavia has imposed some constraints on system adaptability.

What was not clear in 1987 was that the winds of change would come not in a matter of years, but months, and that Czechoslovakia and even Bulgaria would feel them. Still, by late 1988 Czechoslovak officials were treating the subject seriously. Josef Kempný, a member of the Czechoslovak party central committee, hinted at the gravity of the challenge in a September 1988 article for *Rudé pravo*: "Restructuring [*perestroika*] requires that we fundamentally change many things in politics, the economy, the social and cultural spheres, ideology, education, in ethics, and attitudes to[ward] society—simply everywhere."[105]

Gorbachev's genius lay in his having understood both that all-embracing change had become inevitable and that it need not work to Soviet disadvantage. On the contrary, by staking out a position in the forefront of change, Gorbachev became a symbol of hope in Eastern Europe and thus minimized the risk that pressures for democratization would be associated with anti-Soviet feeling. Moreover, as the United States and Germany step in with credits and trade offers, some of the economic pressure is taken off of Moscow, and to the extent that the transformation of Eastern Europe will include its economic recovery, that recovery will likewise redound to Soviet advantage. And finally, by pushing the East German, Czechoslovak, and Bulgarian parties to adapt, and allowing the communist parties to transform themselves, Gorbachev at least opened up the possibility of finding stable paths to pluralization, and of finding a more satisfactory basis for mutually beneficial relations between the USSR and the East European states.

14 The Great Transformation

The LDPD is, if I can put it this way, in favor of a socialism that is fun. That means that it does not merely proclaim joy in life, but makes it possible. — Manfred Gerlach, chairman of the Liberal Democratic Party of Germany (31 October 1989)

In the space of little more than a year, the one-party monopolies of Eastern Europe crumbled, and instead of dissolving into fratricidal chaos, as some pessimists had feared, these societies quickly gave rise to a welter of new political formations. By early 1990 there were 17 political parties operating in East Germany, 80 in Poland, 35 in Czechoslovakia (22 appearing on the June 1990 ballots), 22 in Hungary, 78 in Romania, 35 in Bulgaria, and more than 86 in Yugoslavia (3 in Bosnia, 31 in Croatia, 6 in Kosovo, 2 in Macedonia, 13 in Montenegro, 6 in Serbia, 19 in Slovenia, and 6 in Vojvodina). Many of these are embryonic parties with little power and few prospects. Some are little more than special interest associations, such as the Liberal Sexual Party in Hungary, the Friends of Beer Party and the Union of Rabbit-Raisers in Czechoslovakia, and the Hungarian Health Party.[1]

The rapid disintegration of communism—poignantly evinced in the rapid closure of party organizations in enterprises and communities—raised a new set of elites to prominence. Suddenly, politics was dominated by a number of literary and artistic figures: nine of the thirteen members of the Hungarian cabinet were historians, including the prime minister (a specialist in the history of medicine) and the foreign minister (a specialist in Hungarian-British relations); the prime minister of East Germany was a former orchestral musician (a viola player); the prime minister of Poland was a Catholic intellectual and journalist; the president of Czechoslovakia was a playwright; the president of Lithuania was a music professor; the leader of East Germany's new Social Democratic Party (Ibrahim Böhme) was a historian; the incumbent director of the New York Philharmonic (Kurt Masur) was a guiding spirit in the New Forum opposition movement; Kiril Marichkov, leader of the Shturtsi (Crickets—Bulgaria's no. 1 rock 'n' roll band) was elected to parliament; the Czechoslovak head of protocol (Pavel Kantor) was a rock singer; Michal Kočab, once a "heart-throb," was an MP in Czechoslovakia; and in fact, the entire Czechoslovak administration in particular was filled with rock musicians, DJs, rock writers, and journalists. Other slots were taken by other intellectuals, including priests and ex-dissidents. It appeared unlikely that these literary and artistic figures could play more than a transitional role before professional politicians and lawyers would take the reins. But their rise to power, even if transitory, showed where legitimacy was vested after four decades of communism.

The Great Transformation also excited hopes among advocates of restorationist politics, and a string of monarchs reappeared and offered to return to the throne—including Crown Prince Alexander of Serbia/Yugoslavia, King Michael of Romania, Tsar Simeon of Bulgaria, and a collective Union of the Nobility of Russia organized by Prince Golitsyn.[2] In Bulgaria local monarchists were registering 30,000 signatures a day (as of June 1990) in support of monarchical restoration, while in Hungary, in a striking contrast, seventy-seven-year old Otto von Habsburg, scion of the dynastic house that once ruled Austria and Hungary, declined the nomination of the Independent Smallholders Party for the post of president of the republic.[3]

In Romania the fascist Iron Guard was revived in early 1990. In February the organization issued a short proclamation:

> The armed anticommunist organization, the Iron Guards, the Legion of the Archangel Michael, is being set up again after 45 years. The Iron Guards will fight against all those who advocate any leftist ideology. We will not stop until we have eliminated all communists, socialists, and other leftist monsters. Force is our creed. . . . Our time has come at last. The country will be ours again. Heil Hitler! We will prevail![4]

There was no clue as to the membership of the Iron Guards, but it seemed to be headquartered in the city of Bacău in eastern Romania.

Overnight, Eastern Europe has been transformed and the old political-economic order has passed from the scene. In taking stock of this transformation, one may say that there are at least four preconditions for the stabilization of a political-economic order: (1) some level of efficacy of formal institutions; (2) a modicum of correspondence between the actual behavior of administrative and legal institutions, and the normative rules which govern their behavior; (3) the satisfaction of the basic economic and adjudicative needs of the population; and (4) a basic acceptance of the legitimacy of the "rules of the political game" by the populace. The greater the shortcomings with respect to these four criteria, the greater the decay of formal institutions and the greater the tendency for informal, underground, countercultural, and dissident-type organizations to arise.

There are many questions which an informed observer must ask herself or himself, including: Why now? Why not earlier? Why everywhere at once? And how important was Gorbachev in unleashing the furies of headlong change?

Why now? Societies, like individuals, have psychological states, and are psychological beings, which accordingly pass through stages. The quickening rhythm of crisis in the region (1956, 1968, 1976, in several Polish cities in 1980–81, and finally 1989) was a sign that the equilibrium was unstable, and that the pressures for change were becoming steadily less containable. The development of dissident networks and samizdat information channels were vital in preparing the way for revolution, as was the example set by Solidarity in 1980–81.

Why not earlier? In actual fact, the people of Eastern Europe attempted to resist many times in the past. In Poland, in particular, anticommunist guerrillas fought the new communist regime for a few years, but without success. In East Germany in 1953 and Hungary in 1956, popular uprisings proclaimed the overthrow of communism. But in each of these cases, resistance was smashed by overwhelming military force. Gorbachev signalled very clearly that he considered the use of force unacceptable; in this way he changed the rules of the game and, ultimately, the game itself.

At first sight it may seem that my answers to these first two questions are diametrically opposed. The synthesis which I see is that the use of military force became unacceptable in large part because of changes in society, and not simply because Gorbachev had a different outlook. The change had been evolutionary, and Gorbachev simply recognized what Brezhnev had refused to allow.

Why everywhere at once? Despite initial imperviousness, ultimately even Albania has followed the pack, at least in part. Why? Because once populations see that change is possible, unstable equilibria become completely untenable, and illegitimate elites are simply washed away in a tidal wave. It is not that Romania or Albania, for example, should be expected to adopt multiparty parliamentary systems along Czechoslovak and Hungarian lines, but that these countries have also experienced change.

This points to a fact sometimes denied by ultra liberals: In political and economic terms, Eastern Europe was very much a "set." These countries had similar systems, similar policies, similar elites, and, as a result, similar problems and similar fates. The one case which was always hugely divergent—Yugoslavia—is even now divergent, and pursues pluralization at its own fragmented pace.

How important was the Gorbachev factor? In a word, it was *catalytic*. I have tried to show how the pressures for change built up steadily in sundry social sectors, but Gorbachev clearly quickened the process, as I explained in the preceding chapter.

In the remainder of this chapter, I will discuss the most recent developments in the eight countries of the region, basically from November 1989 to October 1990. They will be taken in alphabetical order for the sake of convenience.

Albania

The first on my list, it was the last to feel the winds of change. One of the earliest hints of change came in May 1989 at a plenary session of the Union of Writers and Artists. In what was a surprisingly daring speech (by Albanian standards), author Kico Blushi, editor-in-chief of the literary monthly *Nentori*, told his listeners that "civilized debate" and public criticism of policies were essential to Albania, and urged the state to show tolerance of criticism. Only a few months later, the state publishing house in Tiranë published Neshat Tozaj's *Knives*, a novel that contained harsh and explicit criticism of the *Sigurimi*, the state security police. Soon thereafter, Ismail Kadare, considered Albania's most successful author, gave an interview to the magazine *Zeri i Rinise*, in which he echoed Tozaj's criticism of the *Sigurimi*, asserting that the *Sigurimi* had fostered "a criminal psychosis . . . that [drove the] country toward crime."[5]

Meanwhile, it was proving impossible to insulate Albanian society from at least some awareness of the processes of change sweeping the rest of Eastern Europe. Albanians were tuning in to Yugoslav and Italian radio stations, and were hearing reports about the Great Transformation. Inevitably, the Albanian media had to address the subject. *Zeri i Popullit* did so in October 1989, with a page 4 story headlined "Fruit of the Ideology of Counterrevolutionary Reformism." Although the article heaped abuse on reform-minded politicians in Hungary, it also admitted that Hungarian politics was repluralizing, that the Hungarian Democratic Forum had won three times as many votes in the regional parliamentary elections as the Hungarian Socialist Workers Party, and that the HSWP had committed itself to the restoration of economic free enterprise.[6] The considerable Albanian interest in these events was conceded by party leader Ramiz Alia at a meeting of the Trade Unions Council in December 1989, although he categorically ruled out the possibility that anything similar could happen in Albania because the country's political evolution was historically different.

Yet, in January 1990 there were Greek and Yugoslav reports of unrest in northern Albania, and of the imposition of harsh security measures in Shkodër, Albania's second largest city. Although Albanian officials denied the truth of these rumors, the government passed a series of liberalizing measures in early May 1990 that among other things, restored freedom of religion and freedom to travel abroad.[7] Alia also called for further reforms, including an easing of price controls, to encourage collective farm workers to sell more fresh produce in the towns.[8] Albania also announced that it now wanted a role in the Conference on Security and Cooperation in Europe, and that it was prepared to resume diplomatic relations with both the United States and the Soviet Union.

These changes were important, but they were, all the same, slight and late in coming. Albanian society has been much weaker than the other societies of Europe, and as of spring 1990 most informed observers predicted only modest reforms within the context of the preservation of a one-party system.

Throughout 1990, there were large protests in various Albanian cities, including Tiranë, Shkodër, and Kavajë, and at least one person was shot dead by police in a July demonstration (in Kavajë). During July, more than 6,000 Albanian citizens took refuge in foreign embassies accredited to Tiranë, and succeeded in obtaining asylum in Australia, the United States, and a number of West European countries. Under the impact of this pressure, the Albanian government sacked a number of reputed hardliners, including Interior Minister Simon Stefani, Defense Minister Prokop Mura, and Politburo members Rita Marko, Manush Myftiu, and Lenka Cuko.[9] The government also took the first step toward the reprivatization of agriculture by allowing farmers to have private plots, and passed a new law allowing foreign investment in Albania.[10] In the sphere of foreign relations, Albania resumed diplomatic ties with the USSR in late July, and by October was actively exploring the possibility of opening diplomatic and other cooperative ties with Israel.[11]

Bulgaria

Bulgaria has been unique in another way—by giving the communists their first electoral victory in free elections in Eastern Europe in June 1990.

The drama of Bulgaria's transformation can be dated to November 1989. An important meeting of the central committee had been scheduled for 11 November, but on 10 November Petar Mladenov, long-time foreign minister, was in Moscow as the guest of the Soviet government. The Soviets evidently urged the dismissal of party secretary Todor Zhivkov for, upon returning to Bulgaria the next day, Mladenov quickly engineered Zhivkov's removal—a move sanctioned at the scheduled meeting.[12] Even before the month was out, the trade unions would declare their independence.[13] Later, the Bulgarian Communist Party would rename itself the Socialist Party, repudiate the disciplinary principle of democratic centralism,[14] and promise the end of press censorship. Other changes quickly followed.

In the wake of Zhivkov's ouster, the Bulgarian Writers' Union posthumously readmitted Bulgarian émigré writer Georgi Markov to its ranks. Markov had been excoriated by the regime and then assassinated with a poison-tipped umbrella in London in 1978. Now he was being granted a full rehabilitation: his memoirs were serialized in the trade union daily *Trud* and in the monthly journal *Otechestvo*, and Markov's widow, Annabel, was received in January 1990 by Politburo member Aleksander Lilov (later party secretary), who promised her that there would be a judicial investigation into Markov's murder.[15] At the same time, various writers involved in opposition activities, such as Blaga Dimitrova, Markov Ganchev, Georgi Mishev, and Stefan Prodev, suddenly found it possible to publish their works in Bulgaria.

Nor was Markov the only figure to be posthumously rehabilitated. Traicho Kostov, a prominent Politburo member executed in 1949 on fabricated charges of antiparty activity, was fully rehabilitated in mid-December 1989, when the party central committee adopted a resolution declaring that all the charges against Kostov had been "slanderous and untrue."[16] Various other party figures persecuted under Zhivkov were rehabilitated in early January 1990. Bulgaria also published figures of the number of people executed without trial, imprisoned, and otherwise repressed after 1944, and in December 1989 issued a formal apology for taking part in the Warsaw Pact invasion of Czechoslovakia in 1968.

By this point the party was suffering an internal crisis of confidence. Symptomatic of this crisis of confidence was its admission that socialist property relations were just as alienating as capitalist property relations. In particular, the army newspaper *Narodna armiya* noted, "State property in Bulgaria has never been managed by the people. Its management was a privilege of the government departments that control this property in the name of the state."[17]

There started to be some response from the public, who participated in public rallies throughout the country, demanding democracy and an end to one-party rule. In late February 1990, for example, 200,000 people packed Sofia's central square to demonstrate against the communist party. People started to talk about a return to monarchy. Tsar Simeon II, who lived in exile in Madrid, was interviewed on Bulgarian television, but despite his evident popularity, a poll of 3,128 Bulgarians showed that only 6 percent favored a restoration of the monarchy.[18] Despite the poll, the issue came to occupy a niche on the public agenda, and the Christian Republican Party, although committed to a republic, considered it appropriate to call for a public referendum on the question, monarchy or republic.[19]

In a matter of months, sundry independent social and political associations came into being, including a Gypsy union, an independent Jewish organization, the Independent Committee for the Defense of Religious Rights, an independent union, and several social democratic parties. The Agrarian Union, freed of communist dominance and reorganized as an independent centrist party, claimed 136,000 members by February 1990.[20] And an opposition press gradually emerged, with such publications as *Svoboden Narod* (organ of the Social Democratic Party), *Narodno Zemedelsko* (organ of the Agrarian Party), *Ekopolitika* (organ of the Green Party), and *Dano*, an unaffiliated magazine devoted to power, business, and sex.[21]

Bulgarian society was awakening—but only belatedly and slowly. A *Der Spiegel* interview probed this issue with opposition figure Petko Simeonov:

> *Der Spiegel*: Why has the Bulgarian opposition woken up only now and has not moved for 40 years?
> Simeonov: Our opposition was and is weak. In addition, it consists almost exclusively of intellectuals, and we lack the responsibility of the intellectuals toward society. . . . [Now] according to a recent poll by the newspaper *Trud*, about half of [the] population are in favor of implementing *perestroika* and *glasnost*.
> *Der Spiegel*: Why not more?
> Simeonov: Because the people are still afraid and because they are busy the whole day long trying to ensure their very existence. The Bulgarians spend more time standing in line than educating their children. In

rural areas, the shelves are empty: no bread, no eggs, no sausage. This does not leave any time for political philosophies.[22]

By January 1990 the communist party was sitting down for talks with leading figures of the opposition, following a pattern already set in Czechoslovakia, Hungary, and Poland. That same month, parliament abolished the communist party's political monopoly, and declared Bulgaria a *democratic* rather than a socialist republic. In the universities, Marxism-Leninism ceased to be a required subject. The Office for Church Affairs, long entrusted with the task of controlling the legal religious establishments, was dismantled. The censorship office was closed. And Department Six, the police unit hitherto entrusted with the surveillance of dissidents, was dissolved.

Finally, in mid-June, after two rounds of elections that some observers said were tainted by fear, the ex-communist party (renamed the Bulgarian Socialist Party) won an absolute majority in the 400-seat unicameral parliament (211 deputies), with 144 deputies elected by the Union of Democratic Forces (a 16-party coalition), 23 by the Turkish Movement for Rights and Freedom, 16 by the Agrarian Party, and 6 by independents. The communists claimed to have won 48 percent of the vote,[23] but the opposition soon charged fraud and manipulation.[24]

Postelection polls found that young people had preferred the opposition Union of Democratic Forces (UDF) to the Bulgarian Socialist Party by a margin of 49.5 percent to 33.8 percent (with the rest of the vote splintered among smaller parties), and that the popularity of the socialists was sinking steadily, even as that of the UDF continued to rise.[25]

The socialists quickly developed problems. In early July Petar Mladenov was forced to resign as president of Bulgaria after a videotape showed him discussing the use of tanks to suppress an antigovernment protest. The parliament chose Zhelyu Zhelev, the fifty-nine-year-old head of the UDF, to replace him as president. Meanwhile, the socialists fell into disarray, amid squabbling between the liberal and conservative wings of the party. Prime Minister Andrei Lukanov (a socialist) was reconfirmed by Zhelev, and attempted to put together a coalition government with the UDF. When the UDF refused to consider a coalition, Lukanov eventually proposed an all-socialist cabinet in September, extending an invitation to the opposition to engage in talks about economic reform and land reform.[26]

Gradually, signs of change emerged. The embalmed body of Georgi Dimitrov, the founder of Bulgarian communism, was removed from its mausoleum in July and cremated. In August thousands of anticommunist protesters stormed Socialist Party headquarters, ransacked it, and set it on fire; thousands more demonstrated in protest of this action. In September, Bulgaria's first privately owned bank—appropriately named the First Private Bank—started operations. And in October 1990 the government outlined a comprehensive economic reform that would include the reprivatization of the economy and the marketization of prices, and the parliament began to consider a bill to depoliticize the army, police, law courts, prosecuting magistracy, and ministry of foreign affairs, removing these agencies from socialist party control.[27]

Meanwhile, Bulgaria confronted the results of a decline in production, and braced for food shortages, price hikes, and electricity shortfalls.[28] In these conditions, the crime rate soared, stirring expressions of concern in the media.[29]

Czechoslovakia

Change in Czechoslovakia was adumbrated in the cultural sphere, especially in the theater and in the film industry, but also in literature. In January 1989 the Czech ministry of culture ordered the return to library shelves of the works of more than 100 banned authors. At the same time, the Union of Czech Writers convened a meeting at which speakers criticized literary policy and upbraided the censorship applied in the cultural sphere. In spring 1989 two Czech writers, Petr Prouza and Ondrej Neff, held talks in West Germany with Czech émigré writers, and in September 1989, the Czech and Slovak writers' unions participated in a conference in Franken, West Germany, with their émigré cohorts. Writers and critics talked of undoing what exiled writer Milan Kundera called the "massacre of Czech culture" in the post-1968 era of "normalization."

In early 1989 several new films tackled subjects that had previously been taboo. Films made in the liberal era of the late 1960s, and not seen since then, were cleared for release; these included *The Joke* (based on Kundera's novel), *All My Good Countrymen*, and *A Coach to Vienna*. Also cleared was Karel Vachek's *Related through Choice*, a documentary dealing with behind-the-scenes political activities of Dubček and other politicians in 1968. In May there was even a Kafka festival in Prague. Since Kafka had always been the *bête noire* of the communists, this was in itself an important barometer of change. And in October communist authorities agreed to a new law, changing the way in which theaters would be managed and essentially dismantling the censorship apparatus in the theater.

By summer 1989 tension in Czechoslovakia was rising, and there was a sense that things were coming to a head. František Cardinal Tomášek of Prague, then ninety years old, addressed just this question in a letter to government officials dated 4 August, in which he warned of a "dangerous tension [between the authorities and] a growing number of citizens demanding a say in how society is run."[30]

The political infrastructure was also starting to crumble, and usually docile politicians started to speak out without fear. The Czechoslovak People's Party (CPP) issued repeated calls for internal renewal. In June 1989, for example, CPP deputy Chairman Bohumil Svoboda told a session of the municipal committee,

> They try to make us believe that criticism of the party's leadership amounts to antiparty activity. In such a case we have to ask ourselves who the party is: those in the upper echelons, about whom the people laugh or cry, or the regular members? And then they tell us that the party is not in a critical state. . . . Events of the recent weeks have, unfortunately, illustrated that the People's Party leadership is apparently not able to handle the critical situation in which the party finds itself. Thousands of letters from members and a number of documents prove that. It is, moreover, questionable whether the current leadership is able to face our present problems. Not one member of the Central Committee even considers stepping down for the sake of the party. Instead, they seek police protection at the party's regional meetings "to ensure order." Or do they need protection for themselves?[31]

On 14 October seventy-three CPP members and officials met in Prague and formed an internal reform movement called the Stream of Rebirth, dedicated to re-Christianizing the party. Within the CPP there were also signs of internal fissure.

Meanwhile, Soviet President Gorbachev was losing patience with Prague's old-style communism. As early as late 1988, General Alois Lorenc, head of the Czechoslovak secret police, met secretly with certain prominent party officials to work out a plot to remove party secretary Miloš Jakeš. The plan, code-named Operation Wedge, was worked out in cooperation with the Soviet KGB and called for replacing Jakeš with Zdenek Mlynar, a member of Dubček's reform government of 1968, who was living in exile in Vienna (though Mlynar reportedly was not willing to cooperate). The plan called for the organization of mass unrest and the simulation of the death of a student to turn people against Jakeš.[32]

Secret police officer Ludek Živčak infiltrated the student leadership and helped to radicalize it. On 17 November Živčak led crowds of demonstrators to Wenceslas Square for what proved to be the first of several days of protest. Some 20,000 people demanded that Jakeš be fired, chanting "Into the rubbish bin with Jakeš!," "Long live Havel!," and "Down with the monopoly of the Czechoslovak Communist Party!"[33] From the tone of the slogans, it was clear that the secret police could not control the demonstrators. The authorities called in the riot police, who used tear gas and clubs to disperse the demonstrators, and arrested scores of participants, including Alexander Dubček.[34]

The police brutality proved counterproductive. It failed to deter people, who took part in demonstrations across Czechoslovakia in the succeeding weeks, in numbers up to 200,000. The CPP issued a sharp protest against the police repression, thus signalling the party's clear decision to break ranks with the communist regime.[35] Charter 77 likewise condemned the suppression of the 17 November demonstration and called for the party and state leaderships to resign. The Czechoslovak Democratic Initiative, which had declared itself a political party on 11 November, also demanded that the government resign. The Movement for Civil Liberties called for the immediate resignation of the minister of internal affairs and all those involved in the decision to use the police. The suppression of the 17 November demonstration proved to be a catalytic event for Czechoslovakia, just as the August 1988 strikes had been for Poland or the opening of Hungary's borders had been for East Germany. Overnight it changed the way people viewed the balance of political forces.

On 26 November communist Prime Minister Ladislav Adamec entered into negotiations with the Civic Forum, an opposition group formed only a week earlier but associated with Václav Havel. On 3 December Adamec tried to assuage the opposition with what were largely cosmetic changes; he proposed a new twenty-one-member cabinet, in which communists retained sixteen seats, including the defense and interior ministries. The Civic Forum immediately rejected this, and demanded a true coalition government. Four days later Adamec resigned, and was succeeded by his erstwhile deputy, Marian Čalfa. On 9 December the two sides finally came to an agreement, swearing in a new coalition government of "national understanding" the following day. Husák resigned as president, and the hugely popular Václav Havel was elected president. Alexander Dubček, the hero of 1968, became chairman of Parliament.

Within a matter of weeks, several dozen political parties announced themselves, though some amounted to little more than lobby groups or political circles. Among the new parties were the Green Party, the Social Democratic Party, the Free Bloc (adhering to conservative economic liberalism), the Alliance of Farmers and the Countryside, the Czechoslovak Democratic Forum (a left-wing group), the Christian and Democratic Union (uniting the old People's Party and a new Christian Democratic Party), the Movement for Autonomous Democracy in Moravia and Silesia, the Friends of Beer Party (in the Czech republic only), the Public Against Violence (the Slovak sister organization of the Civic Forum), the Slovak Nationalist Party, the Slovak Democratic Party (also nationalist), the Freedom Party (yet another Slovak nationalist party), the Czechoslovak Party for Social Justice, the Liberal Democratic Party in Slovakia, the Republican Party (which modeled itself on American parties and focused on program rather than on recruiting members), a Gypsy party, the Party of Czechoslovak Neutrality (aiming for permanent neutrality on the Swedish and Swiss models), and the Transnational Radical Party (which declared itself the champion of "all minorities"—national, religious, cultural, and sexual).[36] The Slovak Independence Movement, a hitherto émigré organization based in Munich, announced in March 1990 that it would relocate its headquarters to Bratislava and register with the ministry of the interior; the party advocates Slovak independence.[37] The communists also split. First, a group of expelled communists convened in Bratislava in November 1989 and formed a new Democratic Socialist Party. Subsequently, in February 1990 a group of reform-minded communists met in Brno and established a new Czechoslovak Democratic Forum. Even the anarchists revived, and in March 1990 announced the formation of the Czechoslovak Anarchist Association, dedicated to "searching [for] and asserting various forms of autonomy and direct democracy."[38] But perhaps the most innovative of all is the Party of Constructive Destruction established in Hradec Králové in March 1990. *Smena* reported that "its main program is permanent opposition to all other political parties that might grow to form a system similar to the former totalitarian power. Constructive destroyers do not seek political power, have no apparatus, do not own any assets, and, for the time being, do not publish anything of their own."[39]

As for the communist party, it hastily convened an extraordinary congress on 21 December in an effort to take stock and devise a new strategy. In a wide-ranging resolution the congress annulled the existing party statutes and called for the drafting of new statutes; disbanded the People's Militia; appealed to former members expelled after 1968 to rejoin the party; and charged the central committee with the task of objectively assessing the 1968–69 period and subsequent "normalization," and to assess the political responsibility for the crisis.[40]

Change swept the Czechoslovak political landscape with rapidity. By the end of November the Prague government announced that it would dismantle its fortifications along the Austrian border. The secret police was abolished in January, and in February new laws were passed guaranteeing citizens the rights of assembly, association, and petition. A report in the Bratislava daily *Pravda* noted in particular, "No one can be forced to become a member of any association. No one must suffer prejudice because she or he is a member of a certain organization, because she or he participates in its activity, because she or he supports it, or because she or he remains outside of it."[41] Independent newspapers popped up like mushrooms after a rainstorm, beginning with the transformation of the monthly samizdat publication *Lidové Noviny* into a legal daily newspaper. In Prague, Václav Havel's play *Audience* was given its Prague premiere sixteen years after the play was written. The Catholic church benefitted by being allowed to fill the various empty episcopal seats, including the seat of the Prešov Eparchy of the Greek Catholic church, vacant for more than forty years.[42] And the Prague periodical *Prače* published statistics on Stalinist victims in Czechoslovakia, conceding that more than 100,000 persons had been imprisoned and 178 persons had been executed for political crimes between 1948 and 1953. In addition, *Prače* noted, some 8,000 persons were beaten to death during interrogations, were shot at the border, or lost their lives in jails or uranium mines.[43]

The government also closed down the Marxism-Leninism Institute of Charles University, thus ending decades of official indoctrination of that political ideology. And in April 1990 Czech and Slovak jurists and constitutional scholars hosted a conference attended by two dozen of their counterparts from America and Europe. Their objective: to learn from Westerners how to frame a new constitution for Czechoslovakia.

Meanwhile, Prague moved rapidly on the economic front to reintroduce a market economy, stimulate private enterprise, and attract Western capital. One token of this was an agreement signed by Continental AG of West Germany in June 1990 with Czechoslovakia's largest tire company, the Barum Group.[44]

The new government's program of repluralization received an overwhelming endorsement from Czechoslovak voters in June elections, with the Civic Forum (associated with President Havel) capturing some 50 percent of the votes in a crowded field. By contrast, the communists drew only 13 percent of the vote. In late June 1990 President Havel named a new noncommunist coalition government led by the Civic Forum. Headed by Prime Minister Marian Čalfa (who had in the meantime resigned from the communist party), the new government also included Civic Forum's Slovak sister organization, Public Against Violence, and the Slovak-based Christian Democratic Movement.[45]

This new government began immediately to dismantle the state structure organized by the communists. The secret service was depoliticized and stripped of any repressive functions.[46] A new law on joint ventures allowed foreigners to hold *more* than 49 percent of the capital stock in an enterprise.[47] In late October the parliament approved a law to auction off some 100,000 small shops and enterprises that the communists had nationalized, with the ultimate objective of achieving the remarketization of the economy by 1992.[48] A potent symptom of the new atmosphere was the fact that Radio Free Europe, the American anticommunist radio station, was allowed to open an office in Prague in August 1990.[49] Havel himself was confirmed as president by Czechoslovakia's freely elected parliament in July 1990, amid reports that the Civic Forum was splitting into left and right wings.[50]

By September 1990 there were rumors that members of the dissolved secret police were plotting a putsch,[51] and the communist party excited widespread fears the following month, when party general secretary Vasil Mohorita said that the government's reprivatization program "signal[led] an end to national understanding and the beginning of a hard and uncompromising struggle."[52] A few days later, tens of thousands of anticommunist demonstrators crowded into the Old Town Square in a show of solidarity against the discredited communists.

East Germany

Political transformation in East Germany was propelled by the exodus of several hundred thousand East Germans during the summer and early autumn of 1989, by huge protests and demonstrations involving as many as 200,000–500,000 people in Berlin and Leipzig, and by the strengthening of opposition confidence through such methods as the circulation of various petitions (like the appeal by the New Forum signed by 200,000 people within the first twelve days of its legalization.)[53] Unable to cope with these new challenges, two high-ranking SED officials committed suicide: fifty-seven-year-old Helmut Mieth, the party chief of Bautzen; and Gerhard Uhe, the party chief of the city of Perleburg, near Schwerin.[54]

Meanwhile, East Germany introduced freedom of travel and opened its borders on 9 November. Within the first eleven days of the new policy, the East German police issued 10,299,107 visas for private trips, and 17,738 permits for permanent emigration.[55]

With labor shortages created by the sudden exodus of large numbers of East Germans, members of the police and the army were deployed to help staff the state railway, the ministry of health and social services, the Red Cross, and various economic enterprises.[56]

By the beginning of December there was open talk of bringing ex-president Honecker to trial for his responsibility for ruining the country. Arrest warrants were issued for 12 prominent party officials including Erich Mielke (former minister of state security), Günter Mittag (former economic secretary of the SED), Harry Tisch (former trade union chair), and Gerhard Müller (former first secretary of the Erfurt party organization).[57] Fearing further repercussions, police officials started burning their files. Seeing clouds of smoke rising from the windows, citizens occupied police offices in various East German cities to prevent the police from destroying any more files.

Before the end of December 1989 the state security police had been disbanded,[58] with nearly half of its estimated 22,000 employees suddenly thrown out of work. The other half were given jobs in two smaller offices: an intelligence agency and an antisubversion office.

On 3 December, after just forty-nine days in power, Egon Krenz resigned as party chief and chair of the Council of State. Hans Modrow, one of the few communists who still enjoyed some credibility because he had been criticized for reformism by Honecker, remained prime minister, and Liberal Party leader Manfred Gerlach became president. Meanwhile, the SED re-named itself the Party of Democratic Socialism and elected Gregor Gysi, a forty-one-year-old Jewish lawyer who had defended East German dissidents in court, as the new party leader. On 7 December the communists came to an agreement with the democratic opposition to hold free elections on 6 May 1990.

East Germany now experienced the same kind of repluralization that had manifested itself earlier in Hungary and Poland, and would later be seen in Czechoslovakia. Among the new parties and associations that emerged in early 1990 were the Christian Social Party, the German Youth Party, the Potentialist People's Party, the Independent Social Democratic Party, the Ecological-Democratic Party, the Carnations Party (uniting reform Marxists dedicated to a market economy and to preserving a sovereign and separate East Germany),[59] the Entrepreneurs' Association, and an independent police trade union. Many leading communists switched political parties, like Wolfgang Berghofer, the reformist mayor of Dresden who resigned from the communist party to join the Social Democratic Party.[60] Overnight membership in the SED/PDS became stigmatized. *Neues Deutsch-*

land reported in December 1989 that factories were posting signs: "Job vacancies. . . . No SED members need apply."[61]

As in other countries of Eastern Europe, independent newspapers and magazines began publication in early 1990. In the East German context one may mention the *Leipziger Andrea Zeitung* and *Die Andere*, both launched in January 1990, and the *Thüringer Anzeiger*, which started in February.

There were also small signs of change, such as the restoration of text in the national anthem,[62] the disclosure for the first time of the number of East German suicides (5,005 in 1987; 4,768 in 1988),[63] the revelation that the SED had seriously considered building extensive additional internment camps in the 1970s in order to lock up thousands of political dissidents and other opponents,[64] and the political rehabilitation of exiled dissident Rudolf Bahro in June.[65]

In late January the government and the opposition agreed to advance the elections to 18 March. The results came as a surprise to most observers. The Social Democrats, expected by many to take first place, garnered only 22 percent of the vote, while the conservative Alliance for Germany, led by the CDU, took 48 percent. The New Forum, which had emerged during the demonstrations of October and November 1989, collected only 3 percent of the vote. The CDU's strong commitment to early reunification and West German Chancellor Helmut Kohl's strong backing were said to have accounted for the CDU's strong showing (it took 41 percent of the 48 percent for the Alliance as a whole). Lothar de Maizière, viola player and new chair of the CDU-East, became prime minister. The church's strong contribution to the opposition was reflected in three of its pastors being named to the new cabinet: Markus Meckel, leader of the Social Democratic Party, became foreign minister; Rainer Eppelmann, leader of the Democratic Awakening Party, became minister of defense and disarmament; and Hans-Wilhelm Ebeling, leader of the conservative German Social Union, became minister of development aid.

As early as 9 November 1989 the East German government (still controlled, at that point, by the SED) dismantled sections of the Berlin Wall and allowed free movement between East and West Berlin. Germans danced on the wall, and, hungry for souvenirs and mementos, people knocked out pieces of the Wall to take home. In a matter of a few months, the Wall had been largely chipped away.

Popular support for reunification gained strength rapidly, and the movement toward reunification quickly gathered momentum. On 19 May the two Germanys signed a state treaty agreeing to establish economic and monetary union, effective only seven weeks later, on 2 July. The treaty established that West Germany's central bank, the Bundesbank, would control monetary affairs, promised massive West German assistance ($85 billion) to East Germany's flagging economy (with forecasts that it will take at least a decade to bring real per capita income in the east close to what it is in the west), and established a basic conversion rate of two ostmarks (OM) for one deutsche mark (DM). East Germans would be able to convert OM4,000 at the rate of 1-to-1, and beyond that at a rate of 2-to-1. East Germans aged sixty and up would be allowed to exchange up to OM6,000 at the rate of 1-to-1, and children fourteen or younger would be allowed to exchange a maximum of OM2,000 at the special rate.[66] On 1 July the deutsche mark became the national currency of East Germany and the intra-German border was dismantled. On 3 July the East German government agreed to hold all-German parliamentary elections on 2 December 1990.[67] At the same time plans were announced to reorganize East Germany's seventeen provinces into five federal states, in effect restoring the traditional jurisdictional borders which had existed before communism.

The superpowers gave German reunification their blessing, and as of July 1990 it appeared that a reunited Germany would be able to retain membership in the NATO alliance by agreeing to limit its armed forces. West Germany and the United States proposed a nine-point plan to the Soviets, which, inter alia, would guarantee that a united Germany would not develop nuclear, chemical, or biological weapons; would entail German renunciation not merely of Polish territories but also of territories lost to the USSR in World War II; would guarantee that no NATO troops would be stationed in the territory of what was East Germany; and would allow Soviet troops to remain in the area of East Germany for a transition period at German expense. To sweeten the deal, the West German government unilaterally extended a $2.9 billion credit to the Soviet Union to help Gorbachev's economic reform program—the largest Western credit ever made available to the USSR.[68] Ironically, the loan was approved on 22 June, the forty-ninth anniversary of the Nazi invasion of the Soviet Union.

One of the cultural side effects of German reunification was the sudden infusion of Anglicisms, long current in West Germany, into German speech in the eastern territories. Among the loan words currently fashionable in West Germany and now infiltrating East Germany: *dress shirt, city shirt, trend colors, jeans dressing, cash management, after-sales service, skin scent, cleansing scrub, razor burn relief*, and *disco hip-hop*. Also noted on the signs of a sock shop: *on wings of fantasy*.[69]

Oddly, after years of claiming that Bonn was not a "real" capital and that the only city conceivable as a permanent German capital was Berlin, in summer 1990 many West Germans started to express a preference for keeping the capital in Bonn.[70] For their part, the East Germans were counting on the capital moving to Berlin, since they banked on that to fuel the economic revival of eastern Germany. The controversy lasted until early August, when agreement was finally reached that Berlin was to be the capital. But uncertainty remained because it was stipulated in the unification treaty that the all-German legislature to be elected in December 1990 would determine where to locate the various ministries. The implication was that most ministries could well remain in Bonn.[71]

On 23 August the East German parliament agreed to 3 October as the date for German reunification, and the new Germany's united parliament held its first session on 4 October 1990—symbolically in the old *Reichstag* building.

Hungary

After the removal of János Kádár from power in May 1988, Hungary was unambiguously in transition. The HSWP took the lead in advocating reform, and at first seemed able to control the process of democratization. But that process itself reinforced the strength of the HSWP's competition, eventually forcing the HSWP to lose control of the process and, ultimately, the reins of power. It was thus in November 1988 that the parliament passed a democratization package designed to broaden "socialist pluralism," and approved the introduction of a multiparty system by 1990 at the latest.[72]

A more decisive step toward repluralization was taken on 18 October 1989, when the Hungarian National Assembly adopted a series of amendments that prepared the way for multiparty elections. Among other things, the amendments abolished the principle of the leading role of the communist party, abolished the 21-member presidential council that had served as the collective head of state, created a strong presidency (with the incumbent to be elected to a four-year term by the National Assembly), created the Constitutional Court to review the constitutionality of disputed laws, and provided guarantees for human and civil rights. The amendment package also gave political parties the right to organize and operate provided they observed the constitution. Two days later the assembly voted to disband the Workers' Guard, a paramilitary organization of the HSWP whose members were seen as largely hostile to democratization, as well as the party organizations in the army. By November 1989 some party leaders were becoming fed up with this headlong retreat, however, and in November 1989 they began to talk about a possible coup. Ironically, they counted on military assistance from the hard-line governments of Czechoslovakia and Romania—governments within weeks of falling. Hungarian Premier Miklós Németh received a tip about the plans and alerted the ministry of the interior. The conspirators knew that the ministry was on their tracks, became frightened, and called a halt to their plans.[73]

With the new legal guarantees, political parties registered themselves in rapid succession. By mid-December 1989 thirteen parties had been registered, with applications submitted by another fifteen parties.[74] Among the newly emerging parties were the Independent Social Democratic Party, the Christian Democratic People's Party, the Hungarian Democratic Forum, the Hungarian Social Democratic Party, the Social Democratic Party, the Social Democratic Party of Hungarian Gypsies, the Homeland Party, the Free Democratic Party, and the Green Party. At the end of December the Independent Smallholders' Peasant Party split in two, giving rise to the National Bourgeois Smallholders' Party.[75] The Pan-Magyar Body, an organization operating underground since 1953, came out into the open, expressing concern about the fate of Hungarian culture both within and outside Hungary (that is, among Hungarians living in Romania and other neighboring states).[76] And finally, there were rather confused reports that the old fascistic Arrowcross Party was being revived.[77]

As Hungary's first free elections in forty years drew closer, it became obvious that anticommunist sentiment was in high fever. All the bitterness and resentment accumulated below the surface for four decades was openly expressed.[78] Miklós Haraszti, the leader of the Free Democrats, drew the logical conclusion: "The communists are finished. They can never win a free election [in Hungary]."[79]

Finally, in March 1990 Hungarians went to the polls to elect all 386 members of the National Assembly. Some 70 percent of eligible voters went to the polls. The result was a resounding victory for the center-right, and a decisive end to communist fantasies about retaining the reins. The Democratic Forum, which supports Hungarian neutrality and the achievement of a market economy in gradual, measured steps, won 24.7 percent of the vote. The Free Democrats, who want a faster transition to a market economy and are active supporters of Hungarian membership in the European Common Market, came in second with 21.4 percent of the vote. The Independent Smallholders' Party, which emphasizes the need to return farmland to families who owned it before collectivization, came in third with 11.8 percent. The ex-communists (Hungarian Socialist Party) took fourth place with 10.9 percent.[80] Democratic Forum leader József Antall, a former librarian and scholar of medical history, became prime minister, and began to put together a coalition with several other parties—specifically, the Smallholders, the Christian Democrats, and the Young Democrats, thus bypassing the second-place Free Democrats and the fourth-place ex-communists.[81] Arpad Goncz, a founding member of the Free Democrats, was elected president. On 26 June the new Parliament voted unanimously (with four abstentions) to negotiate Hungary's withdrawal from the Warsaw Pact.[82]

Westerners quickly identified Hungary as one of the more promising investment opportunities in the new Eastern Europe, and, as already noted in chapter 12, independent newspapers made an appearance, buoyed up by foreign capital. A private, English-language radio station also began operation in March 1990. Meanwhile, General Electric, Suzuki Motors, General Motors, US West Communications, and other Western companies signed major deals, involving automobiles, the modernization of the Hungarian telephone system, commercial and residential development in Budapest, and major transportation and manufacturing opportunities. On the lighter, more sybaritic side, a sex club opened in Budapest, publishing six sex magazines, and with two pornographic films to its credit by July 1990. The club announced plans to set up two "sex cruises" on Lake Balaton, to open brothels across Hungary, to establish a fleet of "sex taxis" to provide transport for call girls, and to market sex tours to Thailand, Greece, and other countries.[83]

In July 1990 Hungary reprivatized agriculture, returning nationalized farmlands to the original owners or their heirs.[84] Where shops, restaurants, and small businesses were concerned, however, the Hungarian parliament decided against returning them to the original owners, and opted instead to sell, in this case, some 10,000 such outlets to the highest bidders, starting in spring 1991. The privatization law, adopted on 18 September 1990, allowed that major chains, large department stores, hard-currency shops, pharmacies, and pawn shops would remain in state hands for the foreseeable future.[85]

Meanwhile, as of October 1990 there were warnings that Hungary was in for a difficult transition. Inflation had reached 30 percent by then, energy supplies were expected to dry up by December (because of the USSR's failure to meet agreed oil deliveries), and Hungary's streets became home to thousands of the homeless, many of them new immigrants from Romania, Bulgaria, and various Third World countries.[86]

Poland

As of mid-1990 Poland was a noncommunist country with a communist president (Jaruzelski), ruled by a group of politicians associated with a trade union, rather than a party, who, in turn, governed an emergent free enterprise system in which more than half of Poland's 7,600 state enterprises will still be in state hands even in 1993.[87] There are other paradoxes too. For example, the communist party (renamed Social Democracy), which long fulminated against private enterprise, has now lost its state subsidies and has therefore gone into business: the party converted a members-only guest house into a hotel, opened trade companies, rented office space, turned the Gdańsk party canteen into a public restaurant, opened a laundry and a shoe store, and even began offering driving lessons for an appropriate fee. As of January 1990 the party also hoped to open its own banks (in a joint venture with a Western bank), break into the tourist industry, and—with Swiss and German help—get into pharmaceuticals.[88]

In this land of paradoxes, some eighty political parties contested in local elections in May 1990.[89] Yet none of these parties had accumulated any real power. With the communist party shattered and in disarray, the ad hoc political arm of Solidarity functioned as "the only real political institution in Poland."[90] Power was dispersed between two rival groups, both tied to Solidarity: one associated with Prime Minister Tadeusz Mazowiecki, who had been essentially picked by Lech Wałęsa to assume that office, but who had alienated Wałęsa by not consulting the latter as he assembled his cabinet; another associated with Solidarity chair Wałęsa, who accused Mazowiecki of being too slow in carrying out necessary economic changes. The conflict between Mazowiecki and Wałęsa became sharp enough to inspire the Warsaw daily *Trybuna* to suggest that Solidarity divide itself, and spawn two political parties: a center-left and a center-right party.[91]

Economic reconstruction has been more urgent than in Bulgaria, Czechoslovakia, or Hungary (or, for that matter, Albania). The Mazowiecki government concentrated on converting to a free enterprise system, curbing inflation, and making the zloty a convertible currency. To advance reprivatization Mazowiecki established the Agency for Ownership Changes, which was charged with drafting a privatization plan and identifying enterprises in good fiscal health for sale to private investors.

With the government removing price subsidies and hiking prices, at least part of the inflationary spiral was a direct result of government policy: in December 1989, for example, the Ministry of Finance announced that the retail prices of electricity, central heating, warm water, and gas would go up an average of 400 percent effective 1 January 1990.[92] Inflation in 1989 was estimated at 700–900 percent, but started to come down in 1990—70 percent in January, 24 percent in February, and 5 percent in March.

The government also approved twelve devaluations of the zloty in its first 100 days in power, and by January 1990 the official rate was close to the unofficial rate, and it was conceivable that the zloty would eventually become a hard currency.

But this economic medicine has been hard on Poles. Industrial sales slumped 27 percent. Farmers complained that rising prices of machinery and fertilizer exceeded their capacity to cope. And by the end of May 1990 some 443,000 people registered as unemployed, in a country which had long been committed to the principle of full employment.[93]

On the political front, the Mazowiecki government also confronted the complicated task of creating a legal framework for a pluralist democracy. Censorship was abolished in January 1990, the police force was depoliticized in February, and public control over the Ministry of Internal Affairs (as opposed to communist party control) was also instituted in February. Later, in July, Mazowiecki fired three of the four communist ministers who had been included in the government as the price for Solidarity's assumption of power: Czesław Kiszczak was ousted from the Ministry of the Interior, Florian Siwicki from the Ministry of Defense, and Franciszek Wieladek from the Ministry of Transport.[94] The government also passed a law providing that any group could declare itself a political party and obtain full legal status, and that the authorities could not be empowered to make any decision affecting this process. The law also established that no political party could obtain any financial aid or subsidization from the government, and that no party could establish cells in workplaces, government offices, the police, or the military. The media were likewise depoliticized, with the result that coverage of the affairs of the Polish United Workers' Party (or, as renamed, Social Democracy) plunged.

As it became patently obvious that the old regime had passed, police and security offices started destroying files and official records. Bonfires of police and communist party records were reported in cities throughout the country before the government finally took steps to halt the destruction.[95]

As for the puwp, its self-confidence was essentially shattered. By December 1988, for example, 38 percent of party members polled said they were ashamed to admit that they were members of the communist party.[96] In late January 1990 the party voted to dissolve itself, reconstituting itself as the "new" Social Democracy Party. Some 100 delegates immediately broke away and formed a rival organization, the Union for Social Democracy, led by reformist communist Tadeusz Fiszbach.

Between January and September 1990, the government returned some 12,000 enterprises to private hands. And as of September, Polish authorities expressed their intention of literally giving away a major part of the state-owned economy to Polish citizens by distributing share vouchers to employees and selling additional shares (with discounts for employees).[97] Wałęsa, however, insisted that change could, and should, be faster, having demanded earlier that the government be granted special temporary powers to speed up reprivatization.[98] Wałęsa also criticized the Mazowiecki government for retaining functionaries—from factory foremen to school principals to government bureaucrats—who owed their positions to the communists. All such people, he demanded, should be fired. "Privatization is revolution," said economist Adam Glapinski, a Wałęsa-supporter. "It means 400,000 people will lose their jobs."[99]

In June Wałęsa formed a new political organization, the Center Alliance, to serve as his political machine, and in August he announced his candidacy for the Polish presidency. In July Mazowiecki's supporters, including Zbigniew Bujak and Władysław Frasyniuk, set up an organization known as Democratic Action, to advance the incumbent prime minister's political fortunes. Mazowiecki also declared his candidacy for the presidency. In these circumstances Poland's appointed president, Jaruzelski, announced that he would step down before the constitutional expiration of his term (which would have been in 1995).

In late September, after lengthy debate, the Polish parliament passed a constitutional amendment providing for the direct popular election of the president—a formula preferred by most Poles.[100] Elections were set for 25 November. Wałęsa's victory in those elections promised a radicalization of strategy in Poland's path back to pluralism.

Meanwhile, democratization seemed to have unleashed a new wave of chauvinism, as reports surfaced of waxing anti-Semitism,[101] a rise of Belorussian nationalism,[102] the taunting of Protestant and agnostic children for not enrolling in "voluntary" Catholic religious instruction,[103] and voluble Polish outcry against a Soviet decision to allow German families forcibly exiled by Stalin to Central Asia to return to the family homesteads in the former East Prussian district.[104]

Romania

"No matter how one arrives in Romania," Celestine Bohlen recounted in the *New York Times* in May 1990, "the country looks as if it is falling apart. Bucharest's airport would be a disgrace anywhere. Water drips from the ceiling, floor tiles are cracked, plants are dead or dying in their pots and the first word of greeting for a visitor, passing an armed sentry at a makeshift checkpoint, is a whispered, 'Cigarettes.'"[105] The scene reflects the legacy of nearly twenty-five years of rule by Ceauşescu—a rule characterized by megalomania, self-glorification, corruption, nepotism, persecution, terror, and an economic policy that combined fallacy with exploitation.

Even as communism was collapsing in the rest of Eastern Europe, Ceauşescu refused to believe that change would come to Romania. On the eve of his overthrow, the party daily *Scînteia* published a lengthy article rejecting political pluralism.[106] In late November the Romanian CP held its fourteenth congress in Bucharest, and continued to sing the party secretary's praises as if nothing were wrong; and yet the atmosphere in Romania had been tense and there was a sense that people were stretched to the breaking point.

In summer 1989 a group of high-ranking communist party members hostile to the Ceauşescu regime formed an opposition group called the Council of National Salvation. The French embassy in Bucharest, and probably also the Soviet embassy, were informed at that time.[107] But the Council was shrouded in so much secrecy that as late as 14 December a Radio Free Europe report expressed uncertainty as to whether the organization really amounted to anything more than wishful thinking.[108]

On 15 December demonstrations broke out in Timişoara when local citizens rallied to prevent security forces from arresting a Reformed clergyman, László Tökés, who had been active in promoting the rights of Hungarians in Romania. Demonstrations and clashes between citizens and security forces, who charged the crowds with fixed bayonets, continued for days, and fighting spread to Arad, Braşov, Sibiu (Hermannstadt), and Bucharest. Romania closed its borders with Hungary and Yugoslavia on 18 December, and its borders with Bulgaria and Moldavia on 19 December. By then demonstrators were shouting, "Wake up Romanians!," "Down with the communists!," and "Death to the dictator!"

Ceauşescu then summoned Defense Minister General Vasie Milea, and ordered him to send troops to fire on the demonstrators. Milea refused, and shot himself in the heart in protest. His suicide helped to turn the army against Ceauşescu, and for several days, army troops did battle with security forces loyal to Ceauşescu. Nicolae and Elena Ceauşescu tried to flee, but were captured on 23 December, and executed on 25 December. Estimates of the number of dead ranged from 5,000 (Red Cross estimate) to 12,000 (Tanjug estimate) to 60,000 (official figure).

The National Salvation Front (NSF) quickly assumed control of the situation. The NSF leader was Ion Iliescu, a longtime communist who had been close to Ceauşescu in the 1970s. The NSF soon published its program, which called for the establishment of a multiparty system, free elections by April 1990, restructuring the economy on a free enterprise basis, halting the destruction of villages in Transylvania, and the establishment of freedom of religion.[109]

The new government immediately put Ceauşescu's closest accomplices on trial, including Emil Bobu (a former party secretary), Tudor Postelnicu (the former minister of the interior), Marin Meagoe (chief of security), Dumitru Popescu (former director of the Sociopolitical Academy), Ceauşescu's sons Nicu and Valentin, and various members of the old Securitate forces. The communist party was disbanded and banned. And a decree issued on 6 February 1990 permitted the establishment of private profit-making businesses with up to twenty employees. The new government also authorized the registration of alternative political parties. By mid-January thirteen new parties had registered, and by the end of the first week of February the number had reached 32. Fresh antigovernment demonstrations in late January forced the NSF to agree to form a new transitional government in which the major opposition parties would be represented. And in the midst of this mêlée, the former King Michael, who had abdicated under pressure in 1947, issued a statement, "If Romanians ask me to return, I am always ready to resume my constitutional responsibilities."[110]

Hungarian-Romanian relations were an obvious policy area of centrality. And the new regime wisely announced that the educational system would be reformed to provide more Hungarian-language instruction in all grades. An early move was the restoration of Hungarian-language instruction at the Tirgu Mureş Medical-Pharmaceutical Institute.[111] The regime also promoted discussion of the possibility of providing "cultural" autonomy for Transylvania's Hungarian population.[112]

Several political parties catering to ethnic Hungarian interests were also founded, including the Magyar Independent Party headquartered in Tirgu Mureş, the Democratic Union of Magyars in Romania (under General Secretary Geza Szocs), the Union of Hungarian Democratic Youth, and a movement dedicated to easing interethnic tensions, the Hungarian-Romanian Democratic Association, created on the joint initiative of members of both national groups.

But on 15 March 1990, when the Democratic Union of Magyars staged some commemorative events, such as laying a wreath at a monument to Hungary's national poet, Sándor Petőfi, the Romanian nationalist organization Vatra Romaneasca (Romanian Hearth) replied with counterdemonstrations, leading to three days of bloodshed in Transylvania and the declaration of a state of emergency in Tirgu Mureş. Tanks cordoned off access roads and observers spoke of the danger of imminent civil war.

In these conditions—a bankrupt economy, a disintegrated political infrastructure, the dangers of civil war, and squabbling among aspiring politicians—the provisional government made preparations for the democratic elections, which had been postponed to 20 May in order to give the new parties more time.

By the time the elections were held, there were seventy-eight parties competing,[113] including the National Peasant Party (under Ion Ratiu), the Liberal Party (under Radu Campeanu), the Social Democratic Party, the Democratic Agrarian Union, the Free Democratic Youth Party (aiming at recruiting young people), the Humanist Ecological Party, the Democratic Unity Party of Moldavia, the Free for the Change Party (emphasizing safeguards for freedom of speech), and the Romanian Ecologist Movement. During the campaign there were frequent complaints by "opposition" parties that the NSF was using violence to harass and intimidate them. The National Peasant Party claimed that sixty local offices had been attacked or damaged, and both leading opposition parties (Ratiu's Peasants, and Campeanu's Liberals) said that organized squads had disrupted some of their rallies.[114]

When the results were tallied, the NSF claimed that its presidential candidate, Ion Iliescu, had won with 86.5 percent of the vote, with only 9.8 percent going to Campeanu, and 3.7 percent to Ratiu. In parliamentary voting, the official tally was: National Salvation Front, 69.0 percent; Democratic Union of Magyars, 6.9 percent; National Liberal Party, 6.0 percent; Green Party, 2.5 percent; National Peasant Party, 2.0 percent; and Vatra Romaneasca, 2.0 percent.[115] This gave the NSF 354 seats in the 506-member parliament; the Democratic Union of Magyars had the second largest bloc of deputies, with 41 seats.[116]

But amid charges of fraud and accusations that the NSF was dominated by communists, rioting erupted in Bucharest in mid-June. When the army refused to respond to President Iliescu's call for help, he appealed to the country's miners, a reliable bloc of NSF support. Within a matter of hours, thousands of miners from northern Romania, wearing dirty workclothes and brandishing shovels, pick-axes, and rubber hoses, descended on the capital and seized control of downtown Bucharest. By evening, the miners had beaten up large numbers of citizens, cleared the university square where the antigovernment demonstration had taken place, and restored a kind of order.[117] A grateful Iliescu praised the miners as "a strong force with much civic discipline."[118] But in relying on vigilantes rather than institutionalized forces to restore order, Iliescu unwittingly betrayed the fact that Romania was still in a revolutionary state.

Yugoslavia

In Yugoslavia, despite an early start on the road to repluralization, the entire process was made vastly more complex by the national question, and more specifically, by the decentralization of power to rival wings of the party, representing discrete nationality groups and sometimes advocating diametrically opposed political platforms. Thus, at the close of the 1980s, while the Slovenian communist party advocated a further loosening of the federation, full republic status for Kosovo, the introduction of a multiparty system in the country as a whole (or minimally in Slovenia), and the reduction of Slovenia's economic obligations to the federation, the Serbian communist party (captured in summer 1987 by the Serbian nationalist demagogue Slobodan Milošević) advocated a recentralized federation with reduced powers for the federal units,[119] the scaling back of Kosovo's autonomy, the retention of political monopoly by the communist party, and the maintenance of existing interregional economic obligations. In pursuit of the second of these objectives, the Serbian party held a referendum on 1 July 1990 asking Serbs to approve a program that essentially eliminated what little autonomy Kosovo still retained at that point.[120]

In the course of 1989 polemics intensified between Slovenia and Serbia over Kosovo, the constitution, and the country's federal arrangement. There were also renewed polemics between Croats and Serbs over the status of Croatia's Serbian minority, which has, at times, sought to establish a Serbian autonomous province within Croatia. Within Bosnia, ethnic frictions—especially between Serbs and non-Serbs—became serious enough that Bosnian party officials gingerly conceded the existence of problems. And then there was Kosovo. As a result, the national question dramatically overshadowed, and, for a while, even preempted, the issue of democratization.

But the various independent groups and associations which had emerged in Yugoslavia in the course of the 1980s continued to press for repluralization. A decisive turn (already noted in chapter 12) came with the trial of Janša, Borstner, Tasić, and Zavrl for their magazine article revealing a military conspiracy to arrest various liberal politicians in Slovenia and restore "socialist order" in that republic.[121] The repluralization of Slovenia was powerfully reinforced and quickened by the fallout from the trial.[122]

As alternative political associations announced their formation in one republic after another, the communist authorities eventually had to adjust, and by June 1990 the communist party organizations of all six republics had endorsed the establishment of a multiparty system. Indeed, two of the parties had been voted out of power (the Slovenian and the Croatian), and had changed their names and foresworn Marxism.[123]

The Slovenian party also walked out of the fourteenth extraordinary congress of the LCY in January 1990, causing it to adjourn, and declared that it no longer recognized any organizational links with, or material obligations to, the LCY.[124] The LCY lacked the will or the ability to do anything about this action. Some Slovenian politicians announced their commitment to seeing Slovenia have its own currency, its own army, and its own foreign ministry[125]—whether as a fully independent state or as a sovereign member of a Yugoslav confederation.

Meanwhile, the infrastructure of party control disintegrated as party members turned in their membership cards, party organizations in economic enterprises and government offices closed up, newspapers severed their connections with party organizations, and pressure was exerted for the disbandment of party organizations in the army as well as the people's general defense and social self-protection committees, also under party control. Symptomatic of this disintegration was the decision, taken in the Serbian republic in June 1990, to remove Marxism from the high school curriculum, and to replace it with courses on religion.[126]

The army, long a bulwark of the one-party system, belatedly gave the green light to a multiparty system through an interview with Assistant Defense Secretary Colonol-General Simeon Bunčić. Interviewed by the Sarajevo daily *Oslobodjenje* in February 1990, Bunčić said that Yugoslav society had reached a "consensus" that the country needed a multiparty system, and indicated that the army would not seek to prevent this.

In spring 1990 free elections were held in two of Yugoslavia's six republics, Slovenia and Croatia. The result was a resounding victory for noncommunist political forces that left Yugoslavia a political anomaly, with communists temporarily still in control in four republics and center-right groups in control in two republics. In Slovenia the election was taken by Demos, an opposition alliance of Social Democrats, Christian Democrats, Liberals (the former youth organization), and others, while in Croatia, the Croatian Democratic Community, headed by retired General Franjo Tudjman, handily won control of the Croatian Assembly with 205 of the 356 seats, and elected Tudjman—whom the communists had for years denounced as a "fascist" and had even imprisoned at one point—president of Croatia. One of the new Croatian government's first acts was to remove the word "socialist" from the name of the republic, and to remove the red star from the flag and coat of arms of the republic.[127]

Both Demos and the Croatian Democratic Community shared a common vision of a confederal Yugoslavia, in which the constituent republics cooperate as sovereign, self-governing states. To this end, the new governments of these two republics jointly coordinated a strategy to press for the earliest possible inception of negotiations on the confederalization of Yugoslavia.[128] Support for this program was strong, with some 51.9 percent of Slovenes favoring confederation in a March 1990 poll, 28 percent preferring secession, and no one expressing support for a unitary Yugoslavia.[129] The drive for confederalization received a further boost on 2 July, when the provincial government of Kosovo declared its independence from Serbia.[130]

In July Slovenia and Croatia proclaimed their sovereignty, followed on 1 August by Bosnia. In October Slovenia and Croatia presented a joint proposal for the restructuring of Yugoslavia as a confederation, as the Slovenes opened liaison offices in Brussels, Vienna, Luxemburg, Washington, D.C., and Moscow.[131] The proposal called for confederation member states to raise their own armed forces, but to coordinate their foreign policy and participate in a joint "advisory" parliament.[132] Slovenia was allegedly planning to raise a peacetime army of 16,000–17,000, an air force of 2,500, and a navy of 1,000, with 40,000–60,000 troops in reserves.[133]

Within Croatia itself, an illegal referendum conducted among local Serbs from 19 August–2 September resulted in an overwhelming vote in favor of a Serbian autonomous district in Croatia. In the wake of this vote, the Serbs declared their autonomy and armed themselves, raiding at least one police station and burglarizing local gun shops.[134] Federal troops were rushed to the Knin region, where most of this was taking place,[135] but as September wore on, there were clashes between local Serbs and Croatian riot police in several Croatian cities.[136] In early October there were reports that Serbs had shot and wounded two Croatian police. The Croatian government belatedly tried to assuage Serbian temper by offering Serbs "cultural" autonomy.[137] But Serbs had earlier indicated that in the event of confederalization, they wanted full political autonomy, if not actual secession from Croatia.

Elsewhere around the country, civil order continued to disintegrate. The otherwise promising news that there were some 30,000 private businesses in operation in Yugoslavia by mid-September[138] seemed almost irrelevant as ethnic tensions flared throughout the country, generally pitting Serbs against non-Serbs. In Bosnia, Muslims organized a political party, while Serbs and Croats began to talk of taking parts of Bosnia for themselves. In Vojvodina, there were calls for a republic. In Serbia itself, Muslims in the region of Novi Pazar began demanding separation from Serbia and an administrative link with Bosnia. And in Kosovo, the Serbian government dissolved the provincial assembly and closed down the Albanian-language daily, *Rilindja*. When the now-dissolved provincial assembly defiantly met in a secret session on 7 September and adopted a constitution proclaiming Kosovo a "republic" within a Yugoslav "confederation,"[139] Serbian authorities ordered the arrest of the members of the dissolved assembly and eliminated most of the few remaining vestiges of Kosovar autonomy.[140] By October 1990 Yugoslavia was on the brink of civil war, and it appeared increasingly unlikely that Yugoslav politicians would find a way to pull back from the brink. Much of the problem stemmed from the demagogic mass manipulation by Serbia's nationalist leadership.

Between December 1990 and January 1991, Serb-Croat relations continued to disintegrate. Serbia's Slobodan Milošević worked in coordination with the army to set up a revived Communist Party (placing his wife, Mirjana, in the leadership of this new party). In mid-January, the army, 70 percent of whose officers are Serbs, put pressure on Slovenia and Croatia to disarm their newly created paramilitary forces, threatening invasion if the two republics did not comply. Slovenia and Croatia refused, placed their military forces on high alert status and signed a bilateral agreement to coordinate security and defense matters.[141] Late January produced a kind of truce in the gathering crisis, and an agreement among the republics to enter into a series of summit talks to search for an exit from the impasse. Slovenia served notice that it was proceeding with the establishment of infrastructure necessary to independent existence, and promised that if there should be no confederal pact by June, Slovenia would secede unilaterally from the Yugoslav federation and apply for membership in the UN and other international bodies.[142] Croatia indicated that if Slovenia seceded, it would follow suit.[143] And Bosnia made it clear that under no circumstances would it remain part of a truncated Yugoslavia, and that it might even joint a prospective Slovenian-Croatian confederation, as a third member. The fifth round of interrepublic talks were held in Sarajevo on 22 February, but failed to reach any agreement. Serbia and Montenegro continued to press for a tight federation. Slovenia and Croatia held fast to their position that the only basis for a "Yugoslav" solution was confederation. Bosnia suggested a compromise, with Serbia and Montenegro regulated tightly by a central government and Slovenia and Croatia enjoying confederal status, with Bosnia and Macedonia enjoying some undefined intermediate status.[144] This compromise was designed to serve Bosnia's economic interests, and to prevent the delicate political balance in that republic (amid gathering frictions between Serbs and non-Serbs) from coming unglued. This compromise was, however, completely unsatisfactory to the Macedonians, who restated their long insistence[145] on the absolute equality of the republics as a prerequisite for any overall solution. The sixth round of summit talks were held in Belgrade on 1 March, but as before, Croatia refused to attend any talks held in Belgrade. By the beginning of March it was difficult to imagine how Yugoslavia could avoid civil war, and the dispatch of federal army troops to the village of Pakrac in Croatia on 2 March was an ominous symptom of the escalation of localized violence.[146]

Conclusion

Social systems reflect and presume specific modal behavior systems, but collective behavior systems themselves reflect and presume consensual clusters of social values, expectations, and assumptions. These values, expectations, and assumptions extend over a wide array of areas, but are interrelated all the same. As values and assumptions change, behavior changes, and over time, changes in behavior produce changes in social systems —whether evolutionary or revolutionary. The creation of Solidarity culminated several years of change in expectations and assumptions, and modifications in values, and proved to be arguably the single most important engine for political change in Eastern Europe. On another level, rock 'n' roll, which began in the 1950s and early 1960s with a focus on sexual liberation, expanded (arguably beginning with *Sgt. Pepper's Lonely Hearts Club Band*) into a force for broadly conceived personal liberation, and projected notions of liberation through music, dance, lyrics, and even garb. Again, feminism ought not to be conceived narrowly; both as a force for independent political thought and action, and more substantively as a force for human equality, feminism is a "modernizing" phenomenon.

At any given point in history, there are various countervailing social forces, which support quite opposed value systems. One need only think of the East European religious scene—the conservative Christian neo-Protestants, the liberal Lutheran establishment, "restorationist" Catholicism, male chauvinist cults like the Hare Krishnas, spiritualism, satanism—to appreciate the point. As a result, cultural shifts in society are necessarily mixed (as in the difference between the city and the countryside), and incomplete.

The repluralization of Eastern Europe did not occur merely because the populations of that region became fed up with communism, or even merely because institutional weapons such as Solidarity became available to them. The precondition for the political repluralization of Eastern Europe was the *broadly conceived repluralization of culture*, and with it, the creation of stable poles of cultural, spiritual, social, and political activity and value formation. The process of repluralization had multifaceted sources—including economics, high politics, trade unionism, intellectual dissent, human rights issues, youth culture, feminism, and rock counter-culture—and will have multifaceted consequences, affecting these spheres and others.

Appendixes: Public Opinion Polls

The direction of popular pressure for change can often be gauged from public opinion polls. Such polls have been taken for years in Hungary, Poland, and Yugoslavia and have been reported since late 1989 in Bulgaria, East Germany, and Romania. Some of the results from recent polls are presented in the following appendixes.

Appendix 1 Bulgaria

November 1989

Do you approve of the latest National Assembly session?

Yes—60 percent
Other responses—40 percent

Do you approve of the election of Petar Mladenov as president of the State Council?

Yes—48.5 percent
Other responses—51.5 percent

Do you approve of the merging of three central committee departments into a single ideological department?

Yes—47.7 percent
Other responses—52.3 percent

Sources: First two responses reported in *Rabotnichesko delo*, 23 Nov. 1989, summarized in BTA (Sofia), 23 Nov. 1989, in FBIS, 1 Dec. 1989, 18; third response based on a survey of 405 persons and reported in *Rabotnichesko delo*, 30 Nov. 1989, 3, summarized in FBIS, 12 Dec. 1989, 18.

15 December 1989 (percentages)

Do you approve of the following political organizations?

	Yes	No
Bulgarian communist party	49	31
Bulgarian Agrarian National Union	36	32
Dimitrov Komsomol	30	50
Fatherland Front	27	48
Bulgarian trade unions	26	48

Do you approve of the following independent associations?

	Yes	No
Club for Glasnost and Democracy	55	12
Podkrepa Labor Federation	47	15
Independent Association for Defense of Human Rights	57	13
Eco-Glasnost	77	6
Progress Committee	24	12
Independent Student Association	52	14
Social Democratic Party	24	19
Nikola Petkov Bulgarian Agrarian National Union	28	20
Union of Democratic Forces	46	16

Source: Survey conducted among 1,512 people (ages 15–60) on 15 December 1989, as reported in *Narodna Mladezh*, 20 December 1989, 2, as summarized in FBIS, 18 Jan. 1990, 16.

January 1990

Do you approve of the decision to restore rights to the Muslim and Turkish-speaking population in Bulgaria?

Yes—89 percent
No—11 percent

Source: Survey conducted among 182 residents of Sofia, reported in BTA (Sofia), 11 Jan. 1990, in FBIS, 16 Jan. 1990, 28.

Appendix 2   Czechoslovakia

November 1989

Do you consider the people leading the restructuring process (communists) a guarantee of success?

No—58 percent
Other responses—42 percent

Should the restructuring process be continued?

Yes—85 percent
Other responses—15 percent

Which information media do you most trust?

Czech—25 percent
Western—23 percent
Neither—52 percent

Source: Opinion poll conducted by the Institute for Public Opinion Research, 23–24 November 1989, among 450 people from the whole of Czechoslovakia, and 260 from Prague, reported in CTK (Prague), 25 Nov. 1989, in FBIS, 1 Dec. 1989, 47.

January 1990

Are you satisfied with the political developments in the past two months (i.e., the overthrow of communism)?

Yes—86 percent
Other responses—14 percent

Are changes in the political system and economic system necessary?

Yes, political—83 percent
Yes, economic—84.3 percent

Will economic reform have any negative consequences?

Yes, short-term deterioration in the living standard—40 percent
Yes, rise in unemployment—25 percent

Source: Opinion poll conducted by the Group for an Independent Social Analysis, 9–19 Jan. 1990, among 2,350 citizens aged 15–69, reported in CTK (Prague), 29 Jan. 1990, in FBIS, 1 Feb. 1990, 24.

January 1990

What are the country's most urgent problems?

State of the environment—55 percent
Obsolescence of industry and technology—37 percent
State of public morale—30 percent
Liquidation of the CP organization—25 percent
Health care and cost of living—24 percent

Which problems should the government tackle first?

Preparation of free elections and the democratization of society—52 percent
Economic reform—44 percent
Solving environmental problems—42 percent
Social and health issues—30 percent
Supplying the domestic market—26 percent

Source: Opinion poll conducted by the Research Institute of Trade and the London branch of the Gallup Institute, 18–27 Jan. 1990, among 1,500 citizens from the whole of Czechoslovakia, reported in *Rudé pravo*, 13 Feb. 1990, 1, 3, in FBIS, 16 Feb. 1990, 22.

February 1990

What sectors of the economy should return to private ownership?

Small workshops and businesses—96 percent
Small farms—79 percent
Restaurants and shops—75 percent
Industrial enterprises—24 percent
Large agricultural enterprises—17 percent

Source: Opinion poll conducted by the Institute for Public Opinion Research, reported in *Zemědělské noviny*, 23 Feb. 1990, 2, in FBIS, 9 Mar. 1990, 24.

February 1990

Whom do you trust?

Václav Havel—88 percent yes, 9 percent no
Federal government—83 percent yes, 11 percent no
National governments—79 percent yes, 13 percent no
Federal Assembly—76 percent yes, 19 percent no
National committees—31 percent yes, 58 percent no
National Security Corps—35 percent yes*
Courts—34 percent yes*
Trade unions—28 percent yes*

*The figures for the negative responses for the last three institutions were not reported.
Source: Opinion poll conducted by the Institute for Public Opinion Research, late February 1990, among 1,325 citizens from throughout the country, reported in Rudé pravo, 2 Mar. 1990, 3, in FBIS, 29 Mar. 1990, 15–16.

March 1990

Did either Czechs or Slovaks receive preferential treatment in official policy during the past 20 years?

Slovaks—4 percent of Czechs
Not Slovaks—71 percent of Slovaks
Czechs—68 percent of Slovaks
Not Czechs—1 percent of Czechs

Source: Opinion poll conducted by the Prague Institute for Public Opinion Research, reported in Prače, 16 Mar. 1990, 2, in FBIS, 23 Mar. 1990, 26.

Appendix 3   Hungary

May 1989

Do you have faith in the following institutions? (Percent answering yes):

Hungarian Socialist Workers' Party—24 percent
National Assembly—44 percent

Do you trust the following political figures? (Percent answering yes):

Imre Pozsgay—69.6 percent
Miklós Németh—69.0 percent
Rezsö Nyers—61.7 percent
Karóly Grósz—50.0 percent

If elections were held today, for which party would you vote?

Hungarian Socialist Workers' Party—36.5 percent
Social Democratic Party—13.0 percent
Democratic Forum—11.4 percent
Alliance of Free Democrats—5.6 percent
Smallholders' Party—5.4 percent
Other—28.1 percent

Source: Study carried out by the Social Science Institute and the Sociological Institute, reported in Budapest Domestic Service, 6 May 1989, in FBIS, 8 May 1989, 25.

June 1989

Is it necessary to have other parties, besides the Hungarian Socialist Workers' Party?

Yes—80 percent
No—17 percent
Don't know—3 percent

Will the HSWP preserve or lose its leading role when other parties also function alongside the HSWP?

Will preserve—35 percent
Will lose—47 percent
Don't know—18 percent

Source: Poll conducted by the Hungarian Public Opinion Research Institute among 300 residents of Budapest, reported in *Magyar Hírlap*, 15 June 1989, 6, in FBIS, 23 June 1989, 51.

Appendix 4   Poland

July 1988

Does the activity of the Catholic church serve the interests of society?

Yes—74.1 percent
No—12.9 percent
No opinion—12.9 percent

Source: Survey conducted by the Public Opinion Polling Center, reported in PAP, 28 July 1988, in FBIS, 29 July 1988, 38.

August 1988

Is the church trying to increase its influence over what is happening in Poland?

Definitely yes—12 percent
Probably yes—28.7 percent
Probably no—15.3 percent
Definitely no—2.5 percent
No opinion—41 percent

Source: Survey conducted by the Public Opinion Research Center, as reported in *Trybuna Ludu*, 2 Aug. 1988, 3, in FBIS, 5 Aug. 1988, 15.

February 1989

How will the standard of living change over the next three years?

It will improve—29 percent
It will not change—36 percent
It will get worse—26 percent
No opinion—9 percent

Which public institution(s) do you trust?

Sejm—61 percent
Government—51 percent
Polish United Workers' Party—26 percent
Armed forces—75 percent

Is the economic situation good?

Yes—4 percent
No—95 percent
No opinion—1 percent

How would you describe the supply of foodstuffs?

Poor—57 percent
Mediocre—30 percent
Good—10 percent
Other responses—3 percent

Should Solidarity be relegalized?

Yes—78 percent
No—8 percent
No opinion—14 percent

What effect would the relegalization of Solidarity have on the economy?

Economy would improve—57 percent
Economy would deteriorate—4 percent
Economy would be unchanged—21 percent
Other responses—18 percent

What effect would the relegalization of Solidarity have on social frictions and tensions?

They would decrease—58 percent
They would increase—10 percent
They would be unchanged—21 percent

What effect would the relegalization of Solidarity have on Poland's relations with its socialist neighbors?

Relations would improve—19 percent
Relations would deteriorate—10 percent
Relations would be unchanged—52 percent
Other responses—19 percent

Source: Poll conducted by the Polish Television and Radio's Center for Public Opinion Research, reported in *Trybuna Ludu*, 20 Feb. 1989, 5, in FBIS, 24 Feb. 1989, 34–35.

July 1989

Who is your preferred candidate for the Polish presidency?

1st: Wojciech Jaruzelski
2nd: Lech Wałęsa
3rd: Bronisław Geremek
4th: Czesław Kiszczak

5th: Aleksander Gieysztor & Mieczysław Rakowski (tie)
[54 per cent had no opinion]

Who is your preferred candidate for the prime ministership?

1st: Mieczysław Rakowski
2nd: Bronisław Geremek
3rd: Witold Trzeciakowski
4th: Ryszard Bugaj
5th: Jacek Kuroń
Others (not rank-ordered): Lech Wałęsa, Ireneusz Sekula, Władysław Baka, Aleksander Kwasniewski, Czesław Kiszczak, Adam Michnik
[61 per cent had no opinion]

Source: Poll conducted by *Gazeta Wyborcza* (Solidarity weekly), as reported by Warsaw Television Service, 9 July 1989, in FBIS, 10 July 1989, 44.

September 1989

How significant is the nomination of Tadeusz Mazowiecki for the prime ministership?

Historic breakthrough—54 percent
Significant but not a breakthrough—34 percent
Not of major importance—3 percent
Insignificant—2 percent
No opinion—7 percent

Will Mazowiecki be a good prime minister?

Definitely yes—23 percent
Probably yes—53 percent
No—4 percent
No opinion—20 percent

Will Mazowiecki effect a radical reform of the economy?

Yes—54 percent
Other—46 percent

Source: Poll conducted by the Polish Radio and TV Committee, as reported in PAP, 18 Sept. 1989, in FBIS, 19 Sept. 1989, 53.

September 1989

If elections were held today, for which party would you vote?

Solidarity—65 percent
Polish United Workers Party—3 percent
Other responses—32 percent

Are you satisfied with Prime Minister Tadeusz Mazowiecki?

Yes—89 percent
No—2 percent
Other responses—9 percent

Source: Opinion poll conducted by the Public Opinion Research Center, reported by Warsaw Television Service, 27 Sept. 1989, in FBIS, 3 Oct. 1989, 42.

October 1989

Which institutions do you trust?

The church—87 percent
The Sejm—71 percent
The army—70 percent
The government—68 percent
Solidarity—66 percent
Democratic Party—34 percent
United Peasants Party—33 percent
Polish United Workers Party—11 percent

Sources: Opinion poll conducted by the OBOP Center for Public Opinion Research, reported in PAP, 20 Oct. 1989, in FBIS, 2 Nov. 1989, 74; and also in PAP, 15 Nov. 1989, in FBIS, 20 Nov. 1989, 78–79.

March 1990

Should the two German states be allowed to (re)unite?

Yes—48 percent
No—39 percent
Other responses—13 percent

Will German reunification be good for Poland?

No—67 percent
Yes—13 percent (2 percent said *very* good)
Other responses—20 percent

Will a future united Germany threaten Polish borders?

Yes—69 percent
No—31 percent

Source: Opinion poll conducted by the Public Opinion Polling Center of Polish Radio and Television, 5–6 Mar. 1990, reported in PAP, 28 Mar. 1990, in FBIS, 29 Mar. 1990, 30–31.

March 1990

Should Soviet troops be withdrawn from Poland?

Yes, as soon as possible, regardless of the situation in Germany—23 percent
Yes, but the date of their pullout should depend on developments in Germany—47 percent
No, they should stay in Poland—23 percent
Other responses—5 percent

Source: Opinion poll conducted by the OBOP TV Center for Public Opinion Research, 4–5 Mar. 1990, reported in PAP, 29 Mar. 1990, in FBIS, 30 Mar. 1990, 44.

Appendix 5   Yugoslavia

December 1988

Are you satisfied with the political situation in the country?

Satisfied—4 percent
Somewhat satisfied—51 percent
Predominantly dissatisfied—35 percent
Completely dissatisfied—8 percent
Other responses—2 percent
By ethnic group, 40.1 percent of Croats and 63.4 percent of Serbs said they were "satisfied" or "somewhat satisfied" with the situation.

Who is to blame for the foreign debt?

Federal officials—33 percent
Everyone—23 percent
Republican and provincial authorities—8 percent
Don't know—25 percent
Other responses—11 percent

How does the position of Croatia compare with that of other republics?

Better—7 percent
Worse—16 percent
The same—57 percent
Other responses—20 percent
By ethnic group, 6 percent of Croats and 15.6 percent of Serbs said that Croatia's position is better, while 1.6 percent of Serbs and 18.8 percent of Croats said it was worse than that of other republics.

Source: Poll conducted by Štefica Bahtijarević and Mladen Zvonarević among 2,000 citizens of Zagreb and surrounding commmunities, reported in *Borba*, 1 Dec. 1988, 5, in FBIS, 6 Dec. 1988, 74–75.

February 1989

Which, in your view, is the best political system for Yugoslavia?

	Self-management	Real socialism	Bourgeois democracy of a parliamentary type	Dictatorship	Monarchy	Other or don't know
Bosnia	85	5	5	—	—	5
Maced.	85	10	5	—	—	—
Slovenia	50	10	30	—	5	5
Serbia	70	15	15	—	—	—
Croatia	40	5	20	5	—	30
Monten.	85	10	5	—	—	—

Source: Poll conducted by and reported in *Borba*, 13 Feb. 1989, 5, summarized in FBIS, 22 Feb. 1989, 76.

April 1989

When will Yugoslavia emerge from its crisis?

In 5 years—41.5 percent
In 10 years—30.0 percent
"In a long time"—6.0 percent
In 2 years—5.0 percent
In 15 years—3.0 percent
When the old leadership has been replaced—3.0 percent
There is no way out—2.0 percent
By the year 2000—2.0 percent
In 20 years—2.0 percent
In 30 years—0.5 percent
In 50 years—0.5 percent
After the congress—0.5 percent
Don't know—3.0 percent

Source: Poll conducted among 120 people by *Borba*'s public opinion research center and reported in *Borba* 10 Apr. 1989, 5, as summarized in FBIS, 24 Apr. 1989, 60.

Slovenia, March 1990

What kind of political future do you favor?

Confederation—51.9 percent
Secession of Slovenia—28 percent
Efficient federation—7.9 percent
A unitarian Yugoslavia—0 percent
Don't know—12.2 percent

Which parties do you trust more?

Slovenian-based parties—79 percent
Yugoslav parties—6 percent
Neither—7 percent
Don't care, don't know—8 percent

What is your political persuasion?

Democrat—25.4 percent
Green—10.3 percent
Liberal—7.3 percent
Socialist—6.8 percent
Communist—5.6 percent
Communist-reformist—5.3 percent
Undecided—31.4 percent
Other responses—7.9 percent

Source: Opinion poll conducted by *Delo* among 532 citizens of Slovenia, reported in *Delo*, 15 Mar. 1990, 1, 3, summarized in FBIS, 20 Mar. 1990, 73–74.

Notes

1   Social Currents and Social Change

1   Quoted in *Financial Times* (London) 12 Apr. 1988, 3.

2   Herbert Blumer, "Social movements," in *Studies in Social Movements: A Social Psychological Perspective*, ed. Barry McLaughlin (New York: Free Press, 1969), 9.

3   Ibid., 8.

4   Irena Grudzińska-Gross, "Culture as Opposition in Today's Poland," *Journal of International Affairs* 40, no. 2 (Winter/Spring 1987): 389.

5   Angela A. Aidala, "Social Change, Gender Roles, and New Religious Movements," *Sociological Analysis* 46, no. 3 (Fall 1985): 287.

6   Milan Komnenić, "The Kosovo Cataclysm," *Serbian Literary Quarterly*, nos. 1–3 (1989): 67.

7   See, for example, Tihomir Djordjević, "Kossovo, 1389," *Serbian Literary Quarterly*,

nos. 1–3 (1989): 36–37. For a more scholarly discussion of Kosovo, see Miloš Mišović, *Ko je tražio republiku Kosovo, 1945–1985* (Belgrade: Narodna knjiga, 1987).

8   Anthony F. C. Wallace, "Revitalization Movements," in *Studies in Social Movements: A Social Psychological Perspective,* ed. Barry McLaughlin (New York: Free Press, 1969), 31–32.

9   Defined and discussed in Pedro Ramet, "Apocalypse Culture and Social Change in Yugoslavia," in *Yugoslavia in the 1980s,* ed. Pedro Ramet (Boulder, Colo.: Westview, 1985).

10   Samuel P. Huntington, *Political Order in Changing Societies* (New Haven, Conn.: Yale University Press, 1968), 5, 53, 79, 196.

11   Ibid., 197.

12   Zygmunt Bauman, "Social Dissent in the East European Political System," *Archives Européennes de Sociologie* 12, no. 1 (1971): 50.

13   See esp. Ibid., 37.

14   Huntington, *Political Order,* 299.

15   Actually no. 5 on his list. His no. 4 is fifth in my account.

16   Bauman, "Social Dissent," 46.

17   Ibid., 47.

18   Leszek Kołakowski, "A Pleading for Revolution: A Rejoinder to Z. Bauman," *Archives Européennes de Sociologie* 12, no. 1 (1971): 58.

19   "Democratic Opposition in Hungary Today: Exclusive Interview with János Kis," *Across Frontiers* (Fall 1986): 44.

20   James C. Davies, "Toward a Theory of Revolution," in *Studies in Social Movements: A Social Psychological Perspective,* ed. Barry McLaughlin (New York: Free Press, 1969); Ted Robert Gurr, *Why Men Rebel* (Princeton, N.J.: Princeton University Press, 1972).

21   On this point, see also Robert Coles, "Social Struggle and Weariness," in *Studies in Social Movements: A Social Psychological Perspective,* ed. Barry McLaughlin (New York: Free Press, 1969), 324–27.

22   See Gabriel Bar-Haim, "The Meaning of Western Commercial Artifacts for Eastern European Youth," *Journal of Contemporary Ethnography* 16, no. 2 (July 1987): 205–26; and Gabriel Bar-Haim, "The Westernization of East European Youth Culture as a Grass Roots Social Movement: A General Overview," *International Journal of Politics, Culture, and Society* 2, no. 1 (Sept. 1988).

23   Bauman, "Social Dissent," 48–49.

24   Ibid., 49.

25   See Jan Vladislav, ed., *Václav Havel, or Living in Truth* (London: Faber & Faber, 1987).

26   Crane Brinton, *The Anatomy of Revolution,* rev. and expanded ed. (New York: Vintage, 1965).

27   Davies, "Toward a Theory of Revolution," 86–103.

28   Gurr, *Why Men Rebel.*

29   Charles Tilly, *From Mobilization to Revolution* (Reading, Mass.: Addison-Wesley, 1978), as summarized in Jim Seroka, "Contemporary Issues and Stability in Socialist Yugoslavia," *Journal of Communist Studies* 2, no. 2 (June 1986): 140.

30   See Henry Spetter, "The New Economic Reform in Bulgaria," *Crossroads,* no. 9 (Autumn 1982); Ilse Grosser, "Wirtschaftsreformen in Bulgarien," *Europäische Rundschau* 13, no. 1 (Winter 1985).

31   Thomas Brey, "Bulgarien im Blickpunkt," *Osteuropa* 36, no. 2 (Feb. 1986): 142.

32   Wolfgang Höpken, "Wirtschaftsreform in Bulgarien," *Südost-Europa* 36, no. 1 (Jan. 1987): 45; Bulgarian Situation Report, *RFER*, 8 Mar. 1988, 20.

33   *NIN* (Belgrade), no. XXXX (27 July 1986).

34   Bulgarian Situation Report, *RFER*, 8 Mar. 1988, 21.

35   *Danas* (Zagreb), no. 294 (6 Oct. 1987): 59.

36   Bulgarian Situation Report, *RFER*, 8 July 1987, 3.

37   *Rudé pravo* (Prague), 31 Jan. 1988, quoted in Czechoslovak Situation Report, *RFER*, 15 Feb. 1988, 29.

38   *Danas*, no. 294 (6 Oct. 1987): 59.

39   Ibid., no. 281 (7 July 1987): 62.

40   *Financial Times* (London), 9 June 1988, 2.

41   Vladimir V. Kusin, "Husak's Czechoslovakia and Economic Stagnation," *Problems of Communism* 31, no. 3 (May-June 1982): 27.

42   Ivan Volgyes, "Hungary: Before the Storm Breaks," *Current History* 86, no. 523 (Nov. 1987): 374; Ivan Volgyes, "Ungarn: Steht eine Krise bevor?," *Osteuropa* 37, no. 5 (May 1987): 334.

43   *Financial Times*, 18 Feb. 1987, 2; *Chicago Tribune*, 6 Dec. 1987, sec. 7, 3; Hungarian Situation Report, *RFER*, 30 Mar. 1988, 26; *New York Times*, 19 Apr. 1989, 3.

44   Hungarian Situation Report, *RFER*, 6 Apr. 1985, 29–30; *Christian Science Monitor*, 29 Apr. 1985, 12; *Süddeutsche Zeitung* (Munich), 18–19 Feb. 1989, 7.

45   Hungarian Situation Report, *RFER*, 12 Aug. 1988, 37.

46   Quoted in *New York Times*, 17 Sept. 1987, 2.

47   Volgyes, "Ungarn," 329.

48   *New York Times*, 23 Oct. 1987, A3.

49   Hungarian Situation Report, *RFER*, 15 Feb. 1988, 23–27.

50   Ibid., 30 Mar. 1988, 31–35.

51   Ibid., 11 Jan. 1988, 19–23.

52   MTI (Budapest), 4 Sept. 1989, in FBIS, 7 Sept. 1989, 38.

53   *Danas*, no. 294 (6 Oct. 1987): 59; Arthur R. Rachwald, "The Polish Road to the Abyss," *Current History* 86, no. 523 (Nov. 1987): 372.

54   *New York Times*, 15 Nov. 1987, 1.

55   *The Times* (London), 4 Sept. 1985, 12.

56   See Vlad Georgescu, "Romania in the 1980s: The Legacy of Dynastic Socialism," *Eastern European Politics and Societies* 2, no. 1 (Winter 1988): 73, 77.

57   Romanian Situation Report, *RFER*, 25 Nov. 1987, 15; *Seattle Times*, 27 Mar. 1988, A10.

58   *Seattle Post-Intelligencer*, 9 Oct. 1983, 28.

59   Georgescu, "Romania in the 1980s," 74; *Washington Post*, 24 Aug. 1987, A12.

60   *Scînteia* (Bucharest), 10 Oct. 1981, 1, in FBIS, 13 Oct. 1981, H1.

61   *Christian Science Monitor*, 26 Oct. 1989, 9.

62   *Financial Times*, 16 Apr. 1988, 2.

63   Charles Bukowski, "Politics and the Prospects for Economic Reform in Yugoslavia," *Eastern European Politics and Societies* 2, no. 1 (Winter 1988): 94.

64   *Christian Science Monitor*, 26 Oct. 1989, 9.

65   *Financial Times*, 16 May 1988, 2.

66   *Danas*, no. 286 (11 Aug. 1987): 8.

67   Labin strike reported in *Washington Times*, 23 Apr. 1987, 10A; Skopje protests reported in *Christian Science Monitor*, 18 Nov. 1987, 2, and *NIN*, no. 1925 (22 Nov. 1987): 12–15. For other reports on strikes in 1986 and 1987, see Yugoslav Situation

Report, *RFER*, 15 Dec. 1986, 9–14; *Danas*, no. 259 (3 Feb. 1987): 9–13; *Borba* (Belgrade), 18 Mar. 1987, 5, in FBIS, 20 Mar. 1987, 16; *Corriere della Sera* (Milan), 21 Mar. 1987, 11, and 25 Mar. 1987, 10; *Washington Post*, 26 Mar. 1987, A29, A31; Yugoslav Situation Report, *RFER*, 4 June 1987, 23–28; *Süddeutsche Zeitung*, 21–22 Nov. 1987, 8.

68 *Frankfurter Rundschau*, 20 June 1988, 1; *Die Welt* (Bonn), 20 June 1988, 12; Tanjug, 22 June 1988, in FBIS, 23 June 1988, 68; *Der Tagesspiegel* (West Berlin), 26 June 1988, 6; Belgrade Domestic Service, 11 Aug. 1988, in FBIS, 12 Aug. 1988, 27; and Tanjug, 16 Aug. 1988, in FBIS, 17 Aug. 1988, 22.

69 Tanjug, 6 July 1988, in FBIS, 7 July 1988, 60.

70 Yugoslav Situation Report, *RFER*, 18 Dec. 1987, 25.

71 *Borba* (Belgrade), 15 July 1988, 5, in FBIS, 5 Aug. 1988, 34.

72 *NIN*, no. 1868 (19 Oct. 1986): 19.

73 Ibid., no. 1903 (21 June 1987): 11.

74 Seroka, "Contemporary Issues," 138.

75 For elaboration, see Sabrina P. Ramet, *Nationalism and Federalism in Yugoslavia, 1962–1991*, 2nd ed. (Bloomington: Indiana University Press, forthcoming).

76 See Pedro Ramet, "Yugoslavia 1987: Stirrings from Below," *South Slav Journal* 10, no. 3 (Autumn 1987).

77 *New York Times*, 16 Nov. 1987, 3.

78 *Christian Science Monitor*, 30 July 1986, 8; Yugoslav Situation Report, *RFER*, 16 Mar. 1987, 17–19.

79 *Intervju* (Belgrade), 7 Nov. 1986, 36.

80 Tanjug, 6 June 1988, in FBIS, 7 June, 1988, 47.

81 William E. Griffith, "The Pitfalls of the Theory of Modernization," *Slavic Studies* 33, no. 2 (June 1974): 248.

82 *Ifjúkommunista* (Budapest), April 1984, in JPRS, no. EPS-84-121 (1 Oct. 1984): 25.

83 *Financial Times*, 13 May 1988, 22.

84 *New York Times*, 16 May 1988, 2; *Financial Times*, 17 May 1988, 2.

85 *Financial Times*, 27 Apr. 1988, 2.

86 *Danas*, 8 July 1986, 65–66, in JPRS, no. EER-86-117 (4 Aug. 1986): 85.

87 *Danas*, 17 June 1986, 60, 65, summarized in JPRS, no. EER-86-112 (29 July 1986): 85.

88 Belgrade Domestic Service, 20 Nov. 1986, in FBIS, 21 Nov. 1986, 14.

89 For details, see Ramet, "Yugoslavia 1987."

90 Quoted in Tomaz Mastnak, "Politics and New Social Movements in Yugoslavia," *Across Frontiers* (Spring 1987): 13.

91 *Financial Times*, 2 Sept. 1988, 2.

92 *Badeshte* (Paris), no. 7 (Sept. 1985): 76–82, summarized in Bulgarian Situation Report, *RFER*, 27 May 1986, 3–7.

93 Bulgarian Situation Report, *RFER*, 14 July 1988, 17–18.

94 Ibid., 27 May 1988, 12.

95 See Zygmunt Bauman, "Intellectuals in East-Central Europe: Continuity and Change," *Eastern European Politics and Societies* 1, no. 2 (Spring 1987).

96 See George Schöpflin, "Opposition in Hungary: 1956 and Beyond," in *Dissent in Eastern Europe*, ed. Jane Leftwich Curry (New York: Praeger, 1983), 76–77.

97 Romanian Situation Report, *RFER*, 29 Oct. 1985, 27–30.

98 Ibid., 15 Oct. 1987, 31–33.

99 Vladimir Socor, "Dissent in Romania: The Diversity of Voices," *RFER*, 5 June 1987, 3.

100 *Christian Science Monitor*, 3 Mar. 1987, 9.

101 Romanian Situation Report, *RFER*, 6 Nov. 1986, 27–29. See also the discussion of Bujor Nedelcovici's novel, *The Tamed Heretic*, in Ibid., 13 Aug. 1985, 21–23.

102 *Neue Zürcher Zeitung*, 24 Dec. 1986, 3.

103 *Vjesnik* (Zagreb), 2 Oct. 1987.

104 For details, see Pedro Ramet, "Yugoslavia's Troubled Times," *Global Affairs* 5, no. 1 (Winter 1989–90).

105 Quoted in Bulgarian Situation Report, *RFER*, 27 May 1988, 5.

106 See René de Flers, "Socialism in One Family," *Survey* 28, no. 4 (Winter 1984): 165–74.

107 Quoted in *Los Angeles Times*, 27 Aug. 1980, pt. I-A, 3.

108 Extract from *Večernik*, 20 Nov. 1981, 8, in FBIS, 25 Nov. 1981, D9.

109 *Pravda* (Bratislava), 12 Jan. 1983, 4, and 31 Mar. 1983, 2; *Rudé pravo* (Prague), 29 Mar. 1983, 1.

110 *Neue Zürcher Zeitung*, 18 May 1985, 1; *The Times* (London), 19 Oct. 1985, 4.

111 Reuter, 16 Mar. 1986, in RFE telex.

112 *Christian Science Monitor*, 29 Apr. 1985, 12.

113 *Wall Street Journal*, 14 Sept. 1987, 16; *Frankfurter Allgemeine*, 2 Oct. 1987, 14.

114 *Neue Zürcher Zeitung*, 26 Mar. 1982, 4.

115 *Financial Times*, 10 Mar. 1987, 4.

116 See Stephen Ashley's excellent report in Bulgarian Situation Report, *RFER*, 8 Apr. 1988, 3–7.

117 Quoted in *Financial Times*, 11 Mar. 1988, 2.

118 *Rzeczywistość* (Warsaw), 2 Feb. 1986, 2, in FBIS, 28 Feb. 1986, G6.

119 I deliberately exclude Yugoslavia here, which has a formula all its own. For explanation and elaboration, see Pedro Ramet, "The Yugoslav Press in Flux," in *Yugoslavia in the 1980s*, ed. Pedro Ramet (Boulder, Colo.: Westview, 1985); Ramet, "Yugoslavia 1987," 27–28; and Sabrina P. Ramet, "The Role of the Press in Yugoslavia," in *Yugoslavia in Transition: Choices and Constraints*, ed. John B. Allock, John J. Horton, and Marko Milivojevic (forthcoming, St. Martin's Press).

120 Daniel N. Nelson, "Worker-Party Conflict in Romania," *Problems of Communism* 30, no. 5 (Sept.-Oct. 1981): 45.

121 Re Czechoslovakia, see *Die Welt*, 17 Feb. 1987, 10; Czechoslovak Situation Report, *RFER*, 6 Mar. 1987, 3–6; and Vlad Sobell, "Czechoslovakia: the Legacy of Normalization," *Eastern European Politics and Societies* 2, no. 1 (Winter 1988). Re Hungary, see *Financial Times*, 2 Mar. 1988, 2; 11 Mar. 1988, 2; 6 Apr. 1988, 2; 8 Apr. 1988, 3; and 3 May 1988, 2. Re Poland, see *Frankfurter Allgemeine*, 13 Nov. 1985, 2; and *Corriere della Sera*, 14 Nov. 1985, 10. Re Yugoslavia, see Pedro Ramet, "Yugoslavia's Debate over Democratization," *Survey* 25, no. 3 (Summer 1980): 43–48; Pedro Ramet, "Jugoslawien nach Tito: Zerbrechliches Gleichgewicht und Drang nach Legitimation," *Osteuropa* 32, no. 4 (Apr. 1982): 292–302; *Neue Zürcher Zeitung*, 3 Oct. 1987, 5, and 11–12 Oct. 1987, 6; and Yugoslav Situation Report, *RFER*, 22 Oct. 1987, 19–22.

122 See Pedro Ramet, "The Limits to Political Change in a Communist Country: The Yugoslav Debate, 1980–1986," *Crossroads*, no. 23 (1987).

123 Brinton, *The Anatomy of Revolution*.

124 *New York Times*, 2 Sept. 1987, 5; Polish Situation Report, *RFER*, 17 Mar. 1988, 25–26.

125 *New York Times*, 6 Feb. 1988, 5; *Corriere della Sera*, 3 Mar. 1988, 4.

126 See Ramet, "Apocalypse Culture"; Wolfgang Höpken, "Jugoslawien: Von der

Wirtschaftskrise zur Systemkrise?," *Südost-Europa* 31, nos. 11–12 (Nov.-Dec. 1982).

127   See Davies, "Toward a Theory," 86, 103, 106.

128   Quoted in *New York Times*, 4 May 1988, 1.

129   *Polityka* (Warsaw), 9 Jan. 1988, as cited in Polish Situation Report, RFER, 25 Feb. 1988, 3.

130   *Luceafărul*, 8 Feb. 1986, excerpted in Romanian Situation Report, RFER, 20 Mar. 1986, 20.

131   See Csába Gombar, "Politisches Denken und die Alternativen einer politischen Reform in Ungarn," *Südost-Europa* 36, no. 10 (Oct. 1987).

132   Quoted in *Financial Times*, 11 Mar. 1988, 2.

133   Quoted in *Pravda* (Moscow), 1 Mar. 1989, 4.

134   Fred W. Riggs, *Administration in Developing Countries: The Theory of Prismatic Society* (Boston: Houghton Mifflin, 1964).

135   *New York Times*, 21 May 1988, 1, 4.

136   For statistics, 1951–81 (except Yugoslavia): Jan Vanous, "East European Economic Slowdown," *Problems of Communism* 31, no. 4 (July-Aug. 1982): 2–3. Other statistics: *Yearbook of National Accounts Statistics for 1961–62* (New York: UN, 1962), 309; *Yearbook of National Accounts Statistics for 1976* (New York: UN, 1977), 2:242; *Yearbook of National Accounts Statistics for 1981* (New York: UN, 1983), 2:342; Romanian Situation Report, RFER, 22 Jan. 1985, 9; Ljuben Georgiev, "Bilanz und Perspektiven der Wirtschaftsreform in Bulgarien," *Europäische Rundschau* 13, no. 1 (Winter 1985): 134; *Anuarul Statistic al Republicii Socialiste România 1986* (Bucharest: Directia Centrala de Statistica, 1986), 57; *Rocznik Statystyczny 1987* (Warsaw: Głowny Urzad Statystyczny, 1987), 88; calculations from *Statistički Godišnjak Jugoslavije 1987* (Belgrade: Savezni Zavod za Statistiku, 1987), 34:92; *Financial Times*, 18 Feb. 1987, 2, and 10 Mar. 1987, 4; UN Economic Commission for Europe, *Economic Survey of Europe in 1986–1987* (New York: UN, 1987), 116; *Countries of the World and Their Leaders, Yearbook 1988* (Detroit: Gale, 1988), 1:302; Paul G. Hare, "Industrial Development of Hungary since World War II," *Eastern European Politics and Societies* 2, no. 1 (Winter 1988): 143; Romanian Situation Report, RFER, 12 Feb. 1988, 5; Czechoslovak Situation Report, RFER, 15 Feb. 1988, 29; Bulgarian Situation Report, RFER, 8 Mar. 1988, 19; Hungarian Situation Report, RFER, 30 Mar. 1988, 25; Warsaw PAP, 26 Jan. 1989, in FBIS, 2 Feb. 1989, 47; BTA (Sofia), 22 Feb. 1989, in FBIS, 23 Feb. 1989, 7; and Hungarian Situation Report, RFER, 1 Sept. 1989, 29.

137   For statistics, 1971–81 (except Yugoslavia): Vanous, "East European Economic Slowdown," 3. Other statistics: "Economic Development, 1971–1975," *Yugoslav Survey* 17, no. 3 (Aug. 1976): 68; Henry Spetter, "The New Economic Reform in Bulgaria," *Crossroads*, no. 9 (Autumn 1982): 122; Bulgarian Situation Report, RFER, 17 Feb. 1986, 18; *Industrial Statistics Yearbook 1985* (New York: UN, 1987), 1:65, 127, 243, 461, 479, and 599; *Statistički Godišnjak 1987*, 100; Wolfgang Höpken, "Wirtschaftsreform in Bulgarien," *Südost-Europa* 36, no. 1 (Jan. 1987): 45; UN Economic Commission for Europe, *Economic Survey of Europe in 1986–1987* (New York: UN, 1987), 143; Romanian Situation Report, RFER, 12 Feb. 1988, 5; Czechoslovak Situation Report, RFER, 15 Feb. 1988, 29; Hungarian Situation Report, RFER, 30 Mar. 1988, 26; Romanian Situation Report, RFER, 29 Dec. 1988, 3; Warsaw PAP, 26 Jan. 1989, in FBIS, 2 Feb. 1989, 48; and Czechoslovak Situation Report, RFER, 16 Feb. 1989, 8.

138   For statistics, 1971–81 (except Yugoslavia): Vanous, "East European Economic Slowdown," 3. Other statistics: "Economic Development, 1971–1975," 69; Spetter, "The

New Economic Reform," 122; *Anuarul Statistic*, 147; Bulgarian Situation Report, *RFER*, 17 Feb. 1986, 18; Romanian Situation Report, *RFER*, 20 Mar. 1986, 14; UN Economic Commission for Europe, *Economic Survey of Europe in 1985–1986* (New York: UN, 1986), 142; UN Economic Commission for Europe, *Economic Survey of Europe in 1986–1987*, 133; *Statistički Godišnjak 1987*, 239; calculations from *OECD Economic Surveys 1986/1987—Yugoslavia* (Paris: OECD, Jan. 1987), 85; Höpken, "Wirtschaftsreform," 45; Romanian Situation Report, *RFER*, 12 Feb. 1988, 5; Polish Situation Report, *RFER*, 25 Feb. 1988, 3; Bulgarian Situation Report, *RFER*, 8 Mar. 1988, 21; Romanian Situation Report, *RFER*, 29 Dec. 1988, 3; Warsaw PAP, 26 Jan. 1989, in FBIS, 2 Feb. 1989, 48; Czechoslovak Situation Report, *RFER*, 16 Feb. 1989, 9; and BTA, 22 Feb. 1989, in FBIS, 23 Feb. 1989, 7.

139   *Danas*, no. 294 (6 Oct. 1987): 59; Vladimir Sobell, "Eastern Europe's Debts: Heavy Burden, Little Benefit," *RFER*, 22 Mar. 1988, 2.

2   Disaffection and Dissent in East Germany

This chapter is a revised and updated version of an essay originally published in *World Politics* 37, no. 1 (Oct. 1984). Copyright © 1984 by Princeton University Press. Reprinted with the permission of Princeton University Press.

1   Relevant studies include Zygmunt Bauman, "Social Dissent in the East European Political System," *Archives Européennes de Sociologie* 12, no. 1 (1971): 25–51; Archie Brown and Jack Gray, eds., *Political Culture and Political Change in Communist States* (New York: Holmes & Meier, 1977); Walter D. Connor, "Dissent in Eastern Europe: A New Coalition?," *Problems of Communism* 29, no. 1 (Jan.-Feb. 1980); Walter D. Connor, "Social Change and Stability in Eastern Europe," *Problems of Communism* 26, no. 6 (Nov.-Dec. 1977); Andrzej Korbonski, "Conformity and Dissent in Eastern Europe," in *Politics and Participation under Communist Rule*, ed. Peter J. Potichnyj and Jane Shapiro Zacek (New York: Praeger, 1983); Alfred G. Meyer, "Political Change through Civil Disobedience in the USSR and Eastern Europe," in *Political and Legal Obligation*, ed. J. Roland Pennock and John W. Chapman, Yearbook of the American Society for Political and Legal Philosophy, vol. 12 (New York: Atherton, 1970); and Peter Veres, "Alienation: A Hungarian View," *East Europe* 14 (Mar. 1965). As treated here, disaffection is a specific type of cognitive dissonance. In this connection the general literature on this theory is also relevant, in particular: Elliot Aronson, "The Theory of Cognitive Dissonance: A Current Perspective," in *Advances in Experimental Psychology*, ed. Leonard Berkowitz (New York: Academic Press, 1969), 1–34; Leon Festinger, *A Theory of Cognitive Dissonance* (Evanston, Ill.: Row, Peterson, 1957); and Leon Festinger, ed., *Conflict, Decision, and Dissonance* (Stanford, Calif.: Stanford University Press, 1964).

2   *Bild* (Hamburg), 20 Nov. 1982, in FBIS, 23 Nov. 1982.

3   Otto Ulč, "Social Deviance in Czechoslovakia," in *Social Deviance in Eastern Europe*, ed. Ivan Volgyes (Boulder, Colo.: Westview, 1978), 28.

4   Paul H. Shapiro, "Social Deviance in Eastern Europe: On Understanding the Problem," in *Social Deviance in Eastern Europe*, ed. Ivan Volgyes (Boulder, Colo.: Westview, 1978), 15.

5   *Neue Zürcher Zeitung*, 23–24 Jan. 1983).

6   See Leonard Binder, "Crises of Political Development," in *Crises and Sequences in Political Development*, Leonard Binder et al. (Princeton, N.J.: Princeton University Press, 1971), 3–72.

7   See Ivan Volgyes, "Political Socialization in Eastern Europe," *Problems of Communism* 23, no. 1 (Jan.-Feb. 1974): 52.

8   See Arthur M. Hanhardt, Jr., "Political Socialization in Divided Germany," *Journal of International Affairs* 27, no. 2 (1973): 188, 192, 196.

9   Otto Luchterhandt, *Die Gegenwartslage der Evangelischen Kirche in der DDR* (Tubingen: J. C. B. Mohr, 1982), 3; Ernst Alfred Jauch, "Katholiken in der DDR," *Kirche in Not* 26 (1978): 66–67; Kurt Sontheimer and Wilhelm Bleek, *The Government and Politics of East Germany*, trans. Ursula Price (London: Hutchinson University Library, 1975), 189.

10 See Reinhard Henkys, "Kirche in der Deutschen Demokratischen Republik," in *Religionsfreiheit und Menschenrechte*, ed. Paul Lendvai (Graz: Verlag Styria, 1983), 165–79; and Pedro Ramet, "Church and Peace in the GDR," *Problems of Communism* 33, no. 4 (July-Aug. 1984), reprinted in revised form in Pedro Ramet, *Cross and Commissar: The Politics of Religion in Eastern Europe and the USSR* (Bloomington: Indiana University Press, 1987), chap. 5.

11 Werner Volkmer, "East Germany: Dissenting Views during the Last Decade," in *Opposition in Eastern Europe*, ed. Rudolf L. Tökes (London: Macmillan, 1979), 114–15. In an interview with a Polish newspaper in 1989, East German dissident Wolfgang Templin sounded a cautionary note on reunification: "There are no political forces at present in the East or the West that would tolerate the unification of Germany. [But] we are demanding the right of GDR society to have its sovereign say on the matter." *Gazeta Wyborcza* (Warsaw), 12 Sept. 1989, 6, in FBIS, 18 Sept. 1989, 38.

12 "Interview with Robert Havemann," trans. Jack Zipes, *New German Critique*, no. 15 (Fall 1978): 41–42, 45; Günter Minnerup, "East Germany's Frozen Revolution," *New Left Review*, no. 132 (Mar.-Apr. 1982): 27–28.

13 *New York Times*, 26 Feb. 1984. See also *Los Angeles Times*, 19 Feb. 1983; *Washington Post*, 21 Jan. 1984, and 28 Jan. 1984.

14 DPA (Hamburg), 18 Apr. 1989, in FBIS, 18 Apr. 1989, 20.

15 Hans-Jürgen Grasemann, "Zwischen Ideologie und Realität: Jugendkriminalität in der DDR," *Deutsche Studien* 14 (Dec. 1976): 368–69.

16 By 9 percent in the 1977–78 period: Ibid., 371; *Frankfurter Allgemeine*, 10 July 1973); *New York Times*, 6 May 1980.

17 *The Times* (London), 10 Oct. 1977.

18 Herbert Prauss, "Jugend in der DDR," *Kirche in Not* 21 (1973): 81.

19 *Die Zeit* (Hamburg), 17 June 1983; *Forum* (East Berlin), Dec. 1982, 3, in JPRS, no. 83252 (13 Apr. 1983).

20 Klaus Ehring and Martin Dallwitz, *Schwerter zu Pflugscharen* (Hamburg: Rowohlt Taschenbuch Verlag, 1982), 90–92.

21 From the East Berlin magazine *Melodie und Rhythmus*, quoted in *Frankfurter Allgemeine*, 15 Sept. 1982, in JPRS, no. 81941 (7 Oct. 1982).

22 *Iwe-Tagesdienst* (Bonn), 26 Mar. 1983, in JPRS, no. 83359 (28 Apr. 1983).

23 *Vjesnik* (Zagreb), 28 Oct. 1983.

24 Norbert Haase, Lothar Reese, and Peter Wensierski, eds., *VEB Nachwuchs. Jugend in der DDR* (Hamburg: Rowohlt Verlag, 1983), 192–93.

25 Euphemistically translated: "legal, illegal, all the same."

26 Quoted in *Der Spiegel*, 3 Jan. 1983, 44.

27 Ibid., 122.

28 See Haase et al., *VEB Nachwuchs*, 243–44.

29 *Der Spiegel*, 3 Jan. 1983, 131.

30 Quoted in Henkys, "Kirche in der Deutschen Demokratischen Republik," 176.

31 Luchterhandt, *Die Gegenwartslage*, 68; Jauch, "Katholiken," 71, 73–74.

32 Quoted in Luchterhandt, *Die Gegenwartslage*, 66. See also Gerald Götting, *Beitrag christlicher Demokraten zu Gegenwart und Zukunft: Reden und Aufsätze, 1981–1986* (East Berlin: Union Verlag, 1987).

33 Luchterhandt, *Die Gegenwartslage*, 71–72; "Notes on Church-State Relations," *Journal of Church and State* 23 (Winter 1981): 166.

34 *Frankfurter Allgemeine*, 4 Jan. 1983, and 7 Jan. 1983.

35 See *Leipziger Volkszeitung*, 1 Feb. 1962, as cited in Ehring and Dallwitz, *Schwerter*, 14–15.

36 *Süddeutsche Zeitung* (Munich), 8 Sept. 1982, in JPRS, no. 81941 (7 Oct. 1982); Ehring and Dallwitz, *Schwerter*, 20–25. See also Timothy Garton Ash, "Swords into Ploughshares: The Unofficial 'Peace Movement' and the Churches in East Germany," *Religion in Communist Lands* 11 (Winter 1983): 245–46.

37 *Wiener Tagebuch* (Vienna), Oct. 1982, in JPRS, no. 82210 (10 Nov. 1982).

38 Ehring and Dallwitz, *Schwerter*, 59, 70; *Die Welt* (Bonn), 21 June 1982).

39 Günter Krusche, *Bekenntnis und Weltverantwortung. Die Ekklesiologiestudie des Lutherischen Weltbundes: Ein Beitrag zur ökumenischen Sozialethik* (Berlin: Evangelische Verlagsanstalt, 1986), 146.

40 *Wall Street Journal*, 22 June 1983); *Facts on File*, 1 July 1983, 490; *Neue Zürcher Zeitung*, 2 Sept. 1983, and 4 Jan. 1984; and *Frankfurter Allgemeine*, 24 Oct. 1983, and 5 Nov. 1983.

41 Interview with clergyman, Berlin, 30 June 1988.

42 Interview with clergyman, Eisenach, 12 July 1988.

43 Ulrike Enders, "Erziehung zu Hass: Zum staatlichen Erziehungsprogramm für kindergarten," *Kirche im Sozialismus* 13, no. 2 (Apr. 1987): 52–53.

44 "Program fur die Erziehungsarbeit im Kindergarten," *Kirche im Sozialismus* 13, no. 2 (Apr. 1987): 55, 56.

45 Interview with clergyman, Berlin, 29 June 1988; *Frankfurter Allgemeine*, 26 June 1987, 2, and 29 June 1987, 5; *Die Zeit* (Hamburg), 10 July 1987, 2.

46 Interview with clergyman, Erfurt, 12 July 1988; and interview source cited in note 45.

47 *Die Welt* (Bonn), 7 June 1988, 10, in FBIS, 8 June 1988, 36; *Neue Zürcher Zeitung*, 10 June 1988, 6.

48 *Frankfurter Rundschau*, 27 June 1988, 1, 3.

49 DPA (Hamburg), 12 June 1988, in FBIS, 13 June 1988, 29–30.

50 DPA 16 Sept. 1988, in FBIS, 21 Sept. 1988, 17; *Neue Zürcher Zeitung*, 22 Sept. 1988, 1.

51 *Frankfurter Allgemeine*, 20 June 1988, 1, in FBIS, 21 June 1988, 20; *Die Welt*, 5 July 1988, 1, in FBIS, 6 July 1988, 29; *Frankfurter Allgemeine*, 9 Aug. 1988, 3, and 10 Aug. 1988, 1.

52 Richard Schröder, "Was kann 'Kirche im Sozialismus' sinnvoll heissen?," *Kirche im Sozialismus* 14, no. 4 (Aug. 1988): 135–37.

53 Barbara Donovan, "East German Churches Demand Justice," *RFER*, 10 May 1989, 2.

54 Cited in *Frankfurter Allgemeine*, 22 Sept. 1989, 3.

55 East Germany actually allows a limited number of conscientious objectors to serve in a uniformed construction brigade. But since the brigade works largely on projects of military importance, some objectors have refused even this.

56 Henry W. Degenhardt, *Political Dissent: An International Guide to Dissident, Extra-*

Parliamentary, Guerrilla, and Illegal Political Movements (Detroit: Gale, 1983), 16–17.

57 "East Germany's Democratic Movement: 'Human Rights GDR,'" *Across Frontiers* (Spring 1986): 13.

58 *Frankfurter Allgemeine*, 23 Sept. 1989, 1–2.

59 *Neue Zürcher Zeitung*, 26 Jan. 1988, 3; 31 Jan.-1 Feb. 1988, 3; and 6 Feb. 1988, 3. See also *Süddeutsche Zeitung*, 6–7 Feb. 1988, 1–2; *Frankfurter Allgemeine*, 8 Feb. 1988, 1.

60 Zelime Amen Ward, "Minority Politics in the German Democratic Republic: Problematics of Socialist Legitimacy and National Autonomy," in *The Politics of Ethnicity in Eastern Europe*, ed. George Klein and Milan J. Reban (Boulder, Colo.: East European Monographs, 1981), 98, 101–2.

61 Quoted in Peter Jokostra, "Ein Archipel von Sprachinseln: Bericht uber die Literatur der sorbischen Minderheit in der DDR," *Deutsche Studien* 15 (Sept. 1977): 279.

62 For details, see Frithjof Heller, "Schön, bemerkenswert und traditionell: Die Sorben zwischen Kruzifix und Thälmannbild," *Kirche im Sozialismus* 13, no. 3 (June 1987): 103–4.

63 ADN, 21 Nov. 1989, in FBIS, 21 Nov. 1989, 37.

64 ADN, 17 Nov. 1989, in FBIS, 21 Nov. 1989, 37.

65 ADN, 20 Nov. 1989, in FBIS, 21 Nov. 1989, 37.

66 *Der Spiegel*, 25 July 1983, in JPRS, no. 84155 (19 Aug. 1983).

67 Wolfgang Buscher and Peter Wensierski, *Null Bock auf DDR. Aussteigerjugend im anderen Deutschland* (Hamburg: Spiegel Verlag, 1984), 39.

68 *Neue Zürcher Zeitung*, 5 July 1983, in JPRS, no. 84084 (10 Aug. 1983); *Süddeutsche Zeitung*, 5 July 1983. See also *Die Welt*, 2 Aug. 1983.

69 Christel Sudau, "Women in the GDR," trans. Biddy Martin, *New German Critique*, no. 13 (Winter 1978): 70–71; David Childs, *The GDR: Moscow's German Ally* (London: George Allen & Unwin, 1983), 251; Sharon L. Wolchik, "Ideology and Equality: The Status of Women in Eastern and Western Europe," *Comparative Political Studies* 13 (Jan. 1981): 459.

70 Childs, *The GDR*, 259.

71 Ibid., 252.

72 *Armeerundschau* (Apr. 1982): 55–56; *Christian Science Monitor*, 5 Jan. 1984. See also *Neue Zürcher Zeitung*, 6 Jan. 1984.

73 Text of letter given in *Der Spiegel*, 6 Dec. 1982, 117, in FBIS, 7 Dec. 1982.

74 Michael Waller, *The Language of Communism* (London: The Bodley Head, 1972), 32.

75 Bauman, "Social Dissent," 46.

76 David Childs, *East Germany* (London: Ernest Benn, 1969), 38; Volkmer, "East Germany: Dissenting Views," 128.

77 Horst Sindermann, at fifth session of the central committee, SED, Feb. 1964, as quoted in Childs, *The GDR*, 74.

78 Bruce Allen, *Germany East: Dissent and Opposition* (Montreal: Black Rose, 1989), 63.

79 Peter Lübbe, *Der staatliche etablierte Sozialismus: Zur Kritik des staat-monopolischen Sozialismus* (Hamburg: Hoffman & Campe, 1975), as cited in Jeffrey Lee Canfield, "Marxist Revisionism in East Germany: The Case of Rudolf Bahro," *The Fletcher Forum* 4 (Winter 1980): 47.

80 Rudolf Bahro, *Die Alternative: Zur Kritik des real existierenden Sozialismus*

(Cologne: Europäische Verlagsanstalt, 1977).

81 Michael J. Sodaro, "Limits to Dissent in the GDR: Fragmentation, Cooptation, and Repression," in *Dissent in Eastern Europe*, ed. Jane Leftwich Curry (New York: Praeger, 1983), esp. 97; Hugh Mosely, "The New Communist Opposition: Rudolf Bahro's Critique of the 'Really Existing Socialism,'" *New German Critique*, no. 15 (Fall 1978): 28, 32.

82 David Bathrick, "The Politics of Culture: Rudolf Bahro and Opposition in the GDR," *New German Critique*, no. 15 (Fall 1978): 20.

83 Canfield, "Marxist Revisionism," 32.

84 Ibid.

85 Günter Bartsch, "Mehr als Alternative: Ein Durchbruch und Neubeginn," *Deutschland Archiv* 11, no. 5 (May 1978): 474. See also Fritz Shenk, "Rudolf Bahro und das Dilemma des Marxismus-Leninismus," *Deutschland Archiv* 11, no. 5 (May 1978): 470–71.

86 When Bahro was jailed, Wolf Biermann commented, "What brings them [the SED] to a complete rage and makes them crazy is the inherent criticism that comes from within" (*Die Welt*, 3 July 1978, quoted in Canfield, "Marxist Revisionism," 28.

87 *Der Spiegel*, 24 Aug. 1981, 35.

88 *Wall Street Journal*, 17 Nov. 1989), A10.

89 Jan Vanous, "East European Economic Slowdown," *Problems of Communism* 31, no. 4 (July-Aug. 1982): 3; *Business Week*, 24 May 1982, 170, 181; *Neue Zürcher Zeitung*, 23–24 Jan. 1983.

90 Richard Portes, "Effects of the World Economic Crisis on the East European Economies," *World Economy* 3 (June 1980): 26; *Frankfurter Allgemeine*, 2 Jan. 1984; *Neue Zürcher Zeitung*, 12 Jan. 1984.

91 Martin McCauley, "Storm Signals in East German Economy," *Soviet Analyst* 11 (10 Feb. 1982): 5; *Der Spiegel*, 3 Oct. 1983), 126; "Interview with Robert Havemann," 43.

92 Volkmer, "East Germany: Dissenting Views," 119–20; *New York Times*, 3 Aug. 1981; *Christian Science Monitor*, 20 Aug. 1981.

93 Roger Woods, *Opposition in the GDR under Honecker, 1971–85* (London: Macmillan, 1986), 14–15.

94 *Bild*, 20 Nov. 1982, in FBIS, 23 Nov. 1982.

95 *Der Spiegel*, 8 Nov. 1982, 16–17, and 10 Jan. 1983, 16–17.

96 Report in DPA, 11 Jan. 1983, in FBIS, 11 Jan. 1983; *Stern*, 13 Jan. 1983, 17, 126–27. Denied in ADN, 11 Jan. 1983, in FBIS, Jan. 11, 1983.

97 *Neue Zürcher Zeitung*, 11 Jan. 1985, 13.

98 *Financial Times*, 11 Mar. 1988, 2; also *Neues Deutschland*, 12 Jan. 1988, 1.

99 *Financial Times*, 10 Jan. 1989, 2.

100 *Wall Street Journal*, 29 Jan. 1988, 12; *Financial Times*, 11 Mar. 1988, 2; *Frankfurter Allgemeine*, 13 Apr. 1988, 6, and 18 Apr. 1988, 13; Barbara Donovan, "Is the East German Economy Running into Trouble?," *RFER*, 14 Apr. 1988, 1–2.

101 *Wall Street Journal*, 17 Nov. 1989, A1.

102 Barbara Donovan, "Plans for a Coordinated Opposition Movement in the GDR," *RFER*, 18 Aug. 1989.

103 *Frankfurter Allgemeine*, 27 Sept. 1989, 4, and 9 Oct. 1989, 4; *New York Times*, 16 Oct. 1989, A4; DPA, 24 Sept. 1989, in FBIS, 25 Sept. 1989, 22.

104 *Frankfurter Allgemeine*, 18 Sept. 1989, 5; 8 Oct. 1989, 1–2; and 9 Oct. 1989, 4.

105 For the Luther revival, see Robert F. Goeckel, "The Luther Anniversary in East

Germany," *World Politics* 37, no. 1 (Oct. 1984); Dan Beck, "The Luther Revival: Aspects of National *Abgrenzung* and Confessional *Gemeinschaft* in the German Democratic Republic," in *Religion and Nationalism in Soviet and East European Politics*, ed. Pedro Ramet, rev. and expanded ed. (Durham, N.C.: Duke University Press, 1989), 223–40.

106   General secretary Walter Ulbricht was eager to suppress the Prague Spring, but East German youth were deeply alienated by East German participation in the Warsaw Pact invasion of Czechoslovakia in 1968, and some offspring of SED elite openly protested against the invasion. See Childs, *The GDR*, 79–80.

3   Underground Solidarity and Parallel Society in Poland

1   "Parallel Polis, or An Independent Society in Central and Eastern Europe: An Inquiry" (Comments by Václav Benda), *Social Research* 55, nos. 1–2 (Spring/Summer 1988): 217.

2   See Jakub Karpiński, "Polish Intellectuals in Opposition," *Problems of Communism* 36, no. 4 (July-Aug. 1987).

3   See Pedro Ramet, "Poland's 'Other' Parties," *The World Today* 37, no. 9 (Sept. 1981): 332–38.

4   Quoted in *Reinventing Civil Society: Poland's Quiet Revolution, 1981–1986* (New York: Helsinki Watch, 1986), 7.

5   "The Strategy is to Keep Pressing: An Interview with Wiktor Kulerski," *Uncaptive Minds* 1, no. 2 (June-Aug. 1988): 16.

6   *Reinventing Civil Society*, 9.

7   Roman Dumas, "Poland's 'Independent Society,'" *Poland Watch*, no. 8 (1986): 65.

8   *Profil* (Vienna), 11 May 1987, 53.

9   Jan B. de Weydenthal, "The Story behind Martial Law in Poland," *RFER*, 14 Apr. 1987, 2; *New York Times*, 17 Apr. 1987, A9; *US News & World Report*, 20 Apr. 1987, 33. For discussion and analysis of Soviet thinking about Poland in 1980 and 1981, see Pedro Ramet, "Innenpolitische Determinanten der Sowjetischen Interventionspolitik. Zu den Auswirkungen der Tschechoslowakischen und Polnischen Krise auf den Westen der UdSSR," *Osteuropa* 35, no. 3 (Mar. 1985).

10   Lech Wałęsa, *A Way of Hope: An Autobiography*, trans. Marete B. Zaleski et al. (New York: Henry Holt & Co., 1987), 211–12.

11   *Tu i Teraz*, 29 Aug. 1984, 3, in FBIS, 7 Sept. 1984, G3–5; AFP, 8 Mar. 1985, in FBIS, 9 Apr. 1985, G1.

12   *Christian Science Monitor*, 8 Jan. 1988, 10.

13   *La Vanguardia* (Barcelona), 29 Aug. 1988, 6, in FBIS, 8 Sept. 1988, 36.

14   Interview with a former Silesian Solidarity leader, Munich, 4 June 1987. See also PAP (Warsaw), 11 Feb. 1982, in FBIS, 12 Feb. 1982, G17.

15   Warsaw Domestic Service, 12 Jan. 1982, in FBIS, 13 Jan. 1982, G10.

16   Interview source cited in note 14.

17   *Le Monde* (Paris), 30 Apr. 1982, 1, 4, in FBIS, 5 May 1982, G31.

18   Interview with a former Solidarity activist from Toruń, Munich, 1 June 1987.

19   Interview source cited in note 14.

20   Interview source cited in note 18.

21   *Los Angeles Times*, 18 Mar. 1982, 4.

22   Ibid., 20 June 1982, 1.

23   Quoted in Ibid., 28 Aug. 1982, 4.

24   Ibid., 21 May 1982, 4.

25   *Süddeutsche Zeitung* (Munich), 24–25 July 1982, 7.

26   From the full text of the statement in *Le Monde*, 12 Oct. 1982, 4, in FBIS, 13 Oct. 1982, G8.

27   Quoted in Jan B. de Weydenthal, *The Communists of Poland: An Historical Outline*, rev. ed. (Stanford, Calif.: Hoover Institution Press, 1987), 210.

28   *Die Welt* (Bonn), 25 May 1985, 7, in JPRS, no. EPS-85-097, (23 Sept. 1985): 17–19.

29   Janusz Bugajski, "Polish Security Service Operations against the Solidarity Underground," *RFER*, 10 Apr. 1984, 4.

30   Ibid., 6–7; Dumas, "Poland's 'Independent Society,'" 69.

31   Quoted in *Die Welt*, 25 May 1985, 19.

32   Wałęsa, *A Way of Hope*, 237.

33   PAP, 9 Mar. 1983, in FBIS, 10 Mar. 1983, G3.

34   *Los Angeles Times*, 2 May 1983, 1.

35   Quoted in *Christian Science Monitor*, 25 Aug. 1983, 7.

36   At a press conference for foreign journalists, Hipolit Starszak, deputy prosecutor general, said that if Bujak surrendered, the charges of high treason would be dropped and he would be amnestied. See *Rzeczpospolita*, 3 Aug. 1984, 5–6, in FBIS, 8 Aug. 1984, G10–14.

37   *Gazeta Robotnicza*, as cited in AFP, 17 Aug. 1984), in FBIS, 20 Aug. 1984, G10.

38   Jan Józef Lipski, interview with *Der Spiegel*, 30 July 1984, 90–92, in FBIS, 1 Aug. 1984, G5–6.

39   Col. Zygmunt Rybacki, interview with *Żołnierz Wolności*, 8 Aug. 1984, 4–5, in FBIS, 15 Aug. 1984, G6–10.

40   Warsaw Domestic Service, 24 Aug. 1984, in FBIS, 27 Aug. 1984, G1.

41   AFP, 20 Aug. 1984 (FBIS, 20 Aug. 1984, G11), and 31 Aug. 1984) (FBIS, 4 Sept. 1984, G11); Warsaw Domestic Service, 23 Aug. 1984, (FBIS, 23 Aug. 1984, G5), and 31 Aug. 1984 (FBIS, 4 Sept. 1984, G12).

42   Quoted in *Seattle Times*, 1 May 1984, A2.

43   AFP, 31 July 1984, in FBIS, 1 Aug. 1984, G2; *Washington Post*, 1 Sept. 1984, A21.

44   AFP, 31 July 1984); AFP (Hong Kong), 29 Aug. 1984; AFP, 3 Sept. 1984; and AFP, 20 Sept. 1984—respectively in FBIS, 1 Aug. 1984, G9–10; 30 Aug. 1984, G10; 4 Sept. 1984, G12–13; and 21 Sept. 1984, G3.

45   AFP, 1 Oct. 1984, in FBIS, 2 Oct. 1984, G1.

46   AFP, 7 Sept. 1984, in FBIS, 10 Sept. 1984, G5; ZDF Television Network (Mainz), 31 Oct. 1984), in FBIS, 6 Nov. 1984, G2–3.

47   *Expresso* (Lisbon), 3 Nov. 1984, 25–27B, in FBIS, 13 Nov. 1984, G8.

48   AFP, 3 Aug. 1984, in FBIS, 6 Aug. 1984, G8; Vienna Television Service, 21 Dec. 1984, in FBIS, 24 Dec. 1984, G6–7.

49   ORF Teletext (Vienna), 31 Oct. 1984, in FBIS, 1 Nov. 1984, G1; Vatican City International Service, 11 Nov. 1984, in FBIS, 11 Nov. 1984, G1–2; AFP, 12 Nov. 1984), in FBIS, 23 Nov. 1984, G2.

50   See Warsaw Domestic Service, 14 Nov. 1984, in FBIS, 14 Nov. 1984, G1–3; Warsaw Television Service, 16 Nov. 1984, in FBIS, 19 Nov. 1984, G1–2; ORF Teletext 20 Nov. 1984, in FBIS, 20 Nov. 1984, G1; and *Le Figaro* (Paris), 20 Nov. 1984, 4, in FBIS, 28 Nov. 1984, G10.

51   *Czas* (Poznań), no. 1 (2), 1985, excerpted in "Extracts from Polish Underground Publications," *RFER*, 11 Sept. 1985, 9–10.

52 Władysław Frasyniuk, "An Open Letter to Solidarity Members and Sympathizers," *Tygodnik Mazowsze*, no. 112 (10 Jan. 1985), in "Recent Articles from Underground Publications in Poland," *RFER*, 20 Mar. 1985, no. 54, 3.

53 *New York Times*, 13 June 1990, A8.

54 Michał Kołodziej, "The Underground Structure of Solidarity," *RFER* 11 Apr. 1985, 7–18.

55 "Underground Solidarity in Silesia—Interview with a Member of the Silesian Regional Executive Committee," *Across Frontiers* (Winter/Spring 1985): 21.

56 Kołodziej, "The Underground Structure," 6; corroborated in Dumas, "Poland's 'Independent Society,'" 68–69.

57 Francis Michalski, "The Rise of a Political Opposition in Poland," *Poland Watch*, no. 8 (1986): 94–95.

58 Quoted in Ibid., 95.

59 *Obserwator Wielkopolski*, no. 117, in *UPNB*, no. 8/88 (29 Apr. 1988): 15.

60 *Süddeutsche Zeitung*, 10–11 Sept. 1988, 2.

61 Michalski, "The Rise of Political Opposition," 105; also Teresa Hanicka, "Political Groups in the Polish Underground," *RFER*, 14 Oct. 1985, 21.

62 *KOS*, no. 20 (29 Nov. 1982), quoted in Hanicka, "Political Groups," 12.

63 Hanicka, "Political Groups," 13.

64 Quoted in Michalski, "The Rise of Political Opposition," 98.

65 Hanicka, "Political Groups," 17.

66 *Christian Science Monitor*, 18 Nov. 1987, 2.

67 *Zeszyty Dokumentacji Politycznej*, no. 60 (Oct. 1985), quoted in Polish Situation Report, *RFER*, 18 Dec. 1987, 23.

68 *Dziennik Polski* (London), 21 Nov. 1987, trans. into German as "Polen: Wiederbegrundung der Polnischen Sozialistischen Partei," *Osteuropa* 38, no. 5 (May 1988): A259. For thorough discussions of their respective subjects, see Arthur F. McGovern, S.J., "Catholic Social Teachings: A Brief History," and George H. Williams, "Karol Wojtyla and Marxism: His Thought and Action as Professor, Prelate and Supreme Pontiff"—both in *Catholicism and Politics in Communist Societies*, ed. Pedro Ramet (Durham, N.C.: Duke University Press, 1990), respectively 28–45 and 356–81.

69 Quoted in *New York Times*, 2 Jan. 1988, 3.

70 Quoted in Ibid.

71 *UPNB*, no. 6/88 (22 Mar. 1988): 10, and no. 13/88 (8 July 1988): 7.

72 Michalski, "Rise of Political Opposition," 103.

73 "Today's Attitudes Are More Christian, More Catholic" [an interview with Leszek Moczulski], *Frontier* (May-June 1987): 6.

74 Polish Situation Report, *RFER*, 4 Apr. 1986, 19.

75 Warsaw Domestic Service, 9 Mar. 1985, in FBIS, 11 Mar. 1985, G3; Warsaw Domestic Service, 11 Mar. 1985, in FBIS, 12 Mar. 1985, G3; *The Times* (London), 23 Apr. 1986, 9; *UPNB*, no. 11/86 (3 June 1986): 26–29.

76 AFP, 4 Aug. 1988, in FBIS, 5 Aug. 1988, 16.

77 Quoted in *UPNB*, no. 13/86 (1 July 1986): 18 (*my emphasis*).

78 *From Below: Independent Peace and Environmental Movements in Eastern Europe and the USSR* (New York: Helsinki Watch, 1987), 77; Czechoslovak Situation Report, *RFER*, 6 Apr. 1987, 21.

79 *UPNB*, no. 3/86 (30 Jan. 1986): 25.

80 *Washington Post*, 4 Nov. 1986, A1; *From Below*, 78.

81 *From Below*, 78; *Washington Post*, 11 Jan. 1987, A27; *Corriere della Sera* (Milan), 7
     Sept. 1987, 7; Gareth Davies, "Conscientious Objection and the Freedom and Peace
     Movement in Poland," *Religion in Communist Lands* 16, no. 1 (Spring 1988): 11.
82 *From Below*, 87–88; *New York Times*, 14 May 1987, 5.
83 Michał Kołodziej, "The Freedom and Peace Movement in Poland," *RFER*, 13 Apr.
     1987, 26.
84 *Trybuna Ludu* (Warsaw), 23 June 1988, 3, in FBIS, 21 July 1988, 37–38.
85 *UPNB*, no. 24/88 (31 Dec. 1988): 12.
86 Ibid., no. 2/88 (22 Jan. 1988): 16–17.
87 Ibid., 15.
88 *The Economist* (London), 21 May 1988, 54; *UPNB*, no. 6/88 (22 Mar. 1988): 18.
89 *UPNB*, no. 2/88 (22 Jan. 1988): 14.
90 *Die Welt*, 21 June 1988, 2.
91 *UPNB*, no. 2/88 (22 Jan. 1988): 16.
92 Ibid., no. 6/88 (22 Mar. 1988): 18.
93 Ibid., no. 2/88 (22 Jan. 1988): 17.
94 *The Economist*, 21 May 1988, 54.
95 *Die Welt*, 21 June 1988, 10.
96 *UPNB*, no. 2/88 (22 Jan. 1988): 16.
97 Quoted in *The Economist*, 21 May 1988, 54.
98 *UPNB*, no. 2/88 (22 Jan. 1988): 16.
99 *New York Times*, 9 Oct. 1988, 6.
100 *Financial Times*, 8 Nov. 1988, 2.
101 See Hanicka, "Political Groups"; *Homek*, no. 21 (June 1985), in "Extracts from
     Polish Underground Publications," *RFER*, 3 Oct. 1985, 23; *UPNB*, no. 1/88 (8 Jan.
     1988): 9–10; Warsaw Domestic Service, 4 Nov. 1982, in FBIS, 5 Nov. 1982, G2; and
     Wojsko Ludowe (Warsaw), no. 3 (Mar. 1983), in JPRS, no. 84028 (2 Aug. 1983): 63–73.
     See also Stefan Malski, "Political Groups in the Polish Underground," *RFER*, 8 Sept.
     1983).
102 *Die Presse* (Vienna), 22 Sept. 1988, 2, in FBIS, 23 Sept. 1988, 28; *Süddeutsche Zeitung*,
     8–9 Oct. 1988, 13. For further details about the Polish Ecological Club, see *UPNB*,
     no. 13/88 (8 July 1988): 12–13.
103 De Weydenthal, *The Communists of Poland*, 113; Warsaw Television Service, 17
     Nov. 1984, in FBIS, 19 Nov. 1984, G1.
104 Quoted in *Reinventing Civil Society*, 24.
105 Quoted in Ibid., 27.
106 Ibid., 31–32; "OKN: Organizing Underground Education, Culture and Science,"
     East European Reporter 1, no. 2 (Summer 1985): 12.
107 Teresa Hanicka, "The Independent Education Movement in Poland," *RFER*, 16 Aug.
     1984, 2.
108 *Reinventing Civil Society*, 40–41.
109 *Tygodnik Mazowsze*, no. 114 (24 Jan. 1985), in "Extracts from Polish Underground
     Publications," *RFER*, 21 May 1985, 5.
110 *Reinventing Civil Society*, 72–73.
111 *Tygodnik Mazowsze*, no. 114 (24 Jan. 1985): 7.
112 *Süddeutsche Zeitung*, 20–21 Feb. 1988, 8; Polish Situation Report, *RFER*, 25 Feb.
     1988, 5–7; *Frankfurter Allgemeine*, 9 Mar. 1988, 1, and 12 Oct. 1988, 3; *Neue
     Zürcher Zeitung*, 26 Mar. 1988, 1; *Financial Times*, 12 Oct. 1988, 2.
113 *Frankfurter Allgemeine*, 7 Oct. 1988, 6.

114 *Reinventing Civil Society*, 44–45.

115 Ibid., 47.

116 Ted Kamiński, "Underground Publishing in Poland," *Orbis* 31, no. 3 (Fall 1987): 318.

117 Quoted in *Washington Post*, 4 Apr. 1987, A13.

118 Warsaw Television Service, 7 Dec. 1984, in FBIS, 11 Dec. 1984, G7; AFP, 14 Mar. 1985 and 15 Apr. 1985—respectively in FBIS, 15 Mar. 1985, G9–10, and 16 Apr. 1985, G7–8.

119 For details, see Polish Situation Report, *RFER*, 5 Mar. 1986, 8.

120 See *Christian Science Monitor*, 8 July 1987, 11.

121 *Reinventing Civil Society*, 54.

122 Kamiński, "Underground Publishing," 322.

123 "*Tygodnik Mazowsze* Interviews Itself," *Tygodnik Mazowsze*, no. 100 (4 Oct. 1984), in "Recent Articles from Underground Publications in Poland," *RFER*, 7 Jan. 1985, 5.

124 Polish Situation Report, *RFER*, 5 Mar. 1986, 20; confirmed in *Reinventing Civil Society*, 65.

125 *UPNB*, no. 7/86 (3 Apr. 1986): 41.

126 Warsaw Domestic Service, 15 Feb. 1985, in FBIS, 19 Feb. 1985, G8–9; AFP, 14 May 1985) and 21 May 1985—respectively in FBIS, 14 May 1985, G6–7, and 22 May 1985, G2–3.

127 *New York Times*, 9 Dec. 1984, 7.

128 AFP, 23 May 1985 and 25 May 1985—respectively in FBIS, 24 May 1985, G2, and 28 May 1985, G1; *Seattle Times*, 13 Oct. 1985, 2.

129 *The Times* (London), 18 Feb. 1985, 7; confirmed in AFP, 9 Mar. 1985, in FBIS, 11 Mar. 1985, G2.

130 AFP, 30 Apr. 1985, 1 May 1985, and 7 May 1985—respectively in FBIS, 1 May 1985, G1; 2 May 1985, G6–7; and 8 May 1985, G2–3.

131 Quoted in *Washington Post National Weekly Edition*, 30 Dec. 1985, 6.

132 *KOS*, no. 78 (18 Aug. 1985), in "Extracts from Polish Underground Publications," *RFER*, 10 Mar. 1986, 19.

133 *Replika*, no. 48 (Spring 1986), excerpted in "Polish Independent Press Review," *RFER*, 12 Dec. 1986, 13–15.

134 *New York Times*, 1 June 1986, 1; *Stampa Sera*, (Torino), 1 Sept. 1986, 14; *Christian Science Monitor*, 3 Oct. 1986, 9; *The Economist*, 4 Oct. 1986, 50.

135 On the Polish opposition's attitude toward Gorbachev, see Adam Michnik, "Der grosse Gegenreformator," *Der Spiegel*, 18 May 1987, 154–55.

136 *News Solidarność*, Coordinating Office Abroad of NSZZ "Solidarnosc," Brussels, 30 Sept. 1986, 1.

137 *KOS*, no. 102 (6 Oct. 1986), excerpted in "Polish Independent Press Review," *RFER*, 12 Dec. 1986, 18–19.

138 *News Solidarność*, 31 Mar. 1987, 1.

139 *New York Times*, 27 Oct. 1987, 2.

140 Jan B. de Weydenthal, "Solidarity Reviews its Options," *RFER*, 20 Oct. 1987, 1; *New York Times*, 18 Oct. 1987, 8.

141 Polish Situation Report, *RFER*, 4 Nov. 1987, 11; *New York Times*, 6 Nov. 1987, 7; *Neue Zürcher Zeitung*, 14 Nov. 1987, 4.

142 AFP, 7 June 1988, in FBIS, 7 June 1988, 37.

143 Quoted in *Wall Street Journal*, 23 July 1987, 1. See also *Washington Post*, 5 Feb. 1987, A25, A31.

144 *Washington Post*, 1 Feb. 1988, A19.

145 *Financial Times*, 9 Mar. 1988, 1.

146 Ibid., 26 Apr. 1988, 3.
147 According to the *New York Times*, 28 Apr. 1988, 1; confirmed in AFP, 7 June 1988, in FBIS, 7 June 1988, 37.
148 Twelve to fifteen thousand according to *Süddeutsche Zeitung*, 30 April–1 May 1988, 2; seventeen to eighteen thousand according to the *New York Times*, 29 Apr. 1988, 1.
149 *New York Times*, 30 Apr. 1988, 1; *Financial Times*, 3 May 1988, 1; *Frankfurter Allgemeine*, 3 May 1988, 1, and 10 May 1988, 5.
150 *New York Times*, 1 May 1988, 1.
151 *Frankfurter Allgemeine*, 28 Apr. 1988, 1, and 29 Apr. 1988, 1; *Financial Times*, 29 Apr. 1988, 1, and 9 May 1988, 16; *New York Times*, 3 May 1988, 1.
152 Quoted in *New York Times*, 5 May 1988, 1.
153 Ibid., 6 May 1988, 1; *Financial Times*, 6 May 1988, 1, and 9 May 1988, 16; *Frankfurter Allgemeine*, 6 May 1988, 1; *Washington Post*, 6 May 1988, A1, 7 May 1988, A1, and 11 May 1988, A1, A30.
154 *Wall Street Journal*, 9 May 1988, 19; Polish Situation Report, *RFER*, 13 May 1988, 25.
155 *Przegląd Wiadomosci Agencyjnych*, no. 20 (147), 18 May 1988, quoted in "Polish Independent Press Review," *RFER*, 4 July 1988, 4.
156 *Le Monde*, 21 June 1988, 3, in FBIS, 22 June 1988, 49–50.
157 *New York Times*, 25 Aug. 1988, 7.
158 Ibid., 18 Aug. 1988, 3, 20 Aug. 1988, 4, and 25 Aug. 1988, 7; *Financial Times*, 19 Aug. 1988, 2, and 20 Aug. 1988, 2; AFP, 18 Aug. 1988, in FBIS, 19 Aug. 1988, 12.
159 *Trybuna Ludu*, 19 Aug. 1988, 2, in FBIS, 24 Aug. 1988, 43.
160 Quoted in *New York Times*, 23 Aug. 1988, 1.
161 AFP, 25 Aug. 1988, in FBIS, 25 Aug. 1988, 34. See also PAP, 18 Aug. 1988, in FBIS, 19 Aug. 1988, 15.
162 *Financial Times*, 22 Aug. 1988, 14.
163 *New York Times*, 25 Aug. 1988, 1.
164 Warsaw Domestic Service, 22 Aug. 1988, in FBIS, 23 Aug. 1988, 11; Warsaw Television Service, 22 Aug. 1988, in FBIS, 23 Aug. 1988, 12; *Financial Times* 30 Aug. 1988, 2; *New York Times*, 16 Sept. 1988, 3; PAP, 16 Sept. 1988, in FBIS, 19 Sept. 1988, 27.
165 Cited in *New York Times*, 14 Sept. 1988, 8.
166 *Tygodnik Mazowsze*, no. 181 (24 Sept. 1986), excerpted in "Polish Independent Press Review," *RFER*, 10 Nov. 1986, 11.

4 Independent Activism in Czechoslovakia, Hungary, and Romania

1 The Yugoslav experience is less well known. For an excellent account, see Vojislav Koštunica and Kosta Čavoški, *Party Pluralism or Monism: Social Movements and the Political System in Yugoslavia, 1944–1949* (Boulder, Colo.: East European Monographs, 1985).
2 Dimitrije Bogdanović, *Knjiga o Kosovu* (Belgrade: Srpska Akademija Nauka i Umetnosti, 1985), 244–46.
3 Zygmunt Bauman, "Social Dissent in the East European Political System," *Archives Européennes de Sociologie* 12, no. 1 (1971): esp. 49–50.
4 Vladimir V. Kusin, "Overview of Dissent in Eastern Europe," *RFER*, 10 Dec. 1987, 1.
5 See Klaus Ehring and Martin Dallwitz, *Schwerter zu Pflugscharen* (Hamburg: Rowohlt Taschenbuch Verlag, 1982).

6 For a detailed description of the Yugoslav scene, see Pedro Ramet, "Yugoslavia 1987: Stirrings from Below," *South Slav Journal* 10, no. 3 (Autumn 1987).

7 "Democratic Opposition in Hungary Today: Exclusive Interview with János Kis," *Across Frontiers* (Fall 1986): 22.

8 *Washington Post*, 14 Mar. 1987, A19.

9 Hungarian Situation Report, RFER, 15 Feb. 1988, 8–9.

10 Two useful lists of activist groups in Eastern Europe, together with brief descriptions of their size, origin, purposes, and activity may be found in Jiří Pehe, "Independent Movements in Eastern Europe (An Annotated Survey)," *RFER*, 17 Nov. 1988, and Jiří Pehe, "An Annotated Survey of Independent Movements in Eastern Europe," *RFER*, 13 June 1989.

11 Ludvík Vaculík, *A Cup of Coffee with My Interrogator*, trans. George Theiner (London: Readers International, 1987), 14–16.

12 See Otto Ulč, "The 'Normalization' of Post-Invasion Czechoslovakia," *Survey* 24, no. 3 (Summer 1979); Vlad Sobell, "Czechoslovakia: The Legacy of Normalization," *Eastern European Politics and Societies* 2, no. 1 (Winter 1988).

13 Janus Bugajski, *Czechoslovakia: Charter 77's Decade of Dissent*, Washington Papers No. 125 (New York: Praeger, 1987), 8–9.

14 There is a voluminous literature dealing in whole or in part with Charter 77. Among the most useful recent publications are H. Gordon Skilling, *Samizdat and An Independent Society in Central and Eastern Europe* (Columbus: Ohio State University Press, 1989), esp. chap. 3, and *A Decade of Dedication: Charter 77, 1977–1987* (New York: Helsinki Watch, 1987).

15 Quoted in Bugajski, *Czechoslovakia*, 12.

16 For a complete list of Charter 77 spokespersons during its first ten years of existence, see Vilém Precan, "Charter 77 Spokesmen, 1977–1986," *RFER*, 11 Feb. 1987.

17 Czechoslovak Situation Report, RFER, 17 Jan. 1987, 3.

18 H. Gordon Skilling, "Independent Currents in Czechoslovakia," *Problems of Communism* 34, no. 1 (Jan.-Feb. 1985): 34.

19 Vilém Precan, "An Annotated List of Charter 77 Documents (1977–1986)," *RFER*, 6 Aug. 1987, 2–3.

20 "The Right to History," Charter 77 Document No. 11/1984 (20 May 1984), excerpted *RFER*, 29 Aug. 1984, 11.

21 Bugajski, *Czechoslovakia*, 47–48.

22 Ibid., 30–32.

23 Interview by Charter 77 spokespersons with Norwegian journalists, 12 Mar. 1984, in *Informacé o Chartě* (Mar. 1984), in *RFER*, 29 Aug. 1984, 5–6.

24 *Los Angeles Times*, 15 Sept. 1981, 7. For reports of arrests, see, for example, *Stuttgarter Zeitung*, 6 June 1981; *Los Angeles Times*, 17 Dec. 1981, 14; AFP, 18 Apr. 1982, in FBIS, 22 Apr. 1982; AFP, 6 Jan. 1983, in FBIS, 7 Jan. 1983, D1; *Frankfurter Allgemeine*, 14 Mar. 1985, 1, and 18 Jan. 1988, 1.

25 Vaculík, *A Cup of Coffee*, 20.

26 Marie Winn, "The Czechs' Defiant Playwright," *New York Times Magazine*, 25 Oct. 1987, 80.

27 *Süddeutsche Zeitung* (Munich), 23–24 July 1988, 8.

28 *Kurier* (Vienna), 12 June 1988, 3, in FBIS, 14 June 1988, 13; Kevin Devlin, "Soviet Pressure behind Bilak's Ouster, Czechoslovak Dissident Tells *L'Unità*," *RFER*, 12 Jan. 1989).

29 Bugajski, *Czechoslovakia*, 52.

30 Josef Škvorecký, "Hipness at Noon," *New Republic*, 17 Dec. 1984, 28.

31 Ibid., 29; Patrick Hunt, "Jazz Defektors," *New Socialist*, Dec. 1986, 12.

32 Škvorecký, "Hipness at Noon," 30.

33 Kenneth Roth, "Prague and the Perils of Jazz," *Commonweal*, 5 June 1987, 352.

34 Quoted in Ibid., 353.

35 Josef Škvorecký, "Hipness at Dusk," *Cross Currents* 6 (1987): 54.

36 One sign of this credibility was the appeal signed by more than 1,000 Czechs and Slovaks in November 1987 for the early release from prison of Karel Srp.

37 On the early period, see Ludvík Něméc, *Church and State in Czechoslovakia* (New York: Vantage, 1955), esp. 253. Regarding the 1970s, see Alexander Tomsky, "Der Katholizismus in der Tschechoslowakei," in *Religionsfreiheit und Menschenrechte*, ed. Paul Lendvai (Graz: Verlag Styria, 1983), esp. 131. For more general discussions, see Pedro Ramet, "Christianity and National Heritage among the Czechs and Slovaks," in *Religion and Nationalism in Soviet and East European Politics*, ed. Pedro Ramet, rev. and expanded ed. (Durham, N.C.: Duke University Press, 1989), 264–85; Pedro Ramet, "Catholics under Communism: The Case of Czechoslovakia," *Christian Century*, 22 Feb. 1989; Milan J. Reban, "The Catholic Church in Czechoslovakia," in *Catholicism and Politics in Communist Societies*, ed. Pedro Ramet (Durham, N.C.: Duke University Press, 1990), 142–55.

38 For further discussion of the underground church in Czechoslovakia, see Pedro Ramet, *Cross and Commissar: The Politics of Religion in Eastern Europe and the USSR* (Bloomington: Indiana University Press, 1987), chap. 8.

39 For summary and discussion, see *Priestervereinigung "Pacem in terris": Eine kritische Analyse* (Munich: Sozialwerk der Ackermann-Gemeinde, 1983), 122–24.

40 Skilling, "Independent Currents," 44–45.

41 Not December, as some reports have suggested. See *Keston News Service*, no. 293 (4 Feb. 1988): 3.

42 Ibid.; *New York Times*, 21 Feb. 1988, 10.

43 The thirty-one points are detailed in Czechoslovak Situation Report, *RFER*, 21 Jan. 1988, 45–48.

44 *New York Times*, 27 Mar. 1988, 6.

45 Bugajski, *Czechoslovakia*, 535–54; AFP, 18 Nov. 1982), in FBIS, 19 Nov. 1982, D5.

46 See the report in Hungarian Situation Report, *RFER*, 15 June 1987, 9–12.

47 *Die Presse* (Vienna), 3 Sept. 1985, 2, in FBIS, 5 Sept. 1985, D5.

48 Czechoslovak Situation Report, *RFER*, 12 Mar. 1988, 15–16.

49 Quoted in Czechoslovak Situation Report, *RFER*, 3 June 1988, 7.

50 *Neue Zürcher Zeitung*, 24 June 1988, 4.

51 Skilling, "Independent Currents," 39.

52 "Political Opposition in Czechoslovakia Today: Exclusive Interview with Jiří Pelikan," *Across Frontiers* (Winter 1985): 8.

53 For details, see Czechoslovak Situation Report, *RFER*, 10 Aug. 1987, 15–16, 19 Aug. 1987, 15–16.

54 *New York Times*, 23 Feb. 1988, 7; Czechoslovak Situation Report, *RFER*, 2 Mar. 1989, 22.

55 *Kurier*, 29 Aug. 1988, 3, in FBIS, 7 Sept. 1988, 5.

56 Václav Havel, "Reasons of Doubt and Sources of Hope," in *RFER*, 1 Mar. 1988, 3. See also Jan Vladislav, ed., *Václav Havel, or Living in Truth* (London: Faber & Faber, 1987).

57 *Die Presse*, 17 July 1986, 2, in FBIS, 18 July 1986, D3; Czechoslovak Situation Report, *RFER*, 31 July 1986, 17.

58   *Profil* (Vienna), 28 Oct. 1985, 65, in JPRS, no. EER-86-007 (17 Jan. 1986): 108.

59   *Magyarország* (Budapest), 1 June 1986, 20, in JPRS, no. EER-86-134 (5 Sept. 1986): 67.

60   *New York Times*, 20 Dec. 1987, 14.

61   *Magyar Nemzet* (Budapest), 14 Nov. 1987), in Hungarian Situation Report, *RFER*, 28 Nov. 1987, 13.

62   *New York Times*, 5 May 1988, A25; *Süddeutsche Zeitung*, 10–11 Sept. 1988, 10; *Financial Times*, 11 Oct. 1988, 3.

63   *Demokrata*, no. 3 (1987), summarized in Hungarian Situation Report, *RFER*, 22 July 1987, 25–26.

64   Jiří Pehe, "Independent Civic Activity in Eastern Europe," *RFER*, 4 Jan. 1989, 3.

65   See Budapest Domestic Service, 22 Oct. 1988, in FBIS, 1 Nov. 1988, 33–34.

66   Ferenc Kőszegi and István Szent-Iványi, "The Peace Movement in Eastern Europe," *Praxis International* 3, no. 1 (Apr. 1983): 24.

67   *Kurier*, 22 Nov. 1982, 2, in FBIS, 24 Nov. 1982, F1; *Die Tageszeitung* (Berlin), 3 Dec. 1983), 8, in JPRS, no. EPS-84-008 (18 Jan. 1984): 57.

68   *Journal de Genève* (Geneva), 22 Feb. 1984, in JPRS, no. EPS-84-045 (5 Apr. 1984): 101.

69   *Christian Science Monitor*, 17 June 1986, 15; "*Vízjel*: Hungary's Samizdat Environmental Journal," *Across Frontiers* (Fall 1987): 13.

70   Gyula Denes, "The Politics of Environmental Protection," *Across Frontiers* (Summer/Fall 1987): 10.

71   Quoted in *Christian Science Monitor*, 16 Nov. 1987, 10.

72   Quoted in Ibid., 17 June, 1986, 15.

73   This analysis derives from András Körösenyi, "The Emergence of Plurality Trends and Movements in Hungary's Society in the Mid-1980s," *Südost-Europa* 37, nos. 11-12 (Nov.-Dec. 1988).

74   Zoltán D. Barany, "Hungary's Independent Political Groups and Parties," *RFER*, 12 Sept. 1989, 1.

75   Interview with Miklós Haraszti, "Hungary in 1989: The Transition to a Post-Communist Society?," *Uncaptive Minds* 2, no. 1 (Jan.-Feb. 1989): 6.

76   Quoted in Steven Koppany, "Hungarian Opposition Groups Hold Meeting to Discuss Nation's Future," *RFER*, 13 Feb. 1986, 2.

77   *Magyar Nemzet*, 14 Nov. 1987, quoted in Hungarian Situation Report, *RFER*, 28 Nov. 1987, 16.

78   Hungarian Situation Report, *RFER*, 28 Nov. 1987, 11.

79   Alfred Reisch, "Hungarian Media Fails to Publish Appeal for Political Reform," *RFER* 10 Feb. 1988, 3.

80   Budapest Domestic Service, 3 Sept. 1988, in FBIS, 6 Sept. 1988, 26–27; *Kurier*, 8 Sept. 1988, 5, in FBIS, 19 Sept. 1988, 25–26.

81   Quoted in Ibid., 5.

82   "FIDESZ: Hungary's Independent Youth Movement," trans. Maria Nagy, *Across Frontiers* 5, no. 2 (Summer 1989): 35.

83   *Magyar Hírlap*, 5 June 1989, 3, in FBIS, 14 June 1989, 43.

84   "The Republican Circle," *Uncaptive Minds* 2, no. 1 (Jan.-Feb. 1989): 9.

85   MTI (Budapest), 3 June 1989, in FBIS, 7 June 1989, 33.

86   *Neue Zürcher Zeitung*, 20 Sept. 1988, 4.

87   Interview with Nyers and Fekete, Budapest Domestic Service, 17 Sept. 1988, in FBIS, 23 Sept. 1988, 22.

88   Hungarian Situation Report, *RFER*, 19 May 1988, 13–14; *Wiener Zeitung*, 17 Sept. 1988, 3, in FBIS, 19 Sept. 1988, 26.

89 On the latter, see *Süddeutsche Zeitung*, 14–15 Feb. 1987, 11.

90 *Washington Post*, 16 Mar. 1987, A13, A16.

91 *New York Times*, 16 Mar. 1988, 2; *Frankfurter Allgemeine*, 17 Mar. 1988, 1; Hungarian Situation Report, *RFER*, 21 Mar. 1988, 3–4.

92 Emil Freund, "Nascent Dissent in Romania," in *Dissent in Eastern Europe*, ed. Jane Leftwich Curry (New York: Praeger, 1983), 60–61.

93 Vladimir Socor, "Eyewitness on the 1977 Miners' Strike in Romania's Jiu Valley," *RFER*, 13 Aug. 1986, 2.

94 Ibid., 4.

95 Freund, "Nascent Dissent," 62; confirmed in Romanian Situation Report, *RFER*, 25 Nov. 1987, 6.

96 Romanian Situation Report, *RFER*, 6 Feb. 1987, 9; Romanian Situation Report, *RFER*, 25 Nov. 1987, 7.

97 Romanian Situation Report, *RFER*, 6 Mar. 1987, 18–19.

98 Ibid., 19.

99 *New York Times*, 30 Dec. 1987, 19.

100 Vlad Georgescu, "Romania in the 1980s: The Legacy of Dynastic Socialism," *Eastern European Politics and Societies* 2, no. 1 (Winter 1988): 73–77.

101 Daniel Chirot, "Romania: Ceausescu's Last Folly," *Dissent* 35, no. 3 (Summer 1988): 271–75.

102 *Neue Zürcher Zeitung*, 24 Nov. 1987, 1, and 25 Nov. 1987, 1; *Frankfurter Allgemeine*, 4 Dec. 1987, 5; Vladimir Socor, "The Workers' Protest in Braşov: Assessment and Aftermath," *RFER*, 4 Dec. 1987, 1–2.

103 *Neue Zürcher Zeitung*, 6 Jan. 1988, 4.

104 *Christian Science Monitor*, 16 Dec. 1987, 7.

105 Quoted in *New York Times*, 22 Nov. 1987, 9.

106 Crane Brinton, *The Anatomy of Revolution*, rev. and expanded ed. (New York: Vintage, 1965).

107 *Frankfurter Allgemeine*, 27 Dec. 1985, 5.

108 Quoted in Socor, "The Workers' Protest," 3.

109 *Christian Science Monitor*, 16 Dec. 1987, 7.

110 *Neue Zürcher Zeitung*, 10–11 Jan. 1988, 2.

111 Quoted in *Liberation* (Paris), 19 Jan. 1987), 17, in JPRS, no. EER-87-022 (17 Feb. 1987): 74. Also *Corriere della Sera* (Milan), 18 Mar. 1987, 10; *Frontier* (Mar.-Apr. 1987): 25.

112 Vladimir Socor, "Romanian Democratic Action," *RFER*, 2 Mar. 1988, 1–2.

113 Romanian Situation Report, *RFER*, 23 June 1988, 41–42.

114 Vladimir Socor, "Romanian and Hungarian Dissidents Find Common Ground," *RFER*, 22 Mar. 1988, 4.

115 *Mladina* (Ljubljana), 15 Jan. 1988, in JPRS, no. EER-88-016 (29 Feb. 1988): 39.

116 Romanian Situation Report, *RFER*, 20 July 1988, 23.

117 *Die Presse*, 20 Sept. 1988, 2, in FBIS, 20 Sept. 1988, 49.

118 Romanian Situation Report, *RFER*, 2 Feb. 1989, 37.

119 Vladimir Socor, "Are the Old Political Parties Stirring in Romania?," *RFER*, 22 July 1985, 5–6.

120 Georgescu, "Romania in the 1980s," 89. For further discussion of the National Peasant Party, see Romanian Situation Report, *RFER*, 6 Nov. 1986, 33–34.

121 See Pedro Ramet, "Gorbachev's Dilemmas in Eastern Europe," in *Gorbachev and the Soviet Future*, ed. Lawrence W. Lerner and Donald W. Treadgold (Boulder, Colo.: Westview Press, 1988).

122   Quoted in *Christian Science Monitor*, 16 Oct. 1987, 1, 10.

123   Quoted in *New York Times*, 4 Jan. 1987, sec. 4, E2.

124   *Die Presse*, 24–25 Nov. 1984, 2.

125   From the complete text, reprinted in Vladimir Tismaneanu, "Dissent in the Gorbachev Era," *Orbis* 31, no. 2 (Summer 1987): 235.

126   Ibid., 240.

127   *Washington Post*, 2 Feb. 1988, A10.

128   *New York Times*, 22 Mar. 1988, 7.

129   Czechoslovak Situation Report, *RFER*, 5 Sept. 1986, 3.

130   Ibid., 15 July 1987, 9.

131   From the complete text, in Polish Situation Report, *RFER*, 1 Sept. 1987, 29–30.

132   See also Socor, "Romanian and Hungarian Dissidents."

133   *Frankfurter Allgemeine*, 12 Jan. 1988, 6.

134   Vladimir Socor, "Independent Groups in Eastern Europe Urge Support for People of Romania," *RFER*, 25 Feb. 1988, 4.

135   *The Economist*, 21 May 1988, 53; *UPNB*, no. 8/88 (29 Apr. 1988): 17–18; *Neue Zürcher Zeitung*, 13 July 1988, 4.

136   Complete text published in *South Slav Journal* 10, no. 4 (Winter 1987/88): 70–71.

137   Quoted in Ibid., 5.

138   Havel, "Reasons of Doubt," 3.

5   Religious Change and New Cults in Eastern Europe

1   Karel Dobbelaere, "Secularization Theories and Sociological Paradigms: Convergences and Divergences," *Social Compass* 31, nos. 2–3 (1984): 200.

2   Peter L. Berger, *The Sacred Canopy: Elements of a Sociological Theory of Religion* (Garden City, N.Y.: Doubleday, 1967), chap. 5.

3   Thomas Luckmann, *The Invisible Religion: The Problem of Religion in Modern Society* (New York: Macmillan, 1967), 101, quoted in Dobbelaere, "Secularization Theories," 202.

4   G. K. Nelson, "Cults and New Religions: Towards a Sociology of Religious Creativity," *Sociology and Social Research* 68, no. 3 (Apr. 1984): 303. See also Masamichi Sasaki and Tatsuzo Suzuki, "Changes in Religious Commitment in the United States, Holland, and Japan," *American Journal of Sociology* 92, no. 5 (Mar. 1987): 1056.

5   *Život Strany*, no. 12 (1983): 49–51, as cited in Czechoslovak Situation Report, *RFER*, 26 July 1983, 5–6.

6   *Życie Partii* (Warsaw), 8 June 1983, 11, and 9 Nov. 1983, 16, 17, both in JPRS, no. EPS-84-016 (3 Feb. 1984): 83–91; confirmed in Polish Situation Report, *RFER*, 5 Feb. 1986), 17–18.

7   *Musca de Partid* (Bucharest), June 1982, 92–94, in JPRS, (29 July 1982): 54–55.

8   *Vjesnik* (Zagreb), 12 Oct. 1983, as cited in *AKSA*, 14 Oct. 1983; *Intervju* (Belgrade), 4 Jan. 1985, as cited in *AKSA* 18 Jan. 1985; *AKSA*, 22 Feb. 1985.

9   See Spas T. Raikin, "The Bulgarian Orthodox Church," in *Eastern Christianity and Politics in the Twentieth Century*, ed. Pedro Ramet (Durham, N.C.: Duke University Press, 1988), 160–82.

10   Todor Stojtschew, "Volksrepublik Bulgarien," in *Religion und Atheismus Heute*, ed. Olof Klohr (Berlin: Deutscher Verlag der Wissenschaften, 1966), 81.

11   Wolf Oschlies, *Kirchen und religioses Leben in Bulgarien* (Cologne: Berichte des Bundesinstituts für ostwissenschaftliche und internationale Studien, 1983, no. 15),

23; "Religious Trends in Eastern Europe," *RFER*, 1 Oct. 1986, 12.

12 For elaboration, see Pedro Ramet, "Christianity and National Heritage among the Czechs and Slovaks," in *Religion and Nationalism in Soviet and East European Politics*, ed. Pedro Ramet, rev. and expanded ed. (Durham, N.C.: Duke University Press, 1988), 264–85.

13 Erika Kadlecová, "Tschechoslowakische Sozialistische Republik," in *Religion und Atheismus Heute*, ed. Olof Klohr (Berlin: Deutscher Verlag der Wissenschaften, 1966), 148, 151–52.

14 Aleš Sekot, in *Sociologia*, no. 1 (1984): 18–19, as summarized in Czechoslovak Situation Report, *RFER*, 16 Feb. 1984, 11–12.

15 Otto Luchterhandt, *Die Gegenwartslage der Evangelischen Kirche in der DDR* (Tubingen: J. C. B. Mohr, 1982), 3; *Archiv der Gegenwart* (Bonn-Bad Gödesberg), 29 June 1983, 26770.

16 Zlatko Frid, *Religija u samoupravnom socijalizmu* (Zagreb: Centar za društvena djelatnosti omladine RK SOH, 1971), 33.

17 *Borba* (Zagreb), 6 Feb. 1986, 3.

18 "Zur Lage der Kirchen in Ungarn," *Osteuropa* 27, no. 7 (July 1977): A429; Miklós Tomka, "A Balance of Secularization in Hungary," *Social Compass* 28, no. 1 (1981): 28.

19 *Új Ember* (Budapest), 25 Nov. 1984, 2, in JPRS, no. EPS-85-018 (5 Feb. 1985): 1.

20 *Contemporanul* (Bucharest), 27 June 1986, 6, in JPRS, no. EER-86-133 (2 Sept. 1986): 95–96.

21 Ten percent are "undecided," and 7 percent are atheists, as of 1986. *ITD* (Warsaw), 12 Oct. 1986, 14–15, in JPRS, no. EER-87-028 (26 Feb. 1987): 107.

22 See Vincent C. Chrypiński, "Church and Nationality in Post-War Poland," in *Religion and Nationalism in Soviet and East European Politics*, ed. Pedro Ramet (Durham, N.C.: Duke University Press, 1989), 241–63.

23 Barbara Strassberg, "Changes in Religious Culture in Post–World War II Poland," *Sociological Analysis* 48, no. 4 (Winter 1988): 347, 353–54.

24 "'The Hope of the Church': Basic Groups in Hungary," *Frontier* (Mar.-Apr. 1987): 18.

25 Tomka, "A Balance of Secularization," 33.

26 See Pedro Ramet, *Cross and Commissar: The Politics of Religion in Eastern Europe and the USSR* (Bloomington: Indiana University Press, 1987), chap. 8.

27 *Skola da Tskhovreba* (Tbilisi), no. 6 (1986), in JPRS, *USSR Report*, no. UPS-86-046 (23 Sept. 1986): 55.

28 Re the Evangelical-Lutheran church, see Theo Mechtenberg, "Die Friedensverantwortung der Evangelischen Kirchen in der DDR," *Deutsche Studien* 19, no. 74 (June 1981). The best discussion of the Catholic Church in English is Robert F. Goeckel, "The Catholic Church in East Germany," in *Catholicism and Politics in Communist Societies*, ed. Pedro Ramet (Durham, N.C.: Duke University Press, 1990), 93–116.

29 Władysław Piwowarski, "Continuity and Change of Ritual in Polish Folk Piety," *Social Compass* 29, nos. 2–3 (1982): 128–32. For examples, see Chrypiński, "Church and Nationality."

30 Paul Keim, "Light-Life: Oases of Renewal," *Occasional Papers on Religion in Eastern Europe* 3, no. 7 (Nov. 1983): 18.

31 Cited in "The Hope of the Church," 18.

32 *Ifjúsági szemle* (Budapest), no. 6, (1987), trans. in JPRS, no. EER-88-027 (31 Mar.

1988): 55–56.

33 "The Hope of the Church," 19.

34 *Új Ember*, 2 Nov. 1986, 11, in JPRS, no. EER-87-008 (16 Jan. 1987): 75–76.

35 "The Hope of the Church," 19.

36 See J. V. Eibner, "Zoltán Káldy: A New Way for the Church in Socialism?," *Religion in Communist Lands* 13, no. 1 (Spring 1985): esp. 41; Vilmos Vajta, "Debatable 'Theology of Diaconia': Hungarian Example of 'the Church in Socialist Society,'" *Occasional Papers on Religion in Eastern Europe* 4, no. 1 (Jan. 1984).

37 *Keston News Service*, no. 255 (24 July 1986): 14, and no. 268 (5 Feb. 1987): 10–11.

38 Ibid., no. 274 (30 Apr. 1987): 18–19, no. 288 (19 Nov. 1987): 13, and no. 289 (3 Dec. 1987): 10.

39 *AKSA*, 21 Sept. 1983; *Glas koncila* (Zagreb), 4 Dec. 1983; and *AKSA*, 20 Jan. 1984.

40 *Keston News Service*, no. 298 (14 Apr. 1988): 16.

41 The Madonna was also said to have appeared in the village of Serednia in Ukraine in 1954. For details, see Bohdan R. Bociurkiw, "Religion and Nationalism in the Contemporary Ukraine," in *Nationalism in the USSR and Eastern Europe*, ed. George W. Simmonds (Detroit: University of Detroit Press, 1977), 86–87.

42 For background, see Pedro Ramet, "The Miracle at Medjugorje: A Functionalist Perspective," *South Slav Journal* 8, nos. 1–2 (Spring/Summer 1985).

43 *Ilustrovana politika* (Belgrade), no. 1484 (14 Apr. 1987): 14–15; *Večernji list* (Zagreb), 27 June 1987, 10; *Top* (Zagreb), 6 July 1987, 11; *Ilustrovana politika*, no. 1496 (7 July 1987): 28–33.

44 *New York Times*, 13 Oct. 1987, 1.

45 *Frankfurter Allgemeine*, 21 Aug. 1987, 5; *Glas koncila*, 13 Aug. 1987, 3.

46 *AKSA*, 4 Dec. 1987, as summarized in *AKSA Bulletin* (prepared by Stella Alexander and Kresimir Sidor), no. 8 (26 Jan. 1988): 13. For further discussion, see chap. 7; and Pedro Ramet, "Religion and Nationalism in Yugoslavia," in *Religion and Nationalism in Soviet and East European Politics*, ed. Pedro Ramet (Durham, N.C.: Duke University Press, 1989), 299–327.

47 "Religious Trends," 4.

48 See Dionisie Ghermani, "The Orthodox Church in Romania," *Religion in Communist Dominated Areas* 27, no. 1 (Winter 1988).

49 Janice A. Broun, "Religion in Romania: The Truth behind the Image," *Freedom at Issue* (Mar.-Apr. 1984): 12.

50 *Keston News Service*, no. 282 (20 Aug. 1987): 10.

51 Ibid., no. 292 (21 Jan. 1988): 11.

52 Figures from the West German institute, Kirche im Sozialismus.

53 *Keston News Service*, no. 280 (23 July 1987): 23.

54 Ibid., no. 303 (23 June 1988): 15; confirmed in Paul Bock, "Protestantism in Czechoslovakia and Poland," in *Protestantism and Politics in Eastern Europe and the Soviet Union*, ed. Sabrina P. Ramet (manuscript under review).

55 Interview, Zagreb, June 1987.

56 "Religious Trends," 12.

57 Joseph Pungur, "Protestantism in Hungary," in *Protestantism and Politics in Eastern Europe and the Soviet Union*, ed. Pedro Ramet (forthcoming, Duke University Press).

58 *Glaube in der 2. Welt* 8, no. 9 (Sept. 1980): 2.

59 Joseph Ton, "Romania: Persecution of the Protestants," *Religion in Communist*

Dominated Areas 25, no. 3 (Summer 1986): 133. See also Earl A. Pope, "The Contemporary Religious Situation in Romania," in *Religion and Communist Society*, ed. Dennis J. Dunn (Berkeley, Calif.: Berkeley Slavic Specialties, 1983), 140.

60   Ton, "Romania," 133.

61   Lindsey Davies, "Pentecostals in Bulgaria," *Religion in Communist Lands* 8, no. 4 (Winter 1980): 299.

62   "A Declaration of Romanian Christians" (Aug. 1974), in *Religion in Communist Dominated Areas*, 13, nos. 10–12 (Oct.-Dec. 1974): 150.

63   "'Freedom to Serve the Lord': Fresh Hope for the Bulgarian 'Church of God,'" *Frontier* (Nov.-Dec. 1987): 2.

64   See *Keston News Service*, no. 281 (6 Aug. 1987): 6.

65   Pope, "The Contemporary Religious Situation," 143; Romanian Situation Report, *RFER*, 11 Sept. 1986, 23.

66   Figures from the West German institute, Kirche im Sozialismus.

67   "'We Have Something to Offer Society': Adventists in Poland," *Frontier* (Sept.-Oct. 1987): 17.

68   Bock, "Protestantism in Czechoslovakia and Poland."

69   Rudolf Grulich, "The Small Religious Communities in Yugoslavia," *Occasional Papers on Religion in Eastern Europe*, 3, no. 6 (Sept. 1983): 5.

70   Janice Broun with Grazyna Sikorska, *Conscience and Captivity: Religion in Eastern Europe* (Washington, D.C.: Ethics and Public Policy Center, 1989), 55.

71   *Keston News Service*, no. 291 (7 Jan. 1988): 16. See also *Intervju* (Belgrade), 7 Nov. 1986, 22; *Keston News Service*, no. 280 (23 July 1987): 22.

72   Interview with *Rzeczpospolita* (Warsaw), 3 Oct. 1985, 4, in JPRS, no. EER-86-023 (18 Feb. 1986): 135–36.

73   Quoted in *Keston News Service*, no. 287 (5 Nov. 1987): 14.

74   Romanian Situation Report, *RFER*, 11 Sept. 1986, 23.

75   MTI (Budapest), 24 June 1988, in FBIS, 6 July 1988, 45.

76   Pope, "The Contemporary Religious Situation," 146–47.

77   *Keston News Service*, no. 296 (17 Mar. 1988): 13–14.

78   Pope, "The Contemporary Religious Situation," 145.

79   *Keston News Service*, no. 281 (6 Aug. 1987): 15.

80   *Glaube und Heimat* (Jena), as cited in *Keston News Service*, no. 282 (20 Aug. 1987): 15.

81   Grulich, "The Small Religious Communities," 7.

82   *Keston News Service*, no. 284 (24 Sept. 1987): 15.

83   Ibid., no. 269 (19 Feb. 1987): 13–14.

84   Ibid., no. 296 (17 Mar. 1988): 13–14.

85   For further discussion of Yugoslav Jehovah's Witnesses, see Pedro Ramet, "The Dynamics of Yugoslav Religious Policy: Some Insights from Organization Theory," in *Yugoslavia in the 1980s*, ed. Pedro Ramet (Boulder, Colo.: Westview Press, 1985), 178–79.

86   *Keston News Service*, no. 281 (6 Aug. 1987): 15.

87   See chap. 3.

88   *Keston News Service*, no. 332 (24 Aug. 1989): 19.

89   Ibid., no. 281 (6 Aug. 1987): 17, and no. 286 (22 Oct. 1987): 11.

90   *NIN* (Belgrade), no. 1893 (12 Apr. 1987): 28–29; *Ilustrovana politika*, no. 1484 (14 Apr. 1987): 50–51.

91   *Keston News Service*, no. 267 (22 Jan. 1987): 16, and no. 282 (20 Aug. 1987): 15;

New Religious Movements: Secretariat for Promoting Christian Unity (St. Paul Editions, 1986), 2; William D. Dinges, "The Vatican Report on Sects, Cults, and New Religious Movements," *America*, 27 Sept. 1986), 145–47, 154.

92   Thomas Robbins and Dick Anthony, "New Religious Movements and the Social System," *Annual Review of the Social Sciences of Religion* 2 (1978): 6–9; James T. Richardson, "New Religious Movements in the United States: A Review," *Social Compass* 30, no. 1 (1983): 86, 89–90, 95–96.

93   Edward A. Tiryakian, *On the Margin of the Visible: Sociology, the Esoteric, and the Occult* (New York: Wiley, 1974), 273, as cited in Robbins and Anthony, "New Religious Movements," 15.

94   Rodney Stark and William Sims Bainbridge, "Secularization, Revival, and Cult Formation," *Annual Review of the Social Sciences of Religion* 4 (1980). See also Roy Wallis, "Figuring Out Cult Receptivity," *Journal for the Scientific Study of Religion* 25, no. 4 (Dec. 1986).

95   Angela A. Aidala, "Social Change, Gender Roles, and New Religous Movements," *Sociological Analysis* 46, no. 3 (Fall 1985).

96   José Casanova, "The Politics of the Religious Revival," *Telos*, no. 59 (Spring 1984): 16–17.

97   For further discussion, see William Sims Bainbridge and Rodney Stark, "Cult Formation: Three Compatible Models," *Sociological Analysis* 40, no. 4 (Winter 1979); also Janet Jacobs, "Deconversion from Religious Movements: An Analysis of Charismatic Bonding and Spiritual Commitment," *Journal for the Scientific Study of Religion* 26, no. 3 (Sept. 1987).

98   *Wall Street Journal*, 19 Apr. 1988, 1, 22.

99   *New York Times*, 14 May 1988, 1, 4.

100   Nelson, "Cults and New Religions," 305, 307.

101   Anson D. Shupe, Jr., and David G. Bromley, "The Moonies and the Anti-Cultists: Movement and Countermovement in Conflict," *Sociological Analysis* 40, no. 4 (Winter 1979); Alan L. Berger, "Hasidism and Moonism: Charisma in the Counterculture," *Sociological Analysis* 41, no. 4 (Winter 1980): 383–89; Rainer Flasche, "Hauptelemente der Vereinigungstheologie," in *Das Entstehen einer neuen Religion: Das Beispiel der Vereinigungskirche*, ed. Günter Kehrer (Munich: Kosel-Verlag, 1981).

102   *Kontakty*, no. 26 (Oct. 1985), in "Extracts from Polish Underground Publications," *RFER*, 17 Jan. 1986, 14; and conversations in Belgrade, July 1988.

103   Interview with Jim Berman, graduate student at the University of Washington, Seattle, 28 Feb. 1989.

104   Yordan Kerov, "Lyudmila Zhivkova: Fragments of a Portrait," *RFER*, 27 Oct. 1980, 16.

105   Bulgarian Situation Report, *RFER*, 7 July 1986), 27–28.

106   Ibid., 28.

107   *Keston News Service*, no. 296 (17 Mar. 1988): 14; *Kontakty* [note 102], 14.

108   *Vikend* (Belgrade), no. 1047 (17 June 1988): 12–13.

109   Mia Za Czoj [Ch'oe Myong-jong], "P'ollandù esò ui Han-gukhak paljoù kwajòng yòn-gu" [A Study of the Development of Korean Studies in Poland], in *Papers of the 5th International Conference on Korean Studies: Korean Studies, Its Tasks and Perspectives* (1988), 2:607–14. I am indebted to Clark Sorensen of the University of Washington for translating this from Korean for me.

110   Summarized in Baltic Situation Report, *RFER*, 18 July 1986, 30. Also *Izvestiia*, 20 Dec. 1986, 6, summarized in JPRS, *USSR Report*, no. UPS-87-005 (26 Jan. 1987): 82;

and Moscow Television Service, 23 Jan. 1987, in JPRS, *USSR Report*, no. UPS-87-015 (15 Mar. 1987): 36.

111 *Danas* (Zagreb), no. 267 (31 Mar. 1987): 66.

112 Ibid., 68.

113 Angus Hall and Jeremy Kingston, *Mysterious Cults* (London, 1981), 120, as cited in Julia Wishnevsky, "Persecution of the Hare Krishna Movement in the Soviet Union," *Radio Liberty Research*, 14 Nov. 1985), 9.

114 Valentin Yurov, in interview with *Russkaia Mysl'* (Nov. 1985), in *Keston News Service*, no. 243 (6 Feb. 1986): 17.

115 Ibid., 18; *Trud*, 28 Aug. 1983, 4, in *CDSP* 36, no. 9 (28 Mar. 1984): 25; John Anderson, "The Hare Krishna Movement in the USSR," *Religion in Communist Lands*, 14, no. 3 (Winter 1986): 316–17; *Izvestiia*, 20 Aug. 1986, 6; *Keston News Service*, no. 278 (25 June 1987): 19, and no. 285 (8 Oct. 1987): 3.

116 Bulgarian Situation Report, *RFER*, 7 July 1986, 27; *Przegląd Tygodniowy* (Warsaw), 14 Oct. 1984, 5, in JPRS, no. EPS-84-145 (28 Nov. 1984): 135.

117 *Keston News Service*, no. 302 (9 June 1988): 6–7.

118 *Danas*, no. 268 (7 Apr. 1987): 68.

119 Ibid., 67.

120 *Przegląd Tygodniowy* [note 115], 135; *UPNB*, no. 2/88 (22 Jan. 1988): 19; *Kontakty* [note 102], 14.

121 Helmut Obst, *Neureligionen, Jugendreligionen, destruktive Kulte* (Berlin: Union Verlag, 1984; 2nd ed., 1986).

122 *Nauka i religiia*, no. 10 (Oct. 1976), abstracted in *CDSP* 29, no. 3 (16 Feb. 1977): 17.

123 *Danas*, no. 264 (10 Mar. 1987): 66–68.

124 Marcello Truzzi, "The Occult Revival as Popular Culture: Some Random Observations on the Old and the Nouveau Witch," *Sociological Quarterly* 13, no. 1 (Winter 1972): 21.

125 See Geoffrey K. Nelson, "The Spiritualist Movement and the Need for a Redefinition of Cult," *Journal for the Scientific Study of Religion* 8, no. 1 (Spring 1969): 152ff.

126 *Keston News Service*, no. 267 (22 Jan. 1987): 16; *Danas*, no. 263 (3 Mar. 1987): 66.

127 Oral source, 25 May 1988.

128 Personal observation, Leipzig, 7 July 1988.

129 Interview with Michał Szymczak, in *Sztandar Młodych*, 9 Apr. 1987, 3, in JPRS, no. EER-87-122 (7 Aug. 1987): 34.

130 *Gość Niedzielny* (Katowice), 10 May 1987, 1, 5, in JPRS, no. EER-87-120 (4 Aug. 1987): 119–20.

131 *Sztandar Młodych* [note 128], 35.

132 *Gość Niedzielny* [note 129], 120.

133 *Informacé o cirkvi* (1988): 17, trans. for me by Dan Beck.

134 *Danas*, no. 318 (22 Mar. 1988), 67–70; *NIN*, no. 1943 (27 Mar. 1988), 27; *Danas*, no. 319 (29 Mar. 1988), 76–77.

135 See the reports in *Glas koncila*, 3 Apr. 1988, 6, and 10 Apr. 1988, 6; *Danas*, no. 319 (29 Mar. 1988): 76.

136 Tomislav M. Petrović, *Rešenje misterije 666* (Sabac: Dragan Srnic, 1989).

137 *Keston News Service*, no. 290 (17 Dec. 1987): 13.

138 Truzzi, "The Occult Revival," 29.

139 Berger, *The Sacred Canopy*, 134.

6 Church and Dissent in Praetorian Poland

1 Jan Szczepański, "Próba Diagnozy," *Przegląd kulturalny*, no. 36 (Jan. 1957), cited in Alexander Matejko, *Social Change and Stratification in Eastern Europe: An Interpretive Analysis of Poland and Her Neighbors* (New York: Praeger, 1974), 207.

2 See, for example, *Washington Post*, 5 May 1988, A32.

3 Samuel P. Huntington, *Political Order in Changing Societies* (New Haven, Conn.: Yale University Press, 1968), chap. 4, esp. 195–97. On Poland, see Robin Alison Remington, "Polish Soldiers in Politics: The Party in Uniform?," in *Dictatorships in Retreat*, ed. Constantine Danopoulos (Boulder, Colo.: Westview, 1988).

4 Huntington, *Political Order*, 229.

5 Giuseppe Garampi, the papal nuncio in Poland from 1772 to 1776, was disappointed when the Polish *Sejm* passed a bill revoking recourse to mutilation or execution as punishment for "apostasy," substituting instead mere exile. Lawrence Wolff, *Poland and the Vatican in the Age of the Partitions: European Enlightenment, Roman Catholicism, and the Development of Polish Nationalism*, Ph.D. dissertation, Stanford University, 1984, 113.

6 Primate Józef Glemp, in a message read in all churches on 20 December 1981, as quoted in Jonathan Luxmoore, "The Polish Church under Martial Law," *Religion in Communist Lands* 15, no. 2 (Summer 1987): 129–30.

7 Primate Józef Glemp, in an interview with *Die Zeit* (Hamburg), 12 June 1987, 6.

8 Vincent C. Chrypiński, "The Catholic Church in Poland, 1944–1989," in *Catholicism and Politics in Communist Societies*, ed Pedro Ramet (Durham, N.C.: Duke University Press, 1990), 138; *New York Times*, 28 Dec. 1987, 6.

9 Jerzy Turowicz, "Kilka uwag o dyskryminacji," *Tygodnik Powszechny*, 16–19 Apr. 1987, trans. into German as "Diskriminierung der katholischen Presse in Polen," *Osteuropa* 37, no. 12 (Dec. 1987): A682–83. A new periodical, *Znak Czasu*, began publication in March 1986 under the editorship of Andrzej Micewski. Authorized by primate Glemp, the quarterly is published in Vienna. See the report in *Die Presse* (Vienna), 12 Mar. 1986, 2. For a list of Catholic religious publications, see *Slowo Powszechne* (Warsaw), 15–17 Feb. 1985, 7, in JPRS, no. EPS-85-045 (15 Apr. 1985): 68–78.

10 *Washington Post*, 26 July 1987, A1, A22; *Keston News Service*, no. 295 (3 Mar. 1988): 13.

11 Article by Jan Rem (pen name of government spokesperson Jerzy Urban), in *Trybuna Ludu*, 22–23 Nov. 1986, 5, in JPRS, no. EER-86-195 (24 Dec. 1986): 78.

12 *Christian Science Monitor*, 8 Jan. 1988, 17.

13 Vincent C. Chrypiński, "Church and Nationality in Postwar Poland," in *Religion and Nationalism in Soviet and East European Politics*, ed. Pedro Ramet (Durham, N.C.: Duke University Press, 1984), 130.

14 AFP, 5 Apr. 1985, and *The Guardian*, 29 May 1985—both in RFE telex.

15 *Die Welt* (Bonn), 15 Dec. 1984; *Keston News Service*, no. 290 (17 Dec. 1987): 14.

16 Quoted in *Christian Science Monitor*, 8 June 1987, 10.

17 Justine De Lacy, "Someone from Cracow," *Atlantic Monthly* (Nov. 1986): 95, 97.

18 Ewa Celt, "A Larger Role for the Church," *RFER*, 31 Dec. 1983).

19 Bogdan Szajkowski, *Next to God . . . Poland: Politics and Religion in Contemporary Poland* (New York: St. Martin's Press, 1983), 11–12; also Andrzej Micewski, *Katholische Gruppierungen in Polen: Pax und Znak, 1945–1976*, trans. Wolfgang Grycz (Munich: Kaiser; Mainz: Grunewald, 1978).

20 Bogdan Szajkowski, "The Catholic Church in Defense of Civil Society in Poland,"

in *Poland After Solidarity*, ed. Bronisław Misztal (New Brunswick, N.J.: Transaction Books, 1985), 72.

21 Ronald C. Monticone, *The Catholic Church in Communist Poland 1945–1985: Forty Years of Church-State Relations* (Boulder, Colo.: East European Monographs, 1986), 18.

22 On 12 September 1945.

23 Oscar Halecki, ed., *Poland* (New York: Praeger, 1957), 215.

24 Zdzisława Walaszek, "An Open Issue of Legitimacy: The State and the Church in Poland," *Annals of the American Academy of Political and Social Science* 483 (Jan. 1986): 130.

25 Adam Nowotny (pseud.), "Fortress Catholicism: Wojtyła's Polish Roots," in *The Church in Anguish: Has the Vatican Betrayed Vatican II?*, ed. Hans Kung and Leonard Swidler (San Francisco: Harper & Row, 1987), 30.

26 Jan Nowak, "The Church in Poland," *Problems of Communism* 31, no. 1 (Jan.-Feb. 1982): 11–12; Monticone, *The Catholic Church*, 69.

27 Adam Bromke, "A New Juncture in Poland," *Problems of Communism* 25, no. 5 (Sept.-Oct. 1976): 15–16.

28 For further discussion, see Pedro Ramet, "Poland's 'Other' Parties," *The World Today* 37, no. 9 (Sept. 1981): 332–38.

29 Monticone, *The Catholic Church*, 108–10.

30 Ibid., 115.

31 See his comments in *Tygodnik Powszechny*, 21 June 1981, as reported in Nowak, "The Church in Poland," 14.

32 Quoted in Luxmoore, "The Polish Church," 127.

33 Quoted in Ibid., 134–35.

34 Reprinted in *Communist Affairs* 2, no. 1 (Jan. 1983): 106.

35 *New York Times*, 13 Sept. 1987, 3; also Grażyna Sikorska, "To Kneel Only before God: Father Jerzy Popiełuszko," *Religion in Communist Lands* 12, no. 2 (Summer 1984): 153.

36 *Los Angeles Times*, 28 June 1982, 4.

37 *Słowo Powszechne*, 30 Aug. 1982, 4, in FBIS, 8 Sept. 1982, G15.

38 Tadeusz Kamiński, "Poland's Catholic Church and Solidarity: A Parting of the Ways?," *Poland Watch*, no. 6 (1984): 79.

39 Luxmoore, "The Polish Church," 149.

40 For further discussion, see Pedro Ramet, *Cross and Commissar: The Politics of Religion in Eastern Europe and the USSR* (Bloomington: Indiana University Press, 1987), chaps. 8 and 9.

41 *The Times* (London), 22 Feb. 1984, 6; *Washington Post*, 22 Feb. 1984, A15.

42 John Moody and Roger Boyes, *The Priest and the Policeman: The Courageous Life and Cruel Murder of Father Jerzy Popiełuszko* (New York: Summit, 1987), 131.

43 *Keston News Service*, no. 213 (22 Nov. 1984): 5, and no. 214 (6 Dec. 1984): 8; *New York Times*, 2 Dec. 1984, 5.

44 *EFE* (Madrid), 22 Feb. 1984, in JPRS, no. EPS-84-041 (28 Mar. 1984): 93.

45 *UPNB* (London), 30 Jan. 1986, 13.

46 Ibid., 23 Sept. 1986, 25, and 20 Feb. 1987, 18.

47 *New York Times*, 21 Sept. 1987, 4. See also Zimon's sermon on the ecological disaster, in *UPNB*, 14 July 1986, 29.

48 *New York Times*, 16 Sept. 1985, 1.

49 ORF Teletext (Vienna), 17 Sept. 1984, in FBIS, 17 Sept. 1984, G1–2; *New York*

Times, 30 Dec. 1985, 5; *Washington Post*, 14 Dec. 1986, A1.

50 *The Economist* (London), 25 Feb. 1984, 44.

51 Kamiński, "Poland's Catholic Church," 83.

52 Irena Korba, "Five Years Underground: The Opposition and the Church in Poland since Martial Law," *Religion in Communist Lands* 15, no. 2 (Summer 1987): 172.

53 *KOS*, 27 Feb. 1984, quoted in Korba, "Five Years Underground," 180.

54 Korba, "Five Years Underground," 175–76.

55 Ibid., 176–77.

56 Quoted in *New York Times*, 25 Nov. 1984, sec. 4, 4.

57 Tadeusz Walendowski, "The Pope in Poland," *Poland Watch*, no. 3 (Spring/Summer 1983): 5–8; Karl Hartmann, "Politische Bilanz des zweiten Papstbesuches in Polen," *Osteuropa* 33, nos. 11–12 (Nov.-Dec. 1983): 897, 900.

58 Polish Situation Report, *RFER*, 10 July 1987, 5; *Glas koncila* (Zagreb), 21 June 1987, 3.

59 *Washington Post*, 11 June 1988, A33.

60 *Corriere della Sera* (Milan), 12 June 1987, 15, and 13 June 1987, 12.

61 *Tygodnik Powszechny*, 28 June 1987, trans. into German as "Die dritte Papstreise nach Polen," *Osteuropa* 37, no. 12 (Dec. 1987): A679–80. See also "Papstbesuch in Polen: Was bleibt für die Gastgeber?," *Herder Korrespondenz* 41, no. 7 (July 1987).

62 *Corriere della Sera*, 16 June 1987, 21.

63 See, for example, the report in *Frankfurter Allgemeine* 4 Apr. 1985, 2, and 16 Apr. 1985, 6.

64 Quoted in *Washington Post*, 21 Sept. 1987, A1.

65 AFP, 7 Aug. 1988, in FBIS, 8 Aug. 1988, 16.

66 *UPNB*, 31 Oct. 1988, 5.

67 *Slowo Powszechne*, 29 Aug. 1988, 1, 2, in FBIS, 1 Sept. 1988, 36–37. See also *Süddeutsche Zeitung*, 27–28 Aug. 1988, 1.

68 *Frankfurter Allgemeine*, 6 May 1989, 12, and 18 May 1989, 6; *Keston News Service*, no. 326 (25 May 1989): 2; *Tygodnik Powszechny* (Kraków), 25 June 1989, 1, 3, in FBIS, 12 July 1989, 39–42. See also PAP (Warsaw), 28 June 1989, in FBIS, 29 June 1989, 43.

69 AFP, 22 Jan. 1989, in FBIS, 23 Jan. 1989, 67; *New York Times*, 27 Jan. 1989, A4; Warsaw Domestic Service, 7 Mar. 1989, in FBIS, 8 Mar. 1989, 52.

70 AFP, 31 Jan. 1989, in FBIS, 1 Feb. 1989, 38.

71 *Keston News Service*, no. 330 (20 July 1989): 9; *Glas koncila* (Zagreb), 30 July 1989, 3.

72 Further discussion in Sabrina P. Ramet, "The New Church-State Configuration in Eastern Europe," *East European Politics and Societies* (in press).

73 *New York Times*, 6 Nov. 1990, A1.

74 *New York Times*, 15 Apr. 1988, 15.

75 Scot J. Paltrow, "Poland and the Pope: The Vatican's Relations with Poland, 1978 to the Present," *Millennium* 15, no. 1 (Spring 1986): 10.

76 *Życie Warszawy* (Warsaw), 13–14 July 1985), in JPRS, no. EPS-85-098 (27 Sept. 1985): 133.

77 Quoted in *New York Times*, 9 Sept. 1986, 4.

78 *New York Times*, 13 Nov. 1986, A20.

79 Polish Situation Report, *RFER*, 2 Dec. 1986, 3.

80 *Niedziela* (Częstochowa), 7 Dec. 1986, 6, in JPRS, no. EER-87-035 (10 Mar. 1987): 99.

81 Ibid., 100.

82 AFP, 31 Aug. 1984, in FBIS, 4 Sept. 1984, G10–11; AFP, 16 Sept. 1984, in FBIS, 17

Sept. 1984, G2; AFP, 22 Sept. 1984, in FBIS, 24 Sept. 1984, G2.
83 Huntington, *Political Order*, 5.

7   Why Albanian Irredentism in Kosovo Will Not Go Away

An earlier version of this chapter originally appeared in *Canadian Review of Studies in Nationalism* 16, nos. 1–2 (1989): Reprinted by permission.

1   See, for example, the statement of the League of Communists Municipal Committee of Titova Mitrovka, 31 January 1990, reported by Tanjug, in FBIS, 1 Feb. 1990, 78–79.
2   E.g., Rainer Joha Bender, "Die Krisenprovinz Kosovo: Ein jugoslawischer Peripherraum im Lembruch," *Zeitschrift fur Balkanologie* 20, no. 1 (1984): 17; Michael T. Kaufman, *New York Times*, 5 Oct. 1984).
3   E.g., Jens Reuter, *Die Albaner in Jugoslawien* (Munich: R. Oldenbourg Verlag, 1982), 10; Dennison I. Rusinow, "Nationalities Policy and the 'National Question,'" in *Yugoslavia in the 1980s*, ed. Pedro Ramet (Boulder, Colo.: Westview, 1985), 145.
4   Tanjug, 12 Jan. 1990, in FBIS, 16 Jan. 1990, 100.
5   Tanjug, 29 Jan. 1990, in FBIS, 30 Jan. 1990, 85.
6   *Rilindja* (Priština), 8 July 1988, 6, and *Politika* (Belgrade), 10 July 1988, 1—both in FBIS, 13 July 1988, 60–63.
7   Dimitrije Bogdanović, *Knjiga o Kosovu* (Belgrade: Srpska Akademija Nauka i Umetnosti, 1985), 10–28; Viktor Meier, "Träume von einer albanischen Zukunft?," *Südosteuropa Mitteilungen* 24, no. 4 (1984): 54.
8   Ivo Banac, *The National Question in Yugoslavia: Origins, History, Politics* (Ithaca: N.Y.: Cornell University Press, 1984), 298.
9   Ivan Babić, "U službi Srpske okupacione vojske u Makedoniji i Kosovu," *Hrvatska revija* (Barcelona) 28, no. 3 (Sept. 1978): 476–77.
10 Banac, *The National Question*, 298–99.
11 Quoted in Ibid., 299.
12 Ibid., 300.
13 Bender, "Die Krisenprovinz," 6.
14 Alex N. Dragnich and Slavko Todorovich, *The Saga of Kosovo* (Boulder, Colo.: East European Monographs, 1984), 138.
15 Bogdanović, *Knjiga o Kosovu*, 244–46.
16 Miloš Mišović, *Ko je tražio republiku Kosovo, 1945–1985* (Belgrade: Narodna knjiga, 1987), 91–110. Also *Intervju* (Belgrade), 19 June 1987, 10–11.
17 Elez Biberaj, "The Conflict in Kosovo," *Survey* 28, no. 3 (Autumn 1984): 42.
18 See Dušan Bilandžić, *Jugoslavija poslije Tita (1980–1985)* (Zagreb: Globus, 1986), 73–74.
19 For further discussion of the economic fortunes of Kosovo, see Sabrina P. Ramet, *Nationalism and Federalism in Yugoslavia, 1962–1991*, 2nd ed. (Bloomington: Indiana University Press, forthcoming).
20 Reuter, *Die Albaner*, 52.
21 Ibid.
22 Biberaj, "The Conflict in Kosovo," 46.
23 Dragoslav Marković, "Ostvarivanje Platforme SKJ o Kosovu," *Socijalizam* 26, no. 12 (Dec. 1983): 1691.
24 Tanjug, 4 Dec. 1980, as quoted in Mark Baskin, "Crisis in Kosovo," *Problems of Communism* 32, no. 2 (Mar.-Apr. 1983): 65.

25   "Rates of Employment and Unemployment, 1980–1987," *Yugoslav Survey* 29, no. 4 (1988): 35.

26   *Borba*, 2–3 Mar. 1985, in JPRS, no. EPS-85-053 (6 June 1985): 133–34.

27   Dragnich and Todorovich, *The Saga of Kosovo*, 161.

28   Ibid., 169.

29   See further discussion and documentation in Ramet, *Nationalism and Federalism*, chapter 9.

30   *Frankfurter Allgemeine*, 4 Apr. 1981); Elez Biberaj, "Albanian-Yugoslav Relations and the Question of Kosovë," *Albanian Catholic Bulletin* 4, nos. 1–2 (1983): 83; *NIN*, 27 June 1982, as cited in Jens Reuter, "Der XII. Kongress des BdKJ," *Südost-Europa* 31, nos. 7–8 (1982): 383.

31   Tanjug, 31 Jan. 1986, in FBIS, 4 Feb. 1986, 16; *Intervju* 29 Mar. 1985, in JPRS, no. EPS-85-066 (11 June 1985): 84; *Danas*, 1 June 1982, 11; Yugoslav Situation Report, *RFER*, 19 Nov. 1987, 7.

32   *The Times* (London), 9 June 1985, as cited in Peter R. Prifti, "Kosovë Stalemate Deepens: An Updated Report," *Albanian Catholic Bulletin* 6 (1985): 82.

33   Tanjug, 11 June 1985, in FBIS, 13 June 1985, 15.

34   *Borba*, 16 Mar. 1983, in FBIS, 29 Mar. 1983, 110.

35   Peter R. Prifti, "Struggle for Ethnic Rights in Kosovo Continues," *Albanian Catholic Bulletin* 5, nos. 1–2 (1984): 68. See also Ramet, *Nationalism and Federalism*, chapter 9.

36   CMD, 20 Mar. 1986; confirmed in Tanjug, 20 Mar. 1986.

37   *Vjesnik*, (Zagreb), 26 July 1982.

38   Ibid.; Sinan Hasani, *Kosovo: Istine i zablude* (Zagreb: Centar za informacije i publicitet, 1986), 181–91.

39   Tanjug, 12 Jan. 1983, in FBIS, 13 Jan. 1983, 122; and Tanjug, 2 Mar. and 31 Mar. 1983—respectively in FBIS, 4 Mar. 1983, 19, and 4 Apr. 1983, 114.

40   Richard F. Staar, ed., *Yearbook on International Communist Affairs 1985* (Stanford, Calif.: Hoover Institution Press, 1985), 371.

41   *The Times*, 30 Dec. 1985; confirmed in *Christian Science Monitor*, 9 Jan. 1986,

42   *New York Times*, 3 May 1986; *Süddeutsche Zeitung* (Munich), 31 May-1 June 1986,

43   *The Times*, 30 Dec. 1985; South-East European Service, 25 Jan. 1986; *Večernje novosti* (Belgrade), 18 Feb. 1986.

44   Jens Reuter, "Unruheherd Kosovo: Resultat einer erfolglosen Politik," *Südost-Europa* 35, nos. 11–12 (Nov.-Dec. 1986): 637–38.

45   Quoted in *New York Times*, 1 Nov. 1987, 6.

46   Prifti, "Struggle for Ethnic Rights," 67.

47   *Politika*, 25 Dec. 1981.

48   *Christian Science Monitor*, 4 Jan. 1983; confirmed in *New York Times*, 5 Oct. 1984,

49   *Pravoslavlje*, 15 May 1982. For further discussion, see Pedro Ramet, "Religion and Nationalism in Yugoslavia," in *Religion and Nationalism in Soviet and East European Politics*, ed. Pedro Ramet rev. and expanded ed. (Durham, N.C.: Duke University Press, 1989), 316–17.

50   *Los Angeles Times*, 15 Mar. 1984.

51   Tanjug, 25 June 1985, in FBIS, 26 June 1985, 13.

52   Re the Macedonians, see *Borba*, 6 Feb. 1986, in FBIS, 14 Feb. 1986, 13–4. Re the Montenegrins, see Marko Špadijer, "Nacionalizam u Crnoj Gori," *Socijalizam* 29, no. 4 (Apr. 1986). See also Hasani, *Kosovo*, 252–53.

53   *Los Angeles Times*, 15 Mar. 1984,

54   Portions of the remainder of this section appeared previously in my earlier paper,

"Concern about Serbian Nationalism," *RFER*, 27 Mar. 1986.

55   *NIN*, no. 1836 (9 Mar. 1986): 22.
56   Ibid., no. 1904 (28 June 1987): 12, and no. 1941 (13 Mar. 1988): 16.
57   South-East European Service, 25 Jan. 1986.
58   *Nedeljna borba*, 23–24 Nov. 1985, and 28–29 Dec. 1985.
59   Tanjug, 24 Feb. 1986, *my emphasis*.
60   Ibid., 24 Dec. 1985, in FBIS, 9 Jan. 1986, 16–7.
61   *Frankfurter Allgemeine*, 5 Feb. 1986.
62   "The Serbian Kosovo Petition," *South Slav Journal* 9, nos. 1–2 (Spring/Summer 1986): 108.
63   *NIN*, no. 1835 (2 Mar. 1986): 28–29, and no. 1836 (9 Mar. 1986): 22.
64   Priština Domestic Service, 3 Apr. 1986, in FBIS, 4 Apr. 1986, 19.
65   *Frankfurter Allgemeine*, 24 June 1986; *The Times*, 29 July 1986.
66   *Die Welt*, 14 Feb. 1986.
67   *Politika*, 16 Mar. 1986.
68   Milan M. Miladinović, "Pojam i suština jugoslovenskog patriotizma danas," *Obeležja* 7, no. 6 (Nov.-Dec. 1977): 1153.
69   Ibid., 1165–66.
70   *Frankfurter Allgemeine*, 11 July 1986.
71   Tanjug, 8 June 1985, in FBIS, 10 June 1985, 110.
72   Priština Domestic Service, 2 Nov. 1985, in FBIS, 12 Nov. 1985, 16; *Politika*, 3 Jan. 1986.
73   *Politika*, 28 Apr. 1986. For a breakdown of ethnic distribution in Kosovo in successive censuses, including 1981, see Bogdanović, *Knjiga o Kosovu*, 252.
74   Lazar Vujović, chairman of the LC Serbian Commission for the Development of Intranational Relations, in Tanjug, 17 Feb. 1982, in FBIS, 18 Feb. 1982, 13.
75   Tanjug, 2 Apr. 1981, in FBIS, 3 Apr. 1981, 13.
76   *Borba*, 9 Jan. 1983, in FBIS, 18 Jan. 1983, 116.
77   Tanjug, 19 Dec. 1984, in JPRS, no. EPS-85-012 (27 Jan. 1985): 32.
78   Tanjug, 4 Apr. 1985, in FBIS, 9 Apr. 1985, 14.
79   Ibid., 15.
80   See Stevan Nikšić, *Oslobodjenje štampe* (Belgrade: Oslobodjenje, 1982).
81   See *NIN*, no. 1836 (9 Mar. 1986): 9–10, and no. 1838 (23 Mar. 1986): 53.
82   Belgrade Domestic Service, 29 Apr. 1985, in FBIS, 30 Apr. 1985, 120.
83   Tanjug, 4 Apr. 1985, in FBIS, 9 Apr. 1985, 14.
84   7 October 1985 session of the Commission for Information and Propaganda, LC Kosovo, as reported in Tanjug, 7 Oct. 1985, in FBIS, 17 Oct. 1985, 14.
85   Tanjug, 11 Jan. 1986, in FBIS, 15 Jan. 1986, 111.
86   Most of these can be found in Azem Vlasi, "Neki oblici antisocijalističkog delovanja u SAP Kosovu," *Socijalizam* 29, no. 4 (Apr. 1986).
87   *NIN*, no. 1871 (9 Nov. 1986), 12.
88   *Vjesnik*, 17 Jan. 1987, 3; *Večernji list* (Zagreb), 8 July 1987, 4.
89   Quoted in *NIN*, no. 1904 (28 June 1987): 9.
90   *Politika ekspres* (Belgrade), 27 June 1987, 1.
91   Quoted in Yugoslav Situation Report, *RFER*, 30 Sept. 1987, 3.
92   *Borba* (Zagreb), 26 Oct. 1987, 1.
93   *The Economist* (London), 23 July 1988, 44.
94   Zagreb Domestic Service, 23 June 1988, in FBIS, 28 June 1988, 61.
95   *Eastern Europe Newsletter*, 31 Aug. 1988, 1.
96   *Politika*, 31 Aug. 1988, 10.

97   Interview with Goran Bregović, leader of White Button, Sarajevo, 14 Sept. 1989. The song comes from an album released in 1987.

98   *Politika*, 17 June 1988, 5.

99   Dragana Roter-Crkvenjakov, "Pokrajinska štampa o promenama ustava SR Srbije," *Novinarstvo* 24, nos. 1–2 (1988): 60.

100 Tanjug, 24 Feb. 1989, in FBIS, 27 Feb. 1989, 59; Belgrade Domestic Service, 25 Feb. 1989, in FBIS, 27 Feb. 1989, 65; Tanjug Domestic Service, 4 Mar. 1989, in FBIS, 6 Mar. 1989, 60.

101 *Politika*, 30 Oct. 1989, 6, and 4 Nov. 1989, 5. For further discussion of Milošević's strategies, see Sabrina P. Ramet, "Slobodan Milošević and the Future of Yugoslavia," in *Orbis* 35, no. 1 (Winter 1991).

102 Quoted in *New York Times*, 19 Jan. 1990, A5.

103 Quoted in Ibid.

104 Belgrade Domestic Service, 31 Jan. 1990, in FBIS, 1 Feb. 1990, 75.

105 AFP, 31 Jan. 1990, in FBIS, 1 Feb. 1990, 76.

106 AFP, 1 Feb. 1990, in FBIS, 2 Feb. 1990, 75.

107 *New York Times*, 8 Feb. 1990, A13.

108 *Politika ekspres*, 1 Feb. 1990, as summarized in Tanjug, 1 Feb. 1990, in FBIS, 2 Feb. 1990, 84.

109 AFP, 1 Feb. 1990, in FBIS, 2 Feb. 1990, 76; and Tanjug, 1 Feb. 1990, in FBIS, 2 Feb. 1990, 80; *Politika*, 18 Feb. 1990, 6.

110 *Intervju*, 29 Mar. 1985, in JPRS, no. EPS-85-066 (11 June 1985): 81.

111 See Wolfgang Höpken, "Party Monopoly and Political Change: The League of Communists since Tito's Death," in *Yugoslavia in the 1980s*, ed. Pedro Ramet (Boulder, Colo.: Westview Press, 1985), 39–41.

112 *New York Times*, 28 Apr. 1986.

113 Samuel P. Huntington, *Political Order in Changing Societies* (New Haven, Conn.: Yale University Press, 1968).

114 Prifti, "Kosovë Stalemate," 82.

8   Feminism in Yugoslavia

1   Blaženka Despot, *Žensko pitanje i socijalističko samoupravljanje* (Zagreb: Čekada, 1987).

2   Interviews with officials, Belgrade, 14 July 1982; with a high-ranking Slovenian official and former partisan, Ljubljana, 19 July 1982; and with members of the editorial board of *Žena*, Zagreb, 2 July 1982. See also Barbara Jancar, "The New Feminism in Yugoslavia," in *Yugoslavia in the 1980s* ed. Pedro Ramet (Boulder, Colo.: Westview Press, 1985).

3   The remainder of this section draws heavily upon my earlier article, "Gleichberechtigung der Geschlechter, Parteipolitik und Feminismus in Jugoslawien," *Osteuropa* 33, no. 7 (July 1983): 539–46

4   V. kongres KPJ, stenografske bilješke (Kultura, 1949), 891, quoted in Nevenka Petrić, "Ravnopravnost žene i muškarca u završnim dokumentima poslijeratnih kongresa KPJ-SKJ," *Žena* 38, no. 1 (Jan.-Feb. 1980): 74.

5   Petrić, "Ravnopravnost žene," 76.

6   For a more detailed survey of this aspect of the question, see Pedro Ramet, "Women, Work, and Self-Management in Yugoslavia," *East European Quarterly* 17, no. 4 (Jan. 1984): 459–68.

7   Olivera Burić, "Položaj žene u sistemu društvene moći u Jugoslaviji," *Sociologija* 14, no. 1 (1972): 68.

8   Ibid., 65–68; Savka Dabčević-Kučar, "Problemi društvenog položaja žene—problemi našeg samoupravnog socijalističkog društva u cjelini," *Žena* 26, no. 2 (1970): 6.

9   Some statistics for this can be found in Olivera Burić, "Izmena strukture društvene moći—uslov za društvenu ravnopravnost žene," *Sociologija* 17, no. 2 (1975).

10 Djura Knezević, "Izbor žena u svjetlu kadrovske politike Saveza komunista," *Žena* 36, no. 55 (1979): 76.

11 Vladimir Bakarić, "Promjene društveno-ekonomskog položaja žene treba vezati uz opći preobražaj našeg društva," *Žena* 36, no. 4 (1979): 2.

12 *Mladost*, no. 38 (Mar. 30–April 12, 1987): 20.

13 All statistics from Lydia Sklevický, "Reluctant Feminists: the 'Woman Question'—A New Approach in Yugoslavia," unpublished paper, 1987.

14 *1987 Yearbook of Labour Statistics*, no. 47 (Geneva: International Labour Office, 1987), 578.

15 *Politika*, 15 Mar. 1981 and 22 Mar. 1981.

16 Nataša Djurić, "Emancipacija na pola puta," *Borba*, 1 June 1980.

17 Radivoje Ivković, "Žena un procesu odlučivanja u osnovnoj organizaciji Saveza komunista," *Opredjeljenja* 6, nos. 3–4 (Mar.-Apr. 1978): 87–88; "Zaključci Predsjedništva CK SKJ o zadacima Saveza komunista na daljem unapredjenju društvenog pitanja i uloge žene danas" (25 June 1980), *Žena* 38, nos. 4–5 (1980): 4; *Politika*, 28 June 1980.

18 Ivković, "Žena u procesu," 87–88; Mirjana Poček-Matić, "SK se mora boriti za afirmaciju marksističkih stavova o ulozi žene u društvu," *Žena* 35, no. 6 (1977): 6; Gabi Čačinović-Vogrinčić, "Socijalizacija za samoupravne odnose zahtijeva ostvarenje nehijerarhijskih odnosa u obitelji," *Žena* 38, nos. 4–5 (1980): 153.

19 Interviews, Zagreb, July 1982 and July 1987.

20 Jancar, "The New Feminism," 218.

21 *Komunist*, 6 Mar. 1981.

22 Interview with a sociologist and member of the Alternative Movement, Ljubljana, 3 July 1987.

23 Interview with two members of Woman and Society, Zagreb, July 1982.

24 See Lydia Sklevický, "Konji, žene, ratovi, itd.: Problem utemeljenja historije žena u Jugoslaviji," in *Žena i drustvo: Kultiviranje dijaloga* (Zagreb: Sociološko-društvo Hrvatske, 1987).

25 Interview with feminist free-lance writer, Belgrade, 7 July 1987.

26 Tanja Prića, "Što je to: 'Žensko pitanje'?," *Polet* 6 Nov. 1978, 4; Rada Iveković, "Klevete i istina," *Književna rec*, 10 Dec. 1978, 3; *NIN*, no. 1453 (12 Nov. 1978), 24–25.

27 Interview with feminist psychotherapist, Belgrade, July 1987.

28 Interview with a member of Lilith, Ljubljana, 1 July 1987.

29 Interview with a member of the editorial staff of *Start*, Zagreb, 22 July 1982.

30 Interview with a high-ranking Slovenian official, Ljubljana, 19 July 1982.

31 Interview with a feminist, Belgrade, 10 July 1987.

32 Vlasta Jalusić, as cited in *Danas*, no. 308 (12 Jan. 1988): 73.

33 Interview source in note 27.

34 Ibid.

35 Susan L. Woodward, "The Rights of Women: Ideology, Policy, and Social Change in Yugoslavia," in *Women, State, and Party in Eastern Europe*, ed. Sharon L. Wolchik and Alfred G. Meyer (Durham, N.C.: Duke University Press, 1985), 247–48.

36 Željka Šporer, "Feminizacija profesija kao indikator položaja žena u različitim društvima," *Sociologija* 27, no. 4 (Oct.-Dec. 1985): 602–5.

37 Vjeran Katunarić, *Ženski eros i civilizacija smrti* (Zagreb: Naprijed, 1984), 235–40.

38 Interview with feminist journalist and author, Zagreb, 26 June 1987.

39 Slavenka Drakulić-Ilić, *Smrtni griješi feminizma: Ogledi o mudologiji* (Zagreb, Znanje, 1984), 59–73.

40 Interview source in note 25.

41 Interview, Belgrade, 10 July 1987.

42 Interview, Zagreb, 22 July 1982.

43 Jancar, "The New Feminism," 211

44 Interview source in note 38.

45 *Danas*, no. 308 (12 Jan. 1988): 72.

46 *Vjesnik—Sedam dana*, 11 Apr. 1987, 8.

47 Tanjug, 22 Mar. 1990, in FBIS, 23 Mar. 1990, 89.

48 See, for example, Magdalena Sokolowska, *Frauenemanzipation und Sozialismus: Das Beispiel der Volksrepublik Polen* (Hamburg: Rowohlt Verlag, 1973); also Magdalena Sokolowska, "The Role and Status of Women in Poland," *Studies in Comparative International Development* 10, no. 3 (Fall 1975).

49 Barbara Jancar, "Neofeminism in Yugoslavia: A Closer Look," *Women in Politics* 8, no. 1 (1988): 3.

50 AFP, 31 July 1981, in FBIS, 3 Aug. 1981, G27.

51 Warsaw Domestic Service, 8 July 1981, in FBIS, 9 July 1981, G10.

52 *The Guardian*, 5 Nov. 1981.

53 "Ciljevi feministkinja," trans. into Serbo-Croatian by Vera Vukelić, *Gledišta* (Belgrade) 22, nos. 5–6 (May-June 1981): 103.

54 *Pravda* (Bratislava), 26 Jan. 1990, 2, in FBIS, 8 Feb. 1990, 31.

55 *ROMPRES* (Bucharest), 31 Jan. 1990, in FBIS, 1 Feb. 1990, 62; Sofia Domestic Service, 17 Mar. 1990, in FBIS, 19 Mar. 1990, 16.

56 Bratislava Domestic Service, 29 Sept. 1990, in FBIS, 2 Oct. 1990, 9.

57 PAP (Warsaw), 27 Sept. 1990, in FBIS, 28 Sept. 1990, 38.

58 Quoted in *Wall Street Journal*, 24 July 1990, A11.

59 *Życie Warszawy*, 6 Jan. 1986, 3, in JPRS, no. EER-86-029 (1 Mar. 1986): 72–75.

60 Jancar, "Neofeminism in Yugoslavia," 7.

61 Interview, Belgrade, 22 Sept. 1989.

62 "Taj mračni predmet želja" [Interview with Nada Sofronić-Ler], *Valter* (Sarajevo), 10 Mar. 1989, 10.

9 Rock Music and Counterculture

This is a completely revised and updated version of "Rock Counterculture in Eastern Europe and the Soviet Union," *Survey* 29, no. 2 (Summer 1985): Reprinted by permission.

1 Interview with Goran Bregović, leader of White Button, Sarajevo, 14 Sept. 1989.

2 Sidney Verba, "Comparative Political Culture," in *Political Culture and Political Development*, ed. Lucian W. Pye and Sidney Verba (Princeton, N.J.: Princeton University Press, 1965), 513.

3 Joel J. Schwartz, "The Elusive 'New Soviet Man,'" *Problems of Communism* 22, no. 5 (Sept.-Oct. 1983); Wolfgang Mleczkowski, "In Search of the Forbidden Nation: Opposition by the Young Generation in the GDR," *Government and Opposition* 18, no. 2 (Spring 1983): 175–93.

4   Archie Brown, "Introduction," in *Political Culture and Political Change in Commu-
    nist States*, ed. Archie Brown and Jack Gray (New York: Holmes & Meier, 1977), 4.
5   See Stephen White, *Political Culture and Soviet Politics* (New York: St. Martin's,
    1979), 143–65.
6   Andrzej Korbonski, "The Pattern and Method of Liberalization," in *Comparative
    Socialist Systems: Essays on Politics and Economics*, ed. Carmelo Mesa-Lago and
    Carl Beck (Pittsburgh: University of Pittsburgh Center for International Studies,
    1975), 201–2.
7   For a discussion of this point, see Brown, "Introduction," 7–8.
8   For example, see *Dissent in Eastern Europe*, ed. Jane Leftwich Curry (New York:
    Praeger, 1983); Rudolf L. Tökes, ed., *Opposition in Eastern Europe* (London: Mac-
    millan, 1979).
9   See Bohdan R. Bociurkiw and John W. Strong, eds., *Religion and Atheism in the
    USSR and Eastern Europe* (London: Macmillan, 1975); Norbert Greinacher and
    Virgil Elizondo, eds., *Churches in Socialist Societies of Eastern Europe*, Concilium:
    Religion in the Eighties (New York: Seabury, 1982); and Pedro Ramet, ed., *Religion
    and Nationalism in Soviet and East European Politics*, rev. and expanded ed. (Dur-
    ham, N.C.: Duke University Press, 1989).
10 See Ivan Volgyes, ed., *Social Deviance in Eastern Europe* (Boulder, Colo.: Westview,
    1978).
11 This list omits the culture of indigenous ethnic minorities—which may be viewed
    with hostility and distrust (as in the cases of Bulgaria, Romania, and the Soviet
    Union), but which could not ordinarily be viewed as "counterculture."
12 Derrick F. Wright, "Musical Meaning and its Social Determinants," *Sociology* 9, no.
    3 (Sept. 1975): 419–23, 425, 431; Richard A. Peterson, "Taking Popular Music Too
    Seriously," *Journal of Popular Culture* 4, no. 3 (Winter 1971): 592; Leonard B. Meyer,
    Emotion and Meaning in Music (Chicago: University of Chicago Press, 1956), 5.
13 S. Frederick Starr, *Red and Hot: The Fate of Jazz in the Soviet Union, 1917–1980*
    (New York: Oxford University Press, 1983), 5.
14 Ibid., 49, 61–62.
15 Ibid., 295.
16 Quoted in *Christian Science Monitor*, 5 Aug. 1983, 3. See also *Komsomol'skaya
    pravda*, 16 Sept. 1984, 4; and *Soviet Analyst* 13, no. 15 (25 July 1984): 3.
17 *Los Angeles Times*, 8 Feb. 1988, 1, 10.
18 James M. Curtis, "Toward a Sociotechnological Interpretation of Popular Music in the
    Electronic Age", in *Technology and Culture*, 25, 1 (January 1984), pp. 94, 96–97.
19 *Tribuna* (Prague), 6 June 1984, in JPRS, no. EPS-84-090 (23 July 1984): 6.
20 Quoted in *The Times* (London), 18 June 1984, 6.
21 Trans. into Serbo-Croatian as "Njezni seksi krikovi," *Start*, no. 294 (30 Apr.-14 May
    1980): 66–67.
22 See, for instance, Peter Yakovlevich Chaadayev, *Philosophical Letters and Apology
    of a Madman*, trans. Mary Barbara Zeldin (Knoxville: University of Tennessee Press,
    1969).
23 Mleczkowski, "In Search of the Forbidden," 181.
24 *Scînteia* (Bucharest), 7 Aug. 1983, 4.
25 *Tribuna* 16 Feb. 1983, 5, in FBIS, 22 Feb. 1983, D9.
26 *Literaturen Front* (Sofia), 26 Jan. 1984, in JPRS, no. EPS-84-031 (1 Mar. 1984): 9;
    Serzhant (Sofia), no. 2 (1983), in JPRS, no. 83252 (13 Apr. 1983): 2.
27 A play on the Beatles' album, *Sergeant Pepper's Lonely Hearts Club Band*.
28 *International Herald Tribune*, 22 Sept. 1978, 8.

29 *NIN*, no. 1663 (14 Nov. 1982); and interview with Pero Lovšin, lead singer of the Bastards, Ljubljana, 30 June 1987.

30 For further discussion, see Pedro Ramet, "Apocalypse Culture and Social Change," in *Yugoslavia in the 1980s*, ed. Pedro Ramet (Boulder, Colo.: Westview Press, 1985).

31 Quoted in Peter J. Prifti, *Socialist Albania since 1944: Domestic and Foreign Developments* (Cambridge: MIT Press, 1978), 187.

32 *Tribuna*, 23 Mar. 1983, 5, in JPRS, no. 83438 (10 May 1983), 21. Along the same lines, *Komsomol'skaya pravda*, 16 Sept. 1984, charged that "the implantation of complete social and political passivity, indifference to the most acute problems of the present day, and the cult of the 'good life'—these are the basic postulates of Western propaganda." Trans. in JPRS, *USSR Report*, no. UPS-84-091 (19 Oct. 1984): 15.

33 *Tribuna*, 23 Mar. 1983, 22, 23. *Tribuna* added that punk music was "encourag[ing] young people to fight against our system." Quoted in *Klassekampen* (Oslo), 19 Oct. 1984, 5, in JPRS, no. EPS-84-150 (6 Dec. 1984): 6.

34 Prifti, *Socialist Albania*, 187.

35 Quoted in *Soviet Analyst* 13, no. 15 (25 July 1984): 3.

36 See *Der Spiegel*, 28 May 1984, 165–71.

37 Polish Situation Report, *RFER*, 28 Sept. 1984, 10.

38 ZOMO is the Polish secret police.

39 Quoted in Polish Situation Report (note 37), 9.

40 Quoted in *Christian Science Monitor*, 20 Sept. 1983, 7.

41 Quoted in *Der Spiegel*, 28 May 1984, 171.

42 Quoted in Polish Situation Report (note 37), 9.

43 Maanam, *Night Patrol*, album released by Arctic, no. 6.25728-BL.

44 Ibid.

45 *UPNB*, no. 2/88 (22 Jan. 1988): 19.

46 *Die Tageszeitung* (Berlin), 24 Jan. 1984, 9.

47 Quoted in J. B., "Poland's Alienated Youth," *RFER*, 7 Apr. 1984, 17.

48 Quoted in *Seattle Times*, 29 Nov. 1987, 3.

49 *Kurier Polski* (Warsaw), 5 Aug. 1986, 1–2, in JPRS, no. EER-86-196 (30 Dec. 1986): 116; *Sztandar Młodych* (Warsaw), 9 Apr. 1987, 3, in JPRS, no. EER-87-122 (7 Aug. 1987): 34; *Gość Niedzielny* (Katowice), 10 May 1987, 1, 5, in JPRS, no. EER-87-120 (4 Aug. 1987): 119; "Najveći tradicionalni skup poljskog roka: Jaročin '87," *Rock* (Belgrade), Sept. 1987, 51.

50 Quoted in Czechoslovak Situation Report, *RFER*, 10 Aug. 1984, 16.

51 Quoted in Wolf Oschlies, *Jugend in der Tschechoslowakei. Kurzer Frühling, lange Winter* (Cologne: Bohlau Verlag, 1985), 317.

52 Timothy W. Ryback, *Rock Around the Bloc* (Oxford: Oxford University Press, 1990), 58–59, 70.

53 Ibid., 76–77.

54 *Gegenstimmen* (Vienna), Winter 1983, 2–6, in JPRS, no. EPS-84-023 (10 Feb. 1984): 5.

55 Otto Ulč, "Social Deviance in Czechoslovakia," in *Social Deviance in Eastern Europe*, ed. Ivan Volgyes (Boulder, Colo.: Westview, 1978), 29.

56 *Gegenstimmen* [note 54], 2.

57 Ibid., 3.

58 *Tribuna*, 23 Mar. 1983, 5, in JPRS, no. 83438 (10 May 1983): 21, 22.

59 Czechoslovak Situation Report, *RFER*, 13 Sept. 1983, 10, 12.

60 *Tribuna*, 12 Oct. 1983, 6, in JPRS, no. 84956 (15 Dec. 1983): 25.

61 *Tribuna*, 16 Nov. 1983, 4, excerpted in JPRS, no. 85003 (22 Dec. 1983): 7.

62   *Klassekampen,* 19 Oct. 1984, 5, in JPRS, no. EPS-84-150 (6 Dec. 1984): 4–5.

63   *Washington Post,* 18 May 1984, A29.

64   *Rudé pravo,* 3 July 1986, 5, in JPRS, no. EER-86-127 (19 Aug. 1986): 104.

65   Ibid., 105.

66   Czechoslovak Situation Report, *RFER* (21 Jan. 1988), 43.

67   Max Stirner, *The Ego and His Own,* trans. Steven T. Byington, ed. James J. Martin (New York: Libertarian Book Club, 1963). See also John Henry Mackay, *Max Stirner: Sein Leben und Sein Werk* (Freiburg: Mackay-Gesellschaft, 1977), and R. W. K. Paterson, *The Nihilist Egoist: Max Stirner* (London: Oxford University Press, 1971).

68   Stirner, *The Ego and His Own,* 217.

69   Ibid., 216.

70   Ibid., 166.

71   Ibid., 354.

72   Andrew R. Carlson, *Anarchism in Germany* (Metuchen, N.J.: Scarecrow, 1972), 1:66.

73   Olaf Leitner, *Rockszene DDR: Aspekte einer Massenkultur im Sozialismus* (Hamburg: Rowohlt Verlag, 1983), 46.

74   Ibid., 47–54.

75   Victor Grossman, "Von der 'Hootenanny' zum Oktoberklub," *Musik und Gesellschaft,* no. 5/88: 238–40.

76   Peter Wicke, *Anatomie des Rock* (Leipzig: VEB Deutscher Verlag für Musik, 1987), 161–64. See also Peter Wicke, *Rockmusik* (Leipzig: Verlag Philipp Reclam jun., 1987).

77   *15. Festival des politischen Liedes 1985,* album released by Amiga (GDR), no. 8-45-296; and "18. Festival des politischen Liedes in Berlin," *Musik und Gesellschaft,* no. 5/88: 243.

78   Wicke, *Anatomie des Rock,* 185, 194.

79   Wolfgang Martin, *Musikalisches Porträt: Karussell* (Leipzig: VEB Harth Musik Verlag, 1988), 2, 12.

80   Quoted in Leitner, *Rockszene DDR,* 389.

81   Silly, *Liebeswalzer,* album released by Amiga, no. 8-56-069.

82   Günter Mayer, "Popular Music in the GDR," *Journal of Popular Culture* 18, no. 3 (Winter 1984): 153.

83   *Informationen* (Bonn), 11 Nov. 1983, 17–18, in JPRS, no. EPS-84-007 (16 Jan. 1985): 42.

84   Fritz Bachmann, "Aktuelle Beispiele unserer Rock- und Popmusik einbeziehen," *Musik* 39, no. 6 (1988): 177.

85   *Vjesnik* (Zagreb), 7 May 1984, 5; *Duga* (Belgrade), 2–16 June 1984, 51; Nenad Neoričić, "Brejkdens parti," *Reporter* (Belgrade), no. 930 (29 Jan. 1985): 5; Goran Lisica, "Suze Erosove," *Reporter,* no. 946 (28 May 1985): 45.

86   Quoted in *Vjesnik,* 29 Dec. 1984, 11.

87   Interview with Darko Glavan, Zagreb, 28 Aug. 1989.

88   Interview with Vlada Janković (chief editor of *Hit nedjelje,* Radio Belgrade), Belgrade, 6 July 1987; interview with Goce Dimovski (director) and Pande Dimovski (music manager), Dom na Mladite, Skopje, 26 Sept. 1989.

89   Interview with Petar Popović, International Label Manager for RTB PGP and founder of *Rock* magazine, Belgrade, 16 June 1987.

90   For further discussion, see Pedro Ramet, "The Rock Scene in Yugoslavia," *East European Politics and Societies* 2, no. 2 (Spring 1988).

91   Laibach, *Rekapitulácija 1980–84,* Walter Ulbricht Schallfolien, WULP-001 & WULP-002, SPK-AUTO-DA-FE, & WULP-003/4.

92 Works include *Ravnodušan prema plaću* (Belgrade: Niro književne novine, 1985); *Hej Sloveni* (Belgrade: Glas, 1987); *Prvih deset godina je najteže* (Belgrade: Dereta, 1988); and *Neću* (Belgrade: Književna zadruga, 1989).

93 Ozren Kanceljak, "Majstor verbalnog terorizma," interview with Bora Djordjević, *Start*, no. 478 (16 May 1987).

94 *Ujed za dušu*, album released by RTB PGP, no. 2320436.

95 Djordjević, *Hej Sloveni*, 114.

96 "Svi su pametni i bez mene: Bora" (interview by Vladimir Stakić), *Rock*, Mar. 1987, 7–9; "Vanguard of Rock Protest: An Interview with Bora Djordjević" (by Pedro Ramet), *South Slav Journal* 10, no. 4 (Winter 1987/88): 44–48; "Svi bi hteli u nušice," *Ana* (Belgrade), July 1988, 24; *Vjesnik*, 31 July 1988, 9.

97 *Večernje novosti* (Belgrade), 30 Dec. 1987); interview with Dragan Todorović, coeditor of *Rock* magazine, Belgrade, 18 July 1988; interview with Bora Djordjević, Belgrade, 18 July 1988.

98 Interview with Tanja Petrović (Radio Studio B), Belgrade, 23 Sept. 1989.

99 *Pop-Rock*, no. 123 (3 May 1989): 20.

100 *Vjesnik*, 21 July 1988, 7, and 24 Aug. 1988, 13.

101 Vesna Perić-Zimonjić, "Rock: Generacijski parastos," *Reporter*, no. 947 (14 June 1985): 10.

102 *Vjesnik*, 8 Dec. 1984, 11.

103 Bulgarian Situation Report, *RFER*, 7 July 1986, 26; interview with Stephen Ashley, Bulgarian Research Service, Radio Free Europe, Munich, 4 June 1987; Gabriel Bar-Haim, "The Meaning of Western Commercial Artifacts for East European Youth," *Journal of Contemporary Ethnography*, 16, no. 2 (July 1987): 218.

104 *Munca* (Budapest), 2 Mar. 1984, 4; *The Economist* (London), 7 July 1984, 45.

105 *Narodna Kultura*, 24 Feb. 1984, quoted in Bulgarian Situation Report, *RFER*, 30 Mar. 1984, 12.

106 "Rock u Bugarskoj i Rumunji: U potrazi za identitetom," *Rock* (Belgrade), June 1987, 52; Bulgarian Situation Report, *RFER*, 12 Aug. 1988, 21.

107 Interview with Stephen Ashley [note 103]; *Index on Censorship* 12, no. 1 (Feb. 1983): 7; Bulgarian Situation Report, *RFER*, 17 Feb. 1986, 28–29.

108 Interview with Stephen Ashley [note 103].

109 Bulgarian Situation Report, *RFER*, 12 Aug. 1988, 20.

110 Ibid.

111 Stephen Ashley, "Rock Music in Bulgaria," in *Rocking the State: Rock Music and Politics in Eastern Europe and the Soviet Union*, ed. Sabrina P. Ramet, ms. in progress.

112 Interview with Annali Gabanyi, Romanian Research Service, Radio Free Europe, Munich, 4 June 1987. See also Trond Gilberg, "Ceausescus 'Kleine Kulturrevolution' in Rumänien," *Osteuropa* 22, no. 10 (Oct. 1972): 717–28

113 "Rock u Bugarskoj i Rumuniji," 53.

114 Quoted in *Christian Science Monitor*, 31 May 1990, 11.

115 *Pop Rock* (Belgrade), 7 Mar. 1990, 14.

116 *Christian Science Monitor*, 8 Feb. 1982, 2.

117 Edith Markos, "'Stephen the King' or Stephen the Superstar," *RFER*, 19 Sept. 1983, 15.

118 *Magyar Nemzet*, 3 Mar. 1984, 9, in JPRS, no. EPS-84-044 (5 Apr. 1984): 13.

119 *Christian Science Monitor*, 30 Nov. 1983, 14.

120 László Kürti, "Rocking the State: Youth and Rock Music Culture in Hungary, 1976–1988," in *Rocking the State: Rock Music and Politics in Eastern Europe and the Soviet Union*, ed. Sabrina P. Ramet, ms. in progress.

121 Letter to the author from László Kürti, 18 Apr. 1990.

122 Solaris, *Marsbéli Krónikák*, album released by Start, no. SLPM-17819.

123 Quoted in Hungarian Situation Report, *RFER*, 30 Aug. 1983, 17.

124 Ibid.

125 *Mozgó Világ* (Budapest), no. 12 (1984), in JPRS, no. EPS-85-048 (22 Apr. 1985): 48–55.

126 Quoted in Zsolt Krokovay, "Politics and Punk [in Hungary]," *Index on Censorship* 14, no. 2 (Apr. 1985): 20.

127 Quoted in Kürti, "Rocking the State."

128 Quoted in Krokovay, "Politics and Punk," 20.

129 Quoted in Kürti, "Rocking the State."

130 *Sztandar Młodych* (Warsaw), 25 Oct. 1983, 3, in JPRS, no. EPS-84-006 (11 Jan. 1985): 94.

131 S. Frederick Starr, "The Rock Inundation," *The Wilson Quarterly*, 7, no. 4 (Autumn 1983): 62.

132 Quoted in *Christian Science Monitor*, 31 May 1990, 10.

133 Quoted in Artemy Troitsky, *Back in the USSR: The True Story of Rock in Russia* (Boston: Faber & Faber, 1987), 127.

10 Young People—The Lost Generation

1 See Klaus Ehring and Martin Dallwitz, *Schwerter zu Pflugscharen* (Hamburg: Rowohlt Taschenbuch Verlag, 1982).

2 *Życie Warszawy* (Warsaw), 30 Sept. 1986, 3, in JPRS, no. EER-86-192 (18 Dec. 1986): 97.

3 *Polityka* (Warsaw), 10 Jan. 1987, 5, in JPRS, no. EER-87-057 (9 Apr. 1987): 94.

4 *Magyar Ifjúság* (Budapest), 28 Dec. 1984, 7–9, in JPRS, no. EPS-85-017 (2 Feb. 1985): 19.

5 Wolf Oschlies, *Jugend in der Tschechoslowakei: Kurzer Frühling, lange Winter* (Cologne: Bohlau Verlag, 1985), 209.

6 *Kontakty*, no. 26 (Oct. 1985), in "Extracts from Polish Underground Publications," *RFER*, 17 Jan. 1986, 13.

7 Quoted in Gabriel Bar-Haim, "The Meaning of Western Commercial Artifacts for Eastern European Youth," *Journal of Contemporary Ethnography* 16, no. 2 (July 1987): 212–13.

8 Quoted in Ibid., 214.

9 *Sturshel* (Sofia), 7 Dec. 1984, 1, 2, in JPRS, no. EPS-85-023 (19 Feb. 1985): 8.

10 See, for instance, Tanjug (Belgrade), 3 Feb. 1986, in JPRS, no. EER-86-025 (25 Feb. 1986): 158.

11 PAP, 20 Apr. 1982, in FBIS, 21 Apr. 1982, G20.

12 *Magyar Hirek* (Budapest), 16 June 1984, suppl., 4–5, in JPRS, no. EPS-84-095 (3 Aug. 1984): 39.

13 *Rheinische Merkur*, 14 Oct. 1988, 25; *Frankfurter Allgemeine*, 26 Nov. 1988, 1.

14 *Nepszava* (Budapest), 25 July 1988, 5, in JPRS, no. EER-88-075 (9 Sept. 1988): 23.

15 Bulgarian Situation Report, *RFER*, 7 Aug. 1989, 23; *Rabotnichesko delo* (Sofia), 5 Feb. 1989, 3, in FBIS, 9 Feb. 1989, 3–4.

16 Wolf Oschlies, *Der Jargon osteuropaischer Jugendlicher. Zur sprachsoziologischen, lexikalischen und politischen Einordnung eines Sozialdialekts* (Cologne: Bundesinstitut für ostwissenschaftliche und internationale Studien, report no. 28, 1979), 1.

17 Ibid., 32.

18 Ibid, 34.

19 Ibid, 42, 44.

20 Quoted in Ibid., 41.

21 Ibid., 65.

22 *Danas* (Zagreb), 6 Dec. 1983, 21–22, in JPRS, no. EPS-84-016 (3 Feb. 1984): 180.

23 *Sztandar Młodych* (Warsaw), 18–20 Nov. 1983, 3, in JPRS, no. EPS-84-005 (9 Jan. 1984): 117.

24 Wolf Oschlies, *Rumäniens Jugend—Rumäniens Hoffnung* (Cologne: Bohlau Verlag, 1983), 153; Wolf Oschlies, *Jugendprobleme in Jugoslawien* (Cologne: Bundesinstitut für ostwissenschaftliche und internationale Studien, report no. 5, 1977), 1.

25 Wolf Oschlies, *"Verlorene Generation." Polens Jugend im "Kriegszustand," 1981–1983* (Cologne: Bundesinstitut für ostwissenschaftliche und internationale Studien, report no. 23, 1983), 11.

26 *Karima* 15, no. 12 (26 Nov. 1987): 14–17, cited in Hungarian Situation Report, *RFER*, 15 Feb. 1988, 11.

27 *Felsooktatasi Szemle* (Budapest), Nov. 1984, 662–67, in JPRS, no. EPS-85-017 (2 Feb. 1985): 14, 16.

28 Josip Županov, "Radnička omladina i društvena stabilnost," in Vlasta Ilišin, Furio Radin, and Josip Županov, *Kultura radničke omladine* (Zagreb: Centar društvenih djelatnosti saveza socijalističke omladine Hrvatske, 1986), 169, 183.

29 *Borba* (Belgrade), 1 Dec. 1989, 3, in FBIS, 12 Jan. 1990, 76.

30 Quoted in Norbert Haase, Lothar Reese, and Peter Wensierski, eds., *VEB Nachwuchs. Jugend in der DDR* (Hamburg: Rowohlt Verlag, 1983), 59.

31 Oschlies, *"Verlorene Generation,"* 12.

32 Furio Radin, "Vrijednosti i vrijednose orijentacije," in Ilišin et al., *Kultura radničke omladine*, 136.

33 *Przegląd Tygodniowy* (Warsaw), 14 Oct. 1984, 5, in JPRS, no. EPS-84-145 (28 Nov. 1984): 131; Czechoslovak Situation Report, *RFER*, 6 Mar. 1987), 21; Hungarian Situation Report, *RFER*, 8 Nov. 1985, 23.

34 Hungarian Situation Report, *RFER*, 3 June 1988, 39.

35 *Krytyka*, no. 16 (1983), in "Polish Samizdat Extracts," *RFER*, 6 June 1984, 1, 3.

36 Quoted in *Christian Science Monitor*, 2 June 1988, 11.

37 *Danas*, 28 Jan. 1986, 22–25, in JPRS, no. EER-86-061 (18 April 1986): 76–83.

38 *Die Zeit* (Hamburg), 13 May 1988, 3.

39 Quoted in Jim Seroka and Radŏs Smiljković, *Political Organizations in Socialist Yugoslavia* (Durham, N.C.: Duke University Press, 1986), 157.

40 Quoted in *Svijet* (Sarajevo), 24 Aug. 1981, 10–11, in JPRS, no. 79299 (26 Oct. 1981): 31.

41 Romanian Situation Report, *RFER*, 26 June 1985, 35.

42 Hungarian Situation Report, *RFER*, 11 July 1986, 40–41; Hungarian Situation Report, *RFER*, 21 Mar. 1988, 9–10.

43 *Narodna Armiya* (Sofia), 4 Nov. 1986, 3, in JPRS, no. EER-87-006 (12 Jan. 1987): 78–79.

44 *Christian Science Monitor*, 26 Nov. 1984, 16.

45 For Yugoslavia, see the data in Srečko Mihailović, "Društveno-politički aktivizam mladih," in *Položaj, svest i ponašanje mlade generacije Jugoslavije: Preliminarna analiza rezultata istraživanja* (Zagreb: IDIS, 1986), 176.

46 Quoted in Tomaz Mastnak, "Politics and New Social Movements in Yugoslavia," *Across Frontiers* (Spring 1987): 13.

47 Tanjug, 28 July 1988, in FBIS, 4 August 1988, 51.

48 Život Strany, no. 1 (3 Jan. 1987): 37–38, quoted in Czechoslovak Situation Report, RFER, 6 Mar. 1987, 21.

49 Wolf Oschlies, Kinder der "Solidarität." Zu Geschichte und Gegenwart der Jugendbewegung in Polen (Cologne: Bundesinstitut für ostwissenschaftliche und internationale Studien, report no. 24, 1981), 19.

50 Trybuna Robotnicza (Katowice), 1 Mar. 1982, 2, summarized in FBIS, 16 Mar. 1982, G20.

51 Roman Dumas, "Poland's 'Independent Society,'" Poland Watch, no. 8 (1986): 72.

52 Polish Situation Report, RFER, 12 Mar. 1987, 13.

53 Tribuna, 21 May 1988, 17, cited in Czechoslovak Situation Report, RFER, 28 June 1988, 29.

54 Czechoslovak Situation Report, RFER, 20 Dec. 1984, 25.

55 Vera Gavrilov, "The Komsomol and Bulgarian Youth in the Post-Zhivkov Era," Radio Free Europe: Report on Eastern Europe 1, no. 11 (16 Mar. 1990): 2, 5.

56 Velimir Tomanović, "O idejnim i vrednosnim opredeljenjima omladine," in Mlada generacija danas: Društveni položaj, uloga i perspektive mlade generacije Jugoslavije (Belgrade: Mladost, 1982), 180.

57 Ibid., 176–77.

58 Quoted in Christine Lemke, "Youth and Youth Policy in GDR Society," in Studies in GDR Culture and Society, ed. Margy Gerber (New York: University Press of America, 1983), 3:102–3.

59 Oschlies, Rumäniens Jugend, 124, 138–39; Oschlies, Jugend in der Tschechoslowakei, 313.

60 Oschlies, Jugend in der Tschechoslowakei, 220; Oschlies, Rumäniens Jugend, 217; Furio Radin, "Vrijednosti jugoslavenske omladine," in Polozaj, svest i ponašanje mlade generacije Jugoslavie: Preliminarna analiza rezultata istraživanja (Zagreb: IDIS, 1986), 58.

61 Quoted in Życie Warszawy, 25 May 1983, 1, as cited in Oschlies, "Verlorene Generation," 21.

62 Ibid.

63 Quoted in Oschlies, "Verlorene Generation," 23.

11   Bulgaria: A Weak Society

1 Bulgarian Situation Report, RFER, 24 Sept. 1980.

2 Paul Marer, "The Economies and Trade of Eastern Europe," in Central and Eastern Europe: The Opening Curtain?, ed. William E. Griffith (Boulder, Colo.: Westview, 1989), 40.

3 Index on Censorship 11, no. 4 (Aug. 1982): 38.

4 In Zemedelsko Zname, as reported in Bulgarian Situation Report, RFER, 8 June 1984, 11–12.

5 Bulgarski Zhurnalist (Sofia), no. 7 (1983), in JPRS, no. 84227 (30 Aug. 1983): 13.

6 Los Angeles Times, 1 May 1977, pt. 5, 4.

7 Bulgarian Situation Report, RFER, 14 Apr. 1989, 18.

8 Among the first public opinion polls published in the Bulgarian press were a poll on the National Assembly session, published in Rabotnichesko delo (Sofia) on 23 Nov. 1989, and a poll on the decisions of the Politburo, published in the same newspaper on 30 Nov. 1989.

9 Robert Sharlet, "Human Rights and Civil Society in Eastern Europe," in *Central and Eastern Europe: The Opening Curtain?*, ed. William E. Griffith (Boulder, Colo.: Westview, 1989), 171; Bulgarian Situation Report, *RFER*, 24 Oct. 1988, 15.

10 Bulgarian Situation Report, *RFER*, 9 Mar. 1989, 17.

11 *Keston News Service*, no. 333 (7 Aug. 1989): 3.

12 Sofia Domestic Service, 17 Jan. 1990, in FBIS, 18 Jan. 1990, 8.

13 *Rabotnichesko delo*, 1 Dec. 1989, 2, in FBIS, 7 Dec. 1989, 21.

14 BTA (Sofia), 28 Sept. 1989, in FBIS, 2 Oct. 1989, p. 10.

15 Full text in Bulgarian Situation Report, *RFER*, 22 May 1989, 16–18.

16 See the interview with Nedjo Gendzhev, chief mufti of Sofia, in *Trud* (Sofia), 31 Aug. 1989, 1–2.

17 See Horst Dieter Topp, "Die türkische Minderheit in Bulgarien," *Wissenschaftlicher Dienst Südosteuropa*, 27, no. 5 (May 1978): 142–43.

18 *The Guardian of Liberty (Nemzetör)* (Munich), May–June 1989, 10; *New York Times*, 24 May 1989, A8.

19 *Süddeutsche Zeitung* (Munich), 27–28 May 1989, 6; Bulgarian Situation Report, *RFER*, 5 Oct. 1989, 9.

20 *Rabotnichesko delo*, 16 Sept. 1989, 2.

21 *Keston News Service*, no. 333 (7 Aug. 1989): 3.

22 Sofia Domestic Service, 17 Nov. 1989, in FBIS, 20 Nov. 1989, 6.

23 BTA, 18 Nov. 1989, in FBIS, 20 Nov. 1989, 7.

24 BTA, 30 Dec. 1989, in FBIS, 4 Jan. 1990, 13.

25 BTA, 4 Jan. 1990, in FBIS, 4 Jan. 1990, 11.

26 *Rabotnichesko delo*, 8 Jan. 1990, 1, 2, in FBIS, 12 Jan. 1990, 10.

27 *New York Times*, 1 Jan. 1990, 7, and 3 Jan. 1990, A6.

28 Quoted in *Christian Science Monitor*, 18 Jan. 1990, 3.

29 *Keston News Service*, no. 346 (22 Mar. 1990): 11.

30 Both quoted in *New York Times*, 12 June 1990, A8.

31 Quoted in Ibid., 7 Oct. 1989, 5.

32 *Anteni* (Sofia), no. 2 (25 Jan. 1989): 8.

33 *New York Times*, 4 Nov. 1989, 4.

34 See his interview in *Süddeutsche Zeitung*, 27–28 May 1989, 11.

35 Yana Bozhina, an English teacher from Sofia, quoted in *New York Times*, 13 Nov. 1989, A9.

36 Deyan Kiuranov, quoted in Ibid.

12 Strong Societies: Hungary, Poland, and Yugoslavia

1 Paul Marer, "The Economies and Trade of Eastern Europe," in *Central and Eastern Europe: The Opening Curtain?*, ed. William E. Griffith (Boulder, Colo.: Westview, 1989), 40.

2 Władysław Markiewicz, "Change in Social Structure and the Increased Significance of the Working Class," in *The Polish Dilemma: Views from Within*, ed. Lawrence S. Graham and Maria K. Ciechocinska (Boulder, Colo.: Westview, 1987), 77–78.

3 The Committee for the Protection of Artistic Freedom (organized in 1982) and the Committee for the Protection of Humanity and the Environment (organized in 1986) are associated with the Serbian Association of Writers. The Committee for the Defense of Freedom of Thought and Expression (organized in 1984) is associated with the Serbian Academy of Sciences.

4 Interview with Miklós Haraszti, "Hungary in 1989: The Transition to a Post-Communist Society?," *Uncaptive Minds* 2, no. 1 (Jan.-Feb. 1989): 2.

5 R. Nyers, "Efficiency and Socialist Democracy," *Acta Oeconomica* 37, no. 1–2 (1986): 1, 2.

6 "Hungary: Grósz and Company," *Eastern Europe Newsletter* 2, no. 20 (Oct. 1988): 7; "Hungary: Battle Lines Drawn," *Eastern Europe Newsletter* 2, no. 22 (9 Nov. 1988): 4–5.

7 Quoted in Hungarian Situation Report, *RFER*, 17 Nov. 1988, 4, my emphasis.

8 *Süddeutsche Zeitung* (Munich), 17–18 Dec. 1988, 8.

9 Hungarian Situation Report, *RFER*, 15 Dec. 1988, 18.

10 MTI (Budapest), 16 Nov. 1988, in FBIS, 17 Nov. 1988, 31.

11 The New March Front describes itself as a movement, not a party, and does not maintain a membership roster. MTI, 11 Jan. 1989, in FBIS, 11 Jan. 1989, 46.

12 The average monthly wage in the industry is about 7,000 forints ($130).

13 Budapest Domestic Service, 18 Feb. 1989, in FBIS, 21 Feb. 1989, 23; *Süddeutsche Zeitung*, 25–26 Feb. 1989, 11; Budapest Domestic Service, 12 Apr. 1989, in FBIS, 13 Apr. 1989, 19; MTI, 28 Apr. 1989, in FBIS, 1 May 1989, 37; *Keston News Service*, no. 330 (20 July 1989): 9; Budapest Domestic Service, 22 July 1989, in FBIS, 24 July 1989, 19.

14 Budapest Domestic Service, 18 Feb. 1989, in FBIS, 21 Feb. 1989, 24.

15 MTI, 31 Dec. 1988, in FBIS, 9 Jan. 1989, 25.

16 *Népszabadság* (Budapest), 16 Feb. 1989, 3, in FBIS, 22 Feb. 1989, 20, 21.

17 *Financial Times* (London), 17 Feb. 1989, 16.

18 Budapest Television Service, 19 Feb. 1989, in FBIS, 24 Feb. 1989, 19.

19 *Pravda* (Moscow), 4 Mar. 1980, 4.

20 *New York Times*, 2 Apr. 1989, 4.

21 Ibid., 17 Apr. 1989, 7.

22 Ibid., 13 Oct. 1989, A6.

23 Ibid., 25 Apr. 1989, 4.

24 MTI, 17 Apr. 1989, in FBIS, 20 Apr. 1989, 27.

25 *New York Times*, 20 May 1989, 6.

26 Radio Budapest, 6 May 1989, as reported in Hungarian Situation Report, *RFER*, 17 May 1989, 3.

27 *New York Times*, 14 Feb. 1990, A9.

28 *Frankfurter Allgemeine*, 8 Oct. 1988), 3.

29 *Berlingske Tidende* (Copenhagen), 24 Sept. 1988, 8, in FBIS, 5 Oct. 1988, 27.

30 *New York Times*, 9 Feb. 1989, 5.

31 *Süddeutsche Zeitung*, 11–12 Feb. 1989, 6; *New York Times*, 13 Feb. 1989, 4.

32 *New York Times*, 7 May 1989, 4.

33 *Keston News Service*, no. 330 (20 July 1989): 4.

34 *Süddeutsche Zeitung*, 25–27 Mar. 1989, 6; *Glas koncila* (Zagreb), 13 Aug. 1989, 1.

35 Budapest Domestic Service, 1 June 1989, in FBIS, 6 June 1989, 25.

36 Budapest Domestic Service, 3 Aug. 1989, in FBIS, 7 Aug. 1989, 19.

37 *New York Times*, 24 July 1989, A2.

38 MTI, 22 Apr. 1989, in FBIS, 26 Apr. 1989, 36; MTI, 15 Aug. 1989, in FBIS, 17 Aug. 1989, 23. By coincidence, the first elected chairman of the new Democratic Youth Federation was a thirty-two-year-old mathematician with the name, Imre Nagy.

39 See summaries in Budapest Domestic Service, 18 Aug. 1989, in FBIS, 24 Aug. 1989, 31–32; and MTI, 18 Aug. 1989, in Ibid., 32–33.

40 *New York Times*, 7 Nov. 1989, A7.

41 *Frankfurter Allgemeine*, 9 Oct. 1989, 1, 10 Oct. 1989, 1, and 11 Oct. 1989, 1–2; *Christian Science Monitor*, 10 Oct. 1989, 4; *New York Times*, 19 Oct. 1989, A8, 20 Oct. 1989, A10, and 21 Oct. 1989, 3.

42 Warsaw Domestic Service, 31 Dec. 1988), in FBIS, 3 Jan. 1989, 49; *Christian Science Monitor*, 13 Feb. 1989, 19.

43 *News Solidarność* (Brussels), 1–15 Sept. 1988, 4.

44 Ibid., 1–15 Jan. 1989, 1.

45 Ibid., 16–30 Nov. 1988, 2–3.

46 Abraham Brumberg, "Poland: State and/or Society," *Dissent* 36, no. 1 (Winter 1989): 49.

47 Quoted in *Christian Science Monitor*, 22 Nov. 1988, 13.

48 Quoted in Ibid., 26 Aug. 1988, 9.

49 David Ost, "The Transformation of Solidarity and the Future of Central Europe," *Telos*, no. 79 (Spring 1989): 94.

50 John Tagliabue, "Lech! Lech! Lech!," *New York Times Magazine*, 23 Oct. 1988, 37.

51 *News Solidarność*, 15–31 Oct. 1988, 1; *Süddeutsche Zeitung*, 29–30 Oct. 1988, 2.

52 *News Solidarność* 1–15 Oct. 1988, 1.

53 *La Repubblica* (Rome), 4 Mar. 1989, 12.

54 Quoted in *Christian Science Monitor*, 13 Apr. 1989, 6.

55 Quoted in *New York Times*, 27 July 1989, A1.

56 *Corriere della Sera* (Milan), 12 Aug. 1989, 1.

57 Quoted in *New York Times*, 24 Aug. 1989, A1.

58 Quoted in Ibid., 25 Aug. 1989, A4.

59 Quoted in Ibid.

60 Quoted in Ibid.

61 Warsaw Television Service (May 25, 1989), in FBIS, 26 May 1989, 30; *Süddeutsche Zeitung*, 27–28 May 1989, 6.

62 Warsaw Television Service, 13 Dec. 1988, in FBIS, 14 Dec. 1988, 53; *Trybuna Ludu* (Warsaw), 13 Feb. 1989, 2; Warsaw Domestic Service, 25 Feb. 1989 and 8 May 1989, respectively in FBIS, 27 Feb. 1989, 32, and 9 May 1989, 39; AFP, 5 Mar. 1989, in FBIS, 6 Mar. 1989, 33; Warsaw Television Service, 17 May 1989, in FBIS, 18 May 1989, 34; Warsaw Domestic Service, 22 June 1989, in FBIS, 23 June 1989, 53; PAP, 15 Sept. 1989, in FBIS, 18 Sept. 1989, 47.

63 *Süddeutsche Zeitung*, 11–12 Feb. 1989, 6, and 25–27 Mar. 1989, 6.

64 Warsaw Domestic Service, 15 Sept. 1989, in FBIS, 18 Sept. 1989, 47.

65 *New York Times*, 7 Oct. 1989, A2.

66 *Christian Science Monitor*, 12 Sept. 1989, 4.

67 *New York Times*, 21 Oct. 1989, 4.

68 Paul Shoup, "Crisis and Reform in Yugoslavia," *Telos*, no. 79 (Spring 1979): 141.

69 Some of these groups are described in Pedro Ramet, "Yugoslavia 1987: Stirrings from Below," *South Slav Journal* 10, no. 3 (Autumn 1987).

70 Interview, Ljubljana, 4 Sept. 1989.

71 *Independent Voices from Slovenia* 5, no. 1 (Jan. 1989): 8.

72 Interviews in Ljubljana with France Tomšić, 4 Sept. 1989; Hubert Požarnik, 6 Sept. 1989; and Dimitrij Rupel, 6 Sept. 1989.

73 *Independent Voices from Slovenia* 5, no. 1 (Jan. 1989): 7.

74 *Svet* (Belgrade), special issue Sept. 1989: 7.

75 Interview with Marija Markes, secretary of the Slovenian Peasant Alliance, Ljubljana, 1 Sept. 1989.

76 Interview with Dušan Semolić, secretary of the Republican Committee of SAWP-Slovenia, Ljubljana, 5 Sept. 1989.

77 Interview, Zagreb, 13 Sept. 1989.

78 Interview, Zagreb, 29 Aug. 1989.

79 As cited in Slaven Letica, *Četvrta Jugoslavija* (Zagreb: CIP, 1989), manuscript, chap. 3.

80 Ibid., and interview, Zagreb, 11 Sept. 1989. For a full account of the circumstances leading up to the closure of Matica hrvatska, see Sabrina P. Ramet, *Nationalism and Federalism in Yugoslavia, 1962–1991*, 2nd ed. (Bloomington: Indiana University Press, forthcoming).

81 Quoted in Yugoslav Situation Report, *RFER*, 26 May 1989, 36.

82 Ibid.

83 For details, see Pedro Ramet, "Yugoslavia's 'Troubled Times,'" *Global Affairs* 5, no. 1 (Winter 1989–90).

13   Dominoes: East Germany, Czechoslovakia, and the Future of Europe

1 Conversations, East Germany, summer 1988.

2 *Welt am Sonntag* (Hamburg), 4 June 1989, 1, in FBIS, 5 June 1989, 6.

3 Ending with the large-scale Albanian riots in Kosovo in April 1981.

4 Quoted in *New York Times*, 7 Nov. 1987, 4.

5 *Rinascita*, 18 Apr. 1987, quoted in Kevin Devlin, "Italian Communist on Contradictions and Crisis in Eastern Europe," *RFER*, 5 June 1987, 2.

6 As of November 1989, I would still place East Germany in this category, rather than in the category with Poland and Yugoslavia.

7 Boris Rumer, "Realities of Gorbachev's Economic Program," *Problems of Communism* 35, no. 3 (May-June 1986): 25; *New York Times*, 1 Aug. 1988; *Financial Times* 3 Aug. 1988, 16.

8 *Christian Science Monitor*, 29 Aug. 1988, 7; Bohdan Nahaylo, "Interview with Tat'yana Zaslavskaya," *Radio Liberty Research*, 15 Sept. 1987, 6.

9 *Chicago Tribune*, 20 Mar. 1990, 9.

10 *Frankfurter Rundschau*, 21 June 1988, 3; *New York Times*, 22 Oct. 1988, 3.

11 *New York Times*, 24 May 1988, 8.

12 *Christian Science Monitor*, 19 Feb. 1988, 32.

13 See Edward Kardelj, *Democracy and Socialism*, trans. Margot and Boško Milosavljević (London: Summerfield, 1978).

14 Quoted in *New York Times*, 6 Feb. 1990, A6.

15 *Financial Times*, 14 June 1988, 2.

16 Cited in *Seattle Times*, 7 Oct. 1988, B2.

17 *Pravda*, cited in *Süddeutsche Zeitung* (Munich), 27–28 Aug. 1988, 6.

18 Reported in *Vjesnik* (Zagreb), 26 Dec. 1987, 3; *New York Times*, 4 Feb. 1989, 1.

19 Vasily Selyunin, "Istoki," *Novyi Mir*, no. 5 (May 1988): 162–89.

20 Julia Wishnevsky, "Grossman's Exposé of Lenin to be Published in USSR," *Radio Liberty Research*, 3 Aug. 1988, 1–2.

21 *Izvestiia*, 3 Apr. 1988, 6, excerpted in Josephine Woll, "Fruits of Glasnost," *Dissent* 36, no. 1 (Winter 1989): 26.

22 *New York Times*, 6 Apr. 1989, 6, and 18 Aug. 1989, A6.

23 *New York Times*, 25 July 1989, A4; *Corriera della Sera* (Milan), 12 Aug. 1989, 4; *New York Times*, 19 Aug. 1989, 1.

24 Quoted in *New York Times*, 19 Feb. 1988, 1, 4.

25 *New York Times*, 7 Apr. 1990, 5.

26 *Washington Post*, 9 Nov. 1986), H5.

27 Quoted in *New York Times*, 31 Oct. 1986, A11.

28 *Washington Post*, 8 Jan. 1987, A1, and 13 Feb. 1987, A35.

29 Mikhail Shatrov, "Dal'she . . . dal'she . . . dal'she," in *Znamya*, no. 1 (January 1988): 3–53.

30 For further discussion, see Pedro Ramet and Sergei Zamascikov, "The Soviet Rock Scene," *Journal of Popular Culture* (Summer 1990).

31 See *Washington Post*, 9 May 1988, B1, B11. For further discussion of Gorbachev's effect on cultural policy, see John B. Dunlop, "Soviet Cultural Politics," *Problems of Communism* 36, no. 6 (Nov.-Dec. 1987).

32 Details in Pedro Ramet, "Gorbachev's Reforms and Religion," in *Candle in the Wind: Religion in the Soviet Union*, ed. Eugene B. Shirley, Jr., and Michael Rowe (Washington, D.C.: Ethics and Public Policy Center, 1989).

33 See Christine Engel, "'Pamjat.' 'Gedenken und Erinnern' als zentrale Begriffe im kulturellen Leben der heutigen Sowjetunion," *Osteuropa* 37, no. 12 (Dec. 1987): 891–903.

34 *New York Times*, 10 May 1988, 7.

35 Ibid., 9 Oct. 1987, 4, and 19 Oct. 1987, 8.

36 *Frankfurter Rundschau*, 24 June 1988, 3.

37 *New York Times*, 19 May 1988, 6. See also AFP, 12 Dec. 1987, in FBIS, *Daily Report* (Soviet Union), 17 Dec. 1987, 57.

38 *New York Times*, 24 Aug. 1988, 6.

39 Ibid., 19 May 1989, 1.

40 Bohdan Nahaylo, "Political Demonstration in Minsk Attests to Belorussian National Assertiveness," *Radio Liberty Research*, 26 Nov. 1987, 1.

41 *Vjesnik*, 19 July 1988, 3.

42 *Christian Science Monitor*, 17 June 1988, 9.

43 *New York Times*, 8 Sept. 1988, 8.

44 Vladimir A. Rubanov, "Ot 'Kul'ta sekretnosti': K informatsionnoi Kul'ture," *Kommunist*, no. 13 (Sept. 1988): 24–36.

45 *Financial Times*, 3–4 Sept. 1988, 1.

46 *New York Times*, 23 May 1989, A7.

47 Reported in *Chicago Tribune*, 5 Nov. 1989, 12.

48 *New York Times*, 4 Nov. 1989, 5.

49 Ibid., 23 July 1988, 3; *Frankfurter Allgemeine*, 27 July 1988, 2.

50 Quoted in "Weekly Record of Events," *RFER*, 22–28 Oct. 1987, 6.

51 *Neues Deutschland*, 6 Oct. 1987.

52 Ibid., 6 Sept. 1988, 2.

53 Czechoslovak Situation Report, *RFER*, 27 Nov. 1987, 11.

54 *New York Times*, 30 July 1988, 4.

55 See Pedro Ramet, "Self-Management, Titoism, and the Apotheosis of Praxis," in *War and Society in East Central Europe*, ed. Wayne S. Vucinich, vol. 10, *At the Brink of War and Peace: The Tito-Stalin Split in a Historic Perspective* (New York: Brooklyn College Press, 1982), 169–94.

56 That is, of course, the purpose behind his export of *perestroika* to Eastern Europe and his restructuring of COMECON. See Pedro Ramet, "Gorbachev's Dilemmas in Eastern Europe," in *Gorbachev and the Soviet Future*, ed. Lawrence W. Lerner and Donald W. Treadgold (Boulder, Colo.: Westview, 1988).

57 Later, at the 28th CPSU Congress in July 1990, Gorbachev had to defend himself against charges that he had "lost" Eastern Europe.

58 *Party Preferences in Hypothetical Free Elections in Czechoslovakia, Hungary, and Poland* (Munich: Radio Free Europe/Radio Liberty, August 1981).

59 Re Romania, see Trond Gilberg, "Ethnic Minorities in Romania under Socialism," *East European Quarterly* 7, no. 4 (Jan. 1974): 435–58; and Hans Hartl, "Nationalitätenpolitik und Nationalismus in Rumänien," in *Nationalitätenprobleme in der Sowjetunion und Osteuropa*, ed. Georg Brunner and Boris Meissner (Cologne: Markus Verlag, 1982), 151–64. Re Bulgaria, see Wolfgang Höpken, "Modernisierung und Nationalismus: Sozialgeschichtliche Aspekte der bulgarischen Minderheitenpolitik gegenüber den Türken," in *Nationalitätenprobleme in Südosteuropa*, ed. Roland Schonfeld (Munich: R. Oldenbourg Verlag, 1987); and Zachary T. Irwin, "The Fate of Islam in the Balkans: A Comparison of Four State Politics," in *Religion and Nationalism in Soviet and East European Politics*, ed. Pedro Ramet, rev. and expanded ed. (Durham, N.C.: Duke University Press, 1988), 378–407.

60 DPA (Hamburg), 13 Mar. 1989, in FBIS, 14 Mar. 1989, 23.

61 *Süddeutsche Zeitung*, 22–23 October 1988, 5; *Die Welt* (Hamburg), 24 Nov. 1988, 4; *Christian Science Monitor*, 23 Jan. 1989, 18, and 24 Feb. 1989, 3; *Der Standard* (Vienna), 15 Mar. 1989, 3, in FBIS, 15 Mar. 1989, 15.

62 For example, Alfred Kosing, "Zur Dialektik der weiteren Gestaltung der entwickelten sozialistischen Gesellschaft," *Deutsche Zeitschrift für Philosophie* 36, no. 7 (1988): Also Johannes Becher's article in *Sinn und Form*, no. 3 (1988), analyzed in Manfred Jäger, "Anti-stalinistisches aus dem Johannes R. Becher-Archiv," *Deutschland Archiv* 21, no. 7 (July 1988): 695–98.

63 For example, Mainz ZDF Television Network, 7 July 1989, and DPA 8 July 1989—both in FBIS, 10 July 1989, 22; *Süddeutsche Zeitung*, 9–10 Sept. 1989, 1.

64 *Die Welt*, 16–17 Sept. 1989, 4; *Frankfurter Allgemeine*, 21 Sept. 1989, 2; *Glas koncila* (Zagreb), 24 Sept. 1989, 1, 4; *Neue Zürcher Zeitung*, 24–25 Sept. 1989, 3.

65 *Frankfurter Allgemeine*, 23 Sept. 1989, 2; 28 Sept. 1989, 5; and 4 Oct. 1989, 3.

66 Ibid., 18 Sept. 1989, 5.

67 *Politika* (Belgrade), 21 Oct. 1989, 1.

68 For the composition of the new Politburo, see *New York Times*, 9 Nov. 1989, A1, A8.

69 *Politika*, 28 Oct. 1989, 2.

70 *Lidova Demokracie* (Prague), 3 May 1989, 1, in FBIS, 9 May 1989, 24; Czechoslovak Situation Report, RFER, 14 July 1989, 3.

71 Czechoslovak Situation Report, RFER, 18 May 1989, 7–10.

72 Ibid., 30 Sept. 1988, 27.

73 Ibid., 16 Feb. 1989, 21.

74 *Rudé pravo* (Prague), 5 May 1989, 5.

75 Ibid., 21 July 1989, 1.

76 Quoted in *Christian Science Monitor*, 13 Dec. 1988, 7.

77 Radio Hvezda, 14 June 1989, quoted in Czechoslovak Situation Report, RFER, 21 June 1989, 3.

78 Quoted in *New York Times*, 24 Nov. 1989, 1.

79   *New York Times*, 14 Nov. 1989, A9.

80   *Politika*, 1 Nov. 1989, 3.

81   Agerpress (Bucharest), 14 Sept. 1989, in FBIS, 15 Sept. 1989, C2.

82   *Scînteia* (Bucharest), 1 Sept. 1989, 1, 4, in FBIS, 7 Sept. 1989, 51.

83   Quoted in Romanian Situation Report, *RFER*, 4 Aug. 1989, 11.

84   *Frankfurter Allgemeine*, 3 Oct. 1989, 6.

85   *New York Times*, 11 July 1989, A3.

86   Ibid., 24 Nov. 1989, A11.

87   *Newsweek*, 16 Oct. 1989, 46.

88   Quoted in *New York Times*, 18 Nov. 1989, 4.

89   *Christian Science Monitor*, 3 Nov. 1988, 1, 8.

90   *The Economist* (London), 12 Aug. 1989, 7; *Wall Street Journal*, 17 Nov. 1989, A10.

91   *Wall Street Journal*, 8 Nov. 1989, A12.

92   *Handelsblatt*, 25 July 1990, 8.

93   On Hungary, see MTI, 17 Feb. 1989, in FBIS, 23 Feb. 1989, 25–26.

94   *Chicago Tribune*, 3 Nov. 1989, 4; *New York Times*, 10 Nov. 1989, A19. Re the Alpine-Adriatic group, see *Frankfurter Allgemeine*, 6 Dec. 1988, 6.

95   *Süddeutsche Zeitung*, 1 Aug. 1990, 6, and 3 Aug. 1990, 10.

96   *New York Times*, 23 May 1990, A6.

97   *Rudé pravo*, 19 Jan. 1990, 15; *Der Standard* (Vienna), 25 Jan. 1990, 2.

98   *Die Welt*, 25 July 1990, 5; *Süddeutsche Zeitung*, 27 July 1990, 8, 31 July 1990, 6, and 22–23 July 1990, 9; *Neue Zürcher Zeitung*, 24 Jan. 1991, 3; *Daily Telegraph* (London), 7 Feb. 1991, 9, and 13 Feb. 1991, 10; *The* Independent (London), 25 Feb. 1991, 13.

99   CTK (Prague), 4 Jan. 1990, in FBIS, 5 Jan. 1990, 1; *New York Times*, 11 Jan. 1990, A8; *Rzeczpospolita* (Warsaw), 12 Jan. 1990, 1 in FBIS, 25 Jan. 1990, 1; *Neues Deutschland*, 2 Oct. 1990, 1; *The Times*, 25 Feb. 1991, 12.

100 *Newsweek*, 16 Oct. 1989, 51.

101 Quoted in *New York Times*, 14 June 1990, A6.

102 Quoted in Ibid.

103 *Neue Zürcher Zeitung*, 8 Sept. 1990, 13; *Wall Street Journal*, 14 Sept. 1990, A8.

104 Pedro Ramet, "Dissaffection and Dissent in East Germany," *World Politics* 37, no. 1 (Oct. 1984): 109, 110.

105 *Rudé pravo*, 5 Sept. 1988, 3, in FBIS, 13 Sept. 1988, 12.

14   The Great Transformation

1   "Political Parties in Eastern Europe," *RFER*, 10 Feb. 1990; Tanjug, 16 Mar. 1990, in FBIS, 19 Mar. 1990, 84; ROMPRES, 28 Mar. 1990, in FBIS, 29 Mar. 1990, 47; *New York Times*, 8 June 1990, A5.

2   *Tineretul Liber* (Bucharest), 11 Jan. 1990, 1; BTA (Sofia), 17 Jan. 1990, 6, in FBIS, 25 Jan. 1990, 6; *New York Times*, 31 Jan. 1990, A6, and 11 May 1990, A4.

3   Budapest Domestic Service, 12 Oct. 1989, in FBIS, 13 Oct. 1989, 44.

4   Blending of translations in ROMPRES, 21 Feb. 1990, in FBIS, 22 Feb. 1990, 78; *Adevarul* (Bucharest), 23 Feb. 1990, 1, in FBIS, 5 Mar. 1990, 61.

5   Quoted in *New York Times*, 11 May 1990, A4. Also Louis Zanga, "Significant Albanian Cultural Plenum," *RFER*, 19 May 1989; Louis Zanga, "Novel Criticizes Albanian Security Services," *RFER*, 15 Nov. 1989, 1.

6   *Zeri i popullit* (tiranë), 11 Oct. 1989, 4, in FBIS, 25 Oct. 1989, 2.

7 *New York Times*, 13 Jan. 1990, 5, and 10 May 1990, A1.
8 *The Economist* (London), 31 Mar. 1990, 49.
   9 *Die Welt* (Bonn), 9 July 1990, 1; *Corriere della Sera* (Milan), 9 July 1990, 4.
10 *Die Welt*, 28–29 July 1990, 8; *Süddeutsche Zeitung* (Munich), 2 Aug. 1990, 7, 28.
11 *Frankfurter Allgemeine*, 1 Aug. 1990, 1; *Süddeutsche Zeitung*, 1 Aug. 1990, 2, and 13–14 Oct. 1990, 8.
12 Charles Gati, *The Bloc That Failed: Soviet-East European Relations in Transition* (Bloomington: Indiana University Press, 1990), 182–83, 187.
13 BTA, 27 Nov. 1989, in FBIS, 5 Dec. 1989, 5.
14 Sofia Domestic Service, 1 Feb. 1990, in FBIS, 2 Feb. 1990, 4.
15 Simon Simonov, "New Face of the Bulgarian Writers' Union," *Radio Free Europe: Report on Eastern Europe* 1, no. 9 (2 Mar. 1990): 4–5.
16 BTA, 13 Dec. 1989, in FBIS, 14 Dec. 1989, 9.
17 *Narodna armiya* (Sofia), 5 Dec. 1989, 1, 2, in FBIS, 14 Dec. 1989, 20.
18 *New York Times*, 3 Apr. 1990, A6.
19 BTA, 6 Feb. 1990, in FBIS, 7 Feb. 1990, 20.
20 BTA, 27 Feb. 1990, in FBIS, 7 Mar. 1990, 11.
21 Re *Dano*, see *Trud* (Sofia), 29 Mar. 1990, 3, summarized in FBIS, 2 Apr. 1990, 9.
22 *Der Spiegel*, 4 Dec. 1989, in FBIS, 12 Dec. 1989, 12.
23 *Frankfurter Allgemeine*, 12 June 1990, 1.
24 Petar Mladenov resigned the presidency on 6 July after stirring controversy with remarks about using tanks against an antigovernment rally. His resignation was celebrated by more than 20,000 jubilant Bulgarians in downtown Sofia the following day. See *Frankfurter Allgemeine*, 16 June 1990, 2; *Süddeutsche Zeitung*, 23–24 June 1990, 8; *Los Angeles Times*, 7 July 1990, A1, and 8 July 1990, A6.
25 BTA, 14 Aug. 1990, in FBIS, 15 Aug. 1990, 7; BTA, 18 Aug. 1990, in FBIS, 20 Aug. 1990, 14.
26 Lukanov's proposed cabinet line-up was reported in *Frankfurter Allgemeine*, 22 Sept. 1990, 5. See also *International Herald Tribune* (Paris), 8 Aug. 1990, 2; *Welt am Sonntag* (Bonn), 23 Sept. 1990, 6.
27 BTA, 20 Sept. 1990, in FBIS, 24 Sept. 1990, 23; BTA, 5 Oct. 1990, in FBIS, 9 Oct. 1990, 4; BTA, 10 Oct. 1990, in FBIS, 11 Oct. 1990, 1.
28 *Süddeutsche Zeitung*, 24 July 1990, 7; *Die Welt*, 26 July 1990, 6; *Frankfurter Allgemeine*, 20 Sept. 1990, 16; *New York Times*, 21 Sept. 1990, A3.
29 *Mladezh* (Sofia), 10 Oct. 1990, 1–2, in FBIS, 16 Oct. 1990, 5–6.
30 Quoted in Czechoslovak Situation Report, *RFER*, 24 Aug. 1989, 17.
31 Quoted in Ibid., 27 Oct. 1989, 9.
32 *Seattle Post-Intelligencer*, 30 May 1990.
33 AFP, 17 Nov. 1989, in FBIS, 20 Nov. 1989, 19.
34 AFP, 18 Nov. 1989, in FBIS, 20 Nov. 1989, 20.
35 *Lidova demokracie* (Prague), 21 Nov. 1989, 1, in FBIS, 28 Nov. 1989, 25.
36 Re the Transnational Radical Party, see *Večerni Praha* (Prague), 20 Feb. 1990, 5, summarized in FBIS, 7 Mar. 1990, 29–30.
37 *Večernik* (Bratislava), 16 Mar. 1990, 1, in FBIS, 22 Mar. 1990, 25.
38 CTK (Prague), 17 Mar. 1990, in FBIS, 19 Mar. 1990, 34.
39 *Smena* (Bratislava), 8 Mar. 1990, 2, 3, in FBIS, 19 Mar. 1990, 34.
40 *Rudé pravo* (Prague), 22 Dec. 1990, 1989, 2, in FBIS, 13 Mar. 1990, 21.
41 *Pravda* (Bratislava), 27 Feb. 1990, 1, 2.
42 Ibid., 19 Feb. 1990, 2.

43 *Prače* (Prague), 16 Feb. 1990, 1, 2, in FBIS, 23 Feb. 1990, 19.

44 *Wall Street Journal*, 20 June 1990, A16.

45 *Los Angeles Times*, 28 June 1990, A11.

46 CTK (Prague), 14 Sept. 1990, in FBIS, 19 Sept. 1990, 27.

47 *Eurobusiness*, June 1990, 46.

48 *Neue Zürcher Zeitung*, 6 Sept. 1990, 15; *Wall Street Journal*, 26 Oct. 1990, A8.

49 *Süddeutsche Zeitung*, 3 Aug. 1990, 7.

50 *Narodna obroda* (Bratislava), 18 Sept. 1990, 2, in FBIS, 28 Sept. 1990, 14; confirmed in *New York Times*, 16 Oct. 1990, A6.

51 *Welt am Sonntag*, 23 Sept. 1990, 6.

52 Quoted in *New York Times*, 12 Oct. 1990, A3.

53 ADN International Service (Berlin), 20 Nov. 1989, in FBIS, 20 Nov. 1989, 47.

54 *Bild* (Hamburg), 9 Nov. 1989, 3.

55 ADN International Service, 20 Nov. 1989, in FBIS, 20 Nov. 1989, 49.

56 Ibid., 1 Dec. 1989 and 4 Dec. 1989, both in FBIS, 5 Dec. 1989, 41.

57 Ibid., 4 Dec. 1989, in FBIS, 4 Dec. 1989, 40; *New York Times*, 5 Jan. 1990, A5.

58 Doubts about the successful completion of the abolition of the Stasi were expressed in June 1990. See *Süddeutsche Zeitung*, 23–24 June 1990, 5.

59 *Neues Deutschland* (Berlin), 15 Jan. 1990, 2.

60 *New York Times*, 20 Jan. 1990, 5.

61 As reported in ADN International Service, 12 Dec. 1989, in FBIS, 12 Dec. 1989, 32.

62 Ibid., 5 Jan. 1990, in FBIS, 8 Jan. 1990, 57.

63 *Neues Deutschland*, 7 Mar. 1990, 5.

64 *Toronto Star*, 20 May 1990, H2.

65 *Frankfurter Allgemeine*, 5 June 1990, 4.

66 The treaty is published in *Neue Zürcher Zeitung*, 23 May 1990, 7–8. See also *Christian Science Monitor*, 22 Dec. 1989, 8; *New York Times*, 3 May 1990, A6, and 12 June 1990, A6; *Wall Street Journal*, 11 May 1990, A9; *Globe and Mail* (Toronto), 19 May 1990, A2.

67 *Frankfurter Allgemeine*, 13 June 1990, 1; *Corriere della Sera*, 1 July 1990, 1, 4, and 2 July 1990, 2; *Los Angeles Times*, 4 July 1990, A8.

68 *New York Times*, 5 June 1990, A7, 13 June 1990, A1, and 23 June 1990, 1, 4; *San Francisco Examiner*, 23 June 1990, A20; *Süddeutsche Zeitung*, 23–24 June 1990, A20.

69 *Der Spiegel*, 7 May 1990, 278, 280.

70 *Frankfurter Allgemeine*, 9 July 1990, 5.

71 *Die Welt*, 26 July 1990, 1; *Süddeutsche Zeitung*, 27 July 1990, 6, and 2 Aug. 1990, 2; *New York Times*, 1 Nov. 1990, A9.

72 Kathrin Sitzler, "Die Anfänge eines politischen Pluarlismus in Ungarn," *Südost-Europa* 38, nos. 11–12 (Nov.-Dec. 1989): 679.

73 Budapest Domestic Service, 3 Mar. 1990, and Budapest Television Service, 3 Mar. 1990, both in FBIS, 5 Mar. 1990, 47–48.

74 *Népszabadság* (Budapest), 14 Dec. 1989, 5, in FBIS, 29 Dec. 1989, 58.

75 Budapest Domestic Service, 7 Jan. 1990, in FBIS, 19 Jan. 1990, 49.

76 Budapest Television Service, 3 Dec. 1989, in FBIS, 7 Dec. 1989, 79.

77 Ibid., 29 Oct. 1989, in FBIS, 1 Nov. 1989, 43–45.

78 *Christian Science Monitor*, 3 Jan. 1990, 6.

79 Quoted in Ibid., 12 Feb. 1990, 6.

80 *Chicago Tribune*, 25 Mar. 1990, 6; *The Economist*, 31 Mar. 1990, 47.

81 *New York Times*, 31 May 1990, A7.
82 *Los Angeles Times*, 27 June 1990, A8.
  83 Budapest Domestic Service, 15 Mar. 1990, in FBIS, 19 Mar. 1990, 62–63; *Bloc* (Feb.-Mar. 1990): 21–22; *New York Times*, 12 May 1990, 4.
84 *Frankfurter Allgemeine*, 24 July 1990, 11; *Süddeutsche Zeitung*, 24 July 1990, 1, and 25 July 1990, 7.
85 Károly Okolicsanyi, "Privatization: Two Cautious Steps," *RFER*, 19 Oct. 1990, 24.
86 *Neue Zürcher Zeitung*, 17 Oct. 1990, 16; *Daily Telegraph*, 2 Nov. 1990, 11.
87 Louisa Vinton, "Privatization Plan Prepared," *Radio Free Europe: Report on Eastern Europe* 1, no. 14 (6 Apr. 1990): 29.
88 *Christian Science Monitor*, 26 Jan. 1990, 4.
89 *New York Times*, 28 May 1990, 5.
90 Ibid., 19 June 1990, A1.
91 *Trybuna* (Warsaw), 2 Mar. 1990, 1, in FBIS, 7 Mar. 1990, 63.
92 Warsaw Domestic Service, 30 Dec. 1989, in FBIS, 2 Jan. 1990, 45.
93 *The Economist*, 21 Apr. 1990, 51; *Wall Street Journal*, 5 June 1990, A1.
94 *Los Angeles Times*, 7 July 1990, A19.
95 *New York Times*, 1 Feb. 1990, A9.
96 The results were published seven months later. See Louisa Vinton, "Disintegration of Polish Communist Party Continues Unabated," *RFER*, 28 Nov. 1989, 3–4.
97 *Neue Zürcher Zeitung*, 6 Sept. 1990, 17; *Financial Times*, 7 Sept. 1990, 6.
98 *New York Times*, 14 Aug. 1990, 14, in FBIS, 6 Sept. 1990, 36–37.
99 Quoted in *Wall Street Journal*, 31 Aug. 1990, A8.
100 *Süddeutsche Zeitung*, 29–30 Sept. 1990, 7.
101 *New York Times*, 17 Sept. 1990, A4.
102 *Polityka*, 14 July 1990, 14, in FBIS, 6 Sept. 1990, 36–37.
103 *New York Times*, 14 Aug. 1990, A2.
104 *Welt am Sonntag*, 9 Sept. 1990, 3.
105 *New York Times*, 17 May 1990, A4.
106 *Scînteia*, 1 Nov. 1989, excerpted in AGERPRES, 1 Nov. 1989, in FBIS, 7 Nov. 1989, 65.
107 *New York Times*, 4 Jan. 1990, A8.
108 Romanian Situation Report, *RFER*, 14 Dec. 1989, 15.
109 Bucharest Domestic Service, 28 Dec. 1989, in FBIS, 29 Dec. 1989, 68.
110 Quoted in AFP, 19 Dec. 1989, in FBIS, 20 Dec. 1989, 66.
111 ROMPRES, 9 Mar. 1990, in FBIS, 12 Mar. 1990, 67; ROMPRES, 23 Mar. 1990, in FBIS, 26 Mar. 1990, 47.
112 ROMPRES, 24 Feb. 1990, in FBIS, 27 Feb. 1990, 67.
113 *Sunday Star* (Toronto), 20 May 1990, A1.
114 *Globe and Mail* (Toronto), 18 May 1990, A7.
115 *Neue Zürcher Zeitung*, 24–25 May 1990, 2.
116 *New York Times*, 2 June 1990, 9.
117 Ibid., 15 June 1990, A1, A6, and 16 June 1990, 4.
118 Quoted in Ibid., 18 June 1990, A1.
119 See the argument in Radoslav Stojanović, *Jugoslavija nacije i politika* (Belgrade: Nova knjiga, 1988), esp. 171-207.
120 *Los Angeles Times*, 2 July 1990, A10.
121 Interview, Ljubljana, 4 Sept. 1989.
122 Interview, Ljubljana, 1 Sept. 1989.
123 Re the Croatian party, see Tanjug, 10 Mar. 1990, in FBIS, 12 Mar. 1990, 80.

124 Belgrade Domestic Service, 4 Feb. 1990, in FBIS, 7 Feb. 1990, 67.

125 Tanjug, 27 Mar. 1990, in FBIS, 29 Mar. 1990, 52.

126 *Süddeutsche Zeitung*, 23–24 June 1990, 8.

127 Ibid.

128 *Frankfurter Allgemeine*, 15 June 1990, 8.

129 Tanjug, 15 Mar. 1990, in FBIS, 22 Mar. 1990, 84.

130 *Los Angeles Times*, 3 July 1990, A6; *Süddeutsche Zeitung*, 23–24 June 1990, 8.

131 Telephone interview with Peter Millonig, official representative of the Republic of Slovenia (in the United States), 2 Mar. 1991.

132 Zagreb Domestic Service, 11 Oct. 1990, in FBIS, 12 Oct. 1990, 51.

133 Tanjug, 11 Oct. 1990, in FBIS, 12 Oct. 1990, 53.

134 More on this in Sabrina P. Ramet, "Serbia's Slobodan Milošević: A Profile," *Orbis* 35, no. 1 (Winter 1991).

135 *Die Zeit* (Hamburg), 31 Aug. 1990, 6.

136 *Welt am Sonntag*, 30 Sept. 1990, 3.

137 *Daily Telegraph*, 4 Oct. 1990, 15; *Politika*, 25 Oct. 1990, 10.

138 *Politika*, 12 Sept. 1990, 14.

139 *Vjesnik*, 14 Sept. 1990, 1.

140 Tanjug, 14 Sept. 1990, in FBIS, 17 Sept. 1990, 51; *Süddeutsche Zeitung*, 29–30 Sept. 1990, 7.

141 *New York Times*, 16 Jan. 1991, A3, 20 Jan. 1991, 7, 21 Jan. 1991, A2, and 22 Jan. 1991, A3.

142 Telephone interview with Peter Millonig [note 131].

143 *Neue Zürcher Zeitung*, 8 Feb. 1991, 2.

144 *Los Angeles Times*, 24 Feb. 1991, A1, A28; *Richmond Times-Dispatch*, 23 Feb. 1991, A9.

145 See the earlier articulation of the Macedonian position in *Borba*, 8 Nov. 1990, 3.

146 For further discussion of Yugoslavia's descent into chaos, see Sabrina P. Ramet, "The Breakup of Yugoslavia," in *Global Affairs*, scheduled for publication in Spring 1992.

Select Bibliography

Sources consulted in connection with the research for this book are cited in the notes. The following is a brief guide for further reading, organized on a country-by-country basis, with subsequent heads for dissent, religion, and general discussions. I have deliberately limited myself to no more than three books per category, a limitation which will necessarily exclude many noteworthy books, but will also simplify the use of this bibliography.

Albania. The classic treatment of postwar Albania is still Peter R. Prifti's *Socialist Albania since 1944: Domestic and Foreign Developments* (Cambridge: MIT Press), first published in 1978. Its scope includes both political and social issues, including religion and women's issues. Also useful is Anton Logoreci's oft-cited volume, *The Albanians* (London: Gollancz, 1977), which includes much material on the labor camp and prison system established under Enver Hoxha. One of the newest studies of note is Elez Biberaj's *Albania: A Socialist Maverick* (Boulder, Colo.: Westview, 1990).

Bulgaria. John D. Bell wrote an excellent history of the Bulgarian ruling party, *The Bulgarian Communist Party from Blagoev to Zhivkov* (Stanford, Calif.: Hoover Institution Press, 1986). It remains one of the best political treatments on Bulgaria to date. R. J. Crampton's *A Short History of Modern Bulgaria* (New York: Cambridge University Press, 1987) is a good overview and covers a lot of ground. John R. Lampe's *The Bulgarian Economy in the Twentieth Century* (New York: St. Martin's Press, 1986) is perhaps the most solid Western treatment of Bulgarian economic issues.

Czechoslovakia. No list of books about Czechoslovakia can omit H. Gordon Skilling's mammoth magnum opus, *Czechoslovakia's Interrupted Revolution* (Princeton, N.J.: Princeton University Press, 1976), which discusses the Dubček period. The pressures leading up to that period are the subject of Galia Golan's 1971 study, *The Czechoslovak Reform Movement: Communism in Crisis, 1962–68* (Cambridge: Cambridge University Press). Her research covers both political and cultural aspects of the transformative processes. Although dated, Eugen Steiner's *The Slovak Dilemma* (Cambridge: Cambridge University Press, 1973) remains a fine study for understanding the Czech-Slovak relationship and Slovakia's special problems.

East Germany. The best books on East Germany are surely yet to be written. Now that that state has been incorporated in the Federal Republic of Germany, archival materials hitherto inaccessible to researchers will surely become available. In the meantime, David Childs' two studies—*East Germany* (New York: Praeger, 1969) and *The GDR: Moscow's German Ally* (Boston: Allen and Unwin, 1983)—impress me as the best works on this country. A more recent collection of articles, *The Quality of Life in the German Democratic Republic,* edited by Marilyn Rueschemeyer and Christiane Lemke and published in 1989 (Armonk, N.Y.: M. E. Sharpe), has been touted as the finest treatment of social issues in the German Democratic Republic.

Hungary. Peter F. Sugar spent more than five years putting together what will surely establish itself as one of the definitive histories of Hungary. *A History of Hungary* (Bloomington: Indiana University Press, 1990) is the product of American-Hungarian collaboration, organized by Sugar. Charles Gati's *Hungary and the Soviet Bloc* (Durham, N.C.: Duke University Press, 1986) probes Hungarian foreign policy and won the Marshall Shulmann prize. Bennett Kovrig's *Communism in Hungary from Kun to Kádár* (Stanford, Calif.: Hoover Institution Press, 1979) traces the history of Hungary's communists from the 1920s to the end of the 1970s.

Poland. Many excellent studies of Polish politics have come out, perhaps especially in the course of the last decade. Three rather special books are: *The Black Book of Polish Censorship,* trans. and ed. Jane Leftwich Curry (New York: Random House, 1984), a collection of guidelines and decisions taken by the censor's office in Poland over a period of more than a decade; Teresa Toranska's *"Them": Stalin's Polish Puppets* (New York: Harper and Row, 1987), which brings together interviews carried out by the compiler with five of the most important figures of Poland's Stalinist era, including Julia Minc, Edward Ochab, and Jakub Berman; and *Konspira: Solidarity Underground* (Berkeley: University of California Press, 1990), by Maciej Lopinski, Marcin Moskit, and Mariusz Wilk, which brings together a vast amount of interview material with Solidarity activists.

Romania. Trond Gilberg's *Nationalism and Communism in Romania* (Boulder, Colo.: Westview, 1990) is the most comprehensive and perhaps the best treatment of the Ceauşescu era in English, and has the virtue of completeness. Robert R. King's earlier *A History of the Romanian Communist Party* (Stanford, Calif.: Hoover Institution Press, 1980) traces the story of the Romanian communists from the founding, through the period of illegality, as far as the end of the 1970s. Mary Ellen Fischer's *Nicolae Ceauşescu: A Study in Political Leadership* (Boulder, Colo.: L. Reinner, 1989) is the first biography of the Romanian dictator in English.

Yugoslavia. Ivo Banac's *The National Question in Yugoslavia: Origins, History, Politics* (Ithaca, N.Y.: Cornell University Press, 1984) is the best work in English on interwar politics in Yugoslavia. For the years from the expulsion of Yugoslavia from the Cominform (1948) to the adoption of the fourth postwar constitution (1974), the best source is Dennison I. Rusinow's now classic *The Yugoslav Experiment, 1948–1974* (Berkeley: University of California Press, 1977). For the most recent period, I refer the reader to my own *Nationalism and Federalism in Yugoslavia, 1962–1991,* second edition (forthcoming in 1992 from Indiana University Press).

Dissent. Rudolf L. Tőkés's *Opposition in Eastern Europe* (Baltimore: Johns Hopkins University Press, 1979), though old, is still a magnificent collection of essays by different authors. Also worth reading is Jane Leftwich Curry's *Dissent in Eastern Europe* (New York: Praeger, 1983). H. Gordon Skilling's *Samizdat and an Independent Society in Central and Eastern Europe* (Columbus: Ohio State University Press, 1989) is masterful, focusing principally on Czechoslovakia but including also discussion of the other countries in the region.

Religion. My own three-volume set covering the three important Christian branches brings together the works of a number of scholars. The volumes are: *Eastern Christianity and Politics in the Twentieth Century* (1988), *Catholicism and Politics in Communist Societies* (1990), and *Protestantism and Politics in Eastern Europe and the Soviet Union* (under review), all from Duke University Press.

General. A useful short history of the region is Robin Okey's *Eastern Europe, 1740–1980* (Minneapolis: University of Minnesota Press, 1982). Joseph Rothschild's mistitled *Return to Diversity: A Political History of East Central Europe since World War II* (New York: Oxford University Press, 1989) actually devoted one-third of its space to events taking place between the end of World War I and the outbreak of World War II. It is perhaps the best short account of twentieth-century Eastern Europe currently available. Zbigniew Brzezinski's *The Soviet Bloc: Unity and Conflict,* rev. and enl. ed. (Cambridge: Harvard University Press, 1967) is still the standard reference for the period from the late 1940s to the 1960s.

Index

About the Author. Sabrina P. Ramet is Associate Professor of International Studies at the University of Washington. She is the author of *Nationalism and Federalism in Yugoslavia, 1963–1983* (1984; second ed., forthcoming, 1992), *Cross and Commissar: The Politics of Religion in Eastern Europe and the USSR* (1987), and *The Soviet-Syrian Relationship since 1955: A Troubled Alliance* (1990), and the editor of five books on international politics and religion. Professor Ramet has contributed chapters to several major works, and her articles have appeared in many prominent journals, including *Orbis* and *Global Affairs.* Recently, Professor Ramet received the Golden Key Award for outstanding teaching (1989–90) and the Henry M. Jackson School of International Studies Student Service Award for outstanding service to students in international affairs.

Library of Congress Cataloging-in-Publication Data
Ramet, Sabrina P., 1949–
Social currents in Eastern Europe: the sources and meaning of the great transformation / Sabrina P. Ramet.
Includes bibliographical references.
ISBN 0-8223-1129-1 (cloth). —ISBN 0-8223-1148-8 (paper)
1. Europe, Eastern—Social conditions.   2. Europe, Eastern—Politics and government—1945–1989.   I. Title.
HN373.5.R36   1991
306'.0947—dc20   90-24049 CIP

Anne Heal

390 4813

Exit 1)
to 4
to North
Libert
(or ses),
Food)
Store.